DICTIONARY
OF
LABOUR BIOGRAPHY

Volume 1

DICTIONARY
OF
LABOUR BIOGRAPHY

Volume I

JOYCE M. BELLAMY
Senior Research Officer, University of Hull

and

JOHN SAVILLE
Professor of Economic and Social History, University of Hull

First edition 1972
Reprinted (with alterations) 1978

Published by
THE MACMILLAN PRESS LTD
London and Basingstoke
Associated companies in Delhi Dublin Hong Kong
Johannesburg Lagos Melbourne
New York Singapore Tokyo

ISBN 0 333 13180 0

Printed in Great Britain by
UNWIN BROTHERS LTD
The Gresham Press, Old Woking, Surrey

To Dame Margaret Cole and
in Memory of the late G. D. H. Cole
with respect and affection

Contents

Introduction

THE idea of a Dictionary of Labour Biography originated with G. D. H. Cole. During the year before Cole's death, Professor Asa Briggs and I were planning a volume of essays in honour of his seventieth birthday. He died, however, early in 1959 and the volume became a memorial. After his death Dame Margaret Cole offered us a number of MS volumes which G. D. H. had been putting together for many years. They consisted of many hundreds of names with a few lines of biographical information attached to each; and the original volumes have now been deposited with the Cole Collection at Nuffield College, Oxford. It was agreed between us that if research funds became available I should take over the work of editing a biographical dictionary, using the MS volumes as my starting-point; and largely because of Cole's association with the Institute of Social History, Amsterdam, and through the good offices of Margaret Cole and Professor Braunthal, the Institute very generously put a research grant at my disposal. It will now be clear to readers why this first volume is very properly dedicated to the Coles, and I would add my further tribute to Margaret Cole for her constant encouragement to this project and for her general understanding and sympathy.

It was at first intended to produce a single large volume on the lines of *Who's Who*, but the scope and range of the Dictionary grew as work progressed, and the present plan, for more than one volume, was finally decided on only a few years ago. There were many false starts, not least because it was always planned to include not only the national personalities of the British labour movement but also the activists at regional and local level; and this presented problems of a new kind for which there were few precedents in other biographical compilations. In this particular respect – the inclusion of the rank and file of the labour movement – the present Dictionary is similar to the *Dictionnaire Biographique du Mouvement Ouvrier Français* published by the Paris Institut d'Histoire Sociale.

The principles upon which the Dictionary is now organised are, we hope, reasonably straightforward, and we trust that they will be recognised as founded upon common sense. Its time span is broadly that of the labour movement in the period of industrialism, from 1790 or thereabouts to the present day, excluding always the living. It has been planned to include everyone who made a contribution, however modest, to any organisation or movement, provided that certain basic details of their career can be established. The question of definition, who was to be included and who left out, was solved for the great majority of persons by their membership of a trade union, co-operative organisation or working-class party or movement; but there remained, and will always remain, a quite considerable number of people about whom argument can legitimately develop. Middle-class radicals without any definite connection with the movements of working people have in general been excluded, so that Cobden and Bright are

out while Beesly, Frederic Harrison and Tom Hughes are just as obviously in.
There remain, however, more difficult cases than these straightforward examples,
and in the last resort it will come down to a matter of editorial judgement rather
than of precise definition. It is not necessary, of course, that an individual should
have remained all his life within the context of the labour movement, since this
would exclude many whose youthful enthusiasm and commitment were transformed in later life into different political and social attitudes; and it would also
exclude the other category of those who came relatively late in life to a labourist or
socialist commitment. The Dictionary, then, will include all who at any time in
their lives were part of what we understand in general terms as the labour movement in Britain, either as members of particular organisations or because of their
ideological attitudes and approach. It is a formula which must remain flexible
enough to include within its terms of reference those like Dr Josiah Court, whose
entry will be found in this first volume, who remained a staunch Tory all his life
while filling for a long period the position of medical adviser to the Derbyshire
Miners' Association.

It became clear as work went forward that one or two volumes would be quite
insufficient to encompass the many hundreds of names for whom detailed information was being accumulated. The present editors, let it be said at once, see no end
to the Dictionary, and if they themselves can count upon something approaching
the biblical span of life, they estimate that eight or ten volumes might be produced
under their auspices. Even then, at least as many again will be needed to clear
arrears down to 1914. Given, then, that the Dictionary is planned as a many-
volumed project, the problem was how to organise the first and succeeding volumes.
The most acceptable method, and the one most commonly used in other biographical works, is to begin with the early letters of the alphabet and work through to the
letter Z in subsequent volumes. Such an approach is not, however, practicable in
the present case for there are too many gaps in our knowledge in terms of individuals, movements and localities. Had the Dictionary been concerned only with
national figures, it would no doubt have been reasonably easy to use the customary
alphabetical structure of most biographical dictionaries, but our emphasis upon
those below the top leadership of organisations and movements meant that far too
many individuals would be missed in the early volumes.

Each volume will, therefore, be organised on a self-contained A to Z basis, and
we have given much thought to the ways in which the volumes can be integrated.
The first requirement is a consolidated name index in all volumes after the first.
A second is a liberal interpretation of the 'See also' column, which gives cross-
references to other relevant entries, including names in other volumes; and where
these latter occur the names in question are asterisked. And finally, we have tried
to compile the general index – itself something of an innovation in a biographical
dictionary – in ways that will allow readers to follow through the headings in all the
subsequent volumes.

There is a further question that relates to the biographical content of any one
volume. Again our starting-point was the unevenness of research that has so far
been published or is to be found in unpublished theses. There are still many towns
for which no adequate social history exists; there are many organisations, especially
trade unions, whose history remains unwritten; and there are many individuals

for whom our knowledge is still quite insufficient. There are also many individuals, it should be added, who remain to be discovered by their biographers. We have been obliged, therefore, to take what is to hand, and to supplement existing knowledge from our own research resources. The first volume contains a large number of miners' leaders and co-operators: the former because mining is the best-documented trade union field and we were able to draw upon the generous help of a number of scholars in this field, and in particular upon Robin Page Arnot; and co-operators because the Co-operative Union kindly made available research monies for use by the Co-operative College at Stanford Hall, Loughborough. Mr H. F. Bing, to whom we are much indebted, has been their main research worker. But while this first volume is heavily weighted with miners and co-operators we have also tried to include a fair selection of other types of radicals, reformers and trade unionists, and our general plan for the first three volumes is to cover the majority of the miners' leaders, to have a large sample of co-operators, to include all the Lib-Lab MPs and all the Labour MPs down to 1914; to have begun making inroads into the Chartist movement, the Christian Socialists of 1848 and of the later nineteenth century, and to have started working systematically through at least one other major union. Such a plan, broad though it is in scope, does not in any way exclude other types of entries supplied either by the editorial research team or by outside contributors whose special interests allow them to offer adequate documentation on this or that individual. It is certainly our hope that with the publication of this first volume we shall be offered an increasing number of entries from scholars who are working within the general terms of reference of the Dictionary. Obviously, the more entries there are from outside contributors, the more quickly succeeding volumes will appear. Our present plans are to publish the next two volumes within three to four years from the date of publication of this first volume.

At the end of the first stage of this project my co-editor and myself have begun to understand the remark by Sir John Clapham about the advantages, were time to allow, of 'another ten years at a finishing school'. We have constantly been overtaken by the discovery of new material, and at the other end of the line we have been surprised how quickly quite prominent personalities can fall into obscurity. On this last matter we hope in the years ahead to persuade as many of the living as possible to set down at least some of the basic facts of their lives; but such documentation is exceedingly time-consuming and cuts sharply into current research. The most grievous problem for all who work in this field is the continuous loss of original records, those belonging to Robert Smillie being only the latest example of thoughtless destruction. The education of members of the labour movement as to the importance of documents, correspondence and the like is no doubt a long-term matter, but a more positive attitude on the part of national leaders, industrial and political, would greatly help research workers in this field. We ourselves have been much encouraged by the assistance we have received from the families, friends and colleagues of those individuals for whom we have sought information, but there are still a quite extraordinary number of people who have died only in the past few decades whose biographical details remain meagre and inadequate. Our search for material would have been far less rewarding had it not been for the co-operation we have received from the librarians and staffs of our magnificent public library system. But despite all the help we have been given from individuals and from those working in public institutions, there is no doubt that users of this Dictionary will discover errors of fact and obtuse interpretations as well as omissions and gaps in knowledge. We can only ask for the co-operation of our readers in making known to us their findings, and in a later volume – which is not likely to be before the fifth or sixth – we will publish full corrigenda and addenda to all the entries up to that point.

It would be otiose for me to indicate even in the most general way the historical perspectives which emerge from a study of a large number of biographical entries. It is, however, already clear that to collect biographical information on the present scale does offer, if not new perspectives, then at least some new emphases within labour movement historiography. The involvement, for example, of working men and women in the development of more democratic political institutions at the local and county level is most striking; and it provides a new dimension to the analysis of the labourist tradition. Another example, of less importance, but one which has greatly surprised us, is the quite large number of working men who became Freemasons in the closing decades of the nineteenth century and throughout the twentieth century; and it may be that here is a subject which is worth further investigation. There is one aspect of our research in this first volume with which we remain especially dissatisfied. It is usually fairly easy to determine parents' occupations; what are much more difficult to discover are the occupations of the children of the individual for whom the main entry has been prepared. For the social historian, and particularly for anyone working on the problem of social mobility, these are important questions. We are far from satisfied at the amount of information we have been able to collect under this heading for this present volume, and we ask our readers to accept that it is a problem we shall try to solve more adequately in the future. For the rest, we have tried to set out for each individual entry the usual kind of biographical detail expected: background of the parents, education, occupation, the membership of organisations and movements, formative intellectual, social and political influences, social and political attitudes and the changes over time, religion, and so on, ending with the details of any estate left at death. Apart from other uses it may have, we have always envisaged this Dictionary as a research tool for scholars in the field of labour history, and to this end we have taken special care with the bibliographies attached to each entry. In addition to bibliographical references specific to particular entries we have also provided consolidated bibliographies for certain periods or movements; and these will be added to in subsequent volumes. A list of these specialist bibliographies is given in the Notes to Readers at the beginning of this volume and there are cross references under individual entries. We do not claim that we have been able to provide fully comprehensive coverage but we trust that what we have been able to put together will prove useful. It will be obvious that in the course of our work we have accumulated a very large mass of information, from which the entries have been written, and we wish to make it clear to all who work in this field that our files are at all times open to research workers and to scholars everywhere. Those making inquiries should write in the first instance to Dr Joyce Bellamy, Dictionary of Labour Biography, University of Hull.

It will be appreciated by readers that length of entry in this volume is not necessarily commensurate with political, industrial or social importance measured on a national scale. And this has been deliberate. While we have naturally considered it necessary to offer reasonable justice to the national figures of the movement, in the matter of length of entry, we have felt it even more desirable to write as fully as possible about those individuals who are either footnotes in national histories or who are not mentioned at all except in local chronicles. From the outset we have understood this Dictionary as an extension to knowledge as well as a summation of existing information and for this reason we have encouraged our contributors and ourselves to write at length on individuals whose names today have often been forgotten, or whose careers are known only dimly, but who in their lives made a not insignificant contribution to the radical politics or the reform movements of their own times. E. T. Craig, Margaret Llewelyn Davies and Frederick Rogers, to mention only three examples from this first volume, are not particularly well known at the present time except to the specialist historian, but their individual histories add a useful dimension to the national story of the movements they served. Inevitably there has been a degree of arbitrariness in all this since for many people of the second and third rank the details of their lives remain meagre and sparse; and a number of entries record little more than a statement of positions held. But the general principle – of writing fully where material is available about relatively minor personalities – remains.

I have exercised my privilege as the older of the two editors to submit this Introduction in my own name not least because this allows me to express my deep sense of gratitude to my co-editor, Dr Joyce Bellamy. No one could wish for a more selfless or more efficient colleague; and it is much more than the usual acknowledgement of a working partnership that I wish to record here.

Finally I wish to offer my personal thanks to a number of friends who, over the years, have offered me both encouragement and hospitality. Work on this Dictionary inevitably involves much travel, and I have been sustained by the warmth and kindness with which I have been received by friends upon whose domestic hearths I have stood on so many occasions. To Chimen and Miriam Abramsky, Ed and Ruth Frow, Professor Margot Jefferys, Miss Joan Knott, Ralph and Marion Miliband, Edward and Dorothy Thompson, and Professor Victor Kiernan, I offer my gratitude for their many individual and collective kindnesses.

University of Hull,
May 1971
JOHN SAVILLE

Acknowledgements

THE Dictionary began with a substantial financial grant from the Institute of Social History, Amsterdam. We are much indebted for this assistance to the late Professor A. J. C. Rüter, who was Director of the Institute at the time, and Prof. Julius Braunthal, a member of the board of the Institute, who has throughout given unfailing support to the project. We owe him a special debt of gratitude. For other financial help we are grateful to: A. S. Horsley Esq., Hessle, East Yorkshire; the Amalgamated Union of Foundry Workers (now part of the Amalgamated Union of Engineering Workers); the National Union of Mineworkers (Durham Area); the Plumbing Trades Union (now part of the Electrical, Electronic, Telecommunication and Plumbing Trades Union); and the Union of Shop, Distributive and Allied Workers.

We owe a great deal to the help and encouragement of Dame Margaret Cole; and among others who have given us special assistance and help we would particularly mention: Chimen Abramsky Esq., University College, London; G. S. Aitken Esq., Amalgamated Union of Engineering Workers; the Hon. Ada M. Ammon, Haywards Heath; Dr Robin Page Arnot, London; Harold F. Bing Esq., Loughborough; I. C. J. Corkindale Esq., General Register Office, London; Miss Pauline W. Gee, Scottish Record Office, Edinburgh; Dr A. R. Griffin, Nottingham University; Lord Peddie of Kingston upon Hull; Harold Smith Esq., Putney, London; Mrs Dorothy Thompson, Birmingham University; Mrs Irene Wagner, Librarian, Labour Party; and Dr J. E. Williams, Leeds University.

There is a special debt we must acknowledge to Dr Philip Larkin, Librarian of the Brynmor Jones Library, Hull University, and his staff, among whom we should particularly mention Miss Maeve M. Brennan, Miss Wendy P. Mann, Alan Marshall Esq., Peter Sheldon Esq. and Miss Lila S. Wijayatilake, in addition to Norman Higson Esq., Archivist, East Riding County Council, and part-time archivist to Hull University Library. Two members of the University Library staff, V. J. Morris Esq. and G. D. Weston Esq., have compiled the index and we are most grateful to them for the care and understanding they have given to the work. We have also greatly appreciated the assistance given by T. Balme Esq., Barnsley Public Library; Messrs C. E. Makepeace and T. Walsh, Local History Librarians, Manchester City Library; and Miss D. M. White, Chief Librarian of Ipswich CB.

Over the years we have been fortunate to have the services of a number of full-time and part-time research assistants and we particularly thank: Miss Mai Alman (Mrs Allwood), Mrs June Butt, Mrs Valerie Gribbin, Dr R. H. C. Hayburn, Dr Dorothy Pockley and Bryan H. Sadler Esq. We are especially grateful to David E. Martin for his careful and conscientious work on this first volume.

We have received help from a large number of individuals to all of whom we offer our gratitude: the Marquess of Ailesbury; Professor W. H. G. Armytage,

Sheffield University; H. Atkinson Esq., Fleetwood; David Ayerst Esq., Burford; Bernard Barker Esq., Cheshunt; J. M. Bayley Esq., Botany, Australia; Mrs E. Brown, Old Brumby, Scunthorpe; H. Campbell Esq., Enfield; R. G. Cant Esq., St Andrews University; Dr S. Coltham, Keele University; Miss Lilian Darch, Par, Cornwall; Fergus D'Arcy Esq., University College, Dublin; Daniel J. Doyle Esq., Williamsport, USA; Miss T. E. Dudley, Runcorn; Mrs G. L. Dye, Sporle, King's Lynn; Dr E. W. Evans, Hull University; Edmund Frow Esq. and Mrs Ruth Frow, Manchester; Mrs Mary Gallacher, Dungloe, Donegal; Mrs O. Harris, New Malden, Surrey; Dr Brian H. Harrison, Oxford University; Professor J. F. C. Harrison, Sussex University; Professor Royden Harrison, Warwick University; Miss D. K. Hines, Ipswich; Harold Hobson Esq., Hilton, Hunts; Dr Patricia Hollis, University of East Anglia; E. N. Hughes Esq., Ruthin; Miss A. Jenkins, Abertridwr, Caerphilly, South Wales; Alan R. Jones Esq., University of East Anglia; J. H. C. Jones Esq., Pontfadog; Ald. J. Knight, Bristol; R. C. Lang Esq., Renfrew; Mrs N. E. Lefèvre, Aberdeen; Herr W. Leist, University of Giessen, Germany; G. G. Lerry Esq., Wrexham; Mrs L. E. Lewis, Ipswich; Miss I. Lobb, Bristol; J. McConville Esq., London Polytechnic; Miss C. McGhee, Sheffield; J. A. Mahon Esq., London; Mrs A. Marlow, Kettering; A. N. Marlow Esq., Manchester; David Marquand Esq., MP, London; W. H. Marwick Esq., Edinburgh; Mrs Lucy Middleton, London; J. P. M. Millar Esq., Dartmouth; Miss Iris Minor, Bristol University; G. M. H. Morris Esq., London; Dr D. Stark Murray, London; H. Newton Esq., Fircroft College; A. E. Pattison Esq., Long Eaton; Dr. Henry Pelling, St John's College, Cambridge; H. G. Perkins Esq., Winchester; Miss G. F. Polley Croydon; Mrs C. Rabinovich, London; Mrs E. Radnedge, Bristol; R. Ratcliffe Esq., Ipswich; Sir Frank Schon, London; the late Mrs Mabel Scott; L. P. Scott Esq., Manchester; Mrs J. Sims, Kettering; Mrs M. Le Blanc Smith, Albury, Surrey; Ald. Dr S. H. Smith, Hessle; Dr John Spencer, Loughton, Essex; Mrs M. K. Starkey, Scunthorpe; Fergus Stevens Esq., Narborough; Eric Taylor Esq., Wolverhampton; Dr C. H. Thompson, London; E. P. Thompson Esq., Leamington Spa; Mrs D. A. Topham, Stockport; Miss T. Topham, Oadby; Mrs E. Twigg, London; A. Vigodny Esq., Millom; J. A. Walker Esq., Nottingham; P. N. Wilson Esq., Kendal; Mrs N. Wood, Cheadle Hulme; Baroness Wootton of Abinger; Mrs Elsie Wyld, Yaddlethorpe, Scunthorpe; R. L. Wyllie Esq., Whitehaven.

Like all who work in the fields of biography and bibliography we have leaned heavily upon the public libraries of Britain. We record here our grateful thanks for the never-failing co-operation we have received. Those we name below refer only to the work of this first volume: Aberdare, Accrington, Ayr, Barnsley, Barrow, Battersea, Birmingham, Blackburn, Bolton, Brighton, Bristol, Bury, Cambridge, Cardiff, Carlisle, Carnforth, Cheltenham, Chesterfield, Consett, Coventry, Cumberland County, Denbigh County, Derby, Derbyshire County, Dewsbury, Dudley, Durham, Durham County, Eccles, Edinburgh, Exeter, Fife County, Gateshead, Glasgow, Gloucester, Greenock, Greenwich, Halifax, Hanley, Haringey, Huddersfield, Ipswich, Kettering, Kilmarnock, Kingston upon Hull, Kirkcudbright, Lanark County, Lancashire County, Leeds, Leicester, Lewisham, Liverpool, London: Guildhall, Long Eaton, Macclesfield, Manchester, Middlesbrough, Newcastle upon Tyne, Newham, Northumberland County, Nottingham, Nottingham County, Plymouth, Port Talbot, Rochdale, Rugby, Runcorn, St Helens, Scunthorpe, Sheffield, Southampton, Southwark, Stoke on Trent, Stratford (London), Sunderland, Tower Hamlets, Walsall, Warwick, West Riding County, Westmorland and Kendal, Wigan, Winchester, Woolwich, Workington, York. Our thanks are also due to the following archivists and their staffs: B. C. Jones Esq., Counties of Cumberland and Westmorland and the City of Carlisle; G. W. Oxley Esq., Kingston upon Hull CB; Dr W. A. L. Seaman, Durham County; R. Sharpe France Esq., Lancashire County; and to the staff of the Liverpool Record Office.

We should like to record our appreciation of the assistance given to us by the late D. Flanagan Esq., Librarian of the Co-operative Union; by his successor, R. Garratt Esq.; and by A. L. Sugar Esq., Publications Manager, Co-operative Union. We wish also to thank the staffs of the following co-operative organisations: Co-operative Press, Manchester; Co-operative Productive Association, Leicester; Co-operative Union, Manchester; Industrial Co-partnership Association, London; International Co-operative Alliance; and the following co-operative societies: Brighton, Gloucester and Severnside, Hartlepools, Ipswich, Leicester, North Midland (Burslem), Nottingham, Oldham, Oxford, Plymouth, Runcorn and Widnes, Sheffield and Ecclesall. To the Secretaries and staffs of the following trade unions we are also indebted for help in various ways: Amalgamated Union of Engineering Workers; Chainmakers' and Strikers' Association; National Union of Journalists; National Union of Mineworkers (especially the following areas: Cumberland, Derbyshire, Durham, North Western, Midlands, Northumberland, North Wales, Nottingham, Scotland, South Wales and Yorkshire); and the National Union of Post Office Workers. We wish to acknowledge further the assistance given by the Town Clerks' Departments of Leicester and Workington, by the Clerks to the Cumberland County Council and Ennerdale RDC and by the Secretary of the Cumberland Development Council. Other help has been given by the following persons and organisations: British Museum and Colindale Newspaper Library; Chris. Cook Esq., Director, LSE Political Papers Project; Hearts of Oak Benefit Society; Manchester Ship Canal Co.; National Peace Council; Oxford University Press; Peace Pledge Union; H. T. Willcock Esq., Southampton Labour Party.

We acknowledge the careful and patient help we have received from a succession of Hull University typing-pool supervisors and their staffs, among whom we would especially like to mention: Mrs M. Barker, Miss A. Caley, Mrs M. Greatorex, Miss L. Hargreaves, Miss P. Matthews, Mrs J. Naylor, Mrs G. Stern, Mrs V. Townsend, Miss J. Walker, Miss J. Walton and Mrs P. Wilkinson. We also wish further to acknowledge the typing assistance given by Mrs B. Brown of Hessle, and Mrs E. Harrison and Miss P. Readymartcher, both of Hull University. For photo-copying services we are indebted to M. J. Oxtoby Esq., of the Hull University printing staff. Finally we acknowledge the assistance in proof-reading given by Messrs H. Inglis, D. E. Martin, D. Parker and R. V. Saville and Mrs J. Ward.

J. M. B.
J. S.

List of Contributors

Miss Mai Alman (Mrs Allwood)	Formerly Jubilee Research Scholar, Co-operative College, Stanford Hall, Loughborough.
Dr R. Page Arnot	London.
Professor P. N. Backstrom	Department of History, College of Liberal Arts, Northeastern University, Boston, Mass., USA.
Ron Bean Esq.	Lecturer, Department of Economics, Liverpool University.
Dr Joyce M. Bellamy	Senior Research Officer, Department of Economic and Social History, Hull University.
H. F. Bing Esq.	Lecturer, Co-operative College, Stanford Hall, Loughborough.
Frank Carruthers Esq.	Features Writer, Cumberland Newspapers Ltd, Cockermouth.
Dr E. W. Evans	Senior Lecturer in Economics, Hull University.
Edmund Frow Esq.	Manchester.
K. G. E. Harris Esq.	Librarian, Newcastle upon Tyne Polytechnic.
Dr Brian H. Harrison	Fellow of Corpus Christi College, Oxford.
Dr Ralph H. C. Hayburn	Lecturer, Department of History, Otago University, NZ.
Dr Alan J. Lee	Lecturer, Department of History, Hull University.
James Macfarlane Esq.	Lecturer, Department of Extra-Mural Studies, Sheffield University.
David E. Martin Esq.	Research Assistant, Department of Economic and Social History, Hull University.
Dr Anthony Mason	Lecturer in Social History, Warwick University.
Mrs Valerie Mason	Kenilworth
The late Professor Charles Loch Mowat	Formerly of the Department of History, University College of North Wales, Bangor.

Dr John Osburn

Head of the Department of History, Central State College, Edmond, Oklahoma, USA.

I. J. Prothero Esq.

Lecturer, Department of History, Manchester University.

Dr E. Royle

Fellow of Selwyn College, Cambridge.

Dr David Rubinstein

Lecturer in Social History, Hull University.

Bryan H. Sadler Esq.

Lecturer in Economic History, Warwick University.

John Saville Esq.

Reader in Economic History, Hull University.

Eric Taylor Esq.

Senior Lecturer in Modern History, Wolverhampton Polytechnic.

R. E. Tyson Esq.

Lecturer in Economic History, Aberdeen University.

Dr J. E. Williams

Reader in Economic History, Leeds University.

List of Abbreviations

AAM	Amalgamated Association of Miners
ACE	*Annals of Collective Economy*
AFL	American Federation of Labor
AMWU	Amalgamated Marine Workers' Union
Anon.	Anonymous
APCE	*Annals of Public and Co-operative Economy*
App.	Appendix
ASE	Amalgamated Society of Engineers
Assn	Association
BAPCK	British Association for the Promotion of Co-operative Knowledge
BBC	British Broadcasting Corporation
Blackw. Mag.	*Blackwood's Magazine*
BLPES	British Library of Political and Economic Science, London School of Economics
BM	British Museum
Boase	F. Boase, *Modern English Biography*, 6 vols (1965)
BSP	British Socialist Party
BSU	British Seafarers' Union
Bull. Soc. Lab. Hist.	*Bulletin of the Society for the Study of Labour History*
Canad. J. Econ. Pol. Sc.	*Canadian Journal of Economic and Political Science*
CIS	Co-operative Insurance Society
CMG	Companion of the Order of St Michael and St George
Coll.	Collection
Cont. Rev.	*Contemporary Review*
Co-op.	Co-operative
Co-op. Rev.	*Co-operative Review*
COPEC	Conference on Politics, Economics and Christianity
CP	Communist Party
CPF	Co-operative Productive Federation
CPGB	Communist Party of Great Britain
CPS	Co-operative Printing Society
CSU	Complete Suffrage Union
CWS	Co-operative Wholesale Society
DLB Coll.	Dictionary of Labour Biography Collection, Hull University
DMA	Durham Miners' Association

DNB	*Dictionary of National Biography*
Dod	*Dod's Parliamentary Companion*
Econ. Hist. Rev.	*Economic History Review*
Econ. J.	*Economic Journal*
Econ. Rev.	*Economic Review*
ed.	editor
et al.	*et alii* (Lat.): and others
Fortn. Rev.	*Fortnightly Review*
I. and P. Acts	Industrial and Provident Acts
ICA	International Co-operative Alliance
ICB	*International Co-operative Bulletin*
idem	(Lat.) the same; author as mentioned in previous entry
IFTU	International Federation of Trade Unions
ILP	Independent Labour Party
Int. Co-op. Bull.	*International Co-operative Bulletin*
Int. Lab. Rev.	*International Labour Review*
Int. Rev. Social Hist.	*International Review of Social History*
Int. Soc. Rev.	*International Socialist Review*
J.	*Journal*
J. Mod. Hist.	*Journal of Modern History*
JP	Justice of the Peace
JPE	*Journal of Political Economy*
JRSS	*Journal of the Royal Statistical Society*
Kelly	*Kelly's Handbook to the Titled, Landed and Official Classes* (in 1938 only: *Handbook of Distinguished People*)
Labour Mag.	*Labour Magazine*
Lab. Mon.	*Labour Monthly*
Landw. Jahrb.	*Landwirtschaftliche Jahrbücher*: Berlin
LCC	London County Council
LCMF	Lancashire and Cheshire Miners' Federation
Lect.	Lecture
Lib-Lab	Liberal-Labour
LP	Labour Party
LRC	Labour Representation Committee
LSE	London School of Economics
LWMA	London Working Men's Association
Macmill. Mag.	*Macmillan's Magazine*
MFGB	Miners' Federation of Great Britain
MNU	Miners' National Union
M. of E.	Minutes of Evidence
MP	Member of Parliament
MS(S)	Manuscript(s)
NAPSS	National Association for the Promotion of Social Science

Nat.	National
N. Brit. Rev.	*North British Review*
NCFS	National Community Friendly Society
n.d.	no date
NMA	Northumberland Miners' Association
n.p.	no pagination
n.s.	new series
NSP	National Socialist Party
NUDAW	National Union of Distributive and Allied Workers
NUM	National Union of Mineworkers
NUR	National Union of Railwaymen
NUS	National Sailors' and Firemen's Union
NUSMW	National Union of Scottish Mineworkers
NUWC	National Union of the Working Classes
19th C.	*Nineteenth Century*
Obit.	Obituary
OUP	Oxford University Press
P	pamphlet
P.C.	Privy Councillor
PLP	Parliamentary Labour Party
Pol. Q.	*Political Quarterly*
Pop. Studies	*Population Studies*
pp.	pages
PRO	Public Record Office
Proc.	*Proceedings*
pt.	part
Q(s)	Question(s)
QJE	*Quarterly Journal of Economics*
Q. Rev.	*Quarterly Review*
RAF	Royal Air Force
R.C.	Royal Commission
RCA	Railway Clerks' Association
RDC	Rural District Council
Rev.	Reverend
Rev.	*Review*
RIC	*Review of International Co-operation*
RRA	Radical Reform Association
sc.	*scilicet* (Lat.): namely
S.C.	Select Committee
SCWS	Scottish Co-operative Wholesale Society
SDF	Social Democratic Federation
ser.	series
SNDC	Socialist National Defence Committee
Soc. Rev.	*Socialist Review*

s.v.	*sub voce* (Lat.): see under
SWMF	South Wales Miners' Federation
SYMA	South Yorkshire Miners' Association
Trans.	*Transactions*
TSSA	Transport Salaried Staff Association
TUC	Trades Union Congress
UCSRR	Universal Community Society of Rational Religionists
UDC	Union of Democratic Control
UMS	United Mineworkers of Scotland
UPW	Union of Post Office Workers
USDAW	Union of Shop, Distributive and Allied Workers
WEA	Workers' Educational Association
West. Rev.	*Westminster Review*
WMA	Working Men's Association
WMC	Workers' Municipal Committee
WW	*Who's Who*
WWW	*Who Was Who*
YMA	Yorkshire Miners' Association
YMCA	Young Men's Christian Association

Notes to Readers

1. Place-names are usually quoted according to contemporary usage relating to the particular entry.
2. Where the amount of a will, estate value or effects are quoted, the particular form used is normally that given in *The Times*, or the records of Somerset House, London or the Scottish Record Office, Edinburgh. For dates before 1860 the source will usually be the Public Record Office.
3. Under the heading **Sources**, personal information relates to details obtained from relatives, friends or colleagues of the individual in question; biographical information refers to other sources.
4. The place of publication in bibliographical references is London, unless otherwise stated.
5. P indicates a pamphlet whose pagination could not be verified. Where it is known, the number of pages is quoted if under sixty.
6. The *See also* column, which follows biographical entries, includes names marked by asterisks and these refer to entries to be included in later volumes.
7. The subject bibliographies attached to certain entries are the responsibility of the editors. The list of such bibliographies and the entries under which they will be found are as follows:

British Labour Party, 1914–31 HENDERSON, Arthur (1863–1935)

Co-operative Education HALL, Fred (1878–1936)
Co-operative Party ALEXANDER, Albert Victor (1885–1965)
Co-operative Production JONES, Benjamin (1847–1942)
Co-operative Union HAYWARD, Fred (1876–1944)
Co-operative Wholesaling REDFERN, Percy (1875–1958)
Co-partnership GREENING, Edward Owen (1836–1923)
International Co-operative
  Alliance MAY, Henry John (1867–1939)
Irish Co-operation GALLAGHER, Patrick (1871–1966)
Retail Co-operation
  Nineteenth Century HOLYOAKE, George Jacob (1817–1906)
  1900–45 BROWN, William Henry (1867/8–1950)
  1945–70 BONNER, Arnold (1904–66)
Scottish Co-operation MAXWELL, William (1841–1929)

Mining Trade Unionism
  1850–79 MACDONALD, Alexander (1821–81)
  1880–99 PICKARD, Benjamin (1842–1904)
  1900–14 ASHTON, Thomas (1844–1927)
  Welsh Mining Trade ABRAHAM, William (Mabon) (1842–
  Unionism 1922)

New Model Unionism ALLAN, William (1813–74)

ABBOTTS, William (1873–1930)
CO-OPERATOR

Born at Brierley Hill, South Staffordshire, in 1873, William Abbotts spent the whole of his working life in Walsall and its neighbourhood. He left school at the age of ten and his first job was selling newspapers. Then followed thirty-one years' service with the London and North Western Railway Company in various positions connected with the passenger and signalling services. During the railway strike of 1911 he was chairman of the local strike committee.

Early in life he became a member of the Walsall Co-operative Society and in 1902 was elected to the education committee, soon becoming its chairman. Later he was elected to the management committee and in 1910 became president of the society. In 1918 he left railway employment to become from January 1919 full-time publicity agent and adviser of Walsall Society which, like many other co-operative societies, had experienced great difficulties during the war years. In 1920 he was appointed adviser, later being known as the chief executive officer, and held this post till his death. During the 1920s he took a prominent part in the negotiations which led to the amalgamations of the Cannock and Wednesbury Societies with the Walsall Society, and was the moving spirit behind many new developments. A fluent and impressive speaker, he had no faith in tame meetings or conferences, and was noted for being provocative in his speeches.

In 1920 he was elected a member of the Midland sectional board of the Co-operative Union and subsequently served on most of the committees of the Co-operative Union, including the United Board, and at the time of his death he was a member of the agricultural committee. He served as secretary of the Stafford District Hours and Wages Board and the Birmingham District Bakery Board.

In addition to his co-operative activities Abbotts engaged in much public and political work. He was made a JP in 1915. He was a very active worker in the local Labour Party, of which he was chairman for a number of years, and on several occasions he sat on the Walsall Council as a Labour member. He was a councillor for Leamore ward from 1920 to 1923 and was again elected for the same ward in 1927, and during this last period on the council he was made chairman of the electric supply committee. In his life outside the labour and co-operative movement Abbotts was connected with various organisations for social and civic improvement and in particular gave much time to work on behalf of the blind.

He was taken ill in February 1930 and died suddenly on 19 March 1930. He was survived by a wife, four sons and two daughters and left an estate valued at £1590.

Sources: F. Hall, *From Acorn to Oak: history of the Walsall and District Co-operative Society, 1886–1936* (Birmingham, 1936); G. D. H. Cole, *A Century of Co-operation* [1945?]; P. Bagwell, *The Railwaymen: the history of the National Union of Railwaymen* (1963). OBIT. *Walsall Observer*, 22 Mar 1930; *Co-op. News*, 29 Mar 1930; *Co-op. Congress Report* (1930).

H. F. BING

See also: W. H. BROWN, for Retail Co-operation, 1900–45; F. HAYWARD, for Co-operative Union.

ABRAHAM, William (Mabon) (1842–1922)
MINERS' LEADER AND LIB-LAB MP

Born on 14 June 1842 at Cwmavon, Glamorganshire, the fourth son of Thomas Abraham, a miner and coppersmith, and his wife Mary. His father died when William was young, and the greatest influence in the early years of his life was his mother, a deeply religious and well-read woman. William had a primary education at the Cwmavon National School, and at the age of ten he began work in the mines as a doorboy. He added to his formal education through private study, Sunday school classes, the Mechanics Institute, and the Eisteddfod. The family belonged to the strict Calvinistic Methodist Connexion, in which William became a lay preacher, being noted for his considerable oratorical ability as well as a powerful singing voice. He began to use the Bardic name Mabon in his early adult years, and it was this name by which he was always known in his long trade union career.

In the mid-1860s Abraham was one of a dozen Welshmen who set out for South America, lured by the prospect of a well-paid three-year contract in the Chilean copper mines. They sailed in the *Hawkeye* and after an eventful four-month voyage, having rounded Cape Horn, they ran the blockade by the Spaniards of the Chilean ports and reached Valparaiso, which had been bombarded by a Spanish squadron. Disappointed with conditions, Abraham came back, and after just thirteen months away from home went first to a tinplate works, and then in 1870 found work as a collier in the Caercynydd pit at Waunarl-wydd near Swansea. He soon became involved in trade union activity – the early 1870s being years of considerable boom – and he helped establish a lodge of Tom Halliday's Amalgamated Association of Miners. In 1873 Mabon became a full-time agent for the Loughor district. A five months' lock-out by the coalowners in 1875 resulted in a defeat for the miners, the rapid disintegration of the AAM and the establishment of the first joint committee to operate a sliding scale of wages regulated by the selling price of coal. The expenses of the committee on the workmen's side were met by a levy of 2*d* per month deducted from wages by the coal companies themselves, and the miners' agents, to whom the money was given, were thus placed in a somewhat equivocal position. Genuine trade unionism was impossible under the conditions of successive sliding-scale agreements; and effectively the further growth of trade union organisation in the whole coalfield was delayed for another quarter of a century.

Mabon championed the sliding-scale principle, and was its most fervent advocate; and the question of the sliding scale versus collective bargaining became a major theme of the miners' countrywide discussions on tactics and strategy in the 1880s. The establishment of the MFGB in 1889 was founded on the rejection of sliding scales, and this greatly strengthened the hands of those in South Wales who were becoming disillusioned with the general principle and its local applications. In particular William Brace, who had organised a small non-sliding-scale union in Monmouthshire, carried on a campaign throughout the valleys of Glamorgan against Mabon and the sliding-scale principle. Mabon dismissed Brace as a tool of the MFGB and as an alien 'English' influence, and in 1893 sued Brace for slander. Damages amounting to £500 were awarded against Brace, who, however, had no intention of paying, and who used the case most effectively against Mabon.

The years of the sliding scale were to be numbered in this decade of the 1890s. There was a growing dissatisfaction with Mabon's industrial leadership, and the hauliers' strike of 1893 further weakened his authority. But it was the strike of 1898 which effectively created the South Wales Miners' Federation and marked the rebirth of a genuine trade unionism in the South Wales coalfield. The SWMF, which elected Mabon as its first president, affiliated to the MFGB in 1899, and the sliding-scale agreements finally came to an end in 1903.

Despite growing criticism of Mabon, from traditional Lib-Lab unionists as well as from the growing number of young Socialists, Mabon remained influential during the first decade of the twentieth century. He became chairman of the Conciliation Board that replaced the sliding-scale committee, and his influence continued to be exercised in the direction of compromise and the peaceful settlement of outstanding questions between coalowners and miners. Isaac Evans in the 1890s made a bitter criticism of Mabon to the Webbs, and went so far as to accuse him of taking bribes from the employers [Page Arnot, *South Wales Miners*, 37 n. 2]. Whether this accusation can ever be proved is doubtful, but it is certainly true that Mabon was on excellent personal terms with the leading Welsh coalowners. It was the Cambrian Combine strike and lock-out of 1910–11 that marked the end of Mabon's influence in the SWMF. Following the ending of the strike the elections for three South Wales representatives on the executive of the MFGB revealed the new mood of militancy. In the autumn of 1911 Brace, Onions and Richards – all three officials of the SWMF – were replaced by Hartshorn, Stanton and Barker. Mabon himself was under constant criticism. At a full meeting of the executive council on 18 November 1911, with Mabon in the chair, the following extract appeared in the minutes: 'Mr W. Abraham's MP Article. Attention was called to an article by Mr William Abraham, MP in the *South Wales Weekly News and Cardiff Times* of 25 November. Resolved: That this Council dissociate itself from this Article, as it is entirely opposed to our declared policy on the Minimum Wage Question, and that we ask Mr Abraham to refrain from making any further statements of this kind.' Mabon himself resigned the presidency of the Federation at the next annual conference in 1912. He continued, however, to participate in mining affairs at the national and international levels. He had served on the executive of the MFGB from 1899 to 1903 as an ordinary member but early in 1904 was appointed treasurer of the Federation. In 1902 the International Miners' Congress had elected him as general treasurer and he held both these posts until 1918.

Mabon was also prominent in national politics. His prestige among the miners had been enhanced when he was elected in 1885 to represent the Rhondda in Parliament. Although he regarded himself as a labour representative, his political convictions were essentially Liberal even after the affiliation of the MFGB to the Labour Party in 1909, so that although he was officially in Parliament as a Labour member, he continued to act with the stalwart Lib-Labs, Burt and Fenwick. In 1906, however, the LRC had endorsed his candidature – an indication of his acceptance as a representative of the workers. He was never an outstanding parliamentarian – his speeches were too oratorical – but his main concern was with mining legislation. He served as a member of three Royal Commissions: Mining Royalties (1890–3), Labour (1891–4)

and Mines (1906–11), playing an important role in all three. The minority report of the Labour Commission regarding sweated industries was prepared by Mabon, Tom Mann and others, published as a pamphlet and praised by Sidney Webb. Mabon was also joint author of a separate report prepared at the time of the 1906 Mines Commission which aroused widespread attention. In 1911 he was made a Privy Councillor and in 1918 awarded an honorary degree of the University of Wales. Even when the miners opposed his industrial policy the general electorate never hesitated in returning him as their MP. Members of the Cambrian Combine Committee planned to replace him by R. B. Cunninghame Graham, but whether the latter accepted nomination is not known. Mabon continued to represent the Rhondda Valley constituency of Glamorganshire until 1918 and from that year to 1902 was MP for the Rhondda West Division.

He had married in 1860 Sarah Williams by whom he had twelve children. His wife predeceased him in 1900 and he himself died at Pentre on 14 May 1922, being survived by several of his children. He left an estate valued at £32,777 (net). This considerable fortune occasioned very hostile comment among trade union circles in South Wales. On the other side the *Western Mail*, while noting that 'Mabon was not a frugal liver; nor was he ungenerous in his lifetime', thought his example a splendid demonstration of thrift. Mabon accumulated his capital from a number of sources. At different times and sometimes the same time in his career he had four paid positions: as MP (being paid from the Rhondda Labour and Liberal Association fund); as salaried official of the Rhondda miners; as president of the South Wales Miners; and as treasurer of the MFGB. Most of his money, however, came from private enterprise: he drew some income from allowing his name to be used in advertisements; he became a director of at least one insurance company; and he invested in ordinary shares, the most lucrative being an investment of £400 in a non-mining industrial enterprise which, because of wartime prosperity, realised £19,000 after the conclusion of hostilities.

Writings: *Political Education and the Education of the Working Classes* (1883) P.

Sources: *Dod* (1886, 1919); S. and B. Webb, *History of Trade Unionism* (1920); *WWW* (1916–28); *DNB* (1922–30); E. W. Evans, *Mabon: William Abraham 1842–1922* (Cardiff, 1959); *Dictionary of Welsh Biography* (1959); R. Page Arnot, *The South Wales Miners: a history of the South Wales Miners' Federation 1898–1914* (1967). OBIT. *South Wales News, Times* and *Western Mail*, 15 May 1922; *Times* and *Western Mail*, 3 Oct 1922.

E. W. EVANS
JOHN SAVILLE

See also: Thomas ASHTON, for Mining Trade Unionism, 1900–14; Alexander MACDONALD, for Mining Trade Unionism, 1850–79; Benjamin PICKARD, for Mining Trade Unionism, 1880–99; *Robert SMILLIE, for Scottish Mining Trade Unionism; and below for Welsh Mining Trade Unionism.

Welsh Mining Trade Unionism: A. Dalziel, *The Colliers' Strike in South Wales: its cause, progress and settlement* (Cardiff, 1872); C. A. H. Green, 'The South Wales Coal Strike', *Econ. Rev. 3* (Oct 1893) 556–62; H. Read, 'South Wales Sliding Scale: its advantages and its defects', *Econ. J. 4* (June 1894) 332–5; 'Onlooker', 'Strike of Colliers in South Wales', *West. Rev. 150* (Sep 1898) 297–300; D. L. Thomas, *Labour Unions in Wales: their early struggle for existence* (Swansea, 1910); D. Evans, *Labour Strife in the South Wales Coalfield, 1910–11* (Cardiff, 1911); T. Smith, *The Mid-Rhondda Miners Fight for the Right to Live* (Tonypandy, 1911) 24 pp.; D. A. Thomas, *The Industrial Struggle in Mid-Rhondda: some points in the case for the owners* (Cardiff, 1911); G. R. Carter, 'The Coal Strike in South Wales', *Econ. J. 25* (Sep 1915) 453–65; idem, 'The Sequel of the Welsh Coal Strike and its Significance', *Econ. J. 25* (Dec 1915) 521–31; E. J. Thomas, 'The Present and Future Prospects of the South Wales Miners', *Communist Rev.*

2 (Jan 1922) 206–24; N. Edwards, *The Industrial Revolution in South Wales* (1924); idem, *The History of the South Wales Miners* (1926); B. Francis, 'Lessons of the Strike in South Wales', *Lab. Mon. 13* (Mar 1931) 175–82; G. Williams, 'South Wales and the Miners' Struggle', *Lab. Mon. 13* (Jan 1931) 17–28; N. Edwards, *History of the South Wales Miners' Federation* (1938); B. L. Coombes, *These Poor Hands: the autobiography of a miner working in South Wales* (1939); P. Massey, *Industrial South Wales: a social and political survey* (1940); E. Ginzberg, *Grass on the Slag Heaps: the story of the Welsh miner* (New York, 1942); R. Page Arnot, *The Miners: a history of the Miners' Federation of Great Britain, 1889–1910* (1949); idem, *The Miners: Years of Struggle: a history of the Miners' Federation of Great Britain from 1910 onwards* (1953); L. J. Williams and J. H. Morris, 'The Discharge Note in the South Wales Coal Industry', *Econ. Hist. Rev. 10* ser. 2 (1957–8) 286–93; idem, *The South Wales Coal Industry, 1841–1875* (Cardiff, 1958); E. W. Evans, *Mabon: William Abraham, 1842–1922* (Cardiff, 1959); E. D. Lewis, *The Rhondda Valleys: a study in industrial development, 1800 to the present day* (1959); J. H. Morris and L. J. Williams, 'The South Wales Sliding Scale, 1876–79: an experiment in industrial relations', *Manchester School 28* (1960) 161–76 [reprinted in *Industrial South Wales 1750–1914*, ed. W. E. Minchinton (1969)]; R. Page Arnot, *The Miners in Crisis and War* (1961); E. W. Evans, *The Miners of South Wales* (Cardiff, 1961); K. O. Morgan, *Wales in British Politics 1868–1922* (Cardiff, 1963); R. Page Arnot, *The South Wales Miners: a history of the South Wales Miners' Federation, 1898–1914* (1967); P. N. Jones, *Colliery Settlement in South Wales Coalfield 1850–1926* (University of Hull, 1969); C. Parry, *The Radical Tradition in Welsh Politics* (University of Hull, 1970); H. Francis, 'Welsh Miners and the Spanish Civil War', *J. Contemporary History 5* (1970) 177–91; J. H. Porter, 'Wage Bargaining under Conciliation Agreements, 1860–1914', *Econ. Hist. Rev. 23* ser. 2 (1970) 460–75; *Men of no Property: historical studies of Welsh trade unions*, ed. G. A. Hughes (Caerwys, Flintshire, 1971).

ACLAND, Alice Sophia (1849–1935)
FOUNDER AND FIRST SECRETARY OF
WOMEN'S CO-OPERATIVE GUILD

Alice Sophia, daughter of the Rev. Francis Macaulay Cunningham, was born on 3 February 1849 at Petersfield, Hampshire, on the edge of the South Downs and was educated in her father's Church school with her brothers and other village children. Later her father became rector of Witney, Oxfordshire, and it was during this period that she married Arthur Herbert Dyke Acland, at that time an Oxford don who later became well known for his services to education and social welfare.

With her husband, Mrs Acland travelled among the workers in the North of England and met many co-operative leaders and their wives. Mr and Mrs Acland believed fervently that co-operation could benefit the working classes and Mrs Acland was convinced that women should have outlets for activities other than those specifically associated with their household duties. As a friend of Samuel Bamford, editor of the *Co-operative News*, the weekly organ of the co-operative movement, she was able to start a 'woman's corner' in the paper which she edited from 1883 to 1886. In her introductory article she wrote:

And now this woman's corner has been opened, in which all matters which lie chiefly in the province of women are to be treated of week after week. We hope to have articles on all sorts of topics which may interest women. We will have discussions about health, about furniture, about cooking, about children, their food, their clothes, their exercise, their education, their going out into the world. . . . We will try to get accounts of foreign countries and of how women get on there. . . . We will hope as time goes on to notice and give some account of the various Acts which affect women's labour; the Married Women's Property Acts and various other matters which concern us most deeply.

The opening of this women's feature on 6 January 1883 included a spirited column appealing to women to take an active part in the life of the movement beyond their role as buyers of Co-op. goods. Responsive letters and suggestions, especially from Mary Lawrenson of Woolwich, led to the formation of a Woman's League. This was inaugurated at the Co-operative Congress in Edinburgh in June 1883 with Mrs Acland as secretary and fifty members, many of whom volunteered to become local secretaries *pro tem.* and start branches in their own districts. Mrs Acland gave them as a motto: 'Study to be quiet and do your own business.' This might seem a strange policy for the new movement but, as she explained later, she did not wish to arouse the antagonism which had been engendered by the dress and manners of some of the contemporary advocates of women's rights.

In 1884 Alice Acland resigned the secretaryship on account of ill-health and became the first president of the League, a position she held until 1886, having by correspondence through the 'woman's corner' gathered round her a central committee of Miss E. H. J. Allen (secretary) and five others who included Miss Greenwood, Mrs Ben Jones and Mrs Lawrenson. When the rules were under consideration in August 1884, it was decided to adopt the name Women's Co-operative Guild, a title suggested by Miss Greenwood. In 1886 Mrs Acland read a paper on 'Guild Organisation' at the annual meeting in Plymouth.

Mrs Acland became Lady Acland when her husband succeeded to the baronetcy, as the thirteenth baronet, in 1919. He died in 1926. She maintained her interest in the Guild and its activities to the last, though she no longer played an active part in its affairs. Ill-health had for many years prevented her from participating directly in the work of the Guild or in other voluntary service and during the last twelve years of her life she was a complete invalid. One of her most treasured possessions was the framed certificate of 'The Freedom of the Guild' presented to her in May 1931 which hung upon the wall of her bedroom where she could see it as she lay in bed. She was eighty-seven when she died on 5 July 1935. A memorial service was held at St Martin-in-the-Fields on 11 July following her cremation on 8 July at Golders Green. Her ashes were interred at Columb John Chapel on the Killerton, Devon, estate where her husband's were buried. She had two children who survived her, a son, Sir Francis Acland, Liberal MP for North Cornwall, who died in 1939, and a daughter who was deeply interested in child welfare work. A grandson, Richard Thomas Dyke Acland, succeeded to the title. Lady Acland left £403 in her will.

Writings: 'Guild Organisation', A.G.M. Women's Co-operative Guild (1886).

Sources: M. L. Davies, *The Women's Co-operative Guild, 1883-1904* (Kirkby Lonsdale, 1904); C. Webb, *The Woman with the Basket* (Manchester, 1927); *DNB* (1922-30) s.v. Acland, Sir Arthur Herbert Dyke. OBIT. *Times, Western Morning News,* 9 July 1935; *Co-op. News,* 20 July 1935.

JOYCE BELLAMY
H. F. BING

See also: A. H. D. ACLAND; Miss M. L. DAVIES; *Mrs M. LAWRENSON.

ACLAND, Sir Arthur Herbert Dyke (1847-1926)
LIBERAL POLITICIAN, EDUCATIONALIST AND CO-OPERATOR

Born at Holnicote, Devon, on 13 October 1847, the third son of Sir Thomas Dyke Acland, eleventh baronet of Columb John, Devon, by his first wife, Mary, daughter of Sir Charles Mordaunt, Bt. There was a long family tradition of public service and Sir Thomas was a pioneer of and active worker in the field of secondary education. Arthur, therefore, was brought up in a home where liberal reforming ideas were freely discussed. After attending Rugby School he went to Christ Church, Oxford, whence he graduated in 1870 with a BA in law and modern history; he was ordained in 1872 and took his MA in 1873. After holding various positions as lecturer and tutor, he was appointed in 1875 as head of the military academy at Cowley, near Oxford, and two

years later became steward of Christ Church. While at Oxford he had brought together a group of students and young Fellows interested in social reform who were known as the 'Inner Circle'; he was also closely associated with Arnold Toynbee in the development of university extension lectures and served as secretary of the Oxford University Extension Delegacy. Having come to realise that his natural vocation for social reform lay outside the confines of the Anglican Church, he resigned his holy orders in 1879.

Acland's political career, and especially his work for educational reform, have been written about in considerable detail [*Times* obit.; *DNB* (1922-30); G. M. Holmes (1964)] and this entry will be restricted mainly to a brief account of his co-operative interests and his contacts with the emerging labour movement. It was through his university extension work in the 1870s that he first came into close touch with working-men co-operators in Lancashire and Yorkshire. Through these, and certain of the former Christian Socialists, and in particular E. V. Neale whom he much admired, Acland came to appreciate the part which voluntary co-operation could play in improving working-class living standards. It was largely due to his efforts that the Co-operative Congress of 1882 was held at Oxford and in the following year he joined the central board of the Co-operative Union. At the Edinburgh Congress in 1883 he read a paper on 'The Present Position and Future Development of Co-operation'. In the same year a small committee of members of Oxford University was appointed by the United Board of the Co-operative Union to assist the Union's southern sectional board on education matters. Acland was a member along with A. Sedgwick and Arnold Toynbee and he also served as secretary of the committee. The interest aroused in the need for co-operative education gave rise to the establishment of scholarships tenable at Oxford; these included the Hughes Testimonial Fund established in 1884 and tenable at Oriel College. Another scholarship at a later date in memory of E. V. Neale was also tenable at Oriel. Acland presented the

Board's first educational report in 1884, which marked the beginning of an extensive educational programme for the co-operative movement. In the same year he was appointed senior bursar of Balliol College.

He was elected Liberal MP for the newly formed Rotherham division of the West Riding of Yorkshire in 1885, but he continued his interests in the co-operative movement and presided on the second day of the Plymouth Congress in 1886. When he spoke in support of a vote of thanks to Professor A. Marshall, the economist, for his presidential address at the 1889 Congress at Ipswich, Acland was introduced as 'our Co-operative Member of Parliament'. In his speech Acland emphasised the value and importance of links between the universities and the co-operative movement. He presided on the first day of the Lincoln Congress in 1891 and dealt with the problem of leadership and democracy in the co-operative movement in his address. By the early nineties Acland was also well known in the labour movement generally. Haldane wrote to Gladstone in 1892 that Acland 'has the personal respect of not only prominent leaders like Tom Mann and Burns, but of the great body of artisans of the northern and midland counties' [Sommer, *Haldane of Cloan* (1960) 88].

He collaborated with Professor C. Ransome of Leeds University in the writing of an outline of English political history which was published in 1882. His next major literary work was written at the request of the central board of the Co-operative Union and in conjunction with Arnold Toynbee and Benjamin Jones. It comprised a scheme of education for co-operators, was published in 1884 as *Working Men Co-operators* with Acland and Jones as joint authors and reprinted on several subsequent occasions. Acland continued to give active support and encouragement to co-operators in several parts of the country but after his election to Parliament his time became increasingly devoted to political activities especially in the field of education. He was much involved in educational legislation at the end of the 1880s, and in 1892 became vice-president of the Committee of Council

in Education in Gladstone's fourth administration, with a seat in the Cabinet. He was a considerable success in the office. Ill-health at the end of the decade compelled Acland to resign from Parliament in 1899 but he retained his deep interests in both education and co-operatives and maintained a close contact with political life until his death. Beatrice Webb [*Our Partnership*, 77] revealed that after the First World War Acland showed a growing interest in the emergence of the Labour Party as the alternative administration to the Tories. He helped finance young university men who contested elections in the Labour interest between 1918 and 1924; and a generous donation from Acland enabled the National Labour Club to be established in 1919.

Acland succeeded his brother, Charles Thomas Dyke Acland, as the thirteenth baronet in 1919. He had married in 1873 Alice Sophia, daughter of the Rev. Francis Macaulay Cunningham, rector of Witney, Oxfordshire, by whom he had two sons and a daughter. Lady Acland shared her husband's enthusiasm for the co-operative movement and played an important part in the foundation of the Women's Co-operative Guild. Arthur Acland died at his London home on 9 October 1926. Following a private family funeral, where no service was held, he was cremated at Golders Green Crematorium. In his will, the gross value of which was £23,749, he left £10,000 to four scholarship trustees, to be appointed by the Central Co-operative Board and the executive committee of the Labour Party, to enable young men and women to study industrial or social or educational conditions in countries outside the UK, a bequest to be known as the Acland Memorial Fund. His wife, a son and daughter survived him, and his papers were left to his wife and daughter.

Writings: (with C. Ransome) *A Handbook in Outline of the Political History of England* (1882; 9th ed. 1906; new ed.1 913); (with B. Jones) *Working Men Co-operators* (1884; 6th ed., Manchester, 1932); 'Land, Labourers and Association', *Cont. Rev.* 50 (July 1886) 112–27; (with others) 'Industrial Value of Technical Training', *Cont. Rev.* 55

(May 1889) 771–96; editor of *A Guide to the Choice of Books* (1891); (with H. L. Smith) *Studies in Secondary Education* (1892); editor of *Memoir and Letters of the Right Hon. Sir Thomas Dyke Acland* (1902); *The Patriotic Poetry of William Wordsworth*: a selection with introduction and notes (1915).

Sources: *Co-op. Congress Reports* (1883, 1889, 1891); H. B. Binns, *A Century of Education being the Centenary History of the British and Foreign School Society 1808–1908* (1908); Viscount Morley, *Recollections*, 2 vols (1917); *DNB* (1922–30); B. Webb, *My Apprenticeship* (1926); *Devon and Exeter Gazette*, 19 Jan 1927; R. B. Haldane, *Autobiography* (1929); J. W. Adamson, *English Education 1789–1902* (Cambridge, 1930); F. Hall and W. P. Watkins, *Co-operation* (1934); M. Thomson, *David Lloyd George: the official biography* [1948]; B. Webb, *Our Partnership*, ed. B. Drake and M. I. Cole (1948); T. Jones, *Lloyd George* (1951); F. Owen, *Tempestuous Journey: Lloyd George his life and times* (1954); W. P. McCann, 'Trade Unionist, Co-operative and Socialist Movements in Relation to Popular Education, 1870–1912' (Manchester PhD, 1960); D. Sommer, *Haldane of Cloan* (1960); G. M. Holmes, 'The Parliamentary and Ministerial Career of A. H. D. Acland, 1886–97', *Durham Research Review* 4 no. 15 (Sep 1964) 128–39; R. Jenkins, *Asquith* (1964). OBIT. *Express and Echo*, *Times*, *Western Morning News*, 11 Oct 1926; *Devon and Somerset News*, 14 Oct 1926; *Sunday Times*, 17 Oct 1926; *Devon and Exeter Gazette*, 19 and 20 Oct 1926; *Co-op. Congress Report* (1927).

JOYCE BELLAMY
H. F. BING

See also: Mrs Alice S. ACLAND; Fred HALL, for Co-operative Education; G. J. HOLY-OAKE, for Retail Co-operation – Nineteenth Century.

ADAMS, John Jackson 1st Baron Adams of Ennerdale (1890–1960)
TRADE UNIONIST AND COUNTY ALDERMAN

Born at Arlecdon, Cumberland, on 12 October 1890, 'Jack' Adams was one of thirteen children. His father, Thomas Adams, an overman in the Parkside Mining Company's iron-ore mine at Winder, Frizington, was killed in a cage accident when Jack was four and the manner of his father's death and the hardships that followed were to colour the rest of his life. At the inquest on Tom Adams a verdict of 'found dead' was recorded after the village midwife had given evidence of the injuries – a broken neck, possibly due to Adams sticking his head out as the cage started to move upwards. Mrs Adams received no compensation apart from a mangle presented to her by the management, perhaps with the intention that she should bring up her family on the proceeds of taking-in washing. However, Mrs Adams worked as a cleaner at Arlecdon County School where Jack was educated until he was thirteen years old when he went to work on a local farm. His half-yearly pay was £3 but when he was fourteen he went to work at Oatlands Colliery, Pica, as an underground haulage hand. A fellow worker at Oatlands was Robert Harlin, who was to become a miners' leader in the USA and later an administrator of Marshall Aid. Adams also worked for a spell at the Margaret Mine, Winder, which was owned by the same firm his father had worked for. As a very young man he came under the influence of Robert Newall, one of the founders of the Cumberland Iron-Ore Miners' Association and a fervent disciple of Keir Hardie.

In 1909, like many others from the district, which was undergoing a period of recession, he emigrated to New Zealand where he worked as a coalminer at Runanga. In New Zealand Adams's interest in politics developed as he made the friendship of men like Paddy Webb, later a trade union leader; Harry Holland, who edited the *Maoriland Worker*; and Bob Semple, who had formed the first Miners' Federation at Runanga and about 1908 assisted in the formation of the first Miners' Federation of New Zealand. Semple became MP for Wellington South in 1918–19 and Wellington East from 1928 to 1954 and held several ministerial posts in the New Zealand Governments between 1935 and 1949. Adams later referred to New

Zealand as his university and these men as his teachers. After four years Adams returned to England and took a job as an iron-ore miner. In 1914 he married Agnes Birney; their only child, Thomas, died a few days after being born in 1923.

When he was twenty-four Adams was chosen as a miners' delegate and quickly made his mark, making many friends among the miners and several enemies among the management. At about the same time as his union work began, he became active in politics. He joined the ILP and obtained a seat on the Arlecdon Parish Council. In February 1916 he became a member of the Arlecdon and Frizington Urban District Council and was elected its chairman in 1919. It was one of the first all-socialist councils in Britain and under Adams's chairmanship his own region and the County Council were left without any doubt about the attitude of the Urban District Council on questions such as Irish Home Rule, unemployment and poor relief. Adams had opposed the war not as a pacifist but on the grounds that it was imperialist and should be ended by negotiation, while future wars were to be prevented by the democratisation of foreign affairs. He supported meetings against the war addressed by Tom Richardson, MP for Whitehaven, C. P. Trevelyan, the Rev. H. Dunnico and Anderson Fenn of the National Council against Conscription. In this opposition to the war Adams was going against the mainstream of public opinion, and he was stoned and sodded off sevetal platforms in various parts of the district; but he never wavered in his conviction that the war should be settled by negotiation.

His progress in local government went side by side with his trade union activities. In 1919 he was vice-president of the Cumberland Iron-Ore Miners' Association and in March of that year was elected to the Cumberland County Council. After a period of unemployment because of victimisation, Adams became full-time organising secretary of the Cumberland Colliery Winding Enginemen's Association and continued in this post when, after amalgamation, it formed part of the Cumberland Enginemen's

and Boilermen's Association. This office allowed him to give more time to his local government activities; he was vice-chairman of the Cumberland County health committee from 1922 to 1943 and its chairman from 1943 to 1948. As a member of the public assistance committee he was tireless in his efforts for the welfare of those on assistance, while as a member of the highways committee he pressed for road improvement schemes which would give jobs to the unemployed. He was elected as a county alderman in 1931 and retained his seat until his death. From November 1923 to November 1931 Adams sat on the Workington Borough Council and for four of these years was chairman of the public health and welfare committee. He was always imaginative and resourceful in his local government work. In his early days on the Arlecdon and Frizington Council he pushed through a sixpenny increase in the rates, using threepence of that for the provision of a new recreation ground for children, twopence to provide jobs for ex-soldiers at £2 10s a week, and a penny for further education.

When West Cumberland was declared a 'Special Area' in 1935 Adams gave up his safe union post and pension rights to become secretary of an *ad hoc* Cumberland Development Council and in 1936 was appointed manager of the West Cumberland Industrial Development Co. Ltd. It was in this field that Adams won acclaim; he approached the task with great energy and enthusiasm, using the full force of his personality in persuading industrialists to open factories in Cumberland, and he allowed no obstacle to stand in the way of their development once they had been established.

As a result of this work Adams received the OBE in 1944 and was appointed Deputy Regional Controller of the Board of Trade for the Cumberland and Westmorland Sub-Region in the same year by Hugh Dalton. Dalton, then President of the Board of Trade, later described it as 'an odd but most successful appointment'. On leaving this post in 1948 Adams received an honorary MA from Durham University and in the 1949 New Year's Honours List was created a baron. He took the title Baron Adams of Ennerdale, almost certainly because his birthplace was in the Ennerdale Rural District. During this period he was also a member of the BBC Advisory Council. In 1949 he became a member of the North Regional Gas Board and in 1950 of the Northumberland and Cumberland Division of the National Coal Board, retiring from both in 1954. He was appointed vice-chairman of the West Cumberland Industrial Development Corporation in 1950. Further recognition of his work came with the Honorary Freedom of Workington and Whitehaven in 1953 and shortly before his death it was announced that an endowment of more than £25,000 was to be made to the Newcastle Division of Durham University to commemorate the services of Adams to his native county. The idea originated with Sir Frank Schon, one of his closest friends; it was subscribed to mainly by Cumberland industrialists; and there was established a Lord Adams Fellowship at King's College, Newcastle, now the University of Newcastle. He was further commemorated some ten years after his death, by the 'Lord Adams Room' in an extension to the Postgraduate Medical School in the West Cumberland Hospital opened in February 1971.

Essentially a practical rather than a theoretical Socialist, Adams devoted the greater part of his life to the improvement of schools, hospitals and employment opportunities in West Cumberland. He lived modestly in Whitehaven and later in Workington with his wife, who died in 1970. In all things he was a dynamic, elemental force. A remarkable tribute was paid to him by a close colleague after his death [*Times*, 7 Sep 1960]:

Jack Adams was a really powerful personality. Wherever he went he made an immediate impact, felt inwardly with an almost physical force. If he was angry the effect was pulverising; if he was pleased his high spirits were bewildering and intoxicating. He was never negative, neutral, or dull. The words poured out of him like a cataract; as a Canadian visitor to West Cumberland once said, he had heard nothing like it since his last visit to Niagara.

The words flowed noisily and ceaselessly in the full richness of the West Cumberland dialect and vocabulary. He did not tolerate interruptions, he overrode your questions, he shouted and coughed and laughed 'with no mitigation or remorse of voice'. He was not a ready listener, but he quickly picked up from you all he needed to know and added it to his cram-full storehouse of fact and information.

His memory for detail was prodigious. He garnished it as he pleased and threw it continuously and breathlessly in the face of his bemused and awe-stricken questioner. He talked for victory, not in a dialectical argument which he would have despised, but over some practical project which he intended to drive through whatever mountains of obstruction lay in his way.

A squat four-square man, a large powerful head and rough features, untidy, at times almost uncouth, but filled in every part of him with a burning restless energy to drive on to his goal and to drive everyone else with him. He boasted and he bullied. He could seem ferocious, unkind, insensitive – but mostly to those who in his opinion were retarding the revival of West Cumberland by lack of courage, lack of zeal, or for some selfish end.

At heart he was tender and affectionate and his life was full of 'little nameless unremembered acts of kindness and of love'. His judgement of men was shrewd and penetrating, if not always unerring. He admired what was admirable and despised what was mean and cheap and prejudiced and narrow. He had no envy or contempt for gifts which were not his.

He gave much honour to learning and learned men. His own formal education had been brief and restricted, but by his own efforts his knowledge and interests were wide and far-ranging, and his belief in education profound.

He died on 23 August 1960, and his ashes were buried at St Michael's Churchyard,

Arlecdon, following a memorial service on 30 August at the Arlecdon Parish Church. Lord Adams, who was a director of John Crowther and Sons (Milnsbridge) and of West Coast Associated Tanneries, left £22,000 net before duty was paid.

Sources: H. Dalton, *The Fateful Years: Memoirs 1931–1945* (1957); *Whitehaven News*, 5 Nov 1959; *WWW* (1951–60); *WW* (1960); a twelve-part serial on Adams by Frank Carruthers appeared in the *West Cumberland Times and Star* between 4 May and 20 July 1968; personal information: Prof. G. H. J. Daysh, University of Newcastle; Sir F. Schon. OBIT. *Guardian, News Chronicle, Times*, 24 Aug 1960; *West Cumberland News*, 27 Aug 1960; *Times*, 31 Aug 1960; *Whitehaven News*, 1 Sep 1960; *Times*, 5 and 7 Sep 1960.

FRANK CARRUTHERS
DAVID E. MARTIN
BRYAN SADLER

ADAMS, William Thomas (1884–1949)
TRADE UNIONIST, CO-OPERATOR AND
LABOUR MP

William Adams was born on 10 September 1884 at Oxshott, near Leatherhead, Surrey, the son of a bricklayer and his wife Annie (née Otway). He was educated at a London board school in the St Luke's area and left at the age of twelve and a half to become a messenger earning 5s a week. His subsequent employment embraced a variety of clerical posts and he was working as a clerk when he was elected to Parliament in 1945. He had joined the ILP in 1906 and held many offices in his local organisation before he resigned from it in 1933, following the disaffiliation of the ILP from the Labour Party. He worked actively in trade union affairs, holding a number of offices in the National Union of Clerks which he had joined in 1910, and his interests also spread to the co-operative movement which he joined in 1914. After three unsuccessful attempts he was elected to the Hammersmith Borough Council in 1934 and was an alderman of the borough from 1938 to 1945, being leader of the council in 1944–5. His first attempt to enter Parliament was for the South Hammersmith constituency which he unsuccessfully contested in 1935. At the 1945 general election he obtained a 3000 majority over his Conservative opponent when he fought as a Co-operative and Labour candidate for the same constituency. Until shortly before his death he was chairman of the North Hammersmith Co-operative Party and at the time of his death he was a member of the London Co-operative Society's political committee. He had been a JP since 1940. William Adams (known as Bill to everyone with whom he had contact) had devoted his life to the labour cause in various spheres: as Labour Party worker, trade unionist, local government representative, co-operator and parliamentarian.

Adams was involved in a serious road accident in 1947 and although he made a good recovery he became seriously ill in November 1948. He died on 9 January 1949 at his Hammersmith home and was cremated following a rationalist service conducted by Mr H. S. Blackham of the Rationalist Association. He had married in 1909 Florence, daughter of Richard L. Nightingale, and they had three sons. His wife and sons survived him and he left an estate valued at £1258.

Sources: *Kelly* (1949); *WWW* (1941–50). OBIT. *Times*, 10 Jan 1949; *West London Observer*, 14 Jan 1949; *Labour Party Report* (1949).

JOYCE BELLAMY

See also: A. V. ALEXANDER, for Co-operative Party; *C. R. ATTLEE, for Labour Party, 1931–51.

ALEXANDER, Albert Victor (Earl Alexander of Hillsborough) (1885–1965)
CO-OPERATOR AND POLITICIAN

Born at Weston-super-Mare, Somerset, 1 May 1885, the fourth child and only son of Albert Alexander, an engineer's smith. His father died at the age of thirty-three of galloping consumption contracted at his work, when Albert was only fifteen months old, leaving his widow aged twenty-eight, penniless, to support the four children. She returned to her work as a corset-maker which she continued for most of the rest of her life. Albert was educated at Barton Hill elementary school, Bristol, leaving at the age of thirteen to become an office boy in a leather company. He declined his mother's offer to pay for his secondary education but attended St George's technical evening classes. At fifteen he became clerk to the Bristol School Board at a wage of 5s a week and in 1903 transferred to the Somerset County Council where he rose to be chief clerk for higher education. For some time during these years he was secretary of the Somerset branch of the National Association of Local Government Officers.

In 1908 he married Esther Chapple, a Bath schoolteacher and an active worker in the Baptist Church. Alexander joined that church, took an increasing interest in religious affairs and became a well-known Baptist lay preacher. At the time of his marriage he was earning only £2 a week and originally he joined the Weston-super-Mare Co-operative Society as a means of saving. Within five years he became a member of the management committee of the society and, after the war, vice-president. During his wartime military service he rose from private to captain, being, in 1919, education officer to the South-Western District of Army Command.

In 1920, at the age of thirty-five, Alexander's political career began. He was appointed, out of 104 applicants, secretary to the parliamentary committee of the Co-operative Congress and soon showed the administrative ability, capacity for mastering facts and dogged persistence which were to mark his public career. He was soon involved in the struggle to resist the corporation profits tax which the Lloyd George Coalition Government tried to impose in 1920 on the undistributed surplus of co-operative societies.

In 1922 he entered Parliament as a Co-operative Party member for the Hillsborough Division of Sheffield which he represented until 1931 and then again from 1935 to 1950. There were four Co-operative Party members in the 1922 Commons and they at once formed a Co-operative Group, while maintaining at the same time close liaison with the PLP. In the first Labour Government (1924) he held the office of parliamentary secretary to the Board of Trade, Sidney Webb being President. Alexander's acceptance of office was formally sanctioned by the Co-operative Parliamentary Committee and the board of the Co-operative Union, thus underlining the fact of the Labour Party–Co-operative Party alliance in Parliament. In the second Labour Government (1929–31) he became First Lord of the Admiralty, and was in part responsible for the Naval Treaty of 1930, the restrictive clauses of which were to be much attacked in the years which followed. Alexander, however, always strongly defended the treaty, which he believed could have led towards the goal of a more general disarmament agreement. From this time he maintained a close interest in naval affairs and when Churchill formed his coalition government in May 1940 Alexander was appointed First Lord for the second time; and he remained at the Admiralty for the rest of the war. He was replaced by Brendan Bracken for the few weeks of the 'caretaker' Government before the general election of 1945, and then once again he returned to the Admiralty. In October 1946 Attlee replaced all three heads of the Service departments and Alexander became Minister without Portfolio. Late in December 1946 he was appointed to the newly-created position of Minister of Defence; and there began a highly controversial period of his career, some part of the story of which has been told in the memoirs of Lord Montgomery of Alamein. He was given a peerage in 1950 and in the new Attlee Government of that year Emanuel Shinwell replaced him as Minister of Defence. Alexander became Chancellor of the Duchy of Lancaster (1950–1). He was deputy leader of the Labour Peers (1951–5) and leader of the Labour Peers from November 1955 in succession to Earl Jowitt. He had been a Privy Councillor since 1929, an Elder Brother of Trinity House since 1941 and was made a Companion of Honour in the same year. In 1963 he was created an Earl and made a Knight of the Garter.

Throughout his political career Alexander was always vigorous in his support of co-operative ideals inside Parliament and outside. In 1934, while out of the House of Commons, he led a lively opposition to Lord Beaverbrook's campaign in the *Daily Express* against the co-operative movement; and he was indefatigable in these years in stumping the country in support of co-operative principles. Alexander was not a striking personality but he possessed stubborn and tenacious qualities as a politician; as he got older he became increasingly moderate in his socialist beliefs. He was among the group of ministers, led by Arthur Henderson, who opposed the cut in unemployment benefits in the critical days of August 1931 which led to the downfall of the second Labour Government. He was always an orthodox member of the Labour leadership, opposed to the United Front and Popular Front policies of the late 1930s, but after 1936 he was a strong critic of non-intervention in the Spanish Civil War. He became increasingly interested in foreign affairs and there are suggestions (by Hugh Dalton) that he would have welcomed the position of Foreign Secretary in the later years of the Attlee Government. He was a member of the Cabinet Commission to India in February 1946, the other members being Sir Stafford Cripps, who led the mission, and Lord Pethick-Lawrence – and reluctantly accepted the inevitability of Indian independence. Later in 1946 he was a member of the British Government's delegation to the Paris Peace Conference and for a short time, in early August, was temporary leader of the delegation.

A. V. Alexander was always keenly interested in sport, having been an active footballer in his youth. In 1954 he was elected president of Bristol City Football Club Supporters' Club. His early religious beliefs remained with him throughout his life, and in 1956 he was president of the UK Council of Protestant Churches. In 1943 he received the Freedom of his native town of Weston-super-Mare, and in 1948 that of the city of Sheffield. In 1945 he received an honorary degree from Bristol University, conferred by the then Prime Minister, Winston Churchill, in his capacity as chancellor of the University, and in 1947 a further honorary degree from Sheffield University.

In his later years he bought a farm at West Mersea, near the Essex coast. He died on 11 January 1965, leaving a widow and one daughter, and an estate valued at £51,228 net [*Times*, 3 Apr 1965].

Writings: *Educational Policy: an address* (Manchester, 1922) 12 pp.; *The Business Value of Political Action to the Co-operative Movement* (Manchester, 1925) 10 pp.; *Is Co-operation a Social Menace? A Reply to Attacks on the Co-operative Movement* (Manchester, 1925) 19 pp.; *Parliament and the Consumer* (Self and Society Series, 1929) 32 pp.; 'Co-operative Societies and Income Tax', *Labour Mag. 11* (Oct 1932) 255–7; 'Security and Naval Disarmament', *New Statesman and Nation*, 30 Jan 1932, 138; 'New Attack on Working Class Savings', *Labour Mag.* (Apr 1933) 539–41; 'Marketing Schemes and Quotas', *People's Year Book* (1935) 166–70; *The World Court – the Way to Peace* (John Clifford Lect. [1935]) 29 pp.; *The Monopoly Menace: present tendencies of legislation and their effects on the co-operative movement* (Manchester, [1936]) 23 pp.; 'Changing Forces in the Pacific: impressions of the sixth conference of the Institute of Pacific Relations', *International Affairs, 16* (Jan 1937) 94–109.

Sources: H. W. Richmond, 'Mr Alexander', *National Rev. 118*, no. 711 (May 1942) 452–5; G. D. H. Cole, *History of the Labour Party from 1914* (1948); H. Nicolson, *King George the Fifth: his life and reign* (1952); H. Dalton, *Memoirs: 1887–1931* (1953); C. L. Mowat, *Britain between the Wars* (1955); H. Dalton, *Memoirs: 1931–1945* (1957); B. L. Montgomery, *The Memoirs of Field-Marshal the Viscount Montgomery of Alamein* (1958); A. Bullock, *The Life and Times of Ernest Bevin*, vol. *1: 1881–1940* (1960); H. Dalton, *Memoirs: 1945–1960* (1962); M. Foot, *Aneurin Bevan* (1962); V. Brittain, *Pethick-Lawrence: a portrait* (1963); *Illustrated London News*, 8 Apr 1964 (with portrait);

WW (1964); Co-operative Press records, Manchester. OBIT. *Guardian, Times*, 12 Jan 1965; *Co-op. News*, 16 Jan 1965; *Co-op. Rev.* (Jan 1965); *Co-op. Party Monthly Letter* (Feb 1965); *Platform*, no. 37 (Nov 1968).

H. F. BING
JOHN SAVILLE

See also: W. H. BROWN, for Retail Co-operation, 1900–45; and below, Co-operative Party.

Co-operative Party: J. Leakey, *Co-operators and the Labour Platform* [c. 1905] 16 pp.; T. Tweddell, 'Direct Representation in Parliament', *Co-op. Congress Report* (1905) 415–41; E. Abbott, *Co-operators and the Labour Party* [1906?] 14 pp.; C. F. G. Sixsmith, 'Co-operators and Labourism', *Socialist Rev.* 7 (July 1911) 356–8; T. W. Mercer, *The Relation of Co-operative Education and Co-operative Politics* (Manchester, 1921) 14 pp.; L. Woolf, *Socialism and Co-operation* (1921); W. P. Watkins, *The Co-operative Party: its aims and work* (1921) 14 pp.; A. Barnes, *The Co-operator in Politics* (Fabian Tract no. 206, 1923) 26 pp.; T. W. Mercer, *Co-operative Representatives in Parliament* (Manchester, 1924) 37 pp.; A. Barnes, *The Political Aspect of Co-operation* (Manchester, 1926); Special Correspondent, 'Co-operation and Labour in Politics', *Labour Mag.* 6 (July 1927) 104–6; idem, 'Co-operators and Politics', *Labour Mag.* 7 (July 1928) 117–19; ILP, *The Co-operative Movement in the Progress towards Socialism* [1928] 39 pp.; W. Mellor, *The Co-operative Movement and the Fight for Socialism* [1934?] 16 pp.; Co-operative Party, *Britain Reborn: work and wealth for all* (Manchester, 1935); Labour Party, *The Labour Party and the Co-operative Party* [1938] 8 pp.; Anon., 'Constitution of the Co-operative Party', *Co-op. Congress Report* (1938) 233–5; F. Longden, *Co-operative Politics inside Capitalist Society* – a reply to *Consumers' Co-operation in Great Britain* [by A. M. Carr-Saunders *et al.*] (Birmingham, 1941); Co-operative Party, *Co-operative MPs Work for Victory: activities of the Co-operative Parliamentary Group in 1940* (Manchester, [1941]) 30 pp.; idem, *23 at Westminster* (1945) 8 pp.; G. D. H. Cole, *The Co-ops. and Labour* (1945) 24 pp.; J.

Bailey, *Facing the Future Together: the Co-operative–Labour agreement explained* (1946) 11 pp.; Co-op. Reorganisation Inquiry, 'The Co-operative Party', *Co-op. Congress Report* (1946) 159–65; J. Bailey, *This is your Freedom* (1947) 17 pp.; G. D. H. Cole, *Co-operation, Labour and Socialism* (Leicester, 1947) 15 pp.; J. Bailey, 'Co-operators in Parliament', *RIC 42* (July 1947) 160–3; idem, *Co-operators in Politics* (Manchester, 1950) 18 pp.; Co-operative Party, *Building the New Britain* [1950] 18 pp.; idem, *Constitution of the Co-operative Party, as approved by the Annual Co-operative Congress, 1951* (Manchester, 1951) 16 pp.; idem, *The Organisation of the Co-operative Party* [1953] 49 pp.; J. Bailey, *Three Movements – One Purpose* [on the trade union and co-operative movements and the Labour Party] ([Manchester], 1954); Co-operative Party, *Co-operation for Trade Unionists* (1957) [13] pp.; idem, *Co-operation and Modern Socialism* (1958); J. Bailey, *Democratic Politics: a co-operative contribution* (1960) 24 pp.; G. W. Rhodes, *Co-operative–Labour Relations, 1900–1962* (Co-operative College Papers, no. 8, 1962); T. F. Carbery, *Consumers in Politics: a history and general review of the Co-operative Party* (Manchester, 1969); S. Pollard, 'The Foundation of the Co-operative Party', in A. Briggs and J. Saville, *Essays in Labour History*, vol. 2: *1886–1923* (1971) 185–210.

ALLAN, William (1813–74)
TRADE UNION LEADER

William Allan was born of Scottish parents in Ulster in 1813 (either in August or early September), but soon after his birth his parents moved back to Scotland. His father was manager of a cotton-spinning mill. William started work at the age of twelve as a cotton piecer but when he was fifteen he was apprenticed to Holdsworth's, a large engineering firm in Glasgow. At the age of nineteen, before his apprenticeship was completed, he married Holdsworth's niece, and in 1835 moved to Liverpool where he was employed by a Mr Bury. He subsequently joined the Grand Junction Railway Company and it was with this company that he later moved to Crewe. He first joined the Manchester Society of Mechanics and later the Journeymen Steam Engine and Machine Makers' Friendly Society, known more popularly as the 'Old Mechanics'. This union had been formed in 1826 by John White, and by the early 1840s, when Allan applied for membership, it was the strongest engineering trade union, with some 3000 members. While William Allan was at Crewe, the secretary of the 'Old Mechanics', Henry Selsby, was arrested at the offices of the union in Manchester, for collecting subscriptions for engineering strikers at a nearby locomotive works, and altogether twenty-seven members of the union were arrested. W. P. Roberts, the famous radical lawyer, was engaged in their defence, and at the first trial in March 1847 eight members, including Selsby, were found guilty. The case was taken to a higher court and the verdict referred, but it was one more indication of the doubtful status of trade unions in the eyes of the law, despite the legalising act of 1825 (6 Geo. IV, c. 129). Selsby resigned in 1848 and Allan became general secretary. He was already a well-known advocate of amalgamation of the engineering unions, and in this case he was ably assisted by the energetic secretary of the union in London, William Newton. There were already a number of iron trade amalgamation committees in existence in certain industrial centres, and with the election of Allan as general secretary of the 'Old Mechanics' the amalgamation movement received a considerable impetus. In the spring of 1850 the executive committee of the 'Old Mechanics' took the initiative in calling a preliminary conference to discuss the general problem of amalgamation, and a second conference, with Allan in the chair, was convened in Birmingham on 9 September 1850. Sixty delegates from thirty-seven societies attended the conference, which lasted seventeen days. The details of the proposed new union were thoroughly discussed and a provisional committee, with Allan as secretary, was given the responsibility of forming the new society at the beginning of 1851.

On 6 January 1851 the Amalgamated Society of Engineers, Machinists, Smiths, Millwrights, and Patternmakers (known as the Amalgamated Society of Engineers – ASE) came into being. Its membership numbered only 5000, a smaller figure than the membership of the 'Old Mechanics' in 1850, and thirty-three branches, which had refused to come into the new organisation, approached Henry Selsby to act as their general secretary. A few branches of other engineering unions had joined. But Allan, Newton and their colleagues did not falter and throughout 1851 there was a striking accession of strength, so that by November 1851 the total membership of the new union was 10,841 and its future looked assured.

The establishment of what later became known as the 'New Model' was an important stage in the history of British trade unionism. While there was less of a break with traditional ideas and practice than has sometimes been supposed, the strength and solidity of the new type of union was to exercise a profound influence upon the future development of trade unionism and the Amalgamated Society of Engineers was to be the example which many unions were later to try to follow. The 'Old Mechanics' had pioneered the way in which the new unions were to develop, with their emphasis upon a centralisation of power in the hands of the executive, strict rules regarding union finance, and high contributions matched by a system of grants and benefits for travel, accidents, sickness and death. Weekly contributions to the new society were at 1s per week and it extended the list of benefits which members could obtain. William Allan was above all else an efficient administrator, immensely hard-working with a great capacity for detailed administration. His major contribution to his own union and to the trade union movement in general was to put the day-to-day union affairs on an efficient working basis. In industrial matters he was cautious and conciliatory, yet he never lost sight of the aims and objectives for which the unions were organised. The famous statement that Allan made to the Royal Commission on Trade Unions in 1867 is typical of his general approach. He was asked the question: 'Is not the interest of the employer and the employed to work together?' 'There I differ', Allan replied. 'Every day of the week I hear that the interests are identical. I scarcely see how they can be while we are in a state of society which recognises the principle of buying in the cheapest and selling in the dearest market. It is in their interest to get the labour done at as low a rate as possible, and it is ours to get as high a rate of wages as possible, and you can never reconcile these two things.'

The new union was faced with a major crisis within a year of its foundation. The ASE had specifically adopted most of the policies which had long been accepted; systematic overtime was to be repudiated; piecework was to be resisted; the number of apprentices must be restricted. The executive of the ASE decided in November 1851 to instruct its members to refuse to work systematic overtime and piecework after 31 December 1851, and in the early days of the new year first the Lancashire employers and then most firms over the country locked out their workers. It was a major industrial dispute on both sides, and public opinion was thoroughly aroused. After three months the union admitted defeat and ordered their members who had remained in support of their executive committee back to work. It was a considerable setback for the union, but the leadership of Allan and Newton surmounted without serious difficulty the inevitable short-term loss of members and the very sharp decline in their finances. By the beginning of 1852 membership was already higher than the total reached before the strike and union funds had accumulated even faster.

The union had been much assisted during the strike of 1851 by *The Operative*, a weekly journal which William Newton first published on 4 January 1851, as well as by the support of some middle-class sympathisers and notably certain of the Christian Socialists. For a time after the defeat of the strike the executive of the ASE experimented on a small scale with the co-operative ideas which the Christian Socialists were advocating; but the main lesson drawn by Allan was the need to build a union on an even more solid foundation, and this he accomplished in a most striking way. When, during

the building strike of 1859–60, the Amalgamated Society of Engineers donated £1000 for three successive weeks to the building unions, the strength of the new type of union was abundantly demonstrated.

During the 1860s Allan took a leading part in most of the trade union and political developments of the decade, although his central concern was always the interests of his union. It was Allan who had proposed, in August 1859, the establishment of the London Trades Council and he was a consistent supporter of the Council throughout the rest of his life. By the end of 1866 the ASE numbered just over 33,000 members in 305 branches, with accumulated funds of £138,113. During the 1852 lock-out an office-boy had been engaged and in the same year a Vacant Book officer was appointed in Manchester. But although Allan's salary was increased to £3 10s per week in 1860 he was not given an assistant general secretary until 1863; and a third national official was added in 1866. Allan's capacity for work was extraordinary, and it was his personal qualities of integrity and industry as much as the union he represented which gave him stature in the general trade union movement in the crucial years of the 1860s. Allan was a kind-hearted and generous man although he could be devastatingly blunt in his comment, and his interests were somewhat narrow; but he was 'a keen working-class politician' [S. and B. Webb (1894) 217] and he supported all the attempts in this decade to improve the social and political position of the working man. While the Webbs' emphasis upon the Junta – the group of leading trade unionists in London, including Allan – has been considerably modified by later historians [G. D. H. Cole (1937); B. C. Roberts (1958); V. L. Allen (1963)], the general influence which Allan himself exerted was nevertheless considerable.

He joined the Reform League in 1865 and in December 1866 moved a strong resolution at the London Trades Council denouncing the 'treachery' of the House of Commons to Reform measures (while adding, characteristically, that 'we have no desire to make our societies channels for political action': a statement that was vigorously reaffirmed later by the executive of the ASE). When the legal position of the unions came in question as a result of the *Hornby* v. *Close* decision, Allan was among those who formed the Conference of Amalgamated Trades, which first met on 28 January 1867; and throughout the life of the Conference he remained an important influence. He was assiduous in supplying Frederic Harrison and Tom Hughes with information for their use as members of the Royal Commission on Trade Unions in 1867–9 (although he was probably less important in this respect than Applegarth) and he himself was an important witness before the Commission. He shared the Junta's hostility to George Potter, and was apparently resentful of those who brought about the convening of the first Trade Union Congress in 1868; but for rather complex reasons the years 1869 and 1870 were to see a change of attitudes. The Labour Representation League, established in the summer of 1869, had R. Marsden Latham as president, Allan as treasurer, Lloyd Jones as secretary, with Potter a member of the executive committee. When the *Bee-Hive* ran into financial difficulties, the leaders of the amalgamated trades agreed to help on condition that the Rev. Henry Solly should be appointed joint editor with Potter, responsible to a committee with Allan as chairman. The newspaper first appeared in its new form in February 1870.

In the last years of his life Allan was a victim of Bright's disease and he endured much suffering, but he continued to work at his ASE duties without pause. His other interests were undiminished although his attendances at outside committees tended to decline. He spoke in 1869 at the first Co-operative Congress, urging the delegates to accept the principle of co-operative banking and reminding them of the needs of trade unions; he became treasurer of the TUC in 1871 and of the newly established parliamentary committee in the same year. He died at his home in Blackfriars Road on 15 October 1874, still in his union office. He had been re-elected without opposition as general secretary of the ASE at every election between 1850 and his death, and in his life and work he must be counted as an important influence in the history of modern trade unionism. He was untheoretical in general, hard-headed in union affairs and in his politics a typical middle-of-the-road working-class radical of the third quarter of the century. A poor speaker, often ungrammatical, often blundering, but a man of sterling honesty – the phrase Applegarth used of him – and a shrewd judge of his peers, Allan had little time for activities outside his union work; but for many years he had been a member of the St Saviour's Board of Works and he was vice-president of the National Sunday League at the time of his death. In religion he was one of the few prominent London unionists who was a practising Anglican and for some years he served as churchwarden for the parish of Christchurch. In his will he left precise instructions concerning his estate, which was to be put in trust for his five children, and he asked for a plain burial in the family grave at Norwood Cemetery. His effects were valued at under £3000.

The funeral was an impressive ceremony with delegates from all corners of the kingdom, and the funeral procession was headed by Tom Hughes, Professor Beesly, Frederic Harrison, J. M. F. Ludlow and all the leading trade unionists of the day. The obituary notice in the *Bee-Hive* gave voice to what it is reasonable to believe were widely held sentiments: 'In politics Mr Allan was a sound and consistent liberal, not given to political quackery in any form. On social questions he was inclined to Robert Owen's school, knowing as he did from experience how much depends upon man's surroundings and external influences. In his life and character he was truthful, upright, and honest, a hater of shams and trickery in any shape and form. In his conversation he was plain even to bluntness, but he always hesitated to wound an adversary. He was kind and generous in his nature, open-handed and open-hearted in act and deed, trusting and trusted, one of nature's own noblemen; not courting favours or fearing frowns he pursued his duty and died at his post. . . .'

Sources: For MS material see below under New Model Unionism. The standard history of the engineers' union is J. B. Jeffery's *The Story of the Engineers* [1945]. The ASE *Monthly Reports*, in which Allan wrote continuously, are a primary source, as are *The Operative* (1851–2) and *The Bee-Hive* (1861–74). See also: *Trades Societies and Strikes* (1860; reprinted New York, 1968); S. and B. Webb, *History of Trade Unionism* (1894); F. Harrison, *Autobiographic Memories*, vol. *1: 1831–1870*; vol. *2: 1870–1910* (1911); A. W. Humphrey, *A History of Labour Representation* (1912); B. C. Roberts, *History of the Trades Union Congress* (1958); Royden Harrison, *Before the Socialists* (1965). OBIT. *Times*, 21 Oct 1874; *Bee-Hive*, 24 Oct 1874 [with portrait]; *South London Press*, 24 Oct 1874; ASE, *Monthly Report* (Nov 1874); *Free Sunday Advocate* (Nov 1874); ASE, Southwark Branch, *Quarterly Report* (Oct–Dec 1874); *Ironworkers' J.*, 15 Nov 1874; ibid., Dec 1874 [by J. M. Ludlow].

JOHN SAVILLE

See also: *Robert APPLEGARTH; *E. S. BEESLY; *Henry BROADHURST; *Edwin COULSON; *Daniel GUILE; *Frederic HARRISON; *Tom HUGHES; *George HOWELL; *J. M. F. LUDLOW, for Christian Socialism, 1848–54; *George NEWTON; *William NEWTON; *George ODGER; *George POTTER; and below: New Model Unionism.

New Model Unionism: (1) MSS: Webb trade union collection, LSE; Frederic Harrison papers, LSE; George Howell collection, Bishopsgate Institute, London; ASE correspondence, executive committee minutes, etc., Amalgamated Engineering Union, London. (2) Theses: D. R. Moberg, 'George Odger and the English Working Class Movement' (London PhD, 1954); S. W. Coltham, 'George Potter and the *Bee-Hive* Newspaper' (Oxford DPhil., 1956); P. J. Head, 'The Status, Functions and Policy of the Trade Union Official, 1870–1930' (Cambridge MLitt., 1956); R. A. Buchanan, 'Trade Unions and Public Opinion, 1850–75' (Cambridge PhD, 1957); A. D. Bell, 'The Reform League from its Origins to the Passing into Law of the Reform Act of 1867' (Oxford DPhil., 1961). (3) Other:

S.C. on Councils of Conciliation, 1856 XIII; R.C. on Trade Unions, 1867 XXX; 1867–8 XXIX; 1868–9 XXXI; T. J. Dunning, *Trades Unions and Strikes: their philosophy and intention* (1860; 2nd ed. 1873); E. S. Beesly, 'Trades' Unions', *West. Rev. 20* (Oct 1861) 510–42; J. M. Ludlow, 'Trade Societies and the Social Science Association', *Macmill. Mag. 3* (Feb and Mar 1861) 313–25, 362–72; F. Harrison, 'The Good and Evil of Trade Unionism', *Fortn. Rev. 3* (Nov 1865) 33–54; T. Hughes, 'Trades' Unions, Strikes and Co-operation', *Macmill. Mag. 13* (Nov 1865) 75–80; E. S. Beesly, *The Amalgamated Society of Carpenters and Joiners . . . reprinted with appendices from the Fortnightly Review* (1867); [W. G. Blaikie], 'The Policy of Trade Unions', *N. Brit. Rev. 7* (Mar 1867) 1–46; J. Waley, 'On Strikes and Combinations with Reference to Wages and the Conditions of Labour', *JRSS 30* (Mar 1867) 1–20; [C. Mackay], 'Strikes and Trade Unions', *Blackw. Mag. 101* (June 1867) 718–36; E. S. Beesly, 'The Trades Union Commission', *Fortn. Rev. 8* (July 1867) 1–18; Comte de Paris, *The Trades Unions of England* (1869); H. Crompton, 'Arbitration and Conciliation', *Fortn. Rev. 11* (May 1869) 622–8; G. Potter, 'Strikes and Lock-outs, from the Workman's Point of View', *Cont. Rev. 15* (Aug 1870) 32–54; [L. J. Brentano], 'The Growth of a Trades-Union', *N. Brit. Rev. 53* (Oct 1870) 59–114; J. Burnett, *A History of the Engineers' Strike in Newcastle and Gateshead* (1872); G. Howell, 'The Financial Condition of Trades Unions', *19th C. 12* (Oct 1882) 481–501; G. Howell, 'The Work of Trades Unions: a retrospect review', *Cont. Rev. 44* (Sep 1883) 331–49; J. M. Baernreither, *English Associations of Working Men* (1889); G. Howell, *The Conflicts of Capital and Labour* (2nd ed. 1890); idem, *Trade Unionism, New and Old* (1891); J. Anderson, *Forty Years' Industrial Progress* (1891) P; S. and B. Webb, *History of Trade Unionism* (1894); ASE, *Jubilee Souvenir* (1901); *Henry Broadhurst MP: the story of his life told by himself* (1901); G. Howell, *Labour Legislation, Labour Movements and Labour Leaders* (1902); A. W. Humphrey, *Robert Applegarth* (1913); P. Redfern, *The Story of the C.W.S.* (Manchester, [1913]); R. W.

Postgate, *The Builders' History* [1923?]; F. E. Gillespie, *Labor and Politics in England, 1850–67* (Durham, North Carolina, 1927); G. D. H. Cole, 'Some Notes on British Trade Unionism in the Third Quarter of the Nineteenth Century', *Int. Rev. for Social Hist. 2* (1937) 1–27 [republished in *Essays in Economic History*, vol. *3* (ed. E. M. Carus-Wilson, 1962)]; J. B. Jefferys, *The Story of the Engineers, 1800–1945* [1945]; M. and J. B. Jefferys, 'The Wages, Hours and Trade Customs of the Skilled Engineer in 1861', *Econ. Hist. Rev. 17* (1947) 27–44; *Labour's Formative Years*, ed. J. B. Jefferys (1948); G. Tate, *London Trades Council, 1860–1950* (1950); Amalgamated Engineering Union, *William Newton 1822–1876* (1951) 9 pp. [Tower Hamlets Central Library]; W. H. G. Armytage, *A. J. Mundella* (1951); E. J. Hobsbawm, 'The Tramping Artisan', *Econ. Hist. Rev. 3* ser. 2 (1951) [reprinted in the author's *Labouring Men* (1964) 34–63]; E. C. Mack and W. H. G. Armytage, *Thomas Hughes* (1952); E. J. Hobsbawm, 'Economic Fluctuations and some Social Movements since 1800', *Econ. Hist. Rev. 5* ser. 2 (1952) 1–25 [reprinted in *Labouring Men* (1964) 126–57]; Asa Briggs, *Victorian People* (1954); D. Simon, 'Master and Servant', in *Democracy and the Labour Movement*, ed. John Saville (1954) 160–200; A. E. Musson, *The Congress of 1868* (1955); R. V. Clements, 'Trade Unions and Emigration, 1840–80', *Population Studies 9* no. 2 (1955) 167–80; H. W. McCready, 'British Labour and the Royal Commission on Trade Unions, 1867–9', *Univ. of Toronto Q.* (1955) 390–409; idem, 'British Labour's Lobby, 1867–75', *Canadian J. Econ. Pol. Sc.* (1956) 141–60; B. C. Roberts, *The Trades Union Congress 1868–1921* (1958); H. J. Fyrth and H. Collins, *The Foundry Workers* (Manchester, 1959); S. Coltham, 'The *Bee-Hive* Newspaper: its origins and early struggles' and R. Harrison, 'Professor Beesly and the Working Class Movement' [both in *Essays in Labour History*, ed. Asa Briggs and John Saville (1960) 174–241]; R. V. Clements, 'British Trade Unions and Popular Political Economy, 1850–75', *Econ. Hist. Rev. 14* ser. 2 (1961) 93–104; V. L. Allen, 'Valuations and Historical Interpretation', *British J.*

Sociology, 14 (1963) 48–58; H. Pelling, *A History of British Trade Unionism* (1963); N. C. Masterman, *John Malcolm Ludlow* (Cambridge, 1963); Royden Harrison, *Before the Socialists* (1965); F. M. Leventhal, *Respectable Radical: George Howell and Victorian Working Class Politics* (1971).

ALLEN, Robert (1827–77)
CO-OPERATOR

Robert Allen was born at Newcastle on Tyne in 1827. He was a Wesleyan, well known for his liberal views, who early became an eloquent advocate of temperance, being a frequent speaker on the Sandhill and the Quayside at Newcastle. He often walked ten to twelve miles to address meetings. Later he was appointed a temperance advocate and in that capacity went to Belfast where he stayed for about one and a half years and spoke frequently in various parts of Ireland.

Returning to England, he settled in Oldham where he married the daughter of Mr Chadwick of Oldham and began to take an interest in local and municipal affairs. He joined the local co-operative society (the Oldham Equitable) on 3 April 1872, was elected to the board of management 8 April 1873 and became president on 13 January 1874, a position he held until his death three years later. During his presidency the membership increased from 2468 to 3269 and the sales from £25,879 per quarter to £40,308 per quarter. He had been elected to the board of the Co-operative Wholesale Society in August 1871 and died in office. He joined with J. T. W. Mitchell in opposing proposals to separate the banking department of the CWS from the main organisation and set up an independent co-operative banking institution; and was a representative of the CWS with Mitchell at a conference at Barnsley, 13 September 1873, called by the central board of the Co-operative Union to discuss the proposal.

Allen was a member of the north-west section of the central board of the Co-operative Union and a member of the committee of the Co-operative Newspaper Society. He travelled all over the country addressing co-operative societies and was described by one who knew him as 'a grand speaker, who did much to popularise the CWS, and killed a lot of prejudice that was meat and drink to private traders'. In politics he was always a Liberal and frequently spoke at public meetings of the party.

He died on 2 April 1877 and, at the opening of the Ninth Co-operative Congress at Leicester on that day, E. Vansittart Neale announced the receipt of a telegram reporting his death. At the suggestion of E. O. Greening, who said that Allen did not die a rich man and had left a widow and family (there were six children, the eldest a girl of not more than fourteen), Congress decided to supplement its expression of sympathy by a collection. £50 was collected at the Congress and through a further appeal by the central board to co-operative societies, the fund reached £271 by December 1877.

Robert Allen was buried at Greenacres Hill Cemetery, Oldham, on Thursday, 5 April 1877. The funeral service, both at the chapel and at the graveside, was conducted by the Rev. Dent, a Wesleyan minister, who afterwards invited G. J. Holyoake to add a few words. Holyoake stood on a plank on the edge of the grave and delivered a moving funeral oration the full text of which was printed in the *Co-operative News* of 14 April 1877. Allen was also survived by his mother and his elder brother, Christopher.

Sources: C. Walters, *History of the Oldham Equitable Co-operative Society Ltd from 1850 to 1900* (Manchester, 1900); P. Redfern, *The Story of the C.W.S.* (Manchester, [1913]). OBIT. *Oldham Chronicle*, 7 Apr 1877; *Co-op. News*, 7, 14, 21 Apr 1877, 1 Dec 1877; *Co-op. Congress Report* (1877).

H. F. BING

See also: Fred HAYWARD, for Co-operative Union; Percy REDFERN, for Co-operative Wholesaling.

ALLEN, Sir Thomas William (1864–1943)
CO-OPERATOR

Thomas William Allen was born at Abertillery, South Wales, on 6 February 1864, the son of the Rev. Thomas Allen, a Baptist minister. He himself was deeply religious and became a local preacher in early life. He studied to enter the Civil Service, but ill-health compelled him to abandon the idea and he entered the Tillery Colliery office, later becoming an apprentice in a grocery and provision store. On the completion of his apprenticeship he joined the staff of the Abertillery Co-operative Society which a few years later merged with the Blaina Society. His religious fervour found expression in his co-operative work and by his eloquence he inspired his colleagues and staff with his own idealism and spiritual driving power. He became general manager of the joint society in 1893 and soon made it the outstanding society in South Wales; known as 'Allen of Blaina' he became a recognised and respected leader in the co-operative and business circles of Newport and the surrounding area. As a member of the south-western sectional board of the Co-operative Union, he contributed much to the development of co-operation in an area in which it was relatively backward.

In 1908 Councillor T. W. Allen, as he then was, was chosen to preside over the 40th Annual Co-operative Congress held at Newport, Monmouthshire; and his inaugural address, occupying eighteen pages of the Congress Report, was an able and wide-ranging speech based on practical experience. In 1906 Allen was elected a director of the Co-operative Insurance Society and in 1910 a director of the CWS, holding both offices until his retirement under the age rule in 1933. Elected chairman of the joint parliamentary committee of the Co-operative Congress in 1916, he worked closely with its secretary, H. J. May, to safeguard the interests of the co-operative movement during the First World War and to secure its recognition by the Ministry of Food. In 1917 Allen entered the Ministry of Food as the official co-operative representative, became chairman of the Consumers' Council and confidential secretary to successive Food Controllers. In 1919 he was knighted for his wartime services – the first co-operator to receive this honour.

Allen was always a stalwart internationalist and advocate of peace. He joined the central committee of the International Co-operative Alliance during the First World War and at the Basle Congress of the ICA in 1921 he was elected to the first International Executive, succeeding Alfred Whitehead as vice-president in 1930. His term of office ended with his retirement from the CWS board in 1933 but had covered some of the most important and fateful years in the history of the ICA. In furtherance of the aims of the Alliance he travelled widely and continued after his retirement to follow the work of the Alliance and to give advice.

During the years between the wars Allen was a member of many Government committees and organisations including the Macmillan Committee on Finance and Industry (1929–31) and the R.C. on Private Manufacture and Trading in Arms (1935–6). He was a member of the Empire Marketing Board and this gave him welcome opportunities to encourage the growth of co-operation among the primary producers of Australasia. Until his death he was chairman of the New Zealand Produce Association as well as of the Anglo-Baltic Produce Association.

In politics he was a radically-minded Liberal, especially in his early days, and he remained always a great admirer of Lloyd George. Despite his Liberal sympathies he took a direct interest in the establishment of the Co-operative Party in 1917–18 and was active in its councils in the early years.

He died at his home in Newport, 24 November 1943, at the age of 79: his wife having predeceased him by several years. He left an estate valued at £6095.

Writings: *Co-op. Congress Report* (1908); 'The Humanitarian Basis of Co-operation', *RIC* (Dec 1940) 373–80; 'The Eight-Point Declaration', *RIC* (Oct 1941) 281–3.

Sources: F. H. Collier, *A State Trading Adventure* (Oxford, 1925); P. Redfern, *The New History of the C.W.S.* (Manchester, 1938). OBIT. *South Wales Echo*, 25 Nov 1943; *Times*, 26 Nov 1943; *Western Mail*, 26 Nov 1943; *Co-op. News*, 4 Dec 1943; *RIC* (Nov–Dec 1943).

H. F. BING

See also: A. V. ALEXANDER, for Co-operative Party; H. J. MAY, for International Co-operative Alliance; Percy REDFERN, for Co-operative Wholesaling.

AMMON, Charles (Charlie) George (Lord Ammon of Camberwell) (1873–1960)

LABOUR POLITICIAN AND TRADE UNIONIST

Born on 22 April 1873 in Southwark, South London, the son of Charles George Ammon, a cutler and toolmaker, and his wife Mary (née Kempley) of Thanet. The father, who subsequently worked as a purser on the *Great Eastern*, contracted TB and died in January 1887 in his mid-forties leaving a widow, son and four daughters. Young Charles was educated at a local board school, attended both Sunday school and the Band of Hope, and first began half-time work in a bottle factory at the age of eleven. He had a variety of jobs before he was fourteen when he joined the London South East District of the Post Office as a telegraph messenger. He became a sorter in December 1892 and most of his working life was spent in the Post Office until he entered Parliament. Charles Ammon extended his earlier education through evening classes and private study and taught himself languages, history, theology and economics, subjects which helped to lead him to Socialism. Like his father before him, Ammon supported the radical wing of the Liberal Party in his early youth but when the ILP was formed in 1893 he joined and in the same year became a member of the Fawcett Association, the sorters' trade union. Also in 1893 he made his first public speech when, on behalf of the Fawcett Association, he moved a vote of thanks to Mr Gladstone for granting the right of organisation and full civil rights to government employees. In the previous year the Association's chairman and secretary had been dismissed for their trade union activities but young Ammon was undaunted and became secretary of the local South Eastern branch of the Association. Through his enterprise the branch became one of the most effective in the Association but during the course of his work for it he suffered various forms of reprimand and was frequently threatened with dismissal; but in the end his persistence to obtain improved working conditions won the supervisors' respect.

Ammon edited the Association's magazine, *The Post*, served on the executive committee, was delegate from his union to the Labour Party Conference of 1905 and later years, and became the Association's chairman. In 1916 he was more or less forced to resign from the Post Office because of his political activities by the Postmaster-General, Sir Joseph Pease, afterwards Lord Gainford. After a succession of trade union appointments which included a two-year spell from 1918–20 as general and organising secretary of the Port of London Docks and Wharves Staff Association, he returned to the postal workers in 1920 when the Union of Post Office Workers was formed to bring together, into one organisation, the smaller associations representing different branches of the service. Ammon was appointed as organising secretary of the Union and held this position until his retirement under the age rule in 1928, at which time he was elected an honorary member.

In 1908 he had helped form a Bermondsey branch of the ILP together with Alfred Salter, whom he converted to Socialism. When the West Bermondsey Labour Party was established in 1910, Ammon was the obvious candidate for chairman. He attended his first international socialist conference, as an ILP delegate, in 1911. The delegation included Keir Hardie, W. C. Anderson, Margaret Bondfield, Ramsay MacDonald and his wife, and Fenner Brockway. In these years he was the typical grass-roots activist and his street corner oratory earned him the name of 'Charlie of the Old Kent Road'; but neither his eloquence nor his trade union organising work prevented him from being bottom of the poll when he stood for the LCC in 1913.

Ammon was a man of deep religious conviction and his socialism grew out of his Christian beliefs. He became a Methodist lay preacher in 1902 and continued to preach almost to the end of his life. He was also a Sunday school teacher in his youth. He was a pacifist and during the First World War he adhered firmly to his principles. He joined the Union of Democratic Control soon after it was founded, supported its general viewpoint and served on its executive council in 1918; but during the war years he was more attracted to the No-Conscription Fellowship for which he became parliamentary secretary in 1916, his job being to supply the Fellowship's parliamentary supporters with information on the treatment of conscientious objectors. He became a member of the well-known 1917 Club in Greek Street, Soho. He had developed the political side of the Fawcett Association long before its members were allowed parliamentary interests and so effective was his work that immediately following the First World War a short-lived anti-socialist association of ex-servicemen civil servants was formed to combat the pacifist and labour group around him. Ammon gradually severed his connection with the ILP some time after the First World War (according to one of his daughters), and he served on the national executive of the Labour Party from 1921 to 1926.

In 1915 he attended with Ernest Bevin the American Labor Convention on behalf of the TUC and in 1917 signed the manifesto welcoming the Russian revolution. He helped to organise the famous Leeds Convention of June 1917 but it was in the postwar world especially that he began to make his mark upon the labour movement. He was defeated when he stood for North Camberwell in the general election of 1918 but in the following year was elected to the LCC as a representative of Camberwell and served until 1925; re-elected to the LCC for North Camberwell in 1934 he became an alderman on the Borough Council in the same year. He left the LCC in 1946, having been chairman in 1941–2, and retired from his aldermanic seat in 1953, after having been Mayor of Camberwell during the Festival of Britain year, 1951. He received the Freedom of the Borough at the end of his year of office.

Ammon entered Parliament as Labour MP for North Camberwell, sponsored by the UPW at the general election of 1922 and held the seat at subsequent elections until 1931. After his defeat in 1918 Ammon had nursed the constituency, and his first step was to open an office in the Old Kent Road which developed into a citizens' advice bureau, open to all local people. This was very much an innovation in local politics in the years immediately after the First World War and Hannen Swaffer, the labour journalist, dubbed it 'Ammon's psychological clinic'. He was appointed London Whip for the PLP in 1923 and, rather surprisingly, in view of his pacifist record, he accepted the position of parliamentary secretary to the Admiralty in the first (1924) and second (1929–31) MacDonald governments. His main parliamentary interests were in education and matters relating to the Post Office; he had been a member of the education committee of the LCC in the early 1920s. Like so many of his colleagues in the 1929 parliamentary party, Ammon lost his seat in the landslide election of 1931, but he returned to the Commons as MP for North Camberwell in 1935 and continued to represent the constituency until he accepted a peerage in 1944. During his years in the Commons, Ammon was much sought after as a committee man and as a leader of goodwill missions. He went on to the Opposition Front Bench in 1937 and led parliamentary delegations to West Africa (1938), Newfoundland (1943), the Channel Islands and China (1947); and between 1939 and 1944 he was a member of the Select Committee on National Expenditure.

Ammon became chairman of the National Dock Labour Board from its inception in April 1944 and it was at this point that he accepted a peerage and moved to the House of Lords. When the Labour Party won the general election of 1945 Ammon became a Privy Councillor and was appointed Captain of the Gentlemen-at-Arms, Government Chief Whip in the Lords and Deputy Speaker of the House. But it was his position with the Dock Labour Board that led to the most publicised crisis of his career. The London Dock Strike of the summer of 1949 had already resulted in the proclamation of a state of emergency, and the appointment of an emergency committee. The precise powers of this committee over the activities of the Docks Board were not clearly defined and when Ammon, backed by the Board, issued an order to the men to return to work with the proviso that failure to comply would 'jeopardise the very existence of the scheme which former dock workers, and many present dock workers, have struggled to achieve', the Government regarded this as provocative and issued a disclaimer. Following a Commons debate on the Dock strike on 26 July 1949, Ammon made a statement in the House of Lords on 27 July in which he pointed out inaccuracies in the comments made on the previous day. He was quite unrepentant about his action, which he always considered justified, but at the Prime Minister's request Ammon resigned from all Government positions although he retained his chairmanship of the Dock Labour Board until he was replaced in 1950.

The range of his public interests outside his direct political interests was considerable. As befitted a Methodist of the late nineteenth century he was a total abstainer and at one time was president of the UK Band of Hope Union. He was active in the Brotherhood movement which was especially vigorous in parts of south London; he went as a delegate to its international congress in Washington in 1920 and was national president in 1929 and again in 1945. He was a vice-president of the Metropolitan Association of Building Societies; a director of the Municipal Mutual Insurance and of the Atlas Building Society; a vice-president of the Royal National Lifeboat Institution; a governor of the LSE and of Dulwich College, a member of the Authors Club, a JP, a member of the Royal Arsenal Co-operative Society and at one time president of the National Arbitration League. He was keen on sport, especially cricket, and was for forty years a member of the Surrey Cricket Club.

He married Ada Ellen May, the daughter of a Walworth contractor, in 1898. A son of his marriage died very young and there were two daughters who survived him.

His wife died in 1958 and Ammon on 2 April 1960, in his 87th year, at King's College Hospital, London. The funeral service was held at the Methodist Church, Half Moon Lane, Herne Hill, where he had often preached, and the Rev. Dr Donald Soper gave the address. He left an estate of £15,433 (net) bequeathing several legacies to charitable institutions. A room was named after him at the Methodist Homes for the Aged, Tankerton near Whitstable, and the Southwark Borough also named one of its old people's homes Ammon House. The *Guardian* paid the following tribute to Lord Ammon's life in its obituary:

> Born among the poor he never forgot their needs and his work in the interests of Labour was a crusade as well as a career; the adoption of British Socialism indeed was to him the practical application of his religion.

Writings: His MS autobiography, written a few years before his death, is now deposited with most of his other papers in the library of the University of Hull. Southwark Borough Library has some of his diaries and press cuttings. Ammon was a frequent contributor to the *St Martins Le Grand Magazine*, a journal specialising in articles on historical and literary aspects of the Post Office, in addition to contributions to *The Post*, the journal of the Fawcett Society (which he edited), to labour and methodist publications and to dock and shipping papers. His BBC broadcasts on Russia, Finland, USA, King George V's Spithead Review of the Fleet and others were published in *The Listener*. Books and pamphlets include: *Christianity and Socialism* (reprinted from *Socialist Review* (1909)); (ed.) *Christ and Labour* (1912); *The Conscientious Objector and the Waste of National Resources* (Nat. Lab. Press [1916?]); *Newfoundland, the Forgotten Island* (1944). His articles, apart from those noted above, included 'Unifying the German Socialist Forces', *Lab. Mag. 1* (1922–3) 322–3 and 'Delay is Dangerous', *The Arbitrator* (1954–5).

Sources: W. Ward, *Brotherhood and Democracy* [1911?]; C. Trevelyan, *The*

U.D.C.: its history and policy (1919); *The Post*, 11 Mar 1922; J. W. Graham, *Conscription and Conscience* (1922); S. V. Bracher, *The Herald Book of Labour Members* (1923); *The No-Conscription Fellowship: a souvenir of its work during the years 1914–1919* (n.d.); S. W. Swanwick, *Builders of Peace* (1924); M. A. Hamilton, 'C. G. Ammon JP, MP, LCC', *The Post*, 3 Jan 1925; *The Post*, 2 June 1928; G. Greenwood, 'The Man who organised the P.O. Workers', *Millgate Monthly*, June 1928; *Potted Biographies* (c. 1932); *Evening News*, 1 Jan 1944; *South London Press*, 10 Sep 1948; F. Brockway, *Bermondsey Story* (1949); Hansard, House of Commons, vol. 467 (1948–9) 2263–332; Hansard, House of Lords, vol. 164 (1948–9) 557–66; *South London Press*, 28 Apr 1950; 26 Sep 1950; 16 May 1951; 29 June 1951; *The Advertiser*, 17 Aug 1951; 29 Nov 1951; 30 Nov 1951; 3 July 1952; J. M. Chalmers, *Official Recognition* [1953?]; C. R. Attlee, *As It Happened* (1954); R. W. Lyman, *The First Labour Government 1924* [1957]; R. F. Wearmouth, *The Social and Political Influence of Methodism in the 20th Century* (1957); Union of Post Office Workers, *How we began 1870–1920* [1959]; *WW* (1959); H. Morrison, *Autobiography* (1960); W. H. G. Armytage, *Heavens below: utopian experiments in England 1560–1960* (1961); A. Marwick, *Clifford Allen: the open conspirator* (1964); personal information: The Hon. Ada Ammon, daughter; UPW records, Crescent Lane, Clapham. OBIT. *Daily Telegraph*, 4 Apr 1960; *Times*, 4 Apr 1960; *South London Press*, 5 Apr 1960; *Times*, 13 Apr 1960; *The Post*, 16 Apr 1960.

JOYCE BELLAMY
BRYAN SADLER
JOHN SAVILLE

See also: *C. R. ATTLEE, for British Labour Party, 1931–51; Arthur HENDERSON, for British Labour Party, 1914–31; *George LANSBURY, for British Labour Party, 1900–13.

ANDERSON, Frank (1889–1959)
LABOUR MP

Frank Anderson was born on 21 November 1889 at Hercules Farm, Birtle, Bury in

Lancashire. His father Thomas Anderson was a farm bailiff and his mother, Mary (formerly Tetherington), the daughter of a farmer. At Greenmount school he received an elementary education and while still a boy listened to ILP speakers who met regularly on Friday evenings in the centre of the village of Tottington. What he heard encouraged him to save his pocket money in order to buy a copy of Blatchford's *Merrie England*, which had a lasting impression upon him. Anderson began work at a calico printing factory, but when the works closed down he entered the railway service as a clerk at the age of seventeen. Active in the trade union movement he held many offices, including chairmanship of the Manchester district council of the NUR and for seven years sat on the executive of the Railway Clerks' Association. In the 1920s Anderson was chairman of the North Lancashire Council of the Railway Clerks' Association, which brought him into contact with labour circles in the Whitehaven district. At the Railway Clerks' conference at Dublin in 1915 he had met Mary Elizabeth (Mamie) Thompson, who had been elected by the Oldham branch as the first woman delegate to the conference. They married in 1919. She was appointed one of the first three National Women Organisers by the Labour Party in 1918 and set out to organise women from Manchester to the Border. During the General Strike she and her husband helped to administer the Miners' Wives' and Children's Fund in West Cumberland.

After unsuccessfully contesting High Peak, Derbyshire, in 1922 and 1923 and the Stretford division of Lancashire in 1929 and 1931, Anderson was adopted as prospective candidate for Whitehaven in 1932, won the seat in 1935 in a three-cornered contest, against William Nunn, the sitting Conservative member, and Tom Stephenson, the Cumberland Miners' secretary, who stood as an ILP candidate. He represented the constituency until his death. During his parliamentary career he was much concerned with the problem of unemployment in Cumberland and the attempts being made to attract new industries to the region. He showed extraordinary ingenuity as well as doggedness in encouraging new employment opportunities; was instrumental in bringing a number of refugees from Europe to the Whitehaven area where they established factories; and in all these matters worked closely with J. J. (Jack) Adams, whose own vigour and energy were equally remarkable. In addition to his work on the Cumberland Development Council, Anderson was a director of a number of industrial enterprises set up in the area. Acknowledged as a first-rate constituency MP, in the years after the war Anderson was noted for the number of pension claims which he took up and it was stated that he had created a parliamentary record by fighting 320 successful pension cases and losing only eighty. He was energetic too in pressing for water and electricity supplies and for road improvements in the more remote areas of his constituency. It was in dealing with this type of problem that he excelled; he was described as a realist who, though a convinced socialist, had no use for revolutionary methods.

He never achieved ministerial office although he acted as a Labour Whip from 1937 to 1940, but he was unhappy with the convention that a Whip should never speak in the House and, after breaking this rule, resigned his post. As the senior member of the Chairmen's Panel for Commons Standing Committees during the period of the post-war Labour Government, Anderson was called upon a number of times to preside over the Commons in the absence of the Speaker and his deputies. However, his career was affected by a serious car accident in 1948 which permanently undermined his health. He and his wife took a house in Hertfordshire in 1950 in order to reduce the need to travel, but he kept in close touch with his constituency and in the nine years he lived in the south his files expanded to include copies of over 27,000 letters.

For the last few years of his life Anderson's health was poor and he had announced his intention not to stand for Parliament again. On the morning of 25 April 1959 he collapsed and died at his home in Watford. His funeral took place at Golders Green

Crematorium on 30 April when James Griffiths, the deputy leader of the Labour Party, gave an address. Anderson was survived by his wife, who had resigned her position as organiser with the Labour Party in 1944. They had no children. He left an estate valued at £4293.

Sources: *Dod* (1959); *Labour Party Report* (1959); *WWW* (1951–60); 'The Frank Anderson Story', *North Western Evening Mail*, 10, 11, 12, 13 and 14 Aug 1959 [these articles, although unsigned, were written by Mrs Anderson]; personal information: A. Vigodny, Millom. OBIT. *Times*, 27 Apr 1959; *West Cumberland News*, 2 May 1959.

DAVID E. MARTIN

See also: J. J. ADAMS; *C. R. ATTLEE, for Labour Party, 1931–51.

ARCH, Joseph (1826–1919)
AGRICULTURAL TRADE UNIONIST AND RADICAL POLITICIAN

Born in the village of Barford, Warwickshire, on 10 November 1826, Arch liked to think that he traced his ancestry back to the Roundheads who fought alongside Cromwell. His grandfather was a hedger and ditcher and his father John Arch also laboured on the land. Before her marriage Arch's mother, Hannah Sharard, had been in domestic service at Warwick castle but she was familiar with the Bible and Shakespeare and was noted in her village as a good hand at letter-writing. One of four children, Arch took much of his education from his mother, and her strong character and decided opinions made up for the inadequacies of the village school which he attended between the ages of six and nine. Although his father regularly worshipped at the Anglican church, his mother was a dissenter who rebelled against the petty tyrannies often practised by the 'squarson', and this opinion too was adopted by Arch; throughout his life he was to remain hostile towards the clergy of the established church who in rural areas were generally identified with the landed interest. But Arch remained a man of religious beliefs and later became a

lay preacher among the Primitive Methodists. His speeches on political matters reflected this early experience of public speaking: they were notable for the biblical colour of the language and the way in which metaphors and illustrations were drawn from the Bible.

At the age of nine Arch began to work twelve hours a day for fourpence, as a crow-scarer. After twelve months at this job he became a ploughboy receiving three shillings a week, and went on to acquire the skills of the stable-boy and mower. While still a youth Arch learned how to cut hedges and won a competition to become 'The Champion Hedgecutter of England'. His abilities as an agricultural labourer helped to protect Arch from political victimisation as did also the ownership of the freehold of his cottage. He had, he declared, been a Liberal from the age of eighteen, and once he had adopted this position the speeches of Gladstone and Bright helped to develop his opinions. After travelling widely as a hedge-cutter, Arch returned to Barford where in 1847 he married Mary Ann Mills, a domestic servant and mechanic's daughter, who was to bear his seven children. For some years Arch travelled around the district in which he lived and beyond in order to find 'jobbing work', not only mowing and hedging, but gravel-digging, carpentry, wood-cutting, draining and so forth; and Arch thereby achieved an unusual degree of independence and a familiarity with the general discontent of the agricultural labourer. During these years he decided that poverty and hardship could only be remedied by combination and this he preached to nearly 2000 labourers at the famous meeting at Wellesbourne in February 1872.

The background against which the movement emerged was one of increasing prosperity for the farmer and also, E. L. Jones (1964) has argued, of improvement in the general condition of the labourer. From the 1860s a degree of scarcity was appearing in the agricultural labour market which had encouraged labourers to obtain better terms and start to organise more formal combinations. According to Arch, the deputation of men who asked him to speak at Wellesbourne were anxious about low wages and the high cost of provisions; and following Arch's speech to the labourers assembled at Wellesbourne it was agreed to form a union. Some men enrolled immediately and a few weeks later on 29 March the Warwickshire Agricultural Labourers' Union came into being with Arch as organising secretary and Henry Taylor, a Leamington carpenter, as the Union's paid secretary. For some months the movement mushroomed, helped along by the coverage in the local and national press which dealt sympathetically with the labourers' case. A National Agricultural Labourers' Union was formed which had over 100,000 members by the end of 1873, and of which Arch became president. In addition a number of local unions were set up, although rivalry between the different unions was a source of weakness. For a while wages in Warwickshire were raised to sixteen shillings a week, an increase of about four shillings, a not inconsiderable achievement for traditionally the most cowed of all workers. Many of the Union's leaders, including Arch, hoped not merely for an improvement in wages and conditions but also for the moral regeneration of 'Hodge', the labourer. The Union's meetings often had a revivalist character to them; many speakers had a Primitive Methodist background, and their remarks were likely to be punctuated with cries from the audience of 'Amen' and 'Praise Him'. Wide interest was aroused by the movement and several Liberal MPs voiced their support for Arch, made donations to the Union and spoke on its behalf: Jesse Collings, Sir Charles Dilke, Bradlaugh, Bright, Mundella and Archbishop Manning being among the prominent individuals who gave encouragement. The London Trades Council also gave support and advice, especially in attempting to amalgamate the separate agricultural unions. Arch demanded that the labourer be given access to the land, but he envisaged this principally in terms of allotments, although in his Union there was support too for establishing peasant proprietorships.

In 1873 Arch visited Ireland, returning a convinced Home Ruler, and later that year spent some weeks in Canada, which led him when back in England to advocate emigration. But his influence was now being shaken; the price fall of agricultural products forced the Union on to the defensive; and there was some loss of public sympathy as the Union became more avowedly political. Many farmers began to assert pressure on their labourers and in 1874 farmers in the eastern counties made a determined attempt to smash the Union. Labourers not only faced lock-outs but also summary eviction from their tied cottages and frequently harassment by the parson and magistrate who usually regarded the Union's officials as 'paid agitators'. Moreover, not only were many of its officials barely literate but the leaders of the Union, Arch included, were unbusinesslike in their methods. There were allegations, sedulously fostered by opponents, of mismanagement and criticisms that a large proportion of the Union's funds were being wasted in administrative expenses. From 86,000 members in 1874, the Union's strength fell to 20,000 in 1880 and to only about 5000 in 1889. In November 1887 Arch was ordered by the Court of Chancery to surrender the funds to trustees and many members, believing that its collapse was imminent, left the Union. Despite a brief revival, in common with the other agricultural labourers' unions that had sprung up, by the mid-1890s it had fallen into a deep decline becoming, as Arch wrote in his autobiography, 'practically non-existent'.

Despite this collapse, however, the Union did produce some lasting results even if not in terms of higher wages. It helped to direct attention to rural problems and stimulated the demand for land reform. Campaigns to limit the jurisdiction of magistrates and disestablish the Church drew upon examples of partiality among JPs and clergy thrown up by the 'revolt of the field'. The introduction of a wider parliamentary franchise in the counties also owed much to the demands of Arch and his followers; and the Union leaders constantly emphasised the need for education and tried to ensure that the provisions of the 1870 Act were carried out in the villages.

Meanwhile Arch had entered upon a

parliamentary career. At the general election of 1880 he contested Wilton in Wiltshire, but the seat was regarded as Lord Pembroke's pocket borough and the contest was won by Sidney Herbert, the brother of Pembroke. Arch was later put up for North-West Norfolk where the Union was strong, and standing in the 'Liberal and labouring-class interest' he was elected for that constituency in 1885. Though narrowly losing his seat in 1886, he regained it in 1892 and represented the division until his retirement in 1900. Joseph Chamberlain and Jesse Collings sponsored him when he first took his seat in the Commons. But in Parliament he was not a great success, for his style of speechmaking was better suited to outdoors, and his maiden speech, on 26 January 1886, opposing as inadequate Chaplin's Allotment Bill, was considered to be his best. As a member of the Commons Arch lost touch with the day-to-day affairs of the Union and some of its members felt he had become a victim of his own conceit. He was made use of by the Liberals who organised speaking tours on which Arch's subject was usually the land question. The flattery of the influential appealed to his sense of vanity and he could no longer speak on behalf of the agricultural labourer with the same authority as he had possessed in the 1870s. As the Sandringham estates were in the NW Norfolk division, Arch held that he represented the Prince of Wales whom he was later to entertain in his Barford cottage under the Countess of Warwick's auspices. After the enactment of the Local Government Act (1888), Arch became a member of the Worcestershire County Council and before and after his entry into Parliament gave evidence before several Royal Commissions and Select Committees, including the Richmond Commission on the agricultural depression (1879–81).

At the time of Joseph Arch's birth, Cobbett was idealising the type of rural labourer which Arch became. Honest and of good character; proud of his agricultural background and skills and determined to stand up to the parson and squire, Arch devoted many years of his life to the cause of his fellow workers. He was always willing to argue with a magistrate although some of his opinions, such as his opposition to vaccination, were muddle-headed. Nevertheless, he was loyal to the Crown and patriotic; when he changed his mind on emigration, he urged labourers to go to Canada, 'an English colony, that they may be Englishmen still'. While describing the lot of the labourer as one of poverty, suffering and slavery, Arch opposed solutions involving land nationalisation or socialism. He relied on the principle of self-help and believed his own life had demonstrated that it was a valid principle. The early chapters of his autobiography (1898) give a moving and vivid account of the life of the agricultural labourers in the middle decades of the century.

Arch's wife died in 1894 and he married Miss Miriam Blomfield, who survived him, in 1899. On leaving Parliament some of his political supporters purchased an annuity for him. Arch's later years were politically inactive and spent in retirement in the same cottage in which he had been born and in which he died on 12 February 1919. The funeral took place at Barford Church on 15 February. In his will Arch left £349.

Writings: *Joseph Arch on the Church and the Labourers. A speech delivered at a working men's meeting at Sheffield, February 1, 1876,* 8 pp.; 'The Labourers and the Vote', *19th C. 3* (Jan 1878) 48–52; Evidence before the R.C. on Agriculture [Richmond Commission] 1882 XIV Qs 5837I–660; *Free Trade versus Protection or Fair Trade* (Leamington, 1884) 56 pp.; 'Lords and Labourers', *New Review 8* (Feb 1893) 129–38; *Joseph Arch: The Story of His Life. Told by Himself,* edited with a preface by the Countess of Warwick (1898).

Sources: *DNB* (1912–21) [by A. W. Ashby]; F. S. Attenborough, *Life of Joseph Arch* (Leamington, 1872) 37 pp.; 'The Agricultural Labourers' Strike', *British Q. Rev. 56* (July 1872) 145–78; Rev. E. Girdlestone, 'The National Agricultural Labourers' Union', *Macmill. Mag. 28* (1873) 436–46; 'Aspects of the Agricultural Labour Question', *British Q. Rev. 59* (Apr 1874)

421–38; F. G. Heath, *Joseph Arch . . . A Brief Biography* (1874); A. Clayden, *The Revolt of the Field . . . with a reprint of the correspondence to the Daily News during a tour through Canada with Mr Arch* (1874); Frederick Clifford, *The Agricultural Lock-Out in 1874* (1875); R. J. Hinton, *English Radical Leaders* (New York, 1875) 275–304; J. Evans, *Mr Joseph Arch and the Agricultural Labourers* [1886] 4 pp.; S. and B. Webb, *History of Trade Unionism* (1894); W. T. Stead, 'How Joseph Arch was Driven from the State Church', *Cont. Rev. 73* (Jan–June 1898) 71–83; W. Hasbach, *A History of the English Agricultural Labourer* (1908); Ernest Selley, *Village Trade Unions in Two Centuries* (1919); F. E. Green, *A History of the English Agricultural Labourer 1870–1920* (1920); George Edwards, *From Crow-scaring to Westminster: an autobiography* (1922); Frances, Countess of Warwick, *Life's Ebb and Flow* (1929); L. Marion Springall, *Labouring Life in Norfolk Villages 1834–1914* (1936); N. R. Smith, *Land for the Small Man* (Morningside Heights, New York, 1946); Reg Groves, *Sharpen the Sickle! The History of the Farm Workers' Union* (1949) includes bibliography; George Tate, *London Trades Council 1860–1950: a history* (1950); Josiah Sage, *The Memoirs of Josiah Sage . . .* (1951); Rex C. Russell, *The 'Revolt of the Field' in Lincolnshire* (Louth, Lincs [c. 1956]); O. R. Macgregor, introduction to 1961 ed. of Lord Ernle, *English Farming Past and Present*; J. P. D. Dunbabin, 'The "Revolt of the Field": the Agricultural Labourers' Movement in the 1870s', *Past & Present*, no. 26 (Nov 1963) 68–97; E. L. Jones, 'The Agricultural Labour Market in England, 1793–1892', *Econ. Hist. Rev. 17* (1964) 322–38; P. L. R. Horn, 'Agricultural Labourers' Trade Unionism in Four Midland Counties, 1860–1900' (Leicester PhD, 1968); Alf Peacock, ' "The Revolt of the Field" in East Anglia', *Our History*, no. 49/50 (1968) 37 pp.; Margaret Blunden, *The Countess of Warwick* (1967); P. Horn, *Joseph Arch (1826–1919)* (Kineton, 1971). OBIT. *Times*, 13 Feb. 1919; *Leamington Spa Courier and Warwickshire Standard*, 14 Feb 1919; *Warwick and Warwickshire Advertiser*, 15 Feb 1919.

DAVID E. MARTIN

See also: *George EDWARDS; *Howard EVANS; *George MITCHELL; *George POTTER; *Benjamin TAYLOR; *Henry TAYLOR.

ARNOLD, Thomas George (1866–1944)
CO-OPERATOR

Born in Greenwich on 11 March 1866, Thomas George Arnold was the son of John Arnold, an employee at the marine engineering works of John Penn. Shortly after his birth the family moved to Woolwich, where John Arnold took an active part in the formation of the Royal Arsenal Co-operative Society in 1868. Many years later, T. G. Arnold recalled his father attending a lecture by J. Butcher and, with seven others, joining the Royal Arsenal Co-operative Society on the following Saturday. Business was then carried on in the back room of the secretary's house, with a carpenter's bench as shop counter. He could also remember his father rejoicing when trade reached £100 a week. Brought up in a co-operative atmosphere young Arnold naturally became interested in the movement and, after completing his elementary education at New Road Presbyterian School, Woolwich, under the headmastership of John Russell (founder and first editor of the *Schoolmaster*), he was appointed the first office boy of the Royal Arsenal Co-operative Society in February 1880, just before his fourteenth birthday. In March 1889 he was promoted to the position of assistant secretary and in 1902 became general secretary, retaining that office till his election to the board of the Co-operative Wholesale Society in 1916. He was joint secretary to the reception committee of the 28th Annual Co-operative Congress held at Woolwich in 1896, a member of the special inquiry committee of the CWS in 1908 and a member of the investigation committee on the duties of CWS directors in 1914. In 1913 he was appointed secretary of the joint committee of the London Co-operative Societies.

Arnold was elected to the Plumstead Vestry in 1898 and became chairman of the finance committee. On election to the Woolwich Borough Council in 1900 he was appointed vice-chairman of the works committee. He resigned from the council in 1902 on his appointment as secretary of the Royal Arsenal Co-operative Society. In 1908 he was appointed a member of the first LCC Old Age Pensions sub-committee for Woolwich, Deptford, Greenwich and Lewisham, and four years later he was elected a governor of the Woolwich and Plumstead Cottage Hospital. In 1915 he was appointed a JP for the County of London (Blackheath Division).

On his election to the CWS Board in 1916 he threw himself, with characteristic energy, into his new duties; serving on all the main committees and being chairman of the finance and general purposes committee, and vice-president of the CWS from January 1932 to the time of his retirement, under the age limit, in 1934. In 1919 he was one of a three-man delegation which spent five months touring Nigeria seeking new sources of raw materials (particularly hides, vegetable oils and hardwoods) for the CWS factories. In May 1926 he served on an Emergency Committee to deal with food distribution by the CWS during the General Strike. He was a member of the Board of Trade Census of Production Advisory Committee in 1926 and again in 1931. He also served on the Royal Commission on Licensing for England and Wales to which he was appointed in 1929.

On the occasion of his retirement in May 1934 he referred to his being introduced to Tom Hughes by his father as one of the great moments of his life. At this retirement ceremony he was presented with a cheque which he gave as the nucleus of a scholarship to be named after his father and administered by the Co-operative Union.

He died on 9 November 1944 at his home in Abbey Wood, London, and was buried in Plumstead Cemetery. He was survived by his wife, Mrs Ellen Arnold, whom he had married in 1890. They had no children. Arnold left an estate valued at £13,418.

Writings: (with A. McLeod) *The Origin and Progress of the Royal Arsenal Co-operative Society* (1890: rev. ed. 1896) 47 pp.; *The Benefits of Co-operation* (Manchester, 1900)

15 pp. (in Woolwich Library); *Co-operation in London: proposals for advancement* (1913) 15 pp. (in Woolwich Library); *The Work and Training of Co-operative Employees* (n.d.) 12 pp. (in Woolwich Library).

Sources: *Handbook of the 28th Co-operative Congress* (Woolwich, 1896); W. T. Davis, *History of the Royal Arsenal Co-operative Society Ltd 1868–1918* (Woolwich, 1922); P. Redfern, *The New History of the C.W.S.* (Manchester, 1938); *WW* (1943); G. D. H. Cole, *A Century of Co-operation* (Manchester, [1945?]); Co-operative Press, Manchester. OBIT. *Co-op. News,* 18 Nov 1944; *Kentish Independent and Kentish Mail,* 17 Nov 1944; *Kentish Mercury,* 17 Nov 1944.

H. F. BING

See also: Percy REDFERN, for Co-operative Wholesaling.

ASHTON, Thomas (1844–1927)
MINERS' LEADER

Born 23 March 1844 at Openshaw, Manchester, the son of John Ashton, a miner, and his wife Betty (née Ogden), he began work in coalmining at the age of twelve against his parents' wishes. Self-educated, he had an organising ability which was early recognised and in 1865 was elected secretary of the local miners' lodge at Bradford and Clayton near Manchester. This failed after two years but in 1873 Ashton called the men together again. This action resulted in his victimisation and although immediately appointed checkweighman by the miners, he was without work for seventeen weeks as the employers refused to accept his nomination. He was, however, finally reinstated and continued to fill the position until 1888. In the meantime his union activities had increased. In 1879 he was appointed secretary of the Ashton-under-Lyne and Oldham Miners' Association and two years later became secretary of the Lancashire and Cheshire Miners' Federation when this was established in April 1881, a position he held until 1919.

From the late 1870s Ashton maintained close relations with Ben Pickard of the Yorkshire miners. Both were convinced of the urgent need of a national organisation which, unlike Macdonald's Miners' National Association, would deal with problems of wages and working conditions as well as national legislation. They were the leading spirits in the series of conferences in the 1880s which led to the establishment of the Miners' Federation of Great Britain at Newport in November 1889; and Ashton became secretary of the new organisation with Pickard as president. Their central aim from then on was to uphold the unity of the Federation, which they did throughout their long years of collaboration: through many crises, including the crucially important lock-out of 1893 (which Ashton later vividly described in his book *Three Big Strikes in the Coal Industry*) and through many bitter differences of opinion on tactics and strategy with sectional interests in the Federation. One of the earliest problems the Federation confronted was the refusal of the Northumberland and Durham miners to accept the Federation's policy of legislative action on the eight-hour day: it led to bitter exchanges between Ashton and John Wilson, general secretary of the Durham miners, and to a scathing attack by Ashton on Thomas Burt, whom he accused in 1892 of 'too old and musty views' on the wages and hours question.

Ashton was a taciturn man: he spoke rarely at conferences, but he wrote a flint and steel English and he proved to be an ideal secretary: immensely hard working, methodical, painstaking, careful and exact. He had little sympathy with the Liberalism of many of his mining colleagues, leaning rather to conservatism, but he was universally trusted and respected for his experience and his personal integrity. During the bitter Cambrian Combine strike of 1910–11 he was attacked on personal grounds for his support of a proposed stettlement; and he wrote to Tom Richards (21 May 1911):

We have obtained all in the terms of agreement that we set out for and fully carried out the instructions of the Special Conference, and yet we are told that we have jockeyed and sold the men.

I have worked for the miners 45 years.

I have attended on thousands of deputations and assisted in settling hundreds of large and important disputes. Some of these settlements have not always been satisfactory to myself, but no man has ever said I sold them before yesterday.

At the first international miners' conference at Jolimont in 1890 it had been agreed previously between the executives of the Federation and the Miners' National Union that Burt and Pickard should alternate as presidents and Crawford and Ashton should be the joint secretaries: an arrangement that resulted from the major differences on the wages and hours question between the MFGB and Northumberland and Durham. This conference was the beginning of Ashton's long association with the international movement. When the Belgian miners went on strike on May Day 1891 for the eight-hour day, Ashton and Parrott of Yorkshire went over some two months later to hand over the MFGB's financial help and to draw up the record of victimisation and police oppression. When Pickard died in 1904 Ashton was re-elected as general secretary in the following year and he continued to be elected until the outbreak of war in 1914. It was Ashton who pressed for a resumption of international meetings after the end of the war.

Ashton was at the centre of all the major issues that faced the Miners' Federation from its earliest days to his retirement in 1919; and he was usually chosen to act on behalf of the miners in matters outside the coal industry. Thus it was Ashton who made a first-hand report on the famous strike of the Penrhyn quarrymen at Bethesda in 1897; and when the Liberal government in 1911 decided to accept George Askwith's suggestion of an Industrial Council representative of labour and capital, Ashton was an inevitable choice.

He was made a Privy Councillor in 1917 and was a JP for his own city of Manchester. He married in 1865 and there were two sons and four daughters of the marriage. He died at his Droylsden home, near Manchester, on 13 October 1927, leaving an estate valued at £2400 (net).

Writings: *Three Big Strikes in the Coal Industry* (Manchester, [1894?]).

Sources: W. Hallam, *Miners' Leaders* (1894); P. de Rousiers, *The Labour Question in Britain* (1896); G. Howell, *Labour Legislation, Labour Movements, Labour Leaders* (1902); A. Watson, *A Great Labour Leader: the life of Thomas Burt M.P.* (1908); J. Wilson, *Memoirs of a Miners' Leader* (1910); *Labour Who's Who* (1927); *WWW* (1916–28). Obit. *Times*, 14 Oct 1927; *Wigan Observer*, 20 Oct 1927.

JOHN SAVILLE

See also: William ABRAHAM, for Welsh Mining Trade Unionism; T. BURT; E. COWEY; Enoch EDWARDS; Alexander MACDONALD, for Mining Trade Unionism, 1850–79; Benjamin PICKARD, for Mining Trade Unionism, 1880–99; *RObert SMILLIE, for Scottish Mining Trade Unionism; John WILSON; Samuel WOODS; and below: Mining Trade Unionism, 1900–14.

Mining Trade Unionism, 1900-14: F. J. Metcalfe, *Colliers and I, or, Thirty Years' Work among Derbyshire Colliers* (Manchester, 1903); R. L. Galloway, *Annals of Coal Mining and the Coal Trade* 2 vols (1904); W. Jevons, *The Coal Question* (1906); T. Mann, 'Miners wake up', *The Industrial Syndicalist 1*, no. 8 (Feb 1911) 36; T. Richardson and J. R. Walbank, *Profits and Wages in the British Coal Trade, 1898–1910* (Newcastle, 1911); Unofficial Reform Committee, *The Miners' Next Step: being a suggested scheme for the re-organisation of the Federation* (Tonypandy, 1912) 30 pp.; W. E. Bohn, 'The Great English Coal Strike', *Int. Soc. Rev. 12* (May 1912) 778–80; J. K. Hardie, 'The Lessons of the Strike', *Soc. Rev. 9* (May 1912) 207–16; J. J. Lawson, *A Minimum Wage for Miners: answer to critics in the Durham coalfields* (Manchester, 1912) 14 pp.; T. Mann, 'The Uprising of the British Miners', *Int. Soc. Rev. 12* (May 1912) 711–16; A. W. Humphrey, *A History of Labour Representation* (1912); A. J. Jenkinson, 'Reflections on a Pamphlet entitled "The Miners' Next Step"', *Econ. Rev. 22* (July 1912) 302–12; W. H. Renwick, 'The Coal Crisis', *19th C. 71*

(Feb 1912) 378–84; D. H. Robertson, 'A Narrative of the Coal Strike', *Econ. J. 22* (Sep 1912) 365–87; G. B. Walker, 'The Coal Strike – and After', *19th C. 71* (Apr 1912) 378–84; P. Galichet, *Les Mineurs Anglais et leurs Trade-Unions: 1 Les mineurs des Midlands, 2 Les mineurs du Northumberland* (1913); R. Page Arnot, *The Miners: a history of the Miners' Federation of Great Britain 1889–1910* (1949); idem, *The Miners: years of struggle; a history of the Miners' Federation of Great Britain (from 1910 onwards)* (1953); J. E. Williams, 'The Political Activities of a Trade Union 1906–14', *Int. Rev. Social Hist. 2* (1957) 1–21; R. Gregory, *The Miners and British Politics, 1906–1914* (Oxford, 1968).

ASHWORTH, Samuel (1825–71)
CO-OPERATOR

Born on 15 January 1825, near Rochdale, the son of Miles Ashworth who at one time in his life had been a marine on board the *Bellerophon* taking Napoleon to St Helena. In civilian life Miles was a weaver, and the young Samuel began his working life as a 'doffer' in a cotton mill but later followed the trade of flannel weaver. His father was a keen radical who in his early days had been an advocate of physical force and Samuel grew up in an active political environment. Like his close friend James Smithies, Samuel was a Unitarian, strongly imbued with the community ideas of Owenism and also much influenced by the Chartist movement. He was the youngest of the first group of Pioneers who opened the Toad Lane Store on 21 December 1844, and he and William Cooper were the first shopmen, serving behind the counter for the first three months without pay. Samuel was then taken on as the first paid counter-man.

Ashworth had always been an admirer of Feargus O'Conner and like so many working men he was particularly enthusiastic over the Land Plan. As one of the first 'allottees' under the Plan he went to Minster Lovell and stayed there for six months (1847–8). After this short period as a farmer, he sold his small farm for £60 and returned to Rochdale to take up employment again with the Pioneers, being at a later date appointed as their first buyer and then manager. He was at the centre of the Society's expansion during the 1850s and of the extension of their work to other enterprises: among them the Rochdale Land and Building Society, the Rochdale Corn Mill, and the Bacup and Wardle Co-operative Manufacturing Society. Ashworth left the Pioneers in 1866 and became a buyer for the Co-operative Wholesale Society, in which position he was notably successful.

He married and had four children, two of whom died in infancy, with a daughter and a son reaching adult life and surviving their father. After a long illness he died on 1 February 1871 and was buried in Rochdale cemetery: he left effects valued at under £803.

Sources: MS notes of interview etc. with F. S. Ashworth (Co-operative College library, Loughborough); 'Samuel Ashworth', *The Chimney Corner* (July 1871); G. J. Holyoake, *History of Co-operation in Rochdale* (1879); W. Robertson, 'Rochdale: the birthplace of modern co-operation' in *Handbook of the Co-operative Congress* (Manchester, 1892); G. J. Holyoake, *The History of Co-operation*, 2 vols (1875–9) (complete edition, revised, 1906); P. Redfern, *The New History of the C.W.S.* (Manchester, 1938); G. D. H. Cole, *A Century of Co-operation* (Manchester, [1945?]); A. Bonner, *British Co-operation* (Manchester, 1961). OBIT. *Reasoner* (Mar 1871).

JOHN SAVILLE

See also: William COOPER; James DALY; Charles HOWARTH; William NUTTALL; James SMITHIES.

ASPINWALL, Thomas (1846–1901)
MINERS' LEADER

Born on 29 May 1846 at Bickerstaffe, south-west Lancashire, the son of James Aspinwall, a labourer, and his wife, Margaret (née Rimmer). When he was fourteen the family settled at nearby Skelmersdale where Aspinwall worked in the mines and in 1873 he was elected a checkweighman at the colliery there of Bromilow, Foster & Co.,

whose Ashton's Green collieries over half a century later still had more than 2000 employees. Following a strike in the early 1880s he was victimised but the right of the owners to dismiss a checkweighman was contested by the miners. The employers' claim was supported by the local magistrate for although Aspinwall had been properly elected in accordance with the Coal Mines Regulation Act of 1872, he was not then employed at the same mine as when he was originally elected. This and other similar cases gave rise to the amending Act of 1887 which enabled miners to elect any person they wished as their checkweighman.

At the beginning of the eighties there had been no general organisation in Lancashire. There were at least twenty districts in the county and their membership would not number more than twenty per cent of the men employed at the collieries. On 18 January 1881, at a conference in Manchester called by Thomas Ashton of Ashton-under-Lyne (the only district then connected with the Miners' National Union), Thomas Aspinwall, agent for Skelmersdale, was elected to preside: and a resolution was passed that 'in the opinion of this Conference it is advisable to form one union for all Lancashire'. A month later in mid-February 1881 a further conference passed the resolution, in view of the very defective organisation, 'that Lancashire be organised as a federation of districts, each district to contribute to a central fund for certain objects to be decided upon'. Representatives from ten districts (Ashton-under-Lyne, Oldham, Tyldesley and Leigh, Skelmersdale, Worsley and Little Hulton, Atherton, St Helens, Hindley, Radcliffe, Bolton) assembled in Manchester on 19 April 1881, at a conference which may be considered the inauguration of the Lancashire and Cheshire Miners' Federation. Rules were passed and an Executive Committee appointed. Aspinwall was elected president; Thomas Ashton, secretary; and Robert Isherwood, treasurer.

By 1884 the coal trade was very unsettled. In half a dozen districts many were on strike against reductions in wages (including the Bickerstaffe Coal Company of Skelmersdale) and Federation members were receiving an allowance weekly of 10s plus 1s for each child from levies. By summer 1884 membership was falling off and from under 17,000 on 8 July fell to 11,500 by 2 September, when a conference reduced strike pay to 7s 6d and 9d. Thereafter organisation became more feeble: and finally, in March 1887, the total number of members paying their dues to the Lancashire and Cheshire Miners' Federation was 7529.

It was towards the end of 1887 that Aspinwall succeeded William Pickard as agent to the Wigan, Pemberton, Standish, Aspull and Blackrod Miners' Union, a position he held until his death. At discussions with the employers in 1887 Aspinwall was already one of the leading spokesmen and in the joint meeting between the coal-owners of West Lancashire and the miners' representatives in Wigan on 29 June it was Aspinwall who put the miners' case in a speech of some eloquence [Arnot (1949) 76–7]. Two years later he moved the 1889 resolution that built solidarity between the Lancashire and Cheshire Miners and their neighbours in Yorkshire. Lancashire Federation reckoned some 50,000 underground miners, and by the end of 1889 they had trebled their trade union figure of 1887 which now stood at 22,000. He was among the delegates to the 1889 Newport Conference which established the MFGB, and on the rota established among the districts of Lancashire, Aspinwall repeatedly represented the Lancashire and Cheshire MF on the executive of the MFGB.

On the Miners' Eight Hours Bill and the opposition thereto of the Miners' National Union, Aspinwall at the end of May 1891 said:

It is not the opposition of the Liberal and Tory members that we fear, because we can replace them in the mining districts, but the opposition of Mr Burt, who has been for many years the leader of the miners, and is still respected by everybody in the country. The miners in Northumberland and Durham are working short hours at the expense of the boys and other classes of workmen in these two counties.

As a supporter of the Miners' Eight Hours Bill Aspinwall was one of the sixteen members from Lancashire in the delegation of sixty miners together with a half-dozen members of Parliament which waited on Home Secretary Matthews, then on Lord Randolph Churchill, and finally on W. E. Gladstone in three successive days of mid-February 1890. This method of deputations, listened to very fully and completely, with a minute taken and sometimes a verbatim account of the proceedings, was one of the features of the development of parliamentary government in the latter half of the nineteenth century.

At the Trades Union Congresses Aspinwall was often one of the dozen or so delegates from Lancashire. In 1886 the Lancashire Federation was represented with 8120 members by Aspinwall and Ashton: in 1889 the delegates were Aspinwall, Ashton, Isherwood and Woods; in 1890 these four and eight other delegates claimed a membership of 30,000; in 1891 Aspinwall with six others made up the deputation; in 1892 it was Aspinwall with nine others: the attendances varying according to the location of the TUC, its distance from Lancashire, and the availability of delegates to take their place on the rota of the districts within Lancashire. Aspinwall also attended a number of international miners' conferences, beginning with Jolimont in 1890.

He was active in local affairs: as chairman of the school board at Skelmersdale and of the old Local Board, Urban Council and Liberal Association; he also held the principal lay offices in the local Anglican parish church. In 1892 he contested Wigan as a Lib-Lab candidate and lost by only 110 votes; he stood a second time in 1895 but was again defeated. Aspinwall was a man of calm, reasoning speech, and his quiet style on the platform was most effective. He was married and left a wife and a family when he died on 21 March 1901 at his Skelmersdale home. His estate was valued at £3788.

Sources: T. Ashton, *Three Big Strikes in the Coal Industry* (Manchester, [1894?]); W. Hallam, *Miners' Leaders* (1894) [with photograph]; R. Page Arnot, *The Miners* (1949); NUM (N. West area) records. OBIT. *Times*, 23 Mar 1901; *Wigan Observer*, 23 Mar 1901.

R. PAGE ARNOT
JOYCE BELLAMY

See also: Thomas ASHTON; Benjamin PICKARD, for Mining Trade Unionism, 1880–99; Samuel WOODS.

BALLARD, William (1858–1928)
CO-OPERATOR

Born on 1 March 1858 at the Old Tollgate, near Glendon, Northamptonshire, the son of Edmund Ballard, tollgate keeper, William was early imbued with co-operative ideals. His father had been the first member of the Kettering Industrial Co-operative Society on its establishment in 1866. Shortly after his birth, the family moved to Kettering where Edmund Ballard worked as a handsewn bootmaker for Messrs Gotch and Sons. William's early education was at a dame school but he then transferred to the Boys' National School where he stayed for six and a half years. He was a lively child and won many school and county prizes. While still at school he worked in the Kettering co-operative store during evenings and on Saturdays, and when he was later apprenticed as a shoe clicker his spare time was still spent working for the society. After working seven years in a Kettering boot factory, he transferred to Leicester where he obtained similar employment with the CWS Wheatsheaf Works. At Leicester he attended the Working Men's College for three years and then returned to Kettering in 1881 to an appointment as storekeeper for the co-operative society's second store, opened in 1872. In 1892 William Ballard was appointed secretary and general manager of the Kettering Industrial Co-operative Society, and he held these positions until his retirement in 1921. Two years later he became a director of the Co-operative Permanent Building Society, and remained on the board for some four years.

His interests also extended to co-operative production. On the establishment of the Kettering Co-operative Clothing Manufacturing Society in 1893, he was largely responsible for the assistance given to the Society by the local industrial society. He served as president of the Kettering Clothing Society for sixteen years, retiring from the position in 1916. Although co-operation was the 'passion of his life', he found time for many other local activities: as county councillor (1910–27), JP (1919–27), and governor of the Kettering Hospital (1923–7). He was a member of the Kettering Liberal Association, Nursing Association, Temperance Society, as well as being secretary of the Oakley Street Baptist Mission and a regular attender at Fuller Baptist Church.

He died at his Kettering home on 11 January 1928 and was survived by his wife, whom he had married in 1881, three sons, all of whom were associated with the co-operative movement, and three married daughters. He left an estate valued at £7452.

Sources: S. York (compiler), *Co-operation in Kettering: diamond jubilee illustrated souvenir* (Kettering, [1926]). OBIT. *Kettering Leader*, 13 Jan 1928; *The Kettering Co-operative Magazine*, Feb 1928.

MAI ALMAN
JOYCE BELLAMY

See also: W. H. BROWN, for Retail Co-operation, 1900–45; John BUTCHER (1833–1921); G. J. HOLYOAKE, for Retail Co-operation – Nineteenth Century.

BAMFORD, Samuel (1846–98)
CO-OPERATOR

Born on 21 May 1846 at Wardle, near Rochdale, the eldest son of Edmund Bamford, he was largely self-educated. He worked as a half-timer and attended a village dame school two evenings a week. He later became a woolsorter at the firm of Kelsall and Kemp in Rochdale and attended evening classes instituted by the Rochdale Pioneers' Society in 1874. Here he obtained a certificate of proficiency and served on the education committee, acting also as an examiner in shorthand. In his early youth he preached regularly to crowded congregations and had considered entering the Methodist ministry but, as he was reported to have said, he 'got tired of preaching the gospel of contentment and took up the gospel of discontent'. During his early life in Rochdale, Bamford was secretary of the Workingmen's Club in Brickcroft for three years, becoming acquainted with Arthur Acland MP, who took a keen interest in the club and remained a friend of Bamford until his death.

In 1875 Bamford was appointed editor of the *Co-operative News* at a salary of 35s per week. The *News* had been first published on 2 September 1871 and like its predecessor, the *Co-operator* (for which see Henry PITMAN), it was in financial difficulties from the beginning. The Co-operative Printing Society, itself established only in 1869, had agreed to produce the paper, and it was to the CPS that the *News* was mostly in debt. The first full-time editor appointed was R. Bailey Walker, a former colleague of Henry Pitman – and he was succeeded, early in 1873, by J. C. Farn, a former Owenite. The *News* was controlled by a board of management, formally registered as the Co-operative Newspaper Society in March 1873. Thomas Hayes was the Society's first chairman and Joseph Smith the secretary for many years.

These early years of the *Co-operative News* were marked, to quote Ben Jones, 'by turmoil and agitation'. The co-operative movement was full of internal controversies, among them the collapse of the many attempts at co-operative production in the early 1870s: the vigorous arguments between the advocates of producers' and consumers' control: the debate around the 'bonus to labour principle'. Bamford altered quite radically the editorial policies of his predecessors. Henceforth the *Co-operative News* was to provide a genuine forum for debate and discussion for all shades of opinion within the movement. The motto of the paper became a reality under Bamford's guidance, 'in all things, unity; in things doubtful, liberty; in all things charity'. He remained editor right up to his sudden death in 1898, and under his guidance the

Co-operative News, according to the testimony of Alfred Marshall, the Cambridge economist, was 'the best pennyworth of news in the United Kingdom' [Ben Jones, 1898]. In the years immediately before his death his son, W. M. Bamford, was sub-editor, and he became editor on Samuel's death. Bamford was in all matters an enlightened man and he was to be an important influence behind the establishment of the Women's Co-operative Guild. In this he was much encouraged by his daughter who was to become an active Guildswoman. As editor of the *News* he agreed to allow Mrs Acland (wife of Arthur Acland) to edit a 'woman's corner' column from the beginning of 1883; and at the June 1883 Co-operative Congress, such had been the response, that the Women's League for the spread of co-operation was formally established.

Bamford was as active as his editorial duties allowed him to be in other fields of co-operative endeavour. He served on the north-western section of the Co-operative Union for some years, was a director of the Manchester Equitable Society for nine years and president for three. His main interest outside the co-operative movement was freemasonry – he was a member of four lodges and held office as Master.

He died following a stroke at his home on 6 March 1898, leaving a wife, son and daughter. He was buried in Rochdale Cemetery by the side of his great friend J. T. W. Mitchell, and James Deans and William Maxwell gave the graveside orations. He left effects valued at £429.

Writings: *Overlapping by Co-operative Societies* (Manchester, n.d.).

Sources: Ben Jones, *Co-operative Production*, 2 vols (Oxford, 1894; reprinted one volume, New York, 1968); P. Redfern, *The Story of the C.W.S.* (Manchester, [1913]); W. M. Bamford, *Our Fifty Years* (Manchester, 1921); C. Webb, *The Woman with the Basket* (Manchester, 1927); G. D. H. Cole, *A Century of Co-operation* [1945?]. OBIT. *Co-op. News*, with contributions from W. E. Snell, G. J. Holyoake and Ben Jones, 12 and 19 Mar 1898.

JOYCE BELLAMY

See also: Miss M. L. DAVIES; G. J. HOLY-OAKE, for Retail Co-operation – Nineteenth Century; J. T. W. MITCHELL.

BARKER, George (1858–1936)
MINERS' LEADER AND LABOUR MP

Born at Hanley, Stoke-on-Trent, on 13 March 1858. His father, a handyman, died when he was two years old: his mother was Welsh. He attended the Norwood National School and began work at eight years old pulling a milk-cart for which he earned 1s 6d a week. When he was ten he worked as a door-boy in the mines, receiving 5s a week for an eleven-hour day. In 1876 at the age of eighteen he joined the Army, served in the Buffs for seven years, during which he saw service in South Africa (being shipwrecked on the way there) and taking part in the Zulu war (1879), for which he was decorated. On returning to Britain he went to Wales where he became a miner and was a member of the first executive committee of the SWMF in 1898. He left Wales for China, probably in 1902, where he worked for several years as a store manager in Tientsin and although it is not known exactly when he returned, in November 1908 he replaced Michael Roach as agent for the Western Valleys district of Monmouthshire. In the following year he was again elected to the executive committee of the SWMF.

By the time Barker was elected to the SWMF executive in 1909 he was a Socialist and already associated with many of the younger men who were later to produce *The Miners' Next Step*. He himself was among the first trade union leaders to identify closely with the establishment of the Central Labour College, following the Ruskin strike. He became a governor of the Labour College, was a vigorous supporter of the Plebs League, and together with Noah Ablett, Vernon Hartshorn, Charles Stanton and James Winstone he helped form a South Wales organisation of the League.

Barker was one of the group of militants who were in bitter conflict with the long-established leaders of the South Wales miners, and in the autumn of 1911 Harts-horn, Stanton and Barker replaced William Brace MP, Tom Richards MP and Alfred Onions as the elected representatives of the South Wales miners on the executive committee of the MFGB. It was the aftermath of the Cambrian Combine lock-out and strike, and the verdict of the rank and file went against their old leaders. Barker was to remain on the MFGB executive until January 1921 when he resigned following his election in the previous month as Labour MP for Abertillery, a seat previously held by William Brace (who had resigned from it). Barker held the seat at all subsequent elections until 1929 when he retired just before the general election of that year on grounds of health. He had been gassed while engaged in rescue work at a colliery disaster just before 1914. By the time he retired from the Commons his militancy had largely evaporated, and he gave no trouble to the Party Whips during his years in Parliament.

Barker was a good deal older than most of the other militants in the South Wales coalfield who became prominent in the years before the First World War. It is not known when he was converted to Socialism but after his return from China he became an active propagandist for the Marxism of the Plebs League. He was active in the ILP before 1914, was elected a JP for Abertillery and was a member of the Bedwellty Board of Guardians. He married Margaret Sadler in 1884 who predeceased him by a few years. There were two sons and two daughters of the marriage. He died at Newport on 28 October 1936 and left £1524 in his will.

Writings: 'Should the Workers be organised by Industries?', *Int. Soc. Rev. 16* (Sep 1915) 147–8; (with W. Lawther) 'Should the Powers of the T.U.C. General Council be increased?', *Plebs, 15* (Nov 1923) 485–90.

Sources: S. V. Bracher, *Herald Book of Labour Members* (1923); *Labour Who's Who* (1927); *Dod* (1929); *WWW* (1941–50); R. Page Arnot, *The Miners* (1949); E. W. Evans, *The Miners of South Wales* (Cardiff, 1961); W. W. Craik, *The Central Labour College* (1964); R. Page Arnot, *The South*

Wales Miners: 1898–1914 (1967). OBIT. *Times,* 29 Oct 1936; *Western Mail,* 29 Oct 1936.

JOYCE BELLAMY
JOHN SAVILLE

See also: *N. ABLETT; William ABRAHAM, for Welsh Mining Trade Unionism; Thomas ASHTON, for Mining Trade Unionism, 1900–14; *A. J. COOK, for Mining Trade Unionism, 1915–26; V. HARTSHORN.

BARNETT, William (1840–1909)
CO-OPERATOR

Born on 1 December 1840 at Altrincham, the son of Richard Barnett, a whitesmith. His parents removed to Macclesfield when William was a young child. His first employment was connected with the *Macclesfield Courier,* after which he served an apprenticeship in bookbinding and attended evening classes. While still in his teens, Barnett became interested in the co-operative movement, and in 1857, two years after the Macclesfield Co-operative Society had started, his first official connection with the Society commenced as a trustee, a position he held for six years. He then relinquished his other employment to become secretary and general manager of the Society and remained in this dual capacity until a few years before his death, when the office was divided, with Barnett continuing to hold the position of general manager.

He was also active in other co-operative enterprises. A director of the Co-operative Insurance Society in its early years, Barnett was chairman of the Society from 1881 to 1908 and was responsible for the introduction of a collective scheme of life insurance in 1904 whereby the lives of all members of a co-operative society could be collectively insured with the CIS. He served on the board of the CWS from 1874 to 1882, was largely instrumental in establishing the Macclesfield Silk Manufacturing Society in 1888, being chairman from its foundation, and he also helped to form the North Western Grocery Managers Association.

His interests extended to local affairs, especially in matters of education. He was a member of the Technical Instruction Committee of the town council and later of the Macclesfield Higher Education Committee, which was constituted under the Education Act of 1902. A Congregationalist, he attended the Park Green Congregational Church and was a former teacher in the Macclesfield Sunday school, being made a trustee of that institution in 1892.

He died at his home in Macclesfield on 26 September 1909 following an accident while driving a trap, and was survived by his wife and five daughters. He left an estate valued at £3967.

Sources: P. Redfern, *The Story of the C.W.S.* (Manchester, [1913]); W. H. Brown, *The Silken Glow of Macclesfield* (Manchester, [1938]); D. Flanagan, *Our Hundred Years: Macclesfield's Co-operative Centenary* (Manchester, 1955); R. G. Garnett, *A Century of Co-operative Insurance* (1968). OBIT. *Co-op. News,* 2 Oct 1909; *Macclesfield Courier,* 2 Oct 1909.

MAI ALMAN
JOYCE BELLAMY

See also: Benjamin JONES, for Co-operative Production; Percy REDFERN, for Co-operative Wholesaling.

BARTON, Eleanor (1872–1960)
CO-OPERATOR AND LABOUR PARTY WORKER

Of Mrs Barton's early life little is known except that her maiden name was Stockton and that, according to *Labour Who's Who* (1927), she was born in 1872 in Manchester: it has not, however, been possible to discover the actual date. Her family were actively associated with the early socialist movement in Manchester. 'Nellie', as she was known to relatives, married a studious young man, Alfred Barton, who played a considerable role in his wife's subsequent career. He had been unable to continue his own career at Rylands Library owing to family circumstances and after their marriage in 1894 the Bartons left Manchester for Sheffield. They settled in the city and began a long association with the local co-operative and socialist movements.

Mrs Barton's many years of service to the co-operative movement began when she joined the Women's Co-operative Guild of the Brightside and Carbrook Co-operative Society, Sheffield, in 1901. She was secretary of the Hillsborough branch for seventeen years and progressed from the district committee to the Yorkshire area committee and then to the central committee, of which she was a member from 1912 to 1914 and again in 1920. In November 1910 she gave evidence, along with Miss M. L. Davies, on behalf of the Women's Co-operative Guild before the R.C. on Divorce. In 1913 Mrs Barton became national treasurer of the Guild and, at the Birmingham Congress in 1914, national president. Her presidential year was a difficult one with the beginning of the First World War and one of the most troublesome periods in the Guild's history. Along with other Guild officials she had helped in that year to secure the adoption of a recommendation that co-operative societies should be represented on citizen committees. In the same year also, she became a member of the education committee of the Brightside and Carbrook Co-operative Society and in 1917 one of its directors, both of which offices she held until 1925. In 1919 she toured America on the invitation of the Labor Party of America, lecturing on maternity and child welfare.

When Margaret Llewelyn Davies and Lilian Harris resigned as secretary and assistant secretary of the Women's Co-operative Guild in 1921, A. Honora Enfield was appointed secretary and Eleanor Barton assistant secretary. Miss Enfield acted as secretary both of the British Women's Co-operative Guild and of the International Co-operative Women's Guild and when, in 1925, she resigned the former office in order to devote her whole time to the international work, Eleanor Barton was appointed to succeed her. She held office until 1937 and before she retired was able to show how the Guildswomen, who at one time had been mainly interested in home crafts, were now actively concerned with problems of planning, housing, libraries, education and civic matters in general. An inquiry by the Rowett Research Institute in the mid-1930s into British food habits was assisted by the Guild, which undertook a special budget survey for the Institute and supplied the latter with 700 completed questionnaires. Reference to this work was made by Sir John Orr in his book, *Food, Health and Income*, published in 1936. In 1937 Mrs Barton visited New Zealand to inquire into that country's labour and co-operative movements.

She was also active in local government affairs and served on the Sheffield City Council from 1919 to 1922 as a Labour and Co-operative representative of the Attercliffe Ward, being one of the first two women to be elected. She was also a JP. Mr (later Alderman) Barton, who was an insurance agent, and his wife were the first married couple to sit together on the Sheffield City Council. Alfred Barton was secretary of the Sheffield ILP before 1914, published *A World History for the Workers* (Labour Publishing Co.) in 1922 and was an active Labour Party worker; from 1926 until his death in 1933 he was chairman of the Libraries, Art Galleries and Museums Committee of the City Council. Mrs Barton herself made three unsuccessful attempts to enter Parliament. In 1922 and 1923 she contested the King's Norton constituency, Birmingham, in the Labour interest, coming second in the poll on both occasions. In 1927 she was adopted for the Central Nottingham constituency but was defeated at the 1929 general election although she reduced the Conservative majority by 5000 and again came second in the poll.

Eleanor Barton was always the eloquent spokesman of the ordinary housewife, whose point of view she put in numerous deputations to cabinet ministers. She served on many government committees including those dealing with reconstruction, housing, women police, midwives, welfare of women and children, and nutrition; was a member of the R.C. on Licensing in 1929. She was the first woman candidate to be adopted for election as a director of the Co-operative Permanent Building Society, an event which occurred in 1931, and for many years was one of the Guild's representatives on the Standing Joint Committee of the Industrial Women's Organisation, being chairman in

1934. She presided over the annual conference of Labour women in that year at Cheltenham. She was also the first woman director of the Co-operative Newspaper Publishing Society, now the Co-operative Press Ltd.

An active pacifist, she popularised the Guild white poppy (an alternative to the British Legion's Armistice Day red poppy), worn to show the devotion of the wearers to the cause of peace. She worked for Anglo-Russian friendship and trade, was active in the 'Hands off Russia' movement at the end of the First World War, and joined the Peace Pledge Union as soon as its membership was open to women. She was largely responsible for drafting the Guild's Peace Pledge card, represented the Guild at the conference of the War Resisters' International in Copenhagen in July 1937, and from 1930 to 1936 represented the Guild on the National Peace Council executive.

She had a son and daughter. Her husband and son having predeceased her, she left England in 1949 to live with her daughter, Mrs Linda Bennett, in New Zealand. Before leaving, her last service to the co-operative movement was the presidency of the South Yorkshire Federation of Co-operative Societies, which office she held in 1947 and 1948. Mrs Barton died at Papatoetoe, New Zealand on 9 March 1960 aged eighty-seven. She left effects valued at £1253 in England.

Writings: Evidence before R.C. on Divorce 1912–13 XX Qs 37087–165; *Through Trade to the Co-operative Commonwealth* (Women's Co-operative Guild, 1927).

Sources: C. Webb, *The Woman with the Basket* (Manchester, 1927); *Labour Who's Who* (1927); *Sheffield Independent*, 11 Mar 1931; personal information: H. F. Bing; Mrs N. E. Lefèvre of Aberdeen, daughter-in-law; Mrs N. Wood of Cheadle Hulme, niece; and Sheffield City Libraries.

JOYCE BELLAMY
H. F. BING

See also: *Mrs Cecily COOK; Miss M. L. DAVIES; Miss A. H. ENFIELD; Mrs C. S. GANLEY.

BATES, William (1833–1908)
CO-OPERATOR

Born at Bury, near Manchester, 24 April 1833, of poor parents. The family removed to Pendleton in 1838 but owing to poverty the children received no schooling; and before the age of nine, William was sent to work as a 'tear boy' in a calico printing works. His father died in 1843 after two years' illness leaving the mother and five children to be maintained by the earnings of two. With the help of friends, William learned to read and write and in 1851, at the age of nineteen, he was married in Eccles church to Eliza Pearson of Pendleton.

William began to be involved in social and political questions early in his life and he associated himself with the Chartist movement in its last years. In 1850, while he was working at Armitage and Sons, cotton spinners, a strike took place which lasted fifty weeks. He sought work at Bolton, returning to Pendleton when the strike was over. He joined discussion and elocution classes to qualify for public speaking, and as a member of the Pendleton Mutual Improvement Society he was presented with a volume of poetry for his own poetic efforts. During the American Civil War he was on the committee of the Union and Emancipation Society, along with Ernest Jones and E. O. Greening; and he was active also locally in the reform agitation which led to the passing of the second Reform Act in 1867. He was a member of the committee appointed to receive Garibaldi on his expected visit to Manchester in the spring of 1864 and when Garibaldi was hustled out of the country under Government pressure, Bates took part in protest meetings. He was also active at this time in a campaign for the abolition of capital punishment.

In 1867 Bates moved to Patricroft, near Manchester, where he joined the Eccles Co-operative Society. He was soon on the board of management and was elected president in 1870, retiring in 1873 on his election to the board of the Co-operative Wholesale Society. He remained on the CWS board until he retired in 1907 a year before his death. In the last thirty-five years of his life he spoke on nearly every co-operative platform in the country as well as paying visits on behalf of the CWS to Ireland, the continent of Europe, Canada and USA. He became chairman of the shipping committee of the CWS (which gave rise to his being called 'The Commodore' by his friends and colleagues) and in 1886 gave evidence before the parliamentary committee on the Manchester Ship Canal. He was a promoter, and from 1871 to 1891, a director of the Co-operative Newspaper Society. He was from its beginning a member of the Co-operative Printing Society and for many years one of its directors.

In June 1907 he retired, owing to ill-health, from the CWS board, having been over forty years one of the most genial and popular spirits among its directors and one of the best known figures in the co-operative movement. At the time of his retirement he was the oldest living member of the CWS board. By religion he was a Methodist and active in the local Sunday school.

He died on Monday 16 November 1908 at his home, Poplar House, Cromwell Road, Patricroft, in his 76th year and was buried in the Eccles Borough cemetery, Peel Green, on Friday 20 November. He was survived by his wife, several adult sons and one daughter and left effects valued at £2242.

Sources: *Eccles Co-operative Record*, Dec 1908; P. Redfern, *The Story of the C.W.S.* (Manchester, [1913]). OBIT. *Co-op. News*, 28 Nov 1908.

H. F. BING

See also: G. J. HOLYOAKE, for Retail Co-operation – Nineteenth Century; Percy REDFERN, for Co-operative Wholesaling.

BATEY, John (1852–1925)
MINERS' LEADER

Born on 14 August 1852 at Backworth, nearly seven miles north-east of Newcastle on Tyne, Northumberland. The family was a large one, and Batey began surface work at the age of eleven at one of the three main mines there owned by the Backworth Collieries Ltd, and at fourteen commenced an apprenticeship as a colliery enginewright. After serving his time he had two years' work in Cumberland and four years in different shops on Tyneside, and then returned to Backworth where he worked until 1907. He joined the Colliery Mechanics' Association, becoming treasurer of his branch, and in 1889 he became treasurer of the county Association. Around 1897 he succeeded Nicholas Storey as general secretary of the Northumberland Colliery Mechanics' Association: at first this was only a part-time position but in 1907 it was made full-time, and Batey then moved to Newcastle where he continued to live until his death. The union was growing rapidly in the early years of the century. In 1903 its membership was 2948 and this had increased to 4357 in 1907; and its funds had risen from £3976 at the beginning of 1901 to £17,258 by 1910.

He became well known in the national trade union movement, serving for a period as treasurer of the National Federation of Colliery Mechanics' Associations and attending many national conferences. In his own area he was a governor of the Northumberland Aged Mineworkers' Homes Association and a member of the House Committee of the Royal Victoria Infirmary in Newcastle. He was a Primitive Methodist from his youth, a Sunday school teacher and for some fifty years a lay preacher.

He married the sister of John Johnson MP, and died at his Newcastle home ten days before his wife on 5 February 1925. He left effects worth £2126.

Sources: W. S. Hall, *A Historical Survey of the Durham Colliery Mechanics' Association 1879–1929* (Durham, 1929); R. F. Wearmouth, *The Social and Political Influence of Methodism in the Twentieth Century* (1957). OBIT. *Newcastle Weekly Chronicle*, 7 Feb 1925; NMA, *Monthly Circular* (1925).

ANTHONY MASON

See also: Thomas ASHTON, for Mining Trade Unionism, 1900–14; *John CAIRNS; William CRAWFORD; M. H. LOWERY; Benjamin PICKARD, for Mining Trade Unionism, 1880–99; *William STRAKER.

BAYLEY, Thomas (1813–74)
LIBERAL BUSINESSMAN AND CO-OPERATOR

Thomas Bayley was born on 26 September 1813, the son of John Bayley, fellmonger of Lenton, Nottingham, and his wife, Catherine (née Yates), of Longton, Staffordshire. Thomas entered the family business and extended it considerably so that by the time of his death T. Bayley & Co.'s connections were worldwide. He was a wealthy man, for in addition to his business interests, he was also the owner of the Lenton Abbey estate on which coal deposits were developed. Bayley, in nineteenth-century terms, was a philanthropist and he was particularly interested in the welfare of his employees, being sometimes described as 'a Robert Owen of Nottingham'. With a fellow industrialist, Benjamin Walker, a lace manufacturer, a reading room in Lenton was opened which became known as Mr Bayley's Reading Room. It was in this room in 1858, with Benjamin Walker in the chair, that the Lenton Temperance Society was formed, and at a meeting of this Society in 1863 Bayley and Walker provided the members with information on the co-operative movement, following a visit they had made to Lancashire. Their support for co-operative ideas led to the formation of the Lenton Industrial and Provident Society Ltd (forerunner of the Nottingham Co-operative Society Ltd); and at a general meeting on 12 May 1863, Thomas Bayley was elected the Society's first president. In his report to the members' meeting in September, he was able to show a profit of £26 since the opening of the first shop on 30 May. In 1864 the Society bought a flour mill owned by Thomas Bayley in order to undertake its own milling but this was not a successful venture.

Thomas Bayley was an ardent chapelgoer and a supporter of the Baptist Connexion, building the Circus Street Hall for their meetings. He himself preached regularly in towns and villages in the Nottingham area and contributed to the unsectarian public schools at Lenton. In politics he was a staunch Liberal. He died at his Lenton Abbey home on 9 August 1874. He had been married twice: first to Harriet Turner of St Mary's, Nottingham, in 1837, by whom he had five children, only two of whom survived beyond childhood. His first wife died in 1846 and he married in 1847 Charlotte Readett of Beaumont Cross, Newark, who survived him. His son, Thomas, succeeded him in the family business, and his friend, Benjamin Walker, took over the presidency of the Lenton Society. His effects were valued at under £50,000.

Sources: *Industries of Nottingham* (1889); E. Mellors, *Men of Nottingham and Nottinghamshire* (1924); F. W. Leeman, *Co-operation in Nottingham* (1963); personal information: J. M. Bayley of Botany, Australia, a great-(step) nephew of Thomas Bayley. OBIT. *Nottingham Daily Express*, 11 Aug 1874.

JOYCE BELLAMY
H. F. BING

See also: G. J. HOLYOAKE, for Retail Co-operation – Nineteenth Century; Benjamin WALKER.

BEATON, Neil Scobie (1880–1960)
TRADE UNIONIST AND CO-OPERATOR

Neil Beaton, the son of a Highland shepherd, was born in the village of Buickloch, Assynt, in Sutherland on 18 August 1880. After an elementary school education he went to Edinburgh at about the age of eighteen. He obtained employment there with a multiple grocery firm working from 8 am to 10 pm (midnight on Saturdays) for fourteen shillings a week, out of which he had to pay for his lodgings and keep himself. Later he became an employee of St Cuthbert's Co-operative Association of Edinburgh. As a young man he interested himself deeply in trade union affairs and became one of the best known propagandists of the Shop Assistants' Union, organising branches in Edinburgh and later becoming Scottish organiser, a position he held from 1911 to 1919. He helped raise the membership throughout Scotland to many thousands, was treasurer of the Scottish TUC in 1916–17 and 1920 and president in

1918–19; in 1921–2 he was national president of the Shop Assistants' Union.

But he was always interested in the co-operative movement and in 1919 accepted an appointment as propaganda agent for the Scottish Co-operative Wholesale Society. Among other achievements he started eight new societies in districts where co-operation had previously been unable to gain a foothold. He was especially keen to see co-operation extended in his native Sutherland and achieved this through the establishment of SCWS retail branch services. In 1924 he was elected to the SCWS board and continued his efforts towards establishing co-operative branches throughout the Highlands. In 1932 he was made president of the SCWS and during the fourteen years of his presidency (1932–46) he employed his great energy in furthering the advancement of the co-operative movement on many fronts. He was a fervent advocate of international co-operative trading, and was particularly interested in the establishment of the International Co-operative Petroleum Agency and the former International Co-operative Wholesale Agency. The Americans called him the 'White Knight of Co-operation', his familiar figure and flowing white hair being seen on platforms and at conferences throughout the British Isles and in many countries overseas. In 1942 he was president of the Co-operative Congress in Edinburgh.

In the field of public service Neil Beaton was appointed in 1941 a member of the Committee of Inquiry into Hydro-Electric Schemes for Scotland, and after its report had been accepted by Parliament in 1943 he was made a director of the governing body of the North of Scotland Hydro-Electric Scheme, a position he held until a few years before his death. He served on a number of other government bodies including the Inquiry into Scottish Ferries, the Royal Commission on the Press and various Transport Commissions and Committees. For many years he was one of the selected arbiters for the Scottish Miners' Union and was much trusted by them for his fair-mindedness and sober judgement.

He was active also in local government affairs and became a member of Edinburgh Town Council in 1964 for the South Leith ward, serving for a term of three years. He died at his home in Portobello, near Edinburgh, on Sunday 23 October 1960 and the funeral took place at Warriston Crematorium, Edinburgh, on Wednesday 27 October. At the service, tribute to him was paid by John Douglas, secretary of the SCWS, who had been associated with him continuously for over thirty years in the co-operative movement. Two daughters and a son survived him.

Writings: 'Co-operation in Scotland', *London-Scottish Self Government Commission: the new Scotland* (1942) 74–81.

Sources: *Labour Who's Who* (1927); *Co-op. Congress Report* (1942); P. Hoffman, *They also serve: the story of the shop worker* (1949) 149–50. OBIT. *Edinburgh Evening News*, 24 Oct 1960; *Scottish Co-operator* 29 Oct 1960 and 5 Nov 1960; *RIC 53* no. 11 (Nov 1960).

JOYCE BELLAMY

See also: W. MAXWELL, for Scottish Co-operation; H. J. MAY, for International Co-operative Alliance.

BIRD, Thomas Richard (1877–1965)
CO-OPERATOR AND TRADE UNIONIST

Born in Walthamstow, London, on 21 October 1877 Thomas Bird was the son of Frank Bird, a carpenter who later became a jobbing builder and decorator. Thomas was educated at Morning Lane Board School, Hackney, which he left at the age of thirteen, but subsequently attended evening classes. Originally a painter's and decorator's apprentice, he left to go to a solicitor's office for a short period and then returned to his father's business. Later he moved to Ipswich where he worked as a painter and decorator until 1923.

Thomas Bird joined the Ipswich Co-operative Society in 1903, was a member of the Society's committee of management from 1911 to 1923 and minute secretary to that committee from 1914 to 1923. From 1923 to 1946 he was employed as publicity officer to the Society and was closely identified with the Society's progress during those years. He was one of the founder members of the Co-operative Publicity Managers' Association in 1938 and an honorary member from 1946 until his death.

He was an active trade unionist, joining the Painters' Union in 1908. In 1913 he was vice-chairman of the Ipswich Trades Council and in 1918 honorary secretary of the Suffolk Federation of Trades Councils and Labour Parties. He was one of the early members of the Ipswich branch of the ILP and became the first secretary of the Suffolk Co-operative and Labour Fête committee.

In both World Wars he was a member of the Ipswich Food Control Committee. He was the secretary and main inspiration of the Mayor's Committee for the unemployed during the slump of the 1930s. In the Second World War he represented the Ipswich Co-operative Society on the Ipswich National Savings Committee, and with the advent of the Labour Government in 1945 took on an honorary secretaryship of this committee when people of other political views were unwilling to assist, retaining the office until 1952.

From 1939 to 1945 he was chairman and organiser of the Ipswich Red Cross Penny-a-week Fund and from 1945 to 1960 was an active member of the committee for the Ipswich Sea Cadets. He was one of the founders and a trustee of the Ipswich King George Memorial Homes for Old People and from 1947 to 1954 a member of the Committee of the Suffolk Mission to the Deaf, being for several years its chairman.

His wife, Caroline Bird, who died in 1942, also gave a lifetime's service to the community of Ipswich. She was a member of the Borough Council and of the Board of Guardians, a JP and an active member of the Women's Co-operative Guild, of which she was elected national president in 1926. Thomas Bird died on 15 June 1965 at the age of eighty-seven. A daughter, Mrs M. Cattermole, who survived him, was on the committee of management of Ipswich Co-operative Society at the time of his death. Bird left effects valued at £1518.

Sources: *Through Sixty Years: a record of progress and achievement 1868–1928* (Ipswich Co-operative Society Ltd, Ipswich, 1928); R. Ratcliffe, History of the Working Class Movement in Ipswich (from the nineteenth century to 1935) in four typescript volumes at Ipswich Borough Library and on microfilm at Hull University Library; C. L. Mowat, *Britain between the Wars* (1955); personal information: C. Topple, Ipswich Co-operative Society. OBIT. *East Anglian Daily Times*, 16 June 1965; *Co-op. News*, 26 June 1965.

H. F. BING

See also: W. H. BROWN, for Retail Co-operation, 1900–45; S. FOULGER; R. J. LEWIS.

BLAIR, William Richard (1874–1932)
LABOUR PARTY WORKER AND CO-OPERATOR

Born on 26 June 1874 in Liverpool, the son of John Blair, a book-keeper, he began his working life with a local shipping firm but soon became interested in the labour, trade union and co-operative movements. In 1902 he was elected to the education committee of the former City of Liverpool Co-operative Society and in 1903 to the management committee. In 1905 he was appointed secretary of the society and began a spirited campaign to enlist new support and to effect amalgamations. When he was appointed the society had a membership of just under 3000 and annual sales of £55,000. When he resigned in 1919, on being elected to the board of the Co-operative Wholesale Society, the new Liverpool Society had a membership of 50,000 and sales of £1,500,000.

From 1917 to 1920 Blair was a member of the north-west sectional board of the Co-operative Union and made the local arrangements for the Jubilee Co-operative Congress held in Liverpool in 1918. He was active also in municipal affairs, being elected a Labour member of Liverpool City Council in 1911. He served on the education committee and the committee for training and employing soldiers and sailors and was a leader in the movement for leasehold reform. For some years he gave up public work owing to ill-health and the pressure of business, and when he stood again for the city council in 1927, he was not elected. He favoured municipalisation on a wide scale and the establishment of a municipal bank.

Blair's election to the board of the Co-operative Wholesale Society in 1919, on which he served till his death in 1932, opened up new opportunities for his energy, ability and enthusiasm. He served on the drapery and finance committees and on the wages committee, of which he became chairman in 1924. In this last capacity he had to deal with over seventy unions and with more than sixty of these, as he told the 1926 Co-operative Congress, there had been no dispute in the post-war period. His known labour sympathies and proved integrity lent strength to him in the task of defending the CWS board's decision to reduce wages in 1923 owing to the general trade depression: a decision which led to a prolonged dispute with the National Union of Distributive and Allied Workers and the National Union of Shop Assistants.

His duties were sometimes hazardous and trying. In 1921 he was in Smyrna when the city was captured by the Turks; and in 1922 he just escaped the Italian bombardment of Corfu. He was active in the development of relations between the CWS and the Irish Agricultural Society, 1921–6, which saved the latter from bankruptcy. This involved for him, as the nearest member to Ireland of the CWS board's Finance Committee, frequent night journeys to Dublin. In 1926 he defended the CWS policy of fixed maximum prices for the sale of its goods as likely to promote more co-operative trade. A year earlier, in 1925, he had been appointed one of the representatives of the finance committee of the CWS board to discuss with a deputation of officials the question of a pension scheme, which had been deferred in 1921. After long negotiations a scheme was approved in 1928 providing pensions for all CWS employees, administrative, clerical and manual. He was also one of three CWS directors appointed to a committee of inquiry in 1928 into the basis of election of the CWS board.

His interest in education was shown by his active part in the discussion on a CWS grant to the Co-operative College in 1924, in which he advocated 'not cheap education but diffused education through a number of centres'. In 1927, together with George Hayhurst and Sir Thomas Allen, he was appointed by the finance committee of the CWS to consider the need to extend knowledge of the problems of production and distribution among consumers in general. (This had arisen largely out of difficulties during the General Strike of 1926.) The committee's report (November 1927) led to a programme for publicity for the principles of consumers' co-operation which included the publication by Ernest Benn Ltd of twenty-four *Self and Society* booklets by well-known authors, the penny *People's Papers*, and a short history of the CWS, *Told in Brief*. Blair was also a member and chairman at the time of his death of the joint committee on technical education of the CWS and the Co-operative Union, the report of which he moved at the 1931 Congress.

He was a member of the board of the Co-operative Insurance Society and the Irish Agricultural Wholesale Society. The Labour Government in 1930 nominated him a non-ministerial member of the Economic Advisory Council and later in that year he was appointed, at the request of the Government, a member of the British trade mission to Egypt in company with Sir Arthur Balfour, Sir Alan G. Anderson and Mr Kenneth Lee. At this time also, he was one of the original members of the Society for Socialist Inquiry and Propaganda which had been formed by G. D. H. Cole and his wife during the winter of 1930–1 with the purpose of revitalising the ideals of the labour movement. Other members included C. R. Attlee, Stafford Cripps and Hugh Gaitskell, and for a short time Ernest Bevin served as chairman.

Blair was keenly interested in sport and all forms of recreation and served on the committee of the Holiday Fellowship. The reports of many co-operative congresses bear witness to his creative thought and activity. He died at the age of fifty-six, on 27 January 1932 after a short illness brought on by over-work. A wife and two married sons survived him. He left an estate valued at £2231.

Writings: *National Retail Price Fixing for Co-operative Production and the Desirability of the Mail Order Business for Co-operators* (Manchester, 1925) 11 pp.

Sources: W. H. Brown, *A Century of Liverpool Co-operation* (Liverpool, [1930]); P. Redfern, *The New History of the C.W.S.* (Manchester, 1938); G. D. H. Cole, *A History of the Labour Party from 1914* (1948); C. L. Mowat, *Britain between the Wars* (1955); A. Bullock, *The Life and Times of Ernest Bevin*, vol. *1: 1881–1940* (1960); M. Foot, *Aneurin Bevan: a biography*, vol. *1: 1897–1945* (1962). OBIT. *Liverpool Post and Mercury*, 28 Jan 1932; *Co-op. News,·* 30 Jan 1932; *Co-op. Congress Report* (1932); *Labour Party Annual Report* (1932).

H. F. BING

See also: Thomas ALLEN; Percy REDFERN, for Co-operative Wholesaling.

BLAND, Thomas (1825–1908)
CO-OPERATOR

Born in Lancaster on 30 September 1825 Thomas Bland spent the first eighteen years of his life at Pendleton. After visiting Huddersfield, where his sister resided, he settled in that town and established a rope and twine maker's· business. When still a young man he married his first wife, who refused to let him join the local co-operative society because her father had lost all his savings in the collapse of the first Huddersfield Co-operative Society; but after his wife died he later remarried and then joined the Huddersfield Industrial Co-operative Society. He was soon elected to the committee (March 1871), and in September 1872 he was elected president and held that office till September 1878. He then resigned but was again elected in September 1883 and served for one further year. He was a member of the committee again from February 1886 to August 1892 and then finally severed his official connection with the society, remaining an active member.

Following the Newcastle Co-operative Congress in 1873 he was elected a member of the central board of the Co-operative Union but did not seek re-election in 1874. He was again elected to the central board in 1880 and served for that year, and was subsequently a member of the board from 1882 to 1887. In December 1874 he was elected to the board of the Co-operative Wholesale Society and remained a member till March 1907, when he retired on grounds of ill-health. From the date of his joining the CWS board, of which he became vice-chairman in 1895, the CWS took first place in his interests and he travelled thousands of miles at home and abroad on its business.

At the Co-operative Congress at Huddersfield (3–5 June 1895), Councillor Thomas Bland JP (as he then was) presided over the second day's proceedings. He was active in temperance work for forty years, particularly in his earlier life, serving on the committee of the Huddersfield Temperance Society for many years. For most of his life in Huddersfield he was connected with the Ramsden Street Congregational Church and for some years was superintendent of its Sunday school in South Street.

In politics Bland was a Liberal and active in the local Liberal organisation. He was for nine years a member of the Huddersfield Borough Council, being elected for the Lockwood Ward in November 1887, and he was twice re-elected without contest. In December 1892 he was appointed a JP for the borough of Huddersfield, being the first working man in the town to achieve this position. He sat on the bench regularly until 1907 when his physical strength began to fail.

As noted above he was twice married and had four sons and one daughter. He died on 1 May 1908 at his residence, Lockwood, Huddersfield, at the age of eighty-two and was buried on 6 May at Edgeston Cemetery, Huddersfield. His effects were valued at £1740.

Sources: *Handbook of the Co-operative Congress, Huddersfield* (1895); P. Redfern, *The Story of the C.W.S.* (Manchester, [1913]); OBIT. *Co-op. News*, 9 May 1908.

H. F. BING

See also: Percy REDFERN, for Co-operative Wholesaling.

BLANDFORD, Thomas (1861–99)
CO-OPERATOR

Thomas Blandford was born on 19 August 1861 at Curragh, Kildare, in south-east Ireland, his father's family being Scottish and his mother's Irish. His parents left Ireland to settle for some time in Newcastle, where Thomas obtained employment in a city warehouse. Later he went to London and, anxious to extend his education, he attended in 1881 a course of lectures given by James Bonar at the Men's and Women's College, Queen Square. Blandford studied economics and in his written work at this time expressed a dislike of State interference and misgivings about the Irish Land League, and favoured co-operative production. His enthusiasm for education was boundless, and for a time in these early years in London he temporarily withdrew from his job as a warehouseman in order to study at the British Museum.

In 1883 he joined the newly-formed Labour Association for the Promotion of Co-partnership (which was later to become the Industrial Co-partnership Association). In this organisation he found the fulfilment of his ideas on industrial co-operation and for the rest of his life co-partnership and co-operative production dominated all his activities. Initially working for the Association in a spare-time capacity, he devoted much effort in the 1880s to the Co-operative Festival Society which organised festivals at the Crystal Palace. In the festivals, Blandford saw an opportunity to publicise the co-operative productive movement and he promoted the Crystal Palace Co-operative Productions Exhibition for a number of years, producing annually a well-written and thoughtful handbook, known as the *Co-operators' Year Book*, for distribution at the exhibitions. For two years he was president of the Labour Co-partnership Association and was responsible for encouraging Henry Vivian, a young carpenter, to join the organisation. They became life-long friends and together they published the magazine *Labour Co-partnership*, first issued in 1894.

In 1894 Blandford was appointed full-time secretary of the Co-operative Productive Federation, founded in 1882, and for the last five years of his short life he worked unceasingly for this organisation. Between 1894 and 1899 fourteen new co-operative productive societies joined the CPF. At last he had the opportunity of working directly for the cause that was most dear to him. He linked his efforts for co-operative production with a ceaseless propaganda for co-operative education, in the belief that it was the educational movement which would produce the men and women capable of directing the processes of social change. He was sympathetic to the trade unions in general, was made an honorary member of the Amalgamated Society of Carpenters and Joiners, and he also joined the London Co-operative Builders Committee. This latter was an attempt to establish co-operative productive enterprise in the London building trade. The committee did useful work in London and later in the Garden City movement as well as encouraging tenants' organisations.

Blandford overworked himself in the cause of co-operative production and, although ill, disregarded his friends' appeals to rest completely. After an attack of influenza he died in London on 25 February 1899, being survived by a sister. Henry Vivian spoke at his funeral at Highgate Cemetery on 28 February. A Blandford Memorial Fund was later established to perpetuate his memory and life's work. This provided originally for a travelling scholarship; it was also used to sponsor memorial lectures but in recent years the Blandford Fund has been financed from delegates' contributions at the annual congresses and the funds raised are then used to present gifts to charities in the cities where the congresses are held.

Writings: (With E. W. Greening) *Federation of Productive Societies* (1890); *Co-operation in Great Britain and Ireland* (Report of first International Co-op. Congress: 1895); *Co-operative Workshops in Great Britain* (1895); editions also in 1897 and 1898; (with G. Newell) *History of the Leicester Co-operative Hosiery Manufacturing Society* (Leicester, 1898);

An Account of the Exhibition of Co-operative Products at Crystal Palace (n.d.).

Sources: R. Halstead, *Thomas Blandford: hero and martyr of co-partnership* (reprinted from the *Co-operative Official*, Manchester, 1925) 15 pp.; J. J. Worley, *Thomas Blandford: the man and his message* (Third Blandford Memorial Lect.: 1943) 12 pp.; G. D. H. Cole, *A Century of Co-operation* [1945?]; *Co-op. Congress Report* (1956); A. Bonner, *British Co-operation* (Manchester, 1961); Co-operative Productive Federation records: Hull University Library ref. DCF. OBIT. *Co-op. News*, 4 Mar 1899; *Co-operators' Year Book* (1900).

JOYCE BELLAMY

See also: Benjamin JONES, for Co-operative Production; E. O. GREENING, and for Co-partnership; H. H. VIVIAN.

BOND, Frederick (1865–1951)
CO-OPERATOR

Frederick Bond was born at Oadby, Leicestershire, on 1 October 1865, his parents being probably farmers. He left school at the age of eleven and in 1881 moved to Scunthorpe, Lincolnshire, where he worked as weighbridge clerk in the Parkgate Iron and Steel Company. He married in 1884 and about the same time joined the Scunthorpe Mutual Co-operative and Industrial Society Ltd, which had been founded in 1874. At the first meeting he attended, he was appointed auditor. The earliest surviving balance sheet of the Society, for the quarter ending 16 June 1885, bears his name and that of T. Teall as auditors. He continued to act as auditor till he was appointed part-time secretary in 1889. In 1891 he attended as the Scunthorpe Society's representative the Twenty-third Annual Co-operative Congress, held in Lincoln. When it was decided to appoint a permanent full-time secretary, Frederick Bond was selected, commencing his duties on 29 July 1895, and he continued in the office until his retirement in 1933. To mark the Society's coming-of-age he wrote a short history, *Our Society*, which was published in 1896.

He was in co-operative matters much influenced by Sir William Maxwell, the great internationalist. Under Bond's direction the Scunthorpe Society grew from small beginnings to become a powerful influence in the town and he himself became a well-known local personality. Among other interests, he was a life governor of Hull Royal Infirmary, a member of the local employment committee of the Ministry of Labour and a member of the Scunthorpe Choral Society. He died on 2 July 1951 in Scunthorpe, his wife having predeceased him a year earlier, and was survived by two sons and three daughters. He left an estate valued at £3017.

Writings: *Our Society* [History of the Scunthorpe Co-operative Society] (1896).

Sources: A. Ginns, *Jubilee History of the Scunthorpe Mutual Co-operative and Industrial Society Ltd* (Manchester, 1924); personal information: Mrs M. K. Stark, daughter.

H. F. BING

See also: W. H. BROWN, for Retail Co-operation, 1900–45; Fred CLARK; G. J. HOLYOAKE, for Retail Co-operation – Nineteenth Century; G. WALSHAM.

BONNER, Arnold (1904–66)
LECTURER IN CO-OPERATIVE STUDIES AND AUTHOR

Arnold Bonner was born on 1 October 1904 at Littleborough, near Rochdale, Lancashire, the son of Cecil Bonner, a bricklayer journeyman. He was born into a co-operative family, his parents being related to Nathan Holt, first full-time librarian of the Rochdale Pioneers (1851), and to G. Shepherd, secretary of the Rochdale Co-operative Corn Mill. He served a six-year engineering apprenticeship in Rochdale and attended at the same time the Rochdale Municipal Technical School where in the second-year senior technical course he obtained a first class in engineering drawing and a second class in practical mathematics and engineering science. His first active co-operative association began with attendance at WEA classes in economics, 1924–8, taken by Professor Fred Hall, principal of the Co-operative College. He obtained a scholarship to Ruskin College, Oxford (1928–30), where he was awarded the University's Diploma in Economic and Political Science with distinction. While at Oxford he became a member of Professor G. D. H. Cole's discussion group and he remained on friendly terms with Cole until the latter's death in 1959.

On leaving Oxford in 1930 Bonner was appointed a tutor at the Co-operative College (then established in Holyoake House, Manchester, the headquarters of the Co-operative Union) and thenceforward devoted practically all his time to co-operative education and to the study of co-operation in Europe, especially pre-war Czechoslovakia, Denmark, Germany and Sweden. After the war he developed a great interest in the growth of co-operation in the then colonial countries – due to the increasing number of students from these countries attending the Co-operative College (which in 1945 moved from Manchester to Stanford Hall, near Loughborough, Leicestershire). He paid three visits to the West Indies at the request of the British Council to further co-operative activity in that region.

In his work at Stanford Hall he concentrated on co-operative studies and became one of the recognised authorities in Great Britain on this subject, producing in 1961 a new textbook on the British co-operative movement which at once was recognised as a standard work. In the same year he succeeded Walter Eason, on the latter's retirement, as senior tutor at the college. His last service to the co-operative movement was his membership of the commission appointed by the International Co-operative Alliance to reconsider basic co-operative principles in the light of modern developments. He died before the commission had completed its work.

Arnold Bonner was a charming man who exercised a deep influence on many generations of co-operative students. As a colleague in the Co-operative College he was always helpful. In his youth he had been a keen walker, often taking parties of students for weekend rambles on the fells and mountains of his native Lancashire and the nearby Lake District. Later, cricket was his passion, as a player and, when he became too old for this, as an umpire. He died suddenly, following a stroke a week earlier, on 15 April 1966 and was cremated on 19 April at Loughborough, following a memorial service at Stanford upon Soar parish church, where he had latterly served as secretary to the parochial church council. He was survived by his wife, Constance. They had no children. He left an estate valued at £10,420.

Writings: *What the Rochdale Centenary celebrates* (Manchester, 1944) 12 pp.; *Lessons of Rochdale Co-operation* (Co-operative Discussion Group Outline no. 1, London Co-op. Society Committee: 1945) 32 pp.; *The Co-operative Way to Peace and Social Justice* (Eighth Blandford Memorial Lect.: Leicester, 1948) 16 pp.; (with W. Padley) *Employees and Full Membership Rights* (Manchester, 1948) 16 pp.; *Economic Planning and the Co-operative Movement* (Design for studies ser. no. 2: Manchester, 1950); *British Co-operation: the history, principles and organisation of the British co-operative movement* (Manchester, 1961; revised edition 1970).

Sources: Personal knowledge. OBIT. *Co-op. News*, 23 Apr and 28 May 1966; *Platform*, no. 8 (Apr–May 1966); *Co-op. Rev.*, May 1966.

H. F. BING

See also: Fred HALL, for Co-operative Education; T. W. MERCER; H. J. T. TWIGG; and below: Co-operation, 1945–70.

Co-operation, 1945–70: G. D. H. Cole, *A Century of Co-operation* (Manchester, [1945?]); H. Spaull and D. H. Kay, *The Co-operative Movement at Home and Abroad* (1947); V. Adams, *The British Co-operative Movement* (1948); *The World Co-operative Movement*, ed. N. Barou (1948; rev. ed. 1960); Co-operative Union Ltd, 'The Co-operative Movement in a Collectivist economy', *ACE 20* (Sep–Dec 1949) 282–301; A. Bonner, *Economic Planning and the Co-*

operative Movement (Manchester, 1950); J. A. Hough, 'A Guide to Co-operative Statistics', *JRSS 113* pt 2 (1950) 238–48; B. S. Yamey, 'The Price Policy of Co-operative Societies', *Economica, 17* (n.s.) (Feb 1950) 23–42; G. D. H. Cole, *The British Co-operative Movement in a Socialist Society* (1951); ICA, *Reports on National Co-operative Societies, 4* (1953); P. Greer, *Co-operatives: the British achievement* (New York, 1955); J. Bailey, *The British Co-operative Movement* (1955; 2nd ed. 1960); J. A. Banks and G. N. Ostergaard, *Co-operative Democracy: a study of aspects of the democratic process in certain retail co-operative societies* (Co-operative College Papers, no. 8: March 1955); F. Knox, *The Co-operative Movement and Monopoly in Britain* (Co-operative College Papers, no. 4: 1957); Co-operative Independent Commission, *Report* (1958); A. Bonner, *British Co-operation: the history, principles and organisation of the British co-operative movement* (Manchester, 1961); Co-operative Union, *Portrait of a Movement: a guide to British Co-operation* (Manchester, 1961); D. Flanagan, 'The British Co-operative Movement since the Independent Commission', *APCE 35* no. 4 (1964) 251–63; G. N. Ostergaard and A. H. Halsey, *A Study of the Internal Politics of British Retail Societies* (Oxford, 1965); Joint Re-organisation Committee, *Report* (Reading, 1965); S. Pollard, *The Co-operatives at the Crossroads* (Fabian Research Series, no. 245: 1965) 44 pp.; H. Spaull, *The Co-operative Movement in the World Today* (1965); L. Harrison and J. Roper, *Towards Regional Co-operatives* (Fabian Society research series no. 260: 1967) 18 pp.; J. Jacques (ed.), *Manual on Co-operative Management* (Manchester, 1969).

BOYLE, Hugh (1850–1907)
MINERS' LEADER

Born on 27 November 1850 at Wooler, under the Cheviots in northern Northumberland, the son of an Irish shoemaker, Michael Boyle, and his English wife, Mary (née Shell). While he was still a boy the family left Wooler for Bedlingtonshire and he was educated at a Catholic school four miles away at Cowpen, the seaport of Blyth. For a time he helped his father in the cobbler's shop and it was here that he received his first education in political matters; but between nine and ten years of age he started working in the old Sleekburn pit two miles north-east of Blyth as a trapper. His father died when he was young, his mother remarried and the family left Bedlington to settle eventually in Seghill seven miles north-east of Newcastle where Hugh continued to work at the coal face for many years. He was physically very robust and as a young man occupied himself with the normal pastimes of a young miner: football, boxing, quoits, bowls.

But he was also interested in wider questions and he extended his own education by private study. He had a considerable knowledge of economics, was much impressed by the ideas of Henry George, and he was a member of the well-known Economics Society of Newcastle. His literary tastes were towards the novels of Bulwer Lytton and Charles Dickens. In 1878 he joined the Miners' National Association and later became the delegate of the Seghill colliery to the Northumberland Miners' Association. He served on the wages committee of the NMA and was a member of the Northumberland conciliation board from its inception about 1893. As a member of the Miners' National Association he attended many national conferences: he was president of his local lodge for many years, and in 1896 he succeeded John Nixon as president of the NMA.

Hugh Boyle was a man of strong individuality and independence of thought. Politically he was a radical and a member of the Newcastle East Liberal Club. An active member of the Northern Franchise Association he supported the movement for proportional representation initiated by Albert Grey (later Earl Grey); and this was the method used in election for offices within the NMA. Boyle was also active in the efforts to extend university extension schemes among the miners, and although a practising Catholic he was much more tolerant on the schools question than most of his fellow religionists. Inevitably he had strong sympathies with the Irish nationalist movement and he always vigorously supported the movement for home rule. Among his other activities were his membership of the Seghill school board, election to the local council, of which he ultimately became chairman and which thereby entitled him to sit on the magisterial bench. At the beginning of 1907 he was appointed a JP for Newcastle. Both he and his wife were co-operators, and Boyle became a governor of the Royal Victoria Infirmary at Newcastle.

On mining questions he took the general attitude of the north-eastern leaders towards the eight-hour day and state intervention; and on behalf of the NMA he opposed both at the miners' international congresses of 1893 and 1896. He made a special study of compensation cases for miners and their families, and was generally and warmly regarded as a first-rate committee man and chairman. He died at his Newcastle home on 26 March 1907 and was buried in St Andrew's cemetery where Thomas Burt, a friend and colleague of long standing, paid tribute on behalf of the NMA. He was survived by his wife, seven sons and a daughter and left £101 in his will.

Sources: E. Welbourne, *The Miners' Union of Northumberland and Durham* (Cambridge, 1923). OBIT. *Newcastle Daily Journal*, 27 Mar 1907; *Times*, 27 Mar 1907; Northumberland Miners' Mutual Confident Association, *In Memoriam*, 6 May 1907, 23 pp.

JOYCE BELLAMY
JOHN SAVILLE

See also: T. BURT; Benjamin PICKARD, for Mining Trade Unionism, 1880–99; John WILSON.

BOYNTON, Arthur John (1863–1922)
TRADE UNIONIST AND CO-OPERATOR

Born on 2 April 1863, the son of a cab owner, Boynton was educated at Trippett Street Council School, Hull. Of his early career nothing is known but he became in adult life a painter and decorator and was employed by Hull Corporation as a foreman painter. He was an ardent trade unionist and served the Hull Trades and Labour

Council for six years as its secretary from 1897 to 1903. He was also interested in the co-operative movement and, with T. G. Hall, was one of the early members of the Hull Co-operative Society. He joined the management committee of the Society in 1898 and in the following year was made vice-president, an office he held until 1901 when he became president. He served the society in this capacity until his death in 1922.

In addition to his trades council and co-operative society interests, Boynton was, for eleven years, chairman of the Hull Football Club. He was made a JP in 1914. He was twice married and was survived by his wife, six sons and four daughters. He died on 4 October 1922 and left £1815 (gross).

Sources: *First Annual Yearbook of the Hull Trades and Labour Council* (1903); S. Marshall, *Co-operative Development in Kingston upon Hull and District* (Manchester, 1951); personal information: Ald. S. Smith, MA. LL.D, Hessle. OBIT. [Hull] *Daily Mail*, 4 Oct 1922.

JOYCE BELLAMY

See also: *T. G. HALL.

BRACE, William (1865–1947)
MINERS' LEADER AND LIB-LAB MP

Born at Risca, Monmouthshire, on 23 September 1865, Brace attended the Risca Board School and began work in the mines at the age of twelve. While working as a miner at Risca Colliery and subsequently at mines in Celynen and Abercarn he extended his education through private study, much encouraged by his mother. Among the first books he read was Thorold Roger's *Six Centuries of Work and Wages* and other writers included Henry George, Ruskin, Marshall and Carlyle. He was a Baptist lay preacher and abstainer, and his natural abilities led to his being elected miners' agent for the Monmouth and South Wales District Miners' Association in 1890. It was in this year that Brace became the centre of the controversy over 'small coal' which lasted well into the next century, and was productive of much ill-feeling in industrial relations. As Brace wrote, in a passage incorporated by Arnot (1949), p. 283:

> This small coal the coal-owners confiscated without payment, on the ground that payment was included in the 1s 6d tonnage price plus whatever percentage the sliding scale might award. The name given by the miners to these screens which confiscated the small coal was 'Billy Fairplay'. Brace, when a collier at Abercarn (or Risca), fought an action against the illegality of this small-coal deduction by the coal-owners without payment for it and won in the law courts, but owing to the lack of union power this victory was frittered away.

The actions of *Brace* v. *Abercarn etc. Colliery Company* were in the County Court on 18 July 1890, in the High Court (Queen's Bench) on 30 January 1891, and in the Court of Appeal on 8 and 9 July 1891; but their natural consequences were evaded by the insertion of a 'small coal clause' supinely subscribed to by twenty-one workmen's representatives, in the new sliding-scale agreement of 1 January 1892.

From the beginning of his trade union career he was a vigorous opponent of the sliding-scale method of wage payment introduced into South Wales late in 1875 whereby wages were tied to coal prices. In the early years especially they operated adversely against the miners and had the effect of stifling trade union growth in the South Wales area for nearly twenty-five years. The Monmouthshire district was a small one but under Brace's leadership it developed into a centre of genuine trade union organisation. Brace was a very fluent orator and campaigned outside his district against the sliding scale. The Monmouth district association was affiliated to the MFGB from the start of the Federation in 1889, but the majority of Welsh miners were led by William Abraham (Mabon) who supported the sliding scale, and they were not affiliated since the MFGB did not accept, on principle, unions with sliding-scale arrangements. Intense personal bitterness developed between Brace and Mabon, and

in 1893 Mabon won a slander action against Brace. He was awarded £500 damages plus costs but Brace refused to pay, and used the episode very effectively in his bitter campaign against the policies of Mabon and other advocates of the sliding scale.

On 1 August 1893 the famous hauliers' strike began. The men were confronted not only with the formidable opposition of the well-organised coalowners but with that of ten miners' agents headed by Abraham and Richards, while in addition to police, soldiers were drafted for the first time in half a century into South Wales for an industrial dispute. Brace, at the eastern end of the coalfield, and Isaac Evans in the south-west, were the only agents to support the hauliers. The strike was crushed, and following the strike, Brace proposed the formation of a new union which could be both independent of the MFGB and the sliding-scale committee, as he realised that the scale could not be abolished until the men were strongly organised. He made little progress, however, although an Amalgamated Society of Colliery Workmen of the South Wales Coalfield did come into being in 1894 and continued until 1897, but membership was small. Mounting agitation against the sliding scales culminated in a five-month strike in 1898 which, while not immediately successful, since the miners were forced to agree to the owners' terms which included a sliding-scale agreement, represents the beginning of a new era in the history of mining unionism in South Wales. Mabon and Brace were reconciled and with the formation of the South Wales Miners' Federation later in 1898 all the Welsh miners were organised in one union. Mabon and Brace were elected president and vice-president respectively of the federation, which was pledged to end the sliding scale. In 1899 it was accepted into the MFGB fold and in 1903 the sliding-scale method of payment ceased.

Brace served on the MFGB executive in 1892–3 representing Monmouth and again from 1900–10 when he was one of several from South Wales. In December 1901 he was appointed to the R.C. on Coal Supplies (1901–3). During this decade, however, he was increasingly in conflict with a group of militants in the SWMF led by George Barker. This group later organised an unofficial reform committee, was strongly influenced by Marxist and then syndicalist ideas and was responsible for publication of the famous pamphlet, *The Miners' Next Step*, in 1912.

Discontent among the South Wales miners spread widely during the years 1910 and 1911; and the outstanding issues came to a head during the twelve months of the Ely pit lock-out, and the ten months of the Cambrian Combine strike (which ended August–October 1911). The dissatisfaction with the moderate leaders of the SWMF was reflected in the replacement of Tom Richards MP, Alfred Onions and Brace himself for three seats on the executive of the MFGB by Vernon Hartshorn, C. B. Stanton and George Barker. The election took place just before the October 1911 Conference of the MFGB. For Brace, however, it was only a temporary break, for he was re-elected in 1912 and served until June 1915, and then again throughout 1919–20.

Brace was already a member of the Monmouthshire County Council when he won the parliamentary division of South Glamorgan in the general election of 1906. He entered Parliament with the support of the Liberals and had been vice-president of the Welsh National Liberal Association, but he regarded himself as a Labour representative of the miners' union. His candidature had been endorsed by the LRC but he was personally opposed to the idea of independent Labour representation and tried at the MFGB conference in 1908 to delay a proposal from the miners for affiliation to the Labour Party. This was only temporary, however, for the miners affiliated in 1909 and before the First World War Brace held the seat as a Labour representative: he was vice-chairman of the Labour Party in 1911. During the war, in which he took a patriotic line, Brace was appointed Under-Secretary for Home Affairs in the Asquith Coalition Government in 1915, and a year later became chairman of the committee for the employment of conscientious objectors. He was made a PC in the same year. He

remained in the Lloyd George administration until the Labour Party ordered all its members to withdraw in 1918. In that year he was returned unopposed for Abertillery, but in 1920, unable to cope with the increasing leftward tendency both in the executive council and the delegate conference, Brace resigned from the presidency of the SWMF in the November. He also resigned from Parliament, and took the position of labour adviser to the Ministry of Labour. He retired in 1927 although he still acted on occasion in a consultative capacity to government departments; and he continued writing for the *Western Mail*. A colleague remembered him stealing the limelight at a conference dinner of the SWMF in 1945, when Brace was eighty, with an oration of remarkable power: 'more than that of Arthur Horner and with a voice like a bell'.

He had married Miss Nellie Humphreys in 1890, and he died at his Newport home on 12 October 1947, being survived by a son, Mr Ivor L. Brace, who at the time of his father's death was Chief Justice of North Borneo; and a daughter, Mrs Harold Simpson. He left an estate valued at £14,899.

Sources: *Review of Reviews, 33* (Jan–June 1906) 572; *WW* (1947); R. Page Arnot, *The Miners* (1949); F. Bealey and H. Pelling, *Labour and Politics 1900–1906* (1958); H. A. Clegg et al., *A History of British Trade Unions since 1889*, vol. *1: 1889–1910* (1964); R. Page Arnot, *South Wales Miners 1898–1914* (1967); personal information: Dr E. W. Evans. OBIT. *Times*, 14 Oct 1947; *Western Mail*, 14 Oct 1947.

R. PAGE ARNOT
JOYCE BELLAMY
JOHN SAVILLE

See also: *N. ABLETT; William ABRAHAM, for Welsh Mining Trade Unionism; Thomas ASHTON, for Mining Trade Unionism, 1900–14; George BARKER; Isaac EVANS; David MORGAN; Benjamin PICKARD, for Mining Trade Unionism, 1880–99; John WILSON.

BROWN, James (1862–1939)
MINERS' LEADER AND LABOUR MP

Born on 16 December 1862 at Whitletts, near Ayr, he was the son of a weaver, James Brown of the *quoad sacra* parish of Newton-on-Ayr (who later became a miner and eventually a colliery manager), and his wife Christine. After attending Annbank Public School he started working in the mines when he was twelve and continued at night school until he was sixteen, extending his early education by using the facilities provided by the village library and from books he acquired himself. He worked as a miner until he was forty-three and during these years was active in trade union affairs: at eighteen he was secretary of the Annbank committee of the Miners' Union: in 1895 he was elected president of the Ayrshire Miners' Union and in 1904 appointed a miners' agent for the Ayrshire district. In 1907 he gave evidence before the R.C. on Mines as president of the union and in 1908 became secretary of the Ayrshire Miners' Union, a post he held until his election to Parliament in 1918. He continued to work as an agent, however, and was a member of the executive of the National Union of Scottish Mineworkers until his death. From 1917 to 1936 he was secretary of the NUSMW and represented the Scottish miners on the MFGB executive in 1909, 1916 and 1935.

Brown began his political life as a Liberal but he joined the ILP about 1899 and always professed himself to have been much influenced by Keir Hardie. In 1906 and again in January 1910 he contested North Ayrshire as a Labour candidate but without success. In 1918 he was elected for South Ayrshire, and retained the seat until 1931, being defeated in the general election of that year. He was re-elected in 1935 and served until his death. In the first Labour Government of 1924 and again between 1929 and 1931 Brown was appointed Lord High Commissioner to the Church of Scotland, the first commoner to hold the office for nearly three centuries. As this appointment suggests Brown was an active churchman. In his early youth he had been rather wild and was

also a football enthusiast, but after his religious conversion he no longer played games and became a strict teetotaller. He taught in the Annbank Sunday school for over fifty years, and in the Church of Scotland filled all the offices open to a layman. He was secretary and chief templar for the Annbank district of the Good Templars. He played some part also in local government affairs, being a member and subsequently chairman of the local school board as well as serving on the parish council.

James Brown became one of the best known and most widely respected of Labour Party members in Scotland. He was extraordinarily well read in English and Scottish literature, and his conduct during his periods of office as Lord High Commissioner was widely acclaimed. In politics he was always a moderate but he moved more to the Right in the years after the First World War, and during the bitter factional struggle within the Scottish miners' unions in the late 1920s Brown took up a strong anti-communist position. He was awarded the OBE in 1917; was made a PC in 1930; received the Freedom of Ayr in the same year, the Freedom of Girvan in 1931, and an Hon. LL.D. from Glasgow University also in 1931. He was a Deputy Lieutenant for Ayrshire and a JP for the county.

He married in 1888 Catherine, daughter of Matthew Steele and his wife Kate MacGregor of Kilbarchan in Renfrewshire, by whom he had four sons and a daughter. His wife was the daughter of a shoemaker and she herself before marriage was a mill-girl. James Brown died on 21 March 1939 in an Ayr nursing home and, following a service at Annbank Church, was buried in the local cemetery. His wife and two sons survived him. He left an estate valued at £2309.

Sources: Evidence before R.C. on Mines vol. III 1908 XX Qs 22928–3226; *Dod* (1919), (1931); S. V. Bracher, *Herald Book of Labour Members* (1923); *Labour Who's Who* (1927); G. A. Hutt, 'Democracy in the Scottish Miners' Union', *Labour Monthly 10* (1928) 348; Anon., *The Scottish Socialists: a gallery of contemporary portraits* (1931); A.

Gammie, *From Pit to Palace: the life story of the Right Hon. James Brown, MP* (1931); *WW* (1936); *Kelly* (1938); *WWW* (1929–40); R. P. Arnot, *A History of the Scottish Miners* (1955); A. Moffat, *My Life with the Miners* (1965). OBIT. *Times*, 22 Mar 1939; *Ayrshire Post*, 24 Mar 1939 (with photograph); *Labour Party Report* (1937–9).

JOYCE BELLAMY
JOHN SAVILLE

See also: *William ADAMSON; A. B. CLARKE; *R. SMILLIE, for Scottish Mining Trade Unionism.

BROWN, William Henry (1867/8–1950)
CO-OPERATIVE JOURNALIST AND AUTHOR

William Brown was born in 1867 or 1868 in East London, near Epping Forest, the son of an active co-operator. In his early youth he attended pupil teachers' centres at Toynbee Hall and Oxford House University Settlements. At the age of fourteen he was a pupil teacher with a class of forty boys at an East London school. W.H.B., as he was invariably known, came into close contact, through his father who was on the committee of the Guild of Co-operators, with many of the contemporary leaders of the co-operative movement, including Tom Hughes and E. Vansittart Neale. It was at the instigation of another pioneer, Lloyd Jones, that he made his first public speech in 1888 at a meeting of the old Tower Hamlets Society. In the same year he joined the staff of the *South Hants Evening Star* but by 1889 he had returned to London as assistant editor of the *British Trade Journal*. After gaining further experience in the City of London he became associated with the monthly journal *Architecture*.

His spare time was devoted to the co-operative movement and he worked alongside E. O. Greening in plans for associating co-operators of all nations into a close union: plans which materialised in the International Co-operative Alliance. He became associated with the *Co-operative News* in 1895 and from 1898–1916 worked as London correspondent of this publication.

From 1895 to 1916 he was secretary of the education committee of the Stratford Co-operative Society. As a member of the central board of the Co-operative Union he played a leading role in the formation of the Cambridge Co-operative Society in 1899.

In 1916 he joined the publicity department of the CWS in Manchester, known as the Co-operative Press Agency. The department was managed by James Haslam, and William Brown edited the *Producer* until his retirement in 1934. Even then, he continued to lead an active life in the service of co-operation. A prolific writer from the beginning of the century, he had already published several co-operative society histories before 1934. Thereafter his output of such works increased and he was also a lively contributor to many co-operative journals until the end of his life. Under the pseudonym of Timothy Autolycus he wrote monthly profiles on prominent secretaries and managers in the co-operative movement for the *Co-operative Official* under the heading 'Gallery of Officials'. Even in hospital shortly before his death he was proof-reading and planning new articles for the *Co-operative Review*.

He was associated with the first garden suburb in Ealing in 1901 and with the first co-operative industry at Letchworth, one of his early publications (1909) being concerned with this development. During the First World War he was a member of the War Emergency Workers' National Committee and at the 1918 general election he unsuccessfully contested the Mossley Division of Lancashire as the first Co-operative Party candidate in the constituency. He was a long-serving member of the Manchester branch of the National Union of Journalists, and his other interests included the Home Reading Union, Women's Industrial Council, Social and Political Education League and the International Arbitration League, on whose council he served. A Rechabite, he was also a member of the Unitarian Church and attended the Cross Street Chapel, Manchester.

He died on 15 December 1950, aged eighty-two, in a Manchester hospital and was survived by three daughters. His funeral was on 19 December at the Southern

56 BROWN

Cemetery, Manchester. He left an estate valued at £5395.

Writings: *The Worker's Advance* (Manchester, 1900); (with H. J. May) *Souvenir of the Co-operative Congress at Stratford* (1904); *George Jacob Holyoake* (Leicester, [1906]) 16 pp.; *The Story of the London Branch of the Co-operative Printing Society Ltd* (1907); *An Industrial Republic* (Letchworth, 1909); *Jubilee Retrospect of the Rise and Progress of the Stratford Co-operative and Industrial Society Ltd* (with supplementary chapters by John H. Bate) [1911] 48 pp.; *The Pioneer Co-partnership Suburb. A Record of Progress . . . Brentham Club and Institute of the Ealing Tenants Ltd* (1912) 33 pp.; *A Century of Co-operation in Sheerness: being a chronicle of the oldest Co-operative Society in the United Kingdom* (Manchester, 1916); *The Political Education of Co-operators* (Manchester, 1919) P; *Co-operation in Cambridge: being the Jubilee Chronicle of the Cambridge and District Co-operative Society Ltd 1868–1919* (Manchester, 1920); *Charles Kingsley: the work and influence of Parson Lot* (Manchester, 1924); *The Making of Homes in the People's Own Houses* (1925) 15 pp.; *Pathfinders . . . Brief Records of Seventy-four Adventurers . . . whose Names are inscribed on the Reformers' Memorial, Kensal Green, London* (Manchester, 1925) 47 pp.; *A Century of London Co-operation* [1928]; *A Century of Liverpool Co-operation* (Liverpool, [1930]); *Rochdale Pioneers: the story of the Toad Lane Store, 1844, and the origin of the Co-operative Union, 1869 etc.* (Manchester, 1931) 15 pp.; *Mrs Gaskell* (Manchester, 1932) P; *A Record of Co-operation in London leading to the Official Opening of the C.W.S. London Branch Administrative Offices and Bank Building* [1933] 32 pp.; *The Co-operative Manager, being the Silver Jubilee History, 1912–37, of the National Co-operative Managers' Association* (York, 1937); *The Trek of the Men: history, programme and policy, rules and standing orders of the National Co-operative Men's Guild* (Manchester, [1937]) 24 pp.; *The Fine Art of Living* [Greening Memorial Lecture, 1937] (Manchester, [1937]) 16 pp.; *Brighton's Co-operative Advance, 1828–1938: with the jubilee history of the Brighton Equitable Co-operative Society Ltd 1888–1938* (Manchester, [1938]); *The Silken Glow of Macclesfield with the Jubilee History of the Macclesfield Silk Manufacturing Society Ltd* (Manchester, [1938]); *The Founder of the Co-operative College* (1939) P; *Bath Society – In Co-operation: the jubilee history of the Bath Co-operative Society Ltd* (Bath, 1939); *Co-operation in a University Town: with the seventy years' record of the Cambridge and District Co-operative Society Ltd* [1939?]; *The Co-operative Story of Kent* (Manchester, 1939); *Wigan Welfare and the Jubilee History of the Wigan and District Equitable Co-operative Society Ltd* (Wigan, [1939]); *The Co-operative Advance in Slough, 1892–1942: the jubilee history of the Slough and District Co-operative Society Ltd* [1942]; *The Rochdale Pioneers: a century of co-operation* (Manchester, [1944?]); *Hepworth's Hundred Years of Co-operative Adventure* (Manchester, [1948]); *Eastleigh Co-operation on the Permanent Way, 1892–1948* (Eastleigh, [1949]); *Newmarket's Co-operative Jubilee History, 1899–1949* (Newmarket, 1949) 38 pp.; *Heywood's Co-operative Centenary, 1850–1950: the centenary record of the Heywood Industrial Co-operative Society Ltd* (Heywood, [1950]); *Mansfield's Co-operative Advance, 1864–1950* (Mansfield, [1950]); *Winchester's Co-operative Golden Jubilee: 1900–1950* (Winchester, 1950).

Sources: W. M. Bamforth, *Our Fifty Years: jubilee souvenir of the 'Co-operative News'* (Manchester, 1921); *Co-op. Official*, Dec 1948, Jan, Feb, Mar 1949; *Co-op. Rev.* n.d. Personal information: A. L. Sugar, Publications Manager, Co-operative Union Ltd. Obit. *Manchester Guardian*, 19 Dec 1950; *Co-op. News*, 23 Dec 1950.

JOYCE BELLAMY

See also: E. O. GREENING; James HASLAM (1869–1937); E. V. NEALE; and below: Retail Co-operation, 1900–45.

Retail Co-operation, 1900–45: Anon., *The Christian Socialist Movement and Co-operation* [Manchester, c. 1900] 8 pp.; J. C. Gray, *Self-help for the People: a brief review of some of the benefits which co-operation has conferred on the working classes* (Manchester, 1900) 7 pp.; A. H. G. Grey, *The Co-operative Movement* [1900] 12 pp.; Anon., 'Co-operators and the New Century: a great work to be done', *West. Rev. 156* (Aug 1901) 138–48; Board of Trade, *Report on Workmen's Co-operative Societies in the United Kingdom*, Cd 698 (1901); H. W. Wolff, 'Progress and Deterioration in the Co-operative Movement', *Econ. Rev. 11* (Oct 1901) 445–59; J. C. Gray, 'Co-operation and the Poor', *CWS Annual* (1902) 111–38; H. Vivian, 'The Present Ideals of Co-operation', *Econ. J. 12* (1902) 272–4; X, 'The Present Ideals of Co-operation', *Econ. J. 12* (1902) 29–41; I. Nicholson, *Our Story: a history of the co-operative movement for young people* (1903) 18th ed. (Manchester, 1933); G. J. Duke, 'The Methods of electing Committees of Management for Co-operative Societies', *Co-op. Congress Report* (1903) 348–9; G. J. Holyoake et al., *Anti-boycott Papers* (Manchester, [1903]); idem., *Bygones worth remembering*, 2 vols (1905); idem., *The History of Co-operation*, 2 vols (1906) rev. and completed; H. W. Wolff, 'Neglected Opportunities of Co-operation', *Econ. Rev. 16* (April 1906) 190–206; C. R. Fay, *Co-operation at Home and Abroad*, vol. *1* (1908) 5th ed. (1948), vol. *2: 1908–38* (1939) 2nd ed. (1948); W. Kilner, *A National Co-operative Society: is it practicable?* (1909) 12 pp.; J. Deans, *The Amalgamation of Societies as a Means of Consolidating the Co-operative Movement* (Manchester, 1910) 11 pp.; S. Webb, *The Place of Co-operation in the State of Tomorrow* [c. 1910] 20 pp.; S. B. Fraser, *Three National Reforms necessary for the Development of the Co-operative Movement* (1912) 8 pp.; Board of Trade (Labour Dept), *Directory of Industrial Associations in the U.K. for 1911* (1911) 129–92 [especially 130–55]; idem., *Report on Industrial and Agricultural Co-operative Societies in the U.K. 1912–13* Cd 6045 LXXV; J. Clayton, *Co-operation* (1912); P. Redfern, *Co-operation for All* (Manchester, 1914); H. W. Wolff, 'Ups and Downs in Co-operation', *Econ. Rev. 24* (1914) 70–4; Anon., 'The Fabian Society on Co-operation', *Co-operative Consumer 2* (Sep 1915) 27–30; A. Williams, *The Future Policy of Co-operation: national and international* (Manchester, 1915) 16 pp.; F. Hall, 'The Economic Results of the War and Their Effect upon the Co-operative

Movement', *Co-op. Congress Report* (1916) 641–57; *Foundations: a study in the ethics and economics of the co-operative movement*, ed. T. Hughes and E. V. Neale, rev. by A. Stoddart and W. Clayton (Manchester, 1916); F. Hall, *Co-operation and After-War Problems* (1918) 15 pp.; A. Sonnichsen, *Consumers' Co-operation* (New York, 1919); Anon., *Co-operators and Reconstruction: the need for co-operative action* (1919) 8 pp.; A. H. Enfield, *The Place of Co-operation in the New Social Order* (1920) 12 pp.; T. W. Mercer, *The Proposed National Co-operative Society* (1920) 16 pp.; idem, *The Co-operative Survey Committee and its Work* (1920) 12 pp.; A. C. Pigou, 'Co-operative Societies and Income Tax', *Econ. J. 30* (June 1920) 156–62; W. R. Rae, *Rule by Committee* (1920) 8 pp.; P. Redfern, *The Consumer's Place in Society* (Manchester, 1920); C. Gide, *Consumers' Co-operative Societies*, first English ed. (1921); O. T. Hopkins, *Working Expenses in Retail Distributive Co-operative Societies* with an Introduction by F. Hall (Manchester, 1921) 38 pp.; H. W. Laidler, *The British Co-operative Movement* (New York, 1921) 16 pp.; T. W. Mercer et al., *Co-operative Policy in Relation to the Organisation of Retail Trade* (Manchester, 1921) 20 pp.; Mrs S. Webb, 'The Co-operative Movement of Great Britain and its Recent Developments', *Int. Lab. Rev. 4* (Nov 1921) 227–56; S. and B. Webb, *The Consumers' Co-operative Movement* (1921); G. Williamson, *Rationalisation of the Co-operative Movement* (1921); N. Angell, *Co-operation and the New Social Conscience* (Manchester, 1922) 20 pp.; A. Pickup and W. E. Banister, *The Policy of Societies in Regard to Trade, Dividends, Reserves and Depreciation* (Manchester, 1922) 24 pp.; G. Riddle, *The Financial Position of the Co-operative Movement in Relation to New Forms of Administration in the Retail Trade* (Manchester, 1922) 10 pp.; J. P. Warbasse, *Co-operative Democracy attained through Voluntary Association of the People as Consumers: a discussion of the co-operative movement* (New York, 1923) 5th ed. (1947); F. Hall, *Handbook for Members of Co-operative Committees* (Manchester, 1923) 4th ed. (1931); S. Webb, *The Constitutional Problems of a Co-operative Society*, Fabian Tract no. 202 (1923) 23 pp.; idem, *The Need for*

Federal Re-organisation in the Co-operative Movement, Fabian Tract no. 203 (1923) 27 pp.; S. R. Elliott, *Co-operative Store-keeping etc.*, *Eighty Years of Constructive Revolution* with an introduction by M. L. Davies (1925); G. A. Greenwood, 'The Future of Co-operation', *Socialist Rev.* no. 7 (s. 2) (Aug 1926) 23–6; A. Örne, *Co-operative Ideals and Problems*, translated in English by J. Downie (1926); A. H. Enfield, *Co-operation: its problems and possibilities* (1927); T. W. Mercer, *Co-operative Policy in Relation to Municipal Trading* (Manchester, 1927) 20 pp.; idem, *The Co-operative Press and Its Development* (Manchester, 1927) 18 pp.; H. Clay, *Co-operation and Private Enterprise* (Self and Society Series 1928) 32 pp.; Co-operative Wholesale Society, *Co-operation in Outline: principal figures, history of the consumers' movement* (Manchester, [1928?]) 11 pp.; M. Digby, *Producers and Consumers: a study in co-operative relations* (1928) 2nd ed. (1938); B. Webb, *The Discovery of the Consumer* (Self and Society Series, 1928) 32 pp.; J. J. Worley, *The Producers' Theory of Co-operation and Its Relation to the Development of Co-operation* (Leicester, 1928) 11 pp.; G. E. Griffiths, 'The Structure and Organisation of the Co-operative Movement: I – Great Britain', *RIC 22* (Feb 1929) 50–7; T. W. Mercer, *Steps towards Standardisation in Co-operative Retail Selling* (Manchester, 1929) 16 pp.; idem, *Richard Carlile on Co-operation: a century-old criticism* (Manchester, 1929) 11 pp.; idem, *Our Road to Manhood* (Manchester, 1932) 12 pp.; A. V. Alexander, 'Co-operative Societies and Income Tax', *Labour Mag. 11* (Oct 1932) 255–7; N. H. Cooper, R. A. Palmer and J. S. Simm, *Income Tax as applied to a Co-operative Society by the Provisions of the Finance Act, 1933* (Manchester, 1933) 44 pp.; Committee appointed to inquire into present position of co-operative societies in relation to income tax, *Report* (1933) Cmd 4260; C. R. Fay, 'Co-operators and the State', *Econ. J. 43* (Sep 1933) 414–26; *Co-operation and Charles Gide*, ed. K. Walter (1933); W. H. Brown, 'A Century of Co-operation in London', *RIC 27* (Aug 1934) 265–9; Co-operative Union, *British Co-operation today*, ed. E. Topham (Manchester, 1934); E. C. Fairchild, *Rise and*

Developments of Co-operation: a study in the history and problems of the co-operative movement (Manchester, 1934) 15 pp.; idem, 'The Co-operative Movement', *19th C. 116* (Aug 1934) 175–85; D. Flanagan, *Functions of the Co-operative Press – National and International* (1934) 11 pp.; F. Hall and W. P. Watkins, *Co-operation: a survey of the history, principles and organisation of the co-operative movement in Great Britain and Ireland* (Manchester, 1934); H. J. Twigg, *The Economic Advance of British Co-operation 1913–34* (1934); Royal Arsenal Co-operative Society, *Is Co-operation making headway?: a thirty years' study of seventeen representative co-operative societies* (Manchester, 1938); W. H. Brown, *The Co-operative Way through the Economic Wilderness* (Manchester, [1935]) 2nd ed. (1936); J. A. Hough, *Dividend on Co-operative Purchase with special reference to the British Consumers' Co-operative Movement* (Manchester, 1936); H. J. Laski, *The Spirit of Co-operation* (Manchester, 1936) 23 pp.; W. H. Brown, *The Co-operative Manager: being the silver jubilee history, 1912–1937, of the National Co-operative Managers' Association* (York, [1937]); S. R. Elliott, *England, Cradle of Co-operation* (1937); G. Walworth, 'The Organisation of the Co-operative Movement' in *Public Enterprise*, ed. W. A. Robson (1937) 321–57; A. M. Carr-Saunders et al., *Consumers' Co-operation in Great Britain: an examination of the British co-operative movement* (1938), rev. ed. (1942); J. J. Worley, *A Social Philosophy of Co-operation* (1942); F. Hayward and R. A. Palmer, 'War and Post-War Problems', *Co-op. Congress Report* (1942) 122–38; N. Barou, 'The Co-operative Balance Sheet (1844–1944)', *Fabian Q.* no. 40 (Jan 1944) 3–10; D. J. Flanagan, *The Co-operative Movement's First 100 Years* (1944) 48; R. A. Palmer, 'Co-operation in retrospect and prospect: I – Great Britain', *RIC 37* (Aug 1944) 132–6; J. Reeves, *A Century of Rochdale Co-operation, 1844–1944* (1944); E. Topham and J. A. Hough, *The Co-operative Movement in Britain* (1944) 51 pp.; A. Bonner, *Lessons of Rochdale Co-operation* (1945) 33 pp.; G. D. H. Cole, *A Century of Co-operation* (Manchester, [1945?]); G. L. Perkins and R. A. Palmer, 'Co-operative Reorganisation Inquiry', *Co-op. Congress Report* (1945) 156–87; J. A.

Hough, *Co-operative Retailing, 1914–1945: a statistical analysis of the development of retailing in the British co-operative movement* (1949); International Co-operative Alliance, *International Co-operation: 1937–49*, vol. 4 (London, 1953); B. J. Youngjohns, *Co-operation and the State 1814–1914* (Co-operative College Papers, no. 1: 1954); A. Bonner, *British Co-operation: the history, principles and organisation of the British co-operative movement* (Manchester, 1961; revised edition, 1970); L. Harrison and J. Roper, *Towards Regional Co-operatives* (Fabian Society research series no. 260: 1967) 18 pp.; *Manual on Co-operative Management*, ed. J. Jacques (Manchester, 1969).

BUGG, Frederick John (1830–1900)
LIBERAL BUSINESSMAN AND CO-OPERATOR

F. J. Bugg was born on 19 March 1830 and came to Ipswich from Colchester in his youth, where he obtained employment with a local boot- and shoe-maker. He later went into business on his own, introducing machinery into his works, and he successfully patented his own invention of compressed leather. He also developed branches in other parts of the country, including London. A nonconformist middle-class businessman with a flourishing leather business, he had a genuine sympathy with the workers and was involved in many of the advanced movements of his time, including the temperance movement. Before 1867 for instance he was active on behalf of the non-electors in Ipswich in the agitation for parliamentary reform. In his efforts to improve the position of the workers, he took over the *Ipswich Free Press* in 1878 which he issued weekly in an enlarged form, distributing it free in a systematic way throughout the town for a number of years entirely at his own cost. The idea of forming a co-operative society appealed strongly to him, and with George Hines and Joseph Goody he was instrumental in organising the preliminary meetings which led to the formation of the Ipswich Industrial Co-operative Society Ltd. A resolution to establish the society was passed at a meeting held on 5 November 1867 and a provisional committee, including F. J. Bugg, was appointed; but it was not till 24 March 1869 that the society was able to begin business. F. J. Bugg was elected the first president and held that office from 1868 to 1877. His wise counsel, business experience and considerable financial help were of great value to the society in its early years. Business and public work compelled him to cease active association with the society after 1877 and a few years later ill-health caused him to give up public work. His later years were lived in comparative retirement. He died on 27 October 1900 and was survived by a wife, six sons and two daughters. He left an estate valued at £64,518.

Sources: *Through Sixty Years: a record of progress and achievement 1868–1928* (Ipswich Co-operative Society Ltd, Ipswich, 1928); R. Ratcliffe, History of the Working Class Movement in Ipswich (from the nineteenth century to 1935), in four typescript volumes at Ipswich Borough Library and on microfilm at Hull University Library. OBIT. *East Anglian Daily Times*, 29 Oct 1900.

H. F. BING

See also: George HINES; G. J. HOLYOAKE, for Retail Co-operation – Nineteenth Century.

BURT, Thomas (1837–1922)
MINERS' LEADER AND LIB-LAB MP

Born on 12 November 1837 at Murton Row, a Northumberland colliery village, the elder son of Peter Burt, a miner, an ardent trade unionist, Primitive Methodist and a Rechabite. His mother's family was also in mining and his maternal grandfather, Thomas Weatherburn, a colliery engineman, assisted Thomas's early education. His schooling was often interrupted and was limited to no more than two years at village schools. His father was victimised for taking part in union affairs in 1844 and the family had to move house since they were living in 'tied' accommodation. On 13 November 1847, at the age of ten, Thomas Burt began work as a trapper boy in Haswell pit, County Durham. Then he became a donkey driver and moved to Running Water in 1848, and after two years there worked in a number of local pits. He became a putter and returned to Northumberland where he worked at Sherburn House pit and Cramlington. In the winter of 1851–2 he moved to Seaton Delaval and remained there until 1859 when he was victimised. He then moved to Choppington where he remained until July 1865.

Burt had little opportunity in his early years for self-education. In his late teens he became a coal hewer, working fewer hours than in his younger years; and he was able to indulge his passion for reading. His favourite authors were John Ruskin, Wordsworth and Edward Gibbon, and to obtain books and periodicals he walked to Newcastle, a distance of eighteen miles. He became involved in trade unionism early in his mining career and was always active in the temperance movement. He joined the Choppington branch of the Northumberland and Durham Mutual Confidence Association when it was formed in 1863 and in the following year he was Choppington delegate to a general meeting of the Association. It was Burt who moved the successful resolution which led to the Northumberland miners seceding from the parent association and on 15 July 1865 he was elected secretary and agent of the new Northumberland Miners' Association, in place of William Crawford, who had resigned. At this time the headquarters of the NMA were at Blyth and Burt moved there from Choppington, never to return to pit work. At this time he was the only full-time official of the union. He was always an organiser and a conciliator, and under his leadership the NMA quadrupled its membership in ten years (from 4250 in 1865 to 17,561 in 1875). In 1872 the headquarters of the union moved to Newcastle, and Burt with them.

Throughout his life Burt was to win a respectful hearing from all sides of the coal industry. He was a man of gentle and pacific character, and in striking physical contrast to many of the other miners' leaders of his day, being frail-looking in appearance. But he was an excellent organiser and a first-rate witness on behalf of the coalminers.

Together with Crawford he gave evidence before the 1865 S.C. on the operation of the acts regulating mine inspection and the miners' complaints; he was one of the initiators of the joint meetings in 1871 between coalowners and the miners, and all his life he worked to establish successful conciliation machinery.

A new phase of his life began with his election, on the Liberal Party ticket, as Radical Labour candidate for Morpeth in 1874. The Liberal member for Morpeth for the previous twenty years stood down in Burt's favour, and Burt polled 3332 votes against the Tory candidate's 585. He was returned unopposed in 1880; he continued to be re-elected in subsequent elections and held the Morpeth seat until 1918, by which time he had become Father of the House of Commons. His maiden speech was in support of a Bill for Household Franchise and he spoke in the House on the usual themes of the radical reformers: Irish Home Rule, the game laws, land tenure and the land laws, trade union law, the disestablishment of the Anglican Church in England and Wales. As an MP he received a salary of £500 from the NMA but in 1888 he reduced it to £400 on account of the depression in the coal trade. In the middle 1880s he refused an offer from Sir Charles Dilke, then president of the Local Government Board, of a city inspectorship at a salary of £900 p.a., increasing to £1000, and with a pension. In the Liberal Government of 1892–5 Burt was parliamentary secretary to the Board of Trade, during which office he took no salary from the NMA. He was a member of a number of committees and commissions during his parliamentary career, the most important being the R.C. on Accidents in Mines (1879–86); the R.C. on Mining Royalties (1890–1); and the R.C. on Labour (1891–4). He was made a Privy Councillor in 1906.

During most of his parliamentary career he remained active in the affairs of his own county union and in the wider movement of the miners. He resigned office as secretary of the NMA only in 1905, retired as agent in 1913 and was then appointed adviser to the Association. He wrote the monthly circulars of the NMA from 1891 to 1913, with a break in the years between September 1892 and June 1897. In his early years as secretary of the NMA Burt had been a staunch supporter of the sliding scale, adopted by the Northumberland miners from 1874.

Trade unionism in the coalfields was at a low ebb by the end of the 1870s and the seven years which followed 1880 have been characterised as the lean years by the historian of the mineworkers [Page Arnot, (1949) 62ff]. The objective of a national federation was never, however, lost sight of and Burt was present at a number of conferences in which attempts were made to work out a new basis for a national organisation. It was at Newport, in the county of Monmouth, on 26 November 1889 that the decision was taken to form a Miners' Federation of Great Britain. Burt was present, but the issue of the eight-hour day was soon to split off the county unions of Durham and Northumberland from the majority of the affiliated bodies in the new Federation. It is a well-known story which occasioned immense bitterness at the time.

Burt took an active part in the development of international contacts between miners in Europe and was present at Jolimont in 1890 and at succeeding international meetings. He also was active for many years in the international peace movement, although not a pacifist, being president of the International League for Peace between 1882 and 1914, and was president of the International Arbitration League for an even longer period. In 1911 he received an honorary degree from the University of Durham, and in 1912 was made honorary freeman of Newcastle. In 1893 a Mr Stephens, a well-known Liberal and a fervent admirer of Burt, although he had never met him, left him £2000 in his will.

Burt was always a firm supporter of the co-operative movement; and he remained faithful to liberal principles and to the Liberal Party throughout his life. He deplored the emergence of the Independent Labour Party after 1893 and later refused to sign the constitution of the Labour Party. The Lib-Lab tradition, of which he was the foremost exponent in his county, struck deep roots among the miners in the north-east coalfield.

The career of Thomas Burt illustrates better than almost any other labour leader the phenomenon of the Liberal-Labour alliance in the closing decades of the nineteenth century. His election to Parliament in 1874, along with Macdonald, evoked a deep response among working people, and especially within the mining community; and Burt's victory was celebrated in the well-known poem by Robert Elliot, 'The Pitman gan te Parliament' [in part quoted by Arnot (1949) p. 290]. After Macdonald's death in 1881 Burt was regarded as his successor in general leadership of the coalfields; and in 1887 there appeared a most interesting appraisal of him by someone who clearly rejected the theory and practice of Lib-Labourism, but who was equally full of appreciation and understanding of Burt himself. The *Miner*, a journal for underground workers published by Keir Hardie from Ardrossan, began its second number (February 1887) with a full photograph of Burt followed by an unsigned biography, most of which is given below. The author might have been Cunninghame Graham, then working closely with Hardie, or Hardie himself, though this seems much less likely:

From his boyhood he had sought to 'improve the moments as they fly' and had subjected himself to a course of reading, including the choicest literary productions of the English language. The poetry of Milton, Shakespeare, Tennyson, Wordsworth, Longfellow, Shelley and Burns; the philosophy of Adam Smith, J. S. Mill, Bastiat, Professor Fawcett, Thornton, Emerson, Carlyle, and Channing; the eloquence of Burke, Grattan, and Curran; the fiction of Scott, Thackeray, Dickens, George Eliot, and the history of Macaulay, Gibbon and Hume. How many of our young men know even the names here mentioned! He also, with the aid of a Popular Educator, mastered, to some degree at least, the propositions of Euclid, and the mysteries of shorthand, while French and German came in for a share of attention. Brought up on such mental pabulum, there is little wonder that the Member for Morpeth is strong-minded, in the best sense of that much abused term. In 1874, and when but 37 years of age, the Radicals of Morpeth returned Mr Burt to Parliament by a substantial majority. His election expenses were all defrayed, and he is also paid a salary for attending to his Parliamentary duties.

Mr Burt is the recognised authority on all labour questions. Men have come to learn that he is not a gad-fly, to be driven hither and thither by every political wind that blows. He is slow to make up his mind; but once made up, he is neither to be shaken nor driven from his position. He has great faith in the doctrines of Political Economy; and capitalists knowing this, and trading on his honesty, feel that they are quite safe in following his lead. A kind of set phrase with politicians, when being asked to support measures affecting the interests of the working class, is – I will follow Mr Burt's opinion in the matter. No greater compliment could be paid him than this.

Had Mr Burt been born into a middle class family, the chances are he would have been an honest conscientious Conservative, such as all admit the late Sir Stafford Northcote to have been. As it is, circumstances have made him an extreme Radical in all matters of Reform, but more than half a Conservative on all matters affecting the interest of capitalists.

Mr Burt has never been an advocate for restriction. He does not wholly condemn it, and believes it would do good if it could be carried out. He has never yet been able to see over that *if*. This was, perhaps, his greatest point of difference with the late Alexander Macdonald, MP, whom he respected with a respect almost amounting to veneration. He will give no encouragement – at least he has never yet done so – to any attempt to get Parliament to do for men that which men ought to be able to do for themselves. He will throw the strong arm of the law over women and children, so as to prevent them being kept too long at work; but

he does not think Parliament should interfere with the hours of labour of adult males.

Mr Burt is a man of the most kindly and lovable disposition, and to this is no doubt due in some measure his great popularity. It is just possible that Mr Burt has a little too much of the philosopher about him. A man may be 'cautious overmuch', and experience has shown that theory and practice are two very different things. The rights of property are no doubt very sacred to the owners thereof; but when the rights of property become the wrongs of labour, the time has arrived for their abolition. Mr Burt will no doubt develop in this direction; but with true Scotch caution – he is descended from the East of Scotland Burts – he must needs see all round the subject before coming to a conclusion.

We trust that the familiar form of the 'pitman philosopher' may long adorn the precincts of St Stephen's. That he has not lost in favour with his constituents, after twelve years' service, is shown by the fact that, despite his Home Rule opinions, neither Conservative nor Unionist could be found to oppose him at the last election. Such a man reflects credit on the class from which he sprung, and exercises an influence upon them at once ennobling and refining. Many are the temptations to swerve from the path of duty which have beset him; despite them all, he can still 'look the whole world in the face' as –

> An honest man,
> The noblest work of God.

Burt married Mary Weatherburn, his cousin, in 1860 and there were four sons and four daughters of the marriage. His wife, a most sympathetic woman, was a source of inspiration and help throughout his career. Burt was often assumed to have been a Primitive Methodist, like so many of his mining colleagues from the north-east, but he was not; and he made a number of disclaimers during his working life. Among them is his reply to W. T. Stead [*Review of Reviews*, 1906]: 'I have struck out your entry under "Religion", as it might mislead. I am not a member – nor have I ever been – of the Primitive Methodist body. My father and mother were Primitives. I went to the P.M. Sunday school and chapel as a boy and youth. From the travelling preachers – who often came to our house – I derived intellectual stimulus, and benefit in other ways; but as I have said I never was a member of the denomination.' Burt died on 12 April 1922 at Newcastle, having been bedridden for three years before his death. He was survived by three sons and a daughter and left £5017 (net). He had received an annuity of £1000 under the will of Andrew Carnegie (a close friend), who had died in 1919. Burt was buried at Jesmond Cemetery near his home on 19 April.

Writings: Evidence before S.C. on Regulation and Inspection of Mines and Miners' Complaints 1866 XIV Qs 1–428; 'Working Men and the Political Situation', *19th C. 9* (Apr 1881) 611–22; 'Methodism and the Northern Miners', *Primitive Methodist Q. Rev.* (July 1882) 385–97; article in *The Miner* (Jan 1887); 'Labour in Parliament', *Cont. Rev. 55* (May 1889) 678–91; 'Mr Chamberlain's Programme', *19th C. 32* (Dec 1892) 864–98; 'The House of Lords III: a dangerous anachronism', *19th C. 35* (1894) 547–52; an interesting statement by Burt of the books which influenced him, especially in his youth, in *The Review of Reviews* (June 1906) 569–70; 'Old Age Pensions', *19th C. 60* (Sep 1906) 372–8; *Lecture on the Life and Work of Joseph Cowen* (1911) 22 pp.; *Thomas Burt . . . Pitman and Privy Councillor. An autobiography with supplementary chapters by Aaron Watson* (1924).

Sources: R. Fynes, *The Miners of Northumberland and Durham* (1873; repr. Sunderland, 1923); 'Character and Public Life', *Spectator*, 5 Oct 1907, 478–9; T. C. Meech, *From Mine to Ministry: the life and times of the Right Honorable Thomas Burt* (1908); A. Watson, *A Great Labour Leader: being a life of the Right Honorable Thomas Burt* (1908); S. Webb, *The Story of the Durham Miners (1662–1921)* (1921); E. Welbourne, *The Miners' Unions of Northumberland and Durham* (Cambridge, 1923); *WWW* (1916–28); *DNB* (1922–30);

R. Page Arnot, *The Miners* (1949); G. D. H. Cole and A. W. Filson, *British Working Class Movements: select documents 1789–1875* (1951). Obit. *Evening Chronicle* [Newcastle], 13 Apr 1922; *Newcastle Daily Chronicle, Newcastle Daily Journal, North Mail* and *Times*, 15 Apr 1922; *Co-op. News*, and *Newcastle Weekly Chronicle*, 22 Apr 1922.

H. F. BING
JOHN SAVILLE

See also: Thomas ASHTON, for Mining Trade Unionism, 1900–14; William CRAWFORD; Charles FENWICK; Alexander MACDONALD, for Mining Trade Unionism, 1850–79; Benjamin PICKARD, for Mining Trade Unionism, 1880–99.

BUTCHER, John (1833–1921)
CO-OPERATOR

Born at Brackley, Northamptonshire, on 12 October 1833. His father died when he was three years old, and he was brought up by his grandfather, a shoe manufacturer. He attended Brackley Grammar School and then entered the shoemaking trade. In his early youth he became interested in social questions, from a radical-liberal point of view, and when, for instance, the agricultural labourers began to organise themselves in the early 1870s he was a frequent speaker on their behalf.

After residing in several places, he settled in Banbury in 1863 where he was manager of a boot and shoe business. He was by this time a fervent advocate of total abstinence and he became secretary of the local temperance society. He also enrolled as a member of the Reform League, organised a meeting at Banbury addressed by Ernest Jones and took part in the Birmingham demonstrations of February 1867.

In the previous year he had called a meeting of a few working men in Banbury which led to the establishment of the Banbury Co-operative Society, of which he was the first secretary. This was a retail society but it also developed wholesale trading to supply the small societies around Northampton until the establishment of the

Midland Counties Wholesale Industrial and Provident Society Ltd. At a conference of the co-operative societies in Newcastle in 1872 Butcher advocated the formation of a Midland section; subsequently at a Midland conference at Banbury (?1872), John Butcher read a paper strongly urging the CWS to take up the manufacture of boots and shoes and a resolution to that effect was passed by the delegates present.

In May 1873 he was elected a member of the CWS board and urged upon his fellow members that biscuits (which the CWS was already manufacturing) were a luxury and boots a necessity. Later in 1873 a CWS boot and shoe factory was established in Duns Lane, Leicester; Butcher resigned from the CWS board and also from the secretaryship of the Banbury Society to become its first manager. He subsequently left the CWS factory to become first a director in one well-known private firm and then a partner in another; but, in 1885, on the sudden death of the CWS manager, he was induced to return to his old post, which he held until his retirement in 1904. When the Duns Lane premises became inadequate, Butcher was instructed to prepare a scheme to meet all requirements for the next twenty-five years and this led to the erection of the new Wheatsheaf Works. In 1888 and 1890 he visited America and gained many useful ideas on management and the use of shoe machinery, some of which were incorporated in his plan for the Wheatsheaf Works. The Leicester factory was repeatedly enlarged and the Co-operative Society's premises in High Street were acquired on his initiative.

He was an active propagandist for the Co-operative Union and the first honorary secretary of the Midland section. He was also associated in the promotion of the Mississippi Valley Trading Co., established in 1875, which encouraged direct trading between British co-operators and the Grangers of America, a co-operative organisation.

He was first elected to the Leicester Borough Council in April 1883 as a Liberal and remained on the Council, with some breaks in service, until November 1891. He had founded a Freemasons' Lodge and held high office in the movement. His later years were marred by blindness and he died on 6 March 1921. The funeral service was held on 10 March 1921 at the Anglican Knighton Church, Leicester. He left an estate valued at £3322.

Sources: *Bee-Hive*, 3 July 1875; B. Jones, *Co-operative Production* (Oxford, 1894); H. D. Lloyd, *Labor Co-partnership* (1898); W. T. Pike, *Contemporary Biographies* (1902); P. Redfern, *The Story of the C.W.S.* (Manchester, [1913]); P. Redfern, *The New History of the C.W.S.* (Manchester, 1938); E. C. Mack and W. H. G. Armytage, *Thomas Hughes* (1952); and biographical information from City Librarian and Town Clerk of Leicester.

H. F. BING

See also: Amos MANN; Fred HAYWARD, for Co-operative Union; E. V. NEALE; Percy REDFERN, for Co-operative Wholesaling.

BUTCHER, John (1847–1936)
CO-OPERATOR

John Butcher was born at Leighton Buzzard on 11 January 1847 and left school to commence work before the age of ten. Later he became apprenticed to a carpenter and joiner and in 1865 entered the service of the London and North Western Railway Company. His ability and energy soon earned him promotion and after service in various capacities he was appointed the first inspector of the signals department at Rugby station in 1873. When he took up his appointment he had nine men working under him: when he retired in 1911 there were seventy.

He was responsible for many important projects including the building and commissioning of Rugby No. 1 signal box and a large signal gantry.

John Butcher joined Rugby Industrial and Provident Co-operative Society in 1874 when there were only 100 members. In 1876 he was elected to the board of management on which he served for forty-one years and from 1881 to 1917 he held office as president. It was in the early years of his presidency that the society decided to devote some of its funds to educational purposes, and in 1885 a branch of the Women's Co-operative Guild was opened in Rugby and educational classes and lectures were instituted. During the last years of his presidency he had to cope with wartime difficulties of rationing, call-up of staff, etc. In addition to his work for the local society, John Butcher became well known in co-operative circles in the Midlands and served as a representative of the Midland section on the central board of the Co-operative Union, 1879–1920. At the Perth Congress in 1897 he was elected to the central board of the Co-operative Union. He attended co-operative congresses regularly over a long period of years; including the Torquay Congress in 1929 when he was in his eighty-third year.

Butcher was a member of the Rugby Urban District Council from its formation in 1894 until 1908. He was also a director for some thirty years of the Rugby Land Society, now the Rugby Building Society, a member of the Rugby Philharmonic Society and an active member of the Wesleyan church. He died on 18 October 1936 at his Rugby home. His wife, whom he had married in 1864, predeceased him in 1927.

Sources: *Home Magazine* (Rugby Co-operative Society), July 1963. OBIT. *Advertiser* [Rugby], 23 Oct 1936; *Co-op. Congress Report* (Manchester, 1937).

H. F. BING

See also: W. H. BROWN, for Retail Co-operation, 1900–45; Fred HAYWARD, for Co-operative Union; and G. J. HOLYOAKE, for Retail Co-operation – Nineteenth Century.

CAMPBELL, Alexander (1796–1870)
OWENITE AND TRADE UNIONIST

Born in 1796 near the point of Skipness, in Kintyre, Argyllshire, Alexander Campbell was apprenticed to the Glasgow building trade as a joiner. He was influenced very early in his life by Robert Owen, and he remained to the end of his days one of Owen's most consistent disciples.

When the Orbiston community was established by Abram Combe in 1825, Alexander Campbell soon joined, taking a leading part in running the iron foundry and later successfully helping in the school. When the community collapsed in 1828 Campbell and William Sheddon were imprisoned, having made themselves legally liable for some of the debts. It was an incident which in no wise discouraged Campbell and on his release he became once again an ardent propagandist for Owen's ideas. He helped establish the first co-operative society in Glasgow in 1829, and in the following year the society opened a bazaar in London Street, its object being to carry out Owen's idea of a labour exchange similar to the one which was later established in Gray's Inn Road in London. Campbell published in 1831 the *Address on the Progress of the Co-operative System* in which he later claimed to have anticipated the 'Rochdale Plan' of dividend on purchase. As a claim it is not improbable [see his own statement, *Trans. Assoc. Promotion Social Science, 1860* (1861) 874; and his 1865 letter published in *Co-operative Educator* (October 1920)].

Campbell shared Owen's scepticism as to political action, but like many contemporary Owenites he actively supported trade unionism. In the autumn of 1831 he established the Glasgow and West of Scotland Association for the Protection of Labour, afterwards known as the General Union of Glasgow. The Union was divided into trade sections, and most seem not to have lasted. A Glasgow United Committee of Trades – a trades council in embryo – was in existence by 1830 and actively engaged in agitation for the Reform Bill. Campbell was closely concerned with the United Committee, is occasionally referred to as its secretary and probably edited its journal, *The Herald to the Trades Advocate* (September 1830–May 1831). He may also have been connected with the *Trades Advocate or Scottish Trade Union Gazette* [1833], of which no copies are extant, and he then began *The Tradesman*, a weekly, which was first published on 28 December 1833 and lasted until 31 May 1834. All these papers were unstamped and in the early summer of 1834 Campbell was summoned before the Court of Exchequer in Edinburgh, at the instigation of the Commissioner of Stamps. He was found guilty but not imprisoned on this occasion. Six months later he was gaoled for seven weeks for non-payment of fines, and published a pamphlet describing the case: *Trial and Self-Defence of A. Campbell* . . . (1835).

During his trade union and radical activities Campbell continued to work within the co-operative movement. He was present at the third national Co-operative Congress (London, 1832) and he was secretary of the Glasgow society. In May 1838 he was appointed one of six Owenite missionaries and in the next two years he travelled widely throughout the United Kingdom. He was the spokesman for Owenism in many public debates, the verbatim reports of at least four of these being published at the time. It was during this period that Campbell first met James Pierrepont Greaves, and he fell strongly under Greaves's influence. He spent much time in the company of Greaves and they corresponded at great length. Greaves died in 1842 and Campbell in the following year published the *Letters and Extracts from the MS Writings of James Pierrepont Greaves.*

When the work of Owenite missionaries was ended in the early 1840s, Campbell lived for a time at Alcott House, Ham Common, in Surrey. It was here that Greaves died. Alcott House was first a school, and then the centre of a spartan utopian community. Exactly when Campbell left Ham Common is not known, but he undertook a missionary tour on behalf of the community in August 1843. Later in the decade he was living at Vine Cottage, Hampton Wick, supervising a young children's boarding school.

What distinguished Campbell from many, if not a majority of Owenites, was the range of his radicalism. Throughout the 1830s, while mostly engaged in Owenite activity, he would seem to have participated in many of the movements of the time. In 1836 he helped form the National Radical Association of Scotland, and in September 1837, when a United Trades Association was established to help the Glasgow cotton

spinners in their dispute, Campbell was among the office-bearers. With John Cuthbertson and James McNeish, Campbell toured the country to encourage protests against the sentences of transportation imposed on the five spinners' leaders.

Although like the Owenites generally Campbell deprecated political action (although favourable on the whole to the Charter), he was nominated for Stockport at the election of 1847, but withdrew. In the following year he became editor of *The Spirit of the Age* (from July to October 1848); and from the same office he conducted the Canadian Land and Railway Investment Association, formed in May 1848, and supported among others by Robert Owen and the Duke of Argyll. Its objects were to encourage working-class investment in railway developments in New Brunswick.

The details of Campbell's life in the first half of the 1850s remain obscure. He was still secretary of the Canadian Association in 1851, and in the spring of 1856 he was reported living in Oxford, where he was an original member of the committee of the Oxford Working Men's Institute. He had returned to Glasgow by November 1856 and once again entered the mainstream of the working-class movement. He became editor of the *Weekly Chronicle*, a rather obscure journal mostly devoted to trade union affairs and this was absorbed, in June 1858, by the *Glasgow Sentinel*, the proprietor of which was Robert Buchanan, a former Owenite. Campbell became the industrial reporter of the *Glasgow Sentinel*, and from about 1863 acted as its editor for some years. Alexander Macdonald, the miners' leader, obtained a controlling interest in the *Sentinel* in 1860, and he and Campbell used the paper in their campaign against the Master and Servant Acts.

The *Glasgow Sentinel* also played an important part in the debates and discussions within the British working-class movement concerning the American Civil War. Both before and after Campbell became editor, the *Sentinel* was hostile to the Federal cause, and vigorously argued for peace between North and South. In these matters Robert Buchanan and Campbell shared the views of the veteran trade unionist, T. J. Dunning, secretary of the Bookbinders' Society. The old Owenites had, of course, a tradition of opposition to slavery and of sympathy for the democratic institutions of the American Republic; but they had no confidence in Abraham Lincoln or in his middle-class supporters in Britain, such as John Bright. [See the discussion in Harrison, *Before the Socialists* (1965) ch. 2.]

As soon as Campbell returned to Scotland he played a prominent part in the revival of co-operation. He was an indefatigable propagandist, and in February 1858 Campbell became chairman of a co-operative association. In the years that followed he was the inspirer of many small co-operative societies. As one who never went back on his early ideals, he was always a vigorous advocate of producers' co-operation, and on at least one occasion he was responsible for one such venture, the West of Scotland Painting Company, established in 1860. In April 1864, he helped promote a Glasgow conference to consider a co-operative wholesale organisation and four years later, after continuous discussion in the columns of the *Scottish Co-operator*, whose editor was John McInnes, and further conferences in Glasgow and Edinburgh, the Scottish Co-operative Wholesale Society commenced business on 8 September 1868.

It was, however, his trade union activities in this last decade of his life for which Campbell is most remembered. He was associated with the re-founding of the Glasgow Trades Council in 1858, and it was this body which began the campaign against the Master and Servant Laws. The prime movers in the agitation were Campbell and George Newton, the latter being the secretary of the Trades Council. They began the campaign in February 1863 by enlisting the services of a sympathetic Glasgow lawyer, John Strachan, who drew up a list of suggested amendments to the law. In the late spring and early summer 1863 the Glasgow Trades Council delegates argued the matter through, and in the following year (March 1864) a fully representative meeting of Glasgow trade unionists decided to set up a special committee to carry the

campaign further. Two months later, in May 1864, there took place in London the famous national conference to consider the next steps in a countrywide agitation. In the words of the Webbs: 'For the first time, a national meeting of trade union delegates was spontaneously convened by a trade union organisation, to discuss a purely workmen's question, in the presence of working men alone' [*History of Trade Unionism* (1894) 235]. Newton and Campbell represented Glasgow at the conference, which brought together most of the leading personalities of the trade union movement.

Campbell continued to be active until his last illness. He took part in many meetings in commemoration of Robert Owen; in 1866 he spoke at an Edinburgh reform demonstration; he gave evidence in 1866 before the Select Committee appointed to consider the Master and Servant laws; and in 1868 he submitted a memorandum to the Royal Commission on Trade Unions, in which once more he reaffirmed his belief in co-operative production.

He received more than one presentation in recognition of his services to the working-class movement: from the Glasgow miners in 1863, and from the Eclectic Society, an Owenite group, in 1868. After nearly a year's illness he died at his home at 11 North Coburg Street, Glasgow, on 10 February 1870. He had married when young, and had six children; but little is known of his domestic life. A portrait of him in old age, painted by J. K. Hunter, a local artist, is in the possession of the Co-operative Union in Glasgow.

Writings: *Address on the Progress of the Co-operative System* (1831); *Authentic Report of the Discussion . . . between Mr A. Campbell and Mr W. P. Roberts on the Principles of Robert Owen* (Bath, 1838) 40 pp.; *Socialism. Public Discussion* [on the doctrines of Robert Owen] *between Mr Alexander Campbell . . . and the Rev. J. T. Bannister carefully revised and corrected* (Coventry, 1839); *A Report of the Public Discussion on Socialism, held in the Theatre, Sheffield . . . between Mr Brindley, the Advocate of Christianity, and Mr Campbell, Socialist Missionary* (Sheffield, 1840) 32 pp.;

Letters and Extracts from the Writings of James Pierrepont Greaves, ed. A. Campbell, 2 vols (Ham Common, 1843–5); *Memoir of J. P. Greaves* [1848?]; *Life of Abram Combe* [1848?]; *Handbook for Emigrants* [1860?]; 'Co-operation: its origin, advocates, progress, difficulties and objects', *Trans. NAPSS* (1863) 752; Evidence before S.C. on Contracts of Service between Master and Servant 1866 XIII Qs 283–453.

Sources: (1) MSS: Occasional references in the Robert Owen correspondence, Co-operative Union Library, Holyoake House, Manchester. (2) Secondary: *Trial and Self-Defence of A. Campbell, operative, before the Exchequer Court, Edinburgh, for printing and publishing the 'Tradesman', contrary to the infamous Gagging Act* (1835) 32 pp.; *Trans. NAPSS* (1860) 874; Obituary of Robert Buchanan, *Glasgow Sentinel*, 17 Mar 1866; G. J. Holyoake, *History of Co-operation in England*, 2 vols (1875–9); B. Jones, *Co-operative Production*, 2 vols (1894, repr. in one vol. New York, 1968); S. and B. Webb, *The History of Trade Unionism* (1894); G. Howell, *Labour Legislation, Labour Movements and Labour Leaders* (1902); F. Podmore, *Robert Owen* (1906); W. Maxwell, *The History of Co-operation in Scotland* (Glasgow, 1910); A. Cullen, *Adventures in Socialism, New Lanark Establishment and Orbiston Community* (Glasgow, 1910); J. A. Flanagan, *Wholesale Co-operation in Scotland* (Glasgow, 1920); S. and B. Webb, *The Consumers' Co-operative Movement* (1921); R. W. Postgate, *The Builders' History* [1923]; F. E. Gillespie, *Labor and Politics in England 1850–1867* (Duke University Press, 1927); *Encyclopaedia of Social Sciences 3* (1930) 166–7; G. D. H. Cole, *The Life of Robert Owen* (1930); J. Johnson, *History of the Working Classes in Scotland* (Glasgow, 4th ed. 1946); G. D. H. Cole, *A Century of Co-operation* (Manchester, [1945?]); Daphne Simon, 'Master and Servant', *Democracy and the Labour Movement*, ed. J. Saville (1954); R. Harrison, 'British Labour and the Confederacy', *Int. Rev. Social Hist. 2* pt. 1 (1957) 78–105; W. H. G. Armytage, *Heavens Below* (1961); A. Bonner, *British Co-operation* (Manchester, 1961); W. H. Marwick,

Alexander Campbell (Glasgow Co-op. Assn, 1963) 19 pp.; R. Harrison, *Before the Socialists* (1965); W. H. Marwick, *A Short History of Labour in Scotland* (Edinburgh, 1967); J. F. C. Harrison, *Robert Owen and the Owenites in Britain and America* (1969). OBIT. *Glasgow Sentinel*, 19 Feb 1870; *Co-operator*, 16 Apr 1870.

NOTE: This entry leans heavily upon the research undertaken by Mr W. H. Marwick, formerly of the University of Edinburgh, whose own published work forms an indispensable introduction to Campbell's life.

JOHN SAVILLE

See also: *A. COMBE; *J. Pierrepont GREAVES; G. J. HOLYOAKE; Alexander MACDONALD; *George NEWTON; *Robert OWEN; William PARE.

CANN, Thomas Henry (1858–1924)
MINERS' LEADER

Born on 14 June 1858 in the mining village of Chacewater, five miles west of Truro, in Cornwall, the seventh son of a tin miner. He began work between the age of eight and nine for threepence a day and went underground when he was fourteen. In 1876 he moved to Brotton, Cleveland, in the North Riding of Yorkshire, where he worked as an ironstone miner, and in 1882 emigrated to the United States, and found employment in the iron ore mines of the State of Michigan. He returned to Cleveland, however, after only twelve months' absence and then, in 1888, turned to coalmining, in which occupation he remained for the rest of his working life. He began work at Castle Eden in Durham, becoming successively hewer, storeman and finally deputy. The colliery, which belonged to Hordern Collieries Ltd, closed down in 1893 but before that Cann, who had become closely involved in trade union affairs, was sentenced to two months' imprisonment for intimidation during a strike in May 1892. Between 1893 and 1896 he worked at Handen Hold colliery, one of a couple of dozen mines owned by Lambton, Hetton and Joicey Collieries Ltd, and in the latter year he succeeded James Johnson as treasurer of the Durham Miners' Association.

Cann had already been a member of the executive committee of the DMA since 1890, and he remained treasurer until 1915, when he took over the position of general secretary of the Association on the death of John Wilson. He represented Durham on the executive of the MFGB in 1909, 1911, 1913, 1916, 1918 and 1921. He gave evidence before the Miners' Eight Hour Day Committee and a Departmental Committee on safety regulations in mines.

Cann was a striking-looking man, shrewd and very thorough in his administrative work. He was a fervent Liberal in his younger days and although he formally joined the Labour Party after the affiliation of the MFGB, he remained a typical Lib-Lab in his general outlook. Before he became a full-time agent for the DMA in 1896 he had served for three years as a member for Greatham on the Durham County Council, and he was also a JP for the county, frequently sitting on the bench; but his trade union work increasingly absorbed his energies and he tended to be less involved in local affairs in the last three decades of his life than many of his colleagues. In religion he had been an active member of the Primitive Methodists and had taught as a Sunday school teacher but for many years before his death he was not connected with the church. A few years before he died he was awarded the OBE.

He was married, with two sons and two daughters, and after several years of failing health he died, still secretary of the DMA, on 6 May 1924.

Sources: Evidence before Miners' Eight Hour Day Committee 1907 XV Qs 14433–86 and Departmental Committee on use of squibs for the purpose of firing shots in naked light mines 1913 Cd 6721; C. H. Metcalfe, MS history of the DMA: DMA, Durham; John Wilson, *History of the Durham Miners' Association* (1907); idem, *Memoirs of a Miners' Leader* (1910); S. Webb, *Story of the Durham Miners* (1921); J. Lawson, *The Man in the Cap* (1941); R. P. Arnot, *The Miners*, vols *1* and *2* (1949 and 1953). OBIT. *Durham*

County Advertiser, 9 May 1924; *Newcastle Weekly Chronicle*, 10 May 1924; *NMA Monthly Circular* (1924).

VALERIE MASON

See also: Thomas ASHTON, for Mining Trade Unionism, 1900–14; William CRAWFORD; Benjamin PICKARD, for Mining Trade Unionism, 1880–99.

CARTER, William (1862–1932)
MINERS' LEADER AND LABOUR MP

Born on 12 June 1862 at Mansfield, the son of Thomas Carter, a brick and tile maker, and his wife Mary Ann (née Hemstock), he became interested in trade union activities in his youth and in 1899 formed a branch of the Nottinghamshire Miners' Association. In 1902 he was chosen as a checkweighman at Newstead Colliery and in 1907 elected vice-president of the Nottinghamshire Miners' Association, becoming president in 1909. He continued working at the colliery until 1910, and then, on the death of Aaron Stewart, he was made assistant secretary and a permanent official of the Association. He represented the Nottinghamshire miners on the MFGB executive in 1911, 1914 and 1917 and remained an agent under George Spencer who was appointed general secretary of the union in 1921.

Towards the end of the 1926 miners' lock-out, George Spencer negotiated a local settlement and this being contrary to MFGB policy he was suspended from the Notts Miners' Association. Spencer then quickly established a breakaway union, supported vigorously by the employers. Carter became general secretary of the official Association in place of Spencer and although a moderate man, he spoke very critically, indeed harshly, of Spencer's activities. Carter served until his death as general secretary of the Association in an exceedingly difficult period when in many pits the Association was virtually eliminated by the refusal of the employers to deal with any officials but those of Spencer's company union; and by the early 1930s the Association was in a very weak position.

Apart from his work for the Association

Carter served as Labour MP for the Mansfield Division of Nottinghamshire from 1918 to 1922 when he was defeated by the Liberal candidate and he did not enter another parliamentary contest. He remained, however, active in local affairs: as a member of the Mansfield Town Council for many years, a JP for the county for twenty years, a life governor of the Nottingham General Hospital, and he was for many years prominently associated with the local co-operative movement.

He died on 29 February 1932 in a Northampton nursing home and was survived by his wife, two sons and two married daughters; he left effects valued at £1800.

Sources: *Dod* (1922); *WWW* (1929–40); R. Page Arnot, *The Miners: Years of Struggle* (1953); A. R. Griffin, *The Miners of Nottinghamshire*, 2 vols: *1881–1914* (Nottingham, 1956) and *1914–1944* (1962); J. E. Williams, *The Derbyshire Miners* (1962). OBIT. *Nottingham Guardian*, 1 Mar 1932; *Labour Party Report* (1932); *TUC Report* (1932).

JOYCE BELLAMY

See also: *A. J. COOK, for Mining Trade Unionism, 1915–26; G. A. SPENCER; *F. B. VARLEY.

CATCHPOLE, John (1843–1919)
MINERS' LEADER

Born at Thrandeston, in East Suffolk, on 22 June 1843, the son of Samuel Catchpole, a labourer, and his wife Mary (née Gardener). His parents removed to Chesterfield, Derbyshire, when he was nine and he later worked in the Derbyshire coalfield as a miner. In December 1864 when the Practical Miners held their national conference at Chesterfield he was elected to the credentials committee. Soon afterwards he became active in the rival Miners' National Association, led by Alexander Macdonald and in 1865 was elected secretary of the Derbyshire and Nottinghamshire Miners' Association which was within Macdonald's federation. In the same year he became checkweighman, the first in Derbyshire, at the Staveley Company's Springwell colliery and was later checkweighman at the Ballarat colliery, New Whittington, and at the Locoford colliery, near Chesterfield. After the collapse of the Derbyshire and Nottinghamshire Association, Catchpole became active in the South Yorkshire Miners' Association which attempted to organise the Derbyshire miners in the 1870s. Together with John Normansell and five other delegates from the district of South Yorkshire, he attended the three-day national conference of miners under the presidency of Alexander Macdonald, held in Leeds on 27–29 April 1875 'to consider the best means of preventing the lowering or wages to an undue extent', with attendance (including representatives from the National Association and also the Amalgamated Association of Miners) 'representing in the aggregate some 192,623 members'. Catchpole became a strong supporter of the movement for the secession of the Derbyshire miners from the South Yorkshire Association and was one of the founders of the Derbyshire Miners' Association in 1880; but beyond speaking at one or two meetings and writing an occasional letter to the press he appears to have taken no leading part in the movement after the new union was established. Like many trade unionists of his day who became weary of the constant insecurity arising from the threat of victimisation he left the industry when he saw an opportunity. He started a small business as newsagent, stationer and sub-postmaster at Holywell Cross, Chesterfield, which he carried on for the rest of his life.

Catchpole, like many miners' leaders of his day, was a Primitive Methodist local preacher. He was elected secretary of the Chesterfield Municipal and Parliamentary Electoral Association in 1874 but in 1877 he was censured for neglecting his duty and resigned. Catchpole was also active in promoting the Cambridge University Extension Movement in Chesterfield and was elected a member of the local committee. He died on 31 July 1919 at Holywell Cross, Chesterfield, and left £466 in his will.

Sources: *Derbyshire Times*, 1864–1919; R.C. on Trades Unions, *Minutes of Evidence*, 1867–9; A. R. Griffin, *The Miners of Notting-*

hamshire (Nottingham, 1956); J. E. Williams, *The Derbyshire Miners* (1962). OBIT. *Derby Mercury*, 8 Aug 1919.

J. E. WILLIAMS

See also: Alexander MACDONALD, for Mining Trade Unionism, 1850–79.

CHARTER, Walter Thomas (1871–1932)
CO-OPERATOR

Walter Thomas Charter was born on 30 December 1871 in Cambridge, the son of Walter Charter, a journeyman carpenter. In his youth he worked as a carpenter in the building trade. He joined the Cambridge Co-operative Society quite early in his life and was soon serving on its education committee and, from 1899, on the management committee. In 1910 he was appointed secretary of the Society and in the following year managing secretary; on the division of the functions in 1918 he was made general manager. He had for some years been a member of the southern sectional board of the Co-operative Union and from 1907 to 1920 was a member of the central board of the Co-operative Union. During the First World War he was a member of the committee dealing with retail societies and food control. The Cambridge Society developed rapidly under his leadership, its share capital having more than doubled from the time he became secretary to 1919 when he left office on being elected to the CWS board, a position he held until his death.

He became well known nationally as a speaker and through his membership of the central board, and he served on many important committees. A pioneer of political action, he was a strong advocate of co-operative participation in politics long before 1914. A member of the parliamentary committee of the Co-operative Union and a founder of the National Co-operative Representation Committee, he moved the historic resolution at the Swansea Congress in 1917 which, being carried by an overwhelming majority, took the co-operative movement into politics and led to the formation of the Co-operative Party:

That, in the opinion of this Congress, the time has now arrived for the co-operative movement to take the necessary steps to secure direct representation in Parliament as the only way of effectively voicing its demands and safeguarding its interests.

In 1924 Charter was appointed by the Prime Minister (Ramsay MacDonald) to the Balfour Committee on Industry and Trade on which he served till 1929. He was a member of the Government's Chinese Purchasing Committee and of the Wheat Commission under the 1932 Wheat Act. With Sir Thomas Allen and T. G. Arnold he constituted the CWS board's emergency committee during the General Strike of 1926. At the CWS divisional meeting in the following October he complained bitterly of the arbitrary attitude of the TUC to the co-operative movement during the strike and declared that 'if there is to be collaboration between the trade union and co-operative movements, it must work both ways'. In 1928 he represented the CWS board on the committee of inquiry into the basis of CWS board elections. As a CWS director he served on the joint committee of the CWS and the Co-operative Union, and he travelled widely on behalf of the CWS, visiting many countries all over the world.

He died on 30 June 1932 being survived by a wife and three sons. The funeral service was at the Methodist Chapel in Cambridge. He left an estate valued at £5179.

Writings: *Taxation: present and future* (1919) 16 pp.; *The Trading and Financial Policy of the Wholesale Societies etc.* (Trade and Business Conference Series, no. 7: Manchester, 1924) 12 pp.

Sources: *Co-op. Congress Report* (1917); W. H. Brown, *Cambridge Co-operative Society: 1868–1919* (Manchester, 1920); W. H. Crook, *The General Strike* (North Carolina, 1931) 313–14; W. H. Brown, *Co-operation in a University Town* [1939?]; P. Redfern, *The New History of the C.W.S.* (Manchester, 1938); G. D. H. Cole, *A Century of Co-operation* (Manchester, [1945?]); A. Bonner,

British Co-operation (Manchester, 1961); S. Pollard, 'The Foundation of the Co-operative Party', in A. Briggs and J. Saville, *Essays in Labour History*, vol. *2: 1886–1923* (1971) 185–210. OBIT. *Co-op. News*, 2 July 1932; *Cambridge Chronicle*, 6 July 1932; *Co-op. Congress Report* (1933).

H. F. BING

See also: A. V. ALEXANDER, for Co-operative Party; Thomas ALLEN; Percy REDFERN, for Co-operative Wholesaling.

CHEETHAM, Thomas (1828–1901)
CO-OPERATOR

Born in 1828 at Lowerplace, a village near Rochdale. His father died while he was a child and his grandfather – a small handloom flannel manufacturer – placed him at the neighbouring school of Mr John Kershaw where he was taught the three Rs and also grammar, astronomy, mathematics.

He left school at eleven and when he resumed his studies at seventeen found he had forgotten nearly everything he had learned except reading. This impressed him very much in later life with the need for post-school education and made him a strong advocate of night schools and the science and art classes run by the Rochdale Pioneers' Society. Cheetham was a frequenter of a local library where he met Samuel Tweedale, a Socialist and co-operator, who introduced him to James Smithies, William Mallalieu, Abraham Greenwood and other leading co-operators. This aroused his interest in the co-operative movement. He joined the Rochdale Pioneers' Society in 1852 and after some time was elected a member of its board of management. He agitated actively for the establishment of a branch of the Society in Oldham Road which was opened on 7 October 1856 as No. 1 Branch, in the management of which he took an active part.

In 1859 he was appointed a member of the board of the Mitchell Hey Manufacturing Society, and was still a member of the company at the time of his death. In 1862 he was made president of the Pioneers' Society, when it was decided to secure the ground on which the new central premises were subsequently built. He took an active part in the work of the educational committee until 1865.

Like many others in Lancashire, Cheetham suffered unemployment at the time of the American Civil War, and he became landlord of a public house, the Fullers Arms, which he renamed the Lincoln. During this period he had to withdraw from active participation in the co-operative movement but after eleven years he resumed his co-operative work and he was again elected president of the Pioneers' Society in 1886, holding office until 1895; a longer period than any other president in the Society's history. When the Co-operative Congress met in Rochdale in June 1892, Thomas Cheetham was one of the Rochdale Society's delegates and presided over the Congress on the third day (8 June). In his chairman's address he emphasised the ethical purpose of co-operation and the need for the educational aspect of its work.

Thomas Cheetham was actively associated with the formation of the Co-operative Wholesale Society. He was an early addition to the committee appointed at a conference at Rochdale in November 1860 to discuss the question of wholesaling. He was chairman of the meeting on Good Friday, 3 April 1863, which resolved to establish a wholesale organisation, and was one of the twelve original members of the North of England Co-operative Wholesale Industrial and Provident Society, being elected a member of the committee at its formal constitution on 10 October 1863.

Politically, Cheetham was a strong Liberal of the Cobden and Bright school, and a firm believer in free trade. Before the extension of the franchise in 1867 he was a member of the executive of the Non-Electors Association and on one occasion accompanied Abraham Greenwood and J. T. W. Mitchell on a deputation to John Bright to try to induce him to speak at a public meeting in Rochdale on the injustice of working men being deprived of the franchise. The interview took place in the library of John Bright's residence in Rochdale.

Thomas Cheetham was elected to the Rochdale Borough Council in 1880 as a Liberal representative of Castleton East Ward. His service on the Council remained unbroken until 1898 when he was defeated by a Conservative candidate by a small majority. After his retirement from the Council he was co-opted a member of the Technical School Committee and Free Library Committee. For his services to the Liberal cause during his public career, he was in 1898 elected an honorary member of the Rochdale and District Reform Club.

At one time he was in the habit of attending the Unitarian Church, but for many years prior to his death he was associated with the Secularists. He was on intimate terms with some of the best-known freethinkers of his time, and had on more than one occasion acted as Charles Bradlaugh's host and chairman in Rochdale. He was a great reader and many of his speeches were interspersed with poetical quotations. He knew the Lancashire dialect well, and took a deep interest in the local scheme for the erection of a memorial to four Rochdale dialect writers.

He died on Monday 30 September 1901 at the age of seventy-three and was buried in Rochdale Cemetery on Thursday 3 October, leaving a wife and two daughters, and personal effects valued at £801.

Sources: *Co-op. Congress Handbook* (1892); *Co-op. Congress Report* (1892); P. Redfern, *The Story of the C.W.S.* (Manchester, [1913]); idem, *The New History of the C.W.S.* (Manchester, 1938); A. Bonner, *British Co-operation* (Manchester, 1961). OBIT. *Rochdale Observer*, 2 Oct 1901; *Co-op. News*, 5 Oct 1901.

H. F. BING

See also: G. J. HOLYOAKE, for Retail Co-operation – Nineteenth Century.

CIAPPESSONI, Francis Antonio
(1859–1912)
CO-OPERATOR

Born on 8 February 1859 at Eastbourne, the son of Francis Primo Ciappessoni, a master watchmaker and jeweller. Of his early career nothing is known but he presumably became a teacher, for from 1880 and many years thereafter he was headmaster of St Patrick's Roman Catholic schools, Cleator Moor, Cumberland. He first became associated with the Cleator Moor Co-operative Society in the mid-1880s, on several occasions filling the presidential chair. In 1897 he was a member of the sectional board from which he retired in 1905. He was largely responsible for the resuscitation of co-operation at Wigton and when a new society was formed there by the northern sectional board he became its first president, holding this office until he was elected to the board of the CWS in 1904, and he was still a member of the board when he died. One of his main interests while on the board was the establishment and general welfare of the Gilsland Convalescent Home.

A few years before his death he had removed to Carlisle. Outside the co-operative movement, his interests were in the educational field, and he was a co-opted member of the Carlisle Education Authority, representing the Roman Catholic body, and he served on the School Attendance and School Management Committees.

Following an operation at Carlisle Infirmary he died on 20 February 1912. His wife, two sons and four daughters survived him. He left effects valued at £660.

Writings: 'The Desirability of employing only Certified Auditors and Independent Stocktakers in connection with the Societies' Accounts', *Co-op. Congress Report* (1903) 338–41.

Sources: P. Redfern, *The Story of the CWS* (Manchester, [1913]). OBIT. *Co-op. News*, 24 Feb 1912; *Cumberland News*, 24 Feb 1912; *CWS Annual* (1913) 272.

MAI ALMAN

See also: G. J. HOLYOAKE, for Retail Co-operation – Nineteenth Century.

CLARK, Fred (1878–1947)
TRADE UNIONIST, LABOUR PARTY WORKER AND CO-OPERATOR

Fred Clark, son of William Clark, a master brickmaker, and his wife Charlotte, was born at Brigg, Lincolnshire, on 1 September 1878. He attended Brigg elementary school but left at the age of ten years to work in a brickyard. For a time, in his early youth, he was employed by the Hull Anti-Mill Society, a co-operative flour-milling organisation, so that his connection with the co-operative movement came early. He also worked as an engine driver in Bradford before moving to Scunthorpe about the turn of the century where, in 1902, he joined the Scunthorpe Mutual Co-operative and Industrial Society, being elected to its board of management in 1906. Initially, on his return to Lincolnshire, he worked as a locomotive driver at the Appleby-Frodingham Steel Works and was an active trade unionist. One of the pioneers in North Lincolnshire trade unionism, he represented the enginemen at the steel works, becoming after some years chief works delegate for the district. For three years he served on the executive of the Blastfurnacemen's Federation. He transferred to the Yaddlethorpe Brick Yard Co. in 1922, thus returning to his former trade, and became manager of the company, a position he held until his retirement in 1939.

His activities in the co-operative movement were extensive. He was president of the Scunthorpe Society from 1922 until his retirement on health grounds in 1944. He served on the South Yorkshire district executive committee, 1925–44, was a member of the central board of the Co-operative Union from 1939 to 1946 and of the national committee of the Co-operative Party from 1925 to 1929. He was also a member of the Scunthorpe Co-operative Men's Guild and represented the north-east sectional board of the Co-operative Union on the National Conciliation Board, the sectional meat committee and the South Yorkshire district wages board. On his retirement a memorial scholarship bearing his name was endowed by the Scunthorpe Society.

Fred Clark's interest also extended to the political field. He pioneered the Scunthorpe branch of the Independent Labour Party in 1905; chaired the general election committees of the local Labour Party and remained a member of the Party until his death. He was also very active in local government

affairs. For seven years he represented Crosby on the Rural District Council, served on the Brigg RDC and also on the Brigg Board of Guardians. In 1927 he became a member of the Scunthorpe Urban District Council and subsequently was appointed an alderman; he served as leader of the Labour group on the Council, 1941–4, and was elected mayor of the Borough for the year 1941–2. He was also vice-chairman of the North Lindsey Water Board, a member of the Lindsey County Council from 1940 and served on the Brigg assessment committee. He was appointed a JP in 1936 and also served for eleven years as chairman of the Scunthorpe Council's water committee. He was a lifelong member of the Methodist Church.

He died in Scunthorpe on 28 July 1947. His wife, formerly Miss S. E. Potts, whom he had married in 1903, predeceased him in 1940 but he was survived by a son, Mr Frank Clark, and a daughter, Mrs Elsie Wyld. He left an estate valued at £2901.

Sources: A. Ginns, *Jubilee History of the Scunthorpe Mutual Co-operative and Industrial Society Ltd* (Manchester, 1924); personal information: Mrs Elsie Wyld, daughter. OBIT. *Co-op. News*, 2 Aug 1947; *Star* [Sheffield], 2 Aug 1947.

H. F. BING

See also: A. V. ALEXANDER, for Co-operative Party; *C. R. ATTLEE, for British Labour Party, 1931–51; F. BOND; W. H. BROWN, for Retail Co-operation, 1900–45.

CLARKE, Andrew Bathgate (1868–1940)
MINERS' LEADER AND LABOUR MP

Born on 5 February 1868 at Lawnmarket, Edinburgh, the son of a butcher, John Clark, and his wife Ann (née Murray). Of his early life little is known except that after his father died he went with his mother to America. (It is not known when he first spelt his name with an e.) On his return as a young man to Midlothian, he entered the Newcraighall pit, one of three pits in Portobello belonging to the Niddrie and Benhar Coal Company Ltd. Here he was later elected checkweighman. He joined the ILP and was a friend of Keir Hardie, being associated with him in the early pioneering socialist days in the Scottish coalfield. Clarke was always active in trade unionism and in 1919 he was appointed secretary of the Mid and East Lothian Miners' Association. In the previous year at the Scottish Miners' Conference of 16 August 1918 he had seconded a resolution which protested against the action of the authorities for the imprisonment of John MacLean and called upon the trade union movement for joint action. Soon after his election as county secretary he stood for the secretaryship of the Scottish Miners' Association but received the support only of his own Association. Within the miners' unions Clarke soon took up an outspokenly right-wing standpoint, based upon a firmly committed anti-communist position. He was one of the first general secretaries (other than George Spencer of Nottinghamshire) who was ready in the 1921 lock-out to pronounce publicly against the policy of the MFGB.

With the death of the Scottish president in April 1932 it fell to Andrew Clarke as vice-president to deliver the presidential address at the annual conference at the end of June. He set the habit, followed thereafter, of a carefully prepared speech. On the unemployed he spoke of 'an inquisitionary system called the Means Test that is more degrading in its operation than the Poor Law was a hundred years ago'. By the time his address was delivered there had developed an intense factional struggle within the ranks of the Scottish miners. The story is told in Arnot, The Scottish Miners (1955) 182ff. A result of this internecine war was the setting up of the United Mineworkers of Scotland, headed from 1932 onwards by Abe Moffat. Andrew Clarke became the most vigorous and bitter opponent of the United Mineworkers and continued his opposition to leading members of the UMS after the latter organisation early in 1936 had decided to disband, urging its membership to join the old National Union. Clarke remained president of the Scottish miners until his death. He attended many miners' con-

ferences in Britain and abroad. The concern dearest to him was probably welfare work, and among his contributions to the welfare facilities of the Scottish miners was the joint secretaryship of the Lothian Miners' Welfare Committee.

He was one of nine Scottish miners' candidates to be elected to Parliament in 1923, when he was returned for the North Midlothian constituency, but he lost his seat in the following year. He then regained it at a by-election in 1929 but he was unsuccessful at the general election of the same year, and he also failed again in 1931. During the period of the Spanish Civil War the Scottish miners were vigorous in their condemnation of the Franco régime, and Clarke, in his presidential addresses, consistently took up a strongly democratic position in support of the Spanish Republic. On all domestic matters which concerned the Communists in the years immediately preceding the Second World War Clarke remained implacably hostile to any joint action.

Apart from his trade union work, Clarke was also active in local government and co-operative affairs: for some years he served on the Musselburgh Town Council and was president of the Musselburgh and Fisherrow Co-operative Society. He was a JP for Midlothian, a manager of the Edinburgh Royal Infirmary, and a member of the Heriot-Watt College Committee. He died on 1 February 1940 at the Royal Infirmary, Edinburgh. Following a service at Inveresk Church Hall, Musselburgh, he was buried in Inveresk churchyard. His wife survived him and he left an estate valued at £1267.

Sources: Dod (1924) and (1925); Labour Who's Who (1927); R. Page Arnot, The Scottish Miners (1955); idem, The Miners in Crisis and War (1961); A. Moffat, My Life with the Miners (1965); General Register Office, Edinburgh. Obit. Edinburgh Evening News, 2 Feb 1940; Scotsman, 2 Feb 1940; Labour Party Report (1940).

JOYCE BELLAMY

See also: *W. ADAMSON; *R. SMILLIE, for Scottish Mining Trade Unionism.

CLAY, Joseph (1826–1901)
CO-OPERATOR

Born at Dalbury Lees near Derby on 25 December 1826 of humble parents. His father died when he was very young, leaving his mother to struggle to bring up four children. Joseph started work at a very early age in a silk factory, working from 6 am to 7 pm for 1s 6d a week. Later he was apprenticed to the smithing trade and when out of his time obtained employment in the Midland Railway Locomotive Department at Derby. In 1851 he was transferred to Gloucester where he continued to work for the railway company for thirty years. In 1881, owing to failing health, he retired from his employment on medical advice receiving a handsome retirement present from his fellow employees.

In 1860 he became interested in co-operation through reading a speech made in the House of Commons by John Bright in which, when advocating an extension of the franchise, he spoke of the achievements in co-operation of the working men of Rochdale. Clay discussed the matter with three fellow workers and they decided to start a store. They commenced business with fifty-four supporters and a capital of £19 16s 8d. The first year's sales amounted to £365, the surplus was £34 and the committee declared a dividend of 6d in the £1 to members and 3d to non-members. The creeping-in of credit trading threatened the Society in its early years but after this was abandoned progress was rapid. In 1865 Clay was elected president of the Gloucester Co-operative Society and held this office till his death in 1901. During those years membership rose from 2128 to over 7000, and in 1883 the Society granted him an honorarium of £50 in gratitude for his services. During Clay's presidency, new central stores were erected in Brunswick Road and branches were opened in Gloucester, Cheltenham, Sharpness, and in the surrounding countryside.

Joseph Clay was elected to the western sectional board of the Co-operative Union in 1867 and served until 1896. He was the board's first chairman, an office he retained for many years and was chairman of the united board 1887–8. He was one of the seven original committee members of the London branch of the Co-operative Wholesale Society (1874) and at its first meeting was appointed chairman, which office he held for over twelve years. He spoke at the coming-of-age celebrations of the CWS in Manchester in 1884, and from time to time he visited Spain and the Continent on its behalf and in 1896 Australia and New Zealand. Most of his time was spent visiting the Wholesale's establishments in England. He was a regular attender at co-operative congresses and in May 1893 presided over the second day's proceedings of the Bristol Congress.

Clay was also an active trade unionist. He joined the Amalgamated Society of Engineers as soon as he was eligible and was secretary of the Gloucester branch for sixteen years (1852–68). He remained in membership until his death.

In 1882, Joseph Clay was elected to the Gloucester School Board, being second in the poll. On the next occasion he headed the poll and remained a member till his death. In politics he was a radical and in religion a staunch Baptist. He was made a JP for the City of Gloucester in 1893, the first working-man JP in that city, and when at home was most regular in his attendance on the bench. In his judicial capacity if he erred, so it was said locally, it was on the side of clemency. He took an active part in establishing Penny Banks for children.

He was taken ill on a journey to Greece on behalf of the CWS in August 1901 and had to be brought home from Athens in the care of a doctor and a nurse. He never recovered and died at his home, 20 Stratton Road, Gloucester, on 25 October 1901. He had married in 1851, and his wife survived him. A year after his death a large gathering was present at the unveiling of a memorial over his grave. He had left effects valued at £642.

Sources: *Co-op. Congress Handbook* (1893); *Co-op. Congress Report* (1893); P. Redfern, *The Story of the C.W.S.* (Manchester, [1913]).

OBIT. *Co-op. News*, 2 Nov 1901; *CWS Annual* (1902).

H. F. BING

See also: G. J. HOLYOAKE, for Retail Co-operation – Nineteenth Century; Percy REDFERN, for Co-operative Wholesaling.

COCHRANE, William (1872–1924)
MINER

Born on 19 September 1872 into a mining family at Choppington, Northumberland, and attended Choppington colliery school. In 1884, at the age of twelve, he began work at the local colliery. After several moves he settled at Coxlodge, in the Gosforth Urban District, in 1902 and remained there for the rest of his life; and it was after he began living at Coxlodge that he became involved in trade union affairs. In 1910 he was elected treasurer of the Hazelrigg lodge in Glendale Rural District of the Northumberland Miners' Association and he served until his death. The owners of Hazelrigg mine, with 950 employed at its peak, were the Burradon and Coxlodge Coal Co. Ltd, who also had pits at Burradon and Weetslade.

Cochrane was a religious man but belonged to no one church. He was a member for the last eight years of his life of the Castle Ward RDC and of the Castle Ward Board of Guardians; and he was an active supporter of many charities, including the Coxlodge Aged People's Treat Fund, Gosforth Nursing Association, Dr Barnardo's and the Newcastle Royal Infirmary. A teetotaller and keen sportsman, he died on 29 December 1924 after an attack of pneumonia, leaving a wife, son and daughter.

Sources: OBIT. *Newcastle Weekly Chronicle*, 3 Jan 1925; NMA, *Monthly Circular* (1925).

ANTHONY MASON

See also: Thomas ASHTON, for Mining Trade Unionism, 1900–14; T. H. CANN; *W. P. RICHARDSON; *William STRAKER.

COOPER, William (1822–68)
OWENITE AND ROCHDALE PIONEER

Born in Rochdale in 1822, William Cooper was first a fustian cutter, then a handloom weaver and afterwards a stationer and account book maker. He became a member of the Rochdale Rational Society along with many of those who were to become the pioneers of the Toad Lane Store in 1844; and he was also greatly inspired by O'Connor and the Chartist movement and in particular by the Land Plan. He remained a staunch radical and secularist for the rest of his life and was among the diminishing band of co-operators who retained the Owenite ideal throughout the years when the co-operative movement was becoming prosperous and profitable. Cooper, in G. D. H. Cole's phrase, was 'the handyman of Co-operation' and throughout his life he worked indefatigably for the movement. His correspondence was enormous and he filled the part of a Co-operative Union in answering letters of inquiry. Those of his papers that have survived bear witness to the range and variety of his social and political interests.

He was one of the founders of the Rochdale Society of Equitable Pioneers, his name standing thirtieth in the list of members at the back of the original Purchase Book, where he is described as a weaver of Lower Place. He was employed as cashier for the Society and took alternate nights with Samuel Ashworth, selling two nights a week. They both gave their services free for the first three months and subsequently were paid at a rate of 3*d* per hour. Cooper succeeded James Daly as secretary when the latter went to Texas in 1849 (dying on the voyage); and when the shop was opened all day in 1851, he was appointed superintendent to oversee the two shopmen and watch the checks. When the Rochdale Society undertook wholesaling in 1850 Cooper was one of two members appointed to attend wholesale customers on Mondays at one o'clock. He was one of the founders of the Rochdale District Co-operative Corn Mill Society in 1850 and ten years later he wrote its history. He was also a promoter of the Rochdale Co-operative Manufacturing Society in 1854 and he vigorously opposed those shareholders who began to demand the abolition of the 'bounty to labour'. During the controversy G. J. Holyoake wrote to Cooper asking for a statement of the attitude of the different religious denominations to the question. Cooper replied that the secularists voted for the bounty as one man, and they were generally supported by the Unitarians and mostly, also, by the Anglicans; and that the most hostile to the principle were the Independents from Milton Church as well as the Methodists and certain other nonconformist sects. Cooper's report was published in *The Counsellor* (September 1861) which Holyoake was at that time editing, and the furore which followed led Abraham Howard, the president of the Rochdale Society, both to repudiate Cooper, on the grounds of religious neutrality, and to suspend him temporarily from his office as secretary (to which he was soon restored).

The attempts to develop a Wholesale Society in the 1850s received a setback when the Central Co-operative Agency in London closed down in 1857; but some of the leading Pioneers, among them Cooper and James Smithies, continued to urge the principle. It came to be appreciated that what was needed was a change in the law allowing federal action within the co-operative movement and at the end of the 1850s there began the series of discussions and conferences which led ultimately to the passing of the 1862 Industrial and Provident Societies Act. Cooper was involved in these discussions from the beginning and in the autumn of 1860 he became secretary of the committee, starting a diary in November 1860 which provides a sparse but continuous record until the establishment of the Wholesale Society in 1863. He gave evidence to the parliamentary committee which inquired into the general question of amendments to the 1852 Act and the desirability of the amendments which were being sought. Vansittart Neale and Ludlow were drawn into the campaign and the establishment of *The Co-operator* in 1860, soon to be edited by Henry Pitman, proved an invaluable centre for discussion and information.

Cooper was one of the twelve individual members of the North of England Co-operative Wholesale Society when it was first established in 1863 and in 1867 he received payment of £8 for four years'

work for the Society, recorded in the first balance sheet of preliminary expenses. J. C. Edwards of Manchester took Cooper's place as secretary to the first board of the Society. Cooper also took part in the conference held on Good Friday 1867 which led to the establishment of the Co-operative Insurance Society. He was one of the seven original members who took up four shares each in order to form a limited company; he and Vansittart Neale produced the draft rules; and Cooper was secretary until his premature death in 1868.

He was a strong opponent of Negro slavery in the American South and he supported the abolitionists cause uncompromisingly. In one of his articles in the *Co-operator*, towards the end of 1862, he drew attention to the way in which the Pioneers' Society had helped to cushion the effects of unemployment caused by the Cotton Famine, by the withdrawal of thousands of pounds of share capital to meet current needs.

In addition to being a prolific correspondent he wrote a good deal in the press, especially in Henry Pitman's *Co-operator* during the 1860s. He died rather suddenly from typhus on 31 October 1868. A subsequent quarterly meeting of the CWS voted £20 to a Cooper Memorial Fund. Besides the widow and family, Holyoake, Lloyd Jones, James Smithies and Abraham Greenwood were among the chief mourners. Holyoake spoke at the graveside and wrote the inscription for the tombstone:

In Memory of
WILLIAM COOPER

who died October 31st, 1868 aged 46 years One of the original "28" Equitable Pioneers. He had a zeal equal to any, and exceeded all in his ceaseless exertions, by pen and speech. He had the greater and rarer merit of standing by principle always regardless alike of interests, or friendships or of himself
Author of the
'History of the Rochdale Co-operative
Corn Mill Society'

Writings: *History of the Rochdale District Co-operative Corn Mill Society* (London: Holyoake & Co., [1860?]) sold by Abel and

John Heywood, Manchester; David Green, Leeds; and William Cooper, Rochdale, 12 pp.

Sources: MSS: papers, letters: Holyoake House, Manchester; G. J. Holyoake, *History of Co-operation*, 2 vols (1906); P. Redfern, *The Story of the C.W.S.* (Manchester, [1913]); F. Hall and W. P. Watkins, *Co-operation* (Manchester, 1934); T. W. Mercer, *Towards the Co-operative Commonwealth* (Manchester, 1936); *Some Interesting Facts* [brochure published by the Rochdale Pioneers' Society (reprinted from the *Wheatsheaf Mag.*, 1939)] n.d.; W. H. Brown, *The Rochdale Pioneers* (Rochdale, 1944); G. D. H. Cole, *Century of Co-operation* (Manchester, [1945?]); A. Bonner, *British Co-operation* (Manchester, 1961). Obit. *Rochdale Observer*, 7 Nov 1868; *The Co-operator*, 14 Nov 1868.

H. F. BING
JOHN SAVILLE

See also: J. C. EDWARDS; G. J. HOLYOAKE; E. V. NEALE; James SMITHIES.

COURT, Sir Josiah (1841–1938)
MINERS' MEDICAL ADVISER

Born at Warwick on 17 January 1841, the second son of a druggist and grocer, John Court, and his wife Eliza (née Flicknoe). He was educated at King Henry VIII School, Warwick, and at fourteen he went to work in a Liverpool shipping office where he became friendly with John Brunner who worked in the same office and later founded the great chemical firm, Brunner, Mond and Co. (now Imperial Chemical Industries). But it was his friendship with a young doctor named Lowndes which finally determined his career. After some persuasion Court's father agreed to allow him to study medicine at the Sydenham College of Medicine, associated with the old General Hospital, Birmingham. He then moved to Guy's Hospital, London, where he completed his studies, and qualified as MRCS in 1863 and LRCP in 1864. In the latter year he bought a practice at Staveley in Derbyshire where he was to live for the rest of his long life.

In Court's early years in Staveley it was still a place of green fields and woodland. He led the life of an ordinary country doctor engaged in country practice. Medicine, midwifery and surgery occupied most of his professional time. Major operations were often performed on the kitchen tables of country cottages. Court was a much loved man, full of common sense and plain talk. Birds, dogs and children had his particular affection and his main recreations were fishing and shooting. He was a crack shot and won the Robin Hood cup at Wimbledon in 1880 with seven bulls in seven shots at 200 yards. He took an active part in the formation of the Staveley Company of Volunteers and for some years held the rank of Captain. In religion he was a practising Anglican, and his private benefactions to the Church were many; in politics he was a Conservative. He was chairman of the local Conservative Association in 1868 and for many years afterwards; and on six occasions between 1895 and 1916 he unsuccessfully contested the constituency of North East Derbyshire, although he made substantial inroads into the Liberal, and later the Lib-Lab vote. He was made a JP in 1901 and received a knighthood in 1920 for his work on miners' diseases.

The growing use of safety lamps instead of naked lights in the 1880s led the Derbyshire miners to complain that the poorer light was affecting their earnings as well as their eyesight. Colliery owners, the mines inspectorate and medical opinion were all inclined to dismiss the view that inadequate light was the cause of nystagmus. A dispute between J. Haslam, secretary of the Derbyshire Miners' Association, and Mr A. H. Stokes, H.M. Inspector of Mines for Derbyshire, over the causes of miners' eye disease reached an impasse; and the matter was reported in the local press. It is not clear who made the first approach, but Dr Court and the Union got together and worked very closely from that time on.

The characteristic sympton of nystagmus, involuntary oscillation of the eyeballs, had been described by C. T. Thackrah in his 1832 book. The miners had complained for years about bad lighting, but little interest seems to have been shown by the authorities until the events mentioned above. The increase of miners' eye disease was blamed by the men not so much on the growing use of safety lamps as on the increasing adoption of bonneted Marsaut-type lamps. Dr Court at this time referred almost entirely to Marsaut lamps; his diagrams showed the shadow areas cast by bonnet, base and pillars, and his experiments with the light output of lamps at the start and end of shifts were made only with the Marsaut. During the winter of 1890–1 Court attended many meetings in Derbyshire and examined 573 men working with naked lights and 524 men working with safety lamps. The terms 'nystagmus' and 'miners' eye disease' were often regarded as synonymous, but Court distinguished clearly between photophobia, night-blindness and nystagmus. He found many men who were only suffering from one or two of these afflictions, although most bad cases of nystagmus usually suffered from the other two as well. In May 1891 he reported that 'the want of good light' was the only cause of nystagmus.

One point of particular interest was the form of argument he used to make certain of his points, in that by setting out in figures the number of men affected under different lighting conditions, he was able to show convincingly the relationship between eye disease and bad light. An obvious point, but it gave the men an argument they themselves could understand.

Meanwhile Simeon Snell, a Sheffield ophthalmic surgeon, was advancing a counter-theory that the disease was caused by the way in which miners had to throw their eyes whilst working at the coal face. Court continued his researches by visiting Durham and the Forest of Dean and, in July 1892, read a paper on his work before the British Medical Association at Nottingham. Court's theory was the subject of violent controversy, and there was opposition from the great majority of ophthalmologists, as well as from the Mine Inspectors and the coalowners. But Court was in no way intimidated or discouraged, and he continued quietly with his investigations. In 1901 he gave evidence in an important arbitration case at Nottingham before Judge Smyly which led to an award of an extra 1d a ton on all coal raised by the South Derbyshire miners in places where the use of safety lamps was compulsory. The miners' claim was not made solely because of the health hazard, but because it was argued that not as much work could be achieved with a safety lamp as with a candle. In 1911 Court called the attention of the Home Secretary, Reginald McKenna, to the fact that the accepted theory on nystagmus was responsible for the increase in the number of compensation cases because it was believed that a miner who had suffered from nystagmus was liable to further attacks: 'If the opinions of these expert eye surgeons are allowed to prevail, the disease will be looked upon as a permanent injury and the increase in compensation demanded from the employers will be very great.' J. S. Haldane was asked to investigate the problem and on 22 February 1912 he presented to the Royal Society a paper written by T. Lister Llewellyn which confirmed Court's conclusion that nystagmus was caused by inadequate light. Court's triumph was complete when he read a paper to the Ophthalmological Congress at Oxford on 19 July 1912. After hearing and discussing the paper the Congress endorsed Court's views. Court's discovery gave an impetus to the attempts which were being made to improve the illumination given by the miner's safety lamp. His research on miners' nystagmus had earned him the gratitude of the Derbyshire miners and led to his being admitted in the 1890s to honorary membership of their union. From time to time he acted as consulting surgeon to the union, frequently giving evidence in compensation cases.

Court also gave some attention to another miners' ailment, ankylostomiasis, popularly known as miners' anaemia or worm disease. It appears to have been imported from tropical or sub-tropical countries and was first discovered by J. S. Haldane in England in 1902 among the Cornish tin-miners after an examination of statistics kept by the Miners' Convalescent Hospital at Redruth. At the request of the Derbyshire Miners' Association Court made a report to the executive committee of the Miners' Federation of Great Britain in the spring of 1903. Later in the year he delivered an address on the disease to the annual conference of the MFGB. He also visited Belgium to carry out investigations in hospitals at Mons and Liége, and did much to advise the MFGB on the kind of legislation which was necessary to combat the disease.

In 1924 Court carried out investigations at Warsop Colliery, Derbyshire, into the effects of working in a high temperature. He confirmed the findings of J. S. Haldane and others that the addition of a little salt to the men's drinking water enabled them to withstand fatigue.

Court, despite the differences in political attitudes, always remained on terms of close personal friendship with most of the leaders of the Derbyshire miners; and he was immensely respected by the ordinary miner. On more than one occasion he appeared as a speaker at the miners' annual demonstration. In all things about which he felt deeply Court had a strong missionary zeal: until the age of ninety-one he was to be seen week after week attending the open-air services of the Salvation Army in the main streets of Staveley.

He died in his ninety-eighth year at his Staveley, Chesterfield, home on 8 February 1938. His wife Sarah, daughter of John Hyde of Hampton Lucy, Warwickshire, whom he married in 1865, predeceased him in 1906 but he was survived by three sons. Following a service at Staveley Parish Church he was buried in Staveley Cemetery. He left an estate valued at £12,442.

Writings: 'Defective Illumination as the Cause of Nystagmus and Other Ocular Disorders observed in Miners', *British Medical Journal*, 15 Oct 1892, 836–8; 'A New Form of Disease amongst Miners. The Worm Disease: what it is and how to prevent it', *World's Work 2* no. 12 (Nov 1903) 611–13; 'Miners' Nystagmus: a retrospect', *Ophthalmoscope 10* no. 12, 1 Dec 1912, 684–7; *Miners' Diseases: records of the researches of Dr J. Court* [Sheffield, 1920].

Sources: (1) MSS: Minutes of the Derbyshire Miners' Association, 1890–1938 (NUM, Saltergate, Chesterfield). (2) Printed: C. T. Thackrah, *The Effects of the Principal Arts, Trades and Professions . . . on Health and Longevity: with a particular reference to the trades and manufactures of Leeds* (1831, 2nd ed. 1832); *Derbyshire Times*, 1890–1938; 'Dr Court: *Report on the Examination of Coal Miners in Derbyshire*', *British Medical Journal*, 11 July 1891, 78 [an unsigned review of a pamphlet]; S. Snell, *Miners' Nystagmus and its Relation to Position at Work and the Manner of Illumination* (Bristol, 1892); W. Hallam, *Miners' Leaders* (1894); *Minutes of the Miners' Federation of Great Britain* (1903); *The Investigation of Mine Air: an account by several authors*, ed. C. Le Neve Foster and J. S. Haldane; T. L. Llewellyn, 'The Causes and Prevention of Miners' Nystagmus' (communicated by Dr J. S. Haldane), *Proc. Royal Society*, series B, 85 (1912); A. Court, *Staveley, my native town* (Sheffield, 1946); H. W. Poole, *My Life in Three Counties* (1950). (3) Secondary: J. E. Williams, 'The Political Activities of a Trade Union, 1906–14', *Int. Rev. Social Hist. 2* (1957) 1–21; idem, *The Derbyshire Miners* (1962). We are much indebted to Mr John Foster, of the Safety in Mines Research Establishment, Sheffield, for technical information incorporated in the text. OBIT. *Times*, 9 Feb 1938; *Derbyshire Advertiser*, 11 Feb 1938; *British Medical Journal 1*, 19 Feb 1938, 424–6.

JOHN SAVILLE
J. E. WILLIAMS

See also: W. E. HARVEY.

COWEN, Joseph (1829–1900)
RADICAL REFORMER, POLITICIAN AND CO-OPERATOR

Born at Blaydon Burn on 9 July 1829, the eldest son of Sir Joseph Cowen, industrialist and MP for Newcastle between 1865 and 1873. Most obituaries and other records for the young Joseph place his date of birth in 1831, but the family circle always celebrated 1829, and Joseph's younger brother John was born in June 1831, a record of which is in the Winlaton parish register. Joseph was educated at private schools at Winlaton and Ryton-on-Tyne and then at Edinburgh University where he enrolled as a first-year arts student for the session 1845–6, but did not continue with his studies.

On returning home Cowen entered his father's rapidly expanding brick manufacturing business. He played an active part in local temperance reform, sanitary reform and educational movements; furthering his belief that if the working classes were to improve their lot they must do it themselves. He was opposed to Tories, Whigs, and Manchester School radicals, whose beliefs he condemned as selfish materialism. He considered that helping the working classes was a middle-class duty, but he became more and more disillusioned with middle-class activity in this respect.

Cowen was strongly influenced by his Winlaton background (Blaydon Burn is virtually part of Winlaton). The Crowley ironworks, although closed in 1816, still conditioned local thinking. The Crowley system of social security, including sick benefits and widows' pensions, had something of a twentieth-century flavour about it, and it was imitated by the Cowens. It contrasted sharply with the coalowners' harsh treatment of the Northumberland and Durham miners in the 1844 strike, an event which obviously made a deep impression on the boy in his formative years. In addition, the economic dislocation caused by the Crowley closure had turned Winlaton almost overnight from a Tory village to a stronghold of radicalism and ultimately of physical-force Chartism. Cowen himself never condemned physical force outright; in fact in 1851 he thought it a potential 'servant of moral force' and he became particularly friendly with men like Harney, whom he employed on the *Northern Tribune* in 1854 and later on the *Newcastle Chronicle*.

It was in foreign affairs that Cowen made his first national impact. He had contacted Mazzini in 1845 and he organised with W. J. Linton the first Subscription for European Freedom in 1851. But much more significant was the arrival of the democratic Polish refugees from Hungary late in 1851. Cowen brought twelve of them to Newcastle and through their leader, Konstantine Lekawski, was introduced to revolutionary politics. He used his firm to smuggle agents and propaganda into Europe and was drawn into financing Polish, French and Italian revolutionaries. When Garibaldi visited the Tyne in 1854 he met Cowen and obtained his support. Cowen's contacts with the refugees and his activities as a conspirator will never be fully revealed as he destroyed almost all of his correspondence in 1858 after Orsini's attempt to assassinate Napoleon III, in which he was almost certainly implicated. In 1864, when Garibaldi again visited England, Cowen's influence was so great that he was considered the only man who could effect a reconciliation between Mazzini and Garibaldi.

In home affairs Cowen was to establish a Newcastle school of radicalism which in the 1850s eclipsed both Birmingham and Manchester. This was particularly true of the period of the Northern Reform Union (1858–62) in which Cowen tried to unite the middle and working classes on a programme of manhood suffrage and vote by ballot. Cowen's visits to Yorkshire, Lancashire and London in October 1858 did evoke some response, and led to Bright's reform campaign which Cowen considered a sell-out.

To obtain greater publicity for the Northern Reform Union, Cowen purchased the *Newcastle Daily Chronicle*, an ailing paper, for which the change from a weekly to a daily issue in 1858 had resulted in too great a financial strain. The proprietors were already heavily in debt to Cowen, when, after protracted negotiations in which the expert advice of friends like Holyoake and Slack was sought, he became sole proprietor in December 1859. According to Holyoake, Cowen sunk £40,000 in the paper before it began to show a profit. New premises and new equipment were bought. The political tone of the paper moved to the left, to the extent that the *Chronicle* became the required reading of the politically conscious Durham and Northumberland working classes. It was the *Newcastle Daily Chronicle* which the young Arthur Henderson read to his workmates during the break for dinner.

Having built up a sound local circulation, the *Newcastle Daily Chronicle* soon achieved a national reputation, similar to that enjoyed by the *Manchester Guardian* in the twentieth century. Radical views were expressed fearlessly, and the *Chronicle* developed close relations with trade unionists, co-operators and other working-class leaders. A new *Weekly Chronicle*, intended as a vehicle for extended articles and comment, was begun in 1864. Under the editorship of W. E. Adams, it attracted contributions from men like Holyoake, Howell, Harney, Kropotkin and Lloyd Jones to the extent that today the paper remains an invaluable source for historians interested in the nineteenth century.

As a boy Cowen studied the principles of co-operation and socialism, going so far as to collect the publications of communistic communities such as Icarians. By 1847 he had found these societies futile on the grounds that they had 'no idea of duty, or of organisation or of growth'. Co-operation appealed to him much more directly. As one who was convinced that the working classes must seek their own improvement, the element of self-help in co-operation was immediately attractive. There is no doubt that Cowen was strongly influenced by Holyoake in seeing co-operation as an important means towards a more equitable distribution of wealth, and of working-class social progress in general.

As a result of readings of Holyoake's works at the Blaydon Mechanics' Institute the Blaydon Co-operative Store was set up in 1858. Under Cowen's close supervision it became a model of its kind, described in 1879 by Holyoake as 'the most remarkable store next to that of Rochdale'. An education fund of $2\frac{1}{2}$ per cent of the profits was used to finance classes and scholarships; the library expanded rapidly and included a superb collection of nineteenth-century blue books, assigned to the flames of the Society's central-heating boilers by the post-1945 committee; news-rooms and libraries were provided at branches as well as at Blaydon; and club rooms were built for recreational activities.

The success of the Blaydon Society helped spread co-operation in the north-east. By 1862 sufficient progress had been made for Cowen to suggest a degree of federation to enable bulk-buying and training in business techniques. He was chairman of a committee which made an abortive attempt in 1862 to set up a Northern Union of Co-operative Stores. Further efforts to found a wholesale organisation were made before the Newcastle branch of the CWS was founded in 1872. Cowen presided over the fifth Co-operative Congress held at Newcastle on Tyne in 1873.

Cowen agreed with most north-east co-operators that production was an essential part of co-operative activity. As one of the trustees of the Durham Miners' Association funds he may well have influenced the union to deposit a large sum in the Co-operative Mining Company in 1873. He supported the establishment of the co-operative printing works and Industrial Bank in Newcastle. Unfortunately for north-east co-operation Cowen entered Parliament in 1874 for with his business acumen he might have been able to prevent the fiascos of the Ouseburn Engine Works and the Industrial Bank.

Later Cowen became disillusioned with co-operators. He felt that they had become mere shopkeepers, losing sight of the idealism of the movement. By 1891 in an interview for *Figaro* he had become bitter:

Of all the meannesses in God's creation and the sweating practised therein, the modern co-operator is the worst living embodiment. I know of things done and being done by societies in the North here, of dishonest dealings, of underpaying, of sweating the life's blood out of the employed, of a wanting of the littlest of the doctrines of honest commercialism, that make one despair.

Cowen's contact with trade unionists was very close. He would frequently examine a union's case in a dispute, employ lawyers at his own expense and help in the formulation of policy. Perhaps his most important success was in the Nine Hours' Strike of 1871 when he supported the strikers vigorously in the *Newcastle Chronicle*, acted as representative for the men, was partly instrumental in having foreign workers shipped home, and ultimately played a decisive part in obtaining a settlement. During this period Cowen was also active in the Northern Reform League, in Chamberlain's National Education League and as a member of Newcastle Council.

Cowen was elected MP for Newcastle on the death of his father in 1873. Gladstone dissolved Parliament before Cowen was able to take his seat, but he was re-elected at the general election and remained senior member for Newcastle until 1886 when he retired from public life. Cowen met with a cold reception at Westminster. He was snubbed by Gladstone and abused by Bright, both of whom blamed him, with some justice, for the defeat of the Whig Headlam, who had represented Newcastle continuously from 1852. Gladstone, in particular, was suspicious of a republican revolutionary, whatever his standing in the north-east. Embitterment followed, leading to a showdown in 1878, when Cowen, whose Polish contacts had created in him a Russophobia second only to Urquhart's, supported Disraeli's policy at the Congress of Berlin. Estrangement from the Liberals increased with Cowen's rapidly growing imperialist views.

By 1880 Cowen's relations with Newcastle Liberals were, at best, lukewarm. They reached breaking point in 1881 when Cowen came out strongly against coercion in Ireland and the Cloture Bill. At this time Cowen developed a close relationship with the Irish Parliamentary Party, even to the extent of having letters addressed to him when Irish MPs suspected interference with their mail.

This was the stage at which Cowen's political future lay in the balance. In 1877 he had been a prominent member of a small radical party, including Chamberlain, Dilke, Burt and Macdonald. This had broken up largely because Cowen and Chamberlain could not agree. In 1881 a new opportunity arose as a result of the campaign against coercion in Ireland. Engels, indeed, at one time envisaged Cowen

as the leader of a 'Proletarian-Radical' party. Cowen did become the first chairman of Hyndman's Democratic Federation, but was one of the first middle-class leaders to resign. Later contacts with the left were largely on an individual basis through Cowen's friendships with men like Kropotkin and Hyndman, and he stood bail for the latter in 1886.

From 1881 Cowen became increasingly embittered. He was at loggerheads with the Newcastle Liberal caucus, whom he accused of putting organisation before policy, and of stifling political debate. He became disillusioned with the miners' unions, particularly in 1885 when he backed Lloyd Jones as a working-class candidate in Chester-le-Street against Joicey, a big coalowner. The Durham Miners' Association, having made a pact with the Liberal Party, refused to assist in the opposition even to an unpopular capitalist candidate. Cowen felt all the more betrayed as he had played a crucial role in financing and securing the return of other working-class MPs, and particularly Thomas Burt, the Northumberland miners' secretary, for Morpeth in 1874. Cowen felt that the working classes had nothing to gain from subservience to the Liberals.

The last years were spent in bitter warfare with the Liberal Party. Relations with John Morley, who became the other Newcastle MP in 1883, were vicious. Morley went so far as to warn T. P. O'Connor in the House of Commons about being seen talking to Cowen. Cowen, for his part, attacked Morley mercilessly in the *Chronicle*, to the extent that in 1885 the Liberals felt obliged to start the *Newcastle Leader* as a rival newspaper. Cowen was still returned at the top of the poll at the 1885 election, but it was obvious that he owed his success to Tory and Irish votes. In these circumstances he decided to retire.

His last years were spent in looking after his wide business interests and in conducting the *Newcastle Chronicle*. He became increasingly imperialist, developing a belief in the inevitable supremacy of the British race. His last published statement was one of strong support for the Boer War. He died on 18 February 1900, in the same month as the

Labour Party was to be born, and left an estate valued at £501,927.

Writings: *Speeches on Public Questions and Political Policy delivered during the Parliamentary Contest occasioned by the death of Sir Joseph Cowen with an additional speech on the subject of Mr Gladstone's manifesto* (Newcastle on Tyne, 1874); *The Bishoprics Bill: speech by Joseph Cowen . . . in the House of Commons July 31 1878* [1878] 16 pp.; *The Foreign Policy of England: extract from a speech delivered by Mr Joseph Cowen on January 31 1880* (National Union of Conservative and Constitutional Associations: 1880); *Mr Joseph Cowen MP on the Eastern Question and Spirited Foreign Policy: a few words of advice to modern liberals* [extracts from speeches delivered 1874–80] (1880) 19 pp.; *Speeches delivered by Joseph Cowen as candidate for Newcastle-upon-Tyne at the General Election 1885* (Newcastle upon Tyne, 1885); *Mr Cowen's Speech on the Second Reading of the Government of Ireland Bill in the House of Commons 7 June 1886* (British Home Rule Association Publications Tractates no. 1 [1886]) 4 pp.; *Ireland and Home Rule* (1886) 30 pp.; *Joseph Cowen's Speeches on the Near Eastern Question*, ed. Jane Cowen (1909).

Sources: (1) MSS: Cowen Collection (Newcastle upon Tyne City Libraries); Jane Cowen, Notes on Joseph Cowen (1910); Holyoake correspondence (Co-operative Union Library, Manchester); Holyoake diaries, etc. (Bishopsgate Institute, London); Howell Collection (Bishopsgate Institute, London).

(2) Newspapers and periodicals: *Gateshead Observer*, 1837–86; *Newcastle Chronicle*, 1840–58; *Reasoner*, 1846–66; *Refugee Circular*, 1851–2; *English Republic*, 1851–5; *Monthly Record of the Society of Friends of Italy*, 1853–5; *Republican Record*, 1855; *Northern Tribune*, 1854–5; *National Sunday League Record*, 1856–9; *Newcastle Daily Chronicle*, 1858–1900; *Northern Reform Record*, 1858–60; *Newcastle Council Proceedings*, 1860–1900; *Newcastle Weekly Chronicle*, 1863–1900; *Newcastle School Board Triennial Reports*, 1871–1903; *Mayfair*, 1877; *Monthly Chronicle*, 1887–91.

(3) Theses: W. K. Lamb, 'British Labour and Parliament 1865–1893' (London PhD, LSE, 1933); R. E. Grimshaw, 'The Northern Union of Literary, Scientific and Mechanical Institutions' (Library Association FLA, 1951); D. W. Crowley, 'The Origins of the Revolt of the British Labour Movement from Liberalism 1875–1906' (London PhD, 1952); C. Muris, 'The Northern Reform Union 1858–1862' (Durham [King's College, Newcastle] MA, 1953); P. Darvill, 'Contributions of Co-operative Retail Societies to Welfare within the Social Framework of the North-east Coast Area' (Durham MA, 1954); R. J. Harrison, 'The Activity and Influence of the English Positivists on Labour Movements, 1859–1885' (Oxford DPhil., 1955); A. D. Bell, 'The Reform League, from its Origins to the Passing into Law of the Reform Act of 1867' (Oxford DPhil., 1961); M. R. Dunsmore, 'The Working Classes, the Reform League and the Reform Movement in Lancashire and Yorkshire' (Sheffield MA, 1962); T. J. Nossiter, 'Elections and Political Behaviour in Durham and Newcastle, 1832–1874' (Oxford DPhil., 1968).

(4) Secondary: T. Fordyce, *Local Records* (1867); J. E. Ritchie, *British Senators* (1869); J. Burnett, *The Nine Hours Movement: a history of the engineers' strike in Newcastle and Gateshead* (Newcastle upon Tyne, 1872); R. Fynes, *A Review of Real and Sham Reformers amongst the Miners* (1872) 39 pp.; idem, *The Miners of Northumberland and Durham* (1873); E. R. Jones, *The Engineers' Strike in the North of England* (1873) 15 pp.; W. D. Lawson, *Tyneside Celebrities* (1873); 'Newcastle Critic', *Life of Joseph Cowen* (1874) 14 pp.; R. Welford, *The Tyneside Apocrypha, containing the Epistle to the Cowenites* (1874) 4 pp.; R. J. Hinton, *English Radical Leaders* (New York, 1875); J. D. Morrisson, *Eminent English Radicals* (1879); J. Annand, *A Plain Letter to Joseph Cowen* (1882) 28 pp.; G. Garibaldi, *Epistolario* (Milan, 1885); E. R. Jones, *Life and Speeches of Joseph Cowen* (1885); H. W. Lucy, *A Diary of Two Parliaments* (1885); J. McCarthy, *A History of our own Times* (1879–85); M. Noble, *Short Sketches of Eminent Men in the North of England* (1885);

E. R. Jones, *Heroes of Industry* (1886); T. W. Reid, *Life of the Right Hon. W. E. Forster* (1888); W. W. Bean, *The Parliamentary Representation of the Six Northern Counties* (Hull, 1890); Newcastle Weekly Chronicle, *Gathering of Contributors* (1891); G. J. Holyoake, *Sixty Years of an Agitator's Life* (1892); W. J. Linton, *Memories* (1895); R. Welford, *Men of Mark 'twixt Tyne and Tweed* (1895); W. Bourn, *History of the Parish of Ryton* (Carlisle, 1896); C. B. R. Kent, *The English Radicals* (1899); J. McCarthy, *Reminiscences* (1899); M. Ostrogorski, *Democracy and the Organisation of Political Parties* (1902); W. E. Adams, *Memoirs of a Social Atom*, 2 vols (1903), reproduced in one volume with an introduction by John Saville (New York, 1968); W. Duncan, *Life of Joseph Cowen* (1904); G. J. Holyoake, *Bygones worth remembering* (1905); idem, *The History of Co-operation in England* (1875-7) [another ed. (less useful) 1906]; G. L. Lampson, *A Consideration of the State of Ireland in the Nineteenth Century* (1907); J. McCunn, *Six Radical Thinkers* (1907); R. S. Watson, *National Liberal Federation* (1907); J. Wilson, *A History of the Durham Miners' Association* (1907); J. McCabe, *Life and Letters of G. J. Holyoake* (1908); J. L. McCallum, *James Annand, MP* (1908); J. Wilson, *Memories of a Labour Leader* (1910); T. Burt, *Lecture on the Life and Work of Joseph Cowen* (1911) 22 pp.; H. M. Hyndman, *The Record of an Adventurous Life* (1911); A. W. Humphrey, *History of Labour Representation* (1913); P. Redfern, *The Story of the C.W.S.* (Manchester, [1913]); P. Corder, *The Life of Robert Spence Watson* (1914); J. Morley, *Recollections* (1917); J. A. Oxberry, *A Great Tynesider: Joseph Cowen 1830–1900* (Felling, [1917]) 11 pp.; A. Watson, *A Newspaper Man's Memories* (1925); F. E. Gillespie, *Labor and Politics in England, 1850–1867* (1927); F. W. Hirst, *Early Life and Letters of John Morley* (1927); T. P. O'Connor, *Memoirs of an Old Parliamentarian* (1929); J. L. Garvin, *Life of Joseph Chamberlain 1* (1932); B. Nicolaievsky and O. Maenchen-Helfen, *Karl Marx, Man and Fighter* (1936); M. A. Hamilton, *Arthur Henderson* (1938); G. Mazzini, *Epistolario* (Imola, 1938–43); E. Morelli, *Mazzini in Inghilterra* (1938);

P. Redfern, *The New History of the C.W.S.* (Manchester, 1938); G. D. H. Cole, *A Century of Co-operation* (Manchester, [1945?]); J. H. Gleason, *The Genesis of Russophobia in Great Britain* (1950); S. Middlebrook, *Newcastle-upon-Tyne* (1950); P. Brock, 'Polish Democrats and English Radicals, 1832–62', *J. Mod. Hist.* 25 (June 1953) 139–56; P. Brock, 'Joseph Cowen and the Polish Exiles', *Slavonic and East European Rev.* 32 (1954) 52–69; M. Duverger, *Political Parties* (1954); A. R. Schoyen, *The Chartist Challenge* (1958); M. Partridge, 'Alexander Herzen and the Younger Joseph Cowen', *Slavonic and East European Rev.* 41 (Dec 1962) 50–63; M. W. Flinn, *Men of Iron: the Crowleys in the early iron industry* (1962); D. F. McKay, 'Joseph Cowen e il risorgimento', *Rassegna storica del risorgimento* Anno LI, Fasc. I (1964). Obit. *Times*, 19 Feb 1900; *Newcastle Daily Chronicle*, 19 and 20 Feb 1900.

K. G. E. Harris

See also: *W. E. Adams; *John Burnett; Benjamin Jones, for Co-operative Production; *G. J. Harney; G. J. Holyoake, for Retail Co-operation – Nineteenth Century; J. H. Rutherford.

COWEY, Edward (Ned) (1839–1903)
MINERS' LEADER

Ned Cowey, as he was always called, was born on 9 April 1839 at Longbenton, Northumberland. He entered the mines at the age of ten and when quite a young man he was victimised for taking part in a strike against the yearly bond (for which see Thomas Hepburn) and attempting to form a miners' association in Durham. This was in 1858 and being unable to obtain employment he joined the Royal Navy in the following year. After four years at sea he returned to mining and worked at the Monkwearmouth Colliery in Sunderland. In 1868 at the same colliery there was a further strike to abolish the bond and to obtain a wage advance. After three weeks, despite large-scale arrests of striking miners, the bond was abolished but the strike for an increase in wages went on for many weeks more. It was eventually settled in the men's favour but a similar strike in the following year was lost and Cowey once again found himself victimised. His wife strongly opposed him returning to the sea and the family suffered acutely until, in January 1871, they moved to Yorkshire when Cowey obtained work at Sharleston Colliery four miles south-east of Wakefield. He quickly resumed his union activities, later became checkweigh-man and in 1876 was elected president of the West Yorkshire Miners' Association. From this time he was closely associated with Ben Pickard. In 1881, when the Yorkshire Miners' Association was formed as a result of the amalgamation of the West and South Associations, Cowey was elected president of the new body and held the position until his death.

For ten years he had been on the executive of the Miners' National Association (see Alexander MACDONALD), but both Cowey and Pickard in the second half of the 1880s were recognising the need for a more broadly based national federation; and Cowey was an influential figure at the Newport conference of 1889 which established the MFGB. He was elected to the provisional executive committee and his position was confirmed at the first annual conference in January 1890. He remained on the executive committee until his death. Throughout the 1890s he continued to play a leading part in the affairs of the miners, both within his own county union and at national level. In particular he was a fervent advocate of the legislative eight-hour day, and he took a major part in the fierce controversy with the representatives of Durham and Northumber-land on this question. Because of his eloquence he was often delegated by the executive committee of the MFGB to under-take difficult assignments. Cowey attended the famous Rosebery Conference of 17 November 1893 (Parrott and Frith being the other Yorkshire representatives) which ended the great lock-out of 1893; and Cowey became a member of the Conciliation Board which the Conference established as part of the settlement. He was elected to the parliamentary committee of the TUC in 1893 (replacing John Wilson of Durham)

and again he remained a member until his death. With the Lib-Lab recapture of the TUC in the middle years of the 1890s, together with the adoption of new rules excluding the representation of Trades Councils as well as the block vote, Cowey and Sam Woods, together with other leaders such as cotton spinner Mawdsley, inflicted a setback on the growing socialist influence and ensured the dominance of the coal and cotton unions for several years ahead. Cowey was also a prominent figure at the inter-national conferences of miners, beginning with Jolimont in 1890.

Cowey was a Primitive Methodist, a local lay preacher, a man of commanding and imposing presence. He was a radical in the Lib-Lab tradition and vigorously opposed to the spread of socialist doctrines in general (in which he recognised and dreaded a revival of the theories of Chartism) and among the miners' unions in particular. Cowey supported James Haslam when the latter stood as a Liberal-Radical candidate, against the official Liberal candidate (who was a prominent coalowner), in the general election of 1885; but his political position was best illustrated during the famous Barnsley by-election of October 1897. The Liberal candidate was a coalowner who was in favour of the Eight Hours Bill and he received the support of Pickard and Cowey and other Yorkshire miners' leaders. The ILP entered Pete Curran, supported by Robert Smillie (who had already been a member of the MFGB executive in 1895) and Keir Hardie (who had similarly been a member in 1890). It was an exceedingly bitter contest with Pickard and Cowey in vigorous opposition to Curran. For the ILP, in the short run at any rate, it was a costly failure.

Apart from his life's work for the miners, and his considerable activity on behalf of his chapel, Cowey participated little in public life. He represented the Darton division on the West Riding County Council for a short time but his whole life was within the mining community. His last year of active life was concerned mostly with the difficult and serious consequences of the Denaby Main decision which followed the legal attack on the unions represented by the Taff Vale decision; and his death on 16 December 1903 was to be followed within six weeks by that of his close comrade-in-arms Ben Pickard. Cowey died at his home at Crofton near Wakefield after an illness of nearly a year. He had married early in life but details of his family are not known. He left £1011 in his will.

Sources: Evidence before R.C. on Accidents 1881 XXVI Qs 10143–359; before R.C. on Mining Royalties 1890–1 XLI Qs 7972–8116; W. Hallam, *Miners' Leaders* (1894) [portrait of E. Cowey]; F. Machin, *The Yorkshire Miners* (Barnsley, 1958). OBIT. *Times,* 18 Dec 1903; *Barnsley Independent,* 19 Dec 1903.

JOHN SAVILLE

See also: William ABRAHAM; T. BURT; *P. CURRAN; Alexander MACDONALD, for Mining Trade Unionism, 1850–79; Benjamin PICKARD, for Mining Trade Unionism, 1880–99; John WILSON (1837–1915).

CRABTREE, James (1831–1917)
CO-OPERATOR

Born in Dodworth near Barnsley in April 1831, James was the son of Joseph Crabtree, a working man who later served two years' imprisonment in Wakefield Gaol for his Chartist activities. James Crabtree assisted his mother by winding yarn when he was nine years of age and then worked as a linen weaver until his father removed to Heckmondwike in 1845 to a teaching appointment. James then entered the trade of carpet weaving and ultimately became manager of the local firm of Frith and Co.

His interest in co-operation and social questions generally, much encouraged by his father, was shown in the foundation of the Heckmondwike Co-operative Society in 1860 for which he was largely responsible, and of which he was eleven times president, his last term of office being in 1913. In 1865 when the CWS, at that time confined largely to south-east Lancashire, was anxious to extend its influence particularly among the numerous societies in the West Riding, James Crabtree was persuaded to join its committee. In 1867 the CWS adopted new rules, including an increase in its committee from seven to nine members, but Crabtree remained the only one from outside south-east Lancashire. In 1870 when Abraham Greenwood retired and became cashier, Crabtree was elected the second chairman of the CWS and remained chairman till 1874 when he was succeeded by J. T. W. Mitchell. During Crabtree's chairmanship business expanded rapidly, the annual sales increasing from about £500,000 to nearly £2 million.

Crabtree's guidance of the CWS tended always to be cautious. At the conference on Good Friday 1870 to consider the beginning of banking business by the CWS he seconded what was, in fact, a delaying resolution moved by William Pare approving of the proposal 'provided sufficient capital can be raised'. He adopted a similar attitude at the Bolton Congress at Easter 1872, but when the CWS had established a banking department, he defended that action at the Newcastle Congress in 1873. Later he favoured the proposal (not adopted) that the CWS should transfer its banking function to the Industrial Bank. In 1872 when it was proposed that the CWS should undertake manufacturing as well as wholesaling, he thought this should be done by separate federations and even after the CWS had successfully opened its biscuit factory at Crumpsall, he was dubious about its entering into the boot and shoe making business (1873). He was one of the committee of three who went to London in April 1873 to discuss the establishment of a London branch of the CWS, but a little later opposed the suggestion of a Bristol branch on the ground that they had enough on their hands in getting the London branch started.

Crabtree resigned from the chairmanship of the CWS board when he became associated with the Heckmondwike Manufacturing Co. Ltd, a company formed in 1873 to take over an old firm of carpet, blanket and rug makers whose business had failed. He served as chairman of this company until 1886 but had already rejoined the CWS board in 1885, and he continued a member until 1889. He was one of the speakers at the CWS coming-of-age celebrations in Manchester in 1884 and served as an elected member of the north-west sectional board of the Co-operative Union, 1870–80. Although he ceased to be a member of the CWS board in 1889, he attended CWS meetings as a delegate or visitor for many years afterwards and as late as 1913 was still an occasional visitor at the CWS headquarters in Balloon Street, Manchester. In that year he attended the Co-operative Congress in Aberdeen, being one of the oldest, if not the oldest co-operator then living. When he died 26 June 1917, he was the last survivor of those who had been connected with the early days of the CWS. He left effects valued at £195.

Writings: 'Surplus Funds', *Co-op. Congress Report* (1881); 'The Banking Question', *Co-op. Congress Report* (1882).

Sources: *Bee-Hive*, 22 May 1875; B. Jones, *Co-operative Production* (1894); P. Redfern, *The Story of the C.W.S.* (Manchester, [1913]); idem, *The New History of the C.W.S.* (Manchester, 1938); G. D. H. Cole, *A Century of Co-operation* (Manchester, [1945?]). OBIT. *Co-op. News*, 30 June 1917.

H. F. BING

See also: Percy REDFERN, for Co-operative Wholesaling.

CRAIG, Edward Thomas (1804–94)
OWENITE SOCIALIST AND SOCIAL REFORMER

Born on 4 August 1804 in Manchester. He lost his father at the age of four, and was then sent to live with his paternal grandparents at Lancaster. The family had for many generations been administratively employed in the Courts of Law on the civil side of Lancaster Castle, and among the earliest recollections of young Craig were the arrival of coaches full of Luddite prisoners, guarded by dragoons with drawn swords. On the death of his grandmother, the boy returned to Manchester in 1815, and four years later was present at Peterloo. His grandparents

had been Church and State people, tolerant and easy-going, but his mother's family, to whom he had now returned, were strict Calvinists, and Sunday attendance at chapel in particular was rigidly observed. When Craig joined the Manchester Mechanics' Institution in the year of its establishment, 1825, his reading matter, borrowed from its library, was kept secret from the family. One of the books he read was an account of New Lanark and Craig quickly developed a passionate interest in social questions. He worked at the fustian trade and in 1828 founded a Fustian Manufacturing Society based on the principles of profit-sharing. The lack of a direct market for its goods soon brought the Society to failure but Manchester was at this time developing into the strongest Owenite centre outside London, and there was no lack of sympathetic contacts. In Salford especially the movement struck deep roots. Craig and his friends formed a mutual improvement society, under the name of the Utility Society, meeting on Sundays at the house of Craig's future father-in-law. One result of the Society's discussions was the establishment of the celebrated Salford Sunday School and Social Institute. The Society included a number of young men who were later to become well-known personalities in the radical and co-operative movement: among them James Rigby, James Hole, Lloyd Jones and Robert Cooper; and in 1829 many of the members of the Utility Society supported the breakaway New Mechanics' Institute which had premises in Poole Street, in which Rowland Detrosier became president [Tylecote (1957) 137] and Abel Heywood one of the lecturers.

These years between 1828 and 1832 also saw the foundation of a number of small co-operative societies in the Manchester area. Craig became president of one, established in June 1830, with Abel Heywood as secretary. Much later in his life Craig noted that it was Dr King's *Co-operator* (1828–30) published from Brighton and William Thompson's *Inquiry into the Principles of the Distribution of Wealth most Conducive to Human Happiness* (1824) that had provided the intellectual inspiration among his colleagues and himself for the spread of co-operation in these early years; and although his own society, following common experience, lasted only a short time, the co-operative movement was now an integral if still limited part of working-class experience. Craig helped organise the first Co-operative Congress at Manchester on 26 and 27 May 1831 and later became editor of one of the first northern co-operative journals (*Lancashire Co-operator*, 11 June 1831–20 August 1831: then *Lancashire and Yorkshire Co-operator*, 3 September 1831–October 1832).

The event which made Craig famous in the history of co-operation was the invitation by John Scott Vandaleur to take over the estate at Ralahine (some twelve miles from Limerick) and run it as a co-operative experiment. It was following outbreaks of peasant violence that Vandaleur turned to Owenism as a solution to his troubles and probably through John Finch of Liverpool he was put in touch with Craig. By early November 1831 Craig was ready to outline to the estate peasantry his plans for a community to be known as the Ralahine Agricultural and Manufacturing Co-operative Association. The Association leased the land from Vandaleur (rent was paid in kind) and the estate was worked co-operatively under the direction of an elected committee. Labour notes were introduced, a school was started – which Mrs Craig organised – and the general sobriety of the community, in such marked contrast with what had gone before, impressed an increasing flow of visitors. For two years the community prospered, and then, suddenly, it collapsed. Vandaleur, an inveterate gambler, wagered away his estate and absconded. Craig used some of his own money to cash the labour notes before the estate was sold for the benefit of the creditors, and on 23 November 1833 the Association came to an end. Craig then returned to England with his wife.

Ralahine had an honoured place in the community tradition of the nineteenth century and was more quoted than any other community experiment. John Finch wrote a series of enthusiastic letters in the *Liverpool Chronicle* and these were republished in the *New Moral World* (31 March–29 September 1838); William Pare produced the first extended version in book form in 1870 followed by a furious controversy with Craig over the authorship [Garnett (1963) 144]; and Craig published his own account in 1882, at a time when the Irish land question was to the forefront of British politics. Alfred Russell Wallace, president of the Land Nationalisation Society, warmly commended Ralahine as a successful practising community; and the educational ideas that Craig put into practice were widely commented upon in the decades which followed.

Craig himself was able to develop further his pedagogic theories for in 1834 he was invited to organise an industrial school at Ealing Grove. The school was financially subsidised by Lady Noel Byron and founded by Craig on the principle of Fellenberg's Academy at Hofwyl, which Craig had visited earlier in the same year. Although Craig was to remain at Ealing Grove only until the end of 1835, the system he established continued, and was favourably commented on by a number of later visitors, among whom was Kay-Shuttleworth in 1839. By this time Craig himself, with the ebullient optimism characteristic of the early Owenites, was a member of another community. In 1836 he had become assistant editor of the *Star in the East* published at Wisbech by James Hill. Hill was a wealthy man whose second wife was the daughter of Dr Southwood Smith, the well-known radical medical authority, and whose own daughter, Octavia, was to become as well known a social reformer as her grandfather, Besides working on the *Star in the East* Craig, together with Mrs Craig, started an infants' school which became a great success. Isaac Ironside of Sheffield sent his own daughter, and William Hodson of Manea Fen sent his two sons. The Craigs also began Sunday evening concerts, a rather startling innovation for the rural areas of eastern England. It was Craig, according to George Hines's pamphlet of 1890, who interested William Hodson in community development and which led to the establishment of the Manea Fen community at Christmas 1838. Craig was invited to help found an industrial school. Later Craig was to make serious criticisms of the organisation of Manea Fen but he left only when the experiment was dissolved early in 1841.

This marks the end of Craig's involvement with community building. He took no part in the Owenite developments after the closing down of the *Crisis* in August 1834 nor is there any record of his visiting Queenwood. He now turned to earning his living in more orthodox ways, becoming first a perambulating lecturer for the Yorkshire Union of Mechanics' Institutes and later, for a time, principal of Rotherham and Mexborough Mechanics' Institute (from December 1853); but for most of his later life he was a working journalist. By 1878 he was able to claim that he had been editor of six newspapers, including the *Leamington Advertiser*, *Brighton Times*, *County Express* and the *Oxford University Herald*. He did not, however, abate his concern with social questions, although his activities took rather unusual forms. His most enthusiastic interest was phrenology, which had been popularised in Britain by George Combe in the 1820s, and Craig seems to have been converted after hearing a lecture by J. G. Spurzheim in Manchester in the year 1827. Phrenology claimed to discover innate mental characteristics, diagnosed by a close examination of the skull of individuals, while Owenism insisted that man's character was formed by his environment. Logically, therefore, the two philosophies were opposed to each other but in practice their reconciliation, or at least their working compatibility, apparently proved possible; and many Owenites turned to phrenology in the years after the collapse of Queenwood [Harrison (1969) 239ff].

Craig remained to the end of his days a lively defender of Robert Owen's views and a vigorous advocate of the community as the rational form of social organisation; and during the 1860s he was advocating many sensible ideas, including the revival of co-operative congresses; but after his Owenite period he collected a great variety of reform causes in addition to his enthusiasm for co-operation. He was of a markedly inventive turn of mind, and in 1873 he was awarded a silver medal at the Cambridge Exhibition of Arts, Industry and Manufacture for the greatest number of inventions (twenty-seven) in the catalogue. He became a fanatical advocate of ventilation and fresh air as the way to better health, and during the 1860s wrote many articles in the *Co-operator* on the subject. As the *Co-operative News* wrote in their obituary notice of him: 'His prescription for health, happiness and longevity was fresh air, exercise, slow eating, deep breathing, cleanliness, temperance, contentment and cheerfulness. He banned drugs, vaccination, and the spawn of Pasteurism.'

His long life took him into the years when Socialism once again became a movement in Britain. He was one of nine members who inaugurated the Hammersmith branch of the Democratic Federation in June 1884; a member of the first executive of the Socialist League, and an occasional speaker on their platforms. He had contributed a series of articles to the *American Socialist* between August 1877 and November 1878 and in the first number of *Commonweal* (February 1885) he wrote a reminiscence of Peterloo. May Morris described him in a charming paragraph in her account of her father's socialist days:

. . . there was nothing silent or pathetic about the figure of E. T. Craig, the old Chartist and Co-operator – beyond the melancholy that must always gather increasingly around the aspect of old age and failing powers. Craig had been a sturdy and valiant fighter; he watched the young movement with keen interest and would make speeches at our meetings in a fife-like voice which sometimes recovered its old chest register in a sort of bellow that beat upon one's eardrums. He would come and sit in the garden at Kelmscott House and we would gather round him and hear tell of those old Co-operative days, or listen to his expositions on phrenology. I remember one time when we were having our characters described by bumps on our heads, Shaw, who was one of the company and also undergoing examination, naughtily asked if he had a bump of veneration. 'A bump?' shrieked the old gentleman, 'why it's a 'ole there!' and struck his stick into the ground to emphasise the answer' [May Morris, vol. 2 (1936) 186–7];

and Bruce Glasier, who got to know Craig through William Morris in the last years of Craig's life, remarked on his enormous ear-trumpet and on how 'Craig was now over ninety years old, and though frail in body, was extraordinarily alert in mind, and full of enthusiasm for the new Socialist movement. His queer little cramped-up figure as he sat on the platform with a grey Scottish shepherd's plaid around his shoulders, contrasted drolly with the bulky form of Morris . . .'.

Craig remained active almost until his last days. He attended the 1893 Co-operative Congress in Bristol, moved a resolution there on co-operative agriculture and the Congress report recorded that he 'spoke with surprising energy'. He and his wife had celebrated the fiftieth anniversary of their wedding on 11 July 1883; and Craig died at his Hammersmith home, appropriately called Ralahine Cottage, on 15 December 1894. His wife survived him. What his religious beliefs were no one knew. James Hole and E. O. Greening, both lifelong friends, were among those who attended the funeral.

Writings: MSS: letters, Co-operative Union Library, Manchester. Craig wrote a great deal in journals and in pamphlet form. An incomplete bibliography can be made up from titles listed in W. H. G. Armytage, *Heavens Below* (1961) 112, and R. G. Garnett, 'E. T. Craig . . .', *Vocational Aspect of Secondary and Further Education 14*, no. 3 (Summer, 1963) 145–50. The list below notes the more important of his political and social writings: *Work and Wages: or Capital Currency and Production* (1865); 'Land, Labour and Capital', *Co-op. Congress Report* (1869); 'Associated Healthy Dwellings: or a New Plan of Practical Propaganda', *Co-op. Congress Report* (1876); *American Socialist* (August 1877–November 1878); *The Irish Land and Labour*

Question illustrated in the History of Ralahine and Co-operative Farming (1882); *Lecture at the Chelsea Co-operative Soc. . . . on the principles and aims of the founders of mutual co-operation* (1883) 8 pp.; *Memoir and In Memoriam of H. Travis, English Socialist* [1886?]; *Labouring Capitalists* (n.d.); *Hard Labour and Head Work: or, Industrial Training* (n.d.); *Participations in Management and Profits of Productive Labour as at Ralahine* (n.d.); *The First Example of Profit Sharing and Home Rule. A Letter Addressed to the Rt Hon. W. E. Gladstone* [1892] 16 pp.; *Ralahine, Idealised, or Organised Production, Distribution and Consumption* (1892).

Sources: There are several useful contemporary accounts, in addition to the obituary notices: *Co-op. News*, 1 Feb 1879; 'E. T. Craig . . . A Biographical Sketch', *Phrenological Magazine* (Feb 1883); *Republican* (July/Aug 1883); *Memoir of E. T. Craig* [n.d. 1886?] 15 pp.; G. Hines, *One of the Old (Co-operative) Guard: being a sketch of the life of Mr E. T. Craig* (3rd ed. 1890) 10 pp.; and these are brought together, with new material, in R. G. Garnett, 'E. T. Craig: Communitarian, Educator, Phrenologist', *Vocational Aspect of Secondary and Further Education, 14*, no. 3 (Summer 1963) 133–50, with bibliog. See also: W. Pare, *Co-operative Agriculture: A Solution of the Land Question as Exemplified in the History of the Ralahine Co-operative Association, County Clare, Ireland* (1870); B. Jones, *Co-operative Production*, 2 vols (1894; reprinted in one volume, New York, 1968); A. R. Wallace, *Studies Scientific and Social*, vol. 2 (1900); *An Irish Commune: History of Ralahine*, ed. D. Coffey (1920); J. Bruce Glasier, *William Morris and the Early Days of the Socialist Movement* (1921); May Morris, *William Morris, Artist*, vol. 2 (1936); G. D. H. Cole, *A Century of Co-operation* (Manchester, [1945?]); J. F. C. Harrison, *Social Reform in Victorian Leeds* (Leeds, 1954); E. P. Thompson, *William Morris* (1955); M. Tylecote, *Mechanics' Institutes of Lancashire and Yorkshire before 1851* (1957); A. E. Musson, 'The Ideology of Early Co-operation in Lancashire', *Trans. Lancs. and Cheshire Antiq. Soc. 67* (1958) 117–38; W. H. G. Armytage, *Heavens Below* (1961); J. F. C. Harrison, *Learning and Living, 1790–1960*

(1961); R. G. Garnett, *The Ideology of the Early Co-operative Movement* (Univ. of Kent, 1966); R. G. Garnett, 'Co-operation and the Owenite-Socialist Communities in Britain (1825–1845)' (London PhD, 1969); J. F. C. Harrison, *Robert Owen and the Owenites in Britain and America* (1969). OBIT. *Times*, 17 Dec 1894; *Manchester Guardian*, 18 Dec 1894; *Co-op. News*, 22 Dec 1894; G. J. Holyoake, 'Craig of Ralahine', *Co-op. News*, 5 Jan 1895.

JOHN SAVILLE

See also: John FINCH; Patrick Lloyd JONES; *Robert OWEN; William PARE; Henry TRAVIS.

CRAWFORD, William (1833–90)
MINERS' LEADER AND LIB-LAB MP

Born in 1833 at Whitley in Northumberland, the son of a miner. He had little education in his early years, being sent to work in the pits when about ten years of age, but an early accident allowed him to attend school during convalescence and in consequence he was somewhat better educated than most sons of miners. By the time he married, at the age of twenty-four, he was already a Primitive Methodist preacher, a speaker for the temperance movement and an advocate of social reform. By the early 1860s he was already known for his trade union activity, and when the Northumberland and Durham Mutual Confidence Association was formed in 1863 Crawford both drew up the rules of the new Association and became its first secretary. Later in the same year, at the famous conference of the National Association of Coal, Lime and Ironstone Miners, he rejected the proposal for an Eight Hours Bill as being inapplicable to his district; an opinion that was held by the Durham as well as the Northumberland miners in the decades which followed. In 1864 the Northumberland miners seceded from the joint Association, and Crawford became their secretary, only to resign in the following year when he became acting secretary of Cowpen Quay Co-operative Society. A month before he resigned he had given evidence (with Thomas Burt) before the

S.C. on the Regulation and Inspection of Mines and Miners' Complaints; and Burt replaced him as secretary of the Northumberland miners. Crawford worked for only about a year for his co-operative society and then commenced business on his own account at Bedlington. Soon after the Durham Miners formed a separate organisation in late 1869, and Crawford was appointed one of their full-time agents (4 May 1870). At the end of 1870 he was invited to become president, and on 3 December 1871 he was made general secretary of the DMA, a position he held until his death. Crawford succeeded Tom Halliday as a mining representative on the ten-strong parliamentary committee of the TUC, on which he sat continuously from 1878 to 1890. He was chairman of the parliamentary committee in 1881 and again in 1888.

Under Crawford's leadership membership of the DMA grew rapidly, not least because these early years of the 1870s were years of considerable economic expansion. In 1872, when the membership was 35,000, the DMA secured the abolition of the yearly bond, which was replaced by a fortnightly agreement. This also marked the beginning of a new approach to industrial relations. A conciliation and arbitration board for wage discussions was established, with an independent chairman. Crawford himself was a strong-minded man of moderate opinions, with a considerable flair for settling problems and difficulties. In politics he was a firm Liberal, and was proposed as a candidate by the Franchise Association in 1874 although he withdrew when other candidates came forward. He was elected in 1885 for Mid-Durham and re-elected in 1886. He participated little in parliamentary affairs, never once speaking on the floor of the House but doing some useful committee work.

His central concern, up to the time of his death, remained in mining affairs. He was secretary of the Miners' National Association from 1877 to 1890, and in the same year of his death he summoned and attended the International Miners' Conference at Jolimont, in Belgium. Earlier in his life he had been somewhat influenced by the ideas of

Lloyd Jones, but his general attitudes became more conservative as he became older. He joined the Freemasons in 1878 and was Worshipful Master of his Lodge in 1886. He was also, for some years, an alderman of the Durham County Council. He died on 1 July 1890 and left £204 in his will.

Sources: Evidence before the S.C. on Regulation and Inspection of Mines and Miners' Complaints 1866 XIV Qs 429–602; R. Fynes, *The Miners of Northumberland* (Sunderland, 1873; repr. 1923); J. Wilson, *A History of the Durham Miners' Association, 1870–1904* (Durham, 1907); A. Watson, *A Great Labour Leader: being a life of the Right Honorable Thomas Burt* (1908); S. Webb, *The Story of the Durham Miners (1662–1921)* (1921); E. Welbourne, *The Miners' Unions of Northumberland and Durham* (Cambridge, 1923); R. F. Wearmouth, *The Social and Political Influence of Methodism in the Twentieth Century* (1957); J. Lawson, *Peter Lee* (1949); R. P. Arnot, *The Miners* (1949). OBIT. *Times*, 2 July 1890; *Northern Echo*, 2 July 1890; *Durham Chronicle*, 4 July 1890.

ANTHONY MASON

See also: T. BURT; Alexander MACDONALD, for Mining Trade Unionism, 1850–79; Benjamin PICKARD, for Mining Trade Unionism, 1880–99.

DALLAWAY, William (1857–1939)
CO-OPERATOR

Born on 6 July 1857 at Chiddingly, near Hailsham, Sussex, the son of John Dallaway, an agricultural labourer. Of his early career nothing is known except that as a young man he was one of a small group who met at the old Coffee Palace, in Duke Street, Brighton, to discuss co-operation and socialism. Eventually the first store opened in 1888 and Dallaway's name was the first on the Brighton Co-operative Society's books. He served as education secretary from 1888 to 1902, and from 1893 to 1901 he was chairman of the Society at a time when George Jacob Holyoake was president. Dallaway saw the original store grow to one with an annual turnover of two million pounds and a membership of 50,000. Elected president of the Society in 1922, he held the post with distinction until his death, presiding in the year before he died over the jubilee celebrations of the Society.

An enthusiastic worker for the temperance movement, he was also an early member of the Brighton Volunteer Fire Brigade. He died, after a lifetime of service to the co-operative movement, at his Brighton home on 21 February 1939, his funeral service being held at the Unitarian Church, Brighton, on 25 February. He left effects valued at £1229.

Sources: W. H. Brown, *Brighton's Co-operative Advance* (Manchester, 1938); personal information: C. E. Hall, education secretary, Brighton Co-operative Society, who gave the date of birth as 16 July 1861. As he was eighty-one when he died (Somerset House death register), the 1857 date, also obtained from Somerset House, seems the more accurate. Obituaries gave his age of death as eighty-two or eighty-three. OBIT. *Co-op. News*, 4 and 11 Mar 1939.

JOYCE BELLAMY

See also: G. J. HOLYOAKE, for Retail Co-operation – Nineteenth Century.

DALY, James (?–1849)
OWENITE AND ROCHDALE PIONEER

Born in the north of Ireland where his father was a sergeant of militia, James Daly settled in Rochdale, in Crook Street, and worked as a joiner for William Robinson in Drake Street, and later as a foreman joiner at a salary of £1 a week for Thomas Robinson. He was keenly interested in music and devoted much of his spare time to study, becoming a good grammarian, arithmetician and mathematician. He was a prominent member of the Oddfellows' Society. He became an Owenite probably in the 1830s, for Rochdale at that time was a lively political town, and nonconformist and social sects abounded. When the No. 24 branch of the Universal Community Society of Rational Religionists was opened in Rochdale, Daly became its secretary; and was the author of several reports on the 'Progress of Social Reform' in the *New Moral World*, 1839–41. The Rochdale Owenites had acquired in 1838 the use of an annexe to the Weavers' Arms in Yorkshire Street, and named it the New Social Institution. This now became the centre of Owenite activity in Rochdale and it was the birthplace and first headquarters of the Rochdale Pioneers' Society. When the Owenites opened a day and Sunday school, Daly acted as schoolmaster. He was one of those who met at the house of James Smithies in 1844 to discuss what could be done to alleviate distress. The Rochdale Rational Society took Holyoake's side in the debate over the Queenwood community, and their support is recorded in Holyoake's paper *The Movement* (letter from Daly and others, including Charles Howarth and William Cooper, 12 Feb 1845).

Daly was present at the meeting on 11 August 1844 which formally constituted the Rochdale Society of Equitable Pioneers, and he became its first secretary (1844–9), collaborating with Charles Howarth in drawing up the rules. The original minute book of the Society (still preserved in the Toad Lane Museum) is in Daly's handwriting and in the purchase book his name appears first on the list as James Daly, joiner, John Street. On 27 October 1844 he was appointed with five others to inspect prospective premises for the stores and when the Toad Lane premises were taken, he knocked up rude shelves prior to the opening. In 1849, when the Pioneers obtained possession of the whole of 31 Toad Lane, Daly, a joiner during the day and secretary during the evening, was responsible for the re-fronting of the premises at a cost of £200. But he found it impossible on his small earnings to give a decent start in life to his family of eight children. In 1849 he decided to emigrate with his family to Texas, the Promised Land of many Owenites at that time, where he hoped to start a co-operative community. His fellow Oddfellows and Co-operators raised funds towards the fares and the family sailed from Liverpool on the s.s. *Transit*. He died of cholera in mid-Atlantic on 29 December 1849 and was buried at sea; his wife also died on the voyage. The children were taken to a hospital at New Orleans on their arrival and subsequently adopted by various families.

Sources: W. Robertson, 'Rochdale: the birthplace of modern co-operation', in *Handbook of Twenty-fourth Annual Co-operative Congress* (Manchester, 1892); W. H. Brown, *The Rochdale Pioneers* (Rochdale, 1944); G. D. H. Cole, *A Century of Co-operation* (Manchester, [1945?]); A. Bonner, *British Co-operation* (Manchester, 1961); biographical information: D. J. Doyle Esq., Williamsport Area Community College, U.S.A.

H. F. BING

See also: Samuel ASHWORTH; Charles HOWARTH; James SMITHIES; *J. STANDRING.

DARCH, Charles Thomas (1876–1934)
CO-OPERATOR

Born in Bristol on 17 February 1876, C. T. Darch was a son of Thomas Darch, a tanner, and his wife Charlotte Ellen (née Moore). Thomas Darch attended Avon Vale Board School and, later, evening classes at Castle Green School, Bristol. At fifteen he entered co-operative service as an office boy at the Bristol depot of the Co-operative Wholesale Society. Five years later he was transferred to the Cardiff depot as grocery traveller in the earliest years of its establishment, and for twenty-nine years he was in close association with the co-operative movement in South Wales (industrial and agricultural). He rose to be assistant manager of the CWS Grocery and Provision Department in South Wales. In February 1926, on the nomination of the Cardiff Co-operative Society, he was elected to the board of the Co-operative Wholesale Society, a rare instance of an employee becoming a CWS director.

C. T. Darch served on the CWS board from 1926 until his sudden death in 1934. He was a member of its grocery and wages committees. He represented the CWS on a number of kindred organisations, including the Health Insurance Section, the Western Section Co-operative Convalescent Fund, the Western Section Co-operative Coal Trade Association and the Western Section Milk Trade Association. He also represented the board on the management committees of a number of societies under its supervision.

C. T. Darch always took a keen interest in education and politics, particularly from the co-operative standpoint. He was chairman of the Cardiff Society's education committee for at least nine years. He was a member of the Educational Association of the Co-operative Union (Western Section) from its inception and became its chairman. He was secretary of the Cardiff Council of the Co-operative Party from its beginning and secretary of the district propaganda committee. He represented the western section of the Co-operative Union on the national council of the Co-operative Party and was a member of its national executive. He was the co-operative representative on the Welsh Council of the Workers' Education Association to which he acted as honorary auditor, and also on the Welsh University Colleges Extension Committee.

He was for many years an active member of the Adult School Movement in Cardiff, and became its vice-president; and he was president and then treasurer of the South Wales and Monmouthshire Adult School Union. He was the co-operative representative on the Cardiff Trades and Labour Council, being also treasurer and a trustee of that body. He was Cardiff and District correspondent of the parliamentary committee on India; a co-opted member of the industrial group of the Cardiff and District Committee of COPEC (Conference on Politics, Economics and Christianity); and was appointed a JP for Cardiff in July 1932.

He died suddenly of heart failure when only fifty-eight years of age, at his home in Cardiff on 25 July 1934. He had attended a CWS meeting in Bristol on the previous Saturday and was at the CWS depot in Cardiff on the day before his death. He was to have been a member of a CWS deputation to America the following weekend. He had married Miss Annie Elliott at Cardiff in 1902 and was survived by his wife, a son and three daughters. He left an estate valued at £5950.

Sources: Co-operative Press records, Manchester; personal information: Miss Lilian Darch, daughter. OBIT. *South Wales Echo*, 25 July 1934; *Co-op News*, 28 July 1934; *Western Mail & South Wales News*, 30 July 1934; *Ourselves*, August 1934.

H. F. BING

See also: A. V. ALEXANDER, for Co-operative Party; Fred HALL, for Co-operative Education; Percy REDFERN, for Co-operative Wholesaling.

DAVIES, Margaret Llewelyn (1861–1944)
CO-OPERATOR AND SOCIAL REFORMER

Born on 16 October 1861 in Marylebone, London, where her father, the Rev. John Llewelyn Davies, was Rector of Christ Church, Miss Davies was christened Margaret Caroline but subsequently adopted the family name of Llewelyn which had been given to each of her six brothers. The Rev. Davies was a broad church Anglican who became influenced in his early years by F. D. Maurice and the Christian Socialists of 1848–54; and he remained on close terms with Maurice, Kingsley, Tom Hughes and many others of the group as long as they lived. (He wrote the *DNB* entry for Hughes.) Margaret's mother Mary belonged to the well-known Unitarian family of the Cromptons. On both sides of the family therefore Margaret found herself in an atmosphere of advanced thought and social commitment. One of her mother's sisters married Professor George Croom Robertson, an active worker in the women's suffrage cause and a close acquaintance of John Stuart Mill, and another sister married Professor E. S. Beesly. An aunt on her father's side, Miss Emily Davies, was the founder of Girton College, Cambridge. Her two youngest brothers, Crompton and Theodore, became close friends at Cambridge with Bertrand Russell.

Margaret was educated at Queen's College, London and then at Girton. She early began social work in Marylebone, volunteering as a sanitary inspector, and somewhat later, probably through the influence of her father, became interested in the co-operative movement. She joined the small Marylebone Co-operative Society in 1886, and her enthusiasm for co-operative sausages was a long-standing family joke. A year later she became secretary of the Marylebone branch of the Women's Co-operative Guild, was then elected to the executive committee, and in 1889 became general secretary on the retirement of Mrs Lawrenson. Margaret had now found her life's work.

In the same year that she began her thirty years' work as the guiding figure in the women's co-operative movement, the family moved to the parish of Kirkby Lonsdale in Westmorland. Margaret set up office in a room in the vicarage and she was joined in her work by Lilian Harris who became her closest associate and lifelong friend. Lilian was the daughter of Alfred Harris, a wealthy banker from Bradford who came to Kirkby Lonsdale about 1850, built a large Victorian monstrosity there and regarded himself as the local squire. Altogether he had fourteen children, eight by his first wife, including Lilian, and six by his second. Lilian was appointed cashier of the Guild in 1893 and assistant secretary in 1901 (in which position she was succeeded by Miss Lucy Davenport).

One of Miss Davies's earliest controversies within the movement concerned the attitude towards profit-sharing and co-partnership on the one side, and the ordinary commercial activity of the CWS on the other. In 1888 with her close friend Mrs Vaughan Nash (formerly Rosalind Shore Smith) she undertook a tour of profit-sharing workshops but their opinion, on balance, was against them; and in 1891 they supported the CWS approach against the former Guild secretary, Mrs Lawrenson. At the time the issue was a much debated one in the movement.

Margaret Davies was largely responsible for developing the Women's Guild not only into a social and educational activity for working-class women in their own areas, but as a pressure group of considerable influence for women's rights. The Guild, during her period of office, supported vigorously the campaign for the Suffrage, undertook what ended as a successful struggle for the minimum wage for women and girls within the co-operative movement itself, and was at all times vitally concerned with the problems of women as housewives and mothers. The Guild's campaign around maternity problems was long sustained; and one of its best known contributions was the publication in 1915, edited by Margaret Davies, of the famous *Maternity: letters from working women*. As she herself wrote in 1927 in the foreword to Catherine Webb's history of the Women's Co-operative Guild:

The principal contribution of the Guild to the life of married women has been changing the whole attitude of the nation towards Maternity. Sentimental expressions of admiration, jocose remarks, and want of care and research by the medical profession are giving place to a recognition of the needs of mothers. Though much remains to be done, the foundations have been laid of a dignified and comprehensive national service of help, which is alleviating the sufferings and privations of women and making the lives of children healthier and happier.

These activities did not always meet with the approval of the male side of the movement. In 1910 the Guild was asked to give evidence before the R.C. on Divorce and after conducting an inquiry among its members, Margaret Davies and Mrs Eleanor Barton presented the evidence. The majority of their members were in favour of an equal law for men and women and they especially stressed the need for much cheaper procedures. The Reports of the R.C. were published in 1912, and their basic recommendations were endorsed with large majorities at the Guild Congresses of 1912 and 1913. In October 1913 the Manchester and Salford Catholic Federation began objecting to the Guild taking up the subject, on the grounds that many co-operative members were Catholics and that the Guild received financial help from co-operative societies as well as the Co-operative Union; and after the Guild had rejected the protest the Catholic Federation then approached the Co-operative Union. The central board of the Union advised the Guild to discontinue its propaganda on the question and when the Guild refused to accept this dictation, the subsidy from the central board was ended; and it was not renewed until 1919, by which time the Guild had won its right to independence.

Both Margaret Davies and Lilian Harris retired from their respective positions in 1921. Both were presented with the Freedom of the Guild in the following year at the Portsmouth Congress and a fund of £700 raised by Guildswomen was given over, at the request of Miss Davies and Miss Harris, to encouraging friendship between Guildswomen of all countries. In 1922 Margaret Davies became the first woman to be elected president of the Co-operative Congress which met that year at Brighton. She had, during her years as Guild secretary, served the wider movement in a number of ways, and during the First World War she represented the Guild on the General Co-operative Survey Committee. The committee had been established by the Dublin Congress in 1914 and it made its final report to the Carlisle Congress of 1919 and to a special Congress in February 1920.

She took an active part in the founding of the International Women's Co-operative Guild at Basle in 1921 and always retained her interest in the international links of the movement. After her retirement she and Miss Harris lived for some time in Well Walk, Hampstead, London, and then near Dorking in Surrey. Miss Davies was always on the left of the labour movement. In October 1915 she was elected to the General Council of the UDC. After 1917 she was always a supporter of the Russian Revolution, though never a Communist, and her pro-Russian and pacifist activities occupied much of her time during the 1920s. She was a firm supporter of trade relations between the English and Russian co-operative movements and from the inception in 1924 of the Society for Cultural Relations between the USSR and Britain she was chairman of the Society until 1928 when ill-health compelled her to resign. Her energy and enthusiasm were responsible for the con-

siderable response the Society evoked in its early years. Her great friend, L. T. Hobhouse, Professor of Sociology at the University of London, became its first president and Margaret enlisted a distinguished panel of vice-presidents, including H. G. Wells, Bernard Shaw, Aldous and Julian Huxley, Virginia and Leonard Woolf.

During her years as Guild secretary she lectured widely and wrote much. Her last public appearance before the Women's Guild was at the Guild Jubilee Congress in London in 1933. She was of striking appearance, tall and gracious with a deep pleasant voice and much loved by all who knew her. Her friends remember her as an extraordinarily vivid personality, with an immense vitality and gaiety in all that she did. Her death occurred on Sunday 28 May 1944, and in her will, the net worth of which was £20,725, she made a large number of personal bequests, the most important of which were £3200 to Lilian Harris, and £3000 to Mrs Vaughan Nash. In addition, £1000 was left to the international Co-operative Women's Guild and £500 each to the Peace Pledge Union and the War Resisters' International. There were also a number of smaller bequests to various reforming societies, including the Howard League for Penal Reform and the Commons, Open Spaces and Footpaths Preservation Society. The sum given to the International Co-operative Women's Guild was used to help Guildswomen to take part in educational events organised by the ICA; and the Co-operative Union promoted a further fund, linked with her name, to assist attendance at international meetings organised by the Union's educational department.

Miss Harris, her lifelong friend, died on 12 January 1950. She left effects worth £6761, most of which was divided among a number of personal bequests, but there were also small amounts to organisations, including £200 to the Peace Pledge Union.

In the book Miss Davies published in 1904, *The Women's Co-operative Guild*, there are photographs of herself, Miss Harris, the vicarage at Kirkby Lonsdale and the room which served as the Guild office. Some of these photographs are reproduced in

Catherine Webb's history of the Guild and there is a full-page portrait of Miss Davies as the frontispiece to the 54th Report of the Co-operative Congress (1922).

Writings: *The Co-operative Movement* (Manchester, 1888) 4 pp.; *The Relations between Co-operation and Socialistic Aspirations* (Manchester, [1890]) 8 pp.; *Co-operation in Poor Neighbourhoods* (Kirkby Lonsdale, 1899) 20 pp.; *A Co-operative Relief Column: or how to adapt co-operation to the needs of poor districts* (Kirkby Lonsdale, 1900); *The Three Wheels of a Store's Machinery* (Kirkby Lonsdale, 1901); *The Work of Educational Committees' Associations* (Manchester, 1901); *The Training of Co-operators* (Kirkby Lonsdale, 1902); *The Women's Co-operative Guild, 1883–1904* (Kirkby Lonsdale, 1904); *The Co-operative Store Abroad: a comparison* (Kirkby Lonsdale, 1906) 24 pp.; Evidence before the R.C. on Divorce 1912–13 XX Qs 36961–7086; *The Education of Guildswomen* (1913) 12 pp.; *Motherhood and the State* (n.d.) P; *Maternity: letters from working women*, ed. M. L. Davies (1915); *The vote at last! More Power to Co-operation* (1918) 8 pp.; (with others) *Co-operation versus Capitalism* (1919) 8 pp.; *Women as Organised Consumers* (Manchester, 1921) 12 pp.; *Death or Life* (International Co-op. Women's Guild, 1924); C. Webb, *The Woman with the Basket: the history of the Women's Co-operative Guild, 1883–1927*, with a Foreword by M. L. Davies (Manchester, 1927); *Life as we have known it, by Co-operative Working Women*, ed. M. L. Davies with an Introductory Letter by Virginia Woolf (1931).

Sources: MSS, printed papers, photographs relating to the Women's Co-operative Guild: LSE Miscellaneous Collection 268 M363; Miss M. L. Davies (niece) supplied two typewritten accounts of Miss Davies, one by Mrs Vaughan Nash (8 pp.) and the second by another niece, Dr Katherine Davies (28 pp.): DLB Coll., University of Hull; George Croom Robertson, *DNB 16*; Henry Crompton, *DNB* (1901–11); Rev. John Llewelyn Davies, *DNB* (1912–21); J. J. Worley, *The Women's Co-operative Guild and the Co-partnership Movement* [1911?] 7 pp.;

Anon., *The Women's Co-operative Guild: notes on its history, organisation and work* (1920); *Report of the First Special Co-operative Congress* (Manchester, 1920); *Co-op. Congress Report* (1922); *Millgate Monthly*, June 1922; B. Groombridge, *Report on the Co-operative Auxiliaries* (Co-operative College Papers, no. 7 Oct 1960); *Co-op. News*, 26 Apr 1969; Royden Harrison, 'The War Emergency Workers' National Committee', *Essays in Labour History*, vol. 2: 1886–1923, ed. A. Briggs and J. Saville (1971). Personal information: Mrs O. Harris; Mrs M. Le Blanc Smith; the Librarian, Co-operative Union Ltd; Mrs C. Rabinovich; P. N. Wilson Esq., and Baroness Wootton of Abinger. OBIT. *Co-op. News*, 3 June 1944.

JOYCE BELLAMY
H. F. BING
JOHN SAVILLE

See also: Mrs Alice S. ACLAND; Mrs E. BARTON; *Thomas HUGHES; *J. M. F. LUDLOW, for Christian Socialism, 1848–54; H. J. MAY, for International Co-operative Alliance; *Catherine WEBB.

DAVISON, John (1846–1930)
MINER AND CO-OPERATOR

Born on 19 February 1846 at Old Stone Row, Bedlington Iron Works, he was educated in the works school. At the age of eight he started work in Sleekburn old pit two miles north-east of Blyth and eventually became deputy overman. He played some part in mining unionism, mostly on the welfare side, and he was one of the originators of the Northumberland Aged Mineworkers' Homes Association, being a member of the management committee from the beginning and its chairman in 1923. His main concern, however, was the co-operative movement. For sixty years he was connected with the Bedlington Co-operative Society and for forty years he was its chairman. In 1900 he left the pits to become an agent of the Co-operative Insurance Society. For over three decades he represented the northern section on the board of the Co-operative Union, and he attended a number of international congresses on behalf of the Union.

He was a director of the Gilsland Co-operative Convalescent Home from its founding, and from 1912 he was its president.

Apart from his co-operative interests Davison took a full part in the life of his community. He was an active chapelgoer, and for sixty-three years he was a lay preacher in the Primitive Methodist Connexion. He was for a number of years a member of the Bedlington Council School management, and he also played an active part in the Ancient Order of Foresters, becoming its local secretary in 1910. In politics he was always a Liberal, speaking frequently on public platforms in the Liberal cause and he had been a close personal friend of Thomas Burt. Davison died at his daughter's home in Choppington on 25 August 1930. He left effects valued at £2031.

Sources: R. F. Wearmouth, *The Social and Political Influence of Methodism in the Twentieth Century* (1957). OBIT. *Newcastle Evening Chronicle*, 26 Aug 1930; *NMA* (1930).
ANTHONY MASON

See also: W. H. BROWN, for Retail Co-operation, 1900–45; T. BURT; Benjamin PICKARD, for Mining Trade Unionism, 1880–99.

DEAN, Benjamin (1839–1910)
MINERS' LEADER

Born on 3 July 1839 at Daw End, Rushall, Staffordshire, son of William Dean, a miner, and his wife Jane (née Nuttall). He had almost no formal education as a child and he began work at about the age of ten in the local lime pits, later obtaining similar work near Wednesbury, walking to and from his home at Pelsall, a distance of about six miles, each day. His father died when he was about twelve years old and from then on he was the main economic support of his mother and two sisters. In his youth he led the typical life of an industrial villager – cock-fighting, pigeon-flying and other sports – and it was not until he reached his majority that he began to change his mode of living. It is probable that the change in his style of life was connected with the

acceptance of Primitive Methodism and the chapel, for Dean was a prominent chapelgoer in later life, and such changes have usually been associated, in British mining communities, with religious conversion. He now began to educate himself and to interest himself in trade union affairs, and after a number of years as a local leader he was elected secretary of the Walsall branch. When the Pelsall District Miners' Association was formed in 1887 he became its agent that same year, and he played a major part in encouraging the affiliation of Pelsall to the Midland Miners' Federation, formed in 1886. For many years he was honorary treasurer of the Midland Miners' Federation. From this time he was of national stature: taking part in the inaugural conference of the MFGB in late November 1889 and representing 2500 miners from Walsall at the 1890 TUC. At the second International Congress of Miners at Paris in April 1891, out of ninety-nine delegates from five countries forty-one were British; and Dean was one of ten delegates of the Midland Miners' Federation. He served six terms on the executive committee of the MFGB: 1891, 1893, 1895, 1898, 1904 and 1907.

Years later, with Dean as secretary, the membership of the Walsall District Miners' Association had risen from 1932 in 1903 to 6120 in 1907, at which time it had thirty-one branches. It then fell to 2792 members at the end of 1909 but rose to 4451 members in 1910 when it had twenty-seven branches. At the bitter debate inside the MFGB at the end of 1907 between the Lib-Labs and the Socialists headed by Smillie over the issue of affiliation to the Labour Party, Dean professed himself bewildered and showed that he was unable to move away from the Lib-Lab period of the sixties and seventies in which he had grown up.

He was, indeed, an active Liberal in politics, a fluent and witty speaker, but he never stood for Parliament although he was canvassed on at least two occasions. He took a prominent part in local affairs. He was a member of Rushall School Board, of which he became vice-chairman, was trustee and later chairman of the Pelsall Mining Accident Fund, and was elected to Walsall

Town Council for Birchills Ward in 1890. He became an alderman in 1901 and Mayor in 1906, and throughout his years on the Town Council he accepted a full share of committee work. During his mayoralty he raised £150 for the Walsall hospital by an appeal to the Pelsall and Walsall miners. In 1893 he was made JP for the borough, the first working man to be so appointed.

Some time around 1890, in partnership with his sons, he established the business of Dean and Sons Ltd, tobacconists, in Lichfield Street, Walsall, afterwards taking a shop also in Park Street, and carrying on both a wholesale and retail trade. His health was failing during the last two years of his life, and he died at his home in Borneo Street, Walsall, on 5 March 1910, leaving a widow and eight children, all of whom had reached adult age. He left effects worth £1202.

Sources: W. Hallam, *Miners' Leaders* (1894) [photograph]; R. Page Arnot, *The Miners* (1949). OBIT. *Wolverhampton Chronicle*, 9 Mar 1910 [photograph]; *Walsall Observer*, 12 Mar 1910.

JOHN SAVILLE

See also: Thomas ASHTON, for Mining Trade Unionism, 1900–14; Enoch EDWARDS; S. FINNEY; Benjamin PICKARD, for Mining Trade Unionism, 1880–99; Albert STANLEY; *S. H. WHITEHOUSE.

DEANS, James (1843/4?–1935)
CO-OPERATOR

James Deans was born at Stewarton, near Kilmarnock, probably in 1843 or 1844, for there is no trace in the parochial register of the date of 10 January 1845 quoted by the *Scottish Co-operator* at the time of his death in 1935 aged 91 years. He was the son of James Deans, a bonnet maker, who was a keen politician, and his wife Jean. The family moved to Kilmarnock where Deans's father became a carpet weaver and Deans himself a handloom weaver apprentice when he left school at the age of nine and a half. In his early youth he became familiar with co-operative ideals through local debates on the subject and in his leisure time attended 'venture schools' where he widened his education. He participated actively in the movement for the extension of the franchise in 1865–7 and was a member of the Kilmarnock branch of the Reform League. In 1870 he went to Glasgow where he was among the founders of the Good Templar Lodge in that year. He also joined the co-operative movement in Glasgow, where he married Janet Milroy in 1872.

On returning to Kilmarnock in 1873 he joined the local co-operative society and later in the year was elected assistant secretary and librarian of the society's education committee. Modest and retiring in manner he had nevertheless a powerful personality and devoted himself to the co-operative cause for the remainder of his working life. About 1874 he was chosen secretary of the Ayrshire Co-operative Conference Association, a post he held for over half a century, and in 1881 was also elected to the Scottish Board of the Co-operative Union, of which he became chairman two years later and part-time secretary in 1885. He led the co-operative movement in its first great fight against the boycott by the Trade Defence Association in 1888–9 and a few years later against the Scottish Employers' Association. He served as part-time secretary of the Scottish section of the Co-operative Union until 1891 when the position became a permanent full-time one which Deans continued to hold until his retirement in 1924, after fifty-two years' active service in the co-operative movement. His interests also extended to the international sphere and he was elected to the executive committee of the ICA at the Hamburg Congress in 1910. He was president of the British Congress at Aberdeen in 1913 and regularly attended meetings of the ICA executive during the First World War. He also instigated a Co-operative Defence Association which paid part of the expenses of candidates pledged to safeguard co-operative interests as members of Glasgow City Council. This organisation was a forerunner of the national Co-operative Party founded in 1917.

During his career he served the co-operative cause as adviser, lecturer and writer, and he was an effective platform debater. He visited Ireland in 1896, the first of a series of visits as a propagandist for the movement. His work there helped to establish a branch in Belfast of the United Co-operative Bakery Society, formed in Scotland in 1869, and this new branch became an important factor in the growth of Irish co-operation. Deans also played a prominent role in the establishment of the Scottish Co-operative Convalescent Homes. He contributed articles to the co-operative press, was appointed chairman of the Co-operative Printing Society in 1884, and in 1922, shortly before his retirement, he published *Co-operative Memories* in which he recounted some of his reminiscences of the early period of co-operation, especially in Scotland and Ireland. He died at his Kilmarnock home on 18 April 1935 and was survived by his wife and at least one son.

Writings: *Co-operation versus Private Trading . . . a public discussion held in . . . Glasgow, 1889* between J. Deans and R. Walker (Manchester, 1889) 32 pp.; *The Best Method of Consolidating and Federating existing Productive Effort* (1892) 12 pp.; 'Private Traders' Anti-Co-operative Movement', *CWS Annual* (1899) 269–96; *The Amalgamation of Societies as a Means of consolidating the Co-operative Movement* (Manchester, 1903) 10 pp.; (with others) *Papers on Co-operative Finance* (1906) 16 pp.; *Co-operative Memories: reminiscences of a co-operative propagandist*, with a Foreword by W. Maxwell and an Introduction by R. Murray (Manchester, 1922).

Sources: *Co-op. Congress Handbook* (1905); W. Maxwell, *History of Co-operation in Scotland* (Glasgow, 1910); W. Robertson, *History of Kilmarnock Co-operative Society* (Kilmarnock, 1910); *Co-op. Congress Report* (1913); J. A. Flanagan, *Wholesale Co-operation in Scotland* (Glasgow, 1920); J. Lucas, *Co-operation in Scotland* (Manchester, 1920); J. Deans, *Co-operative Memories* (Manchester, 1922); *Scottish Co-operator*, 12 Aug 1922 and 11 Oct

1924. OBIT. *Scottish Co-operator*, 20 Apr 1935; *Co-op. Congress Report* (1935).

MAI ALMAN
JOYCE BELLAMY

See *also*: W. MAXWELL, for Scottish Co-operation; H. J. MAY, for International Co-operative Alliance.

DEANS, Robert (1904–59)
CO-OPERATOR

Robert Deans was born on 7 January 1904 at Hirst, Northumberland, the son of David Deans, a coalminer. He began work with Newbiggin Co-operative Society, Northumberland, at the age of fourteen. Nearly a decade later he gained a scholarship to the Co-operative College, then at Holyoake House, Manchester, and spent six months there in 1927–8; he was then selected to attend a three months' course at the International High School, Elsinore, Denmark. In 1929, he was appointed manager and buyer of the grocery and greengrocery department of Durham Co-operative Society. From 1931 to 1938 he was general manager of Easington Lane and South Hetton Co-operative Society and in 1945 was appointed manager of Murton Co-operative Society. For many years he served on the management committee of the East Durham Co-operative Dairies; he also served on the committee of the South-east Durham Co-operative Bakery.

Deans was elected to the board of the Co-operative Wholesale Society in 1944 and at the time of his death he was one of the senior members of its grocery committee. As a CWS director he travelled widely and, on behalf of the English and Scottish Joint Co-operative Wholesale Society, he visited India and Ceylon in 1948 and Kenya in 1952. He was a member of the central executive of the Co-operative Union, and chairman of the processing committee of the Pig Industry Development Authority. He was elected a member of the central committee of the International Co-operative Alliance at the Stockholm Congress in 1957 and in 1958 was elected to the executive committee of the ICA.

Deans was a JP for Northumberland and usually sat on the Ashington bench. He died on 19 December 1959 at Monkseaton, leaving a widow and one son, John, aged seventeen. He left an estate valued at £16,110.

Sources: OBIT. *Whitley Bay Guardian*, 24 Dec 1959; *Durham Chronicle*, 25 Dec 1959; *Co-op. News*, 26 Dec 1959; *RIC 53* (Jan 1960); *Co-op. Congress Report* (1960).

H. F. BING

See also: A. BONNER, for Retail Co-operation, 1945–70; W. H. BROWN, for Retail Co-operation, 1900–45; H. J. MAY, for International Co-operative Alliance; and Percy REDFERN, for Co-operative Wholesaling.

DENT, John James (1856–1936)
CO-OPERATOR

Born on 27 January 1856, the son of John Weaver Dent of Northampton, a bricklayer, he began learning the same trade at the age of ten. He later extended his formal education by attending the London Working Men's College. Throughout his life Dent was actively associated with movements for greater freedom of speech and increased opportunities for working-class education. He was a close friend of Sir Charles Dilke and while secretary of the famous Eleusis Club he formed lasting friendships with Charles Bradlaugh, G. J. Holyoake, Tom Hughes, E. V. Neale, Hodgson Pratt and E. O. Greening.

Dent was a pioneer of the co-operative movement in the south of England. He first became officially associated with it in 1875, when he started the Fulham Co-operative Society. At that time and for long afterwards London was regarded as a co-operative backwater. He helped to start other societies, some of which like the Fulham Society failed, but he lived to see co-operation strongly established in the London region. He attended his first Co-operative Congress in 1883 and his fiftieth, at Rhyl, in 1934 (attendance at the last forty-nine having been continuous). At the Rhyl Congress he was presented with some books for his

service to the movement by Sir Fred Hayward who spoke of his long record of distinguished service, both co-operative and public.

Dent was a member of the central board of the Co-operative Union from 1887 to 1893, but for a much longer period he was associated with the Co-operative Union, though not a member of the board. He was one of the founders of the Tenant Co-operators Ltd in 1888 and for forty-seven years was a member of its committee. He was a member, and for a time chairman, of the Co-operative Southern Education Association, and for some years on the southern sectional board of the Co-operative Permanent Building Society.

His real life's work, however, centred around the Working Men's Club and Institute Union of which be became secretary in 1883 and president in 1909 and with which he was connected until 1922. He supported the WEA and among his many honorary duties was his thirty-seven years' service to the Working Men's College; and for over twelve years he was a member of the London University Joint Committee for promoting tutorial classes for workers. Among his other co-operative interests were the Guild of Co-operators, the Convalescent Fund, the Women's Co-operative Guild and the Hodgson Pratt Memorial Fund, initiated by him and subsequently administered by the Co-operative Union. He built up a unique collection of books and periodicals on the early co-operative and socialist movements which he bequeathed to the Co-operative Union and much of which is now the library of the Co-operative College, Stanford Hall, Loughborough.

From 1886 to 1918 Dent was an active member of the managing executive of the Emigrants' Information Office and for his services in this sphere he was made a CMG. He joined the Civil Service in 1893 where he served the Board of Trade as Labour Correspondent until his retirement in 1919. For a further ten years he continued to advise the Development Commission on co-operative and social questions. When Sir Horace Plunkett started the Irish Agricultural Association, Dent was among other leading British co-operators whose advice Plunkett sought and a lasting friendship developed between them. In his later years Dent assisted in the promotion of the Fisheries Organisation Society of which he became a governor.

A modest and retiring man, Dent married in 1883 Alice, daughter of John Henry Chicken of Chelsea, and they had two sons and four daughters. He died at his Camberwell home on 21 February 1936 in his eighty-first year and was cremated at Golders Green on 26 February. He left an estate valued at £9782 (net) and his will included a bequest of £200 to the Working Men's College.

Writings: *The Co-operative Ideals of Dr William King: editor, Brighton 'Co-operator' 1828-30* (Manchester, 1921) 14 pp.; *John Malcolm Forbes Ludlow CB, Christian Socialist and Co-operator, 1821-1911* (Manchester, 1921) 16 pp.; *Co-operation and the Working Men's College: a lecture* (Manchester, 1928) 19 pp.

Sources: *WWW* (1929-40); B. T. Hall, *Our Fifty Years: the story of the Working Men's Club and Institute Union* (1912); *Co-op. Congress Report* (1934); M. Digby, *Horace Plunkett: an Anglo-American Irishman* (Oxford, 1949); A. Bonner, *British Co-operation* (Manchester, 1961). OBIT. *Times*, 24 Feb 1936; *Co-op. News*, 29 Feb 1936; *Co-op. Congress Report* (1936).

H. F. BING

See also: *John BURNETT; Fred HAYWARD, for Co-operative Union; G. J. HOLYOAKE, for Retail Co-operation – Nineteenth Century; *Horace C. PLUNKETT.

DIXON, John (1828-76)
MINERS' LEADER

Born on 24 May 1828 at Briestfield, near Huddersfield, the son of a collier who was also a local Wesleyan preacher and superintendent of the Sunday school. The young Dixon attended Sunday school from an early age and at the age of seven, shortly after the death of his mother, he entered the mine to work as a 'hurrier' with his father. The latter died when John was fourteen and

he later moved to Gomersal, also in the West Riding of Yorkshire, where, in his early twenties, he began his life's interest in trade unionism. He said later that he had been encouraged in this by hearing David Swallow (one of the founders of the Miners' Association of Great Britain and Ireland) speak in the year 1844.

John Dixon married in 1850, at which time he was still illiterate. He moved from Gomersal to Drighlington and in 1858 he became secretary of a miners' lodge. In the following year the 'Miners Organisation of the Adwalton and Drighlington District' was formed with Dixon as its secretary. Three years later, against the advice of Dixon himself, a serious strike occurred and the union collapsed. Dixon was among those victimised and he travelled to West Yorkshire in search of work, and after being unemployed for some fifteen months he finally obtained employment at Snydale near Featherstone. The union re-formed in 1865 with Dixon once again as secretary, and in the next year the District union amalgamated with the West Yorkshire Miners. Dixon became assistant secretary to William Brown, at the rate of 5s 6d a day for three days a week. In the following year, 1867, Dixon replaced Brown as secretary.

He was a firm advocate of amalgamation as the key to bargaining strength. In 1870 when his own Association had fewer than 500 members he proposed the coming together of all the unions in the West Riding of Yorkshire; but parochialism was still too strong and another decade had to pass before a county union in Yorkshire came into being. John Dixon moved around the coalfield in his last years. He lived at Methley in 1868 and some time later moved to Normanton where he was made chairman of the first School Board in 1873. In the same year he gave evidence before the S.C. on Coal. He died on 8 April 1876, being succeeded by Benjamin Pickard, who had been his assistant secretary since 1873.

Sources: Evidence before S.C. on Present Dearness and Scarcity of Coal 1873 X Qs 4949-5167; F. Machin, *The Yorkshire Miners* (Barnsley, 1958); R. Challinor and

B. Ripley, *The Miners' Association: a trade union in the age of the Chartists* (1968).

JOYCE BELLAMY

See also: *William BROWN; Alexander MACDONALD, for Mining Trade Unionism, 1850–79.

DRAKE, Henry John (1878–1934)
CO-OPERATOR AND LABOUR PARTY WORKER

Henry Drake was born on 13 November 1878 at East Stonehouse, Plymouth, the son of William Henry Drake, a labourer. He was educated at Union Street Council School, then at the technical school before becoming a junior clerk at the Liberal Club. He entered the teaching profession where he was first a pupil teacher at St Andrews Boys' School, Plymouth, and later a certificated teacher at the Mount Street Schools. He was at one time chairman of the Plymouth and South Devon branch of the National Union of Teachers.

Drake's father had worked for the co-operative movement and his son participated actively in it at local, regional and national levels. He was a member of the education committee and of the management committee of Plymouth Co-operative Society, becoming chairman of the education committee; only a few months before his death he was elected president of the society in April 1934. For many years a member of the south-west sectional board of the Co-operative Union, he was ultimately its chairman. He was first elected to the central board of the Co-operative Union in 1914 and served in 1914–15, 1927–31 and 1932–4. He was a member of the National Education Board, the executive of the Co-operative Union and the joint committee on technical education of the Union and the CWS. His work for the Plymouth Society was commemorated through the Society's scholarship to the Co-operative College, his name being linked with that of a former president, W. H. Watkins, as the Watkins–Drake scholarship.

Drake worked enthusiastically for the Plymouth Labour Party from its foundation and he always advocated a united front with the co-operative movement. He was at the right hand of Mr J. J. H. Moses when the latter won the Drake Division for the Labour Party in 1929, having also assisted him when he was a candidate in the 1923 and 1924 elections and again in 1931, although on all these occasions Moses was not elected. Drake was a member of the old Board of Guardians at Plymouth (1919–29), being in 1928 the first Labour governor of that body. He was appointed a JP for Devon county in 1929; he was also a member of the Charity Trust Committee, an active member of the Peverell Park Methodist Church and a Freemason.

He died at Tywardreath, Cornwall, on 11 August 1934, where he had gone to recuperate, after months of illness. His wife, who survived him, was also a devoted worker for the co-operative movement. He left £1035 in his will.

Sources: R. Briscoe, *Centenary History: a hundred years of co-operation in Plymouth* (Manchester, 1960); personal information: R. Briscoe, Plymouth. OBIT. *Western Morning News*, 13 Aug 1934; *Co-op. News*, 18 Aug 1934; *Co-op. Congress Report* (1935).

H. F. BING

See also: W. H. BROWN, for Retail Co-operation, 1900–45; Fred HAYWARD, for Co-operative Union; A. HENDERSON, for British Labour Party, 1914–31.

DUDLEY, Sir William Edward (1868–1938)
CO-OPERATOR

William Dudley was born at Runcorn on 29 May 1868, the son of William Dudley, a house painter. He was educated at the local church school and, about 1883, joined the staff of the Bridgewater Navigation Company which was purchased in 1887 by the Manchester Ship Canal Company and subsequently operated by the Bridgewater Department of that company. Born into a co-operative family, Dudley early attended meetings of the local society and in 1894, the year after his marriage to Miss Theresa Sutton of Wem, he was elected to the management committee of the Runcorn and Widnes Co-operative Society at the age of twenty-six. He was president of the society from 1896 to 1911 and, during this time, served on the north-west sectional board and the united board and in 1904 was elected to the central board of the Co-operative Union. He had continued on the staff of the canal company and was head of the engineer's office, but he resigned in 1911 on being elected to the board of the Co-operative Wholesale Society. This was the prelude to a long career in the service of the co-operative movement.

During the First World War, he was particularly active on the home front in connection with food supplies. In 1917 he was one of four representatives of the CWS board who, together with representatives of the Scottish CWS, were given 'full power to deal with all questions arising in regard to food control during the period of the war', with freedom to attend on government departments whenever required. During the war years Dudley served on fourteen departmental committees. In 1918, when the Government set up the Consumers' Council, he was one of the two representatives of the CWS board on that body. He received the OBE in 1920. In 1924 he was made a member of the Royal Commission on Food Prices and was a member of the National Food Council.

In 1925 he received the highest honour in the co-operative movement by being elected president of the 57th Annual Co-operative Congress held at Southport. In introducing him to the Congress, Alderman (later Sir) Fred Hayward spoke of his long and devoted service to the co-operative movement. Dudley, in his address, dealt mainly with improving the business efficiency of the movement. In the following year, 1926, he was knighted and when Runcorn celebrated International Co-operators' Day in the same year, it celebrated also the honour bestowed on a popular Runcorn man as well as a CWS director. In May 1926 he was one of five representatives of the CWS to participate in the jubilee celebration of the New York depot of the CWS, being afterwards received by President Coolidge at the White House. In 1933 he succeeded to the presidency of the CWS on the retirement of Sir Henry Wilkins and served until 1936. At a general meeting of the CWS in January 1934, when it was decided to establish the CWS Retail Society, he made a brief and dignified reply to Lord Beaverbrook who had organised a noisy and ill-informed campaign against this proposal, in defence, it was claimed, of small shopkeepers. In 1936, when the International Peace Congress met in Cardiff, he was one of the two CWS speakers at a reception given to the Congress at the CWS South Wales depot on 15 June.

Following decontrol by the Ministry of Transport in August 1920, the Bridgewater Department of the Manchester Ship Canal Company functioned under the direction of a committee of directors, known as the Bridgewater Committee, on which William Dudley served as chairman for a number of years. He also represented the CWS on the directorate of the Canal Company, his term of office covering the period 1919–38, and was succeeded by Sir William Bradshaw, then president of the CWS. Dudley also represented the CWS on the directorate of Manchester Collieries Ltd. In 1931 he received the order of the Dannebrog (Denmark) and, in 1935, the Order of Mérite Agricole (Quebec) – both in recognition of services to the development of trade with those countries.

William Dudley also worked actively in local affairs in Runcorn. Elected to the Runcorn Urban District Council in 1914, he served as chairman in 1921–3 and subsequently on some of the local council committees. A JP from 1919, he was vice-chairman of the Runcorn bench in 1936. Although not uninterested in politics, Dudley believed that party allegiance was incompatible with the aims and character of the co-operative movement, especially on the business side. In the religious sphere, Dudley served the parish church and its Sunday school for over half a century. He became a teacher in the Sunday school in 1883, his father having also been prominently connected with the school and led a most successful young men's class from the age of twenty-two. In his early youth he learnt shorthand and subsequently taught the subject at evening school.

His health had been failing for some time before he died on 7 May 1938, shortly before his seventieth birthday. Lady Dudley had predeceased him in 1927 but he was survived by a son and daughter. He left an estate valued at £14,583 (net).

Sources: *Co-op. Congress Report* (1925); *Runcorn Weekly News*, 14 Mar 1930; *WW* (1937); P. Redfern, *The New History of the C.W.S.* (Manchester, 1938); personal information: Miss T. E. Dudley JP, daughter, and the Manchester Ship Canal Co. OBIT. *Guardian* (Runcorn), 13 May 1938.

JOYCE BELLAMY
H. F. BING

See also: W. H. BROWN, for Retail Co-operation, 1900–45; Fred HAYWARD, for Co-operative Union; Percy REDFERN, for Co-operative Wholesaling.

DYE, Sidney (1900–58)
LABOUR MP

Born at Wells-next-the-Sea, Norfolk, on 24 August 1900, Sidney Dye was the son of James William Dye, a dairyman, and his wife Daisy (née Walker). He attended Wells elementary school until the age of thirteen when he began to work on the land. At the age of sixteen he joined the National Union of Agricultural Workers and three years later became secretary of the Wells branch. In 1920 he was elected secretary of the Wells Labour Party. Awarded the Buxton Memorial Scholarship he went to Ruskin College, Oxford, and took the University diploma in economics and political science. He afterwards attended the International People's College at Elsinore, Denmark, and in order to study agriculture visited a number of continental countries.

In 1924 Dye was appointed Labour agent to the Dover constituency and two years later became agent to the Cambridgeshire Divisional Labour Party, a post he occupied until 1931. In 1932 he became a tenant farmer at Swaffham, later buying his farm

which he continued to work during the remainder of his life. He was a member of the Norfolk County Council from 1934 and was elected an alderman in 1946; on the Council he was chairman of the Public Assistance Committee and its successor, the Welfare Committee. Appointed as a JP in 1934, he sat on the Swaffham Rural District Council from 1935. At the general election of 1935 Dye unsuccessfully contested South-West Norfolk, but was elected for that constituency in 1945 when he had a narrow majority over the sitting Conservative, Somerset de Chair. Re-elected in 1950, he lost the seat the following year only to regain it in May 1955 when he had the distinction of being the only Labour MP to gain a seat for his party in the election. Dye continued to represent the division until his death.

In Parliament he spoke with authority on agricultural matters and often stressed the importance of food production. In 1948 he accompanied a parliamentary delegation to Eire and the following year was a member of delegations to Holland and Northern Ireland. He visited Poland in 1957 with a party of MPs who had been invited by the Polish Parliament. For a time he was the chairman of the Parliamentary Food and Agriculture Group of the Labour Party. Shortly before his death, Dye made his first speech from the Opposition Front Bench when he wound up for Labour in the debate on the Small Farms Bill. He was a conscientious MP and his farming background may have helped to foster an individualistic approach to politics which did not always find favour with members of his own party. Dye's last speech in the House of Commons was cheered by Government MPs when he condemned demonstrators who had entered the RAF site at North Pickenham and denied the suggestion of Sydney Silverman that the authorities had used undue violence.

Dye was killed in a road accident on 9 December 1958 while driving from his farm to Brandon Station on his return to the Commons. An inquest, after hearing evidence that his car's brakes were defective, returned a verdict of accidental death. Dye was survived by his wife, Grace (née Gidney), whom he had married in 1932, and by a son and a daughter. Since the age of nineteen, Dye had been a Methodist local preacher and he was a founder member of the Parliamentary Socialist Christian Group. In a tribute T. C. Skeffington-Lodge wrote of him:

He won and held the support of his constituents on his own merits, and may well have felt he did not need outside supporters. They might have been out of step with the rugged individualism and independence born and bred in Sidney as a man of the soil and as a local preacher of long experience. His meetings were more like family parties than anything else. He was on Christian name terms with every-one, and always made a simple and sincere appeal to his hearers based on the practical idealism in which he believed. Never willing to toe the party line if he thought it wrong, he brought to Parlia-ment a refreshing glimpse of one at peace with himself and the world.

Dye's funeral took place on 13 December at Swaffham Methodist Church. He left £16,040 gross in his will.

Sources: C. Bunker, *Who's Who in Parliament* [1946]; *WWW* (1951–60); *Dod* (1958); *Labour Party Report* (1959); personal information: Mrs G. L. Dye, widow. OBIT. *Eastern Daily Press*, 10 Dec 1958; *Times*, 10, 15 and 19 Dec 1958.

DAVID E. MARTIN

See also: *C. R. ATTLEE, for British Labour Party, 1931–51.

DYSON, James (1822/3–1902)
CO-OPERATOR

Of Dyson's early life little is known except that he was born in the district between Ashton-under-Lyne and Oldham and his youth was spent in the neighbourhood of Bardsley, near Ashton. By trade he was a silk hatter and with a few kindred spirits he founded a Working Hatters' Co-operative Association at 12 Broughton Road, Salford, in March 1850. There were eleven members working in one room, producing about two

dozen hats a week. J. M. Ludlow reported on them in the *Christian Socialist 2* (1851). At the same date a Working Tailors' Association was begun at 13 Princes Street, Manchester, and in April 1852 the two associations joined together to open a shop in Bridge Street, Manchester, where they remained for the rest of their existence. By 1864 there were six tailors and nine hatters in the community. The Tailors' Association ended in 1872 and the Hatters' in the following year. Dyson was the manager for an unspecified period of the Hatters' Association and probably was still connected with the Association up to the time of its closure.

In March 1856 James Dyson was one of the Manchester representatives at a con-ference at Rochdale to consider the question of a wholesale department. At a meeting at Rochdale on 7 October 1860 he was elected to a committee to further the idea and at Lowlands Farm, Jumbo, near Middleton, on 4 November 1860 he was elected chair-man and was chairman at a subsequent meeting at Middleton. He drew up a five-point charter for the amendment of the Industrial and Provident Societies Acts which would make possible the establish-ment of a wholesale society. All this was reported to a delegate conference in Manchester on Christmas Day 1860.

On Good Friday 1863 was established the North of England Co-operative Wholesale Agency and Depot Society Ltd; and James Dyson was enrolled as one of the twelve 'original members' (i.e. individual members in addition to the Society members). He was elected a member of the first committee along with Abraham Greenwood, James Smithies, Edward Hooson, John Hilton, James Crabtree and Joseph Thomasson. Dyson continued as a member of the committee and acted as its treasurer till May 1867. He was also active in the formation of the Co-operative Insurance Society and when this Society was registered on 29 August 1867 he was one of the seven original members who each took up four shares.

In 1874 Dyson joined the Manchester and Salford Equitable Society, being elected to the committee in 1882. In March 1887 he retired from the society's directorate to become check manager and at once concerned himself with improving the position of his fellow workers in the co-operative movement. Between 1887 and 1890, in collaboration with Thomas Fowe, an employees' association was formed, and although short-lived, organised several conferences and laid the foundations of a more permanent organisation which was established in 1891 under the title of the Manchester District Co-operative Employees' Association. Dyson and Fowe were first president and treasurer respectively. In 1895 the Association became the Amalgamated Union of Co-operative Employees and Dyson contined as president until increasing infirmity compelled his retirement from office in 1897. In 1921 AUCE amalgamated with another trade union, the combined organisation then being known as NUDAW (National Union of Distributive and Allied Workers).

He died on 25 September 1902 at his grandson's home in Ardwick, Manchester, and was buried at Dukinfield Cemetery, Ashton.

Sources: J. M. Ludlow, 'Notes of a Co-operative Tour through Lancashire and Yorkshire', *Christian Socialist 2* (1851) 212–14; P. Redfern, *The Story of the C.W.S.* (Manchester, [1913]); G. D. H. Cole, *A Century of Co-operation* (Manchester, [1945?]); J. Bailey, *The British Co-operative Movement* (1955). OBIT. *Co-op. News*, 11 Oct 1902; Anon., 'Mr James Dyson', *Co-op. Employee* (Dec 1908) 12–15.

H. F. BING

See also: Abraham GREENWOOD; *J. M. F. LUDLOW, for Christian Socialism, 1848–54; J. SMITHIES.

EDWARDS, Enoch (1852–1912)
MINERS' LEADER AND MP

Born on 10 April 1852 at Talk-o'-the-Hill, a mining village in North Staffordshire, the eldest son of James Edwards, a miner. He was educated at a Primitive Methodist day school and commenced work at the Hollinwood Colliery, earning 6d a day at the age of nine. Edwards never forgot his early years as a boy underground and in later years he was vigorous in his support for control of hours of work. He recalled at a public meeting in 1906 (in celebrating his election as MP for Hanley) how at the age of ten he was alone in the pit and discovered a miner who lay dead under a roof fall. These experiences remained with Edwards all his life, and his gentleness of manner concealed an unshakeable determination to improve the lot of the mining community. He always spoke scathingly of those who used the phrase 'the good old days'.

Edwards's formal education had been meagre but he was encouraged to read as a boy in the pit by some of the miners with whom he worked and who lent him books on history, and biographies; and his knowledge was further extended by his work as a Sunday school teacher, there being a small library attached to the Sunday school. He was also a member of the Primitive Methodists' Young Men's Improvement class. In his early youth he joined his local lodge, and was soon made treasurer. In 1869 he went to the Talk-o'-the-Hill Colliery and in 1874 transferred to the Harecastle Colliery company. At both, offers of management jobs were made to him, but he declined. In July 1875 he was elected checkweighman, and in the same year he became treasurer of the North Staffordshire Miners' Association. Three years later, in October 1878, he was made general secretary, a position he held until his death. Edwards was the prime mover in the establishment of the Midland Miners' Federation (which embraced a number of local and district unions in Staffordshire, Shropshire and Warwickshire) and he became president of the Federation in 1886 and treasurer in 1888.

As president of the Midland Federation Enoch Edwards took a prominent part in the series of conferences which preceded the famous Newport conference of November 1889 which formally established the MFGB. Edwards was appointed national treasurer of the MFGB and he held the position from 1889 to 1904, when he succeeded Ben Pickard as president. From the time of Newport, then, Edwards moved into the national stage of the miner's struggle; and, like Pickard's, much of his personal history is the detailed history of the MFGB. He was present at the Rosebery Conference of 1893 and became a member of the conciliation conference which was part of the settlement agreed upon. As president of the MFGB he represented the miners along with William Abraham and Robert Smillie on the R.C. on Mines in 1906. The last years of his life were years of increasing stress and tension. The Cambrian Miners' strike of 1910–11 and the minimum wage strike of 1912 put especial strain upon Edwards, but although increasingly unwell he continued working up to the time of his death. One unfortunate episode which caused him much trouble was his support for a parliamentary bill in August 1911 which sought to impose a 'cooling-off period' for strikes. The bill, tabled in the Commons by Arthur Henderson, Charles Fenwick, George Barnes and Will Crooks, would have made strikes illegal unless thirty days' notice had been given in advance. The bill had not been officially authorised either by the TUC or the Labour Party, and it came under very severe criticism at the TUC at Newcastle on Tyne in September 1911. Enoch Edwards, among others, had difficulty in explaining away his support.

From his early days Edwards was much involved in local affairs. He took a prominent part in the friendly society movement, becoming district secretary of the Ancient Order of Shepherds and being also a member of the Ancient Order of Foresters. He was elected to the Burslem School Board in 1886 (having moved to Burslem in 1884) and he served on the board for nine years. In 1886 also he was elected to the town council, later becoming an alderman, and mayor in 1889. He also served on the Staffordshire County Council, resigning only when he entered Parliament; was a JP for Burslem and later for Stoke, and was also a magistrate for the county. He had unsuccessfully contested Hanley as the official Liberal candidate in 1900 but won a resounding victory in 1906. Edwards was a convinced free trade Liberal in politics and a reluctant adherent to the

Labour Party when the MFGB affiliated in 1909 (the Midland Federation voted against Smillie's resolution at the 1907 annual conference). At the two general elections in 1910 Edwards was now required to stand as a straight Labour candidate; but his new label made no difference to his views. The local newspapers still described him as Lib-Lab, and he was adopted at a joint meeting of the Hanley Trades Council and Hanley Liberal Association. When Edwards died the Hanley constituency became an issue of serious dispute between the Labour Party and the Liberals concerning the political affiliation of the new candidate; and in the immediate event it was a Liberal, R. L. Outhwaite, who won the by-election: a result which undoubtedly helped to widen the breach between the MFGB and the Liberal Party [Gregory (1968) 168–73].

Edwards was moderate in opinion and expression, a man of integrity and thoroughly trusted and loved by his colleagues. 'He had no enemies', wrote Thomas Ashton after Edwards's death; and Robert Smillie, whose own views were very different from those of Edwards, paid a striking tribute at the International Miners' Federation conference very soon after Edwards's death:

To Mr Edwards more than anyone else living today, or anyone connected or who has been connected with the Federation, is due the fact that the miners have been, for some time now, absolutely solidly organised together in one body. To him is due the fact that what at one time were warring branches who had the same interest at stake, were drawn together.

Persons holding extreme views, in all probability, however honest and anxious they might be to establish a great ideal, might through their very extreme views prevent them getting very far in that direction: but Mr Edwards had a desire to see the whole mining movement of Great Britain carried forward together under one banner, and he had that peculiar temperament which could overlook to a great degree the extreme views of others, and could work for the purpose of unity. It was due to a great extent to him that we became united North, South, East and West, under one common banner in the Federation of all miners of the country. [Quoted by Arnot, (1953) 121–2]

Edwards married Elizabeth Alice, daughter of Henry Rathbone, in 1875 and he died at Southport on 28 June 1912. He left effects worth £3192.

Sources: W. Hallam, *Miners' Leaders* (1894) [photograph]; R.C. on Mines vol. III 1908 XX; *Dod* (1912); *WWW* (1897–1915); D. Evans, *Labour Strife in the South Wales Coalfield 1910–11* (Cardiff, 1911); R. P. Arnot, *The Miners: a history of the Miners' Federation 1888–1910* (1949) and *The Miners: years of struggle* (1953); R. Gregory, *The Miners and British Politics* (Oxford, 1968). OBIT. *Staffordshire Sentinel*, 28 June 1912 [photograph]; *Times*, 29 June 1912.
JOYCE BELLAMY
JOHN SAVILLE

See also: Thomas ASHTON, for Mining Trade Unionism, 1900–14; Benjamin PICKARD, for Mining Trade Unionism, 1880–99; Albert STANLEY; *John WARD.

EDWARDS, John Charles (1833–81)
CO-OPERATOR AND RADICAL

Little is known of the early family life of John Edwards. He was born in 1833, presumably in Manchester, and while he was still in his teens became a vigorous advocate of the temperance cause. He worked as a mechanic in his younger days, although whether he ever served an apprenticeship is not known. His interest in the co-operative movement began in the 1850s when he was a founder-member of the Manchester and Salford Equitable Co-operative Society, of which he became the first president. In 1859 he was associated with Edward Hooson and E. O. Greening in drafting amendments to the Industrial and Provident Societies Acts which would make possible the establishment of a wholesale society; and he helped prepare the report to the famous Manchester conference of Yorkshire and Lanca-

shire delegates, on Christmas Day 1860, which decided on the desirability of such amendments. When the CWS was founded in 1863, Edwards became its first secretary and cashier and remained in these positions until 1868, but from this date he ceased to take a prominent part in the co-operative movement.

During the American Civil War (1861–5) Edwards and a few friends in the Manchester Socratic Debating Society were responsible for convening the first large meeting in Lancashire to demonstrate sympathy with the northern cause; and it was from this meeting that came the Union and Emancipation Society. It was Edwards again who persuaded the new society, by a narrow majority, to include the word 'Union' in its title, the large minority arguing that such an inclusion would involve interference in American internal affairs. Edwards was appointed joint secretary with E. O. Greening, and he gave much of his time and energy to propaganda for the Federal cause.

During his whole life Edwards was active in liberal politics, numbering among his friends and correspondents John Stuart Mill, Louis Blanc and George Wilson. He remained to the end of his days a tireless advocate of co-operative principles. For some years before his death he was in a precarious state of health, and he died on 12 March 1881 at his home in Chorlton-on-Medlock, being survived by his wife and one son. His personal estate was under £800.

Sources: P. Redfern, *The Story of the C.W.S.* (Manchester, [1913]); E. O. Greening, *Memories of Robert Owen and the Co-operative Pioneers* (Manchester, 1925) 18 pp.; F. Hourani, *Manchester and Abraham Lincoln* (reprinted from *Manchester Guardian*, 1 Jan 1863 and 11 Feb 1863) [1942] 11 pp.; A. Bonner, *British Co-operation* (Manchester, 1961). OBIT. *Co-op. News*, 19 Mar 1881.
H. F. BING
JOHN SAVILLE

See also: E. O. GREENING; G. J. HOLYOAKE, for Retail Co-operation – Nineteenth Century; Edward HOOSON; Percy REDFERN, for Co-operative Wholesaling.

EDWARDS, Wyndham Ivor (1878–1938)
CO-OPERATOR AND LABOUR PARTY WORKER

Born on 26 July 1878 at Cwm-gilly, Rhymney, Monmouthshire, the son of Edward Edwards, a coalminer, Wyndham Edwards went to live at Cwmavon, near Port Talbot, at the age of five. As a young man he developed an interest in politics and the co-operative movement, and as he was a teacher by profession it was the educational work of the co-operative movement which particularly interested him. He became a member of the Independent Labour Party and his services to both the political and co-operative wings of the labour movement began in the early 1900s. In 1915 he was elected president of the Afon Valley Co-operative Society and held that office until his death. For a period he was chairman of the Mid-Glamorgan District Association, chairman of the Mid-Glamorgan Hours and Wages Board from its inception in 1921, and chairman of the Western Sectional Joint Wages Council for twenty years.

In 1924 he was elected a member of the western sectional board of the Co-operative Union. Later, he became a member of what was then the central education committee, later the educational council, and was appointed to the education executive, succeeding W. R. Rae to the chairmanship of both the council and the executive in 1936. He was also associated with the work of the committee on technical education and in 1937 was elected to serve as the central board's representative on the special committee to examine the co-ordination of co-operative production.

In 1935 he presided over the 67th Co-operative Congress held at Cardiff and impressed all by his skill and courtesy. In his presidential address he appealed especially for closer co-operation between the co-operative, trade union and political wings of the labour movement.

A convinced trade unionist, Edwards passed through most of the offices of the Glamorgan Association of the National Union of Teachers. He was headmaster of Cwmavon Council School and was due to retire on superannuation at the end of the month in which he died. Deeply interested in music, he was president of the Cwmavon Choral Society and conducted the boys' choir at Sandfields School which gained many successes at eisteddfods.

Edwards was an ardent worker for the Labour Party in Port Talbot and at the time of his death was the parliamentary nominee of the Co-operative Party. He was closely associated with various schemes of social welfare work in Port Talbot and served on the Rural District Council. He was made a JP in 1925.

Although apparently in good health at the time, Edwards collapsed suddenly and died on 22 March 1938 while presiding at a committee meeting. He left a wife and a son and daughter. Like her husband, Mrs Edwards was a magistrate for Port Talbot. Edwards left an estate valued at £3640.

Sources: *Co-op. Congress Report* (Manchester, 1935). OBIT. *Co-op. News*, 26 Mar 1938; *Co-op. Congress Report* (Manchester, 1938).

H. F. BING

See also: W. H. BROWN, for Retail Co-operation, 1900–45; Fred HALL, for Co-operative Education; Fred HAYWARD, for Co-operative Union; A. HENDERSON, for British Labour Party, 1914–31.

ENFIELD, Alice Honora (1882–1935)
CO-OPERATOR

Honora Enfield, as she was generally called, was born in Nottingham on 4 January 1882, the daughter of Ernest William Enfield, a banker, and educated at St Leonard's School, St Andrews, Scotland, and Somerville College, Oxford. She took the examination for a degree before degrees were actually awarded to women. Later she taught for several years in a secondary school and also engaged in historical research. In 1913 she took service with the National Federation of Women Workers and for four years worked in the administration of the National Health Insurance Acts (1913–17).

The co-operative movement made a

strong appeal to her from the time that she learned of its scope and ideals and she came to regard it as the surest road to social peace. In 1917 she gladly accepted the invitation to become private secretary to Margaret Llewelyn Davies, secretary of the Women's Co-operative Guild, and succeeded her as general secretary of the Guild when Miss Davies retired owing to ill-health in 1922. Honora had already shown great skill in piloting the campaign of the Women's Guild for improved social benefits for women workers under the State insurance schemes; and the women's battle, which was carried to the House of Lords, was greatly aided by the capacity and determination which she brought to bear upon the negotiations and on the presentation of the case.

In 1921, at the Basle Congress of the International Co-operative Alliance, the formation of an International Women's Co-operative Guild was agreed on by several women, among whom was the dynamic Emmy Freundlich. Honora Enfield was made secretary of the International Guild and held this office along with the secretaryship of the English Guild from 1922 to 1927. She then resigned the English post and devoted herself entirely to the work of the International Women's Co-operative Guild.

From early association with Quaker friends, Miss Enfield absorbed a passionate devotion to the cause of peace, and she was for many years a member of the National Peace Council. During the last ten years of her life she engaged in ceaseless activities for peace and co-operation, travelling all over Europe to encourage and inspire women in the struggle for these ends. As a representative of the International Women's Co-operative Guild, she resided in Geneva from February to July 1932 as a member of the Disarmament Committee of the International Women's Organisations. Her remarkable gift for languages was of great service in this work.

Other official positions held by Miss Enfield were membership of the committee of the Electrical Association for Women, of the International Institute for the Study of Co-operation and of the International Industrial Relations Institute. She wrote many brochures and pamphlets on the co-operative movement.

Exhausted by continuous travel and work, Miss Enfield made a last journey to France in 1935, partly for the physical recuperation she so badly needed but partly also in an endeavour to establish a Women's Guild among French co-operators before the ICA Congress of 1937. She died in Paris on 14 August 1935 and was cremated in that city. Tributes to her great work came from co-operators, and particularly from women, all over the world. She left an estate valued at £6041.

Writings: *Memorandum on Midwifery Services* (Women's Co-operative Guild, 1918); *The Place of Co-operation in the New Social Order* (Women's Co-operative Guild, 1920) 12 pp.; *A Lady of the Salons: the story of Louise Colet* (1922); *International Co-operative Trade* (1924); *Co-operation: its problems and possibilities* (1927).

Sources: C. Webb, *The Woman with the Basket* (1927). Obit. *Times*, 21 Aug 1935; *Co-op. News*, 24 and 31 Aug 1935; H. J. May, 'A. Honora Enfield', *RIC* (Sep 1935) 324–5.

H. F. BING

See also: *Mrs Cecily COOK; Miss M. L. DAVIES.

EVANS, Isaac (1847?–97)
MINERS' LEADER

Born at Garndiffaith, near Pontypool, about 1847. Nothing seems to be known about his early life but around 1877 he was working as a collier in Skewen. In 1880 he was elected miners' agent for the Neath, Swansea and Llanelly miners, but continued to work in the mines until 1887 when he became agent for the whole of the western district of South Wales.

Evans was an unusual man in a number of respects, not least that he seems to have been uncertain about the sliding-scale principle already in the 1880s, although it must be added that he signed the agreements of 1880, 1882 and 1889. He also played a prominent role in organising the enginemen and stokers in this decade. In 1883 at the first meeting of engine and boiler men from all over South Wales which was held at Merthyr, Evans was in the chair and encouraged the men to co-operate in order to improve their conditions. Two years later he was elected president of the Enginemen and Stokers Association for the succeeding twelve months. At the 1889 Newport Conference which led to the establishment of the MFGB Evans welcomed the eight-hour day policy but indicated that it could not be applied in South Wales because of the five-year agreements on the sliding scale. He had previously expressed support for the idea of one national union and for fixing a minimum wage. Although he was one of the signatories to the sliding-scale agreement of 1 January 1892, he rejected this shortly afterwards and refused to sign the final copy; and the Neath, Swansea and Llanelly miners refused to continue to pay the levies required to finance the sliding-scale committee [E. W. Evans (1961) 155].

When the unofficial hauliers' strike (with a first demand for a twenty per cent advance in wages) broke out on 1 August 1893, and was spread throughout most of the coalfields by the 'marching gangs', the coalowners, refusing to negotiate, set up an emergency committee to arrange *inter alia* the quartering of troops from four regiments, under the command of General Harrison. While the ten workmen's representatives on the sliding-scale committee, including Mabon, Onions and Richards, issued a manifesto denouncing the strikers for their violation of agreement, Isaac Evans came to their aid, and was ready to put the hauliers' demands (including an end to the sliding scales and for junction with the MFGB) before the emergency committee. Evans, however, died the year before the SWMF came into existence, the formation of which was the beginning of the end of the sliding-scale agreements.

Evans was described by the Webbs as 'a short, thick-set bulldog-looking sort of man', and in the Webb papers there is a remarkable statement of Evans's attitude to Mabon, whom he despised for his general policies and whom he accused of taking bribes. The

esteem accorded to Evans beyond all other agents in South Wales is evidenced in the constitution and rules of the British Labour League (Pontypool, 1890). Isaac Evans was president. Vice-presidents were: W. Abrahams MP; Alfred Onions of Abercarn; John Jenkins of Cardiff; Henry Davies of Aberaman; Richard McGhee of Glasgow; and Michael Davitt of Dublin. Among the executive council of thirty-six members were: the only Socialist MP, R. B. Cunninghame Graham; two Welsh Liberal MPs (D. Randell of Llanelly and S. T. Evans of Neath); Keir Hardie, John Weir, John Burns, Tom Richards, David Morgan of Aberdare, John Williams of Ynysybwl and J. L. Mahon.

In his activities outside mining proper Evans followed the traditional pattern of miners' leaders. He was active in local government, being elected to the Glamorgan County Council in 1891, later becoming an alderman. He was prominent, too, in co-operative and friendly society bodies, and for three years he was a member of the local Board of Guardians. Unlike most miners' leaders, Evans was an active member of the Church of England and he devoted much of his religious life to the Sunday school movement. He was a skilful and tactful negotiator in trade union affairs, a Liberal in politics and in personal life a man of immense courage. His health is believed to have been much impaired by the many rescue attempts he had led, but the immediate cause of his early death on 12 November 1897 was an operation for the removal of a bone he had swallowed. His family life had been happy, and he was survived by his wife, seven daughters and four sons. He was buried in Skewen Parish Church Cemetery and left £85 in his will.

Sources: Webb Papers vol. 26: LSE [see R. Page Arnot, (1967) 37 n. 2]; Evidence before R.C. on Mining Royalties 1890–1 XLI Qs 10688–845; before R.C. on Labour 1892 XXXIV Qs 4388–957; N. Edwards, *The History of the South Wales Miners* (1926); E. W. Evans, *The Miners of South Wales* (Cardiff, 1961); R. Page Arnot, *South Wales Miners* (1967); biographical information:

Dr E. W. Evans. OBIT. *Western Mail*, 13 and 17 Nov 1897.

JOYCE BELLAMY
JOHN SAVILLE

See also: William ABRAHAM, for Welsh Mining Trade Unionism; W. BRACE.

EVANS, Jonah (1826–1907)
CO-OPERATOR

Jonah Evans was born on 16 August 1826 in Fron Cysyllte, near Llangollen, Wales, and educated at the village school. He left Wales as a young man in search of work and was employed first on the construction of the Chester to Warrington railway line and then as a weighman at Runcorn Docks. Later he took a full-time appointment with the Runcorn and Widnes Co-operative Society.

He was among those who attended the informal meetings in Runcorn in the winter of 1861–2 at which the formation of a co-operative society was discussed. Information about these meetings is derived in part from a manuscript in Evans's handwriting in which he describes himself as a porter. At the meeting on 23 June 1862 which appointed the first committee he was elected assistant secretary and he continued his official connection with the Society until his retirement in February 1905. He was a member of the acting committee which drafted the rules, formally adopted on 13 September 1862, thus inaugurating the Society; and when a new committee of eight members was elected on 4 October (after the rules had been approved by the Registrar under the Industrial and Provident Societies Act 1862), Evans was one of the eight, and was also elected one of two auditors, an office he held until 1867. He was treasurer of the Society from 1868 to 1905 and general manager from 1879 to 1904. On his retirement the Runcorn Society voted him an honorarium of three hundred guineas.

Like many Welshmen, Jonah Evans was musical, and he acted as choirmaster of the thriving Welsh Chapel in Runcorn. Although never taking any prominent part in political affairs he was a vigorous radical in his everyday opinions. He died at Runcorn on 25 September 1907 and left effects valued at £921.

Sources: W. Millington, *Runcorn and Widnes Industrial Co-operative Society Ltd Jubilee History 1862–1912* (Manchester, 1912); personal information: Education Secretary, Runcorn and Widnes Co-operative Society, 1963.

H. F. BING

See also: G. J. HOLYOAKE, for Retail Co-operation – Nineteenth Century.

FENWICK, Charles (1850–1918)
MINERS' LEADER AND LIB-LAB MP

Born on 5 May 1850 at Paradise Row, Cramlington, Northumberland, the son of a miner, John Fenwick. He attended the village school but received little formal education; he began work at nine years of age above ground at the pit, and at ten went underground where he worked a 12–13 hour day. When he was seventeen he became a hewer which meant shorter working hours and enabled him to extend his education through home reading. In 1863 he joined the Northumberland Miners' Association and worked actively in his local association. In May 1876 he attended his first delegate meeting as a representative of Bebside on the River Blyth in Bedlingtonshire and from this time he was often a member of delegations to meet colliery owners. In June 1878 he was elected to the joint committee of the NMA and on a number of occasions was a member of its wages committee; and he was also made a trustee of the Association. He was a delegate to the TUC at Aberdeen in 1884. In the following year he was elected straight from the coal face to become Liberal MP for the Wansbeck Division of Northumberland, a seat which he held through eight successive general elections until his death. Throughout his parliamentary career he continued to be closely associated with miners' activities. He attended the four-day conference of the miners of England, Scotland and Wales in the Oddfellows Hall, Edinburgh, beginning on 11 October 1887, where he represented 26,000 miners. This conference, like that of the previous April, had been called by the Miners' National Union, and was held under the presidency of Thomas Burt MP. At the Miners' National Conference in Newcastle on Tyne on 22 and 24 November 1887, Fenwick was chosen as vice-president of the conference; and the committee of five (empowered to carry out its decision to call another conference on the question of shorter hours) consisted of Ashton of Lancashire, Keir Hardie of Scotland, Frith of Yorkshire, Enoch Edwards of the Midland Federation and Charles Fenwick. In January 1889 he attended the MNU Conference at Leeds and in the same year was a delegate, with Burt, to the international trades union congress at Paris and with him was largely responsible for the formation of the Miners' International which met at Jolimont in 1890, and which he also attended.

Fenwick was a Gladstonian Liberal, resolutely opposed to state intervention, and he retained these attitudes to the end of his life. At the 1887 TUC Keir Hardie – who was attending for the first time – launched a bitter attack on Henry Broadhurst. Broadhurst defended himself vigorously and Fenwick, who naturally supported him, quite wrongly predicted that Hardie's agitation 'like Jonah's gourd' would wither as quickly as it had sprung up [Pelling (1965) 62]. At the same congress Fenwick joined Ben Pickard in making clear their opposition to the idea of an independent Labour Party. In 1890 the TUC voted by the narrow majority of thirty-eight a resolution in favour of the legal eight-hour day; and Broadhurst, who was in any case suffering from ill-health, found it convenient to retire from the position of secretary to the parliamentary committee. Fenwick, although well known for his opposition to compulsory hours legislation, defeated George Shipton and T. R. Threlfall for the secretaryship; and this was the beginning of several years' intense controversy over the eight hours agitation. In 1892 Sam Woods, vice-president of the MFGB, moved a vote of censure at the TUC against the parliamentary committee and its secretary for not carrying out Congress instructions to give full support to the miners' Eight Hours Bill

in Parliament. Fenwick defended himself, pointing out that he had been elected as a Liberal, and that the majority of his own constituents (the Northumberland miners) were not in favour of the Bill. Moreover, Fenwick continued, Congress knew clearly his position when he was elected in 1890. On this occasion and again in 1893 Fenwick was re-elected with large majorities – in 1893 against Keir Hardie, the only other candidate; but in the following year the issue was revived with even more bitterness. The miners' Eight Hours Bill had received a second reading in the House of Commons, after a most vigorous debate in which Gladstone spoke very critically of the Bill and then voted for it; but at the committee stage a clause was introduced which permitted local option, and the promoters withdrew the Bill. The wrecking clause was carried by only five votes, of which Fenwick's was one. At the 1894 TUC all speakers paid tribute to Fenwick's honesty of purpose and his right to vote in the Commons as his conscience dictated; but Congress were at last determined to replace their secretary of the parliamentary committee, and Sam Woods was elected in his place.

Despite these major differences with his own mining colleagues, Fenwick was much respected inside the coal industry and outside in the wider movement; and he became well known in national terms. In 1892 he was a member of the Coal Dust Commission, and in 1894 of the R.C. on Secondary Education in England and Wales. He also served on the Inquiry into the Causes of Injuries to Railway Servants in 1900, and was the first Labour member to serve on the Committee of Selection. Fenwick was supported financially by the Northumberland Miners' Association and always believed that as much could be accomplished by the Labour wing of the Liberal Party as by a separate party. Scarcely known as a political speaker when he entered Parliament, he became deputy chairman of committees and frequently presided over the House when the Speaker left his chair. In Lord Rosebery's administration, Fenwick was selected to second the Address to the Throne in 1894.

In the late nineties there was developing

a close co-operation between a group of radical Liberals, headed by Sir Charles Dilke, and the TUC parliamentary committee, and on 29 March 1899 Sam Woods convened a meeting of Lib-Lab MPs 'to consider the necessity of more common understanding among the Labour members of the House of Commons'; the result was that John Burns and Woods were appointed as a sub-committee with Fenwick as Whip. After the general election of 1906 – Fenwick being endorsed neither by the MFGB nor the LRC – Fenwick became secretary of a loose association of some twenty-one trade union Lib-Lab MPs; and on 8 May 1906, together with William Brace, Fenwick withstood the claim of Keir Hardie and David Shackleton that the newly-constituted Parliamentary Labour Party should alone be represented on all important committees of the House 'directly affecting the working class'. The political tide began to run against Lib-Labs like Fenwick in the next few years. In July 1906 the Northumberland miners voted by a narrow majority for the eight-hour day; and in the same month Keir Hardie spoke from the platform at the annual gala of the NMA and scored what the *Morpeth Herald* (21 July 1906) described as a personal triumph. In August 1907 the NMA voted overwhelmingly to affiliate to the MFGB and their application was accepted later in the same year; and in May 1908 the Northumberland miners recommended affiliation to the Labour Party. All these developments were naturally uncomfortable to both Fenwick and his colleague Thomas Burt; and there now developed a lengthy dispute concerning their position as Northumberland MPs since neither had any intention of signing the Labour Party constitution. In the event both men stood as independent Liberals in the two general elections of 1910, and very sensibly, in view of their personal standing, they were not opposed by either an LRC or MFGB candidate [Gregory (1968) 72ff].

One last incident in Fenwick's career may be mentioned. In the summer of 1911 he put his name to a Labour Disputes Bill designed to impose a 'cooling-off' period of thirty days. The occasion was notice being given of an immediate railway strike in mid-August. The Bill, which had the support also of Arthur Henderson, G. N. Barnes and Will Crooks as well as Liberal and Conservative MPs, was presented on 17 August, the day of the declaration of the national railway strike. When the TUC assembled in Newcastle on Tyne in the first week of September hard words were used about Fenwick and his colleagues. The Bill, which included proposals for fining strikers who did not comply with its regulations, was not however proceeded with; but it was important evidence of the rifts which were developing in the Labour movement in these years.

Fenwick was made a Privy Councillor in 1911. For many years he had been a lay preacher for the Primitive Methodists. When W. T. Stead, editor of *The Review of Reviews*, in 1906 asked the Labour members of the new Parliament to list the books that had influenced them in their lives, Fenwick replied with the letter which follows:

I gladly respond to your request re the books which I have found most helpful to me in fighting my way up from my humble origin: (i) Matthew Henry's *Commentary* [on the Bible] (ii) *European Democracy* and *Faith in the Future* by Joseph Mazzini (iii) The story of Mungo Park and the travels of Dr Livingstone (iv) Macaulay's *History* and *Essays*. Sir Walter Scott, Kingsley and Rosa Carey [a popular writer] are my favourite novelists. I am glad when I can find time for a chat in the 'ingle' with any of them.

Fenwick married Miss Jane Gardner in 1869, and on his death on 20 April 1918 he was survived by her and two sons. He left an estate valued at £2774 gross (£1419 net).

Sources: *Dod* (1886) and (1916); *Times, House of Commons* (1910); *WWW* (1916–28); R. Page Arnot, *The Miners* (1949); H. Pelling, *The Origins of the Labour Party 1880–1900* (1954: 2nd ed. 1965); R. F. Wearmouth, *The Social and Political Influence of Methodism in the Twentieth Century* (1957); B. C. Roberts, *The Trades Unions Congress, 1868–1921* (1958); R. Gregory, *The Miners and British Politics, 1906–1914* (Oxford, 1968). OBIT.

Newcastle Journal, 22 Apr 1918; *Times*, 22 Apr 1918; *NMA* (1918).

ANTHONY MASON
JOHN SAVILLE

See also: T. BURT; Alexander MACDONALD, for Mining Trade Unionism, 1850–79; Benjamin PICKARD, for Mining Trade Unionism, 1880–99; John WILSON; Samuel WOODS.

FINCH, John (1784–1857)
OWENITE

Born in Dudley in 1784, John Finch was the son of a mechanic. He was educated at a local Unitarian school, and at the age of fourteen he was apprenticed as a clerk in a rail warehouse and remained with the firm for twenty years, having in the last years become a partner. He was an active member of the Unitarian chapel and from the age of seventeen a Sunday school teacher. In 1818 he moved to Liverpool to join a firm of iron merchants as a traveller, work which he was able to combine with rigorous proselytising activities for Unitarianism.

He became a member of the influential Unitarian Chapel in Renshaw Street, whose pastor was the Rev. John Hamilton Thom and among whose congregation were the Rathbones and other leading Unitarian families. In 1827, with his eldest son John, he began business on his own, and during most of his subsequent Owenite career he continued as a fairly successful businessman.

The Rathbone family had become interested in Robert Owen's activities as early as 1818, and it is probable that Finch himself became acquainted with Owenite ideas and with Owen himself through the Rathbones. In the winter of 1829 Finch helped found the first Liverpool Co-operative Society and this lasted until December 1832. He attended the Co-operative Congresses at Birmingham in 1831 and at London and Liverpool in 1832. In 1832 he began a short-lived co-operative journal *The Bee*, edited jointly with M. J. Falvey, a Catholic Owenite, and from this time Finch became an enthusiastic advocate of Owen's ideas.

Apart from the co-operative society, Finch's early philanthropic activities mostly stemmed from his enthusiasm for the cause of temperance. In September 1830 he became a founder member of the Liverpool Temperance Society and this led him to work among the dock labourers. The first steps towards the forming of a Dock Labourers' Society were taken at a meeting in September 1830 and for the next twelve months Finch laboured to organise a new system of work-sharing along the waterfront, with the teetotal pledge as the necessary step towards individual self-improvement. It was an ambitious and imaginative scheme which was wrecked on the bitter hostility of the employers, against a background of an ever-increasing supply of labour from both North Wales and Ireland. Finch had the idea of organising the seamen on similar, co-operative lines (letter to Owen, 16 February 1831) but nothing came of his proposals. Failure in no way weakened his belief in the social importance of the temperance movement and in the first half of the 1830s it was his advocacy of total abstinence that occupied most of his abundant energies outside his business interests.

Although Finch came to see temperance 'as the forerunner of an improved Social System' (Finch to Owen, 12 October 1836), it was the full doctrine of Owenism that gradually infused his personality. He was a profoundly religious man who found no difficulty in accepting the doctrines of Owen as being in full accord with Christianity. There was a strong millennial core to Finch's social and spiritual beliefs which found expression in a devotion to Owen as the new Messiah, and an enthusiasm for Socialism as the practical, immediately realisable, Kingdom of Heaven upon earth. His letters to Owen, in the Manchester collection, are suffused with his passionate belief that the millennium was at hand; and this he accepted until the end of his life.

Largely as a result of attacks by Finch in the Liverpool press against both Church and Chapel, he was expelled for his Owenite convictions from the Liverpool Total Abstinence Society in 1837; and from thenceforward he concentrated his energies upon

Socialist propaganda. His radicalism was wide-ranging. In the Liverpool election of 1837 he campaigned for the secret ballot, annual parliaments and universal suffrage; and he vigorously opposed the New Poor Law of 1834. He became secretary of a lively branch of the Association of All Classes of All Nations and in December 1839 there was opened in Liverpool the largest Hall of Science built in the provinces. This was in Lord Nelson Street, although the use of it by the Owenites ceased after May 1842.

In April 1839 the national movement had once again accepted a change of name and 'The Universal Community Society of Rational Religionists' became the new title under which the Socialists now gathered. When Harmony Hall was established at Queenwood, Hampshire, for a community experiment, Finch became one of the trustees and acting governor, with Heaton Aldam as director of agricultural operations. Finch resigned in May 1840 but returned in August 1842 as governor and finally in 1846 superintended its winding-up. Before this, however, he had visited America in 1843, accompanied by his daughter, and his account of the various communities he visited were published in the *New Moral World* between 13 January and 6 July 1844.

His last practical venture into Socialist experiment came in the period of the Christian Socialists. The family business had been concerned solely with the merchanting of iron but about 1850 they obtained control of an important Liverpool ironworks, the Windsor Foundry. In the spring of 1851 the Foundry was offered for sale to the newly-established Amalgamated Society of Engineers as a co-operative workshop, but although negotiations were apparently resumed after the famous lockout of 1852, there is no conclusive evidence that it was in fact ever organised as an experiment in workers' control.

Finch married young and there were six children of the marriage. He wrote much in the local Liverpool press as well as in a succession of Owenite journals. His temperance tracts had a wide circulation and the exposition of his own version of millennial Christianity was published in a number of pamphlets and books of which *The Millennium, or the Wisdom of Jesus, and the Foolery of Sectarianism, in Twelve Letters* (1837) and *The Seven Seals broke open; or the Bible of the reformation reformed*, 3 vols (1853), were the most important. Finch was in close personal touch with all the leading Owenites of his day; he had visited Ralahine and William Thompson's estate at Glandore and was named as one of the trustees of the latter's will. He wrote a series of fifteen letters on Ralahine which were originally published in the *Liverpool Chronicle* and then in the *New Moral World*, 31 March–29 September 1838. To the end of his life he continued to exhibit to an extraordinary devotion to the ideals of Robert Owen. At the conclusion of the Crimean War Mrs Finch wrote to Owen on 12 May 1856: 'My dear husband says your Millennium has begun; and that you have lived to see the close of the last great War which will ever agitate mankind. . . .' Finch died less than a year later on 18 February 1857.

Writings: *Important Meeting of the Working Classes: delegates from fifty co-operative societies* [1831 ?]; Evidence before the S.C. of Inquiry into Drunkenness, 1834 VIII Qs 3772–886; *Temperance Tracts* (Liverpool, 1836); *The Millennium, or the Wisdom of Jesus, and the Foolery of Sectarianism, in Twelve Letters* (Liverpool, 1837); *Moral Code of the New Moral World or Rational State of Society revised, and approved by Robert Owen* (Liverpool, 1840); *A Reformed Established Church: the best means of obtaining mental and religious liberty* (Liverpool, 1841); *The Book of the Inspired British Prophet of the Seventeenth Century, containing the Religion of the Millenium, New Law of Righteousness and most Remarkable Prophesies . . . concerning the Deliverance and Salvation of the Working People . . . and the Immediate and Universal Establishment of the Millennium*, ed. J. Finch ?, Part I (Liverpool, 1842); *Society as it is, and Society as it ought to be; or Social Diseases and Social Remedies . . . by a Liverpool Merchant* (Liverpool, 1847); *Town Dues and Currency, Free Trade and Protection* (Liverpool, 1850); *The Seven Seals broke open; or, the Bible of the reformation reformed*, 3 vols in 7 books (1853).

Sources:
(1) MSS. Rathbone family papers, University of Liverpool; Robert Owen correspondence, Co-operative Union, Manchester; Toxteth Park Chapel papers, Liverpool Record office. (2) Secondary: The most important source book for the history of Owenism, with a comprehensive bibliography, is J. F. C. Harrison, *Robert Owen and the Owenite Movement in Britain and America* (1969); E. Smith, *Report of a Discussion of the Claims of Rome . . . held in the Music Hall* (Liverpool, 1830); *New Moral World*, 15 Feb 1840; J. S. Buckingham, *History and Progress of the Temperance Reformation* (1854); D. P. Thompson, *Guide to Liverpool* (1854); G. J. Holyoake, *The History of Co-operation*, 2 vols (1st eds 1875 and 1879); G. E. Evans, *History of Renshaw St Chapel* (Liverpool, 1887); P. T. Winskill and J. Thomas, *History of the Temperance Movement in Liverpool and District* (Liverpool, 1887); Lloyd Jones, *The Life, Times and Labours of Robert Owen*, 2 vols (1889); P. T. Winskill, *The Temperance Movement and its Workers*, 4 vols (1891–2); W. Pilkington, *Facts about the Origin of the Teetotal Principle and Pledge* (Preston, 1894); W. Rathbone, *A Sketch of Family History during Four Generations . . .* (1894); P. T. Winskill, *Temperance Standard Bearers of the Nineteenth Century*, 2 vols (Liverpool, 1897–8); F. Podmore, *Robert Owen*, 2 vols (1906); W. H. Brown, *A Century of Liverpool Co-operation* (Liverpool, 1929); G. D. H. Cole, *The Life of Robert Owen* (2nd ed. 1930); A. Holt, *Walking Together* (Liverpool, 1938); G. D. H. Cole, *A Century of Co-operation* (Manchester, [1945?]); J. B. Jefferys, *The Story of the Engineers* [1945]; Margaret Cole, *Robert Owen of New Lanark* (1953); R. K. P. Pankhurst, *William Thompson* (1954); R. B. Rose, 'John Finch, 1784–1857', *Trans. Hist. Soc. Lancs. and Cheshire* 109 (1957) 159–84; A. E. Musson, 'The Ideology of Early Co-operation in Lancashire and Cheshire', *Trans. Lancs. and Cheshire Antiq. Soc.* 68 (1958) 117–38; James Murphy, 'Robert Owen in Liverpool', *Trans. Hist. Soc. Lancs. and Cheshire* 112 (1960) 79–103; A. Bonner, *British Co-operation* (Manchester, 1961); W. H. G. Armytage, *Heavens Below* (1961).

JOHN SAVILLE

See also: *J. M. F. LUDLOW, for Christian Socialism, 1848–54; *Robert OWEN; William PARE.

FINNEY, Samuel (1857–1935)
MINERS' LEADER AND LABOUR MP

Born on 22 April 1857 at Audley, near Talke, North Staffordshire, son of Francis Finney, a brickmaker, and his wife Martha (née Humphries). He was educated at a Primitive Methodist day school and, like his parents, he became a regular chapel attender. He began work locally on the pit top at the mine owned by the Talk-o'-the-Hill Colliery Ltd when he was ten years old, and went underground two years later. When he was fifteen the death of his brother James in a pit accident was such a shock to the family that Sam Finney stopped working in the mines for some three months, but then resumed. He became involved in trade union affairs as a young man and after acting as secretary to the local lodge of the North Staffordshire Miners' Federation (which was formed in 1869) he moved to Jamage, one of four mines owned by the Bignall Hill Colliery Ltd, where in 1881 he became checkweighman. In 1888 he was elected president of the North Staffs Miners' Federation and was among the delegation from the Midland Federation who attended the inaugural conference of the MFGB in late November 1889 at Newport. On the death of Enoch Edwards in 1912 he succeeded him as secretary and agent of the Midland Federation, and represented the Federation on the executive committee of the MFGB for seven terms between 1913 and 1924. In this latter year he retired from all trade union positions.

Like so many miners' leaders, Sam Finney was much involved in local affairs. He was elected a member of Burslem Town Council in 1903 (later Stoke-on-Trent Borough Council) and subsequently became an alderman, being especially active in education. He was also a magistrate for Stoke-on-Trent. He first attempted to enter Parliament in 1912 when he unsuccessfully contested in the Labour interest the Hanley constituency previously held by Enoch Edwards. It was a strong Liberal seat and the

Liberal Party were unwilling to continue with the arrangement whereby the constituency was represented by a miner. They put up R. L. Outhwaite, a Liberal land-reformer and single taxer who turned out to be an excellent candidate, much more forceful and energetic than Finney, who apart from his religious zeal was rather uninspiring. Outhwaite easily won with Finney a very poor third after the Unionist [Gregory (1968) 171ff]. During the war, at a by-election in January 1916, Finney was returned unopposed as a Labour member for North West Staffordshire, following the death of another miners' leader, Albert Stanley. There took place a re-arrangement of boundaries immediately after the war, and Finney was returned as the member for the Burslem division of Stoke-on-Trent in the general election of December 1918. He retired from the Commons just before the general election of 1922. Three years earlier he had gone with Margaret Bondfield as a delegate to the AFL conference in Atlantic City, where he met Woodrow Wilson.

Throughout his long life Finney remained an active and ardent Primitive Methodist. He became very well known as a local preacher and as a young man of twenty-four considered seriously the idea of taking up the ministry as a profession. When he moved to Burslem he became secretary, treasurer and class leader of the Hamil Road Primitive Methodist chapel and later went on to the Burslem circuit as a lay preacher. He married the only daughter of James and Harriet Bagnall of Ellesmere, Shropshire, in 1884, and there were four daughters of the marriage. He died on 14 April 1935 at the Codnor home of one of his daughters, being survived by his wife and children. His will showed effects of £3966.

Sources: *Dod* (1922); *Labour Who's Who* (1927); *WWW* (1929–40); R. Page Arnot, *The Miners* (1949) and *The Miners: Years of Struggle* (1953); R. Gregory, *The Miners and British Politics, 1906–1914* (Oxford, 1968). OBIT. *Evening Sentinel* [Staffordshire], 15 Apr 1935.

JOYCE BELLAMY
JOHN SAVILLE

See also: Thomas ASHTON, for Mining Trade Unionism, 1900–14; *A. J. COOK, for Mining Trade Unionism, 1915–26; Benjamin DEAN; Enoch EDWARDS; Benjamin PICKARD, for Mining Trade Unionism, 1880–99.

FISHWICK, Jonathan (1832–1908)
CO-OPERATOR

Born at Bolton in May 1832, Jonathan Fishwick, known to his friends as 'honest Jonathan', was an insurance agent by profession and took an early and active interest in the co-operative movement. He was elected to the board of management of Bolton Co-operative Society in 1862 and served for several years, being twice elected president. He was appointed on two occasions as Bolton representative on the board of management of the Co-operative Wholesale Society in 1871 and 1872; and he was Bolton representative at the 4th Co-operative Congress at Bolton in 1872 and also at the 5th Congress, at Newcastle on Tyne in August 1873.

Jonathan Fishwick was also an earnest advocate of trade unionism. He was one of the founders of the National Union of Life Assurance Agents, his name being no. 5 on the original list of members of the Bolton branch, which was the first branch and the one from which the Union originated. He was the principal founder of the *Assurance Agents' Chronicle* and the largest shareholder in the company owning it. For many years he worked in the insurance office of the Prudential. He was a practising Anglican in religion and in his later years, at any rate, a staunch Conservative in politics. He died on 24 March 1908 and left effects valued at £674.

Sources: F. W. Peaples, *Great and Little Bolton Co-operative Society Ltd Jubilee History* (published by the Society, 1909); P. Redfern, *The Story of the C.W.S.* (Manchester, [1913]). OBIT. *Bolton Chronicle*, 28 Mar 1908.

H. F. BING

See also: G. J. HOLYOAKE, for Retail Co-operation – Nineteenth Century.

FLEMING, Robert (1869–1939)
CO-OPERATOR

Born in Glasgow on 27 March 1869, Robert Fleming was educated at Crookston Street Public School and afterwards at Hutcheson's Grammar School; he was then apprenticed to the engineering trade as a pattern-maker and fitter. Emigrating to Belfast at the age of twenty-two, he became prominent in labour, co-operative and social work. He had become a trade unionist in 1889 at the age of twenty and remained in full membership all his life. From 1893 to 1899 he was a member of the Belfast Trade and Labour Council. In religion he was a member of the Church of Christ.

It was in the co-operative field that he became best known. He was secretary of the Belfast Co-operative Society, 1898–1902, and during critical years retrieved the society from a state of insolvency and placed it on a sound financial basis. He was a director of the Belfast Society, 1902–5, and then again secretary, 1905–8, when a serious illness forced him to resign. In 1898 he had been appointed chairman of the North of Ireland (later Irish) Co-operative Conference Association and he held this office till 1903. In 1903 the Irish executive was reorganised under new Co-operative Union rules and Fleming was appointed chairman of that executive, resigning that office in 1912 to take on the secretaryship till 1917. In 1909 the Co-operative Union decided to appoint an organiser for Ireland, and Fleming, at that time a public auditor under the Industrial and Provident Society Act 1893, was appointed and held office until his election to the board of the Co-operative Wholesale Society in 1917.

Fleming was a member of the central board of the Co-operative Union, 1904–17, and a member of the Co-operative Union Survey Committee, 1915–18. His proudest moment came in 1914 when he was elected president of the Co-operative Congress in Dublin, the first Congress to be held in Ireland. His inaugural address, delivered extempore, occupied fifteen pages of the Congress report. Three years later at the 1917 Congress, before his election to the CWS

board, Fleming made a vigorous plea for the co-operative movement to begin work in agriculture.

In 1917 he was elected to the board of the Co-operative Wholesale Society and from then on played an active part in its affairs, travelling widely in its interests for the next twenty years until his retirement under the age-rule in 1937. He served on the CWS drapery committee and on sub-committees dealing with exports and textiles. He was a member of the committee which controlled the society's activities in West Africa and in 1919 was one of a three-man team which spent five months travelling through Nigeria from the coast up to Kano on the edge of the Sahara in search of new sources of palm kernels, palm oil, hardwood and hides. In addition to two visits to Africa, he paid two visits to Greece and Smyrna and two visits to Russia. His second visit to Russia was on behalf of the English and Scottish Joint CWS, following an invitation from Centrosoyus (the Russian Central Co-operative Organisation) to visit their co-operative tea plantations in Transcaucasia. He was twice received in the White House by American Presidents.

Fleming was sometimes referred to as 'the orator of the Board' and was at one time its vice-president. He was on the committee of the English and Scottish Joint Co-operative Wholesale Society and its chairman in 1935. He represented the CWS on the National Co-operative Authority and on the central committee of the International Co-operative Alliance till 1937. At the time of his retirement he was a director of several local co-operative societies.

He died at Didsbury, Manchester, on 12 October 1939 and was buried at the Southern Cemetery, Manchester, on 16 October. He left an estate valued at £5950.

Sources: *Co-op. Congress Report* (1914); *Leicester Co-op. Congress Handbook* (Manchester, 1915); P. Redfern, *The New History of the C.W.S.* (Manchester, 1938). OBIT. *Co-op. News*, 21 Oct 1939; *RIC*, Oct 1939; *Co-op. Congress Report* (1940).

H. F. BING

See also: W. H. BROWN, for Retail Co-operation, 1900–45; Fred HAYWARD, for Co-operative Union; H. J. MAY, for International Co-operative Alliance; Percy REDFERN, for Co-operative Wholesaling.

FORMAN, John (1822/3–1900)
MINERS' LEADER

Born at Allerton Burn near Ancroft, Northumberland, he spent his early life at Cramlington and Seaton Delaval in the same county. About 1850 he obtained work in the Annfield Plain district of Durham, and a few years later moved to the Crook district where he became checkweighman at Grahamsley colliery near Roddymoor. Forman was one of the founders of the Durham Miners Association in 1869 and he was a member of the first executive committee. He became an agent of the union and in 1874 was appointed permanent chairman, a position which he held until his death. In 1872 he had taken the chair at the first Durham Miners' Gala.

Forman was a quiet, studious man little known outside the mining industry, but he worked hard for the union. He took a leading part in explosion investigations, and was a member of rescue parties at Seaham in 1871 and 1880. He had a theory which later was accepted which dealt with the ignition of coal dust and he may have written a pamphlet on the subject. He read widely, especially on scientific subjects, and was a member of the Board of Examiners for the mine manager's certificate. He died, aged seventy-seven, on 2 September 1900 and left £1205 in his will.

Sources: R. Fynes, *The Miners of Northumberland and Durham* (Sunderland, 1873; repr. 1923); J. Wilson, *A History of the Durham Miners' Association, 1870–1904* (Durham, 1907). OBIT. *Durham Chronicle*, 7 Sep 1900.

ANTHONY MASON

See also: Thomas BURT; William CRAWFORD; Alexander MACDONALD, for Mining Trade Unionism, 1850–79; Benjamin PICKARD, for Mining Trade Unionism, 1880–99.

FOSTER, William (1887–1947)
MINERS' LEADER AND LABOUR MP

Born on 12 January 1887 in the Chapel Lane district of Wigan, one of a large family whose father was a miner, he attended St Thomas's elementary school at Wigan until he was eight. His parents then moved to Haydock where Foster continued his education until he was nearly twelve. Then the family moved once again, going on this occasion to Bryn Gates, Bamfurlong, in the Urban District of Abram, where Foster's elder brother and father worked at the Bryn Hall Colliery. For a short time Foster attended St Luke's school but then started working at the same colliery as his father and brother. On his first pay day he joined the miners' union and attended evening classes to extend his earlier education. At seventeen he was a collier at Low Hall Collieries, Platt Bridge, but three years later was victimised for his trade union activities and had to leave. He subsequently obtained employment at the Arley mine of the Bamfurlong Collieries where he stayed for twenty years. During all this time he was an active member of the Bamfurlong branch of the Lancashire and Cheshire Miners' Federation and succeeded J. A. Parkinson as secretary of the branch. He attended LCMF meetings on behalf of the branch and also served on the Federation's executive committee. For seven years he was secretary of the National Miners' Mutual Indemnity Society which insured colliery workers for any liability under the Workmen's Compensation Acts. By a county ballot held in 1929 Foster was elected miners' agent for the area extending from Wigan to Chorley in the north and to St Helens in the south with a membership of 20,000; in 1932 he was elected vice-president of the LCMF, and he served on the executive committee of the MFGB in 1934 and 1939.

Apart from his work for the miners, Foster was also active in local political and public affairs. He was a member of the Abram Urban District Council for nine years, serving as chairman and as a member of the Wigan magisterial bench. He also served for a time on the St Helens Council and was made a JP for St Helens in 1934. He was very active in labour politics: as chairman of the Abram Labour Party and of the Ince Parliamentary Labour Party when Stephen Walsh represented that constituency in the House of Commons, and also as chairman of the Platt Bridge Labour Club which he helped to establish. At the 1929 general election, Foster was agent to Gordon Macdonald when the latter succeeded Walsh as MP for the Ince Division and in 1942 was himself returned unopposed as MP for Wigan following the death of J. A. Parkinson, the former member, who had been first elected in 1931. Foster retained his seat at the 1945 general election and was appointed parliamentary secretary to the Ministry of Fuel and Power in August of that year but resigned from this post in May 1946. Although he made no public statement, he is believed to have objected to the decision to appoint businessmen to the National Coal Board.

In 1937 he was elected by the TUC to be a fraternal delegate to the Co-operative Congress and was chosen by the TUC to attend the Canadian Labor Congress in Canada in 1942. An expert on workmen's compensation law, Foster was vice-chairman of the National Board for Mining Examinations in 1944.

He had married in 1911 Jane Stringfellow of Wigan and had two sons and a daughter. He died at Providence Hospital, St Helens, on 2 December 1947 and was buried at Abram parish churchyard following a service at Wigan Parish Church. He left effects worth £4697. His wife had predeceased him but his family survived him. He was succeeded as Labour MP for Wigan by R. W. Williams.

Sources: *Dod* (1945) and (1946); *WWW* (1941–50). OBIT. *Wigan Observer*, 6 Dec 1947; *Labour Party Report* (1948).

JOYCE BELLAMY

See also: T. ASPINWALL; *A. J. COOK, for Mining Trade Unionism, 1915–26; *Peter LEE, for Mining Trade Unionism, 1927–44; *J. A. PARKINSON; *Henry TWIST.

FOULGER, Sydney (1863–1919)
CO-OPERATOR

Born on 17 March 1863 at Ipswich, the second son of Hamilton Lazarus Foulger, a shoe factor, who was in business at Ipswich for over thirty years, Sydney entered the manufacturing side of the same industry. In his early youth he was actively engaged in political activities and was joint secretary of the Ipswich Radical Association. He was a member of the Ipswich Co-operative Society from 1885 and a close associate of George Hines. From 1887 to 1901 Foulger was a member of the Society's management committee, serving as president from 1895 to 1901. He left the boot industry to become cashier to the Ipswich Society at the turn of the century, a position he held until his death; and he was also chairman of the education committee at the time of his death. Devoted to the co-operative movement, he addressed many meetings on its behalf and also served on the southern section of the Co-operative Union.

His interests extended to local affairs and he had been elected, just prior to his death, as a co-operative member of the Ipswich Town Council. He had served for seven years on the Ipswich Board of Guardians and was made a JP a few months only before he died. In religion he was a Unitarian, and in later life, at any rate, a member of the Labour Party. He died suddenly on 8 November 1919 at Ely after attending a conference, with his wife, two sons and three daughters surviving him. At the time of his father's death his eldest son was manager and secretary of the Saffron Walden Farmers' Co-operative Society. Foulger left effects valued at £3199.

Sources: *Through Sixty Years: a record of progress and achievement 1868–1928* (Ipswich Industrial Co-operative Society Limited, Ipswich, 1928); R. Ratcliffe, History of the Working Class Movement in Ipswich (from the nineteenth century to 1935), in four typescript volumes at Ipswich Borough Library and on microfilm at Hull University Library. OBIT. *East Anglian Daily Times*, 10 Nov 1919; *Wheatsheaf*, Dec 1919.

JOYCE BELLAMY

See also: T. R. BIRD; F. J. BUGG; J. GOODY; George HINES; G. J. HOLYOAKE, for Retail Co-operation – Nineteenth Century.

FOWE, Thomas (1832/3?–94)
CO-OPERATOR AND RADICAL

Little is known of his early life. He was probably born in Lancashire in 1832 or 1833 and was often referred to as Thomas Fowe of Manchester. He was a member of the Manchester Reform League and its treasurer from 1866 to 1869. In 1867 he became one of the secretaries of the Working Men's Committee on Public Worship and was very active in this movement for some years but later in life allied himself with the secularists. He left Manchester for London in 1869 and a meeting of the Reform League in Manchester on 10 August 1869, presided over by Edward Hooson, passed a resolution thanking him for his services in Manchester and wishing him well for the future.

In London he became active in the co-operative movement and is believed to have been the first secretary of the southern section of the Co-operative Union, a post he held till 1873. In 1874 he became a member of the committee of the London branch of the Co-operative Wholesale Society and was appointed its secretary. On his retirement in 1878 he received from the London branch committee a letter of warm thanks and appreciation. Some time after this he seems to have returned to Manchester for in 1891 he became treasurer of the Manchester District Co-operative Employees' Association which was formed in that year and retained this office till his death. (In 1895 this organisation became a national one and was registered as the Amalgamated Union of Co-operative Employees.)

He was an active member of the Manchester and Salford Equitable Society and died aged sixty-one on 28 March 1894 after a few days' illness. He was buried in Manchester Southern Cemetery, on 30 March.

Sources: P. Redfern, *The Story of the C.W.S.* (Manchester, [1913]). OBIT. *Co-op. News*, 7 Apr 1894.

H. F. BING

See also: Fred HAYWARD, for Co-operative Union; *George HOWELL, for Reform League.

FOX, James Challinor (1837–77)
CO-OPERATOR

Born on 3 January 1837, probably in the Manchester area, of poor parents, Fox had little formal education in his early years but already at the age of twelve he was buying books from his own savings. A born propagandist and lecturer, he addressed a meeting of 2000 people when he was sixteen. An ardent temperance advocate throughout his life, he first became interested in the co-operative movement in 1858 when he joined the Manchester and Salford Industrial Society. This failed, despite much labour on his part, but a few years later he was among the founders of its successor, the Hulme Pioneers' Society, serving as its secretary for the first few years. A member of the CWS board from 1868 to 1871, he also served as secretary of the society when this was an honorary post. From 1872 until his death, except for a break in 1876 on health grounds, he was auditor of the CWS.

Fox was an assiduous lecturer on behalf of temperance and co-operation, and he travelled widely arguing these causes; his speeches always reflecting the early idealism of the co-operative movement: that those who produced wealth by their labour had a right to share in it, and that the co-operative movement was the road to a new social order. He died on 18 October 1877, leaving a widow and daughter, and was buried at Salford Borough Cemetery on 23 October 1877. On Sunday 28 October, the Rev. James Clark of Salford preached a special sermon on Fox's life and death; and Abraham Greenwood became treasurer of a fund to raise a suitable memorial over his grave. Fox left effects valued at less than £1500.

Sources: P. Redfern, *The Story of the C.W.S.* (Manchester, [1913]). OBIT. *Co-op. News*, 27 Oct, 9 Nov and 17 Nov 1877.

H. F. BING

See also: G. J. HOLYOAKE, for Retail Co-operation – Nineteenth Century.

FRITH, John (1837–1904)
MINERS' LEADER

Born on 6 July 1837 at Rawmarsh near Rotherham, his father Joseph Frith being a miner at Messrs Charlesworth's Collieries. After a rudimentary education John Frith was working in the mines at the age of ten under his father and in the next twenty-four years he passed through all types of work from trapper boy to coal getter. He extended his early education through night classes and was one of the original members of the South Yorkshire Miners' Association when this was established in 1858. He formed the Rawmarsh lodge and maintained an official connection with this until his departure about 1873 for Roundwood, where he helped found another lodge. In 1874 he succeeded D. Moulson as president of the South Yorkshire Association, and when John Normansell died in the following year, Frith took over the position of secretary. His assumption of office coincided with a very difficult period for miners' unions everywhere, falling prices and wage cuts being the common experience all over the country. Among his many worries was the Shirland Colliery Company, in which the South Yorkshire Association had invested heavily. The Shirland Colliery is often wrongly described as a co-operative enterprise, and it went into liquidation at the beginning of 1877, the union losing all its invested capital [see Williams, *Derbyshire Miners*]. The South Yorkshire Association also began to lose its Derbyshire members, following a series of strikes and wage-reductions, and by the end of the 1870s its membership, itself much reduced absolutely, was almost entirely limited to miners in South Yorkshire. This was part of the reason for the successful attempt (there had been earlier failures) to amalgamate the West and South Yorkshire Associations in the early 1880s. Frith remained secretary of the latter union until amalgamation on 1 July 1881, when he became financial secretary to the new Yorkshire Miners' Association and he retained this position until 1904, the year of his death. (Edward Cowey became president of the new YMA, and Ben Pickard secretary.)

Frith had a fine reputation in pit rescue work, and he was one of the Yorkshire representatives to give evidence before the R.C. on Accidents in 1881. The last years of his life was a period of great stress for the YMA. Following the Taff Vale decision, the Denaby Main case, which covered a period of four years from 1902 to 1906, placed the YMA's officials in a highly precarious and difficult position [see Bealey and Pelling, *Labour and Politics*]. The uncertainty in which the union found itself from 1902 onwards probably contributed something to the deaths of Cowey, Pickard and Frith, which occurred within less than two years of each other (1903–4), and it was only later, in May 1905, that the Court of Appeal reversed the adverse decision against the YMA.

Frith was also active in local government as a member of Barnsley Town Council and was for some time a member of the Library Committee. He had married twice and left a widow and grown-up family when he died at his Barnsley home on 17 February 1904 after a long illness. He left £456 in his will.

Sources: *Sheffield Mail*, 8 June 1926; F. Bealey and H. Pelling, *Labour and Politics 1900–1906* (1958); F. Machin, *The Yorkshire Miners* (Barnsley, 1958); J. E. Williams, *The Derbyshire Miners* (1962). OBIT. *Barnsley Independent*, 20 Feb 1904.

JOYCE BELLAMY
JOHN SAVILLE

See also: Alexander MACDONALD, for Mining Trade Unionism, 1850–79; Benjamin PICKARD, for Mining Trade Unionism, 1880–99.

GALBRAITH, Samuel (1853–1936)
MINERS' LEADER AND LIB-LAB MP

Born on 4 July 1853 in County Down, Northern Ireland, while his mother was visiting relatives in the area. His father had migrated to Durham and was employed by the Londonderry estate as a mason at Wynyard Park. At the age of ten young Samuel began work as a trapper in the pit at Trimdon Grange, one of two pits later owned by Walter Scott Ltd, and he went through all the grades of work underground – putter, driver, hewer. In 1875 he started work at Browney Colliery and it was here that his trade union activity began. In 1879 he was appointed checkweighman and began to take an active part in county affairs of the union. His early education had been almost entirely lacking and he was twenty-one years old before he could read and write. In 1884 he began attending university extension lectures and he gained a mine-manager's certificate, being one of the first miners' leaders to achieve this. It led to an offer of work on the technical side from a colliery company, but Galbraith declined the invitation, preferring to continue his union activity.

In 1900 he was appointed agent of the Durham Miners' Association, and he held the position until 1915. During these years he represented Durham on the executive committee of the MFGB in 1909, 1911 and 1914. In 1915, on 29 April, he was elected MP for mid-Durham on a Lib-Lab ticket, and this brought him into conflict with the DMA at the time of the general election of 1918 when Galbraith stood for the Spennymoor division. He was firmly against a Labour Party independent of the Liberal Party, and in 1918 he was opposed by Joseph Batey on behalf of the Labour Party. This political conflict caused Galbraith much heart-searching, but although it meant severing his connection with the DMA in any official capacity he stood firm on the matter of principle as he had done much earlier on the issue of state legislation of hours of work. He retired from Parliament at the time of the 1922 election and Batey, again a candidate, easily won the seat.

His political and social interests outside mining trade unionism were numerous. He was among the first group of miners to be elected to the newly constituted Durham County Council in 1889 (later being made an alderman). He was chairman of the Old Age Pension Committee of the County Council; chairman of the Tuberculosis Care Committee; a member of the Durham Board of Guardians; and appointed JP for the county in 1907. He was a founder of the Gilsland and Grange-over-Sands Con-

valescent Homes; a founder of the Johnston School, Durham; a vigorous supporter of the Durham Territorial Association. Throughout his life he was an active co-operator, being for a time chairman of the Brandon Co-operative Society and, from 1890, a member of the Co-operative Wholesale Society's Northern Sectional Board.

He told the story much later in his life of how, as a young man of twenty-one, he had been playing cricket on 25 August 1874. On his way home he and his friend called in at a public house in Brandon, and stayed until closing time. At 11.20 pm a voice spoke to him saying: 'Is it for this that I gave thee thy life? Get thee home and devote thyself to other things.' Galbraith went home, locked himself in his room and fasted for twenty-four hours. At the end of his fast he had taken the decision both to educate himself and to join a church; and for fifty years he was to be closely identified with the Methodist New Connexion in Durham. The Bible became his first book and he always read it through once every year, the New Testament twice. In the year before his death he went back to the field in Brandon where he had first heard the voice, and gave thanks to God who had called him to his service.

After his retirement from Westminster and union affairs Galbraith still kept a lively interest in social and charitable work. He maintained a close connection with the Aged Miners' Homes and for five successive years he provided a free Christmas breakfast to 120 children in Durham. Among his most treasured possessions were letters from the Royal Family, and one especially from the Private Secretary of King Edward VIII, acknowledging verses which Galbraith had composed on the occasion of the King's accession to the throne. He was awarded the OBE after the First World War.

He married in 1885, his wife Helen, who was a daughter of Henry Petty, being at the time a pupil teacher and a Primitive Methodist. He died on 10 April 1936, leaving effects worth £5221.

Sources: J. Wilson, *History of the Durham Miners' Association 1870-1904* (Durham,

1907); R. Page Arnot, *The Miners* (1949); R. F. Wearmouth, *Social and Political Influence of Methodism in the Twentieth Century* (1957); *Durham County Advertiser*, 25 Jan 1935; *WWW* (1929–40). OBIT. *Durham County Advertiser*, 17 Apr 1936.

ANTHONY MASON
JOHN SAVILLE

See also: Thomas ASHTON, for Mining Trade Unionism, 1900–14; T. H. CANN; Benjamin PICKARD.

GALLAGHER, Patrick (Paddy the Cope) (1871–1966)
CO-OPERATOR

Patrick Gallagher was born on 25 December 1871 at Cleendra, Donegal, the eldest of nine children of a peasant farmer, and although he attended Roshine School his early education was constantly interrupted by work in the potato fields. When he was ten he went to the hiring fair at Strabane and a few years later worked in Scotland where he came in touch with Michael Davitt's agitation on behalf of the Irish people. Some of Gallagher's family emigrated to America but he himself returned to Ireland, married a local girl in 1896 and then, with her, returned to Scotland where he worked in coalmining and joined a co-operative store. He had been a member of the United Irish League during his stay in Scotland.

On returning to Ireland at the turn of the century he was determined to bring the benefits of co-operation to his native land. In 1903 he met George Russell ('A.E.') in Dungloe and later other prominent co-operators, and decided to start a small co-operative in his native Cleendra. Short of capital but with an unshakeable faith, and aided by his family and friends, he founded the Templecrone Co-operative Society in 1906. In the beginning the emphasis was on the provision of fertilisers and farm equipment. Sir Horace Plunkett spoke to the members of the Society in the same year of the struggles which he had experienced in getting the co-operative movement started in Ireland. At first the new Society had difficulties in obtaining supplies but they successfully approached the Glasgow CWS for help. The venture succeeded and was extended to include general goods. The Society also began manufacturing and in time controlled almost the entire industrial activities of the neighbourhood. Its turnover in 1965 exceeded £300,000 and it had become one of the foremost in Ireland. From the start it was known as the 'Cope' and its founder as Paddy the Cope.

Gallagher travelled extensively, lecturing and giving advice on co-operative techniques, and the Society's activities attracted visitors from many countries. His autobiography, *My Story*, published in 1939, was translated into several languages; and he lived to see his achievements regarded as an example for co-operative ventures in other parts of the world.

His wife Sally, a loyal companion, predeceased him in 1949 and 'Paddy' himself died on 24 June 1966. They had two sons, one of whom survived his father.

Writings: *My Story: By Paddy the Cope* (1939).

Sources: *My Story* (1939); personal information: Mrs Mary Gallagher, Dungloe, Co. Donegal. OBIT. *Donegal People's Press*, 1 July 1966.

JOYCE BELLAMY

See also: *Horace C. PLUNKETT; and below: Irish Co-operation.

Irish Co-operation: W. Pare, *Co-operative Agriculture: a solution of the Land Question, as exemplified in the History of the Ralahine Co-operative Agriculture Association, County Clare, Ireland* (1870); H. C. Plunkett, 'Co-operative Stores for Ireland', *19th C. 24* (Sep 1888) 410–18; idem, 'Co-operation in Ireland', *Co-op. Congress Report* (1890); E. T. Craig, *The Irish Land and Labour Question illustrated in the History of Ralahine and Co-operative Farming* (1893); T. A. Finlay, 'Agricultural Co-operation in Ireland', *Econ. J. 6* (1896) 204–11; idem, *The Progress of Co-operation* (Statistical and Social Inquiry Society of Ireland) (Sep 1897); J. Dorum, 'Co-operation in Irish Agriculture', *West. Rev. 164*

(1905) 267–72; D. A. MacCabe, 'The Recent Growth of Co-operation in Ireland', *QJE* 20 (1906) 547–74; L. P. Byrne, 'Agricultural Co-operation in Ireland', *International* (1909) no. 20, 236–41; C. O'Brien, *Co-operative Mills and Bakeries* (Dublin, 1915) 50 pp.; L. Smith-Gordon and C. O'Brien, *Co-operation in Ireland* (International Co-operation Series, no. 3: Manchester, 1921); J. Deans, *Co-operative Memories* (Manchester, 1922); Irish Co-operative Women's Guild, *Twenty-one Years' Work: 1907–1928* (Belfast, 1928) 31 pp.; Horace Plunkett Foundation, *Agricultural Co-operation in Ireland: a survey* (1931); R. A. Anderson, *With Horace Plunkett in Ireland* [A History of the Co-operative Movement in Ireland] (1935); C. C. Riddall, *Agricultural Co-operation in Ireland: the story of a struggle* (Dublin, 1950) 48 pp.; J. Johnston, *Irish Agriculture in Transition* (Dublin and Oxford, 1951).

GANLEY, Caroline Selina (1879–1966)
CO-OPERATOR, LABOUR PARTY WORKER AND MP

Caroline Ganley was born on 16 September 1879, at Stonehouse, Plymouth, the daughter of James Blumfield, a tailor. She was first educated at church and national schools in Plymouth and later at Ottershaw School, Chertsey. She married James Ganley in 1901 and went to live in Westminster. She had earlier taken up a position on the Left, was opposed to the Boer War and in 1906 joined the Social Democratic Party. She became one of the first members of the Women's Socialist Circle (later the Women's Labour League) and was secretary in 1907–8. During the First World War she was a member of the Women's International Committee. Mrs Ganley joined the Labour Party in 1918 and was for many years a member of its National Executive Council, serving as its vice-president from 1921 to 1923.

She became interested in the consumers' co-operative movement, and in 1918 was elected to the board of the West London Co-operative Society. When this amalgamated with the London Co-operative Society in 1921, she became a member of the board of the latter and continued in that

office until 1946. In 1942 she was elected first woman president of the London Co-operative Society and played a major part in steering the society through the difficult war years. She was also active in the Women's Co-operative Guild, chairman of the Lavender Hill branch of the Guild and a champion of the woman's point of view in civic, national and international affairs. From 1921 to 1925 she was president of the London Women's Co-operative Guild committee and was also a member of the Standing Joint Committee of Industrial Women's Organisations.

Mrs Ganley's interests were extensive in the political sphere. She was elected to Battersea Borough Council in 1919 and served until 1925 at a time when Shapurji Saklatvala was MP for North Battersea. At the local level Mrs Ganley took a special interest in housing and health problems, serving as chairman for five years on the health and maternity committees. From 1925 to 1929 and again from 1934 to 1937 she was a member of the LCC. In 1920 she was among the first women magistrates to be appointed in London and served on juvenile courts for twenty years. Although unsuccessful in 1935 when she contested the parliamentary constituency of Paddington North, she was elected as Co-operative and Labour member for Battersea South in 1945, retained the seat in 1950 with a small majority (368) but was defeated in the 1951 general election. During her years at Westminster she and her husband celebrated their golden wedding, the first ever seen in the House of Commons, and her women colleagues made her a presentation. Her husband, who predeceased her, had worked for a co-operative society before his retirement.

Her other interests included education and as early as 1912 she had been appointed a school manager; and in later years she served as governor of several schools. In 1953 she returned to the Battersea Borough Council on which she continued to serve until 1965. Mrs Ganley retained to the end of her life her abiding interest in co-operative and labour matters and she was a member of many London committees. In 1936 she had been the only woman to represent England on the Cost of Living Inquiry Committee and in 1941 she was appointed to the London Price Regulation Committee. In the previous year she had presided at the National Congress of Labour Women. She was awarded the CBE in 1953. She died in London at the age of eighty-six on 31 August 1966 and was survived by her two sons and a daughter. She left an estate valued at £3245.

Sources: *Clapham Observer*, 8 June 1945; *Daily Herald*, 20 June 1951; *Evening Standard*, 26 Oct 1951; *South London Press*, 17 Mar 1964; *The Battersea Booklist Quarterly*, Spring 1965. OBIT. *Guardian*, 1 Sep 1966; *Times* 1 Sep 1966; *South Western Star*, 2 Sep 1966; *South London Press*, 6 Sep 1966; *Platform*, 12 Oct 1966; *Co-op. Rev.*, Oct 1966.

JOYCE BELLAMY

See also: *C. R. ATTLEE, for British Labour Party, 1931–51; A. BONNER, for Co-operation, 1945–70; Miss M. L. DAVIES; A. HENDERSON, for British Labour Party, 1914–31; *George LANSBURY, for British Labour Party, 1900–13.

GLOVER, Thomas (1852–1913)
MINERS' LEADER AND LABOUR MP

Born on 25 March 1852 at Prescot, Lancashire, the son of William Glover, a collier who became an underground manager at Black Brook Colliery in 1854. His father's promotion involved a family removal to St Helens where Thomas Glover was educated at Lacey's school (a church school) from the age of six until he began working at Black Brook Colliery when he was ten. At twenty he was working at Laffak Garswood Colliery and was one of the founders of the St Helens district of the Lancashire and Cheshire Miners' Federation. He was secretary for the St Helens district from 1880 to 1884 when, after twenty-two years as a miner, he was appointed agent for the district. Glover was one of five leading miners of Lancashire (including William Pickard and Sam Woods) who on 23 June 1886 signed the agreement on submission to arbitration of the basis for

a sliding scale, then being negotiated on the motion of the workers' side. Glover was also treasurer of the LCMF and represented the Lancashire miners on the executive committee of the MFGB in 1894, 1889 and 1905. At the MFGB special conference in St Martins Town Hall, London, on 22 and 23 August 1893, at the opening of the great lock-out of that year, the question arose as to whether the men at pits where the employers had offered to pay the old rate of wages should continue to work, whereupon Glover moved an amendment (carried by one hundred and twenty to sixty-four votes) 'that no pit in this Federation be allowed to recommence work until a general settlement is made for all to recommence at one and the same time' (Ashton, p. 210). In 1894 he became a member of the national Conciliation Board which was established following the great strike and lock-out of the previous year.

In 1896 there took place a reconstruction of the Lancashire and Cheshire Miners' Federation and the Wigan Conference of 19 December carried resolutions, which in part read: 'That Mr Saml. Woods be appointed president . . . That Mr Thos. Ashton be secretary of the new Federation . . . That Messrs Thos. Aspinwall, Thos. Glover, Thos. Greenall and Jesse Butler be appointed agents'.

At the 1906 general election he contested and won the St Helens constituency as an LRC candidate, defeating the Conservative (H. Seton-Karr) who had held the seat for twenty years and who was the son-in-law of one of the Pilkington partners. The Lancashire and Cheshire Federation was distinct from the other coalfields in its early affiliation to the new LRC five years before the mining unions as a whole affiliated. Consequently while in other counties the mining MPs were Lib-Labs, Glover and Walsh stood at the general election of January 1906 as Labour Party candidates: and the coalfield conference on 27 January 1906 passed the following resolution: 'That this conference desires to heartily thank all those who took any part in assisting in the triumphant victory of Mr T. Glover for St Helens and Mr S. Walsh for Ince; and we rejoice at their splendid victory, and congratulate them on their return to seats in the British House of Commons.' Glover's victory was in part due to the 1903 Gladstone–MacDonald electoral pact [Bealey and Pelling, ch. 6], which cleared the way for a straight fight between Glover and the Conservative candidate. Glover retained the seat in the first general election of 1910 (January) but was defeated in the December election of that year. He was a member of the St Helens Board of Guardians; a borough magistrate from 1893 and a county magistrate from 1909.

He had married in 1872 the daughter of William Seddons of Aston, Birmingham, and they had five children. He died on 9 January 1913 and his funeral service was held at a Congregational Church in St Helens. He left £673 (net) in his will. One of the few personal statements that have been found was in a letter written to W. T. Stead in answer to the latter's inquiry in 1906 regarding the books which had influenced the new Labour MPs. Glover replied [*Review of Reviews* (June 1906)]:

I am sorry to say that I have not gained my experiences out of books, but from the everyday experiences of how the workers have been treated by the employers and the class which do not work, and whose main object has always been to keep the working man as much in the dark as they can. I had to work in the mines from a very early age – nine years old when I started and very long hours – and the little I learned was at the night schools, and then by seeking to get into company always above myself and learning from them, which was most valuable to me.

Sources: MSS: NUM (N. West Area) records; *St Helens Lantern*, 26 Oct 1888, 325–6; *St Helens Newspaper*, 12 Jan 1906; Thomas Ashton, *Three Big Strikes in the Coal Industry* (Manchester, [1894?]); R. Page Arnot, *The Miners* (1949); T. C. Barker and J. R. Harris, *A Merseyside Town in the Industrial Revolution* (1954); F. Bealey and H. Pelling, *Labour and Politics 1900–1906* (1958); H. Pelling, *Social Geography of British Elections*

1885–1910 (1967). OBIT. *Manchester Guardian*, 10 Jan 1913; *Times*, 11 Jan 1913; *St Helens Newspaper*, 14 Jan 1913.

R. PAGE ARNOT
JOYCE BELLAMY

See also: Thomas ASHTON, for Mining Trade Unionism, 1900–14; Alexander MACDONALD, for Mining Trade Unionism, 1850–79; Benjamin PICKARD, for Mining Trade Unionism, 1880–99; Samuel WOODS.

GOLIGHTLY, Alfred William (1857–1948)
TRADE UNIONIST AND CO-OPERATOR

Alfred William Golightly was born in Lincoln on 21 October 1857 though his parents were Tynesiders. His father, William Golightly, was a locomotive engine driver on the north-east coast who moved to Lincoln because of a strike at the North Eastern Railway works. He died when Alfred was twelve and at that age Alfred became an engineering apprentice. The boy had had some education at the Great Northern Railway Company's British School at New England, Peterborough, whither the family had moved from Lincoln, and by his own diligence had added shorthand, mathematics and mechanical science. He served his apprenticeship at the Great Northern Railway Works at Peterborough and Doncaster, finishing off at Manchester and Sheffield and the Lincolnshire Railway works at Sheffield. He joined the Sheffield branch of the ASE as a fitter on 2 February 1878.

Having served his apprenticeship, he married and settled in Manchester where he was employed in the works of Beyer, Peacock and Co. and also of Sir Joseph Whitworth; and he began to take an interest in the affairs of the Amalgamated Society of Engineers. He had transferred to the Openshaw 3rd branch of the Union and in 1892 was elected to the national executive council for the no. 3 division. When the ASE organised a prize-essays competition on trade unionism, he submitted an essay and was bracketed in the first place with George Barnes (later general secretary of the ASE) and George Henderson (of Woolwich). In 1903 he became chairman of the ASE executive council on the death of Alfred Sellicks. He had been a close friend of Sellicks and like him worked for the settlement of trade disputes by peaceful means. Both were closely involved in the lock-out of 1897–8. Golightly was, however, defeated at the 1903 election for the council mainly because he had disapproved of the proposed strike action of the Clydeside engineers in 1902. He retired from union activities in 1929.

Previous to coming to London to serve the ASE, Golightly had been a member of the Droylsden Co-operative Society and on arrival in London threw himself into the life and work of the Stratford Co-operative Society. He was soon elected to the general committee and became president in 1897, an office he was to hold for eighteen years. In 1898 he contested a seat on the Leyton Urban District Council against William Collison, the advocate of free labour, with such success that he was subsequently returned unopposed and after seven years' service was elected vice-chairman of the council and in the following year chairman. He served twenty-one years on the Leyton Urban District Council. In 1938 he was elected to the Chigwell Council. He was a staunch progressive in politics and an able advocate of municipal ownership wherever it could be run successfully and profitably for the community. For eleven years he was an inspector of evening classes in engineering at the People's Palace in the Mile End Road, on the eastern side of London, and responsible for setting the examination papers.

In 1904 Golightly presided over the 36th Annual Co-operative Congress held at Stratford. In his presidential address he referred to the growth of co-operation in the London area (which had formerly been a co-operative desert), to the cause of free trade (then beginning to be challenged by the tariff reform movement) and to that of international arbitration.

He was elected to the board of the Co-operative Wholesale Society in 1915, being at the time employed in the CWS Engineering Department in London. He remained a member of the board, serving its finance committee, until his retirement, under the age limit rule, in 1929. He was also chairman of the International CWS, a member of the central board of the Co-operative Union and a director of the Russo-British Grain Export Company. He was a member of the committee on the duties and remuneration of CWS directors, 1914–15, and of the 1919 committee to investigate the possibility of a pension scheme for all co-operative employees. In 1922 he was one of three CWS directors who visited Russia to re-establish sound commercial relations with the Russian co-operative movement, after the strict Soviet control of that movement had been slightly relaxed.

At a conference in Suffolk in June 1926 he criticised severely the attitude of the Trades Union Council to the co-operative movement during the General Strike of the previous month, which, he said, had gone near to destroying co-operation [see G. D. H. Cole, *A Century of Co-operation* [1945?] 299–300].

After a long retirement, Alfred Golightly died at his Chigwell home on 18 March 1948 aged ninety. He had been a member of the ASE and AEU for seventy years. He left effects valued at £2611.

Sources: *Co-op. Congress Report* (1904); *Handbook of Stratford Co-op. Congress* (1904); *Handbook of Paisley Co-op. Congress* (1905); W. Collison, *The Apostle of Free Labour* (1913); P. Redfern, *The New History of the C.W.S.* (Manchester, 1938); J. B. Jefferys, *The Story of the Engineers, 1800–1945* [1945]; personal information: Librarian, Co-operative Union, Manchester; Amalgamated Union of Engineering and Foundry Workers. OBIT. *Stratford Express*, 26 Mar 1948.

H. F. BING

See also: William ALLAN, for New Model Unionism; *G. N. BARNES; Fred HAYWARD, for Co-operative Union; Percy REDFERN, for Co-operative Wholesaling.

GOODY, Joseph (1816/17–91)
RADICAL AND CO-OPERATOR

Joseph Goody was born in either 1816 or 1817 (being seventy-four years old when he died). His father was a baker, probably in

Sudbury, and Joseph succeeded his father in business only to give it up for employment on the railway. For more than twenty-five years he was the travelling inspector for the Ipswich district, and he retired from this position at the age of seventy, to become stationmaster at the Derby Road station, Felixstowe.

Goody became active in radical politics at the age of seventeen, having been first drawn into political discussion and debate at the time of the 1832 Reform Bill. He was an ardent supporter of the Chartist movement, an admirer of Feargus O'Connor and an investor in the Chartist Land Plan. He was also greatly influenced by the ideas of Robert Owen. With F. J. Bugg and George Hines he was active in 1867 in the third and successful attempt to form a co-operative society in Ipswich, and the Ipswich Industrial Co-operative Society was registered in the following year. He became treasurer for some years, and for twenty-one years sat continuously on the management committee.

In his later years he was a member of the executive committee of the Liberal Association, and was a director of the Ipswich Reform Club. He was a total abstainer. He died on 21 May 1891.

Sources: *Through Sixty Years: a record of progress and achievement, 1868–1928* (Ipswich Industrial Co-operative Society, Ipswich, 1928); R. Ratcliffe, History of the Working Class Movement in Ipswich (from the nineteenth century to 1935), in four typescript volumes at Ipswich Borough Library and on microfilm at Hull University Library. Obit. Notice by George Hines, *East Anglian Daily Times*, 22 May 1891.

H. F. BING
JOHN SAVILLE

See also: T. R. BIRD; S. FOULGER; George HINES.

GRAHAM, Duncan MacGregor (1867–1942)
MINERS' LEADER AND LABOUR MP

Born at Rawyards, Airdrie, in March 1867, the son of Malcolm Graham and Mary

MacGregor, he was educated at Whiterigg, Lochside and Longrigg Board Schools and started work as a miner in 1878 at the age of eleven. Graham first became associated with the trade union movement in 1886, and in 1892 he was elected a checkweighman at the Thankerton Colliery, Holytown, owned by John McAndrew & Co. Ltd, where he stayed until 1897. He worked for the Liberal party in his youth but discovered, when he was a local strike leader in 1894, that there was nothing to choose between Liberal and Tory employers and so decided to join the ILP in that year. He was one of the original seven who formed the first executive of the Lanarkshire Miners' Union which in 1894 replaced the Lanarkshire Miners' Federation. He moved to Eddlewood Colliery Hamilton in 1897 where he also worked as a checkweigher, but in 1908 he was one of several political organisers to be appointed by the Lanarkshire Miners' Union, a position he held until 1918 when he became general secretary of the union. After serving five years as secretary he relinquished his post but remained on its staff as an agent for the rest of his life. He represented his union on the national executive of the Scottish Mineworkers from 1918 to 1930 and served on the executive of the MFGB in 1920 and 1929.

In the factional struggle within the Scottish unions which raged for nearly ten years after their defeat in the 1926 lock-out, Duncan Graham took the side of the old officials who, he hinted, had been displaced by a method of voting 'unrepresentative of the true opinion' of the Lanarkshire miners. As it was on this same method that he himself had been elected many years earlier his charge was felt to be unsubstantiated and his reputation was somewhat diminished.

After the decade of faction was nearly at an end, at the time of the Spanish Civil War he moved at the 1938 Scottish Conference a resolution (which was carried unanimously) denouncing 'the armed intervention by foreign fascist powers in Spain' and deploring 'the action of the present Government in refusing to carry out International Law which gives the right to Constitutional Governments to purchase arms in their own defence'.

Graham acted as political agent in a number of parliamentary elections in South Lanark and Midlothian, and in 1918 entered the House of Commons himself as Labour MP for Hamilton, a seat he held continuously until his death. The 1918 election was unusual as, apart from the usual opposition from Unionist and Liberal, there was a National Democratic Party candidate – none other than David Gilmour, who for several years had been secretary of the Lanarkshire Miners' County Union. The results were:

D. M. Graham (Lab)	6998
H. S. Keith (Coalition Unionist)	4819
D. Gilmour (Nat. Democratic Party)	4297
J. H. Whitehouse (Lib)	504

When he spoke in the Commons, which was not very often, he showed himself to be a formidable exponent of the miners' point of view. He was always a good constituency man, and was especially concerned with pensions and unemployment. For a time he was chairman of the Scottish Labour group, was one of five MPs chosen in 1931 to draft a revised version of the Coal Mines (Minimum Wages) Act of 1912, and he was the only Labour candidate out of seven in the Scottish mining areas to retain his seat at the 1931 general election. At that time, only one other constituency in the whole of Scotland – Govan – had, like Hamilton, consistently returned a Labour member since the First World War. In 1939, in recognition of his services to Hamilton, he was made a freeman of the Burgh.

He was twice married: first in 1897 to Isabella Miller, daughter of Thomas Gillies, of Holytown, a miner; and second, after his first wife's death, to Isabella, daughter of Wm Moore, of Newarthill. He had a family of five sons and two daughters. His death occurred on 19 October 1942 at his Hamilton home and following a service at Cadzow Church he was buried in Brent Cemetery, Hamilton. His wife and family of four sons and two daughters survived him; his eldest son was killed on war service. He was succeeded as Labour MP for Hamilton by Thomas Fraser.

Sources: S. V. Bracher, *The Herald Book of Labour Members* (1923) (with photograph); *Labour Who's Who* (1927); Anon., *The Scottish Socialists: a gallery of contemporary portraits* (1931); *Dod* (1941); *WWW* (1941–50); R. Page Arnot, *A History of the Scottish Miners* (1955). OBIT. *Times*, 20 Oct 1942; *Hamilton Advertiser*, 24 Oct 1942; *Labour Party Report* (1943).

R. PAGE ARNOT
JOYCE BELLAMY

See also: *William ADAMSON; A. B. CLARKE; *Robert SMILLIE, for Scottish Mining Trade Unionism.

GRAY, Jesse Clement (1854–1912)
CO-OPERATOR

Born on 12 July 1854 at Ripley, Derbyshire, the son of a Baptist Minister, William Gray, who moved to a new pastorate at Hebden Bridge in 1860. Jesse Gray attended the local grammar school there and on leaving in 1867 became a clerk in the Manchester audit office of the Lancashire and Yorkshire Railway. In 1874 he was appointed by Joseph Greenwood to the position of assistant secretary of the Hebden Bridge Fustian Society of which Greenwood was one of the founders. Within six months he had been promoted to general secretary, a position he held until 1883, when E. V. Neale appointed him to be his assistant at the Co-operative Union. Like Neale he believed passionately in co-operative production and he had read a paper on this subject at a co-operative sectional conference in 1881: the first of many contributions to the literature of the co-operative movement. In 1886 he read a paper on the same subject at the Co-operative Congress which was awarded first prize and was unanimously adopted, although the CWS abstained from voting: an indication of the differences of opinion between leaders of the co-operative movement on the subject of independent co-operative production on the one hand and the manufacture of goods by the Wholesale Society on the other. Gray succeeded Neale as secretary of the Co-operative Union in 1891 and brought to his new post a vitality and an administrative ability which made him a greatly respected figure.

In addition to his work for the British co-operative movement, his reputation as a leader in co-operative affairs was international and he was well known in many parts of the Continent. He attended at least twenty foreign Congresses and was secretary of the International Co-operative Alliance. He prepared and gave evidence before several House of Commons committees including that dealing with the Industrial and Provident Acts of 1893; on the advisability of establishing army canteens on a co-operative system in 1902; and before the Income Tax Committee appointed in 1904 to consider the position of co-operative societies. But his name is especially associated with his proposal for a National Co-operative Society which he put forward in his presidential address to the Co-operative Congress in Birmingham in 1906. He pointed out the need to overcome the conflict between commercial success and the old co-operative ideals of equality and suggested a blending of the latter with the newer methods. His plan was for a single co-operative society which would bring together the scattered units within the movement on a unitary, and not a federative basis. While this would involve the sacrifice of some individual liberty in running societies he believed it would be for the general good of the whole movement. It was an attempt to convert the existing organisation into one run on parliamentary lines with a general council of 150 members elected by the constituent societies. It created much comment at the time but was regarded as being in advance of the general climate of opinion in the movement and his suggestions were not acted upon.

In addition to his work for the co-operative movement, Gray found time for some outside interests. In 1893 he was appointed a JP for Manchester and for a number of years served on the Licensing Committee. He was a vice-president of the Free Trade League established in Manchester in 1903; was closely associated with the Garden City movement from its beginning and was one of the co-operative representatives on the board of the North Wales Quarries, a trade union

and co-operative venture whose object was to provide employment for slate quarry workers. Ill-health compelled him to retire in 1910 and he died at his home at Gatley, near Manchester, on 24 February 1912. His wife, two sons and a daughter survived him.

Writings: *How to start Co-operative Stores* (Manchester, 1886) 8 pp.; *Co-operative Production in Great Britain*, repr. *Age of Steel*, Jan 1887 (Manchester, 1887) 14 pp.; *Co-operative Production* (Manchester, [1888]) 16 pp.; *Co-operation versus Competition* (Manchester, [1889]) 12 pp.; *The System of Credit as practised by Co-operative Societies* (Manchester, [1889]) 32 pp.; *Loan Capital: how to deal with it* (Manchester, [1892]) 8 pp.; Introduction by J. C. Gray to *The Industrial and Provident Societies Act 1893* (Manchester, 1894); *Deceased members' shares: with some hints on probate and administration* (1898) 10 pp.; *Co-operation in Agriculture* (1898) 16 pp.; *Self-Help for the People: a brief review of some of the benefits which co-operation has conferred on the working classes* (1900) 8 pp.; *Pamphlet on the Foods and Drugs Act and Shop Assistants Act* (Manchester, 1900); *Opinions on the Boycott Tactics of the Grocers* (1902); 'Co-operation and the Poor', *CWS Annual* (1902) 111–38; 'Co-operation in the U.K.', *Reports of the 5th and 6th International Co-operative Congresses* (1902 and 1904); 'Question as to the Policy of expending Large Sums on the Erection of Extensive Central Stores; or on the other hand of having only Central Warehouse Premises and Branch Shops where required', *Co-op. Congress Report* (1903); *Notes of importance for the Use of Committees and Officials* (Manchester, 1903) 12 pp.; *The Boycott of Co-operation* (Manchester, 1903); *An Incident of the Boycott* (Manchester, 1903) 16 pp.; *Co-operative Societies and the Income Tax* (Manchester, 1903) 10 pp.; *Loan Capital: how to deal with it* (Manchester, 1904) 8 pp.; *Competing Co-operators* (Manchester, 1904) 8 pp.; 'Present Status of Co-operation in Great Britain', *Arena, 33* (1905) 258–62; *Co-operation as a Factor in the Education of the Citizen* (n.d.) 12 pp.; Inaugural Address, *Co-op. Congress Report* (1906); *Co-operation: the ideals of its founders; a comparison with present day methods* *and proposals for future consideration* (1914) 12 pp.

Sources: *Co-op. Congress Handbooks* (1894, 1904, 1905, 1906); W. Kilner, *A National Co-operative Society: is it practicable?* (1909) 12 pp.; P. Redfern, *The Story of the C.W.S.* (Manchester, [1913]); T. W. Mercer, *The Proposed National Co-operative Society: summary of inaugural address by J. C. Gray* (Manchester, 1920); S. and B. Webb, *The Consumers' Co-operative Movement* (Manchester, 1921); G. D. H. Cole, *A Century of Co-operation* [1945?]; E. C. Mack and W. H. G. Armytage, *Thomas Hughes* (1952); D. Flanagan, *A Centenary Story of the Co-operative Union of Great Britain and Ireland: 1869–1969* (Manchester, 1969).

JOYCE BELLAMY

See also: Joseph GREENWOOD; Fred HAYWARD, for Co-operative Union; H. J. MAY, for International Co-operative Alliance; E. V. NEALE.

GREENALL, Thomas (1857–1937)
MINERS' LEADER AND LABOUR MP

Born on 5 May 1857 at Tarbuck, Lancashire, the son of Thomas Greenall, a coalminer. Young Tom had only a few years' schooling but he was able to read and write before he started work at the age of eight in a bottle factory. Some years later he began working at the Alexandra Colliery, St Helens, where he hauled tubs of coal by belt and chain – the belt going round the waist and the chain between the legs – and this he did for ten or twelve hours a day, with no half-day on Saturday. Greenall always claimed that he was a trade unionist at the age of twelve, his father being chairman of a local union in St Helens and an elder brother being a committee member. For about twenty years he worked in the pits in various capacities, and then in 1889 he was appointed agent of the Lancashire Miners' Federation, a position he held for forty-one years. He was among those at the founding conference of the MFGB in Newport in 1889, and he represented the Lancashire miners on the MFGB's executive committee at intervals between

the years 1897 to 1924. He was elected president of the Lancashire and Cheshire Miners' Federation in 1908, retiring only in 1929; represented his county on the national Conciliation Board, and attended many mining conferences in Europe and America. He was especially noted, in his own district, for his skilled and painstaking negotiating ability.

Apart from his mining interests he was active in local government affairs: as a member of the Swinton and Pendlebury Urban District Council from 1889 to 1907, of which he was chairman in 1903–4. He made two unsuccessful attempts to enter Parliament, in January 1910 when he contested the Leigh constituency and in 1918 when he fought Farnworth; but he was elected Labour MP for Farnworth in November 1922 and held the seat until he retired from Parliament at the time of the general election of 1929. Appointed a JP for Salford in 1906, he served as a magistrate for thirty years. He also gave active support to the co-operative movement and served his local society as committee man and chairman.

He had married in 1879 Sarah, daughter of William Saunders, and died at his Pendlebury home on 22 December 1937. He left effects valued at £4505.

Sources: S. V. Bracher, *The Herald Book of Labour Members* (1923) [with photograph]; *Labour Who's Who* (1927); *Dod* (1929); *WWW* (1929–40). OBIT. *Bolton Evening News*, 23 Dec 1937; *Times*, 24 Dec 1937.

JOYCE BELLAMY

See also: Thomas ASHTON, for Mining Trade Unionism, 1900–14; *A. J. COOK, for Mining Trade Unionism, 1915–26; and Benjamin PICKARD, for Mining Trade Unionism, 1880–99.

GREENING, Edward Owen (1836–1923)
CO-OPERATOR AND SOCIAL REFORMER

Born on 17 August 1836 at Warrington, the grandson of a Nathaniel Greening who had introduced into the town the trade of wire-drawing. Nathaniel's partner was the father of the later Liberal MP Peter Rylands. The original partnership broke up and Edward Greening's own father also left the business in order to set himself up independently, first at Bedford Leigh and then later in Manchester. Edward's early years were spent at Bedford Leigh where, in 1842, his father's small factory was attacked by the 'Plug Plot' demonstrators. When the family moved to Manchester Edward attended the Quakers' school in Mount Street, and he remained greatly influenced by Quaker teachings throughout his life.

When he was thirteen family circumstances compelled his early withdrawal from school and he was apprenticed to the wire-working trade. Three years later he left the bench for office work and at the same time began to attend evening classes. In the following year, at the age of seventeen, he played an active part in the work of the Anti-Slavery Society: an organisation which raised money in Manchester to assist the work of the abolitionist movement in America to maintain an 'underground railway' by which black slaves from the American South escaped into the free territories of the North. In 1855 Greening's father decided to emigrate to Canada following the failure of his business affairs and Edward began in business himself with one of his brothers; in a few years he was earning a considerable income. In the meantime he had married at the age of twenty-three and had joined both the United Kingdom Alliance – of which he was later to serve on the executive – and the Union and Emancipation Society – of which he was one of the founder members. The Society was established in the early 1860s shortly after the start of the American Civil War, with the object of supporting the Northern cause. Greening was one of the two honorary secretaries of the Society and became increasingly prominent in the campaign against the slave-owning South. He was vigorous in opposition to those in Britain who wished to recognise the South and he wrote constantly in the columns of the *Manchester Examiner* and the *Daily News* and lectured widely all over the country. Like many who took part in this important movement Greening became more committed

to a radical liberalism as the political struggle continued. His colleague as honorary secretary was John C. Edwards, the first secretary of the Co-operative Wholesale Society, and among those with whom he collaborated were Dr John Watts, Edward Hooson and Ernest Jones.

The 1860s were a crucial decade in Greening's intellectual and political development. He helped found the Manchester and Salford Manhood Suffrage League – a section of the Reform League – and he became intensely interested in, and involved with, the co-operative movement: making contact in these years with many of its leading members, including E. T. Craig, G. J. Holyoake, Thomas Hughes, Lloyd Jones and William Pare. For the remainder of his life most of his activities were directly associated with various aspects of co-operation. He was especially interested in the principles of industrial co-partnership and these he introduced into his own business. During this decade of the 1860s, he played a leading part in the establishment of several co-partnership concerns, of which the most important were the Cobden Memorial Mills at Sabden in Lancashire and the South Buckley Coal and Fire Brick Company (this latter, however, quickly failing). In 1868, with the encouragement of Thomas Hughes and other middle-class supporters, he founded in London the Agricultural and Horticultural Association – popularly known as the One and All – and he left Manchester to become its managing director. Its object was to supply agricultural implements, seeds, manures etc. on co-operative principles, and Greening also edited its publications: the *Agricultural Economist* and the *One and All Gardening Annual*. In its early years especially the Association prospered and it remained in existence until the special difficulties of the First World War forced it to close down in 1915. To encourage a wider interest in the co-partnership idea in general Greening founded and edited the *Industrial Partnership Record* in 1867, the journal changing its name to the *Social Economist* in 1868, it being then edited jointly by Greening and G. J. Holyoake.

In 1868 Greening was invited by a group

of radical working men to stand for Halifax at the general election. The two official candidates were a Whig industrialist and James Stansfeld. The latter was fully aware of George Howell's efforts to limit sharply the numbers of genuinely independent working-class candidates and Greening was not supported by the Reform League at national level; but according to *The Times* (1 Oct 1868) the local branch of the Reform League supported his candidature. He was the object of scurrilous attacks upon his personal integrity during the election campaign and was inevitably defeated, despite being publicly supported by John Stuart Mill and Ernest Jones.

Greening's own business failed in 1870, but by this time he was already involved in other ventures, including the One and All Association. For the remainder of his long life he worked almost entirely within the co-operative movement. In 1867 he convened a national Co-operative Conference in Manchester attended, among others, by Thomas Hughes, E. V. Neale, G. J. Holyoake, the Rev. W. N. Molesworth of Rochdale and J. M. Ludlow, who contributed a paper. After his removal to London in 1868 he took an active part in the preliminary meetings for the first national Co-operative Congress in May 1869, out of which developed the Co-operative Central Board and then, more gradually, the Co-operative Union. In 1874 he helped establish the Co-operative Institute in London for lectures, debates and other social activities; and arising out of this organisation came the idea of a National Co-operative Festival which Greening initiated, and which was held annually at the Crystal Palace from 1886 to 1910. Greening warmly encouraged the Co-operative summer schools, was on the committee of the Vacant Land Cultivation Society and was closely associated with Holyoake and Neale in the formation of the International Co-operative Alliance in 1895. He took the chair at the inaugural conference of the ICA. He served on the central board of the Co-operative Union for many years and retired early in 1904, the year when he delivered the opening address at the Stratford Congress.

Greening was an eloquent speaker, a vigorous controversialist and a prolific writer. He was the author of several co-operative society histories, wrote many propaganda leaflets and pamphlets and contributed steadily throughout his life to the co-operative press. He was widely travelled, and his descriptions of visits to co-operative enterprises at home and abroad were collected together in *The Co-operative Traveller* and *The Co-operative Traveller Abroad*. From the late 1860s until his death Greening's influence, while widely diffused and important throughout the co-operative movement in Britain, was in some matters circumscribed. In the great debate of the 1870s concerning 'the bonus to labour', especially in the field of wholesale co-operation, Greening belonged to the minority of Thomas Hughes, Holyoake and E. V. Neale; and in the last years of his life he became vehemently opposed to the idea of separate parliamentary representation for the co-operative movement, and it was he who moved the heavily defeated contrary amendment at the 1917 Congress which brought into existence the Co-operative Party.

Despite, however, the total rejection by the CWS in the 1880s of any concession to co-partnership principles Greening persevered in the cause. He played an important part in the establishment of the Co-operative Productive Federation in 1882 – whose aim was to secure unity of action among organisations run on co-partnership lines – and of the Labour Association in 1884, whose purpose was the promotion of enterprises on co-partnership lines.

In the last years of his life, particularly after the closure of the Agricultural and Horticultural Association in 1915, Greening was in some financial difficulties, and a testimonial fund contributed by co-operative societies raised £1239. Just before his death a further fund raised £853, but before this could be converted into an annuity he had died.

Greening was a man of quite extraordinary energy. In the three years from 1919 to 1922, when he was in his ninth decade, he attended eight congresses, thirty-five conferences, eighty-five public meetings, thirty-two weekend and summer schools as well as other gatherings of a co-operative character. In politics he remained a radically minded, free trade Liberal; and in religion he seems to have been a Unitarian. He was twice married: the first time in June 1860 to Emily Hepworth and there were several children, of whom at least one, E. W. Greening, shared his father's interests in the co-operative movement. Edward Greening died at his Lewisham home on 5 March 1923, and he was buried at Hither Green Cemetery. He was survived by his wife and family and left an estate valued at £474 (net).

Writings: *The Present Position and Prospects of Partnerships of Industry* (Manchester, 1866) 10 pp.; Articles in the *Industrial Partnership's Record* in 1867–8 including: 'Industrial Partnerships: their basis, origin and present position' (Mar, May, Aug 1867 and Jan 1868); 'Partnerships of Industry as Investments for Capital' (Mar 1867) and 'On the Marvellous Profitableness of Co-operation' (May 1867); *Complete Enfranchisement of the Manhood of England* [a speech repr. from *Newark Advertiser* (Newark, 1867)] 8 pp.; 'How far is it desirable and practicable to extend Partnerships of Industry?', *Trans NAPSS* (1870) 485–500; 'Mutual Guarantee', *Co-op. Congress Report* (1872); 'The Future of Labour in Co-operation', *Co-op. Congress Report* (1874); 'A Plea for a Truly Co-operative Press', *Co-op. Congress Report* (1874); 'Co-operative Production', *Co-op. Congress Report* (1875); 'The Failures of Industrial Partnerships', *Co-op. Congress Report* (1877); 'The Future of the Working Classes', *Co-op. Congress Report* (1885); 'Profit-sharing and Co-operative Production', *Industrial Remuneration Conference* (1885); *The Alleged Failure of Co-operative Production* (1885); *Helping Production* (1885); 'Co-op. Agriculture applied to Market Gardening and Fruit Culture', *CWS Annual* (1885) 194–7; *The Co-operative Traveller Abroad* (1888); (with E. V. Neale) *Proposals for an International Alliance of the Friends of Co-operative Production* (1892) 12 pp.; *Co-operative Rights in Public and Private Bills* (1895) 8 pp.; Inaugural Address to 1904 Co-op. Congress, *Co-op. Congress Report* (1904); *How to make Co-opera-tion succeed in Large Centres of Population*, 23 pp.; *Rural Revival* [1905?] 8 pp.; *Garden Making* [1907?] 26 pp.; *Manuring* [1908?] 32 pp.; Introduction to J. MacCabe, *Life and Letters of G. J. Holyoake* (1908); *A Policy of Conciliation for Co-operators. How to reconcile the interests, ideals and work of agricultural, productive and distributive societies* [1915] 7 pp.; *G. J. Holyoake* (1917) 32 pp.; *A Democratic Co-partnership; Wigston Hosiers* (Leicester, 1921); *A Pioneer Co-partnership: being the history of the Leciester Co-operative Boot and Shoe Manufacturing Society Ltd* (Leicester, 1923). Greening contributed many articles to the following journals: *Co-op. News; Co-op. Official; Co-partnership; Millgate Monthly; Scottish Co-operator* and *Wheatsheaf*. In the last years of his life he wrote a short autobiographical sketch (location not known) to which reference is made by his biographer, Tom Crimes, in *Edward Owen Greening: a maker of co-operation* (Manchester, 1923).

Sources: (in addition to T. Crimes above) *Times*, 28 July 1868; 13 Aug 1868; 1 Oct 1868; *Halifax Courier*, 15 Aug 1868 and 3 Oct 1868; *Halifax Guardian*, 15 Aug 1868 and 3 Oct 1868; *Social Economist*, 1 Nov 1868, 142; B. Jones, *Co-operative Production* (1894); G. Hines, 'Is it Coercion?', 30 May 1903, source: Hull University Library (Hines microfilm); A. W. Humphrey, *A History of Labour Representation* (1912); P. Redfern, *The Story of the C.W.S.* (Manchester, [1913]); G. D. H. Cole, *A Century of Co-operation* [1945?]; E. C. Mack and W. H. G. Armytage, *Thomas Hughes* (1952); A. Bonner, *British Co-operation* (1961); R. Harrison, *Before the Socialists* (1965). OBIT. *Co-op. News*, 10 Mar 1923; *Times*, 10 Mar 1923; *Kentish Mercury*, 16 Mar 1923; *Co-op. Congress Report* (1923).

JOYCE BELLAMY
EDMUND FROW
JOHN SAVILLE

See also: Thomas BLANDFORD; G. J. HOLYOAKE, and for Retail Co-operation – Nineteenth Century; *Thomas HUGHES; H. J. MAY, for International Co-operative Alliance; E. V. NEALE; and below: Co-partnership.

140 GREENING

Co-partnership: J. E. Cairnes, 'Co-operation in the Slate Quarries of North Wales', *Macmillan's Mag.* 11 (Jan 1865) 181–90; G. J. Holyoake, 'Partnerships of Industry', *Trans. NAPSS* (1865) 480–7; R. A. Arnold, 'Labour and Co-operation: the future of labour', *Trans. NAPSS* (1866) 687–9; A. Briggs, 'The Whitwood Colliery', *Trans. NAPSS* (1866) 703–8; E. O. Greening, *The Present Position and Prospects of Partnerships of Industry* (Manchester, 1866) 10 pp.; [H.] Briggs, Son & Co., *Report on the ... System of Industrial Partnership adopted by H. Briggs, Son & Co.* (1867) 12 pp.; J. M. Ludlow, *Trade Societies and Co-operative Production* (Manchester, 1867) 10 pp.; G. B. Addison, *Partnership of Industry: some notes, facts and figures in reference to the promotion of Cobden Mills Co.* (Manchester, [1868]); A. Briggs, 'Industrial Partnerships', *Co-op. Congress Report* (1869) 74–7; E. O. Greening, 'How far is it desirable and practicable to extend Partnerships of Industry?', *Trans. NAPSS* (1870) 485–500 (includes discussion); Fox, Head & Co., *The Co-operative Scheme of Messrs Fox, Head & Co.*, 4 vols (1871–4); G. J. Holyoake, 'The Abuse of Industrial Partnerships', *Trans. NAPSS* (1872) 456–60; E. O. Greening, 'On the Failures of Industrial Partnerships', *Co-op. Congress Report* (1877) 69–71; J. A. Fox and S. Taylor, 'What results may be expected to arise from an extension of the system of participation by labour in the profits of manufacturing, agricultural and trading enterprises', *Trans. NAPSS* (1881) 660–90 (includes discussion); S. Taylor, *On Profit-sharing between Capital and Labour: a word to working men* (Cambridge, 1882); idem, *Profit-sharing between Capital and Labour: six essays to which is added a memorandum on the industrial partnership at the Whitwood Colliery (1865–1874) by A. Briggs and H. C. Briggs* (1884); E. O. Greening, 'Profit-sharing and Co-operative Production' (Industrial Remuneration Conference Paper: 1885) 304–11; E. V. Neale, *The Labour Association for promoting Co-operative Production based on the Co-partnership of the workers: its principles, objects and methods* (1885) 12 pp.; N. P. Gilman, *Profit-sharing between Employer and Employee: a study in the evolution of the wages system* (Boston and New York, 1889) 243–95; D. L. Schloss, 'The Labour Problem', *Fortnightly Rev.* n.s. 51 (Oct 1889) 437–47; Board of Trade, *Report on Profit-sharing* 1890 LXXVIII C. 6267; J. S. Nicholson, 'Profit-sharing', *Cont. Rev.* 57 (Jan 1890) 64–77; D. F. Schloss, 'Industrial Co-operation', *Cont. Rev.* 57 (Apr 1890) 552–68; T. W. Bushill and D. F. Schloss, 'List of British Profit-sharing Firms' [with Notes], *Econ. Rev.* 1 (Jan 1891) 92–6; B. Jones, 'Co-operation and Profit-sharing', *Econ. J.* 2 (1892) 616–28; L. L. Price, 'Profit-sharing and Co-operative Production', *Econ. J.* 2 (Sep 1892) 442–62; D. F. Schloss, *Methods of Industrial Remuneration* (1892) rev. (1898); T. W. Bushill, *Profit-sharing and the Labour Question* with an Introduction by S. Taylor (1893); W. Maxwell, *The Relation of Employés to the Co-operative Movement* (1893) 14 pp.; W. E. Snell, 'Co-operators and Profit-sharing', *Econ. Rev.* 3 (Apr 1893) 201–11; H. Vivian, *Evidence before the R.C. on Labour*, 1893–4 XXXIX pt I Qs 7523–688; Board of Trade, *Report on Profit-sharing* 1894 LXXX C. 7458; H. Vivian and A. Williams, 'The Co-partnership of Labour', *Econ. Rev.* 4 (July 1894) 297–317; H. Vivian, *What is Co-partnership?* [1896] 4 pp.; E. C. Gregory, 'The Labour Association for Promoting Co-operative Production based on Co-partnership of the Workers', *Econ. Rev.* 7 (Jan 1897) 100–4; E. V. Neale, *The Principles, Objects and Methods of the Labour Association* [1897?] 16 pp.; Labour Association for Promoting Co-operative Production, *How to start a Co-operative Workshop* [1898?] 4 pp.; H. D. Lloyd, *Labor Co-partnership: notes of a visit to co-operative workshops, factories and farms in Gt Britain and Ireland* (1898); H. Vivian, *Partnership of Capital and Labour as a Solution of the Conflict between them* [1898] 11 pp.; idem, *Co-operative Stores and Labour Co-partnership* (1899) 8 pp.; J. Bonar, *Labour Co-partnership* [1899] 12 pp.; W. H. Lever, 'Prosperity sharing versus Profit-sharing in relation to Workshops Management', *Econ. Rev.* 11 (Jan 1901) 47–64 and (July 1901) 316–21; A. Williams and H. Vivian, 'Recent Progress of Labour Co-partnership', *Econ. Rev.* 11 (Apr 1901) 201–17; A. Williams, *History and Present Position of Labour Co-partnership* (1903) 8 pp.; H. Vivian, *Industrial Democracy*

[1903?] 8 pp.; idem, *The Labour Co-partnership Movement in Gt Britain* [1904] 10 pp.; G. Bisset, *Is Co-operation capable of solving the Industrial Problem?* (Manchester, 1905) 23 pp.; A. Williams, *Twenty-one Years' Work for Co-partnership* (1905) 12 pp.; idem, 'Twenty years of Co-partnership', *Econ. Rev. 15* (Jan 1905) 15–27; H. Vivian, *A New Chapter in the History of Co-operation and Labour: The North Wales Quarries Ltd* (1906) 20 pp.; R. Halstead, *Co-partnership and the Store Movement* [1909?] 11 pp.; F. Maddison, 'The Labour Co-partnership Association', *Econ. Rev. 20* (July 1910) 314–17; E. Jackson, *A Study in Democracy: an account of the rise and progress of industrial co-operation in Bristol* (Manchester, 1911); W. H. Brown, *The Pioneer Co-partnership Suburb* (1912) 33 pp.; C. R. Fay, 'Co-partnership in Industry', *Econ. J. 22* (Dec 1912) 529–41; R. Halstead, *Co-partnership and Modern Labour Troubles* [1912?] 11 pp.; F. Harrison, *Are we ready for Industrial Co-operation?* [1912?] 10 pp.; H. Quelch, *The Co-partnership Snare* (1912); Board of Trade, Labour Dept, *Report on Profit-sharing and Labour Co-partnership in the United Kingdom* 1912–13 Cd. 6496 XLIII [with bibliography]; C. R. Fay, *Co-partnership in Industry* (Cambridge, 1913); H. S. Furniss, 'Co-partnership and Labour Unrest', *Econ. Rev. 23* (Jan 1913) 61–72; L. V. Lester-Garland, 'Co-partnership and Labour', *Econ. Rev. 23* (Apr 1913) 150–7; E. R. Pease, *Profit-sharing and Co-partnership: a fraud and failure?* (Fabian Tract no. 170: 1913) 16 pp.; A. Williams, *Co-partnership and Profit-sharing* [1913]; C. Carpenter, *Co-partnership in Industry with an appendix comprising chronological notes on British Profit-sharing and Co-partnership, 1829–1914* (1914); L. L. Price, *Co-operation and Co-partnership* [1914]; Ministry of Labour, *Report on Profit-sharing and Labour Co-partnership* 1920 XXIII [Appendix F for bibliography]; E. O. Greening, *A Democratic Co-partnership* (Leicester, 1921); idem, *A Pioneer Co-partnership: being the history of the Leicester Co-operative Boot and Shoe Manufacturing Society Ltd* (Leicester, 1923); R. Halstead, *Thomas Blandford, Hero and Martyr of Co-partnership* (Manchester, 1925) 15 pp.; Kettering Clothing Manufacturing Co-operative Society Ltd, *The Story of a Successful Experiment in Co-partnership* (Kettering, [1925]) 24 pp.; G. D. H. Cole, 'Workers' Control in Industry', *Co-operator's Year Book* (1933) 13; Co-operative Co-partnership Propaganda Committee, *Co-operative Co-partnership* 4th ed. (Leicester, 1944) 48 pp.; Conservative Political Centre, *Co-partnership Today: a survey of profit-sharing and co-partnership schemes in industry* (1946, repr. 1955) 46 pp.; G. D. H. Cole, *Co-operation, Labour and Socialism* (Blandford Memorial Lect.: Leicester, 1947) 15 pp.; A. Hemstock, 'Co-operative Co-partnership Production in Great Britain', *ACE 19* (Jan–Mar 1948) 43–51; P. Derrick, *The Co-operative Approach to Socialism* (Socialist Christian League: 1956); idem, *The Company and the Community* (Fabian Research series no. 238: 1964) 33 pp.; A. Flanders, R. Pomeranz and J. Woodward, *Experiment in Industrial Democracy* (1968); *Co-ownership Co-operation and Control: an industrial objective*, ed. P. Derrick and J.-F. Phipps (1969).

GREENWOOD, Abraham (1824–1911)
CO-OPERATOR

Born in 1824 at Wardleworth Fold, Rochdale, Abraham was the son of David Greenwood, a blanket manufacturer, and his wife Martha, both of whom came from Batley Carr, Dewsbury, and had settled in Rochdale about 1819. Abraham was educated first at a dame school, then at a school kept by an uncle at Armley and finally at Rochdale. He trained as a weaver at his father's mill but at the age of sixteen was apprenticed to woolsorting, at which trade he worked for twenty-six years in Rochdale. This occupation could only be conducted in daylight, and in his leisure hours he devoted himself to studying ethics, politics, religion and socialism. David Greenwood was a West Riding freeholder and an active politician, and Abraham inherited his father's political interests. At eighteen he was secretary of the local Chartist Association and acted as part-time librarian of the People's Institute. Some of the members belonged to the Rochdale Pioneers' Society and through them he joined the Toad Lane Store in 1846. He was soon elected to the management committee, originated the education department and eventually became president. He was one of the founders of the Rochdale Corn Mill Society and its first chairman. The success of the Corn Mill encouraged the establishment of the Co-operative Manufacturing Society of which Greenwood was also a promoter.

The need for a wholesale society had been early recognised in the co-operative movement and E. Vansittart Neale was preaching the idea continuously from 1850. Greenwood warmly supported Neale, and in 1859, with Hooson and J. C. Edwards, he began working for amendments to the 1852 Industrial and Provident Societies Act which would remove certain of the legal obstacles to a federal wholesale society. They sought, and obtained, the support of Neale and J. M. Ludlow; and they were further encouraged by the vigorous support of the monthly *Co-operator* which began publication in 1860 (edited first by E. Longfield and then, after the first nine months, by Henry Pitman). The Jumbo tea party (August 1860), the Rochdale conference of November 1860, the Manchester conference on Christmas Day 1860, all took the issue further, and after further conferences in 1861 to discuss the text of the Bill, the 1862 Industrial and Provident Societies Act was passed. The Act *inter alia* allowed societies to hold shares in other societies thereby facilitating the establishment of a federal structure.

In all these developments Greenwood played an active role. On Christmas Day 1862 he read a paper to an Oldham conference setting out a scheme for a co-operative wholesale agency and a further conference on Good Friday 1863 debated Greenwood's scheme in detail. Rules for the new society were submitted in August 1863 and the society was registered as the North of England Co-operative Wholesale Industrial Provident Society Ltd. Greenwood was elected president with Councillor James Smithies (Rochdale) as treasurer and J. C. Edwards (Manchester) secretary. Greenwood held office for seven years, and then from 1874 to 1878 he served just as cashier and afterwards as bank manager to the CWS.

Greenwood had many other co-operative interests. He was one of the founders, a director and for a time manager of the Co-operative Insurance Company (later the CIS); and a promoter of the Co-operative Newspaper Society (which published the *Co-operative News* from 1871) serving on its board until his retirement in 1902, having been chairman for twenty-five years. A member of the central board of the Co-operative Union, he regularly attended co-operative congresses and was president on the second day of the Rochdale Congress in 1892. He was often accompanied to co-operative meetings by his daughter, who in 1883 was one of the founders of the Women's Co-operative Guild.

He spent his last years at Fleetwood, where he died at his Knott End home on 3 May 1911. He was buried at Rochdale Cemetery on 7 May 1911 and was survived by a married daughter, Mrs William Evans, her husband and their two sons. He left £312 in his will.

Writings: 'A Suggestive Paper on the Important Subject of a Wholesale Co-operative Agency', *The Co-operator*, Mar 1863; *The Educational Department of the Rochdale Equitable Pioneers' Society: its origin and development* (Manchester, 1877) 16 pp.; *The Fundamental Principles of Co-operation* (Manchester, [1881]) 8 pp.

Sources: *Bee-Hive*, 24 Apr 1875; P. Redfern, *The Story of the C.W.S.* (Manchester, [1913]); G. D. H. Cole, *A Century of Co-operation* (Manchester, [1945?]); A. Bonner, *British Co-operation* (Manchester, 1961); R. G. Garnett, *A Century of Co-operative Insurance* (1968); biographical information: H. Atkinson, Knott End, Fleetwood. OBIT· *Co-op. News*, 6 May 1911; *Rochdale Observer*, 6 May 1911.

H. F. BING
JOHN SAVILLE

See also: Samuel ASHWORTH; William COOPER; J. DYSON; G. J. HOLYOAKE, and for Retail Co-operation – Nineteenth Century; Charles HOWARTH; E. V. NEALE; Percy

REDFERN, for Co-operative Wholesaling; J.
SMITHIES.

GREENWOOD, Joseph (1833–1924)
CO-OPERATOR

Joseph Greenwood was born at Wadsworth
in the Upper Calder Valley in 1833. His
parents were handloom weavers and while
still very young Joseph assisted the family's
work by bobbin-winding. He learned the art
of fustian cutting when nine years old and
later used this knowledge in establishing a
co-partnership fustian and dyeing works. He
received no formal schooling but in his early
youth travelled long distances to attend
lectures and became keenly interested in the
co-operative and co-partnership movements,
learning of these directly from G. J. Holyoake, Thomas Hughes, Lloyd Jones and
Vansittart Neale. He was also thought to
have heard Robert Owen lecture.

He was one of a small group of journeymen cutters who founded the Hebden
Bridge Fustian Manufacturing Co-operative
Society in 1870, a co-partnership fustian and
dyeing works at Hebden Bridge which was
later taken over by the Co-operative Wholesale Society. He began work in a small room
ten feet square, and at the end of the first
year there were ninety-five members and a
profit of £3. Greenwood was the first secretary and manager and under his control a
large factory was built at Nutclough, ever
extending and employing larger numbers of
workers. It was only in 1909, after forty years'
service, that he retired. Greenwood had
great faith in the principle of co-partnership
and never lost an opportunity of advocating
it. He himself took a personal hand in the
establishment of the Burnley Self-Help
Society, Bradford Cabinet Makers' Society,
and the Leicester Hosiery Society.

He was for years one of the leading spirits
in the Hebden Bridge Co-operative Society
and in 1878 became a member of the north-
western section of the Co-operative Union.
For over thirty years he was secretary of the
Calderdale District Co-operative Association. He was still an honorary member of
the central board at the time of his death,
being by then its oldest honorary member.

He spoke at many meetings and conferences
held under the auspices of the Co-operative
Productive Federation and the Labour Co-
partnership Association. At the Co-operative
Congress in Leicester, 1877, he read a paper
on 'The Place of the Labourer in Co-operation' and at different times wrote several
papers published by the Co-operative Union,
the most important being *The Story of the
Formation of the Hebden Bridge Fustian Manufacturing Society* (1888). He gave evidence in
1892 on co-operative production and especially on the work of the Hebden Bridge
Society before the R.C. on Labour.

Joseph Greenwood's activities were not
confined to the co-operative movement. He
was for thirty-three years a member of
the local council, became the 'Father' of the
Council, was three times chairman of the
local education authority, a JP on the Todmorden Bench, chairman of the governors
of the Hebden Bridge Secondary School,
and one of the prime movers in the establishment of the local co-operative library. He
died on 4 December 1924, at the age of
ninety-one and was buried on 9 December in
the Birchcliffe Baptist Cemetery, near the
grave of J. C. Gray with whom he had been
closely associated in much co-operative and
humanitarian work. He left an estate valued
at £6730 (net).

Writings: 'The Place of the Labourer in
Co-operation', *Co-op. Congress Report* (1877)
66–8; *The Story of the Formation of the Hebden
Bridge Fustian Manufacturing Society* (Manchester, [1889]) 23 pp.; Evidence before
R.C. on Labour, 1893–4 XXXIX pt I Qs
941–1107; *Jubilee of the Luddenfoot Industrial
Co-operative Society Ltd: facts and incidents in
the history of the above society 1860–1910* (Manchester, 1910).

Sources: Co-operative Productive Federa-
tion records: Hull University Library ref.
DCF. OBIT. *Co-op. News*, 13 Dec 1924; *Co-op.
Congress Report* (1925).

H. F. BING

See also: J. C. GRAY; E. O. GREENING, for
Co-partnership; G. J. HOLYOAKE, for Retail
Co-operation – Nineteenth Century.

HALL, Frank (1861–1927)
MINERS' LEADER

Born near Sheffield on 7 July 1861, the son of Wilfred Hall, a file cutter. While he was quite young his parents moved to Derby and afterwards to Trentham in Staffordshire where his father was butler to the chaplain of the Duke of Sutherland. When Hall was nine years of age his father entered the service of Hugh Wood of Swanwick Hall, Derbyshire, a local coalowner. The family were unable to pay the 6d a week required for their son's education and, at the age of eleven, Frank Hall went to work at the Swanwick Collieries. Later he received night school education, being a regular attender at the science and art classes at Ripley, Derbyshire, from their inception. He studied mining and other subjects but when, at the age of twenty, it was suggested to him that he should study for a mine manager's certificate 'he felt that it would not give him the opportunity he desired of doing something to improve the position of his fellow men'. Hall eventually became a checkweighman at the Alfreton Colliery and began to take an active part in the affairs of the Derbyshire Miners' Association. Much of his reputation was based upon his handling of the lengthy disputes and intricate legal and arbitration proceedings which went on for several years at the Alfreton Colliery before his election as vice-president of the Derbyshire Miners' Association in 1906. In the following year he was elected treasurer. In 1913 he became general corresponding secretary and treasurer, and in 1914 general corresponding and financial secretary (in the same year the word 'corresponding' was deleted from his title), an office which he held until his death. Hall served on the executive committee of the Miners' Federation of Great Britain, 1913–21, and again from 1923 until his death in 1927.

Hall was a moderate trade union leader who was opposed to strikes. He was criticised by the rank-and-file members of the union after the 1912 strike. He advocated the ending of the 1920 strike and after the 1921 lock-out a member of the union asserted that a speech made by Hall had been such a valuable asset to the coalowners that one firm had posted it at the pit-head. After the 1926 stoppage Richard Gascoyne, the secretary of the Nottinghamshire and District Miners' Industrial Union (a company union), stated that Hall had worked in collusion with Frank Varley, of the Nottinghamshire Miners' Association, to bring about a Nottinghamshire and Derbyshire settlement. Hall brought an action against Gascoyne for slander but Gascoyne withdrew his allegations at the last minute when witnesses were assembling in the court.

In politics Hall was a loyal supporter of the Labour Party. He played an active part in organising the party in the North-East and Mid-Derbyshire constituencies during the First World War and in 1918 unsuccessfully contested the Clay Cross division of Derbyshire. After the 1921 lock-out the Derbyshire Miners' Association turned its attention from political to industrial action and attempted to discourage its officials from standing for Parliament by ceasing to pay a retaining fee to those who were elected. Hall considered this to be a reactionary move and announced that he would no longer be a candidate for the Clay Cross division.

He died at his Chesterfield home on 1 December 1927, and following a service at the Brewery Hill Baptist Church was buried at Spital Cemetery. A wife, two sons and a daughter survived him. He left an estate valued at £11,065.

Sources: (1) MSS: Minutes of the Derbyshire Miners' Association, 1906–27 (NUM, Saltergate, Chesterfield); (2) Printed: *Minutes of the Miners' Federation of Great Britain*, 1913–27; *Derbyshire Times*, 1906–27; (3) Secondary: R. F. Wearmouth, *The Social and Political Influence of Methodism in the Twentieth Century* (1957); J. E. Williams, 'The Political Activities of a Trade Union', *Int. Rev. Social Hist.* 2 (1957) 1–21; idem, *The Derbyshire Miners* (1962). OBIT. *Times*, 3 Dec 1927; *Derby Mercury*, 9 Dec 1927; *Derbyshire Times*, 10 Dec 1927.

J. E. WILLIAMS

See also: Thomas ASHTON, for Mining Trade Unionism, 1900–14; *A. J. COOK, for Mining Trade Unionism, 1915–26.

HALL, Fred (1878–1938)
CO-OPERATIVE TEACHER AND
EDUCATIONALIST

Born in Rochdale in 1878 of a working-class family closely linked with the Rochdale Society of Equitable Pioneers, Fred Hall attended an elementary school and at the age of thirteen entered the well-known cotton mills of John Bright & Bros; first as an office boy, later becoming a clerk. He then became assistant manager to a printing firm at Wardle, then secretary and traveller and ultimately manager of the North British Eyelet Company. While engaged in commercial occupations in the daytime, he attended university extension classes in Rochdale in the evenings, and the growing interest in the subjects he studied led ultimately to a decision to take up education as a profession. With this object in view he read for the BCom degree of Manchester University. As soon as he had matriculated he began teaching in the evening schools in Rochdale. His first classes under the Rochdale Education Committee were in geography, English, and arithmetic. In 1908 he resigned from business and was appointed teacher of book-keeping and later of business methods at the Bury Technical School, and at the Salford Secondary School for Boys he gave instruction in business methods and typewriting. In 1909 he was in charge of the advanced book-keeping and geography classes at Rochdale Technical School. He was also taking classes organised by the Rochdale Co-operative Society's Education Committee and did much private teaching for several years.

Fred Hall obtained his BCom at Manchester University in 1908 and his MA (Honours in Economics) in 1910, and in the same year was appointed chief lecturer in commercial and industrial organisation at the Belfast College of Technology (then known as the Municipal Technical Institute). Soon he became head of the Department of Commerce with 2000 students and a teaching staff of fifty which enabled him to exhibit his considerable administrative ability. In 1913 he was appointed Professor of Commerce.

In 1907 he married Miss Ada Briggs, a granddaughter of one of the original Rochdale Pioneers, and when he settled in Belfast he became an energetic member of Belfast Co-operative Society and especially of its education department. He was already thinking of a Co-operative College and had raised the question with the Co-operative Union and in the correspondence columns of the *Co-operative News*. In 1911 he explained the proposal more fully in an article published in the Belfast Society's local pages of the Co-operative Union's monthly magazine *The Wheatsheaf*. Invited to submit a paper on the subject to a national conference in Leicester at Easter 1912, he urged the immediate establishment of a Co-operative College and his proposal was heartily approved. He himself then founded an unofficial group called the College Herald Circle to campaign for the idea and in 1913 commenced the publication of *The College Herald*. He put forward as the threefold aims of the College: (1) a centre of higher education in co-operative subjects, (2) a centre for the cultivation of the co-operative spirit, and (3) a centre for research into co-operative principles and practice.

By 1913 the number of students enrolled in classes under the auspices of the Co-operative Union had reached 20,958 and at its meeting prior to the Co-operative Congress in Dublin at Whitsuntide 1914 the central board of the Co-operative Union unanimously approved the appointment of a permanent teacher at Holyoake House (the Union's headquarters in Manchester). It was no doubt inevitable that Professor Hall, who had already organised the first Co-operative Summer School at Castleton in 1913, should be invited to accept the post. Among many candidates his experience, qualifications and strong co-operative sympathies were outstanding and thus in May 1915 he came to the Co-operative Union as adviser of studies. He retained the title of Professor and continued in the educational service of the Co-operative Union until his death.

In 1915, with Britain already at war for a year, plans for the immediate establishment of a Co-operative College had necessarily to be shelved. Instead Hall threw his energies into the work of the General Co-operative Survey Committee, set up by the Dublin Congress in 1914, and took a leading part in the preparation of its voluminous reports. The survey took four years and Hall himself did much of the research involved. Its report of 300 pages presented to the Blackpool Congress in 1920 and covering educational, productive and distributive aspects, did much to enhance Hall's authority in the movement and provided him with a great deal of material for subsequent co-operative courses.

Shortly after his appointment as adviser of studies, Hall submitted a far-reaching plan for the development of all aspects of the education and research work of the movement and for its propaganda and publishing activities. In 1923 he completed his *Handbook for Members of Co-operative Committees* which at once became a standard work. In 1917 he had founded and become editor of *The Co-operative Educator*, in which *The College Herald* was absorbed.

In addition to his work for the survey committee during the war years, Hall never ceased to emphasise the need for a Co-operative College as the apex of the educational work of the movement. In 1919 the College came into existence housed at first in part of Holyoake House. The first full-time student, a young Australian ex-serviceman, was enrolled in April 1919. Holyoake House was non-residential and on his staff as lecturer, Hall had Mr T. W. Mercer as a colleague. The Carlisle Congress (Whitsuntide 1919) passed a resolution in favour of the creation of an independent college and building and in November the central board issued an appeal for £50,000 to provide a suitable building, equipment and an endowment fund. But the post-war depression prevented the full realisation of this scheme and Holyoake House continued for many years to be the centre of college teaching. In 1924 a residential hostel was acquired in Kersal near Manchester and in 1933 the reconstruction of Holyoake House gave the College more adequate accommodation.

Fred Hall made an important social as well as intellectual contribution to the early

co-operative summer schools during 1913–20 and he initiated the International Co-operative summer school, subsequently taken over by the International Co-operative Alliance. He had been a pioneer of the Workers' Education Association (having been secretary of a class in Rochdale organised in 1902 under the leadership of T. W. Price) and for twenty-three years acted as a link between the educational work of the co-operative movement and that of the WEA (in which he was a member of the National Council). He was involved also in the University Extension Movement, in Ruskin College (of which he was a governor) and in the World Association for Adult Education. He served on or gave evidence concerning the co-operative movement before many Government and other Committees and he was a member of the post-war Committee on National Debt and Taxation (1924). He co-operated with W. P. Watkins (a student and then a teacher at the Co-operative College and later Director of the International Co-operative Alliance) in the compilation of the co-operative movement's official textbook, *Co-operation*.

Fred Hall's philosophy may be summed up in a statement he made shortly after the war ended in 1918: 'Co-operation must replace competition in all men's activities . . . and the only force which can succeed in eliminating the undesirable traits in human character is education.' Throughout his life he was an active member of the Unitarian Church. He died suddenly at his home in Rochdale on Sunday afternoon 28 August 1938, after returning from Exeter where he had been lecturing, and he was buried at Rochdale Cemetery. He was survived by his wife. There were no children. Hall left an estate valued at £15,181.

Writings: *Business Letter Writing* (Pitman's first steps in business) [1912]; *Handbook for Commercial Teachers* [1912]; *The Elements of Commercial History* (Pitman's practical primers of business) [1915]; *Sunnyside: a story of industrial history of co-operation for young people* (Manchester, 1919) 3rd ed. (1935); *The History of the Co-operative Printing Society Ltd, 1869–1919* (Manchester, 1920); *A Standard*

Balance Sheet: the uniform classification of expenditure; and the organisation of statistics of a co-operative society (Manchester, 1921); with G. Collard, *The Story of Commerce* (1922); *Co-operators and the Present Crisis* (Manchester, 1922) 18 pp.; *Handbook for Members of Co-operative Committees* (Manchester, 1923; 3rd rev. ed. 1928); *Standard Co-operative Book-keeping*, 3 parts (Manchester, 1925); 'British Co-operation: an analysis of its progress', *People's Year Book* (1932) 46–56; with W. P. Watkins, *Co-operation: a survey of the history, principles and organisation of the co-operative movement in Great Britain and Ireland* (Manchester, 1934); *From Acorn to Oak: being the history of the Walsall and District Co-operative Society Ltd, 1886–1936* (Birmingham, 1936). In addition Hall published many pamphlets on behalf of the Co-operative Union, Manchester. Among those relating to general subjects are: *National Co-operative Men's Guild and its Mission in the Movement* (1914) 20 pp.; *The Study of Business Organisation* (1916) 7 pp.; *Economic Results of the War and their Effect upon the Co-operative Movement* (1916) 14 pp.; *Co-operative Control of Raw Materials and Prices: I Introductory* (1916) 18 pp.; *Ideas of Peace and Reconstruction* (1918) 10 pp.; *Co-operation and After-war Problems* (1918) 16 pp.; *Co-operative Capital: its accumulation and employment with special reference to working expenses and trading results in retail societies* (1920) 20 pp.; *Co-operators and the Present Crisis* (1921) 18 pp.; *The League of Nations and its Co-operative Implications* (1921) 8 pp.; *Co-operation and the Problem of Unemployment* (1921) 16 pp.; *Will Prices and Dividends Fall?: a paper on the economic situation as it affects co-operators, with an estimate of the future in regard to prices, profits, dividends, employment, the state of trade and wages* (1921) 12 pp.; *The Organisation of Retail Distributive Societies in the Face of Present-day Competition* (1922) 16 pp.; *Principles and Organisation of Trade and Commerce: national and international* (1924) 16 pp.; with H. Cox, *Pensions for Employees in the Co-operative Movement* (1925) 12 pp.; *British Co-operation: some recent changes and developments* (1927) 12 pp.; *The Consumer's Theory of Co-operation: is it enough?* (1927) 8 pp.; *Rationalisation and Co-operation* (1929) 12 pp.; *Departmental Trade and Working Expenses* (1929) 20 pp.; *Music*

and the Co-operative Movement (1929) 8 pp.; *The Trade of Dry Goods Departments in Retail Distributive Co-operative Societies* (1931) 15 pp.; see below: Co-operative Education for Hall's pamphlets relating to education in the co-operative movement.

Sources: T. W. Price, *The Story of the W.E.A.* (1924); G. D. H. Cole, *A Century of Co-operation* (Manchester, [1945?]); A. Bonner, *British Co-operation* (Manchester, 1961); Co-operative Press records, Manchester. OBIT. *Times*, 30 Aug 1938; *Co-op. News*, 3 Sep 1938; *Rochdale Observer*, 3 Sep 1938; *RIC*, Sep 1938; *Co-op. Educator 23* no. 4 (Oct 1938); *Co-operator's Year Book* (1939).

H. F. BING

See also: A. BONNER; T. W. MERCER; W. H. WATKINS; and below: Co-operative Education.

Co-operative Education: E. Slater, 'Co-operation and Education', *Co-op. Congress Report* (1870) 57–9; J. Holmes, 'The Necessity of Co-operative Education and on the Desirability of Co-operative Training', *Co-op. Congress Report* (1877) 63–5; A. Greenwood, *The Education Department of the Rochdale Equitable Pioneers Society Ltd: its origin and development* (Manchester, 1877) 16 pp.; J. Holmes, 'Education in Connection with Co-operation', *Co-op. Congress Report* (1880) 63–5; E. V. Neale, *Association and Education: what they may do for the people* (1882) 16 pp.; A. Toynbee, *Education of Co-operators* (1882) 12 pp.; A. H. D. Acland, 'Education of Co-operators and Citizens', *CWS Annual* (1885) 420–4; Miss Amy Sharp, *Co-operative Education* (Manchester, 1886) 12 pp.; T. G. Davies, 'Co-operation and Education', *CWS Annual* (1888) 308–14; R. H. Tutt, *The Duty of a Society to educate its Members in the Principles of Co-operation* (Manchester, 1889); Bishop B. F. Westcott, 'Educational Value of Co-operation', *Econ. Rev. 1* (1891) 5–12; Anon., 'Education in relation to the Co-operative Movement', *Progressive Rev. 1* (1897) 299–308; G. J. Holyoake, *Essentials of Co-operative Education* (1898) 20 pp.; H. Shaw, *Co-operation and Education* (Manchester, 1898) 10 pp.; M. L. Davies, *The Work of Educational*

Committees' Associations (Manchester, 1901);
W. R. Rae, *The Work of an Educational Committee* (Manchester, 1901) 15 pp.; J. C. Gray,
'Instruction in Co-operation in Great
Britain', *Report of sixth Int. Co-op. Congress*
(1904); W. R. Rae, *The Training of Co-operative Managers* (Manchester, 1904); idem,
'How best can Co-operative Societies utilize
their Education Funds in view of the Educational Facilities now provided by Municipal
and Local Authorities?', *Co-op. Congress
Report* (1904) 376–86; W. H. Watkins, *Co-operative Teaching* (1907) 16 pp.; idem, *Present
Co-operative Educational Resources and some
Immediate Needs* (1908) 24 pp.; T. Bank,
Co-operators and Class Work (1909) 16 pp.;
W. Clayton, 'Survey of Co-operative Activities in Education, Production and Distribution', *Co-op. Congress Report* (1914) 557–8;
F. Hall, *A Co-operative College* (1914) 24 pp.;
idem, *The Co-ordination and Extension of Co-operative Education* (1914) 24 pp.; idem, *The
Summer School for Co-operators* (1915) 10 pp.;
W. J. Foster, *The Value of the Educational
Work of the Co-operative Movement* (1917)
12 pp.; F. Hall, *The Work of a Co-operative
Educational Association* (1918) 12 pp.; idem,
*Further Prospective Developments of Co-operative
Education* (1919) 12 pp.; A. T. Wintersgill,
Co-operative Education: some suggestions regarding its Future Organisation and Extension (1919)
10 pp.; T. W. Mercer, *The Relation of Co-operative Education and Co-operative Politics*
(1921) 14 pp.; A. V. Alexander, *Educational
Policy* (1922) 12 pp.; F. Hall, *The Necessity
for Co-operative Education* (1923) 14 pp.; idem,
The Training of Employees, Officials and Committee Members of Co-operative Societies (1924)
16 pp.; H. J. Twigg, *The Organisation and
Extent of Co-operative Education* (Manchester,
1924) 49 pp.; idem, *An Outline History of Co-operative Education* (Manchester, 1924); J. J.
Dent, *Co-operation and the Working Men's
College* (1928) 19 pp.; F. Hall, *The Co-operative College and its Work* (1928) 18 pp.;
idem, 'Co-operative Educational Work: I.
Great Britain', *RIC 24* (Feb 1931) 50–4;
H. J. Laski, 'Co-operative Education', *Co-op.
Consumer 23* (Jan 1937) 4–6; E. C. Fairchild,
*A Scheme of Education for the Advancement of
the Co-operative Movement* [1937] 18 pp.;
G. D. H. Cole, *A Century of Co-operation* (Man-

chester, [1945?]); 'Co-operative Reorganisation Inquiry: recommendations on education', *Co-op. Congress Report* (1946) 146–59;
R. L. Marshall, *Co-operative Education* (1948)
21 pp.; S. M. Scott, *Directory of Co-operative
Training Institutions* (1952) 37 pp.; W. P.
McCann, 'Trade Unionist, Co-operative
and Socialist Movements in Relation to
Popular Education, 1870–1912' (Manchester
PhD, 1960); A. Bonner, *British Co-operation*
(Manchester, 1961; revised edition, 1970).

HALLAM, William (1856–1902)
MINERS' LEADER

Born in 1856, of Hallam's early life nothing
is known. In 1883 he was elected checkweighman at the Markham Colliery,
Staveley, Derbyshire, and later became a
delegate to the council of the Derbyshire
Miners' Association. In 1890 he was elected
president of the Association and held office
until 1898 when he was defeated by Barnet
Kenyon. Hallam closely contested the presidency until his premature death in 1902 at
the age of forty-six.

Unlike many of the other miners' leaders
of this period Hallam was an Anglican. He
was a member of the Staveley Parish Church
choir and clerk to the parish council. He was
never a prominent figure in mining trade
unionism and is best remembered today by
historians of the British labour movement for
his *Miners' Leaders*, which he published in
1894. In commenting on the keen intellect,
sturdy common sense, courage and self-sacrifice of the miners he wrote: 'It would be
surprising, indeed, if a body of Englishmen
possessing such qualities as these, did not find
itself able at all times to produce leaders of
no ordinary calibre. We are not astonished,
therefore, to find that the officers of the
miners' unions have been men, generally of
exceptional and often of quite remarkable
abilities.'

Hallam died from a heart affection on 4
July 1902 at his Staveley home and was
survived by his wife, two sons and two
daughters.

Writings: *Miners' Leaders: thirty portraits
and biographical sketches* (1894).

Sources: (1) MSS: Minutes of the Derbyshire Miners' Association, 1890–1902 (NUM, Saltergate, Chesterfield); (2) *Derbyshire Times*, 1890–1902; J. E. Williams, *The Derbyshire Miners* (1962). OBIT. *Derby Mercury*, 9 July 1902; *Derbyshire Times*, 12 July 1902.

J. E. WILLIAMS

See also: Benjamin PICKARD, for Mining Trade Unionism, 1880–99.

HARDERN, Francis (Frank) (1846–1913)

CO-OPERATOR

Frank Hardern was born at Macclesfield on 25 July 1846, the son of a silk mill steward, John Hardern. His mother was also a silk worker and Frank as a boy was employed as a half-timer in the same trade. Owing to the industry's decline following the Cobden Treaty with France, the Hardern family, like many others, had to seek employment elsewhere. They moved to Manchester, and then in 1861 settled in Oldham where young Frank secured work at a foundry connected with Messrs Platt Bros & Co., textile engineers, although ill-health caused him to give up this strenuous work at the age of twenty. He devoted this enforced leisure to study to which he attributed much of his later success. For three or four years he was employed by the local Gas Meter Company, rising to the position of storekeeper, and was then engaged as timekeeper by Messrs Bradbury & Co. Ltd. In August 1879 he was appointed secretary to the Broadway Spinning Co., and shortly afterwards the duties of salesman were added to the office. Later he became manager and retained this position until his retirement, on account of ill-health, a month or two before his death. At the time of his death he was chairman of the Henshaw Street Spinning Co., chairman of the Commercial Spinning Co., and auditor for the Hollinwood Spinning Co. From March 1896 to February 1911 he was a member of the committee of the Oldham Master Cotton Spinners' Association.

His co-operative career began when he joined the Oldham Industrial Co-operative Society on 28 May 1872. He was elected to its education committee in 1877, to its board of management in 1879, and became president of the Society on 21 August 1882, holding this office till October 1894. He presided on the second day of the fifteenth Co-operative Congress held in Oldham in 1883. In 1889 he was elected a member of the central board of the Co-operative Union and on behalf of that body gave evidence before the Royal Commission on Labour in 1892 and the Shop Hours Act Committee in the same year. For some time he was chairman of the parliamentary committee of the central board, and also chairman of the united board of the Co-operative Union. In 1899 he received the highest honour of the co-operative movement, being elected president of the thirty-first Co-operative Congress at Liverpool. Much of his presidential address related to educational questions.

Frank Hardern was active in the religious, temperance and political life of Oldham, and was made a JP in 1893. He believed that in order to exercise its proper influence the co-operative movement must participate in the industrial politics of the country, apart from party politics. He was a scrutineer of the Co-operative Wholesale Society. During his later years he somewhat slackened his activities in the co-operative movement owing to failing health but for forty years there had been few more familiar figures than his on co-operative platforms. He was a strong supporter of J. T. W. Mitchell during the heated controversies over profit-sharing. He was a staunch Liberal and a lifelong Nonconformist, being a member of the Union Street Congregational Church.

Although he had been in failing health for some time his death came as a surprise. He had a sudden seizure on Sunday night, 28 September 1913, and never regained consciousness, dying on the Tuesday night (30 September); and he was buried on 3 October at Chadderton Cemetery, Oldham. He left a widow – an ardent co-operator and Guild worker – four daughters and two sons. His estate was valued at £5991.

Sources: *Co-op. Congress Report* (1883); Evidence before the S.C. on the Shop Hours

Bill 1892 XVII Qs 4842–5181 and R.C. on
Labour 1893–4 XXXIX pt I Qs 1108–221;
Co-op. Congress Report (1899); J. T. Taylor,
*Jubilee History of the Oldham Industrial Co-
operative Society Ltd, 1850–1900* (Manchester,
1900); personal information: Education
Secretary, Oldham Industrial Co-operative
Society Ltd. Obit. *Co-op. News*, 4 Oct 1913;
Oldham Chronicle, 4 Oct 1913; *Co-op. News*, 11
and 18 Oct 1913.

H. F. Bing

See also: G. J. Holyoake, for Retail Co-
operation – Nineteenth Century; J. T. W.
Mitchell.

HARES, Edward Charles (1897–1966)
TRADE UNIONIST AND CO-OPERATOR

Edward Charles Hares was born at Wood-
borough, near Winscombe, Somerset, on
29 November 1897, the son of Albert Edward
Hares, a farm labourer. The family moved to
Charlton Kings, Gloucestershire, where at
the age of eight, Edward Hares attended the
village school. At thirteen he commenced
work with the Gloucester Co-operative
Society as a van boy on horse-drawn delivery.
After three years' service with the forces
during the First World War, he resumed
service with the Gloucester Society and from
1920 to 1937 was a horse delivery van driver.
In 1937 he became an agent for the Co-
operative Insurance Society and remained in
this employment till his retirement.

Hares took an interest in trade union
affairs from an early age and was for some
years a branch secretary of the Union of
Shop, Distributive and Allied Workers and
served on the South West District Council.

He was appointed a director of Gloucester
Co-operative Society in 1940, became vice-
president in 1956 and held this position till
his death. He served on the Western sectional
board of the Co-operative Union, the sectional wages board, the district council, the
district wages board and on the national
Conciliation Board. As a member of the
central executive of the Co-operative Union
(1956–66) and the General Purposes Committee, he served on many national trade
associations, having a particularly long connection with the dry-goods trade. A keen
supporter of the Co-operative Party, he was
for some years a member of the Party's
national executive.

He retired from the Co-operative Union
at Whitsun 1966 under the age rule. He was
a keen gardener and was rarely seen without
a flower adorning his buttonhole. He continued to live at Charlton Kings, which in
the meantime had become a part of the
borough of Cheltenham, until his death in
the Cheltenham General Hospital, after a
short illness, on 14 August 1966 at the age of
sixty-eight. He left a widow and one son; a
second son had been killed in war service.
For six years Mrs Hares had represented the
co-operative movement on Charlton Kings
Urban District Council. Hares left £1020 in
his will.

Sources: Personal information: L. M.
Jackson, Gloucester and Severnside Co-
operative Society Ltd; *Co-op. Congress Reports*
(1957–65). Obit. *Gloucestershire Echo*, 17 Aug
1966; *Co-op. News*, 3 Sep 1966; *Co-op. Congress
Report* (1966).

H. F. Bing

See also: A. Bonner, for Co-operation,
1945–70; Fred Hayward, for Co-operative
Union.

HARTSHORN, Vernon (1872–1931)
MINERS' LEADER AND LABOUR POLITICIAN

Born on 16 March 1872 at Cross Keys, near
Pont-y-waun, Monmouthshire, the son of
Theophilus Hartshorn, a miner, and his
wife Ellen (née Gregory), the daughter of a
farm labourer. He first worked in the mines
and then in a colliery office before becoming
a checkweighman at Risca; and in 1905 he
was appointed a full-time miners' agent at
Maesteg in Glamorgan. He was associated
early in his life with the Primitive Methodists
and he also became a vigorous propagandist
for the ILP. He proved to be an exceptionally
able miners' leader and his district was one
of the best organised in the South Wales
coalfield. After his appointment at Maesteg,
which became his home for the rest of his life,
Hartshorn joined with other militants in the

South Wales area in challenging the conservative and cautious leadership of Mabon (William Abraham) and his colleagues on the executive of the SWMF. It was this group – which included George Barker, Charles Stanton and James Winstone – which began to displace the established members of the executive after the Cambrian Combine strike of 1910–11 and especially after they were reinforced in the SWMF executive council in the early summer of 1911 by Noah Rees, with two other members of the Cambrian Strike Committee, and by Noah Ablett. When voting took place in the early autumn of 1911 for the South Wales representatives on the executive committee of the MFGB Hartshorn topped the poll, and together with Barker and Stanton, took the place of William Brace, Alfred Onions and Tom Richards. A year later the famous pamphlet *The Miners' Next Step* consolidated the opposition to the older leaders, but at the same time opened up a division between the older Socialists and the younger men of the Miners' Unofficial Reform Committee, whose views were linked with Tom Mann's propaganda of syndicalism. Hartshorn himself by the autumn of 1912 had become a known opponent to syndicalist ideas and policies.

The achievement of position soon began to modify Hartshorn's ideas and attitudes, and he fairly quickly evolved into a moderate, pragmatic leader. Hartshorn's next turning-point was during the First World War when he took a patriotic line, and he was bitterly opposed by certain of his former friends and colleagues among the militants, and in particular by Noah Ablett. Hartshorn's wartime activities included membership of the 1915 Home Office departmental committee on the wartime shortage of manpower in the mines due to (voluntary) over-enlistment (Coal Trade Organisation Committee) and the Coal Controller's Advisory Committee. By Prime Minister Lloyd George he was also appointed Labour representative on the Industrial Unrest Committee in South Wales. He continued to serve on the executive committee of the MFGB during the war years until November 1920 when he resigned from both the executive committees of the MFGB and the SWMF because of sharp differences over the tactics of the miners' strike of October 1920, on which Brace and Hartshorn were of one accord. Earlier in the previous year he had been one of the MFGB leaders to give evidence before the Sankey Commission and he spoke out strongly in the House of Commons against what he regarded as the betrayal of their promises to the miners by the Lloyd George Government. Hartshorn always had a flair for the presentation of detailed facts on the coal industry and his knowledge, as well as his competence as a negotiator, was widely recognised. When James Winstone died in 1921 Hartshorn was elected president of the SWMF (and thus returned to the executive of the MFGB) and he continued as president until he was offered a position in the MacDonald administration of 1924.

Hartshorn made two attempts to enter Parliament before he was finally elected in 1918. The first was as candidate for mid-Glamorgan in March 1910 when he was backed by an *ad hoc* committee representing trade councils, miners' lodges and ILP branches, and he contested the seat again in the general election of December 1910. His candidature as an independent Socialist was in sharp contrast with the position of the three officials of the SWMF (Abraham, Brace and Richards) who, although adopted as MFGB candidates, largely depended on the Liberal Party within their constituencies. Hartshorn's open letter in the by-election addressed to the Rev. Towyn Jones (one of the Liberal 'giants of the pulpit' with his Welsh *hwyl*) brought Hartshorn into national prominence. In the general election of 1918 he was returned unopposed for the Ogmore division of Glamorgan, and he retained this seat in all subsequent elections. He became a well-known speaker on mining questions in the House of Commons and in 1923 he became chairman of the Welsh Parliamentary Labour group. In the following year he became Postmaster-General in the minority Labour Government. In November 1927 he was asked by the Labour Party to join C. R. Attlee on the Indian Statutory Commission, headed by Sir John Simon, and before its work (greeted in India with hostile demonstrations, *hartals* and strikes) had been completed Ramsay MacDonald had formed his second administration. A government reshuffle in 1930 allowed Hartshorn to become Lord Privy Seal and then, a few months later, to take over responsibility for unemployment from J. H. Thomas. After only a few months in this new position he died suddenly at his Maesteg home on 13 March 1931. He had married Mary Matilda Winsor in 1899 and there were two sons and a daughter of the marriage. He left an estate valued at £2278 (£1988 net).

Writings: Articles in the *Western Mail* relating to the Welsh coal trade; Evidence before R.C. on Coal Industry (Sankey Commission) vol. 1 1919 XI Qs 9278-381; 9412-534.

Sources: Pall Mall Gazette Extra, *The New House of Commons* (1911); *Dod* (1912) and (1919); *WWW* (1929-40); *DNB* (1931-40); R. Page Arnot, *The Miners* (1949); idem, *The Miners: Years of Struggle* (1953); idem, *South Wales Miners 1898-1914* (1967); C. L. Mowat, *Britain Between the Wars* (1956); R. W. Lyman, *The First Labour Government* (1957); *Dictionary of Welsh Biography* (1959); K. O. Morgan, *Wales in British Politics 1868-1922* (1963). OBIT. *Times*, 14 Mar 1931; *Western Mail*, 14 Mar 1931; *Labour Mag. 9* no. 12 (Apr 1931) 531-3; *Labour Party Report* (1931).

JOYCE BELLAMY
JOHN SAVILLE

See also: William ABRAHAM, for Welsh Mining Trade Unionism; Thomas ASHTON, for Mining Trade Unionism, 1900-14; *A. J. COOK, for Mining Trade Unionism, 1915-26; Arthur HENDERSON, for Labour Party, 1914-31.

HARVEY, William Edwin (1852-1914)
MINERS' LEADER

Born on 5 September 1852 at Hasland, near Chesterfield, the youngest of a family of five children of James Harvey, a labourer, and his wife Elizabeth (née Gelsthorpe). His father died when he was still a child and his mother had to eke out a living by baking bread. Harvey was educated at the village Church day school and Primitive Methodist Sunday school and when he was ten years of age went to work at the pit. At the age of seventeen he heard a lecture on trade unionism which induced him to join the Hasland lodge of the South Yorkshire Miners' Association. He soon began to take an active and prominent part in the work of the lodge and when he was only twenty-one years old he was elected delegate to the Council meetings of the SYMA at Barnsley. This led to his dismissal by his employers and he found himself blacklisted and refused employment at every other colliery in the neighbourhood. He therefore moved to Sheepbridge where after about six years he again suffered because of his trade union activity and was obliged to move to Morton to obtain employment. Harvey was converted to Primitive Methodism, became a local preacher in his early twenties, and developed strong antipathies to the Established Church.

Harvey was one of the founders of the Derbyshire Miners' Association in 1880, becoming its part-time treasurer. In 1882 he relinquished this office because of difficulties with his employers who expected him to play in the colliery cricket team at the time when union meetings were held. In 1883 he was elected full-time assistant secretary. In 1906 he became financial and corresponding secretary and in 1913 general and financial secretary, an office which he held only for a short time until his death. Harvey was a member of the executive committee of the MFGB in 1891, 1893, 1895-7, 1899-1902, 1904, 1906, 1908 and 1910, and vice-president of the MFGB 1912-14.

In his early years Harvey was a fiery orator but in later life became more cautious and moderate, and was bitterly opposed to Syndicalism. When he was sent with Thomas Ashton to South Wales in 1911 to try to settle the dispute over abnormal places they were followed through the streets of Tonypandy with shouts of 'We want the 20th rule' (i.e. national support from the MFGB). In politics Harvey was a Liberal and became vice-president of the Labour Electoral Association in 1894. A classic expression of the standpoint of mining trade unions in the Midland counties towards political action, and also of the reasons for their adherence to the Liberal Party, was given by Harvey in a speech on 26 February 1889 (reported fully in the *Ilkeston Advertiser* four days later) in reply to a Conservative candidate's speech a month earlier which implied 'that the business of trade unionists was to look solely and entirely to trade matters and not to interfere, either by voice, vote, or anything else, with legislative enactments'. Harvey said:

My reply was that we could not separate politics from trade unions – (hear, hear) – that their history taught us it was by legislation they were made legal, their funds protected by law, and security given to workmen of all trades; that combination punishable by law in the past involving untold suffering, imprisonment and privations by such heroes as the six Dorsetshire labourers, Ernest Jones, etc. has been legalised by law, and that by a Liberal Government, led by the Right Hon. Wm Ewart Gladstone. (Loud cheers)

Harvey then referred to the rejection by the House of Lords of the County Franchise Bill and said:

The country was indignant, large meetings and demonstrations were held all over the country, until the House of Lords, fearing its existence was in jeopardy, gave way and the great emancipation bill was carried safely through by the greatest of all statesmen, W. E. Gladstone (renewed cheers). Now, Sir, I think I have proved that our liberties have come from the Liberal party, and that is why I am found supporting them and not because I am subsidised. (Hear, hear)

Harvey was highly critical of the Independent Labour Party and of Socialism and in 1897 refused to speak from the same platform as Keir Hardie. On all the difficult questions confronting the miners, Harvey took broadly the same position as Ben Pickard, being in favour of the legislative establishment of the eight-hour day and against the sliding scales. Both men opposed

the establishment of the LRC in 1900; and the Derbyshire Miners' Association voted consistently against the affiliation of the MFGB to the Labour Party. In 1907 he was elected MP for North-East Derbyshire, defeating Dr J. Court, and held the seat until his death in 1914.

Harvey played a prominent part in local affairs in Derbyshire. He was a JP on the Ilkestone Bench, 1893–1914; member of the Chesterfield Borough Council, 1897–1914, of the Chesterfield School Board, 1895–1903, and of the Chesterfield Education Committee, 1903–14. In 1894 he became president of the Chesterfield Trades Council.

He married in 1874 and died at his Chesterfield home on 28 April 1914 leaving a son, his wife having predeceased him. After a memorial service at Mount Zion Primitive Methodist Chapel at Brampton, he was buried at Chesterfield General Cemetery. He left an estate valued at £4966 (net).

Sources: (1) MSS: Minutes of the Derbyshire Miners' Association, 1880–1914 (NUM, Saltergate, Chesterfield); (2) Printed: *Minutes of the Miners' Federation of Great Britain*, 1890–1914; W. Hallam, *Miners' Leaders* (1894); *Parliamentary Debates*, 1907–14; *WW* (1913); (3) Secondary: R. Page Arnot, *The Miners* (1949); H. Pelling, *The Origins of the Labour Party, 1880–1914* (1954); R. F. Wearmouth, *The Social and Political Influence of Methodism in the Twentieth Century* (1957); J. E. Williams, 'The Political Activities of a Trade Union, 1906–14', *Int. Rev. Social Hist.* 2 (1957) 1–21; idem, *The Derbyshire Miners* (1962). OBIT. *Times*, 29 Apr 1914; *Derbyshire Times*, 2 May 1914.

J. E. WILLIAMS

See also: Benjamin PICKARD, for Mining Trade Unionism, 1880–99; Thomas ASHTON, for Mining Trade Unionism, 1900–14; Josiah COURT.

HASLAM, James (1842–1913)
MINERS' LEADER

Born on 1 April 1842 at Clay Cross, Derbyshire, the son of Thomas Haslam, a shoemaker, and his wife Mary (née Whaley), and the youngest of a family of ten children. After a meagre education at the Stable School, Clay Cross, he began work on the pit brow at the age of ten earning 10d for a twelve-hour day. When he was sixteen he began work in the pit and during the next twenty-nine years passed through all the different branches of mine work, until he left to become full-time secretary of the Derbyshire Miners' Association in 1881. For a number of years before this he had been interested in trade union activities, becoming secretary of the Clay Cross lodge of the South Yorkshire Miners' Association in October 1875. He continued in this office until October 1879 when the Derbyshire miners broke away from the South Yorkshire Association. Haslam saw the necessity of an independent county organisation, was one of the founders of the Derbyshire Miners' Association in 1880 and was initially part-time secretary. From his appointment as full-time secretary in the following year until his death in 1913 he served the Derbyshire miners in this capacity.

Haslam was a moderate trade union leader, disliking extreme militancy. He was once described as 'a typical trades unionist of the old school . . . more akin in character and personality to Mr Burt than to any other Labour representative in the House . . . as much respected among the colliery officials and employers in Derbyshire as among the miners'. Haslam was called upon to resign along with the other Derbyshire officials on more than one occasion when opposition to the union's leadership began to develop as part of the general tide of industrial unrest from about 1909. In his presidential address to the TUC in 1910 he protested against indiscipline and stressed its injury to collective bargaining. He was opposed to the 1912 coal strike and the six months of national negotiations in which he participated, in spite of failing health and against medical advice, are thought to have hastened his death.

As a member of the central board of the Miners' National Union from 1884, Haslam was reluctant to join the more militant MFGB formed in 1889. However, when the Derbyshire Miners' Association severed its connection with the National Union in 1890 Haslam resigned his seat on the central board and loyally played his part in the Federation. In 1891, as a representative of the Federation, he gave evidence before the Royal Commission on Mining Royalties. He was a member of the executive committee of the MFGB, 1892, 1894–6, 1898, 1900, 1901, 1903, 1905, 1907, 1909 and 1911. In 1890 he represented his county union at the first International Miners' Congress at Jolimont in Belgium, and the next year, representing not Derbyshire but the MFGB, he was a delegate to the International Congress in Paris. In the debate on the question of an international strike to achieve the eight-hour day Hallam quoted the result of the ballot in his own union which voted 95 per cent for a strike; and the stormy debate which followed took up the greater part of the time of the Congress [Arnot (1949) 162ff].

In 1885 Haslam tried unsuccessfully to win the Liberal nomination for Chesterfield, and he went on to contest the seat as an Independent (Liberal Radical) in opposition to the official Liberal and Conservative candidates. He came third. In 1906 he was adopted by the Liberals as the Lib-Lab candidate, and was elected. His candidature had been endorsed by the TUC. In the House of Commons after 1906 Haslam was one of the nine members of the TUC Parliamentary Committee who were also MPs, six of whom had stood under the auspices of the LRC. Haslam retained his seat until his death in 1913. He fought vigorously against the affiliation of the MFGB to the Labour Party and in 1908, when the ballot vote on the question of joining had resulted in a relatively small majority in favour – with Durham not participating in the ballot – Haslam brought forward the following resolution:

That in view of the fact that the number of votes against joining the LRC, together with the number of members of the Federation who did not vote at all, far exceeds the number in favour of joining, this Conference is of opinion that another ballot should be taken, and that nothing less than a two-third membership vote be permitted to finally settle this question.

Conference defeated the resolution by 391,000 votes to 97,000. In the following year, 1909, Haslam was elected chairman of the parliamentary committee of the TUC.

A Primitive Methodist, he remembered with pride the days when the so-called 'Ranters' used to sing and shout through the streets of Clay Cross. Haslam was a member of the Clay Cross School Board and the Chesterfield Board of Guardians and was also active in other local spheres: as a JP for Chesterfield, 1893–1913, on the Chesterfield Borough Council, 1896–1913, and on the Education Committee of the Council from 1903 to 1913. He died on 31 July 1913 and left estate to the net value of £1941.

Sources: (1) MSS: Minutes of the Derbyshire Miners' Association, 1880–1913 (NUM, Saltergate, Chesterfield); (2) Printed: *Minutes of Miners' Federation of Great Britain,* 1890–1913; *Derbyshire Times,* 1880–1913; *Minutes of Evidence,* R.C. on Mining Royalties 1890–1 XLI Qs 8117–242; *Parliamentary Debates,* 1906–13; *TUC Report* (1910); (3) Secondary: W. Hallam, *Miners' Leaders* (1894); R. C. K. Ensor, *England, 1870–1914* (1936); R. Page Arnot, *The Miners* (1949); R. F. Wearmouth, *The Social and Political Influence of Methodism in the Twentieth Century* (1957); J. E. Williams, 'The Political Activities of a Trade Union, 1906–14', *Int. Rev. Social Hist.* 2 (1957) 1–21; idem, *The Derbyshire Miners* (1962). OBIT. *Times,* 1 Aug 1913; *Derbyshire Times,* 2 Aug 1913; *Derby Mercury,* 8 Aug 1913.

J. E. WILLIAMS

See also: Thomas ASHTON, for Mining Trade Unionism, 1900–14; W. E. HARVEY; Alexander MACDONALD, for Mining Trade Unionism, 1850–79; Benjamin PICKARD, for Mining Trade Unionism, 1880–99.

HASLAM, James (1869–1937)
CO-OPERATIVE AUTHOR AND JOURNALIST

James Haslam was born in the Gate Pike district of Bolton in 1869 into a family of handloom weavers (according to his own

entry in *Who's Who* (1930)), but it has not been possible to establish his actual date of birth. Educated initially at an elementary school, at the age of eight he worked part-time at a rope walk and then in a cotton mill as a little piecer. He also sold newspapers in the streets. He later gave up his newspaper work to attend evening classes at the Manchester Technical College and taught himself shorthand, some French and Latin. Fired with enthusiasm for working-class Socialism in its early days he attended street corner debates and demonstrations, and when the little piecers tried to organise themselves he was their first honorary secretary. In this activity he came into contact with Allen Clarke, the Lancashire dialect poet and novelist, and with him and J. R. Clynes attempted unsuccessfully to form a Lancashire Cotton Piecers' Association. He ruined his industrial prospects by this action and at the age of twenty-three left the mill for journalism when Clarke found him a job on a labour weekly – *The Labour Light* – but this failed.

He then joined Clarke on a local satirical weekly which ran for three years and he also contributed to the *Cotton Factory Times,* the organ of the Lancashire cotton trade unions, and the *Clarion.* In the following two years he worked for the *Hyde Reporter, Bolton Evening Echo,* and *Blackpool Gazette and News*; then rejoined Clarke in running the *Northern Weekly* and other papers. The *Northern Weekly* nearly failed during a cotton strike and Haslam secured a vacancy on the *Liverpool Courier* and *Liverpool Evening Express* and began to contribute to London and Manchester papers. After six and a half years in Liverpool, he came to Manchester in 1906 where he edited a textile journal for a year, then became a freelance, contributing to Manchester, Liverpool and London papers, including the *Manchester Guardian, Liverpool Weekly Post, Clarion* and *Labour Leader.* He also compiled some local co-operative histories, wrote articles for special publications on social and industrial questions, and also on Lancashire customs and traditions. His novel, *The Hand-Loom Weaver's Daughter,* published in 1904, was based on his firsthand knowledge of the Lancashire cotton industry.

He fought consistently to improve the pay and conditions of journalists, and he helped to form the National Union of Journalists, of which he was president in 1919, a member of its executive for nearly twenty years and from 1924 until 1937 editor of its own organ, *The Journalist*. In 1915 he had joined the staff of the *Co-operative News* as Special Commissioner and in 1916 was appointed by the CWS, along with W. H. Brown, to form a journalistic section and develop CWS publications. He helped to found the monthly trade and business journal of the movement, *The Producer* (1916 onwards), and in 1926 the three publicity sections of the CWS were organised into one department under his management. He was at his best in the editorial chair with his wide knowledge, cosmopolitan outlook, low-pitched voice and easy command and flow of English. He continued this work in the CWS until retirement in 1933, after which he returned for a short time to the *Cotton Factory Times* as editor.

For many years a member of the Manchester Press Club and the Newspaper Press Fund, he served the former as president and the latter as chairman. After his retirement from the CWS he continued to write as a freelance, especially for co-operative periodicals, but a severe illness in 1937 compelled him to give up work, leave Manchester and retire to St Anne's where he died on 8 October 1937. He was survived by his wife, whom he married in 1899, and a son, Graham, who was also a journalist.

Writings: *The Handloom Weaver's Daughter* (1904); *The Press and the People: an estimate of reading in working-class districts*, reprinted from *Manchester City News* (Manchester, 1906) 20 pp.; *Eccles Provident Industrial Co-operative Society Ltd: history of fifty years' progress 1857–1907* (Manchester, 1907); *Cotton and Competition: striking facts and figures* [1909] 11 pp.; [Accrington and Church Industrial Co-operative Society Ltd.] *History of Fifty Years' Progress: a souvenir in commemoration of the society's jubilee 1860–1910* (Manchester, [1910]); *Woolfold Co-operative Society Ltd Bury: history of fifty years' progress 1865–1915* (Manchester, 1915); 'Women in Industry', *CWS Annual* (1915) 419–48; 'Co-operation and Economic Control', *Labour Mag. 2* (June 1923) 59–61; 'Japan's Rise to Industrial Power', *People's Year Book* (1934) 133–7 and innumerable articles in co-operative and other periodicals and newspapers.

Sources: *Journalist 3* no. 1 (May 1919); *Ourselves* (CWS House Journal: Feb 1929); *WW* (1930); P. Redfern, *The New History of the C.W.S.* (Manchester, 1938); *WWW* (1920–40). OBIT. *Liverpool Echo*, 8 Oct 1937; *Times*, 9 Oct 1937; *Journalist* (Nov 1937) 188.

JOYCE BELLAMY
H. F. BING

See also: W. H. BROWN, for Retail Co-operation, 1900–45; Percy REDFERN, for Co-operative Wholesaling.

HAWKINS, George (1844–1908)
CO-OPERATOR AND TRADE UNIONIST

Born on 13 January 1844 at Hertingford-bury, a village near Hertford, the son of James Hawkins, a miller, who was a Chartist. George was apprenticed to the famous printing firm of Stephen Austin and Sons in Hertford. He married in 1866 and in the same year joined the local co-operative society which, however, soon failed. In 1872 he moved to Oxford as Oriental compositor at the University Press, at that time the largest industrial employer in the town. The local Co-operative Society was founded in the same year and Hawkins immediately joined, being elected to the committee of management two years later. In 1879 he became president, helped to carry the Society through a serious financial crisis in 1881–2, but resigned the presidency in January 1883 because of the unpopularity of some of his decisions. He was re-elected a year later, in January 1884, and continued in the position until 1889 when he resigned owing to increasing CWS duties.

In 1875 he was appointed secretary of the Oxford district of the Co-operative Union, a post he continued to occupy until a few years before his death. In 1881 he was elected a member of the southern sectional board of the Union but retired from this post after one year. In 1885 he was elected a member of the committee of the London branch of the Co-operative Wholesale Society and subsequently became its chairman, retaining this office until his retirement in 1905. He had a wonderful grasp of detail in all matters relating to the CWS and was an exceedingly popular chairman on account of his wisdom and sense of humour. He was one of the clearest, most vigorous and most incisive speakers in the co-operative movement and was at his best when presiding over the quarterly meetings of the CWS in London. At the official opening of the new Leman Street premises in 1887 he presided over a distinguished company which included the Rev. (later Canon) Barnett of Toynbee Hall, E. V. Neale, G. J. Holyoake, J. C. Gray and E. O. Greening. In October 1891, along with J. T. W. Mitchell (chairman of the CWS), he attended the opening of the Cardiff branch of the CWS, and in December 1892 he was present at the coming-of-age celebrations of the Newcastle branch. In April 1895 he presided over a meeting and luncheon to celebrate the growth of the London branch of the CWS which in twenty years (1875–95) had increased its share of the total CWS trade from one-twentieth to one-seventh. His enforced retirement due to ill-health, in the latter part of 1905, was marked by a presentation subscribed to him by the staff at Leman Street. In reply, Hawkins said that he ever liked to be in the forefront of the co-operative fight, believing that fight to be one which, above all others, made for the progress and welfare of the people at large. He presided for the first day over the Co-operative Congress at Bristol in 1893 and was president of the Exeter Congress in 1902.

From the days of his apprenticeship Hawkins was an energetic and ardent trade unionist. His work for the Typographical Association did much to strengthen the Oxford branch, of which he served several terms as president. For some twenty years he was 'Father of the Chapel' at the University Press, where between 500 and 600 workers were employed at the end of the century. He took an active part in the development of social and educational facilities for the University Press employees, being chairman

of the first Council of the Institute built in 1893 to further these purposes. In 1890 he was a founder-member of the Oxford Trades Council, and later became president, and in the same year he was elected as a Liberal Councillor for West Ward, serving for three years. At the end of his term of office on the City Council he was appointed a JP, probably the first Oxford working man to be elected to the Bench.

Hawkins was a remarkable personality with never-failing high spirits and abundant cheerfulness. In all his activities he was greatly helped by his wife, who was also an enthusiastic co-operator. In religion he was a staunch Anglican and for many years he had acted as sidesman at the church of St Philip and St James until the daughter parish of St Margaret was founded. He died at his Oxford home on Sunday 22 March 1908. The first part of the funeral service was conducted at St Margaret's, and he was buried in St Sepulchre's Cemetery, off Walton Street. He left effects valued at £350.

Sources: *Handbook of Co-operative Congress and Guide to Bristol, 1893* (Bristol, 1893); *Souvenir Handbook of the Co-operative Congress at Exeter* (1902); *Co-op. Congress Report* (1902); P. Redfern, *The Story of the C.W.S.* (Manchester, [1913]); *The Clarendonian* (Jan 1919 and Jan 1926 – photograph); *Oxford and District Co-operative Society Ltd: 1872–1947* (1947); biographical information: Education Secretary, Oxford Co-operative Society; Oxford University Press. Obit. *Co-op. News*, 28 Mar 1908.

H. F. BING
JOHN SAVILLE

See also: Percy REDFERN, for Co-operative Wholesaling.

HAYHURST, George (1862–1936)
CO-OPERATOR

Born at Accrington, Lancashire, on 25 September 1862, the son of Hargreaves Hayhurst, an innkeeper, George Hayhurst was left fatherless at the age of fifteen months, and youngest of six children. His early education was at Antley day school and at the age of eight he started work half-time in a cotton mill as a 'reacher', later becoming a 'taper'. He extended his education by attending evening classes and subsequently entered the office of a brickworks where he rose to be secretary of the company. He early became interested in the co-operative movement and was elected to the education committee of the Accrington and Church Co-operative Society at the age of twenty-one; served on the management committee from 1889 to 1907, and was president 1906–7. He was a leading figure in the North East Lancashire District Conference Association and a member of the central board of the Co-operative Union, 1901–8.

He was elected to the board of the Co-operative Wholesale Society in 1907 and remained a member till his retirement under the age rule in 1931. He served on the finance committee and on the committee of the health insurance section. He was a director of the Co-operative Insurance Society and its chairman in 1921, chairman of the English and Scottish Joint CWS, 1921–31, and represented the CWS on the British Cotton Growing Association, the Royal Commission on Decimal Coinage and the Government Committee for Safeguarding Industry. In 1914 he was a member of the committee on CWS auditors' duties and status. In 1919 he he was one of four CWS directors on a committee to inquire into a pensions scheme for all co-operative employees. In 1927 he was appointed, together with W. R. Blair and Sir Thomas Allen, by the finance committee of the CWS to consider the wider diffusion of knowledge of the relation of production and distribution to the masses of consumers. Their report (November 1927) led to a programme for publicity for the principles of consumers' co-operation which included the publication of twenty-four *Self and Society* booklets by prominent authors published by Ernest Benn Ltd, the penny *People's Papers*, and a short history of the CWS, *Told in Brief*, etc. George Hayhurst was opposed to the growing tariff policies of the early 1930s and was one of a committee of three, under the Safeguarding of Industries Act, who presented a minority report against a duty on pottery.

His interests in local affairs included the initiation of a land-owning scheme which enabled local co-operative societies to acquire the Stanhill estate on which the Stanhill Ring Mill Company, the North East Lancashire Laundries and the Co-operative Dairies were erected. He was an originator of the Accrington Mill Building Co., serving for a time as joint secretary and afterwards as a director. A Wesleyan Methodist, he had a lifelong connection with Antley Chapel and school, and was closely associated with many other local organisations in Accrington including the Accrington Industrial Development Council, and the Accrington Stanley Football Club. In 1919 he was made a JP of the town. After a short illness he died on 17 November 1936, being survived by a son, Mr W. Hayhurst.

Sources: J. Haslam, *History of Fifty Years' Progress* [Accrington and Church Industrial Co-operative Society Limited]: *a souvenir in commemoration of the Society's jubilee, 1860–1910* (Manchester, 1910); P. Redfern, *The New History of the C.W.S.* (Manchester, 1938). OBIT. *Accrington Observer and Times*, 21 Nov 1936; *Co-op. Congress Report* (1937).

H. F. BING

See also: Thomas ALLEN; W. R. BLAIR; Percy REDFERN, for Co-operative Wholesalnig.

HAYWARD, Sir Fred (1876–1944)
CO-OPERATOR

Fred Hayward was born in Burslem on 19 February 1876. He was the son of James Hayward, a potter, who for many years was a prominent member of the executive of the Pottery Workers' Society and a director of the Star Mutual Building Society. Before he was a year old Fred's parents moved to Tunstall where he spent his early life. He attended the Central Board School, Tunstall, became a half-time jigger-turner in a local pottery at the age of ten and at twelve left school altogether. After working for two and a half years in a clothing shop, he returned to the pottery trade as an apprentice biscuit placer and remained in it till 1904.

He was one of the founders of the Burslem Co-operative Society in 1901, became its first part-time secretary, 1902–6, full-time secretary, 1906–20, and managing secretary from 1920 until his resignation on health grounds in 1935. The Society had made great progress under his leadership and after his resignation retained his services in an advisory capacity. When he became managing secretary in 1920 the Society was one of the ten largest in the country.

In 1911 Fred Hayward was elected to the executive of the Macclesfield, Crewe and District Conference Association of the Co-operative Union; in 1915 he was elected to the north-western sectional board and, from that time on, the Co-operative Union was, in his own words, 'practically all my life'. He was elected to the central board of the Co-operative Union in 1915 and was chairman 1918–19, 1920–1 and from 1924 to 1932 when the new constitution of the Co-operative Union, which as chairman of the committee of inquiry into the constitution of the Union he had helped to frame, came into operation. Almost as a matter of course he was appointed chairman of the new national authority and of the national executive and occupied these offices until he retired in 1944. He was president of the Carlisle Congress in 1919 and of the special Congress at Blackpool in 1920 called to consider the report of the General Co-operative Survey Committee (1914–19). As chairman of the central board, he was *ex officio* president of the annual congress for a number of years and was elected president of the Edinburgh Congress in 1941, such a second presidency being unique in co-operative history.

He was elected to the joint parliamentary committee of the Co-operative Union in 1922, became its chairman in 1927 and retained this office until he retired from the committee in 1942. He led the campaign against what he regarded as the unjust imposition of income tax on co-operative societies and presided over a special national conference on this issue in London in 1933. He travelled all over the country addressing meetings, frequently interviewing officials of the Treasury and giving evidence before the Raeburn Committee of 1932–3 on the taxation of co-operative societies. At various times he served as chairman of the Co-operative Milk Trade Association and of the Co-operative Meat Trade Association and was chairman of a committee of inquiry into the constitution of the CWS (1921).

He was always interested in the international side of the co-operative movement. In 1927 he was elected to the central committee of the International Co-operative Alliance and in 1931 became a member of its executive. In 1934 he welcomed the ICA Congress when it met in London. In 1936 he and his wife, together with A. V. Alexander MP and Mrs Alexander, attended the Conference of the Institute of Pacific Relations in California and addressed a large gathering of co-operators at Los Angeles. During the Spanish Civil War (1936–9) he helped establish a special fund to send milk to undernourished child war-victims. One of his last public acts was to urge the creation of a freedom fund to help continental co-operators in Nazi-occupied territories when their countries were liberated. This appeal was launched by the Co-operative Union in March 1943 and became part of a world-wide appeal for relief and rehabilitation sponsored by the International Co-operative Alliance. Treasury currency restrictions and food control immediately after the war placed obstacles on the immediate utilisation of the fund. However, as a result of the fund, France secured £50,000 and Belgium, the Netherlands, Poland and Yugoslavia £35,000 each in value (some of the help being in kind). In this way the co-operative movements in Europe were more easily able to resume normal activity, and the balance of the British fund was passed to the ICA Development Fund for assisting the newly-emerging countries.

Although Fred Hayward described the co-operative movement as practically all his life, he found time for much other public work. He was a member of the Wolstanton and Burslem Board of Guardians (1904–10) and a prime mover in the transfer of children from the workhouse to scattered homes. He was first chairman of the scattered homes committee. He worked for the federation of the pottery towns and when this was accom-

plished by the establishment of the new
Stoke-on-Trent County Borough Council in
1910 he was elected a member of that Council and served continuously for twenty years.
In 1913 he was elected an alderman at the
age of thirty-seven and in 1919 he was made
a JP, and often presided over the Burslem
court. For a time he was chairman of the
Labour group on the Council. In 1925 he
was appointed chairman of the overseers of
the city and in the same year was chosen
Lord Mayor of Stoke-on-Trent. Among his
great services to the city of Stoke was in the
sphere of finance. First appointed as chairman of the finance committee in 1928, he
held this position until 1932 and again in
1934–5. He was a member of the Coal Mines
National Industrial Board established under
the Coal Mines Act (1930), received a knighthood in the birthday honours list of 1931 and
in 1933 was admitted a freeman of the city
of Stoke.

Sir Fred Hayward suffered much in his
last years. In 1940 he had a leg amputated
and in 1942 he became blind, but in spite of
these handicaps, he continued much of his
activity. In this, as throughout his life, he
was much helped by his wife (formerly Miss
Mary Hudson) whom he married in 1900.
Lady Hayward was devoted to public work,
especially in connection with the Board of
Guardians and charitable institutions. Fred
Hayward died on 19 November 1944 and
was cremated at Carmountside Crematorium, Stoke-on-Trent, on 21 December.
He left an estate valued at £5417.

Writings: *The Co-operative Boycott and its
Political Implications* (Manchester, [1930])
16 pp.; *Should Co-operative Societies pay Income
Tax on the Amount returned to Members as
Dividend?* (n.d.) 12 pp.

Sources: *Co-op. Congress Reports* (1919) and
(1941); *Kelly* (1938); *Co-op. News*, 3 June
1944; Co-operative Press records, Manchester; Co-operative Union Library, Manchester; personal information: North Midland Co-operative Society, Burslem. Obit.
Evening Standard [Stoke], 19 Dec 1944; *Co-op.
News*, 23 Dec 1944; *Co-op. Congress Report*
(1945).
H. F. BING

See also: W. H. BROWN, for Retail Co-
operation, 1900–45; H. J. MAY, for International Co-operative Alliance; Percy RED-
FERN, for Co-operative Wholesaling; and
below: Co-operative Union.

Co-operative Union: E. V. Neale, 'The
most Efficient and Practical Plan of arranging the Powers and Duties of the Central
Board', *Co-op. Congress Report* (1873) 15–19;
J. Borrowman, R. Kyle, and E. V. Neale,
'The Co-operative Union: its work, duties
and machinery', *Co-op. Congress Report* (1879)
12–18; E. V. Neale, *Central Co-operative
Board: its history, constitution and use* (1880);
Anon., *The Central Board: its use, work and
cost* (1885) 15 pp.; J. Allan, *The Co-operative
Union: its necessity and its advantages* (Manchester, 1893) 20 pp.; C. Webb, *The Machin-
ery of the Co-operative Movement* (Manchester,
1896) 18 pp.; D. McInnes, *Contributions to the
Co-operative Union* (Manchester, 1909) 12 pp.;
H. J. May, *The Co-operative Union Ltd: its
scope and methods of district work* (Manchester,
1910) 12 pp.; C. Webb, 'The Machinery of
the Co-operative Movement', *Co-operation 2*
(Sep 1910) 17–19; (Oct 1910) 28–9; (Nov
1910) 17–19; W. R. Rae, 'The Co-operative
Union and the Unification of its Forces',
Co-op. Congress Report (1912) 441–60; G.
Goodenough, *The Central Board and the Grant
to the Women's Co-operative Guild* (Manchester,
1914) 16 pp.; Anon., *The Women's Guild and
the Co-operative Union Grant* (Manchester,
1915) 8 pp.; D. McInnes, *The Co-operative
Union: its importance to the movement* (Manchester, 1915) 12 pp.; S. and B. Webb, *The
Consumers' Co-operative Movement* (1921); G. E.
Griffiths, 'The Structure and Organisation
of the Co-operative Movement: I Great
Britain', *RIC* (Feb 1929) 50–7; E. Topham,
*Your Co-operative Union: what it does for the
movement and its members* (2nd rev. ed. 1933)
23 pp.; F. Hall and W. P. Watkins, *Co-opera-
tion: a survey of the history, principles and
organisation of the co-operative movement in Great
Britain and Ireland* (Manchester, 1934);
A. M. Carr-Saunders, P. S. Florence, R.
Peers et al., *Consumers' Co-operation in Great
Britain: an examination of the British co-operative
movement* (1938; rev. ed. 1942); G. D. H.
Cole, *A Century of Co-operation* (Manchester,

[1945?]); G. L. Perkins, 'The Co-operative Union's Future Services', *People's Year Book* (1945) 20–45; R. Southern, 'The Co-operative Union and the Future', *People's Year Book* (1949) 13; A. Bonner, *British Co-operation* (Manchester, 1961); D. Flanagan, *A Centenary Story of the Co-operative Union of Great Britain and Ireland: 1869–1969* (Manchester, 1969); Co-operative Union, *Report on integration of the Co-operative Wholesale Society and the Co-operative Union* (Manchester, 1970) 45 pp.

HENDERSON, Arthur (1863–1935)
TRADE UNIONIST AND LABOUR PARTY LEADER

Born on 13 September 1863, Arthur Henderson was the son of David Henderson, a Glasgow labourer who died when the boy was nine. His mother remarried and the family moved to Newcastle, where Arthur attended St Mary's School until he was twelve, when he was apprenticed as an iron-moulder. At sixteen he was converted to Wesleyan Methodism, in which faith he remained all his life, becoming in later years a well-known lay preacher.

In 1883 he joined the Friendly Society of Iron-Founders and was soon secretary of his local lodge, and this was the beginning of his long career in the movement. In 1892 he was appointed district delegate, covering Northumberland, Durham and Lancashire. From his early days in the trade union movement Henderson was a man of moderation. He always strongly upheld methods of conciliation and arbitration in industrial disputes, and he became the first secretary of the North-Eastern Conciliation Board in 1894, the establishment of which he had long supported. In the same year he attended his first Trades Union Congress, at Norwich. His political ideas matched his attitudes to trade union problems. He was a Liberal with moderate radical inclinations, and in 1893 was elected to the Newcastle City Council on the Liberal ticket. Two years later he was selected by the Newcastle Liberal Party executive to stand in the Liberal interest in the 1895 general election; but the decision was overruled, largely because of opposition

to a working-class candidate. The incident made a considerable impression upon Henderson himself and must be rated as one of the factors responsible, in the long term, for moving him towards acceptance of independent labour representation. But this was some years in the future, and in 1896 he accepted the full-time position of Liberal agent to Sir Joseph Pease, MP for Barnard Castle. On this appointment Henderson and his family moved to Darlington, where he became involved immediately in local politics, being elected to the Durham County Council in 1897, and to the local Darlington Council in the following year. He became mayor of his town in 1903.

There was some criticism of Henderson from within his own trade union for his Liberal politics, and especially for the fact that he worked politically for an employer. Henderson, however, supported the affiliation of the Foundry Workers to the Labour Representation Committee, and when in 1903 the union agreed to finance parliamentary candidates, Henderson was elected top of the list with instructions to contest Barnard Castle. The sitting member died in 1903; and although Henderson was still Liberal agent, he refused to stand as the Liberal candidate, but fought under the auspices of the LRC. He won the seat with a majority of forty-seven.

On entering the House of Commons Henderson began the practice of writing monthly accounts of parliamentary developments for the Foundry Workers' *Report*; and he continued these almost to his death. He became treasurer of the LRC, worked with Sir Charles Dilke and Gertrude Tuckwell on behalf of shop assistants, gradually accepted the principle of minimum-wage legislation and became a socialist of the Fabian persuasion. He also vigorously supported the Women's Trade Union League, and became first honorary treasurer of the British section of the International Association for Labour Legislation.

In the 1906 general election he was again returned for Barnard Castle, with an increased majority, and the family moved to Clapham Park, London, where Henderson lived for the rest of his life. He was appointed

Chief Whip to the Parliamentary LP, in 1908 succeeded Keir Hardie as parliamentary leader, and in 1911 was mainly responsible for persuading the PLP to accept J. Ramsay MacDonald as leader, with Henderson himself as general secretary. MacDonald also became treasurer, and at the 1912 LP Conference Henderson successfully proposed an important constitutional change whereby the treasurer was elected by the Conference and not by the executive. During the years before 1914 Henderson was a strong supporter of the moderate group of the women's suffrage movement, and in addition to his parliamentary and temperance work, he continued to be deeply involved in trade union activities, being elected president of the Foundry Workers in 1910.

As general secretary of the LP from 1911 Henderson began slowly to develop international contacts. His first visit abroad was in 1912 (when the familiar mode of addressing him, 'Uncle Arthur', was first used). With the outbreak of war in August 1914 he took a patriotic line, supporting the LP's participation in recruiting campaigns – a cause in which he himself became very active and for which he was made privy councillor in January 1915. He became chairman of the important War Emergency Workers' National Committee on which sat, among others, Robert Smillie, J. A. Seddon, W. C. Anderson, William Brace, J. R. MacDonald, Sidney Webb, Mary Macarthur and H. M. Hyndman. The aims of the committee were to study, and where possible to take action on, the effects of the war on working-class living standards. Henderson's most effective colleague, with whom he became very close, was Sidney Webb. In May 1915 Asquith invited Henderson to become a member of the Liberal Cabinet, junior posts being offered to G. H. Roberts and William Brace. After much controversy a majority of the PLP and the national executive agreed, and Henderson became president of the Board of Education. It was an unpopular decision with important sections of the labour movement, especially the ILP, and after mounting pressures, Henderson resigned in August 1916 and accepted the nominal position of Paymaster-General in

order to become full-time adviser on labour questions to the Cabinet. When the Government was reorganised in December 1916, with Lloyd George as Prime Minister, Henderson, supported by the LP executive and later by the LP Conference, entered the War Cabinet. Opposition to him personally, and to Labour's participation in the Government in general, grew steadily, especially among rank and file trade unionists. After the March 1917 Revolution, Henderson went on an official mission to Russia, the main purpose of which was to persuade Russia to stay in the war. Soon after he returned from his six weeks' visit he resigned from the Government, on 11 August 1917, over the question of the Stockholm Conference; and henceforth devoted all his energies to the building of the LP organisation and elaboration of its post-war policies. In January 1918 there was published *Labour and the New Social Order* (drafted by Sidney Webb); in February 1918 the *War Aims Memorandum* (Henderson, J. R. MacDonald and Sidney Webb); and in two conferences, January and February 1918, Henderson persuaded the LP to adopt a revised constitution, with a Socialist statement of aims, including the famous Clause Four on common ownership, and with provision for individual membership on a constituency basis.

Henderson stood for East Ham South, in East London, in the general election of December 1918, and was heavily defeated; but was elected for the Widnes division in August 1919. He took a leading part in the Berne International Socialist Conference in February 1919, and was elected one of its four vice-presidents. He was chairman of the LP commission of inquiry on Ireland which reported to a special conference on 29 December 1920. He took the initiative on the LP executive in rejecting the application of the Communist Party to affiliate to the Labour Party in 1920, and vigorously defended the decision at the LP Conference in 1921; and he remained an unswerving opponent of the British CP for the rest of his career. His main work, in the immediate post-war years, between 1918 and 1922, was in building and extending the LP organisation, and in this he was remarkably successful.

He was defeated at Widnes in the 1922 general election, when the LP increased its seats to 142, with four and a quarter million votes; but he campaigned vigorously for MacDonald as parliamentary leader. On 18 January 1923 he won a by-election at East Newcastle, but was again defeated at the general election of December 1923 when the LP won 191 seats and took office for the first time as a minority government. Henderson became Home Secretary and returned to the Commons after a successful by-election at Burnley on 28 February 1924. His career at the Home Office was unremarkable. With MacDonald and Snowden he represented the UK at the London International Conference, July–August 1924, and he was the leading member of the British delegation to the League of Nations, autumn of 1924. He was not consulted by MacDonald over the dissolution of Parliament on 9 October 1924, and in the subsequent general election, in which the Zinoviev letter played an important part, Labour's representation fell to 161. Henderson held his seat at Burnley with a reduced majority, and he became the Labour chief whip in the new House of Commons. He continued to give MacDonald his loyalty in the face of many attacks on the latter from the left wing of the movement. He made an extensive tour of Empire countries in 1926, and his political interests became increasingly international. He had maintained his close involvement with the reconstituted Second International and was voted chairman of the executive, of the acting bureau and of the administrative committee in August 1925. He remained in these positions until 1929. His main work at home, between the two Labour Governments, was, as always, the strengthening of the LP organisation. He warmly welcomed the new programme *Labour and the Nation*, mostly drafted by R. H. Tawney, and especially its foreign policy statement.

The general election of late spring 1929 gave the LP 288 seats, thus making Labour the largest party in the Commons. After some hesitation on MacDonald's part, Henderson became Foreign Secretary, with Hugh Dalton as his under-secretary. He remained secretary of the LP, although during the period of the Labour Government most of the administrative work rested upon his deputy, J. S. Middleton. Against the background of an international situation that steadily deteriorated, Henderson achieved some temporary successes, among them the official recognition of the Soviet Union, the settlement of the German–Polish dispute over Upper Silesia, and the agreement at Geneva for a general disarmament conference in February 1932. Although he played little part in domestic policies, he consistently supported MacDonald, until MacDonald himself made the break. When the May economy committee reported on 31 July 1931, Henderson was appointed to the Cabinet sub-committee (with MacDonald, Snowden, Thomas and Graham) to consider proposals for the whole Cabinet. The crisis grew steadily through August 1931, and on 24 August MacDonald agreed to form a National Government with himself as Premier and with Tory and Liberal support. Henderson was then elected leader of the LP in MacDonald's place, although at a later meeting of the LP executive he alone voted against MacDonald's expulsion from the Party. At the general election of 27 October 1931 the Labour representation fell to fifty-two. All the national leaders, Henderson included, lost their seats, with the exception of George Lansbury and C. R. Attlee.

Henderson had already been nominated president of the projected disarmament conference and, although there was a vigorous and often vicious press campaign against him in Britain, the position was confirmed by the League of Nations. The conference opened in late February 1932, but its results were meagre, and Henderson, who had been in ill-health since the general election, was in an especially difficult position because of his relations with the British Government. Lansbury had become chairman and Attlee vice-chairman of the PLP, and in October 1932 Henderson formally resigned as leader of the Party, Lansbury taking his place. Henderson continued his work at Geneva, but in September 1933, on Charles Duncan's death, he was elected for Clay Cross, Derbyshire, in a three-cornered fight against a

Government candidate and the general secretary of the CP, Harry Pollitt. Henderson left Geneva in the spring of 1935 after the total failure of the disarmament conference. He had already resigned the secretaryship of the Party in 1934, a presentation being made to him at the LP Conference in that year. In 1934 also he had taken part in the centenary celebrations of the Tolpuddle Martyrs and had preached in the main church of the Dorchester Methodist circuit. But the most important event for him in 1934 was the award of the Nobel Peace Prize.

Henderson married in 1888 and he had three sons and a daughter, the eldest son being killed in the First World War; both the younger sons became politicians. In his politics Henderson belonged to the Right. He was honest, selfless and unshakeable in his fundamental beliefs. Apart from his religious faith these included the unity of the Party, parliamentarianism at home and collective security in the world. He won the respect and affection of his colleagues, including many, such as G. D. H. Cole and Harold Laski, who often sharply disagreed with his politics. In the shaping and making of the British Labour Party in the first half of the twentieth century no career will repay analysis more than that of Arthur Henderson. He died on 20 October 1935 in London, and George Lansbury spoke at his funeral on 24 October. He left an estate valued at £23,328 (net).

Writings: (with J. Ramsay MacDonald) *Notes on Organisation and the Law of Registration and Elections* (1904); (with G. N. Barnes) *Unemployment in Germany* (1908) 15 pp.; (with J. Ramsay MacDonald) 'Trade Unions and Parliamentary Representation', *Cont. Rev. 95* (Feb 1909) 173–9; 'Religion and Labour', *Constructive Q. 1* (Mar 1913) 183–9; *Child Labour* (1915) P; *The Aims of Labour* (1917); *Prussian Militarism* (1917) P; *The League of Nations and Labour* (1918) 13 pp.; 'The Outlook for Labour', *Cont. Rev. 113* (Feb 1918) 121–30; *Labor's After-War Economic Policy* (New York, 1918) P; (with G. N. Barnes) *The Religion in the Labour Movement* (1919); *International Labour Standards* (1919) 16 pp.; 'An Industrial Parliament', *Labour Mag. 1*

(July 1922) 116–19; 'Labour's Electoral Triumph', *Labour Mag. 1* (Dec 1922) 341–3; 'War against War. Political Action for Peace', *Labour Mag. 2* (Jan 1923) 391–3; 'What the General Election means to the Workers', *Labour Mag. 2* (Dec 1923) 339–41; 'Labour still makes Progress', *Labour Mag. 3* (Nov 1924) 293–5; 'Life and Labour in Australia', *Labour Mag. 5* (Feb 1927) 435–8; 'Matteotti, the People's Martyr', *Labour Mag. 6* (Oct 1927) 242–5; 'The Principles of the Protocol', *Labour Mag. 6* (Nov 1927) 298–300; 'Socialism as a World Force', *Labour Mag. 7* (Sep 1928) 198–203; 'A Progressive International', *Labour Mag. 9* (Oct 1930) 251–3; 'Work for Peace during 1930', *Labour Mag. 9* (Jan 1931) 387–9; 'Labour's Army is unconquered', *Labour Mag. 10* (Nov 1931) 289–92; *Consolidating World Peace* (Oxford, 1932) 27 pp.; 'World Peace can be won', *Labour Mag. 10* (Feb 1932) 437–40; *Labour's Foreign Policy* (1933) 35 pp.; *Labour outlaws War* (1933) 12 pp.; 'The Pursuit of Peace', *19th C.* (Jan 1934) 1–14; *Labour's Peace Policy: arbitration, security, disarmament* (1934) 15 pp.; *Labour's Way to Peace* (1935); *Conference for the Reduction and Limitation of Armaments: preliminary report* (Geneva, 1936).

Sources:
(1) MSS: Labour Party archives, Transport House, London; Webb Coll., LSE; George Lansbury Coll., LSE; Keir Hardie correspondence formerly belonging to Mr Francis Johnson, ILP; Woodrow Wilson papers and John P. Frey papers, Library of Congress, Washington; Richard R. Ely Coll., Madison, Wisconsin; and below: British Labour Party, 1914–31.

(2) Secondary: The standard biography is M. A. Hamilton, *Arthur Henderson* (1938), which needs to be supplemented and corrected by later writings. E. A. Jenkins, *From Foundry to Foreign Office: the romantic life-story of Rt Hon. Arthur Henderson* (1933); H. Tracey, 'Rt Hon. Arthur Henderson', in *The Book of the Labour Party, 3* [1925] 151–64; H. Tracey, 'Twenty-five Years of Political Change', *Labour Mag. 7* (Aug 1928) 146–50; H. Dalton, 'British Foreign Policy, 1929–31',

Pol. Q. 2 (Oct 1931) 485–505; H. J. Laski, 'Ramsay MacDonald', *Harper's* (May 1932) 746–56; *Times*, 21 Oct 1935; *WW* (1935); *DNB* (1931–40); C. M. Lloyd, 'Uncle Arthur', *New Statesman*, 26 Oct 1935; *Survey of International Affairs*, ed. A. J. Toynbee, vols 1929–35; Lord Parmoor, *A Retrospect, looking back over a Life of more than Eighty Years* (1936); H. Dalton, 'Arthur Henderson', *Labour 5* (May 1938) 203; W. N. Medlicott, *British Foreign Policy since Versailles* (1940); Viscount Cecil, *A Great Experiment* (1941); M. A. Hamilton, *Remembering my Good Friends* (1944); Margaret Cole, 'Arthur Henderson', in *Makers of the Modern Labour Movement* (1948) 248–67; J. R. Clynes, 'Arthur Henderson', in *The British Labour Party*, ed. H. Tracey, *3* (1948) 187–99; Margaret Cole, *Growing up into Revolution* (1949); F. P. Walters, *A History of the League of Nations*, 2 vols (1952); Beatrice Webb, *Beatrice Webb's Diaries 1912–1924*, ed. M. Cole (1952); H. Dalton, *Call back Yesterday: memoirs 1887–1931* (1953); H. R. Winkler, 'Arthur Henderson', in *The Diplomats, 1919–1939*, ed. G. A. Craig and F. Gilbert (Princeton, 1953) 311–43; Beatrice Webb, *Beatrice Webb's Diaries 1924–1932*, ed. and with an introduction by M. Cole (1956); H. Dalton, *The Fateful Years: memoirs 1931–1945* (1957); H. J. Fyrth and H. Collins, *The Foundry Workers* (Manchester, 1959); House of Commons, Parliamentary Debates, 1903–35; League of Nations, *Records*, etc. 1929–35; *Documents on British Foreign Policy, 1919–1939*, eds R. Butler and J. P. T. Bury, 2nd ser. *1–8* 1946–60); R. W. Lyman, 'The British Labour Party: the conflict between socialist ideals and practical politics between the wars', *J. of British Studies 5* (1965) 140–52; A. Marwick, 'The Labour Party and the Welfare State in Britain, 1900–1948', *American Historical Rev. 73* (1967) 380–403; T. Jones, *Whitehall Diary*, vol. *1: 1916–1925* (1969), vol. *2: 1926–1930* (1969), ed. K. Middlemas; J. F. Naylor, *Labour's International Policy: the Labour Party in the 1930s* (1969); P. Stansky, *The Left and War: the British Labour Party and World War I* (1969); *Essays in Labour History*, vol. *2: 1886–1923*, ed. A. Briggs and J. Saville (1971).

JOHN SAVILLE

See also: *J. R. CLYNES; *G. D. H. COLE; *Hugh DALTON; *George LANSBURY, for British Labour Party, 1900–13; J. Ramsay MACDONALD; *James MAXTON; *E. D. MOREL; *Philip SNOWDEN; *R. H. TAWNEY; *J. H. THOMAS; *Sidney WEBB; *J. C. WEDGWOOD; *J. WHEATLEY; and below: British Labour Party, 1914–31.

British Labour Party, 1914–31:
(1) For MSS, see individual biographical entries.

(2) Theses: M. Whitney, 'The Attitude of British Labour towards the League of Nations' (Stanford MA, 1930); H. Meynell, 'The Second International, 1914–1933' (Oxford BLitt., 1957); G. A. Ritter, 'The British Labour Movement and its Policy towards Russia from the first Russian Revolution until the Treaty of Locarno' (Oxford BLitt., 1959); M. I. Thomis, 'The Labour Movement in Great Britain and Compulsory Military Service, 1914–1916' (London MA, 1959); E. A. Rowe, 'The British General Election of 1929' (Oxford BLitt., 1960); A. J. B. Marwick, 'The Independent Labour Party, 1918–1932' (Oxford BLitt., 1961); L. J. MacFarlane, 'The Origins of the Communist Party of Great Britain and its Early History, 1920–1927' (London PhD, 1962); R. E. Dowse, 'The Independent Labour Party, 1918–1932, with Special Reference to its Relationship with the Labour Party' (London PhD, 1962); S. Hornby, 'Left-wing Pressure Groups in the British Labour Movement, 1930–1940: some aspects of the relations between the Labour Left and the official leadership, with special reference to the experience of the ILP and the Socialist League' (Liverpool MA, 1966); D. M. Chewter, 'The History of the Socialist Labour Party of Great Britain from 1902 until 1921 with special Reference to the Development of its Ideas' (Oxford BLitt., 1966); J. F. Harbinson, 'A History of the Northern Ireland Labour Party' (Oxford MSc.(Econ.), 1966); R. J. A. Skidelsky, 'The Labour Government and the Unemployment Question, 1929–31' (Oxford DPhil., 1967); R. S. Barker, 'The Educational Policies of the Labour Party, 1900–

1961' (London PhD, 1968); W. Golant, 'The Political Development of C. R. Attlee to 1935' (Oxford BLitt., 1968).

(3) Reference works: Reports of the National Executive Committee and Reports of Annual Conferences, 1914–31; *The People's Year Book*, 1914–31; *The Labour Year Book*, 1916, 1919, 1924, 1925–31; *The Labour International Handbook*, ed. R. Palme Dutt (1921); *The Herald Book of Labour Members*, ed. S. V. Bracher (1923); *The Labour Who's Who* (1927); *Dod* (1914–31); *Potted Biographies: a dictionary of anti-national biography*, 4th ed. (1931); D. E. Butler and J. Freeman, *British Political Facts 1900–1960* (1963).

(4) The most important secondary works are (excluding most biographical works): G. D. H. Cole, *A History of the Labour Party from 1914* (1948) [with statistical appendices, bibliography and chronological lists of Labour Party Programmes, Reports, Pamphlets, etc., 1914–47]; C. L. Mowat, *Britain between the Wars* (1955); R. T. McKenzie, *British Political Parties* (1955; 2nd ed. 1963); S. R. Graubard, *British Labour and Russian Revolution 1917–24* (Harvard, 1956); R. W. Lyman, *The First Labour Government 1924* [1957]; R. J. A. Skidelsky, *Politicians and the Slump: the Labour Government of 1929–1931* (1967). All these volumes have full bibliographies and are especially useful for lists of biographies, autobiographies and periodical literature, including newspapers. See also: G. D. H. Cole, *The World of Labour*, 1st ed. (1913); G. D. H. Cole, *Labour in the Commonwealth* (1918); W. A. Orton, *Labour in Transition* (1921); R. H. Tawney, *The Acquisitive Society* (1921); J. Clayton, *Rise and Decline of Socialism 1884–1924* (1926); E. Wertheimer, *Portrait of the Labour Party*, 1st ed. (1929); G. D. H. Cole, *The Next Ten Years in British Social and Economic Policy* (1929); *The Scottish Socialists: a gallery of contemporary portraits* (1931); R. H. Tawney, *Equality* (1931); G. T. Garratt, *The Mugwumps and the Labour Party* (1932); H. J. Laski, *The Crisis and the Constitution* (1932); J. Scanlon, *Decline and Fall of the Labour Party* (1932); R. H. Tawney, 'The Choice before the Labour Party', *Pol. Q. 3* (1932) 323–5, 521–4; Stafford Cripps,

Can Socialism come by Constitutional Means? [1933?]; W. P. Maddox, *Foreign Relations in British Labour Politics* (Cambridge, Mass., 1934); *Lenin on Britain*, Introduction by H. Pollitt (1934); C. R. Attlee, *The Labour Party in Perspective* (1937); G. A. Hutt, *The Postwar History of the British Working Class* (1937); G. D. H. Cole, *Socialism in Evolution* (Penguin Books, 1938); J. Scanlon, *Cast off all Fooling* (1938); C. F. Brand, *British Labour's Rise to Power* (Stanford, 1941); F. Brockway, *Socialism over Sixty Years: the life of Jowett of Bradford 1864–1944* (1946); G. D. H. Cole and R. Postgate, *The Common People, 1746–1946*, 2nd ed. (1946); F. Brockway, *Inside the Left: thirty years of Platform, Press, Prison and Parliament* (1947); E. Halévy, *Histoire du Socialisme Européen* (Paris, 1948); *The British Labour Party: its history, growth, policy and leaders*, ed. H. Tracey, 3 vols (1948); F. Williams, *Fifty Years March* (1950); W. R. Tucker, *The Attitude of the British Labour Party towards European and Collective Security Problems, 1920–39* (Geneva, 1950); R. Postgate, *George Lansbury* (1951); H. Dalton, *Call back Yesterday: memoirs 1887–1931* (1953); R. Bassett, *1931: Political Crisis* (1958); H. Pelling, *British Communist Party: a historical profile* (1958); P. P. Poirier, *The Advent of the Labour Party* (1958); A. J. P. Taylor, *The Trouble Makers* (1958); C. Landauer, *European Socialism*, 2 vols (University of California, 1959); A. Bullock, *The Life and Times of Ernest Bevin*, vol. 1: *1881–1940* (1960); Margaret Cole, *The Story of Fabian Socialism* (1961); R. Miliband, *Parliamentary Socialism* (1961); H. Pelling, *A Short History of the Labour Party* (1961); Sidney Webb, 'The First Labour Government', *Pol. Q.* (Jan–Mar 1961) 6–44; M. Foot, *Aneurin Bevan: a biography*, vol. 1: *1897–1945* (1962); A. M. McBriar, *Fabian Socialism and English Politics 1884–1918* (1962); C. A. Cline, *Recruits to Labour: the British Labour Party, 1914–1931* (Syracuse, 1963); A. J. P. Taylor, *English History, 1914–1945* (1965); J. F. Naylor, *Labour's International Policy: the Labour Party in the 1930s* (1969); D. Carlton, *MacDonald versus Henderson: the foreign policy of the second Labour Government* (1970); M. Swarz, *The Union of Democratic Control in British Politics during the First World War*

(Oxford, 1971); *Essays in Labour History*, vol. 2: *1886–1923*, ed. A. Briggs and J. Saville (1971); M. Cowling, *The Impact of Labour 1920–1924* (Cambridge, 1971).

HETHERINGTON, Henry (1792–1849)

RADICAL REFORMER

Hetherington was born in Compton Street, Soho, London, in 1792, the son of John Hetherington, a tailor, the eldest of three children. As a young boy he was apprenticed to Luke Hansard, the parliamentary printer. He was out of work when his apprenticeship ended and he went to Belgium for a short time, where he worked at his trade. After he returned to London his first practical experience with radical ideas seems to have been the result of his contact with George Mudie. On 23 January 1821 Hetherington was among a group of printers who met Mudie to discuss the latter's plan for a community; and a committee was appointed for the purpose of raising money. Four days later the first number of the *Economist* appeared: 'a periodical paper', so its sub-title ran, 'explanatory of the new system of Society projected by Robert Owen Esq., and of a plan of association for improving the condition of the working classes during their continuance in their present employments'. What part, if any, Hetherington took in the Spa Fields community is not known, but certainly from this time until his death Hetherington was greatly influenced by Owenite ideas. He was an early member of the London Mechanics' Institution (established in December 1823) and was later on the committee, becoming a close friend of George Birkbeck.

Hetherington had been brought up by his mother in the Anglican faith, and during this first period of his life in London he joined the Freethinking Christians, a sect which attempted to practise a simple rational Christianity, founded in 1798 by Samuel Thompson. The sect split when the Elders refused to admit a free-thinking Jew, and those who opposed the decision, including Hetherington, were expelled. Hetherington used the occasion to publish what was probably his first pamphlet: *Principles and Practice contrasted; or, a peep into 'the only true Church of God upon Earth'*, commonly called *Freethinking Christians*. Only the second edition of 1828 seems extant.

By this time Hetherington had entered the main stream of contemporary working-class politics. According to some sources he joined the London Co-operative Society in 1824 and he was certainly a member of the British Association for the Promotion of Co-operative Knowledge (BAPCK) established in May 1829, intended to be a clearing house and propaganda centre for co-operative ideas and practices. In 1830 he was a member of the First Middlesex Society. On the more directly political front, Hetherington, after being refused entry into Richard Carlile's discussion circle, joined the Civil and Religious Liberty Association in 1828. The Association, a group of Irish and English radicals who had come together on the issue of Catholic Emancipation, turned itself into the Radical Reform Association (RRA) in the spring of 1829 and added certain specific political demands – such as the vote, the ballot and annual parliaments – to its general programme. Hetherington also helped in the founding of the Metropolitan Political Union in 1830.

These political and social developments brought Hetherington into close contact with a remarkable group of (mostly) young radicals, among them William Lovett, James Watson, John Cleave, George Foskett, William Carpenter, John Gast and Julian Hibbert. Like Hetherington many were greatly influenced by Robert Owen, while rejecting what was to become the Owenite denial of the usefulness of political activity. For Hetherington and his radical friends, politics was founded upon the need for men to become educated and thereby politically aware and active, and this would then allow them to obtain political power. To become politically educated, the working class required knowledge, and it was a free press above all else which would give them this knowledge and make them aware of their common interests against their oppressors. Hetherington was in contact with Carlile from the beginning of his own political career and it was Carlile with whom Hetherington had a long and bitter conflict. It was partly because of Hetherington's friendship with Hunt that they quarrelled so violently, but there were other reasons, and the bitterness between them lasted for the whole decade of the 1830s.

Both the Radical Reform Association and the British Association (whose membership overlapped) came to an end during the spring and summer of 1831, but already Hetherington and others had founded the National Union of the Working Classes, itself a development of the Metropolitan Trades Union. The NUWC had the support of many members of both the now defunct RRA and BAPCK. Hetherington had been for some time a regular speaker at the Rotunda and this now became the regular meeting-place for the weekly meetings of the NUWC.

Hetherington had first registered his own press and types in 1822 and by the end of the decade he was already publishing pamphlets, etc., on his own account as well as for others. He began issuing *The Penny Papers for the People, published by the Poor Man's Guardian* on 1 October 1830, preceding what were to become the better known *Political Letters* of William Carpenter by a few days. Most of the *Penny Papers* bore the initial 'M', that of Thomas Mayhew, a young law student, who continued as editor when the *Penny Papers* became the *Poor Man's Guardian* in July 1831. Before the *Guardian* appeared, however, Hetherington had begun the unstamped *Republican* in March 1831, for the second number of which he was prosecuted and fined. The *Poor Man's Guardian*, the first issue of which appeared on 9 July 1831, was the longest lived of all the unstamped papers: it was 'undoubtedly the finest working-class weekly which had (until that time) been published in Britain' [E. P. Thompson (1963) 811–12].

From the outset the *Guardian* was intended to defy the stamp laws, and the opening statement in the first number set the tone of the sustained campaign that was about to begin: 'Defiance is our only remedy; we cannot be a slave in all: we submit to much – for it is impossible to be wholly consistent –

but we will try, step by step, the power of RIGHT against MIGHT, and we will begin by protecting and upholding this grand bulwark and defence of all our rights – this key to all our liberties – THE FREEDOM OF THE PRESS – *the Press, too, of the* IGNORANT *and* THE POOR!' After the second number of the *Guardian* Hetherington was summonsed by the Bow Street magistrates but he left London, announcing his intention in the third number of 21 July 1831. He travelled the country, organising distribution and in particular encouraging his growing army of sellers. Before the struggle was finished over a thousand men, women and children were prosecuted, and either fined or imprisoned. Hetherington himself was convicted in his absence in July 1831, and sentenced to fines of £80 and costs or two years' imprisonment. In August he began the unstamped *Radical*; in September he escaped from the Bow Street officers in Manchester, but in October he was arrested, having come back to London to visit his mother who was dying. In the following March, to his great surprise, he was released from prison [*PMG*, 24 March 1832, 322–3] and he was in time to lead the great London protest demonstration on the day set aside for the National Fast. Hetherington was next arrested in January 1833 and on this occasion he was imprisoned along with James Watson, being released from Clerkenwell in June 1833. Hetherington was indicted again in 1834, both for the *Guardian* and *The Destructive and Poor Man's Conservative* which he had begun publishing on 2 February 1833. The case was heard before Lord Lyndhurst, Hetherington defending himself with great vigour and ability, and the verdict went against him on the *Destructive* but on the *Guardian* he was acquitted. On 21 June 1834 the *Guardian* stated the fact: 'This paper (after sustaining a Government persecution of three years and a half duration, on which upwards of 500 persons were unjustly imprisoned and cruelly treated for vending it) was, on the trial of an *ex-officio* information filed by His Majesty's Attorney-General against Henry Hetherington in the Court of Exchequer, before Lord Lyndhurst and a special jury, declared to be a strictly legal publication.'

It was a notable victory against a militant Establishment; and the campaign was remarkable for the ingenuity as well as the tenacity and self-sacrifice of the unstamped sellers as well as the remarkable solidarity between radicals of all views around the unstamped issue. Hetherington himself used the unlikely disguise of a Quaker on a number of occasions to outwit the police, and among his shop-boys, and later hawkers, was the young Julian Harney. *The Poor Man's Guardian* had, moreover, a much greater significance beyond the important role it played in establishing the principles of a free press. The years of its publication (it ended on the last Saturday in 1835) encompassed a turbulent period in working-class history, including the great trade union upsurge of 1833-4. The editor of the *Guardian* for much of its existence was Bronterre O'Brien and the close collaboration with Hetherington was probably the most fruitful period of all O'Brien's career. Both were concerned to discuss issues of working-class policies within a rational, class-conscious perspective. Both vigorously supported the Owenite trade union movement while at the same time warning against the tendency to ignore, or deprecate, the need for political power; and the polemical discussions between the *Guardian* and James Morrison's *Pioneer* in 1833 and 1834 are among the most interesting debates of this period.

When Hetherington lost his case over *The Destructive and Poor Man's Conservative* in June 1834, his fines amounted to £120, and he thereupon transformed it into a general newspaper, the *Twopenny Dispatch*. To avoid his goods being seized in lieu of fines he made over his bookselling stock to Watson. For a large part of 1835 he lived in Pinner, then a village on the outskirts of London, using the name of Mr Williams, but by August 1835 his debts to the Crown amounted to £200 and his goods were seized. He bought a new printing machine, and the papers continued. He was imprisoned again in February 1836 and not released until his fines were paid in May 1836. When the stamp duty was lowered, in 1836, his press and stocks were returned, and in September 1836 he began the stamped

London Dispatch, at 3½d, which he continued to publish at a loss until September of the following year.

By this time the London Working Men's Association had been formed in June 1836 by Lovett, Cleave, Hetherington and their closest associates; and in February 1837 the famous meeting at the Crown and Anchor tavern passed a series of resolutions which included all the 'six points' soon to become the People's Charter. Hetherington was treasurer of the LWMA on its formation, and during 1837 he went on tour for the Association in the industrial north, the Midlands and Wales. His close working relationship with O'Brien ended in the same year – the result of a series of complicated disagreements, involving among others Daniel O'Connell and the latter's attitude to the Glasgow spinners' strike. Hetherington played an active but secondary role in the early days of the Chartist movement, being always on the side of Lovett rather than O'Connor. He was delegate for London (except Marylebone) and Stockport at the Convention of 1839, and opposed both the idea of a national holiday and the move from London to Birmingham. Hetherington had especially close contacts with Welsh Chartism. Hugh Williams, the Carmarthen solictor who played a central part in the early development of Chartism in Wales, was a close friend; and Hetherington toured central Wales in November 1837 on behalf of the LWMA and had established branches in Welshpool, Newtown and Llanidloes. When the Chartists of Montgomeryshire requested the Convention to send a missionary to their district it was Hetherington who was chosen, and he reached Welshpool during the first week of April 1839. When John Frost was sentenced to death after the Newport Rising, Hetherington was a leading figure in the national campaign to obtain a reprieve.

We have little direct evidence of Hetherington's reactions to the events of 1839 but he was certainly more firmly opposed than ever to O'Connor's leadership. He presided over the dinner given to Lovett and John Collins on their release from prison, and once again began working alongside

Lovett, whose publication of *Chartism* later in 1840 was followed by the establishment of the National Association for Promoting the Political and Social Improvement of the People. Hetherington was secretary at the first meeting of the National Association and printed and published the Association's *Gazette*. He was also a trustee of its Hall in London until 1847. Although Hetherington in 1841 was sympathetic to Joseph Hume's household and lodger plan (Lovett not deviating from universal suffrage), his general support for Lovett's ideas led to a bitter controversy with O'Connor in the columns of the *Northern Star*, and he took part in the discussions which Joseph Sturge initiated early in 1842 between working-class Chartists and middle-class reformers, and which culminated in the abortive Complete Suffrage Union conference at Birmingham in December 1842. Hetherington generally agreed with Lovett throughout these debates and negotiations and found himself more estranged than ever from O'Connor.

At no time, however, did Hetherington turn his back on radical politics. When the Democratic Committee for Poland's Regeneration was established in March 1846, with Julian Harney as secretary, and O'Connor as treasurer, Hetherington became a member; and he joined the Mazzini-inspired People's International League which was founded at a public meeting on 28 April 1847. He became also a member of the Democratic Committee of Observation on the French Revolution when it was established early in 1848 and it was the leading members of this Democratic Committee who decided to form the People's Charter Union on the evening of the same day as the Kennington Common demonstration of 10 April 1848. It was from this organisation, the president of which was Thomas Cooper, now a moral force advocate, that emerged the Newspaper Stamp Abolition Committee in March 1849. Hetherington would no doubt have played a notable part in this new campaign but he was now within a few months of his death. One of his last political acts was to chair a great meeting of protest in June 1849 against the counter-revolution in Hungary and Baden.

During the last ten years of his life Hetherington continued to be centrally concerned with the problems of free speech and especially with the persecution of the free-thought movement. After the collapse of the Grand National Consolidated Trades Union the Owenite movement had built a new organisation with aims and objectives that were a good deal narrower than those of the years of the early 1830s; and to the outside world at least, the Owenites, towards the end of the decade, became increasingly identified with the attack on organised religion. A high point of the counter-offensive by the Anglican church, which led the campaign, was the speech of Henry Phillpotts, Bishop of Exeter, in late January 1840 in the House of Lords; and the publicity which this occasioned was undoubtedly an important contributory factor to the series of prosecutions on charges of blasphemy which were set in train during the next few years. Hetherington was an early victim. In 1838 C. J. Haslam had begun publishing his *Letters to the Clergy of all Denominations*. Cleave was first indicted for selling some of the *Letters*, imprisoned and then, after a few weeks, freed. Abel Heywood, as the original publisher, was then prosecuted but the case, in effect, was dropped. And then it was Hetherington's turn. His trial was held in December 1840 before Lord Denman. Hetherington conducted his own defence, being congratulated by the judge on his presentation of the case, but was found guilty; whereupon he was sentenced to four months' imprisonment. This was only the first of a number of blasphemy trials, the most famous being those connected with the publication of the *Oracle of Reason*, a very aggressive free-thought journal whose first editor was Charles Southwell. The editors of the *Oracle* were successively prosecuted and imprisoned and it was during the prosecution of G. J. Holyoake, who succeeded Southwell in the editorial chair, that M. Q. Ryall founded the Anti-Prosecution Union, later to be known as the Anti-Persecution Union. From the first Hetherington involved himself actively in its affairs, raising money and organising protests. At one such meeting, held at the Literary and Scientific Institute on 10 June 1844 to protest against the treatment of Thomas Paterson (the third editor of the *Oracle of Reason*) in Perth Penitentiary, Hetherington delivered one of his most astringent and witty speeches, very typical of his style, and well worth saving from obscurity [Barker [1938?] 43ff].

Hetherington in this last decade of his life also continued to be active in other spheres of the Owenite movement. He was a constant speaker at the Social Institution in John Street and sat on its administrative committee. He supported Holyoake's criticisms of the Queenwood community (published in the *Movement*) and he was present at the Congress of the Rational Society near Harmony Hall in 1846. He also became, in the last years of his life,. an active vestryman of the parish of St Pancras.

Hetherington, wrote R. G. Gammage in his *History of the Chartist Movement*, was 'possessed of indomitable courage and inflexible perseverance', and he had a 'rough, strong logic [which] struck conviction into every mind, while his dry and essentially English humour, gave to it an agreeable zest'. On one occasion while he was in prison he lectured the chaplain on the absurdity as well as the barbarity of the doctrine of original sin, and quoted text for text. A year and a half or so before his death he composed a last will and testament, a famous document in the history of free thought, and gave copies in his own handwriting to James Watson (his closest friend for many years) and G. J. Holyoake. Two days before he died he signed another copy, as earnest of his firm belief in its principles, and his signature was witnessed by Holyoake, H. A. Ivory and John Kenny. He died from cholera on Thursday 23 August 1849, leaving a widow, a Welsh woman whom he had married c. 1811. (According to Hollis (1969) nine children were born, but only one survived him.) Hetherington at some periods of his life may have been quite prosperous, and in 1837 it was estimated, by Bronterre O'Brien, not always a reliable witness in these matters, that his business was bringing in £1000 a year. But at his death he left only £200 'of goods and chattels' and his two executors (James

Watson and T. Whittaker) had difficulty in meeting the claims on his estate [Hollis (1970) 135–6].

Hetherington was buried in Kensal Green Cemetery, in a plot of land previously purchased by W. Devonshire Saull (a prominent member of the John Street Institute), who himself was buried in the grave next to Hetherington in April 1855. The hearse was covered by a canopy, on each side of which were the words of a frequent phrase of Hetherington's: 'We ought to endeavour to leave the world better than when we found it.' James Watson and Holyoake delivered the funeral orations and Thomas Cooper delivered a lecture on Hetherington and his life and work at the John Street Institute on 26 August.

Writings:

(1) *Principles and Practice contrasted; or, a peep into 'the only true Church of God upon Earth', commonly called Freethinking Christians* (2nd ed. 1828); *Cheap Salvation: or an antidote to priestcraft, being a succinct, practical, essential and rational religion deduced from the New Testament* (2nd ed. 1843).

(2) Hetherington published the following papers and journals: *The Cerberus: or Tartarean Review* (1830); *The Penny Papers for the People* (Oct 1830–July 1831); *The Poor Man's Guardian: a weekly newspaper for the people, established contrary to 'Law' to try the powers of 'might' against 'right'* (1831–5); *The Radical* (1831–2); *The Republican; or Voice of the People* (1831–4); *Every Man's Library of Republican and Philosophical Knowledge* (1832); *The Penny Christ* (June 1833); *The Destructive and Poor Man's Conservative* (2 Feb 1833–); then *The People's Conservative and Trade Union Gazette* (14 Dec 1833–); then *Two Penny Dispatch and People's Political Register* (14 June 1834–); then *London Dispatch* (17 Sep 1836–Oct 1839); *The Odd Fellow* (1839–41). For full details of the unstamped press see J. H. Wiener, *A Descriptive Finding List of Unstamped British Periodicals 1830–1836* (1970) and the list of unstamped papers, 1830–6, in P. Hollis, *The Pauper Press* (1970) 319–27.

(3) Other contemporary journals that are relevant include: *Weekly Free Press* (1829–

30); *Magazine of Useful Knowledge* (1830); *Carpenter's Political Letters* (1830); *Working Man's Friend* (1833); *The Man* (1833); *Weekly True Sun* (1834–5); *Cleave's Weekly Police Gazette* (1836); *London Mercury* (1836–7); *Northern Star* (1837–49); *English Chartist Circular* (1841–3); *Oracle of Reason* (1841–3); *The Movement* (1843–5); *The Circular* (1845).

Sources: MSS: The materials for a full biography of Hetherington are scattered widely in many collections. Among the most important are the Place papers in the British Museum; and the Owen and Holyoake papers, Co-operative Union Library, Manchester; the Lovett Collection, Birmingham Public Library; the Carlile Collection, Huntington Library, San Marino, California; and the Home Office records. For the last group, and for detailed bibliographical references to the work and life of Hetherington in the 1820s and 1830s, there are four secondary works of major importance: E. P. Thompson, *The Making of the English Working Class* (1963; Pelican ed. 1968); Patricia Hollis, introduction to reprint of *The Poor Man's Guardian 1* (1969) vii–xxxix; idem, *The Pauper Press: a study in working-class Radicalism of the 1830s* (Oxford, 1970); J. Wiener, *The War of the Unstamped* (Cornell Univ. Press, 1970). For Hetherington's part in the free press controversies and struggles of the 1840s, the primary and secondary material are more limited: see E. Royle, 'George Jacob Holyoake and the Secularist Movement in Britain, 1841–1861' (Cambridge PhD, 1968). See also: *A Full Report of the Trial of Henry Hetherington on an Indictment of Blasphemy . . . December 1840, for selling Haslam's Letters to the Clergy of all Denominations* (1840) 32 pp.; Anon., *The Trials of Thomas Paterson, Thomas Finlay and Miss Matilda Roalfe for Blasphemy* [1844?]; G. J. Holyoake, *A Visit to Harmony Hall* (reprinted from the *Movement*) . . . (1844); idem, *The Life and Character of Henry Hetherington* (1849); R. G. Gammage, *History of the Chartist Movement . . .* (1854; 2nd ed. of 1894 reprinted New York, 1969, with an introduction by John Saville); Thomas Cooper, *The Life of Thomas Cooper* (1872; reprinted with an introduction by John Saville,

Leicester Univ. Press, 1971); W. Lovett, *Life and Struggles of William Lovett* (1876); W. J. Linton, *James Watson: a memoir* (Manchester, 1880); G. J. Holyoake, *Sixty Years of an Agitator's Life*, 2 vols (1893); W. J. Linton, *Memories* (1895); G. Wallas, *Life of Francis Place* (1898); C. D. Collet, *History of the Taxes on Knowledge*, 2 vols (1899); F. Podmore, *Robert Owen*, 2 vols (1906; reprinted in one volume, New York, 1968); M. Hovell, *The Chartist Movement* (Manchester, 1918); J. West, *History of the Chartist Movement* (1920; reprinted New York, 1968); M. Beer, *History of British Socialism* (1920); J. M. Robertson, *A History of Free Thought in the Nineteenth Century*, 2 vols (1929); Th. Rothstein, *From Chartism to Labourism* (1929); G. D. H. Cole, *Life of Robert Owen* (1930); A. G. Barker, *Henry Hetherington (1792–1849)* [n.d. 1938?] 62 pp.; G. D. H. Cole, *Chartist Portraits* (1941; reprinted with an introduction by Asa Briggs, 1965); idem, *A Century of Co-operation* (Manchester, [1945?]); T. Kelly, *George Birkbeck* (Liverpool, 1957); A. R. Schoyen, *The Chartist Challenge* (1958); D. Williams, 'Chartism in Wales', in *Chartist Studies*, ed. Asa Briggs (1959); W. H. G. Armytage, *Heavens Below* (1961); Dorothy Thompson, 'La Presse de la Classe Ouvrière Anglaise' in *La Presse Ouvrière 1819–1850*, ed. J. Godechot (Paris, 1966); J. F. C. Harrison, *Robert Owen and the Owenites in Britain and America* (1969); Alfred Plummer, *Bronterre* (1971). There is an inadequate *DNB* entry by G. J. Holyoake. OBIT. *Northern Star*, 25 Aug 1849; *Democratic Review*, Sep 1849; *Reynolds Political Instructor*, 2 Feb 1850.

I. J. PROTHERO
JOHN SAVILLE

See also: *Richard CARLILE; *John CLEAVE; G. J. HOLYOAKE; *Feargus O'CONNOR; *James WATSON.

HIBBERT, Charles (1828–1902)
CO-OPERATOR

Born on 29 August 1828 at Newton Heath, Manchester, at an Owenite co-operative store. In early adult life he moved to another district in the Manchester area, Moston, and then to Eccles where he worked as a silk dresser. Co-operation on the Rochdale model was then in its infancy but was spreading in Lancashire in the mid-1850s and a society known as the Eccles Union was purchasing tea in bulk and distributing it privately to members. In 1857 the Eccles Provident Industrial Co-operative Society was established and Charles Hibbert was one of the founder members, contributing towards the capital required to start the business. He was appointed the Society's first chairman and in 1858 became treasurer. In 1860 he took the position of shopman with the Society and later became manager of the Patricroft branch, a position he held for forty-one years and from which he resigned in March 1901, about a year before his death on 2 April 1902. He left effects valued at £2143.

JOYCE BELLAMY

Sources: J. Haslam, *Jubilee History of the Eccles Co-operative Society* (Manchester, 1907); *Eccles Co-op. Record* (n.d.). OBIT. *Co-op. News*, 12 Apr 1902.

See also: G. J. HOLYOAKE, for Retail Co-operation – Nineteenth Century.

HICKEN, Henry (1882–1964)
MINERS' LEADER

Born at North Wingfield, North Derbyshire, on 2 April 1882, the son of Philip Hicken, a miner, and his wife Emily (née Hyde), he left school at twelve years of age and began work as a trammer at the Pilsley Colliery, for which he received 10*d* a day. He stayed there for twelve years and then, after a year at the Parkhouse Colliery, went to the Williamthorpe Colliery where he became a checkweighman. He was also secretary of the Williamthorpe lodge of the Derbyshire Miners' Association, which had between 1700 and 1800 members. Of his eighteen years' experience in the pit, fourteen were spent at the coal face. In May 1920, Hicken was elected treasurer of the Derbyshire Miners' Association and in January 1928 general secretary. In 1928 he also became a member of the executive committee of the MFGB. Earlier in 1924, when Frank Hodges was elected to Parliament as Member for Lichfield, Hicken had been nominated by the Derbyshire Miners' Association for the secretaryship of the MFGB but he was not elected. Thereafter several attempts were made to secure his election to national office. He was nominated for the vice-presidency of the MFGB in 1931, 1932 and in 1934, and for the presidency in 1930 and also in 1939, but on each occasion he was unsuccessful. In 1934 he came top in both the first and second preference vote. The third vote resulted in a tie of 250 votes each between Hicken and Lawther, to whom after the adjournment 253 votes were given against 247 for Hicken. Had he been in one of the larger coalfields he would almost certainly have attained national leadership.

In August 1942 during the Second World War Hicken was appointed Regional Labour Director for Nottinghamshire, Derbyshire and Leicestershire by the Minister of Fuel and Power. Hicken suggested that the council of the Derbyshire Miners' Association might either accept his resignation or grant him leave of absence until the end of the war. The council recommended leave of absence but when the matter was referred to the branches they decided that Hicken should resign. Among some of the men there was the uneasy feeling that their popular leader had 'gone over to the other side'. When the coal industry was nationalised on 1 January 1947, Hicken became Labour Director to the East Midlands Division of the National Coal Board and in 1948 he was awarded an OBE. He remained with the National Coal Board until his retirement in 1956.

Like many of the nineteenth-century miners' leaders in Derbyshire and elsewhere Hicken began life as a Liberal and a Methodist. He gained prominence before the First World War by his activities on the political platform and in the pulpit but he came to intellectual maturity at a time when Socialism and Syndicalism were in the air and he quickly became influenced by more revolutionary creeds. At an early age he became very studious and by the time of his death had built up an extensive library. He soon rejected both Liberalism and Methodism and became profoundly influenced by Marx. In the 1920s he was described as 'trying to make our flesh creep with threats of red revolution' and 'revelling in the anticipation of gore and bloodshed'. His election as treasurer in 1920 was part of the revolt against the older trade union leaders. His powerful oratory, his extreme militancy, his impressive appearance, his long hair, his habit of wearing an immaculate white shirt and collar without a tie (which he continued as an official of the National Coal Board), were all characteristics which endeared him to thousands of miners and made him one of the most colourful and dominating personalities in the history of the Derbyshire Miners' Association.

Hicken combined a revolutionary fervour with practical policies which kept the Association organisationally intact during the late twenties when unions in neighbouring coalfields were crippled by the growth of company unionism. He also played a prominent part in promoting welfare schemes. He was the driving force behind the development of the Derbyshire Miners' Holiday Centre at Skegness and in 1938 was appointed to the Miners' Welfare Committee by the Board of Trade. He died on 20 September 1964 and left an estate valued at £4759.

Writings: Evidence before R.C. on Safety in Coal Mines 1938–9 XIII Qs 28269–911.

Sources: (1) MSS: Minutes of the Derbyshire Miners' Association, 1918–42 (NUM, Saltergate, Chesterfield); (2) Printed: *Minutes of the Miners' Federation of Great Britain*, 1918–42; *Derbyshire Times*, 1918–64; (3) Secondary: J. E. Williams, *The Derbyshire Miners* (1962). OBIT. *Derbyshire Times*, 26 Sep 1964; *Derbyshire Miner*, Oct 1964.

J. E. WILLIAMS

See also: *A. J. COOK, for Mining Trade Unionism, 1915–26; *Peter LEE, for Mining Trade Unionism, 1927–44.

HILTON, James (1814–90)
CO-OPERATOR

James Hilton was born at Hartshead Lees near Oldham, on 14 October 1814, of humble parents. He attended day school for only

one day and learned to write at Sunday school. He started work as a piecer in a cotton mill and later became an apprentice roller turner in a textile machinery factory. He moved to Stockport and then returned to Oldham, to work at Platt Bros & Co., textile engineers. He married Miss Hurst of Lees in 1850 and about that time began to take an interest in social problems.

In 1857 he joined the Oldham Industrial Co-operative Society and served on its management committee in 1861–4, 1865–6, 1867–8 and 1882–9. He was three times president of the Society, in 1863–4, 1865–6 and 1867–8. In July 1869 he was appointed treasurer of the Society and retained this office till age and a comfortable competency enabled him to resign in September 1882. In the following month he was re-elected to the committee of management.

In September 1884, on the nomination of the Oldham Society, he was elected to the board of the Co-operative Wholesale Society and remained on it till his death, serving on the finance sub-committee. He was not widely known because of his reticent disposition and unassuming manner but his colleagues on the CWS board greatly respected his judgement, especially in financial matters, and he was much loved by his associates in the Oldham Society. He died on 18 January 1890, being survived by his wife. He left a personal estate valued at £757.

Sources: J. T. Taylor, *Jubilee History of Oldham Industrial Co-operative Society Ltd 1850–1900* (Manchester, 1900); P. Redfern, *The Story of the C.W.S.* (Manchester, [1913]); personal information: Education Secretary, Oldham Industrial Co-operative Society Ltd. OBIT. *Co-op. News*, 25 Jan 1890.

H. F. BING

See also: G. J. HOLYOAKE, for Retail Co-operation – Nineteenth Century.

HINES, George Lelly (1839–1914)
RADICAL REFORMER AND CO-OPERATOR

Born at Tattingstone, near Ipswich, on 6 June 1839, George Hines was registered in his mother's name at birth. A biography published in the *Bee-Hive* while Hines was still alive suggested that his parents belonged to the agricultural labouring class. He attended St Matthew's School, Ipswich, where he received a good early education; and all his life Hines was passionately interested in books. On leaving school he took a messenger's job and then became a cabin boy on a coasting vessel. After a year he joined the Royal Navy in which he served for six or seven years, buying his discharge in 1861. He worked for eleven years as head goods guard on the railway and then as a fireman. He finally left the railway service to become cashier in the clothing manufacturing firm of F. J. Bugg of Ipswich and later became secretary and accountant.

On his return to Ipswich Hines began to take a leading part in the politics of the town. He was a radical who in the 1860s and early 1870s supported the Liberal Party at municipal and parliamentary levels, but after the second Reform Act Hines moved steadily towards the principle of independent labour representation. He was actively concerned with the formation of the Ipswich Labour Representation League in 1875 and vigorously supported William Newton in a by-election of 1876 against the Conservative candidate. The Labour League was succeeded by the Ipswich Working Men's Political Association, whose chairman was Hines, and he stood as 'non-conformist working man's candidate' for the Ipswich School Board in January 1880, coming third out of eleven places; he continued on the School Board until 1892, when he did not seek re-election. In 1894 he was involved in the formation of a branch of the ILP and was its first president, a position he held for four years. The branch was succeeded by the Ipswich Labour and Social Reform League and then in 1906 a second branch of the ILP was established, Hines becoming president in 1909. He had been appointed to the magistrates' bench in 1893, as the nominee of the Trades Council.

In addition to his political activities Hines was one of the founders of the Ipswich Co-operative Society in 1868 (together with F. J. Bugg and Joseph Goody) and he served on its management committee from that year until 1890. He held office as secretary from 1869 to 1873 and was president from 1877 to 1890. In 1874 when the London branch of the CWS was established he became a member and often accompanied buyers on their visits to foreign depots. He retired from co-operative service in 1907. He represented the CWS at the Industrial Remuneration Conference of 1885 and made a characteristically lively intervention.

Hines was a leading political personality in Ipswich for half a century. He was a frequent contributor to the *East Anglian Daily Times* and other local papers, and he wrote for many years for the *Co-operative News*. He was twice married. By his first wife, who died in 1886, he had three daughters and six sons, and by his second, whom he married in 1889, a son and a daughter. He died at his Ipswich home on 4 April 1914 and the funeral service on 8 April was held at the Unitarian Chapel, of which Hines had been a member for at least twenty years. His wife and nine children survived him, and he left personal effects of £1906.

Writings (apart from newspaper articles): 'Spread of Co-operation in Agricultural Villages', *Co-op. Congress Report* (1879); 'Twelve years of School Work in Ipswich', *CWS Annual* (1885) 411–12; 'Co-operation in its Application to Agriculture', *CWS Annual* (1887) 210–32; (with B. Jones and H. Pumphrey) *Easy Book-keeping for Small Co-operative Societies* (Edinburgh, 1887) 24 pp.; *Co-operative Fairy Tales. Toyla's Salvation: or, a Story of Three Sisters and Giant Sostringe* (1888) 19 pp.; *Co-operation and the Perils of Credit* (Manchester, [1888]) 7 pp.; *One of the old (Co-operative) Guard. Being a sketch of the Life of Mr E. T. Craig ...* (3rd ed. 1890) 10 pp.

Sources: *Bee-Hive*, 25 Sep 1875; *Industrial Remuneration Conference* [1885], Report of Proceedings and Papers: with an introduction by John Saville (New York, 1968) 121–3; *Through Sixty Years* [History of Ipswich Industrial Co-operative Society Ltd] (1928); R. Ratcliffe, four (typescript) volumes on the History of the Working Class Movement in Ipswich (from the nineteenth century to 1935): at Ipswich Borough Library and microfilm at Hull University Library; personal information: Miss D. K. Hines, daughter, of Ipswich, who has a Miscellany volume of newspaper cuttings relating to her father's articles and letters in various publications: microfilm in Hull University Library. OBIT. *East Anglian Daily Times*, 6 Apr 1914; *Co-op. News*, 11 Apr 1914.

JOYCE BELLAMY

See also: F. J. BUGG; J. GOODY; *William NEWTON.

HOBSON, John Atkinson (1858–1940)
ECONOMIST AND JOURNALIST

Born on 6 July 1858 at Iron Gate, Derby, the second son of William Hobson and his wife Josephine Atkinson. William, a printer, bookseller and joint proprietor of the *Derbyshire and North Staffordshire Advertiser* (founded in 1846), was a prosperous and eminent Derby citizen, twice elected mayor, in 1883 and 1885. A Whig in politics, he founded the local branch of the Liberal-Unionist Association in 1886. He died in 1897. His eldest son, Ernest William Hobson (1856–1933), was a distinguished mathematician, friend of the South African statesman J. C. Smuts and mathematics tutor to the young J. M. Keynes. Two of his sons, Oscar and Charles, became economists. William's third son, Henry Mortimer Hobson (1861–1920?), took over the family newspaper, while the eldest daughter Mary Josephine Hobson (d. 1915), married a cousin, the Yorkshire barrister Charles Milner Atkinson.

J. A. Hobson, like his father, uncles and brother before him, was sent to Derby School in 1868, an old grammar school of some eighty boys. He proceeded on an open scholarship to Lincoln College, Oxford, in 1876 having just completed a Cambridge University Extension course in economics. A second in Classics was followed by a disappointing third in Modern Greats but athletically he was more successful and nearly won a blue. On going down in 1880 he began to teach classics at schools in Faversham and Exeter and to lecture in English literature for the Oxford Extension Dele-

gacy. In Exeter he married a rather formidable well-to-do lawyer's daughter from New Jersey, Florence Edgar. He also met there the businessman-mountaineer A. F. Mummery, with whom he eventually produced the *Physiology of Industry* (1889), a book which challenged the validity of Say's Law, that products automatically create their own markets. The cool reception given the work by H. S. Foxwell (to whom it had been handed by Ernest Hobson), F. Y. Edgeworth and L. L. Price led to Hobson's being prevented from lecturing on economics for various extension boards. At a time when economics was becoming professionalised this, together with his failure to secure a teaching post at the new London School of Economics in 1895, virtually ended his academic career. It was almost thirty years before he was offered an honorary chair at Manchester University, which he declined, and his experience as a 'heretic' and outsider made him an acute critic of 'orthodox' opinion in the social sciences and of class-biased educational systems.

In 1887 he had moved to the West End of London to try his hand at journalism, beginning with the 'London Letter' for the family newspaper which he continued until 1897. The early 1890s saw his conversion from a mild Liberal-Unionist into a radical 'new Liberal'. In 1890 he became a member of the Ethical Society in London, which had close links with Oxford and with the Extension movement, but after five years he left because of the Society's too close an association with the individualistic views of the Charity Organisation Society. While still a member, however, he met the Fabian journalist William Clarke, who procured for him the commission to write what was to be one of his most successful books, the *Evolution of Modern Capitalism* (1894), and who may have introduced him to the young Ramsay MacDonald. Hobson, Clarke, MacDonald, the young Oxford Liberal Herbert Samuel and the ethicist Richard Stapley founded the Rainbow Circle, in 1894, and the *Progressive Review* (1896–8) to stimulate informed discussion and to formulate broadly collectivist political principles. The

Circle continued to meet for another thirty years but the *Review*, of which Hobson was a director, folded in only two. It had provided him with experience and contacts, however, including the American radical H. D. Lloyd, whose last work, *A Sovereign People: the Swiss Democracy* (1907), Hobson finished and edited. The London Ethical Society had also prompted Hobson to take up the study of John Ruskin's economic and social theory, with the result that he became the foremost exponent of Ruskin's gospel 'there is no wealth but life', particularly in his *John Ruskin: Social Reformer* (1898). In 1895 he joined the more radical South Place Ethical Society where, first with J. M. Robertson, Joseph McCabe and Herbert Burrows and much later with C. Delisle Burns and S. K. Ratcliffe, he preached the principles of rational democracy every Sunday morning for forty years. It was then in this ethical sub-culture that Hobson first made the acquaintance of labour men, mostly London intellectuals and Fabians. His books, *Problems of Poverty* (1891) and the *Problem of the Unemployed* (1896), and his numerous articles on industrial and labour matters brought him the favourable recognition of the labour movement in general.

Hardly had he moved from London in 1899 and settled in the important Fabian intellectual community at Limpsfield, Surrey, when he was called upon by C. P. Scott, editor of the *Manchester Guardian*, to go as the paper's Special Commissioner to South Africa. It was there that he confirmed the analysis of economic imperialism which he had touched upon in an article of the previous year, namely that it was the direct result of the expanding forces of modern capitalism. He returned to England when war broke out and was welcomed at a special dinner by Sir Robert Reid and David Lloyd George, a prelude to his serving on several peace committees. Together with Cronwright Schreiner, whom he had brought back with him from South Africa, he made a hair-raising speaking tour of 'jingo' Britain, during which meetings were regularly broken up, including those at Edinburgh, Leeds and Scarborough. His books, *The War in South Africa* (1900), the *Psychology of*

Jingoism (1901) and *Imperialism: a study* (1902), were well received in pro-Boer circles and established him as one of the country's leading radicals. *Imperialism* was to be used much later by Lenin, who had reviewed Hobson's *Evolution of Modern Capitalism* in 1899. Hobson was apparently widely read by Russian liberals and radicals at this time.

In 1901 he led a brief and abortive attempt to get Liberals and Labour men into a 'new party' [P. Poirier (1958) 177–8], but much of the next five years of Conservative government was spent in touring and speaking in the United States and in Canada. At home as a member of the Free Trade Union, a liberal anti-protectionist organisation, and as a journalist and economist, he contributed to the fight against tariff reform, a fight which he continued energetically through the First World War and into the 1930s. Unsuccessful in his attempts to procure an editorship, he continued to write for the *Independent Review* and later for the *English Review* and for all the major liberal journals, including leaders for the *Manchester Guardian*, an association cemented by the marriage of his daughter Mabel to C. P. Scott's son Edward. In 1906 he became leader writer for the new liberal daily the *Tribune*, but he found that his health, which for some time had been very frail, would not stand the strain. In 1907 he found a more congenial niche writing 'middles', on economics, literature and the United States, for H. W. Massingham's new *Nation* where he exercised his most effective critical tool, a biting sardonic sense of humour, which was even more effective in the conversation at the *Nation* lunches than in print.

His economic work had been left idle for a time after the rather disappointing reception given to his *Economics of Distribution* (1900) and the *Social Problem* (1901). By 1909, however, he had rethought his analysis and produced the *Industrial System*, which set out a theory of the 'surplus' and its practical applications. He held that the 'surplus' created by the maldistribution of income led, through oversaving and underconsumption, to unemployment and that the remedy lay in eradicating the 'surplus' by the re-distribution of income through taxation and the nationalisation of monopolies. It was taken by some to be the theory behind Lloyd George's 1909 budget, but its more radical implications were reflected neither in the budget, nor in the contemporary analyses of Fabians and other Socialists. He went on to develop a theory of 'human economics', in which, following Ruskin, he insisted upon the qualitative as well as the quantitative side of 'wealth', and in which he put forward a theory of industrial relations based upon an analysis of 'needs' and incentives [*Work and Wealth* (1914)].

His political activities before the First World War included the political chair-manship of the New Reform Club, member-ship of the Secular Education League, and of the National Campaign for the Abolition of the Poor Law, and it is said that he was amongst Asquith's candidates for peers with whom the Government would have swamped the House of Lords in 1911. In 1908 he was deputed by a number of Liberals in the New Reform Club to impress upon his friends J. C. Smuts and J. X. Merriman the necessity of securing the native franchise in any proposed Union of South Africa, but although read and respected by these statesmen his efforts proved fruitless. A close friend of the Quakers Seebohm Rowntree and E. R. Cross, although never himself a pacifist, he became very involved in the peace movement and a leading member of the International Arbitration League. When war seemed imminent in 1914, he helped to found the British Neutrality Com-mittee and then became one of the chief members of the Union of Democratic Con-trol, serving on the executive council for nearly a quarter of a century. He was also associated with the National Peace Council (founded in 1904) and several other minor peace societies during the war. He was a persistent advocate of an international body to prevent wars, a step *Towards International Government*, the title of a book he wrote in 1915; but he was intensely disappointed in the particular scheme for a League of Nations which actually materialised (which owed a lot to his friends J. C. Smuts and

Gilbert Murray), for he considered it little more than a 'New Holy Alliance' of the victors.

It was through the UDC that he began to move towards the Labour Party, for with many other radical Liberals he found it impossible to continue his allegiance to the Liberal Party after the events of 1916. He had always been sympathetic to Labour, a sympathy strengthened by his work for the Board of Trade before the war and by his participation in the Whitley Committee on Industrial Relations and the Ministry of Reconstruction Committee on Trusts, where he worked side by side with Sidney Webb, J. R. Clynes, Ernest Bevin and other labour men and women. In 1919, in evidence to the Sankey Commission, he advocated the nationalisation of the coal industry. In 1918 he contested the Combined Universities seat as an Independent, was narrowly beaten, and soon afterwards joined the ILP. He became a member of the ILP Advisory Committee on International Relations and served on the specially constituted com-mittee which considered and rejected C. H. Douglas's Social Credit proposals in 1922. He was at this time at the forefront of the radical opposition to the reparations clauses of the Versailles Treaty and was working closely with Pethick-Lawrence and Hugh Dalton in the consideration of a capital levy scheme. A form of his underconsumption theory appeared in the Minority Reports of the TUC and Labour Party Parliamentary Committee on the Cost of Living (1920/1).

He was an occasional contributor to the *Socialist Review* and the *New Leader* at this time but his economic work was given its most important recognition in 1924 when he was appointed a member of the ILP Living Wage Committee; and his views were in part reflected in the Report of 1926. This Report displeased many leading members of the Party, including MacDonald, Snow-den and Beatrice Webb, and succeeded in winning little support from the Left of the Party, with the result that it failed to make much political impact. Hobson had already incurred the displeasure of some unionists in 1924 when he had suggested (*New Leader*, 4 April 1924) that the demands of the large and powerful unions could well harm less well-organised labour. He repeated his underconsumptionist analysis of unemployment to the Colwyn Committee on the National Debt and Taxation in 1924 and some semblance of his view could be detected in Mosley's and Strachey's *Revolution by Reason* (1925) but neither the Labour Party nor the Liberal Party adopted his remedy, although, under pressure from Keynes, the self-styled 'new liberals' in 1928-9 made some ground towards it.

Hobson was by this time seventy years of age, and although still remarkably active, he had become rather a father figure who, it was thought, 'might well be made economist "by special appointment" to the British Labour Party'. MacDonald offered him a peerage in 1931 but, a bitter critic of MacDonald's government, he refused and moved even further towards Socialism and planning (see 'A British Socialism', *New Statesman*, 25 January and 1 February 1936). His greatest triumph came in 1936 when Keynes, in his *General Theory of Employment Interest and Money*, acknowledged that Hobson had been at least half right in his analysis of unemployment.

His journalistic work in the 1930s was greatly curtailed and confined for the most part to the *New Statesman* and the New York *Nation* and the occasional article for *Political Quarterly*. His attention turned from unemployment in the early years of the decade to the problem of promoting democracy and peace in a world, as he saw it, threatened by dictatorship and war. To this end he had since the 1920s urged greater American participation in the efforts to secure a lasting peace and his last article in December 1939 expressed the hope that American intervention would shorten the war. Two years previously he had joined with Clifford Allen, Norman Angell and others to reach a compromise solution of the Czechoslovakian crisis.

He died of old age on 1 April 1940, at his Hampstead home. His estate was valued at £2704. His wife died a few years later and his daughter Mabel Scott in 1970. His son Harold was still alive in 1971. Hobson's contribution to 'welfare' thinking and the development of the social and economic policy of the Labour Party was overshadowed to some extent by the Second World War, by Beveridge and by Keynes. His chief impact in Britain had been on G. D. H. Cole and on John Wheatley, but if rather neglected in his own land, he had more of a following in the United States where it is said that his views penetrated into F. D. Roosevelt's 'brains trust'. He had himself been among the first to bring the work of an American 'heretic', Thorstein Veblen, to the attention of the British public. Hobson was a 'socialist' in the Ruskinian sense that he conceived of society as an organic whole and in the way in which he considered social reform to be a matter of social justice and democracy. He had never had much time for the 'Germanic' Marx, however, although he spoke better of him in later years, and he disliked the authoritarianism of the Fabians, the bureaucracy of the USSR and what he considered to be the individualism of the trade unionists and the Guild Socialists. He wished to reform capitalism, not to abolish it, and therefore his 'socialism' was always 'practical' rather than revolutionary. Hobson himself wrote in 1938, 'I can only plead that its [sc. the underconsumptionist thesis] acceptance and embodiment in a public policy of equitable distribution still appears to me the only way of escaping a revolutionary conflict of classes and of nations. How far that equity of distribution requires recourse to Socialism, Communism and other modes of State planning must depend in large measure upon the current economic structure of each nation, and its capacity of skilled, honest and humane regulation of the economic resources in the standardised industries which satisfy the ordinary economic needs of its members' [*Confessions of an Economic Heretic* (1938) 188].

Writings: The bulk of Hobson's journalism appeared in the *Derbyshire and North Staffordshire Advertiser* ('London Letter', 1887-97), the *Ethical World* (1898-1902), the *Speaker* (1899-1907), the *Manchester Guardian* (1899-1928), the *Tribune* (1906-8), the London *Nation* (1907-30) and the New York *Nation* (1908-34). Reports of his South

Place lectures appeared in the *South Place Magazine* (later the *South Place Monthly List* and then the *South Place Monthly Record*), 1901–39. His major economic articles appeared in the *Quarterly Journal of Economics* and the *Journal of Political Economy*. He was also a frequent contributor to the *British Friend, Commonsense*, the *Commonwealth*, the *Contemporary Review*, the Co-operative Wholesale Society's *Annual*, the *English Review, Foreign Affairs*, the *Hibbert Journal*, the *New Age*, the *New Republic, Sociological Papers* (later the *Sociological Review*), the *U.D.C., War and Peace*; and more occasionally to some forty other journals. His major books and pamphlets were *The Physiology of Industry* (1889) [with A. F. Mummery]; *Problems of Poverty* (1891, 8th ed. 1913); *Evolution of Modern Capitalism* (1894, 4th ed. 1926); *Problem of the Unemployed* (1896, 4th ed. 1904); *John Ruskin: Social Reformer* (1898; 4th ed. 1904); *War in South Africa* (1900); *Economics of Distribution* (1900); *Social Problem* (1901); *Psychology of Jingoism* (1901); *Imperialism: a study* (1902); *International Trade* (1904); *Canada Today* (1906); *Fruits of American Protection* (1906); *Crisis of Liberalism* (1909); *Industrial System* (1909); *A Modern Outlook* (1910); *The Case for Arbitration* (1911); *Science of Wealth* (1911, 3rd ed. 1938); *Economic Interpretation of Investment* (1911); *Industrial Unrest* (1912); *Gold, Prices and Wages* (1913, 3rd ed. 1924); *German Panic* (1913); *Work and Wealth* (1914); *Traffic in Treason* (1914); *Towards International Government* (1915); *A League of Nations* (1915); *Labour and the Costs of War* (1916); *New Protectionism* (1916); *Fight for Democracy* (1917); *Democracy after the War* (1917); *Forced Labour* (1917); *1920: Dips into the Future* (1918) [by 'Lucian']; *Richard Cobden: the International Man* (1918); *New Holy Alliance* (1919); *Taxation in the New State* (1919); *Morals of Economic Internationalism* (1920); *Taxation* (Labour Party, 1920); *Obstacles to Economic Recovery in Europe* (1920); *Economics of Reparation* (1921); *Problems of a New World* (1921); *Economics of Unemployment* (1922, 3rd ed. 1931); *Incentives in the New Industrial Order* (1922); *Free Thought in the Social Sciences* (1926); *Notes on Law and Order* (1926); *Conditions of Industrial Peace*

(1927); *Wealth and Life* (1929); *Rationalisation and Unemployment* (1930); *God and Mammon* (1931); *Towards Social Equality* (1931); *The Modern State* (1931); *Poverty in Plenty* (1931); *From Capitalism to Socialism* (1932); *The Recording Angel* (1932); *Moral Challenge to the Economic System* (1933); *Democracy and a Changing Civilisation* (1934); *Veblen* (1936); *Property and Improperty* (1937); *Confessions of an Economic Heretic* (1938); *Le Sens de la Responsabilité dans La Vie Sociale* (1938). He contributed to, edited, introduced and prefaced numerous other works of which the following may be mentioned: *Land, Co-operation and the Unemployed*, ed. J. A. Hobson (1894); 'On Labour', in *Good Citizenship*, ed. J. E. Hand (1899); 'Protection as a Working Class Policy', in *Labour and Protection*, ed. H. W. Massingham (1904); anonymous articles in *Towards a Social Policy*, ed. J. L. Hammond (1906); *William Clarke, a Collection of his Writings*, edited by H. Burrows and J. A. Hobson (1908); preface to J. B. Glasier, *The Meaning of Socialism* (1919). See also *Labour and Social Credit* (Labour Party, 1920) and *The Living Wage* (ILP, 1926). For a detailed bibliography see A. J. Lee, 'A Study of the Social and Economic Thought of J. A. Hobson' (London PhD, 1970).

Sources: *Derby School Register*, ed. B. Tacchella (1902); *Modern Mayors of Derby* (1909); *Parliamentary Papers*, VIII 1918 Cd 9153, XIII 1918 Cd 9236, XII 1919 Cmd 360; *Manchester Guardian*, 14 Oct to 27 Nov 1918; J. A. Hobson, *New Leader*, 4 Apr 1924; *Committee on the National Debt and Taxation* (Colwyn) 1927 Cmd 2800 XI and *M. of E.* 1927 Non-Parl; P. T. Homans, *Contemporary Economic Thought* (1928); J. A. Hobson, 'Sixty Years of England', *South Place Monthly Record*, June 1930; E. M. Forster, *G. L. Dickinson* (1934); W. P. Maddox, *Foreign Relations in British Labour Politics* (1934); H. W. Nevinson, *Fire of Life* (1935); J. M. Keynes, *General Theory of Employment, Interest and Money* (1936); G. D. H. Cole, *Political Quarterly* (1938) 439; J. H. Muirhead, *Reflections of a Journeyman in Philosophy* (1942); M. A. Hamilton, *Remembering my Good Friends* (1944); H. N.

Brailsford, *Lifework of J. A. Hobson* (1948); B. Webb, *Our Partnership* (1948); S. Olivier, *Letters and Selected Writings*, ed. M. Olivier (1948); T. W. Hutchison, *Review of Economic Doctrines 1870-1929* (1953); D. Garnett, *The Golden Echo* (1954); B. Webb, *Diaries, 1924-32*, ed. M. Cole (1956); Hugh Dalton, *Fateful Years* (1957); J. Bowle, *Viscount Samuel* (1957); P. Poirier, *The Advent of the Labour Party* (1958); J. Dorfman, *Economic Mind in American Civilisation*, vols 4 and 5 (1959); A. Bullock, *Life and Times of Ernest Bevin 1* (1960); A. Marwick, *Clifford Allen* (1964); R. K. Middlemas, *The Clydesiders* (1965); R. E. Dowse, *Left in the Centre* (1966); R. Skidelsky, *Politicians and the Slump* (1967); V. I. Lenin, *On Britain* (Moscow, n.d.); J. A. Hobson papers, University of Hull Library; personal information: Harold Hobson and the late Mrs Mabel Scott. OBIT. R. H. Tawney, *DNB* (1931-40); G. D. H. Cole, *Econ. J. 50* (1940) 351-60; *Nature 145* (1940) 770; F. W. Hirst, *Manchester Guardian*, A. G. Gardiner, *News Chronicle*, *Times*, 2 Apr 1940; F. Brockway, *New Leader*, 4 Apr 1940; *Derbyshire Advertiser*, 5 Apr 1940; *Times Literary Supplement*, 6 Apr 1940; S. K. Ratcliffe, *The Standard*, May 1940; C. D. Burns, *South Place Monthly List*, May 1940; A. Creech Jones, *Travel Log*, May 1940; S. K. and K. M. Ratcliffe, *South Place Ethical Society*, July 1958.

ALAN LEE

See also: *Norman ANGELL; *Clifford ALLEN; *H. N. BRAILSFORD; *Herbert BURROWS; *William CLARKE; *Stanton COIT; J. Ramsay MACDONALD; *E. D. MOREL; *G. D. H. COLE; *John WHEATLEY

HOLYOAKE, Austin (1826-74)
SECULARIST, RADICAL PRINTER AND PUBLISHER

Born in Birmingham on 27 October 1826, a younger brother of G. J. Holyoake whose career his own closely followed, Austin Holyoake became a Socialist after hearing Robert Owen's views discussed at home. He learned his trade from his brother-in-law, John Griffith Hornblower, who was the first printer of the *Reasoner*. In 1847 Austin took over Hornblower's presses and acted as G. J. Holyoake's printer until the two brothers went into partnership in 1851. He managed the printing side of the Fleet Street Publishing House, 1853-62, and the publishing side, 1859-62. He then set up on his own as 'Austin & Co.' at 17 Johnson's Court until his death in 1874 when the business was acquired by the National Secular Society for Charles Watts.

During the 1850s Austin was very much overshadowed by his elder brother, but after 1862 he came into his own as Charles Bradlaugh's assistant. He sub-edited the *National Reformer* from 1866 to 1874, and acted as a bridge between the two halves of the Secularist movement. He was a radical leader of the second rank, being a member of many republican committees and secretary of the Garibaldi sub-committee in charge of recruiting the legion in 1860-1. As a member of the Association for Promoting the Repeal of the Taxes on Knowledge and his brother's printer, he was the last man in England to be prosecuted for selling unstamped newspapers. In 1866 he joined the Reform League, and in 1871 chaired the meeting which formed a Republican Committee in London. He also chaired several debates, including that between G. J. Holyoake and C. Bradlaugh at the Hall of Science in 1870.

He was married twice. His first wife Lucy died in childbirth, aged twenty-seven, on 23 September 1855, and he himself died of consumption on 10 April 1874.

Writings: *National Secular Society Almanac*, eds. C. Bradlaugh and A. Holyoake (1869-74) 48 pp. plus supplements; *Secular Ceremonies, A Burial Service* (1870) 8 pp; *Does there exist a Moral Governor of the Universe?: an argument against the alleged universal benevolence in nature* (1870) 8 pp; Preface to *The Existence of God* [report of debate between A. Robertson and C. Bradlaugh] (1870) 2 pp.; *Large or Small Families?: on which side lies the balance of comfort?* (1870) 8 pp.; *Thoughts on Atheism; or, can man by searching find out God?* (1870) 8 pp.; *Facetiae for Freethinkers* [1871?]; *The Secularist's Manual of Songs and Cere-*

monies, eds. A. Holyoake and C. Watts [1872?] of which Holyoake's contributions were: 'The Essentials of Elocution', 'A Marriage Service' and 'A Burial Service' (first published 1870); *The Book of Esther: a specimen of what passes as the inspired word of God* (1873) 12 pp.; *Daniel the Dreamer: a Biblical biography* (1873) 16 pp.; *Heaven and Hell: where situated* (1873) 8 pp.; *Ludicrous Aspects of Christianity: a response to the challenge of the Bishop of Manchester* (in a speech delivered by him . . . in August 1870) (1873) 16 pp.; *Superstition Displayed: being the celebrated letter of William Pitt, Earl of Chatham* (1873) 4 pp.; *Would a Republican Form of Government be suitable to England?* (1873) 12 pp.; *Sick Room Thoughts* (1874) 2 pp.

Sources: Scattered references to him are to be found in the *Reasoner*, in G. J. Holyoake's papers and the writings by and about him. A fragment of autobiography is contained in a letter to the *Eastern Post*, Apr 1871, which is in the Holyoake Papers in Manchester (no. 2005). The main sources are the obituary notices in the *National Reformer*, 19 Apr and 10 May 1874 and the sketch by Harriet Law in *Secular Chronicle*, 24 Feb 1878. The second *National Reformer* article was reprinted by G. J. Holyoake as *In Memoriam. Austin Holyoake, died April the 10th* (1874) which includes Austin's *Sick Room Thoughts*. The substance of the obituary notices is printed in J. M. Wheeler, *A Biographical Dictionary of Freethinkers of all Ages and Nations* (1889) and F. Boase, *Modern English Biography* 5 (1912, repr. 1965). See also references in general works, examples of which are C. D. Collet, *History of the Taxes on Knowledge* (1899), W. E. Adams, *Memoirs of a Social Atom*, 2 vols (1903; reprinted in one volume with an Introduction by John Saville: New York, 1968); F. B. Smith, 'The Atheist Mission, 1840–1900' in *Ideas and Institutions of Victorian Britain*, ed. R. Robson (1967) and D. Tribe, *100 Years of Freethought* (1967).

E. ROYLE

See also: *Charles BRADLAUGH; G. J. HOLYOAKE.

HOLYOAKE, George Jacob (1817–1906)

SECULARIST, CO-OPERATOR AND LIBERAL JOURNALIST

Born in Birmingham on 13 April 1817, the second child and eldest son of George Holyoake, a whitesmith, and Catherine Groves, he was brought up in near-poverty. He had little formal education and at the age of nine went to learn his father's trade at the Eagle Foundry. Between 1834 and 1840 he attended classes at the Mechanics' Institute where he excelled in mathematics. Several of his fellow pupils were followers of Robert Owen, and in 1837 Holyoake gave his first lecture on Socialism. The following year he joined the Association of All Classes of All Nations, which in May 1839 amalgamated with the National Community Friendly Society to become the Universal Community Society of Rational Religionists, administered by a Central Board. In 1839, he married, left the foundry, and started teaching. Two of his friends, F. Hollick and J. L. Murphy, had become Socialist lecturers, and in 1840 he was himself appointed by the Worcester branch. The following May he was sent to Sheffield as stationed lecturer and schoolmaster at the Hall of Science. The pay was thirty shillings a week.

Although the Socialists were usually opposed to Christianity, the Central Board now forbade lectures against the churches. Several social missionaries and lecturers, including Holyoake, resented this, and Charles Southwell of Bristol started his own paper, the *Oracle of Reason*, in November 1841, in which to promulgate atheism. A month later he was arrested for publishing a blasphemous article on the Bible. Holyoake was still a theist, but his youthful Christianity had been modified by Unitarian and Socialist influences and he sympathised with the cause of free speech, so he immediately took over the editorship of the *Oracle*. On the way to visit Southwell in Bristol Gaol he gave a lecture at Cheltenham on Home Colonisation. In reply to a question about the place of God in a Socialist community, Holyoake replied that the people were too poor to have a God, unless, like the soldiers after the late war, he were put on half-pay. This was taken for blasphemy and he was arrested. While on bail, he was helped by the London Radicals, including Richard Carlile. His defence speech lasted over nine hours and he was imprisoned in Gloucester Gaol for six months. While there his theism finally became atheism as he studied orthodox defences of Christianity by Leslie and Paley, and he wrote in reply, *A Short and Easy Method with the Saints* and *Paley Refuted in his own Words*.

On release from gaol in February 1843, Holyoake resumed as a lecturer and teacher in London. He was also a member of the London Atheistical Society and secretary of the Anti-Persecution Union. The *Oracle* closed in November 1843, and with M. Q. Ryall he started the *Movement* which ran till Holyoake went to Glasgow as Socialist lecturer in 1845. After nine months that branch could no longer afford to pay him, so he went to Paisley, and then began looking for a new teaching post in London. James Watson, the radical publisher, suggested a new journal, and in June 1846 Holyoake started the *Reasoner* which he issued weekly until 1861. The paper became the centre of his life and he used it to advance an individualised version of Socialism first put forward in his book on *Rationalism* in 1845. The new organisation was at first called Theological Utilitarianism, but after 1852 was known as Secularism.

The aim of Secularism was to present a theory of life which ignored all concerns except the here and now. Holyoake wished to end the theological strife produced by the older freethinkers and to adopt more refined methods of philosophical attack combined with practical co-operation with sympathisers of all creeds. The major influences on Holyoake in the development of this policy were F. W. Newman, J. S. Mill, W. H. Ashurst, Harriet Martineau, and the circle of intellectuals, including G. H. Lewes and George Eliot, who produced the *Leader* newspaper. Secularism gained national recognition under Holyoake's leadership, especially following two public debates with a Congregationalist

minister, Brewin Grant, in January–February 1853 and October 1854. The *Reasoner* reached a circulation of five thousand, and about fifty provincial and metropolitan branches were formed, many of them supported by former Owenites. But Holyoake's concern not to offend respectable opinion alienated some secularists who began to follow Charles Bradlaugh's more militant leadership, and the latter's paper, the *National Reformer*, replaced the *Reasoner* as the national organ of Secularism in 1861.

After this, Holyoake's other interests gradually supplanted Secularism. He was always active in politics, though in 1848, when he edited with W. J. Linton a Chartist newspaper, the *Cause of the People*, he was only on the fringe of the Chartist movement; and he also edited the first number of Harney's *Friend of the People* (7 December 1850) out of friendship with Harney, when the latter was ill. He was one of the first to advocate co-operation with the middle classes, was a member of Joseph Cowen's Northern Reform Union, the London Political Union and, in 1866, the Reform League, but his advocacy of the 'intelligence franchise' lost him some support. He was a firm advocate of Gladstonian Liberalism and his pamphlets *The Liberal Situation* (1865) and *A New Defence of the Ballot* (1868) were widely acclaimed. Like many contemporary radicals, he took a keen interest in foreign affairs, being among those who welcomed the European refugees to London in 1848, and was on several of the committees set up to help them and their countries. In 1860–1 he was acting secretary to the committee established to finance a British voluntary expedition to support Garibaldi. In domestic politics he was less openly republican and his views on the labour question never outgrew Owenism. For him, trade unions were benefit societies and organisations for maintaining standards oı craftsmanship, and the co-operative movement and emigration were alternatives to strike action and state socialism. He never accepted the need for Labour to break with the Liberals. In 1869 he was responsible for persuading the foreign office to instruct Consulates to include labour information in their reports and in 1879 and 1882 he went to North America to prepare an Emigrant's Guide Book.

Next to Secularism, the co-operative movement is most closely associated with Holyoake's name. He was never an important leader on the organisational side, but he was one of its best-known public figures and its most powerful advocate in print. As an Owenite he knew many of the early co-operators, especially at Rochdale, and his book, *Self Help by the People* (1858), was largely responsible for the international fame of the Rochdale Equitable Pioneers' Society. The book went through ten editions and many reprints in English, and appeared in at least seven foreign languages. Holyoake was recognised as the international leader of Co-operation and attended many Co-operative Congresses both at home and abroad. He was a promoter of the first British Congress in 1869, presided in 1875 and 1887, and was present at the first Italian Congress in Milan in 1886. He was always concerned to stress that Co-operation involved profit-sharing in production as well as consumption, and urged the co-operative movement with little success to promote co-partnership. After the 1884 Congress, a separate co-partnership movement was started, and Holyoake's later efforts went into this.

Holyoake described himself as an agitator and this was his main achievement. He was especially concerned with the freedom of individual activity and expression. In 1851, with his brother Austin, he started a printing business which, with the acquisition of James Watson's stock in 1853, became a publishing house at 147 Fleet Street. In the agitation which led up to the abolition of the newspaper stamp in 1855 Holyoake, as a member of the Association for the Repeal of the Taxes on Knowledge, incurred potential fines of over £600,000 for publishing monthly papers (the *War Chronicles* and the *War Fly* sheets) at weekly intervals. The publishing business was closed in 1862, but he was unable to escape the urge to write his own papers. In 1876 he began the *Secular Review* which rallied the opposition to Bradlaugh over his publication of the

Fruits of Philosophy in 1877. A short-lived British Secular Union was started to rival Bradlaugh's National Secular Society (founded 1866). In 1892, Holyoake was a founder of the Rationalist Press Committee (Association in 1899), of which he was the first president.

His main object as an agitator was to remove the Christian bias in the law. He was prominent in the movements for secular education and the replacement of the oath by affirmation, though he disagreed with Bradlaugh's efforts to enter Parliament (1880–5) because the latter was willing to take the oath. He was also president of the Liberty of Bequest Committee (from 1893), president of the Travelling Tax Abolition Committee (from 1887) and a member of the Peace Society. As a Liberal journalist he edited the *Brighton Guardian* (1878–80) and contributed to a large number of radical papers, including the *Newcastle Chronicle* and the *Birmingham Weekly Post*. He was personally acquainted with many MPs from all parties, was eager to help the Liberal Whips in their increasingly difficult task of finding candidates, and built himself a powerful position as a parliamentary lobbyist. An Oddfellow and member of several political clubs and professional bodies, he was elected an honorary member of the National Liberal Club in 1893. He offered himself for Parliament in 1857 (Tower Hamlets), 1868 (Birmingham) and 1884 (Leicester), but never went to the poll.

As a public speaker, Holyoake triumphed over the disadvantages of slight build and a weak, high-pitched voice. His health was frequently bad, and he suffered periodical blindness after 1847. His main weapons were a barbed wit (which alienated friends), fairmindedness (which disarmed enemies) and obvious sincerity. As a writer he was pedantic, but his journalism was skilful and his pen was always ready to defend the rights of the individual. He was not a good historian, his autobiographies and histories of secularism and co-operation are not seldom misleading, and he frequently overestimated his own importance. He outlived many of the controversies which made his early reputation, and later contemporaries came to regard him as the grand old man of reform.

Holyoake married twice: in 1839, Ellen Williams (died 1884) by whom he had four sons and three daughters, and in 1886, Jane Pearson. He died on 22 January 1906 and his ashes lie in Highgate Cemetery. He left an estate valued at £2206 (net). In 1911 the new headquarters of the Co-operative Union in Manchester were named after him.

Writings: Holyoake's writings are numerous. G. W. F. Goss, *A Descriptive Bibliography of the Writings of George Jacob Holyoake With a Brief Sketch of his Life* (1908), gives an almost complete list with details. He has omitted the following: *Undiscussed Errors which threaten Co-operation* (n.d.) 4 pp.; and from the *Cabinet of Reason* series (edited by Holyoake 1851–4), no. 8. *Gospel Exercises*; no. 9. *Theology for the People*; no. 10. *Essays, Critical and Theological.*

The most important of Holyoake's works are: (1) Biographical: *The History of the Last Trial by Jury for Atheism in England* (1850); *Among the Americans* (1881); *Travels in search of a Settler's Guide Book of America and Canada* (1884); *Sixty Years of an Agitator's Life* (1892); *The Warpath of Opinion* (1896); *Bygones Worth Remembering* (1905). (2) Secularism: *Paley Refuted in his Own Words* (1843) 39 pp.; *Rationalism: a treatise for the times* (1845) 47 pp.; *The Logic of Death* (1850) 15 pp.; *The Philosophic Type of Religion* (1851) 26 pp.; *Secularism, the Affirmative Philosophy of the People* (1854) 16 pp.; *The Trial of Theism* (1858); *The Principles of Secularism briefly explained* (1859) 40 pp.; *The Logic of Life* (1860) 16 pp.; *The Limits of Atheism* (1861) 16 pp.; *Cumming wrong; Colenso right* (1863); *The Origin and Nature of Secularism* (1896). (3) Discussions: *Christianity and Secularism* (with Brewin Grant, 1853); *Report of a Public Discussion* (with Brewin Grant, 1854); *Secularism, Scepticism, and Atheism* (with C. Bradlaugh, 1870). (4) Co-operation: *Self Help by the People: history of co-operation in Rochdale, Part I, 1844–1857* (1858); *Part II, 1857–1877* (1878); *The History of Co-operation in Halifax* (1867); *The History of Co-operation in England, vol. 1: The pioneer period 1812–1844* (1875);

vol. 2: *The constructive period 1845–1878* (1879); *Manual of Co-operation* (1885); *Self-help a Hundred Years ago* (1888); *The Co-operative Movement today* (1891); *A Jubilee History of the Leeds Industrial Co-operative Society* (1897); *History of Co-operation* (revised edition, 1906). (5) Radicalism: *The advantages and disadvantages of trades unions* (1841) 12 pp.; *The Government and the Working-man's Press* (1853) 12 pp.; *The Case of Thomas Pooley* (1857) 32 pp.; *The Workman and the Suffrage* (1859) 16 pp.; *The Social Means of promoting Temperance* (1859) 31 pp.; *The Liberal Situation* (1865) 36 pp.; *A New Defence of the Ballot* (1868) 8 pp.; *The Common People* (1870) 8 pp.; *A Plea for Affirmation in Parliament* (1882) 20 pp. (6) Education: *Practical Grammar* (1844); *Mathematics no Mystery* (1847); *A Logic of Facts* (1848); *Rudiments of Public Speaking and Debate* (1849). (7) Brief biographies: *Richard Carlile* (1849) 40 pp.; *Henry Hetherington* (1849) 16 pp.; *Robert Owen* (1859) 28 pp.; *Charles Bradlaugh* (1891) 16 pp.; *Thomas Burt* (1895) 16 pp.; also nine contributions to *DNB* (see Goss, 81). (8) Periodicals edited: *Oracle of Reason* (1842); *Movement* (1843–5); *Reasoner* (1846–61); *Cause of the People* (1848); *Counsellor* (1861); *Secular World and Social Economist* (1862–4); *English Leader* (1864–6); *Working Man* (1866); *Industrial Partnerships' Record* (1867–8); *Social Economist* (1868–9); *Secular Review* (1876–7); *Brighton Guardian* (1878–80); *Present Day* (1883–6).

Sources:

(1) MSS: Holyoake Papers: Co-operative Union Library, Holyoake House, Manchester; Holyoake Collection, Bishopsgate Institute, London; Local Collection, Birmingham Central Library (some minor items); Museo del Risorgimento, Milan; Harriet Martineau (Add. MSS 42, 726), Charles Babbage (Add. MSS 37, 193), Leigh Hunt (Add. MSS 38, 111) collections, British Museum; Duke University, Durham, N. Carolina.

(2) Secondary: The major sources are J. McCabe, *Life and Letters of George Jacob Holyoake* (1908), G. W. F. Goss, *A De-*

scriptive Bibliography (1908) (cited above) and
E. Royle, 'George Jacob Holyoake and the
Secularist Movement in Britain, 1841–1861',
Cambridge PhD (1968) unpublished. The
most useful additional sources are: R. J.
Hinton, *English Radical Leaders* (New York,
1875) 255–74; C. D. Collet, *History of the
Taxes on Knowledge* (1899); W. E. Adams,
Memoirs of a Social Atom, 2 vols (1903;
reprinted in one volume with an Intro-
duction by John Saville: New York, 1968);
DNB (second supplement, 1912); J. Mc-
Cabe, *A Biographical Dictionary of Modern
Rationalists* (1920); F. E. Gillespie, *Labor
and Politics in England, 1850–1867* (1927);
W. Kent, *London Worthies* (1939); G. D. H.
Cole, *A Century of Co-operation* [1945?];
J. E. McGee, *A History of the British Secular
Movement* (1948); J. Eros, 'The Rise of
Organised Freethought in Mid-Victorian
England', *Sociological Rev.* (July 1954) 98–
118; A. Bonner, *British Co-operation* (1961);
R. Harrison, *Before the Socialists* (1965); S.
Budd, 'Militancy and Expediency – an
account of the Secular Movement in the
Nineteenth Century', paper (unpublished)
read at the *Past and Present* conference on
Popular Religion 7 July 1966; *The Red
Republican and The Friend of the People* with
an Introduction by John Saville, vol. 1
(1966) i–xv; S. Budd, 'The Loss of Faith:
reasons for unbelief among members of the
Secular Movement in England 1850–1950',
Past and Present, no. 36 (Apr 1967) 106–25;
F. B. Smith, 'The Atheist Mission, 1840–
1900', in *Ideas and Institutions of Victorian
Britain*, ed. R. Robson (1967); W. S. Smith,
The London Heretics, 1870–1914 (1967);
D. Tribe, *100 Years of Freethought* (1967);
J. F. C. Harrison, *Robert Owen and the
Owenites in Britain and America* (1969). The
latter lists a number of Holyoake's works
and contains a comprehensive bibliography
of Owenism. OBIT. *Times*, 23 Jan 1906;
Co-op. News, 27 Jan 1906; *Times*, 11 Apr
1906; obituary notices appeared in newspapers throughout Europe and both the
Manchester and London Collections have a
large number of cuttings.

E. ROYLE

See also: *Charles BRADLAUGH; *G. W.

FOOTE; E. O. GREENING; *Thomas HUGHES;
Lloyd JONES; William PARE; James SMITHIES;
and below: Retail Co-operation – Nineteenth Century.

**Retail Co-operation – Nineteenth Cen-
tury:** E. V. Neale, *Scheme for the Formation
of the Working Associations into a General
Union* [1850] 15 pp.; Society for the Forma-
tion of Co-operative Stores, *Laws for the
Government of the Society* (1851) 11 pp.;
L. Jones, 'Co-operative Stores and Co-
operative Workshops: their value in the
social movement', *Trans. Co-op. League*, Part
III (Oct 1852) 88–95; Society for Promoting
Working Men's Associations, *Report* (1852);
Anon., 'Co-operative Trading', *Chambers's
Edinburgh J.* 19, 28 May 1853, 343–5; A. J.
L. St André, *Five Years in the Land of Refuge:
a letter on the prospects of co-operative associa-
tions in England* (1854); J. Holmes, 'The
economic and moral advantages of co-
operation in the provision of food', *Trans.
NAPSS* (1857) 567–9; Anon., 'Progress of
Co-operation', *Chambers's J.* 9, 23 Jan 1858,
70–2; J. Wilson, 'The Liverpool Co-opera-
tive Provident Association', *Trans. NAPSS*
(1858) 579–83 and (1862) 801–3; W.
Chambers, *Co-operation in its Different Branches*
(Social Science Tracts, no. 1 [1860]) 24 pp.;
H. Fawcett, 'How the Condition of the
Labouring Classes may be raised by Co-
operation', *Trans. NAPSS* (1860) 371–3;
idem, 'Co-operative Societies: their social
and economical aspects', *Macmillan's Mag.* 2
(Oct 1860) 434–41; M. D. Hill, 'Co-opera-
tion', *Trans. NAPSS* (1860) 748–55; J.
Watts, 'Co-operative Societies', *Trans.
NAPSS* (1860) 873–4; W. N. Molesworth,
'On the Extent and Results of Co-operative
Trading Associations at Rochdale', *JRSS* 24
(Dec. 1861) 507–14; E. Potter, *Some Opinions
on Co-operative Associations &c.* (1861) 27 pp.;
H. Fawcett, 'On the Present Prospects of
Co-operative Societies', *Macmillan's Mag.* 5
(Feb 1862) 335–42; G. J. Holyoake, 'On
Certain Moral Errors endangering the
Permanence of Co-operative Success', *Trans.
NAPSS* (1862) 804; J. Plummer, 'Co-opera-
tion in Lancashire and Yorkshire', *British
Almanack and Companion* (1862) 58–80; H.
Solly, 'On the Relation of Co-operative

Societies to the Educational and Moral Improvement of the Working Classes', *Trans. NAPSS* (1862) 803–4; A Campbell, 'Co-operation: its origin, advocates, progress difficulties and objects', *Trans. NAPSS* (1863) 752; [A. Hill], 'Co-operative Societies', *Q. Rev. 114* (Oct 1863) 418–48; H. Pitman, 'Co-operative Stores', *Trans. NAPSS* (1863) 624–7; J. Plummer, 'On the Past and Present Aspects of Co-operation', *Trans. NAPSS* (1863) 752–3; Anon., 'The Progress of Co-operation: a chapter of contemporary history', *Good Words* (1864) 660–4; [H. Martineau], 'Co-operative Societies in 1864', *Edinburgh Rev. 120* (Oct 1864) 407–36; *The Co-operator: a record of co-operative progress by working men*, ed. J. Pitman (Manchester, 1864); J. M. Ludlow and L. Jones,' *The Progress of the Working Class, 1832–67* (1867); J. Borrowman, 'National Co-operative Organisation', *Co-op. Congress Report* (1869) 81–3; C. Bray, 'Organisation and Co-operation', *Co-op. Congress Report* (1869) 52–7; R. Harper, N. Wilkinson and J. C. Farn, 'Causes of Failure in Co-operative Stores', *Co-op. Congress Report* (1869) 92–6; G. J. Holyoake, 'Defects of Official Statistics of Co-operation', *Trans. NAPSS* (1869) 594–7; J. T. McInnes, 'Hindrances to Co-operation', *Co-op. Congress Report* (1869) 96–9; W. N. Molesworth, 'The Best Means of making Co-operative Societies mutually helpful', *Co-op. Congress Report* (1869) 62–3; W. Pare, 'Co-operative Organisation and Propaganda', *Co-op. Congress Report* (1869) 79–81; H. Travis, 'Higher Aims of Co-operation and how to realise them', *Co-op. Congress Report* (1869) 49–52; J. Watts, 'Co-operation: how to secure safe progress therein', *Co-op. Congress Report* (1869) 43–7; J. M. Ludlow, 'The Amendment of the Law relating to Co-operative Societies', *Co-op. Congress Report* (1870) 51–7; J. McKendrick, 'Co-operation in the North of England', *Trans. NAPSS* (1870) 543–4; E. V. Neale, 'The State, Prospects and Objects of Co-operation', *Co-op. Congress Report* (1870) 43–8; J. Holmes, 'Co-operation, its progress and present position', *Trans. NAPSS* (1871) 581–6; E. V. Neale, 'On the State of the Law affecting Co-operative Societies', *Co-op*

Congress Report (1871) 64–6; R. B. Walker, 'On the More Complete Organisation of the Co-operative Body', *Co-op. Congress Report* (1871) 8–11; J. Head, 'Retail Traders and Co-operative Stores', *Trans. NAPSS* (1872) 444–56; L. Jones, 'Federative Trading', *Co-op. Congress Report* (1872) 53–5; A Post Office Man, 'The Story of the Civil Service Supply Association by One of the Original Members', *Cornhill Mag. 28* (July 1873) 45–53; G. J. Holyoake, *The Logic of Co-operation* (1873) 16 pp.; J. T. McInnes, 'On the Most Satisfactory Principle and Method of Voting as applicable to Distributive and Productive Societies Respectively', *Co-op. Congress Report* (1873) 21–6; E. W. Bradbrook, 'The Co-operative Land Movement', *JRSS 37* (1874) 327–37; H. Fawcett, 'The Position and Prospects of Co-operation', *Fortnightly Rev. 21* (Feb 1874) 190–208; L. Jones, 'The Progress and Consolidation of Co-operation', *Co-op. Congress Report* (1874) 35–7; G. J. Holyoake, 'The Beginning of the Co-operative Trouble', *Cont. Rev. 26* (July 1875) 269–80; E. V. Neale, *The Principle of Unity, the Life of Co-operation* (Manchester, 1875) 8 pp.; R. B. Walker, 'The Present State of the Co-operative Movement and the Future before it', *Co-op. Congress Report* (1875) 49–50; G. J. Holyoake, 'A Dead Movement which learned to live again', *Cont. Rev. 28* (Aug 1876) 444–61; E. V. Neale, 'The Policy of paying High Dividends', *Co-op. Congress Report* (1876) 13–18; L. Jones, *Co-operation: its position, its policy and its prospects* (1877) 31 pp.; E. V. Neale, *Economics of Co-operation* (1877) 30 pp.; G. J. Holyoake, 'The New Principle of Industry', *19th C. 4* (Sep 1878) 494–511; T. Hughes, *The History and Objects of Co-operation* [1878?] 27 pp.; J. H. Lawson, 'Co-operative Stores: reply to the shopkeepers', *19th C. 5* (Feb 1879) 362–7; T. Lord, 'A Shopkeeper's View of Co-operative Stores', *19th C. 5* (Apr 1879) 733–9; G. J. Holyoake, *The History of Co-operation in England 2: The Constructive Period 1845–78* (1879); S.C. on Co-operative Stores, *Reports* 1878–9 IX (344); 1880 (111) VIII (367); A. Greenwood, *The Fundamental Principles of Co-operation* (Manchester, [1881]) 8 pp.; T. Hughes and E. V. Neale, *A Manual for*

Co-operators (Manchester, 1881); A. H. D. Acland and J. Lockhead, 'The Present Position and Future Development of Co-operation', *Co-op. Congress Report* (1883) 7–11; J. Holmes, 'Upon the Decline of the Early Principles and Practice of Co-operation in Recent Working', *Trans. NAPSS* (1883) 575–6; A. H. D. Acland and B. Jones, *Working Men Co-operators: an account of the co-operative movement in Gt Britain* (1884) 8th ed. (Manchester, 1941); E. V. Neale, *The Economic Aspect of Co-operation* (Manchester, [1884]) 11 pp.; L. Levi and E. V. Neale, 'Condition of the Working Classes', *Trans. NAPSS* (1884) 588–641; L. Feber, 'The Rise and Progress of Co-operation in Oldham', *Co-op. Congress Report* (1885) 55–6; T. Hughes, 'Co-operation in England', *Good Words 26* (1885) 63–7, 161–5; A. H. D. Acland, 'Co-operation among English workingmen', *Harper's Mag. 12* (June–Nov 1886) 923–31; idem, 'Working Men's Co-operative Organisations in Great Britain', *JRSS 49* (Dec 1886) 755–9; B. Jones, *What is meant by Co-operation* (Edinburgh, 1886) 35 pp.; E. V. Neale, *The Common Sense of Co-operation* (Manchester, 1886) 8 pp.; G. J. Holyoake, *The Growth of Co-operation in England* (Manchester, 1887) 22 pp.; V. Nash, *The Relation of Co-operative to Competitive Trading* (Manchester, 1887) 11 pp.; T. Ritchie, *The Relation of Co-operative to Competitive Trading with Special Reference to High and Low Dividends* (Manchester, 1887) 16 pp.; Anon., 'The Crisis in Co-operation', *Spectator, 60* (1887) 760–1; G. J. Holyoake, *The Policy of Commercial Co-operation as respects including the Consumer* [1888] 16 pp.; B. Jones, 'Progress, Organisation and Aims of Working Class Co-operators', *JRSS 51* (1888) 33–53; E. V. Neale, *The Distinction between Joint Stockism and Co-operation* (Manchester, [1888]) 8 pp.; J. C. Gray, *The System of Credit as practised by Co-operative Societies* (Manchester, 1889) 32 pp.; idem, *Co-operation versus Competition* (Manchester, 1889) 12 pp.; G. J. Holyoake, 'The Progress of Co-operation I: England', *New Rev. 1* (Sep 1889) 332–44; M. De Morgan, 'Co-operation in England in 1889', *West. Rev. 133* (May 1890) 532–40; W. A. S. Hewins,

'The Co-operative Movement', *Econ. Rev. 1* (Oct 1891) 537–44; G. J. Holyoake, *Self-help a Hundred Years ago* (1891); idem, *The Co-operative Movement today* (1891: 7th ed. 1921); A. Maskery, 'How best to utilise the Increasing Surplus Capital of the Movement', *Co-op. Congress Report* (1891) 109–10; B. Potter, *The Co-operative Movement in Great Britain* (1891); S. Webb, *The Best Method of bringing Co-operation within the Reach of the Poorest of the Population* (1891) 11 pp.; J. M. Ludlow, 'A Dialogue on Co-operation', *Econ. Rev. 2* (Apr 1892) 214–30; B. F. Dunelm, 'The Co-operative Ideal', *Econ. Rev. 4* (1894) 445–62; H. Vivian, *The Objects and Methods of the Co-operative Movement* (1895) 8 pp.; G. Hawkins, 'Are modifications in the Rochdale System of Co-operation necessary to meet the Needs of the Great Centres of Population?', *Co-op, Congress Report* (1896) 136–40; J. Ackland. 'The Failure of Co-operation', *Econ. Rev. 7* (July 1897) 338–53; J. M. Ludlow, 'Is Co-operation a Failure?', *Econ. Rev. 7* (Oct 1897) 450–9; W. E. Snell, 'Is Co-operation a Failure?', *Econ. Rev. 7* (Oct 1897) 460–7; Lord Brassey, 'The Difficulties and Limits of Co-operation', *19th C. 43* (June 1898) 915–31; R. Halstead, 'Practical Co-operation', *Econ. Rev. 8* (Oct 1898) 446–62; Wholesale Trader, 'Co-operation in Practice', *Econ. Rev. 8* (July 1898) 314–25; M. L. Davies, *Co-operation in Poor Neighbourhoods* (Kirkby Lonsdale, 1899) 20 pp.; E. O. Greening, *How to make Co-operation succeed in Large Centres of Population* (Manchester, 1899) 23 pp.; H. W. Wolff, 'Co-operative Ideals', *Econ. Rev. 9* (Jan 1899) 42–66; A. Hewitt, *The Amalgamated Union of Co-operative Employés* (Manchester, [c. 1900]) 16 pp.; C. Webb, *Industrial Co-operation: the story of a peaceful revolution* (Manchester, 1904); G. D. H. Cole, *A Century of Co-operation* (Manchester, [1945?]); S. Pollard, 'Nineteenth Century Co-operation: from community building to shopkeeping' in *Essays in Labour History*, eds. A. Briggs and J. Saville (1960) 74–112; A. Bonner, *British Co-operation: the history, principles and organisation of the British Co-operative Movement* (Manchester, 1961); R. G. Garnett, 'Co-operation and the Owenite-

Socialist Communities in Britain (1825–1845)' (London PhD, 1969).

HOOSON, Edward (1825–69)
CHARTIST AND CO-OPERATOR

Born on 16 April 1825 near Halifax, where he spent his early years. His formal education was limited and he was apprenticed to the trade of wire-drawing. On becoming a journeyman he went to Manchester where he worked for Richard Johnson who later assisted Hooson and his bench-mate, Whiteley, to start their own wire-drawing business. Hooson, who participated actively in the radical movements of his time, was a close friend and supporter of Ernest Jones both before and after Jones's imprisonment in 1848. After the decline of Chartism, Hooson continued to work within the reform movement, and in the middle 1860s was chairman of the Manchester branch of the Reform League, and it was in this capacity that he signed the resolution thanking Thomas Fowe for his services as treasurer of the branch, on the latter leaving Manchester for London. Hooson was also a founder and active supporter of the Union and Emancipation Society, established in the early years of the American Civil War to support the Northern cause and which was largely maintained financially by the liberal capitalist, Thomas Bayley Potter. The Society was dissolved in 1866. With J. C. Edwards he called the well-known meeting, held in the Free Trade Hall, Manchester, on 31 December 1862 which passed resolutions supporting Abraham Lincoln at the time of the American Civil War.

His interests extended to the co-operative sphere where he was among the early advocates of co-operative wholesaling. In 1859 Hooson, with Abraham Greenwood and John C. Edwards, initiated the demand for amendments to the Industrial and Provident Societies Act to enable a federal wholesale society to be legally formed. In this campaign the help of the Christian Socialists, J. M. F. Ludlow and E. V. Neale, was sought. Edward Hooson and James Dyson represented Manchester at conferences in Rochdale in October 1860 and were appointed members of a committee to consider the establishment of a wholesale agency. A conference of delegates from most Lancashire and Yorkshire co-operative societies, held in Manchester on Christmas Day 1860, heard the committee's report and agreed on definite desirable amendments to the I. and P. Acts. Hooson was enrolled as one of the twelve original individual members (in addition to societies) when the North of England Co-operative Wholesale Agency and Depot Society Ltd (later the CWS) was established on Good Friday 1863, each member taking up a 5s share. He served on the committee until his death. A family man, he was enabled to work so actively in the many reform movements of the time through the assistance of his partner Whiteley, who worked long hours to provide for Hooson's family while the latter was engaged in public speaking and other activities.

Hooson died on 11 December 1869 and was buried in Ardwick Cemetery, Manchester, near to the grave of his friend Ernest Jones, who had predeceased him a few months earlier.

Sources: *The Pioneer: a political handy-sheet for men and women*, 16 Feb 1889; *Co-op. News*, 7 Apr 1894 (obit. of T. Fowe); *Co-op. News*, 11 Oct 1902 (obit. of J. Dyson); P. Redfern, *The Story of the C.W.S.* (Manchester, [1913]); idem, *The New History of the C.W.S.* (Manchester, 1938); F. Hourani, *Manchester and Abraham Lincoln* (reprinted from *Manchester Guardian*, 1 Jan 1863 and 11 Feb 1863) [1942] 11 pp.; G. D. H. Cole, *A Century of Co-operation* (Manchester, [1945?]); John Saville, *Ernest Jones: Chartist* (1952): A. Bonner, *British Co-operation* (Manchester, 1961); information on Union and Emancipation Society: Manchester Local History Library.

JOYCE BELLAMY
H. F. BING

See also: *J. M. F. LUDLOW, for Christian Socialism, 1848–54; Percy REDFERN, for Co-operative Wholesaling.

HOWARTH, Charles (1814–68)
OWENITE AND ROCHDALE PIONEER

Little is known of the early life of Charles Howarth who was one of the most active of the Owenite Socialists in Lancashire and one of the founders of the Toad Lane Store in 1844. His birth is sometimes given as 1818 but 1814 is the more likely as he was recorded as being fifty-four when he died. Rochdale, where presumably he was born and where certainly he lived for most of his adult life, had a vigorous intellectual and political life in the early decades of the nineteenth century. Nonconformist religious sects proliferated and there was a bitter struggle between the Anglican church and the Nonconformists over the payment of church rates; the Ten Hour movement was widely supported, with James' Standring, one of the Pioneers, as secretary to the Rochdale Ten Hours Committee; the campaign against the New Poor Law was as vigorous in Rochdale as it was in Todmorden; and the Chartist movement, getting under way in the late 1830s, evoked a powerful response from the Rochdale working class. There was also an influential group of middle-class radicals in the town: Jacob Bright, John Bright's father, being the local leader of the Society of Friends and active in municipal and educational affairs; and his son followed in his father's path in the 1840s.

An Owenite propagandist society had been established in Rochdale as early as 1830. It sent a delegate to the Birmingham Congress of 1831 and in 1833 a retail shop was opened at No. 15 Toad Lane, a few doors from where the 1844 shop was to be established. The shop managed to survive until 1835, its collapse being due to large debts incurred through excessive credit. Howarth was connected with this venture, although a very young man, and so was James Standring. Despite this failure, the Owenite group continued to keep together. In May 1835 Robert Owen established the Association of All Classes of All Nations; and in May 1839 this association amalgamated with the National Community Friendly Society to form the Universal Community Society of Rational Religionists (which

from May 1842 was known simply as the Rational Society). The Rochdale Owenites established a branch of the Rational Society, no. 24. They had already begun renting in April 1838 an annexe of the Weavers Arms in Yorkshire Street and this they named the New Social Institution. This was to remain the centre of Owenite activity in Rochdale and it was to be the birthplace and first headquarters of the Rochdale Pioneers. Lectures, debates, discussions were held here, and there is extant a letter from Howarth to Robert Owen asking him to come and speak in Rochdale, saying that the Socialists had succeeded in making many converts. This was in December 1839.

In 1839 and the early years of the 1840s the majority of the politically conscious workers in Rochdale were in fact under Chartist leadership; but the small group of Owenites continued their activities. The vigorous debates and discussions of these years, together with the strikes of 1842, and especially the weavers' strike of 1844, formed an essential part of the background out of which came the new co-operation. The meetings and discussions in the year 1844 which led to the opening of the Toad Lane shop on the evening of 21 December 1844 have been described many times. The first formal meeting of the Rochdale Society of Equitable Pioneers was on 11 August 1844 when Miles Ashworth, a weaver, was elected president. He was replaced by Charles Howarth at the next quarterly meeting, and it was Howarth who drew up most of the rules of the Society, including the dividend on purchase, who strongly advocated strict cash trading, and who is credited with suggesting the actual name of their Society. Howarth, who was employed as a warper in a cotton mill (and therefore to be ranked among the better-off among the class of skilled workers) was a man of great common sense, very methodical and careful in his habits, and nicknamed 'the lawyer' from his extensive knowledge of the Friendly Societies Acts and of the general problems of efficient organisation.

From the commencement of the Toad Lane store Charles Howarth remained at the centre of most of the activities of the

Rochdale Pioneers for many years. He became secretary of the Corn Mill Society in 1850; was one of the promoters of the Rochdale Co-operative Manufacturing Society in 1854; and in March 1856 he was one of the Pioneers' delegates at a conference in Rochdale to consider setting up a wholesale department. When the North of England Co-operative Wholesale Society was established in 1863 Howarth was one of the original twelve members and he served on the committee until 1866. In 1867 he was associated with the establishment of the Co-operative Insurance Society, being one of the seven persons who took up four shares each to establish a legal company under the Companies Act.

Howarth moved from Rochdale to Heywood, probably at the end of the 1850s. He represented Heywood on a committee in 1860 which began drafting amendments to the Industrial and Provident Societies Acts. Of his private adult life, little is known. He had married some time in his career and there was a family, and on his death the CWS made a grant of £20 to his widow. He died on 25 June 1868 and was buried in Heywood Cemetery when William Cooper delivered the funeral oration, speaking of Howarth's work for the radical and co-operative movements.

Sources: W. Cooper, *History of the Rochdale District Co-operative Corn Mill Society* [n.d. 1860?] 12 pp.; G. J. Holyoake, *History of Co-operation*, 2 vols (1875–9); idem, *History of the Rochdale Pioneers* (1882); W. Robertson, 'Rochdale: the birthplace of modern co-operation', in *Handbook of Annual Co-operative Congress* (Manchester, 1892); F. Podmore, *Robert Owen* (1906); P. Redfern, *The Story of the C.W.S. 1863–1913* (Manchester, [1913]); E. O. Greening, *Memories of Robert Owen and the Co-operative Pioneers* (Manchester, 1925); W. H. Brown, *The Rochdale Pioneers* (Manchester, 1944); G. D. H. Cole, *A Century of Co-operation* (Manchester, [1945?]); A. Bonner, *British Co-operation* (Manchester, 1961); J. F. C. Harrison, *Robert Owen and the Owenites in Britain and America* (1969). OBIT. *Rochdale Observer*, 4 July 1868.

H. F. BING
JOHN SAVILLE

See also: Samuel ASHWORTH; William COOPER; J. DALY; James SMITHIES; *J. STANDRING.

HUGHES, Hugh (1878–1932)
MINERS' LEADER

Born on 4 November 1878 at Easington Lane, near Hetton-le-Hole, County Durham, he was the son of Edward Hughes, a coalminer, and his wife, Elizabeth, daughter of William and Sarah Hughes of Whitford, Flintshire. He was educated until 1887 at South Hetton Church School after which his father returned to North Wales where Hugh continued his education at Llanasa Church School. He declined a place at Newmarket Grammar School and when he was thirteen or fourteen he assisted his father, who was checkweighman at Point of Ayr Colliery, when the latter was ill. About two years later Hugh was working at the Trelogan lead mine and then was employed as a blacksmith on a farm before returning to Point of Ayr. When his father was appointed agent and general secretary of the Denbighshire and Flintshire Miners' Federation in 1898, the family removed to Wrexham. For a time Hugh worked again as a blacksmith before going to Liverpool where he was employed by the Docks Board. When he married in Liverpool in 1905, however, he was a checkweighman and shortly afterwards moved to a similar position at Coed Talon Colliery. About 1915 he became financial secretary of the North Wales Miners' Association, succeeding his father as agent and general secretary in 1925. He served on the MFGB executive on four occasions between 1925 and 1931.

He made an unsuccessful attempt to enter Parliament when he contested Wrexham in the Labour interest at the 1918 general election. At the following general election in 1922 he stood down in favour of his friend, Professor Robert Richards, who became the first Labour MP for Wrexham. In 1921 he was elected to the Denbigh County Council and was made an alderman in 1925. He was also a county magistrate. He married, in 1905, Eliza Jane, daughter of William and Mary Ann Jones, by whom he had two sons and four daughters. When he died at his Wrexham home on 25 December 1932 He was survived by his wife and family. He was buried at Wrexham Borough Cemetery on 29 December, leaving effects valued at £787.

Sources: Personal information: E. Norman Hughes (son of Hugh Hughes); J. C. H. Jones (nephew), and from E. R. Luke, County Librarian, Denbigh, other biographical details. Obit. *Wrexham Leader*, 30 Dec 1932; *Labour Party Report* (1933).

JOYCE BELLAMY

See also: *A. J. Cook, for Mining Trade Unionism, 1915–26; *Edward Hughes; *Peter Lee, for Mining Trade Unionism, 1927–44.

JACKSON, Henry (1840–1920)
CO-OPERATOR AND RADICAL

Born at Charlestown, Northowram near Halifax, on 22 March 1840, Henry Jackson was the son and grandson of shoemakers and grew up to manage a small boot works. He supported the parliamentary candidature of E. O. Greening for Halifax in 1868 and was active in working-class politics in that town from his youth until he removed to Manchester in 1876. He was an active member of the Halifax Co-operative Society from 1864 and served on its management committee. He became an early delegate to CWS meetings and in 1874 was nominated by his colleagues for a seat on the board of the Co-operative Wholesale Society, was elected and served on the board with energy and initiative for eighteen months till he was appointed boot and shoe buyer for the CWS and manager of the CWS boot department in Manchester. This was in 1876; and he continued in the position until his retirement in June 1920. After forty-four years he found it difficult to leave the department and is said to have been often seen in his old office during the remaining months of his life.

At Manchester he retained his interest in political affairs and was a stalwart worker in the advanced radical movement of the

1880s. For a long time he was on the committee of Blackley Co-operative Society and took a keen part in the battle for the right of co-operators to hold meetings in the Boggart Hole Clough. On his 80th birthday he was honoured by a complimentary dinner by the Boot Buyers' Association.

He died suddenly of heart failure on 22 December 1920 leaving a widow, a son and four daughters, and was cremated on Tuesday 28 December at Manchester Crematorium. He left an estate valued at £11,235 (gross).

Sources: P. Redfern, *The Story of the C.W.S.* (Manchester, [1913]); idem, *The New History of the C.W.S.* (Manchester, 1938). Obit. *Co-op. News*, 1 Jan 1921.

H. F. BING

See also: Percy REDFERN, for Co-operative Wholesaling.

JARVIS, Henry (1839–1907)
MINERS' LEADER

Born on 21 May 1839 at Staveley, Derbyshire. Because of the poverty of his parents he received little education and began work at the age of twelve as a 'trapper'; subsequently passing through all the branches of the miner's trade at various collieries in Derbyshire and Yorkshire. He was first involved in an industrial dispute in 1854 when there was a lock-out of miners at Pilley Green, near Barnsley. In 1866 he was discharged from the Staveley Hollingwood Colliery and also, soon afterwards, from the Aldwarke Main Colliery, because of his trade union activities. By 1883 Jarvis was once again in trouble as a result of his efforts to establish a local base for the Derbyshire Miners' Association which had been formed in 1880. In June 1883 he was receiving victimisation payment and was 'morally certain' that he would not succeed in obtaining employment where he was known. He therefore decided to try his fortune in tea-hawking and asked for a grant from the Association to set him up in business. He pointed out that he would always be willing to hold meetings in the interests of the miners when he was on his rounds. The Association agreed to this proposal and allowed him £5. Jarvis never again worked in a mine but combined work for the union with his tea-hawking until he became a full-time official. In 1884 he was elected president, an office which he held until 1887 when he became part-time treasurer; in 1894 he was elected full-time treasurer. He held the office until his death.

Jarvis was not a conspicuous figure in the trade union world but he appeared on a number of platforms advocating workers' unions and supporting advanced Liberal views. An effective organiser, he carried out the routine work of the Association efficiently. During his period of office as treasurer the membership of the Derbyshire Miners' Association rose from about 2500 in 1887 to 36,087 in 1907. The union's funds rose from about £800 to £249,599 in the same period, despite a deficit of £2836 incurred in the 1893 lock-out. In his later years he suffered greatly from bronchitis. He died on 10 May 1907 and was survived by his wife and a grown-up family. He left £82 in his will.

Sources: (1) MSS: Minutes of the Derbyshire Miners' Association, 1880–1907 (NUM, Saltergate, Chesterfield); (2) *Derbyshire Times*, 1880–1907; W. Hallam, *Miners' Leaders* (1894); J. E. Williams, *The Derbyshire Miners* (1962). OBIT. *Derby Mercury*, 17 May 1907; *Derbyshire Times*, 18 May 1907.
J. E. WILLIAMS

See also: Alexander MACDONALD, for Mining Trade Unionism, 1850–79; Benjamin PICKARD, for Mining Trade Unionism, 1880–99.

JENKINS, Hubert (1866–1943)
MINERS' LEADER

Born on 26 September 1866 at Walford, near Ross, Herefordshire, the son of William Jenkins, a tinworks labourer, and his wife Jane (née Wilks). He was educated at Lea School, near Ross, and left school after passing the highest standard at the age of twelve. For three years, from the age of thirteen, he worked underground in the Wigpool Iron Ore mines, Forest of Dean, and when the mine closed he moved to a colliery near Cinderford. At the end of a six weeks' strike, with no pay, in the early months of 1883 he went to live with relatives in the Rhondda and worked at various coalmines in the area. In August 1884 he and Lewis John of Cowbridge went together to the Caerphilly District where they lived at Bedwas and worked at the Rudry, Cwmglo and Wernddu Collieries. Jenkins was already a committed trade unionist and during this period he acted as delegate to the Caerphilly District of Miners, the secretary of which was Lewis Miles. In August 1887 Jenkins left for America.

He first worked in the anthracite coal region of Skulykill County, Pennsylvania, and then went with Thomas Taylor (who had accompanied him to the United States) to Carmelville, Muskingham County, Ohio. There he joined the Knights of Labor and after moving again helped to form a lodge of the United Mineworkers of America at Nicholson's Mine, Guernsey County, Ohio, and for a short time acted as secretary. He was now twenty-three, and after another migration further west, he decided to return to South Wales in the summer of 1890.

He went back to Bedwas, worked in the Rudry pit until the autumn and then he and William Bull (whom Jenkins had met in America) went to Ynysbwl where they worked at the Mynachdy and Darran Diu Collieries. Here Bull became chairman and Jenkins secretary of the joint lodge of Mynachdy and Blackgrove Collieries which was connected with the Rhondda Coal District Miners' Association. Jenkins acted as delegate to the monthly meetings which were held at Porth. Both he and Bull were victimised and Jenkins moved back to the Caerphilly area where he obtained work at Llanbradach and in 1897 he was appointed secretary of the Caerphilly District. When the big strike of 1898 took place his own pit was a non-associated colliery and he and William Matthews (treasurer) were responsible for the collection of levies to assist the strike fund. The South Wales Miners' Federation was formed in October 1898 and Jenkins acted as the *pro tem.* secretary in establishing the East Glamorgan District. Two years later, in 1900, he took over the District secretaryship and part-time agent's position from E. Morgan, and resigned the lodge secretaryship of No. 1 Llanbradach. In 1905 he was elected full-time agent, the district secretaryship going to Henry Richards of Bedwas. Jenkins had been checkweigher at Senghenydd Colliery since November 1902 and this position he now resigned on his full-time appointment.

His career as a full-time official stretched over a period of just over twenty-seven years. His experience in mining had been wider than most, since he had worked in house coal and steam coal seams and in flat and steep measures; and his knowledge of the variety of mining practice served him in good stead when negotiating price lists. He was a member of the executive committee of the SWMF from 1907 until 1932; gave evidence before the R.C. on Mines (1906–9); and served on the South Wales Conciliation Board. He was always an advocate of settlement by conciliation and negotiation in preference to strikes, but he was not a 'peace at any price' trade unionist. He was vigorous in his efforts to appoint workmen's inspectors following the Coal Mines Act of 1911, and he was a leading figure on behalf of the SWMF in the inquiry into the disastrous explosion at Senghenydd on Tuesday 14 October 1913 when 439 men lost their lives [Arnot (1967) 344ff].

Like so many miners' leaders, Jenkins played an active part in local affairs. He became a member of Caerphilly Urban District Council in 1906, was elected to the Glamorgan County Council in 1907 and remained for many years on the latter body, being made an alderman of the county in 1919, serving on many committees and becoming chairman in 1930. During the 1914–18 war, which he supported, he was a member of the Military Appeal Tribunal and was chairman of Caerphilly and District Mayor's Relief Fund Committee.

He retired from the position of full-time agent in July 1932, and then continued to act as a part-time official responsible for compensation claims arising out of fatal accidents. His public work in no way diminished in the last decade of his life. He had been appointed JP in 1914; at one time was chairman of the Treforest School of Mines; from 1930 was a Traffic Commissioner for South Wales; and at various times was a member of the Council of the University of Wales, the executive committee of the Training College of Domestic Arts, the Advisory Council for Technical Education, the executive of the Federation of Education Committees and a governor of several schools. He was a life member of the management committee of The Beeches, a miners' convalescent home, for several years the chairman of Windsor Workmen's Hall and Institute at Abertridwr and president of the Abertridwr Welfare Association.

In 1930, to celebrate his election to the chairmanship of Glamorgan County Council, he and his wife – also a public worker in her own right – were given a presentation of a roll-top desk, a silver tea and coffee service and a wallet of notes.

Hubert Jenkins was a lifelong Baptist and for many years was a member of Ebenezer English Baptist Church. He was possessed of a nice sense of humour. He married his wife, Catherine, in 1890 and there were eight children of the marriage, two dying in infancy. He died on 28 April 1943 at his Abertridwr home and was buried at Penyrheol Cemetery after a service conducted by the Pastor of the Ebenezer English Baptist Church. His wife, two sons and three daughters survived him and he left effects valued at £1765.

Sources: Evidence before the R.C. on Mines, 1908 XX Qs 35267–371; *Labour Who's Who* (1927); *Western Mail*, 21 Mar 1930 and 6 May 1931; *Who's Who in Wales* (1933); R. Page Arnot, *The South Wales Miners* (1967); biographical information: D. Francis, NUM (South Wales); personal information: Miss A. Jenkins, Abertridwr, daughter; MS diaries; microfilm in Hull University. OBIT. *Western Mail*, 29 Apr 1943.

JOHN SAVILLE

See also: William ABRAHAM, for Welsh Mining Trade Unionism.

JOHN, William (1878–1955)
MINERS' LEADER AND LABOUR MP

Born on 6 October 1878 at Cockett, near Swansea, of a mining family, the son of Evan and Rachel John. He attended the National school at Cockett and entered the mines at the age of thirteen and most of his education was obtained later by his own efforts. He became active in trade union affairs as a young man and he was also among the founders of the ILP in the Rhondda valley. For five years he was secretary of the miners' lodge at Llwyn-y-pia before being elected as checkweighman at Glamorgan Collieries, Pontypridd, in 1909. By this time John was becoming well known among the rank and file of Welsh miners and at the time of the long-drawn-out Cambrian Combine strike he became chairman of the Cambrian Committee. The strike began with the lock-out of colliers at the Ely pit in August 1910. Sympathy strikes followed and this ultimately developed into a full-scale confrontation within the Cambrian Combine group. It was an exceedingly bitter struggle and a landmark in the internal evolution of the South Wales Miners' Federation in that the old leadership began to be displaced in the period following the return to work. John himself was sentenced to one year's imprisonment for alleged involvement with the Tonypandy riots but his sentence, and that of John Hopla, was later reduced to eight months by the Home Secretary, Reginald McKenna [Arnot (1967) 317]. During the time he was in prison John was appointed agent for the Rhondda and he took up this position on his release. From 1912 to 1922 he was a member of the executive committee of the SWMF.

From 1920 until his retirement in 1949 on health grounds he was MP for the Rhondda West constituency, the seat becoming vacant because of the resignation of William Abraham (Mabon). In June 1929 John was appointed parliamentary private secretary to J. J. (Jack) Lawson when the latter became parliamentary secretary to the Ministry of Labour. John kept his seat in the general election of 1931 and at subsequent elections. In November 1935 he was appointed a Welsh Whip and was deputy chief Labour Whip from March 1942 to 1945, and at the same time was appointed Comptroller of H.M. Household, 1942–4, and a Lord Commissioner of the Treasury from October 1944 to July 1945. Although not a frequent speaker in the House of Commons he was respected for his mastery of coalfield matters, and for eighteen of his twenty-nine years in the Commons he was secretary of the Welsh parliamentary party. He was a man of moderate views and in all things a supporter of constitutional procedures. His native eloquence was better suited to the valleys of the Rhondda than to the debating chamber at Westminster and he played an important part in the life of his own region. He was an ardent Welsh nationalist, very knowledgeable about the literature of his country, and he won a number of prizes for recitations and essays at eisteddfods. In religion he was a Baptist and served for a period as president of the Welsh Baptist Union. For all his adult life he was an active co-operator.

He married Anna, the daughter of George and Catherine Brooks, in 1908. There were no children of the union, and he died at his Porthcawl home on 27 August 1955. His wife predeceased him by some five years. He left an estate valued at £2324.

Sources: David Evans, *Labour Strife in the South Wales Coalfield, 1910–1911* (Cardiff, 1911); S. V. Bracher, *The Herald Book of Labour Members* (1923); *The Labour Who's Who* (1927); *Dod* (1921); (1942–6); R. Page Arnot, *South Wales Miners 1898–1914* (1967); Obit: *Western Mail*, 29 Aug 1955; *Times*, 30 Aug 1955; *Labour Party Report* (1956).

JOHN SAVILLE

See also: William ABRAHAM, for Welsh Mining Trade Unionism.

JOHNSON, John (1850–1910)
MINERS' LEADER AND LIB-LAB MP

Born on 1 October 1850 at Wapping near Newcastle, the son of Thomas and Martha Johnson, he was educated first at a village dame school and subsequently by reading books lent to him by Primitive Methodist ministers and others. He commenced work in the mines when nine years old. His first association with trade unionism was in 1869 when he was elected as a delegate to meetings of the Northumberland Miners' Association. Originally at Backworth, some six miles north-east of Newcastle, he left there in 1872 for Netherton Colliery and after a short time transferred to Chopping-ton Colliery near Morpeth where he re-mained until a strike in 1877. At the end of that year he went to Andrew's House Colliery in the Chester-le-Street R.D., Co. Durham, where he worked as a hewer for twelve years and was in due course elected colliery delegate to the Durham Miners' Association. In 1883 he was elected to the DMA committee and in 1890 on the death of W. Crawford was appointed general treasurer. He was made financial secretary of the DMA in 1896, a post he held until 1910. He attended the 1889 conference when the MFGB was established and served on the executive committee of the latter in 1908 and 1910. He was also a member of the arbitration committee of the Durham Colliery Owners' Mutual Protection Asso-ciation and the DMA.

In the years which followed the estab-lishment of the MFGB, Johnson took a full share in representing the Durham case in the much disputed eight-hours question. He attended the famous national conference in January 1893 at Birmingham, held in the Hen and Chickens hotel, where for two days the matter was debated. Johnson seconded the Durham motion, proposed by John Wilson, that the eight-hour day must come from the work and pressures of the county unions; and later in the year (April) Johnson was among those who interviewed H. H. Asquith on the same question, as a counter to the agitation for a Government Eight Hour Bill which came from the majority of the MFGB.

A regular attender at national and inter-national trade union conferences, he also took an active part in the Durham Political Reform Association. He served on the Durham County Council from 1901 to 1907

and in January 1904 was elected to Parliament as a Lib-Lab member for the Gateshead constituency. In Parlia-ment he frequently intervened in debates and was an ardent advocate of old age pensions. Re-elected in 1906 he was defeated in the first election of 1910 when, having agreed to sign the Labour Party constitution, he fought the seat wholly in the Labour interest. Pelling (1967) writes of this episode:

> But he was rather too 'advanced' in his views to please either the miners or the local Liberals; and in particular, he offended the miners by supporting the Miners' Eight Hours Act, which they disliked. In January 1910 the Gateshead Liberals put up a candidate against him; the miners flocked into the town to demonstrate their own hostility to him; and so, in spite of having the official Irish Nationalist vote, he was defeated. Thus the most solidly working-class borough in the whole region reverted to Liberalism (p. 327).

Other activities included membership of the Board of Guardians of Durham Union and the presidency of the Durham City Trades Council. By religion a Primitive Methodist, he had been a local preacher from 1878.

He married a Miss Errington by whom he had four sons; and died on 29 December 1910, leaving £866 in his will.

Sources: W. Hallam, *Miners' Leaders* (1894); *WWW* (1897–1916); *Aldersgate* (1904 and 1906); *Durham Chronicle*, 8 Jan 1904; *Dod* (1905); J. Wilson, *History of the Durham Miners' Association, 1870–1904* (Dur-ham, 1907); Evidence before R.C. on Mines vol. III 1908 XX Qs 35915–69; R. F. Wearmouth, *Methodism and the Struggle of the Working Classes, 1850–1900* (Leicester, 1954); idem, *The Social and Political Influence of Methodism in the Twentieth Century* (1957); H. Pelling, *Social Geography of British Elections 1885–1910* (1967). OBIT. *Durham Chronicle*, 30 Dec 1910; *Times*, 30 Dec 1910.

ANTHONY MASON

See also: Alexander MACDONALD, for Mining Trade Unionism, 1850–79; Benjamin PICKARD, for Mining Trade Unionism, 1880–99.

JONES, Benjamin (1847–1942)
CO-OPERATOR

Born on 9 September 1847 at Salford, Manchester, the son of Reuben Jones, a dyer's labourer whose wife was a power-loom weaver. His early years were spent being looked after by baby-minders, an experience which made him sympathetic in later life towards working men being able to keep their wives at home. After a short education at a National School, he commenced work in a cabinet-maker's shop when he was nine. Two years later he was an errand boy to a small Manchester tradesman, and he later became book-keeper to the firm. In 1866 he entered the Manchester office of the CWS as assistant book-keeper under William Nuttall. He had extended his earlier education by evening classes at Owens College, and at the Mechanics' Institute, to the committee of which he was elected at the age of twenty-one. He helped also to organise evening classes for co-operative societies at Blackley and Failsworth and was a Sunday school teacher at the Ragged School, Harpurhey, Manchester.

In 1871 Jones was appointed as a salesman and assistant buyer at the CWS headquarters in Manchester and in 1873 was chosen to open a London branch which commenced business on a small scale at 118 Minories in 1874. At that time co-operative activities in the south of England and in London especially were largely undeveloped. In association with another Lancashire man, William Openshaw, the business expanded rapidly and Jones and his colleagues laid the foundations of the London CWS on a firm basis. From 1874 to 1902 Jones was general manager of all departments of the CWS London branch with the exception of tea, coffee and cocoa. New premises at Leman Street were opened in 1887 and the annual turnover, which had been £130,752 in 1875, rose to £1½ million in 1892 and was £3¼ million in 1902 when

Jones retired. In 1874 Jones was made honorary secretary of the southern sectional board of the Co-operative Union, a position he held until 1894 during which time he organised the movement along the coast from Dover to Bournemouth.

In addition to his work for the London CWS, he was also actively concerned in other aspects of the co-operative movement. At the Oxford Congress in 1882 he drew attention to the need to extend co-operative education, and in the following year he collaborated with A. H. D. Acland MP, then Bursar of Christ Church, Oxford, to produce a textbook for educational classes entitled *Working Men Co-operators*, first published in 1884 and subsequently reprinted for the eighth time in 1941. He gave lectures on co-operative subjects at Toynbee Hall in the 1880s, and read a paper at the Industrial Remuneration Conference of 1885 of which he was a member of the organising committee. He gave practical assistance to the London branch of the Co-operative Printing Society and served as first chairman of the board. He was a member of the central board of the Co-operative Union and was responsible for registering the Union under the Industrial and Provident Societies Act in 1889. At the Co-operative Congress of that year he presided on the second day and was president throughout the 1896 Congress. His work for the co-operative movement enabled him to travel widely throughout Europe and the Middle East, and in 1896, with J. Clay and W. Stoker, CWS directors, he made a world tour. Among other pioneering aspects of his co-operative career should be included the first secretaryship of the Co-operative Guild. He gave evidence in 1884 before the R.C. on the Housing of the Working Classes in which he favoured a system of joint working-class ownership, and in 1888 founded the Tenant Co-operators' Association which returned to tenants one-eighth of the gross rental of their dwellings and was the first co-operative housing society.

He was an advocate of profit-sharing and interested in the Co-operative Aid Society – an organisation for helping groups of working men to start self-governing workshops. His sympathies leaned even more, however, towards productive activities by wholesale societies, where greater success had been achieved than with the co-operative workshops where the workers shared the profits and ran the business, and where many failures had occurred. His views conflicted in this respect with those of E. O. Greening, T. Hughes and E. V. Neale who favoured workers' co-operation in manufacture. Jones believed in the active participation of the CWS in production and was largely responsible for the establishment of the flour mill at Silvertown, the cocoa works at Luton and CWS depots at Bristol, Cardiff and Northampton. His ideas were shared by Beatrice Potter (Mrs Sidney Webb) whom he assisted when she was collecting material for her history of the co-operative movement, published in 1891, and who described him in *My Apprenticeship* as 'a combination of a high-minded grocer, a public-spirited administrator and a wire-puller. Within the co-operative movement he was all three.' He was, however, sufficiently concerned about the role of co-operation in manufacturing to contribute articles on the subject to the *Co-operative News*, which formed the basis of his major literary work, *Co-operative Production*, published in 1894 and a primary source of information on the early attempts at workers' co-operation.

He inaugurated and was honorary secretary of the first parliamentary committee of the Co-operative Union, and in this capacity was the sole witness on behalf of that body before the Town Holdings Commission in 1887 where his evidence resulted in the Commission's recommendation that co-operative societies should have the right to enfranchise their leaseholds. About 1876, shortly after his arrival in London, he was a member of the Labour Representation League. A resident of Norwood, he participated actively in the Norwood Liberal and Radical Association, serving on its committee and being responsible for the establishment of the Norwood Reform Club. In March 1892, following pressure from trade union organisations and the Royal Arsenal

Co-operative Society, he agreed to become a parliamentary candidate for Woolwich. He unsuccessfully contested this constituency in the Labour interest at the 1892 and 1895 general elections; he again tried to enter Parliament as a Lib-Lab candidate at Deptford in 1900 but was not elected. He was also prospective candidate at Romford and Peterborough but in neither case went to the poll. Among his other interests should be mentioned the London Playing Fields Committee, of which he was one of the founder members.

His wife, formerly Miss Annie White of Lancashire, whom he married at Altrincham in 1870, was an active member of the Women's Co-operative Guild. She became secretary of the Norwood Branch, which was the fourth of the first six to be opened in 1884, the year after the Guild was inaugurated. A member of the first central committee, she read papers at Annual Congresses of the Guild in 1885, 1886 and 1887, was president from 1886 to 1891 and a member of the central committee at the time of her premature death in her 46th year in 1894. When Jones retired from the CWS in 1902 he settled at Bournemouth where he owned an hotel, the Queen, several cafés and a bakery business. He continued to write articles for the co-operative press but his main literary work during his retirement was the publication in 1918 of a philosophical autobiography entitled *Life According to Jones*. Although not a regular attender, he was a Congregationalist by religion.

When Jones died at his Bournemouth home on 25 February 1942 at the age of 94 he was one of the last survivors of the generation of co-operators who knew the original Rochdale Pioneers, among whom were Samuel Ashworth, William Cooper, Charles Howarth and James Smithies, and about whom he often spoke. A Congregational minister officiated at his funeral service which took place at North Cemetery Crematorium, Bournemouth, on 2 March 1942. He was survived by three sons and a daughter, and left an estate valued at £10,011

Writings: Evidence before R.C. on the

Housing of the Working Classes, 1884–5 XXX Qs 13760–847; (with A. H. D. Acland) *Working Men Co-operators: an account of the artizans' co-operative movement in Great Britain* (1884; 8th ed. Manchester, 1941); *What is meant by co-operation?* (Edinburgh, 1886) 35 pp.; Evidence before S.C. on Town Holdings, 1887 XIII Qs 10635–1208; 'Progress, Organisation and Aims of Working Class Co-operators', *JRSS 51* (1888) 33–63; 'Co-operation and Profit-sharing', *Econ. J. 2* (1892) 616–28; *Co-operative Production* (Oxford, 1894); (with L.B.) 'Co-operative Wholesale Societies and their Relations to Retail Co-operative Societies', *CWS Annual* (1896) 209–31; 'Retail Co-operation and the Relations between the Individual and the Store', *CWS Annual* (1896) 199–208; 'The Possibilities of International Co-operative Trade', *CWS Annual* (1898) 257–82; 'The Future Financial Development of the Co-operative Movement', *CWS Annual* (1899) 166–96; 'The Position of Co-operation in Other Lands', *CWS Annual* (1901) 379–98; *Life According to Jones* (1918).

Sources: *Bee-Hive*, 28 Aug 1875; *Illustrated Co-operative Almanack* (1890); J. Arnold, 'Biographical Sketch of Mr Ben Jones', *Report of a Public Meeting 25 March 1892* (copy at Woolwich Library, London); *Co-op. Congress Handbook* (1896); *Manchester Guardian*, 7 Sep 1937; G. D. H. Cole, *A Century of Co-operation* [1945?]; H. C. Jones, *Ben Jones: a great co-operator. His Life* [*According to his son*] [1946?]. OBIT. *Co-op. News,* 6 Mar 1942.

JOYCE BELLAMY

See also: Percy REDFERN, for Co-operative Wholesaling; and below: Co-operative Production.

Co-operative Production: H. [T. Hughes], *History of the Working Tailors' Association* [1850] 11 pp.; J. M. Ludlow, 'Notes of a Co-operative Tour through Lancashire and Yorkshire', *Christian Socialist 2* (1851) 212; Society for Promoting Working Men's Associations, *First Report* (1852); Anon., 'A Curious Experiment at Leeds' [Co-operative Flour Mill], *Chambers's J. 2*, 23 Dec 1854, 401–2; W. Cooper, *History of the Rochdale District Co-operative Corn Mill Society* (Manchester, [1860?]) 12 pp.; W. Chambers, *Co-operation in its Different Branches* (Social Science Tract, no. 1 [1860?]) 16–19; Anon., 'Strikes and Industrial Co-operation', *West. Rev. 25* no. 2 n.s. (1864) 349–83; F. Harrison, 'Industrial Co-operation', *Fortn. 3* (Jan 1866) 477–503; J. M. Ludlow, 'On Some New Forms of Industrial Co-operation', *Good Words*, 1 Apr 1867, 240–8; J. M. Ludlow, *Trade Societies and Co-operative Production* (Manchester, 1867) 10 pp.; M. MacLeod, 'Co-operative Production', *Co-op. Congress Report* (1869) App. II 107–9; J. Borrowman and G. J. Holyoake, 'The Best Means of promoting Co-operative Production', *Co-op. Congress Report* (1873) 49–53; J. M. Ludlow, 'Some Hints on the Problem of Co-operative Production', *Co-op. Congress Report* (1873) 53–5; T. Brassey, 'Co-operative Production', *Cont. Rev. 24* (July 1874) 212–33; J. Borrowman, 'Co-operative Production', *Co-op. Congress Report* (1874) 38–9; E. O. Greening, 'Co-operative Production', *Co-op. Congress Report* (1875) 44–5; L. Jones, 'Trade Societies' Funds and Co-operative Production', *Co-op. Congress Report* (1875) 56–60; E. V. Neale, 'The Management and Best Form of Constitution to be given to Productive Societies formed in connection with a Distributive Centre, so as to secure a True Co-operative Action between the Producers and Consumers', *Co-op. Congress Report* (1875) 46–7; W. Campbell, 'How to diminish the Risks and increase the Benefits of Productive Co-operation', *Co-op. Congress Report* (1876) 53–7; R. Kyle, 'Hindrances to Productive Co-operation', *Co-op. Congress Report* (1876) 52–3; W. Marcroft, *Sun Mill Company Ltd: its commercial and social history from 1858 to 1877* (Oldham, 1877); T. Brassey, *Lectures on the Labour Question: VI Co-operative Production* (1878); J. Odgers, W. Swallow and J. Hepworth, 'Papers on Co-operative Production', *Co-op. Congress Reports* (1879) 37–42; (1880) 44–8; (1881) 57–8; E. Simcox, 'Eight Years of Co-operative Shirtmaking', *19th C. 15* (June 1884) 1037–54; J. C. Gray, *Co-operative Production* *in Great Britain*, repr. from *Age of Steel* (Jan 1887) 14 pp.; T. Hughes, *Co-operative Production* (Manchester, 1887) 12 pp.; J. Greenwood, *The Story of the Formation of the Hebden Bridge Fustian Manufacturing Society Ltd* (Manchester, [1888]) 23 pp.; D. F. Schloss, *Co-operators at work: an account of the Leicester Co-operative Boot and Shoe Manufacturing Society Ltd* (1889) 10 pp.; T. Ritchie, *Our Future Policy in Co-operative Production* (1890) 14 pp.; E. Cummings, 'Co-operative Production in France and England', *QJE 4* (July 1890) 357–86; Co-operative Printing Society, *The Origin, the History and the Services of the Co-operative Printing Society* (1890); J. Deans, *The Best Method of Consolidating and Federating existing Productive Effort* (Manchester, 1892) 11 pp.; R.C. on Labour (1892), *Minutes of Evidence*, 1893–4 XXXIX pt I; B. Jones, *Co-operative Production* (Oxford, 1894); J. C. Gray, *Co-operative Production* (Manchester, [c. 1895]) 16 pp.; idem, *The Future of Productive Co-operation: a plea for unity* (n.d.) 8 pp.; J. M. F. Ludlow, 'Co-operative Production in the British Isles', *Atlantic Mon. 75* (Jan 1895) 96–102; and 'Some Words on the Ethics of Co-operative Production', *Atlantic Mon. 75* (Mar 1895) 383–8; H. W. Wolff, 'Co-operative Production', *Econ. Rev. 5* (Jan 1895) 19–38; H. Vivian, 'A Novel Attempt at Co-operative Production in the Building Trades', *Econ. J. 6* (June 1896) 270–2; T. Blandford, *Co-operative Workshops in Gt Britain, 1897* [1898]; T. Blandford and G. Newell, *History of the Leicester Co-operative Hosiery Manufacturing Society Ltd* (Leicester, 1898); J. Bonar, 'Co-operators of Kettering', *Econ. Rev. 9* (Oct 1899) 528–31; R. Shuddick, 'Co-operative Workshops', *West. Rev. 152* (Sep 1899) 266–70; W. H. Hunt, 'An Interesting Industrial Experiment' [Hadleigh, Essex], *West. Rev. 154* (Sep 1900) 285–97; G. D. Taylor, *Duty of Distributive Societies to Form a Fund out of their Profits to foster Co-operative Production* (1900) 12 pp.; C. Webb, *Industrial Co-operation: the story of a peaceful revolution* (Manchester, 1904; 12th ed. 1929); H. Vivian, *A New Chapter in the History of Co-operation and Labour: the North Wales Quarries Ltd* (1906) 20 pp.; Co-operative Printing Society, *Story of the London Branch of the Co-operative Printing Society* (1907); E. Aves, *Co-operative Industry* (1907); W. H. Brown, *An Industrial Republic* (Letchworth, 1909); Board of Trade (Labour Dept), *Directory of Industrial Associations in the U.K. for 1911*, Cd 5619, 156–60; Co-operative Union, *Industrial Co-operation* (Manchester, 1912); Board of Trade, *Report on Industrial and Agricultural Co-operative Societies in the U.K.* (1912–13) Cd 6045; W. G. Harrison, *The Best Means of Developing the Productive Side of the Movement* (Manchester, 1913) 19 pp.; G. Williamson, *Co-operative Production: its ethical basis* (1914) 12 pp.; A. Mann, *Democracy in Industry: the story of twenty-one years' work of the Leicester Anchor Boot and Shoe Productive Society Ltd* (Leicester, 1914); G. Stanton, *The Story of an Industrial Democracy, 1896–1917* (Leicester, 1918); L. Woolf, *Co-operation and the Future of Industry* (1918); F. Hall, *The History of the Co-operative Printing Society Ltd, 1869–1919* (Manchester, [1920]); Anon., 'Building Guild and the CWS', *Producer 4*, 21 June 1920, 256; R. Halstead, 'The Work of the Co-operative Productive Federation', *Better Business 5* (May 1920) 194–201; G. Cox, 'The English Building Guilds: an experiment in industrial self-government' *JPE 29* (Dec 1921) 777–90; S. G. Hobson, 'The Building Guild and its Growing Pains', *Labour Mag. 1* (Dec 1922) 379–80; C. S. Joslyn, 'The British Building Guilds: a critical survey of two years' work', *QJE 37* (Nov 1922) 75–133; idem, 'A catastrophe in the British Building Guilds', ibid. (May 1923) 523–34; W. T. Charter, *The Industrial Co-operative Movement as a Factor in Industrial and Commercial Efficiency particularly in relation to the Stability of the State* (Manchester, 1929) 16 pp.; T. W. Mercer, *Sixty Years of Co-operative Printing: 1869–1929* (1930); T. W. Mercer, *First Essentials of Co-operative Industry* (1930) 22 pp.; C. E. Tomlinson, *A Survey of Co-operative Production* (Manchester, 1934) 20 pp.; W. H. Brown, *Co-operative Understanding: being the jubilee story of the 'Holyoake' Boot and Shoe* (Leicester, [1938]) 28 pp.; Anon., 'Co-ordination of co-operative production', *Co-op. Congress Reports* (1937) 181–6; (1938) 222–3; (1939) 184–93; (1940) 148–50; G. D. H. Cole, *A Century of Co-operation* (Manchester [1945?]); A. Hemstock, 'Industrial Co-operation' in N. Barou ed., *The Co-operative Movement in Labour Britain* (1948) 64–73; G. D. H. Cole, 'The Future of Producers' Co-operation in Great Britain', *RIC 43* (April 1950) 92–5; R. E. Tyson, 'The Sun Mill Company Limited: a study in democratic investment, 1858–1959' (Manchester MA, 1962).

JONES, Patrick Lloyd (1811–86)
OWENITE, RADICAL REFORMER AND JOURNALIST

Born of Welsh parents at Bandon, Ireland, on St Patrick's Day (hence his forename) 17 March 1811. His father was a fustian cutter who had taken some part in the revolutionary events of 1798 in Dublin and who was later converted to Catholicism, which to him symbolised Irish nationalism. His mother remained Protestant. Lloyd Jones (by which name he was invariably known in Britain) followed his father's trade and emigrated to Manchester by way of Liverpool. In his teens he came under the influence of E. T. Craig and soon rejected his religious faith to become an Owenite rationalist. His father disowned him. In his early years in Britain he was best known for helping to found and run a co-operative store and Owenite free school at Salford between 1829 and 1831 and he quickly established himself as an active Owenite propagandist in the industrial north. Manchester was the strongest Owenite centre outside London and in Salford especially the movement struck deep roots. Lloyd Jones had a good platform presence and by many witnesses was reckoned to be one of the outstanding debaters and lecturers of the nineteenth-century working-class movement.

The Owenite movement during the 1830s had several times broached the idea of full-time organisers – called Social Missionaries – but lack of funds had prevented any appointments. In May 1838 the Manchester Congress of the Association of All Classes of All Nations appointed six as full-time paid officials. Each social missionary was located in a main town with res-

ponsibility for the surrounding district, and Lloyd Jones was appointed to the London district. At this time the connection between Owenism and Trade Unionism was already past; and there was now an increasing anti-clerical emphasis in Owenite lecturing and propaganda, a trend looked upon with disfavour by the central board of the national organisation, who were concerned about the impact upon public opinion, and its effect upon the collection of monies for the Queenwood community in particular. In January 1840 the Bishop of Exeter made his famous attack upon Owenite Socialism in the House of Lords – the starting-point for the legal prosecutions for blasphemy in the 1840s – and Lloyd Jones, with Robert Buchanan, another social missionary, took what Holyoake was later to describe as 'a running leap into the clerical ranks'. In order to be allowed to lecture on Sundays, Jones at once, and Buchanan with some hesitation, obtained licences to preach as dissenting ministers, under the Act of 19 George III, c. 44, having declared on oath that they professed the Protestant faith. There was a strong reaction against them within the Owenite movement, and Holyoake in particular, then a very young man, vigorously attacked the decision. Jones was reappointed as a social missionary to the London district in 1841; he continued as a paid lecturer in 1842; and in 1843 the Central Board once again appointed him as a social missionary. In 1844 the Board sent him to the industrial North as a lecturer but at the 1845 Congress the Central Board recommended that social missionaries should be discontinued 'their services being so seldom required during the past year, and the deficiency of the General Fund' (*New Moral World*, 24 May 1845).

Jones returned to his trade as a fustian cutter, and in the middle forties he moved to Leeds. In 1846 he was a member of the Leeds Redemption Society, which favoured co-operative communities shorn of controversial rationalist religious concepts, and in which James Hole played an active part; and two years later Jones was living in London, working as a small master tailor in Oxford Street.

Lloyd Jones had always been on the side of moral force in the Chartist controversies, and earlier, in 1839, he had dissuaded a large meeting of working people in Manchester from supporting the tactic of the Sacred Month. When the Chartist movement revived in 1848, Jones took the same side. He visited Paris in company with William Lovett, and was much impressed with the national workshops. Together with his former Owenite collegues Robert Buchanan and Alexander Campbell, he helped establish and edit *The Spirit of the Age* in July 1848, but it soon looked like collapsing for financial reasons. It was rescued by W. H. Ashurst, the radically-minded solicitor to the Post Office, who offered the editorship to Holyoake, who unsuccessfully urged upon Ashurst the dismissal of Jones: a further occasion to deepen the antipathy between Jones and Holyoake (which, indeed, lasted all their lives). In November 1848 Jones became a founder of the short-lived League for Social Progress. He also joined Bronterre O'Brien and G. W. M. Reynolds in launching the National Reform League, which added Owenite and radical planks to a Chartist core. In 1849 he wrote letters on labour problems to the *Spirit of the Times* using the pseudonym of 'Cromwell'.

Jones was now, however, on the threshold of becoming involved in a new movement. On 20 April 1849, J. M. F. Ludlow, one of the leading members of the Christian Socialist group around F. D. Maurice, began a series of meetings at the Cranborne Coffee House between a number of London Chartists and the Christian Socialists. Ludlow was already in touch with Walter Cooper, and Jones was among those who attended the early meetings. He was to become Ludlow's closest friend among working men, and he brought to Ludlow and his group much needed experience of the working-class movement, and contacts with both the trade unions and the co-operative movement. Lloyd Jones became one of the leading propagandists of co-operation in the early 1850s; he gave evidence before Slaney's Committee on Investments of the Middle and Working Classes in the summer of 1850; and debated

publicly with Ernest Jones, the most formidable opponent of the co-operative movement in these years: first at Padiham, 28–29 December 1851, and then at Halifax, 26 and 28 January 1852. He vigorously advocated the establishment of a London co-operative store to market the commodities of the various producers' associations and to provide capital for them; and such a store was founded in London in October 1850, with Lloyd Jones as manager. The store latter became a central Co-operative Agency, a development much favoured by E. V. Neale and Jones, as well as by co-operators in the north of England, and vigorously opposed by Ludlow as a betrayal of the ideals of the movement. This controversy, which occupied a large part of the discussions within the Christian Socialist movement in the years 1850–4, is told in detail in most of the co-operative histories, and most clearly by G. D. H. Cole (*A Century of Co-operation*, Ch. 6). Holyoake in his *Reasoner* vigorously criticised the Owenite rationalist Jones for participation in *Christian* Socialism, although it was never an issue between Jones and his associates. Jones replied to Holyoake that he was as interested in practical results as he was uninterested in theoretical dilemmas.

The Christian Socialists began a series of lectures in March 1852 from which was to grow the idea of the Working Men's College. Jones lectured in the series – which were held in the Hall of Association, built by the North London Working Builders in the spring of 1852 – throughout 1853, and on 11 January 1854 he seconded a motion in the Council of Promoters, moved by Tom Hughes, 'to establish a People's College in connection with the Metropolitan Association'. Education was always a central social purpose with Jones, and he continued his educational activity within working-class circles to the end of his days.

When the Christian Socialist movement ended, Lloyd Jones remained active in the co-operative and trade union movements. He attended the Co-operative Conferences of 1853 and 1854, helped form the Co-operative Industrial and Commercial Union in 1854, was on the trade union committee formed to help the Preston strikers in 1855, and then, probably in 1855, he moved to Leeds. In Leeds he was a director of, and lecturer to, the Mechanics' Institute (1855–6) and in 1857 he helped found and was first editor of the *Leeds Express*. He was assisted in the establishment of the paper by Lord Goderich – later the Marquis of Ripon – and by E. Ackroyd and W. E. Forster. Ludlow contributed many articles and Jones's editorial emphasis was concerned especially with the promotion of national education. After two or three years Jones went to live in London but he continued to write for the *Express* on working-class topics in the social, political and educational spheres. His writings were characterised by a clearly defined purpose and he always went straight to the point. Jones never owned another paper but wrote leading articles for the *Glasgow Sentinel* and the *North British Daily Mail* (relinquishing his position from this Glasgow paper in 1863 rather than write against the men during a painters' strike and against the North during the American Civil War). He was one of the editors of the *London Reader* for a time beginning in 1863, and was the most prolific writer of leading articles for the *Bee-Hive* in the seventies and its successor the *Industrial Review* (1877–8). He contributed to the *Co-operative News* in the middle seventies after Holyoake's influence was no longer important and it ceased its sarcastic attacks on Jones, which he rarely received in silence. In 1876 he joined the staff of the *Newcastle Weekly* and *Daily Chronicle*, for which journals he wrote until the end of his life. In January 1878 he became editor of a new paper, the *Miners' Watchman and Labour Sentinel*, but this was a short-lived venture.

Jones's journalistic reputation especially rests upon his voluminous series of leading articles in the *Bee-Hive* and *Industrial Review*, which have been rightly praised by the Webbs. Although Jones's deepest attachment lay with co-operation, trade union matters not unnaturally bulked largest in this series. He sought to interpret events to the working class, to explain to them where, in his view, their best interests lay, and to defend the working class from assaults upon

it by the 'respectable' British press. He would go into the field to examine strike conditions for himself, or examine conditions in a coal-mine. He also sought to explain the meaning of the co-operative movement to trade unionists, and trade unionism to co-operators at a time when considerable anti-union sentiment existed among the latter. Beginning in 1873 he strongly advocated arbitration, and was often chosen by trade unionists to represent them on arbitration panels. With Thomas Burt he represented the miners on the first arbitration board for the Durham coalfield in 1874, and in the following year he served in a similar capacity with William Crawford, secretary of the Durham Miners' Association. He frequently spoke at miners' galas in Durham and Northumberland during this decade, always condemning sliding-scale agreements and advocating a minimum wage. Jones's political articles generally supported the Liberal Party (except for 1873–4, when he favoured independent labour representation through the Labour Representation League) and rarely had anything but invective for the Conservatives. In 1872, for example, he expressed the hope that despite the disappointing policies of the Liberal Government, the newly enfranchised working men could find a comfortable home in 'the great Liberal Party' (*Bee-Hive*, 17 Aug 1872). But he often differed with the Liberals on policies, and the trend of his writings was towards disenchantment with the Liberals. Naturally he wrote in favour of many reforms, such as a new approach to pauperism, secularisation of elementary education, and disestablishment of the Church of England. George Howell as secretary of the Plimsoll and Seamen's Fund Committee enlisted his pen in that cause.

Throughout his life Jones continued his association with Ludlow. Together they wrote *The Progress of the Working Class* in 1867, and in the late sixties they both worked assiduously in the cause of a revision of the labour laws when the trade unions, following the *Hornby v. Close* decision, found themselves in an increasingly precarious legal position. During the 1868 election

Jones worked for the Reform League, in a situation in which a number of compromising deals were made with the Liberal Party [see Harrison, *Before the Socialists*], but Jones only supported candidates who were thoroughly sound on the Labour question, and he himself refused payment, even of expenses, for work in London. In the following year he became the first Secretary of the Labour Representation League; in 1871 he was named a member of the first Parliamentary Committee of the TUC; and in 1873 helped persuade the Miners' National Union to pledge their support for independent labour representation.

He never lost his deep, abiding interest in the co-operative movement. He wrote articles for the *Industrial Partnership Record*, a monthly journal started in 1867 by E. O. Greening which advocated co-partnership in industry; he played a leading role in organising the first Co-operative Congress in 1869, became a member of the first Central Board and read many papers at many subsequent Congresses. In the 1870s he addressed innumerable provincial co-operative groups. He presided over the first day of the 1885 Congress held at Oldham, and among his recommendations were a co-operative bank to provide capital for co-operative enterprises, and a co-operative newspaper in which political views could be expressed. He himself always retained his radical views and was a supporter of Bradlaugh in 1871 when the latter pleaded for the recognition of the French republican government at the time of the Franco-Prussian War; although a year earlier Bradlaugh had criticised in his *National Reformer* the Manchester Committee of the Owen Memorial Fund for deciding to pay Jones for writing a biography of Robert Owen, commenting that Jones 'would do and has done his very best to hinder and misrepresent our Freethought advocacy'.

In the general election of 1885 he experienced what was probably the greatest disappointment of his life when he unsuccessfully contested the Chester-le-Street constituency as an independent miners' candidate. Despite being supported by Joseph Cowen his election campaign lacked adequate finance and he came in second to the Liberal whose party had always carried the seat. The physical effort of electioneering proved a very great strain upon him. He returned to his London home in Lambeth where he died of cancer on 22 May 1886, a few months prior to the Co-operative Congress where it was planned to present him with a testimonial valued at £1159. His wife Mary Dring, whom he had met during his early years as an Owenite and whom he had married in 1837, died on 31 May 1886, only a few days after her husband. Their eldest son Lloyd predeceased them. Two sons and two daughters survived them. Lloyd Jones left a personal estate of £238.

The death of Lloyd Jones brought a remarkable series of witnesses to the affection and respect in which he was held by his contemporaries. In 1863 he had applied, unsuccessfully, for the position of Librarian to the University of Glasgow, and the testimonials which were then written on his behalf (reprinted in the obituary notice of the *Co-operative News*) emphasised his love of learning as well as the integrity of his character. As his lifelong friend J. M. F. Ludlow wrote in the *Spectator* after Jones's death:

And young he was essentially at heart, firing up into youthful wrath against all oppression and wrong, kindling up into youthful enthusiasm for all that is good and true. Behind the powerful speaker and writer, the vigorous politician, there was a loving, charming man, gay and humorous, beloved alike of family and friends, an enthusiastic book-lover and book-collector, deeply read in English literature, especially of the seventeenth century (George Wither was, perhaps, his favourite old author). A more delightful companion could not be found.

Writings: *A Reply to Mr R. Carlile's objections to the five fundamental facts as laid down by Mr Owen. An answer to a lecture delivered in his chapel, November 27th 1837* (Manchester, 1837) 15 pp.; *Socialism examined, a Report of a*

Discussion which took place at Huddersfield on December 13th, 14th and 15th 1837, between the Reverend T. Dalton and Mr Lloyd Jones . . . upon the 'five fundamental facts' and the 'twenty laws of human nature': as found in the Book of the New Moral World by R. Owen Esq. (Manchester, 1838); *The Influence of Christianity: report of a discussion which took place at Oldham, 19th, 20th February 1839 between the Rev. J. Barker and Mr Lloyd Jones* (Manchester, 1839); *Report of the Discussion on Owenism . . . Sheffield . . . March, 1839, between Mr Lloyd Jones . . . and Mr W. Pallister . . .* (Sheffield, 1839) 40 pp.; *Report of a discussion betwixt Mr Troup and Mr L. Jones on the propositions (1) That Socialism is Atheistical and (2) That Atheism is incredible and absurd* (Dundee, 1839); *Christianity versus Socialism: report of a discussion between the Rev. Alexander Harvey, and Mr Lloyd Jones, social missionary, in the Relief Church, Calton, Glasgow, on December 24, 1839, on the vast superiority of Christianity over the Religion of the New Moral World* (Glasgow, 1840) 44 pp.; *The Freaks of Faith; or an account of some of the many Messiahs who have deluded mankind* (2nd ed., Manchester, 1840) 16 pp.; *Report of a Discussion on Marriage as advocated by Robert Owen between L. Jones and J. Bowes in the Queen's Theatre, Liverpool, May 27th 1840* (Liverpool, 1840) 16 pp.; *Minutes of Evidence* before S.C. on Investment for the Savings of the Middle and Working Classes 1850 XIX Qs 962–88; 'Co-operative Stores and Co-operative Workshops', *Trans. Co-op. League*, Part 2 (1852); with J. M. Ludlow, *The Progress of the Working Class 1832–1867* (1867); 'The Workman's Duty as a Voter', *Industrial Partnership Record*, 1 June 1868, 49–50; 'Co-operative Newspaper', *Co-op. Congress Report* (1870); 'Federative Trading', *Co-op. Congress Report* (1872); 'Trade Unions in relation to Co-operation', *Co-op. Congress Report* (1874); 'Trade Societies' Funds and Co-operative Production', *Co-op. Congress Report* (1875); 'Die jüngste Landarbeiterbewegung in England', *Landw. Jahrb.* bd 4 (Berlin, 1875) 805–19; *A Letter from Lloyd Jones to George Jacob Holyoake* [1876?] 8 pp.; *Co-operation: its position, its policy and its prospects &c.* (1877) 31 pp.; *Trade Unions. Two Lectures* (1877); 'How should Labour be paid in Co-operation?', *Co-op. Congress Report* (1877); 'Store Management', *Co-op. Congress Report* (1877); *Co-operation in Danger: an appeal to the British Public* (1880); 'Wholesale Co-operation', *Co-op. Congress Report* (1880); 'The Land Question in connection with Co-operation', *Co-op. Congress Report* (1881); 'Utilisation of Surplus Capital', *Co-op. Congress Report* (1883); 'Alexander Macdonald', *Newcastle Daily Chronicle*, 17 Nov 1883 [quoted in J. M. Baernreither, *English Associations of Working Men* (1893) 409–11]; 'The Struggle for Reform, 1832', *To-day, the monthly magazine of scientific Socialism*, 2 new series (1884), 233–46; *Inaugural Address at the Seventeenth Annual Co-operative Congress held at Oldham . . . 1885* (Manchester, [1885]) 16 pp.; *The Life, Times, and Labours of Robert Owen*, with a short notice of the author by W. C. Jones (1889) [later editions to 1919]. Apart from the above publications Jones was a prolific writer of articles, and the journals and newspapers to which he contributed regularly or edited were: *New Moral World, Spirit of the Times* (as 'Cromwell' in 1849); *Spirit of the Age* (1848–50); *Glasgow Sentinel* (as 'Cromwell' 1850–63); *The Bee-Hive* (1871–6); *Industrial Review* (1877–8); *Leeds Express* (from 1857); *Newcastle Weekly*; *Newcastle Daily Chronicle*; *Miners' Watchman and Labour Sentinel*; *Co-operative News*; *Christian Socialist*; *North British Daily Mail*.

Sources:
(1) MSS: unpublished autobiography of J. M. F. Ludlow in de Graz papers, Cambridge; George Howell Collection, Bishopsgate Institute, London; Holyoake Papers, Co-operative Union Ltd, Manchester; Joseph Cowen Collection, Newcastle Central Library.

(2) Theses: D. C. Morris, 'The History of the Labour Movement in England, 1825–1852. The Problem of Leadership and the Articulation of Demands' (London PhD, 1952); J. D. Osburn, 'Lloyd Jones, Labour Journalist, 1871–1878: a study in British working-class thought' (Oklahoma PhD, 1969).

(3) Secondary: *National Reformer*, 20 Jan

1878; Testimonial Committee, *Lloyd Jones. Notice of his Life* [1885?]; G. J. Holyoake, *Sixty Years of an Agitator's Life* (1892); J. M. Ludlow, 'Some of the Christian Socialists of 1848 and the following years II', *Econ. Rev. 4*, Jan 1894, 24–42; S. and B. Webb, *The History of Trade Unionism* (1st ed. 1894); *DNB 10* [by Holyoake]; *Boase, 2*; W. E. Adams, *Memoirs of a Social Atom* (1903, repr. with an Introduction by J. Saville, New York, 1968); J. McCabe, *Life and Letters of G. J. Holyoake* (1908); A. W. Humphrey, *A History of Labour Representation* (1912); C. R. Raven, *Christian Socialism 1848–1854* (1920); J. West, *History of the Chartist Movement* (1920); E. Welbourne, *The Miners' Unions of Northumberland and Durham* (1923); G. D. H. Cole, *The British Working Class Movement* (1926); G. D. H. Cole, *A Century of Co-operation* (Manchester, [1945?]); F. Higham, *F. D. Maurice* (1947); W. D. Morris, *Christian Origins of Social Revolt* (1949); G. D. H. Cole and A. W. Filson, *British Working Class Movements: select documents 1789–1875* (1951); John Saville, *Ernest Jones: Chartist* (1951); E. C. Mack and W. H. G. Armytage, *Thomas Hughes* (1952); J. F. C. Harrison, *History of the Working Men's College* (1954); idem, *Social Reform in Victorian needs: the work of James Hole 1820–1895* (Leeds, 1954); B. Roberts, *The Trades Union Congress 1868–1921* (1958); A. Briggs and J. Saville, *Essays in Labour History* (1960); A. Bonner, *British Co-operation* (Manchester, 1961); J. F. C. Harrison, *Learning and Living 1790–1960* (1961); T. Christensen, *Origin and History of Christian Socialism 1848–1854* (Copenhagen, 1962); J. E. Williams, *The Derbyshire Miners* (1962); Royden Harrison, *Before the Socialists* (1965); J. F. C. Harrison, *Robert Owen and the Owenites in Britain and America* (1969). OBIT. *Leeds Express*, 24 May 1886; *Leicester Daily Post*, 24 May 1886; *Durham County Advertiser*, 28 May 1886; *Co-op. News*, 29 May 1886; *Newcastle Weekly Chronicle*, 29 May 1886; *Spectator* [obit. by J. M. Ludlow], 29 May 1886; *The Republican 12* no. 6, Aug 1886, 33–4.

JOYCE BELLAMY
JOHN OSBURN
JOHN SAVILLE

See also: William COOPER; Joseph COWEN; G. J. HOLYOAKE; *George HOWELL; *Thomas HUGHES; *J. M. F. LUDLOW; E. V. NEALE; *Robert OWEN.

JUGGINS, Richard (1843–95)
TRADE UNION LEADER

Born on 16 July 1843 in Darlaston, Staffordshire, the son of a miner who was killed in a pit accident when Richard was eleven. He started work in a nut and bolt workshop at the age of seven, and followed this trade for the next twenty years. During this time he acquired some formal education at night school and Sunday school.

In November 1870 the Nut and Bolt Makers' Association was formed, and having played a leading part in its formation Juggins became part-time secretary. Fourteen months later, in January 1872, he was dismissed from his employment for leading an agitation and became full-time secretary of the union. The front room of his home, 60 New Street, Darlaston, became the union office. By this time he was becoming well known locally as a Methodist lay preacher.

The main qualities that Juggins brought to the job of union leadership were integrity, organising ability and a great capacity for hard work. In the second three months of 1876, for instance, he travelled over 1600 miles on union business and was away from home for forty-six days. Under his leadership by 1877 the union had developed into the National Amalgamated Association of Nut and Bolt Makers with thirty-one branches in places as far apart as Newcastle and Cwmbran, Wolverton and Wigan. Membership had been built up to over 2000, and funds to over £3000, and for a short time the *Nut and Bolt Journal* was published. Juggins's success in building up the union is the more noteworthy when it is considered against the national background of unionism at this time, which was one of declining authority and falling membership.

During these years 1872–7, Juggins also had the unique distinction of acting as arbitrator in his own trade. Following a twenty-week strike in 1877 an independent arbitrator was appointed, but when this system began to prove unsatisfactory Juggins took the initiative in developing in the nut and bolt trade a pattern of industrial relations which was to be copied by many other trades in the Birmingham and Black Country area. From a series of meetings between him and the nut and bolt employers in January and February 1885 there emerged the beginnings of the 'alliance philosophy'. Undercutting in what was a time of depression for the trade prevented its practical implementation at that time, but in February 1889 the South Staffordshire Nut and Bolt Wages Board was established. The distinctive feature of its operation was that both sides of the industry contributed to a fund which was used to support strikes in firms which undercut agreed price lists. Juggins and the nut and bolt trade thus anticipated by a number of years the more famous Birmingham Alliances usually associated with the names of W. J. Davis and E. J. Smith.

As the only professional organiser in the Black Country metal trades Juggins was frequently called on to act as spokesman and negotiator for groups other than the nut and bolt workers. The experience so gained convinced him not only of the need for organisation within trades, but also of the need for some wider form of organisation to buttress individual unions in their negotiations with employers, and to seek legislative enactment. To this end he organised a series of mass meetings in various Black Country towns in the spring of 1886, and from these resulted the Midland Counties Trades Federation. Inaugurated on 12 May 1886 with a membership of a few hundred drawn from three societies, this organisation grew to a membership of 20,000 in 1900. Juggins became its first secretary, doubling this position with the secretaryship of the Nut and Bolt Makers' Association, holding both posts until his death. In 1889 the Federation voted him a salary of £52 per year, and in the following year presented him with a purse of 100 gold sovereigns, a clock and an illuminated address in appreciation of his work. Some time later he was presented with a pony and trap to

help in the considerable amount of travelling that his work involved.

Juggins was for over twenty years, in a very real sense, the voice of the Black Country craftsman and in this capacity gave evidence before the Select Committee of the House of Lords on the Sweating System in Industry 1889 and the Royal Commission on Labour 1892. He represented his own union and the Midland Counties Federation at many Trades Union Congresses, and from 1886 onwards was a member of the Labour Electoral Committee of the TUC for the Birmingham area. He was also a delegate to the International Labour Congress several times.

In addition to his union activities Juggins played an active part in local government. He was for many years a member of the Darlaston School Board, the Darlaston Urban District Council and the Walsall Board of Guardians. He was elected to all these bodies as an independent member, though he was a lifelong Liberal. This may have been due to the early influence on him of his Sunday school teacher, Mr James Slater JP, a prominent local Liberal. In 1891 a move was made by a section of the Midland Counties Federation to seek Juggins's adoption as the official Liberal candidate for Dudley, but in the face of opposition from the local party executive, and division within the Federation this came to nothing.

Juggins died at his home on 5 March 1895. He was twice married. His second wife and a number of grown-up children of both marriages survived him. He was buried at James Bridge Cemetery, Darlaston, where in November 1896 a memorial stone was erected over his grave, with money subscribed by members of the Nut and Bolt Makers' Association and the Midland Counties Federation. He had left effects valued at only £47.

No union records of the Juggins period have survived. The Nut and Bolt Makers' Union was dissolved in 1956 when the secretary died and no successor could be found. Membership at the time was about thirty. The union then amalgamated with the Screw and Rivet Society of Smethwick, which had survived from the 1880s.

Sources: Evidence before the S.C. of the House of Lords on the Sweating System, 1889 XIII Qs 17577–20769 *passim*; R.C. on Labour 1892 XXXVI Group A Qs 17770–18096; reports of activities of Nut and Bolt Makers' Association and Midland Counties Trades Federation in *Dudley Herald, Midland Advertiser, Wednesbury Herald, Wolverhampton Chronicle*, 1870–95; G. C. Allen, *The Industrial Development of Birmingham and the Black Country, 1860–1927* (1929); J. A. C. Baker, 'History of the Nut and Bolt Industry in the West Midlands' (Birmingham MCom., 1965) [copies in Birmingham University Library and Wednesbury Public Library]. OBIT. *Midland Advertiser*, 9 Mar 1895; *Wednesbury Herald*, 9 Mar 1895; *Wolverhampton Chronicle*, 13 Mar 1895; memorial to Juggins, *Wolverhampton Chronicle*, 11 Nov 1896.

ERIC TAYLOR

See also: William MILLERCHIP; Thomas SITCH.

KENYON, Barnet (1850–1930)
MINERS' LEADER AND MP

Born at South Anston, Yorkshire, on 11 August 1850, the son of Henry Kenyon, a labourer, and his wife Ann (née Hanson). [In *Who's Who* and *Who Was Who* Kenyon's date of birth is shown as 1853 but *Dod* (1914) and Somerset House Records confirm the earlier date as the correct one.] He began work in a quarry at the age of ten and afterwards became a farm labourer and then a miner in the South Yorkshire coalfield. In 1876 he moved to Clowne, Derbyshire, and after a few years at the Barlborough Colliery was elected checkweighman at the nearby Southgate Colliery in 1880. In 1898 he was elected president of the Derbyshire Miners' Association, a position he held for ten years resigning to become agent and assistant secretary of the union when James Haslam, the senior agent, entered Parliament. Kenyon was a moderate trade union leader who was opposed to strikes and advocated conciliation. He was strongly criticised by rank-and-file members of the Derbyshire Miners' Association for his attitude to the 1912 strike but was greatly respected by the employers as a 'reasonable' trade union leader, and the Duke of Devonshire attended his funeral.

In politics Kenyon was a Liberal. He successfully contested the Chesterfield division of Derbyshire in 1913 but his candidature aroused a storm of controversy. It was at first endorsed by the MFGB and by the Labour Party but both organisations subsequently withdrew their support when they discovered that Kenyon was working closely with the Liberals. At the by-election of 20 August 1913, Kenyon had 7725 votes against 5539 for the Unionist and 583 for the Socialist, John Scurr. In 1918 Kenyon stood again for Chesterfield, this time as a Liberal coalition candidate, and was returned unopposed. In 1924 he had the support of both Liberals and Conservatives against the Labour candidate, George Benson, whom he defeated by 13,071 votes to 9206. He retired from Parliament in 1929. Kenyon's persistent refusal to adhere to the political policy of the MFGB led to constant friction between himself and the Derbyshire Miners' Association. In 1923 he was removed from his position as general agent and given a life pension of £2 a week. In the period of financial stringency which followed the 1926 dispute the decision to pay Kenyon's pension was rescinded.

Kenyon played a prominent part in public life and is said to have won popularity by his general courtesy and able and thoughtful speeches. He was a Primitive Methodist, became a local preacher in 1882 and a class leader in 1886. When the Clowne Co-operative Society was formed in 1889 he became its president and in 1895 he became a member of the Worksop Board of Guardians and of the Clowne Rural District Council. During the First World War, at the request of the Minister of Munitions, he toured the country exhorting munition workers to greater efforts. By September 1917 he had addressed well over 150,000 of them and had an impressive collection of inscribed mementoes. His proudest possession was said to be a six-pound shell which was made by young women who had formerly been milliners.

Representatives of all political parties had started a fund for Kenyon in recognition of his great public services but he died at his Chesterfield home on 20 February 1930 shortly after this had been initiated. He was married and two years earlier he and his wife had celebrated their golden wedding. They had no family of their own but had adopted eight children. He left £819 in his will.

Sources: (1) MSS: Minutes of the Derbyshire Miners' Association, 1898–1930 (NUM, Saltergate, Chesterfield); (2) Printed: *Minutes of the Miners' Federation of Great Britain*, 1898–1914; *Derbyshire Times*, 1898–1930; *Parliamentary Debates*, 1913–29; (3) Secondary: R. F. Wearmouth, *Methodism and the Struggle of the Working Classes, 1850–1900* (Leicester, 1954); idem, *The Social and Political Influence of Methodism in the Twentieth Century* (1957); J. E. Williams, 'The Political Activities of a Trade Union, 1906–14', *Int. Rev. Social Hist. 2* (1957) 1–21; J. E. Williams, *The Derbyshire Miners* (1962). OBIT. *Derbyshire Advertiser*, 21 Feb 1930; *Derbyshire Times*, 22 Feb 1930; *Times*, 24 Feb 1930.

J. E. WILLIAMS

See also: Thomas ASHTON, for Mining Trade Unionism, 1900–14; *A. J. COOK, for Mining Trade Unionism, 1915–26.

KILLON, Thomas (1853–1931)
CO-OPERATOR

Born in Bury, Lancashire, in 1853 (the year usually quoted for his birth), Thomas Killon was the son of an Irish tenant farmer who emigrated from Ireland at the time of the potato famine. Killon belonged to a poor family of five children and when he was seven he worked as an errand boy for a tailor and a year later became a half-timer in a cotton mill. After leaving day school, Killon extended his early education by attending night classes at St Joseph's R.C. School and ultimately rose to be a mill foreman.

Much of his life was devoted to the co-operative movement. He joined the Bury Co-operative Society in 1874, served it in

various capacities for a number of years and maintained a lifelong association with the Society. In addition to serving as a member of the Society's committee, he was also secretary for a time and president on two occasions (1886 and 1888) and represented the Society at the 1889 Ipswich Congress. But it was particularly his work for the CWS by which he became well known. Initially he attended CWS meetings as a delegate from the Bury Society but was elected to the board of the CWS in 1892. The productive side of co-operation was of particular interest to him. He served on the shipping committee for eight years, in the last years as chairman, and also on a number of other CWS committees, including those dealing with drapery, groceries, propaganda, parliamentary affairs, railway rates and the London Tea Department. He maintained an especial interest in the tea-growing side of the business into which the CWS entered in 1902; he attended the Swiss Co-operative Congress in 1904, visited Norway, Sweden, Montreal and New York on the Society's business and in 1913 went to India. He was also a member of a deputation to India and Ceylon in 1919 when additional tea plantations were purchased for the CWS and SCWS. Thomas Killon succeeded Thomas Tweddell as president of the CWS when the latter died in 1916 and he served in this office until ill-health compelled his own retirement in 1920. In November 1917 he was appointed to the important Orders Committee of the Ministry of Food, from which he resigned in 1918. In the latter year he was president of the fiftieth Co-operative Congress held in Liverpool and also presided over the Co-operative 'Greetings to Peace' meeting held in the Mitchell Hall, Manchester, on 19 November 1918.

His interests also extended to the trade union movement and he had a long connection with the Bury Trades and Labour Council. He was a member of the Michael Davitt Club in Bury from its inception and served for many years as its president. He was a staunch Liberal in politics and a Roman Catholic in religion being a member of the limited order of Catholic Brethren.

When he retired, he continued to live in north Manchester, not far from his native town of Bury. He was twice married, his first wife having died in 1888; his second wife, formerly Margaret Roberts, died in 1917, and he left no family when he himself died at his Higher Broughton home on 14 August 1931, in his seventy-ninth year. His funeral took place on 18 August following a Requiem Mass at the Servite Church, Kersal, and he was buried at Bury Cemetery. He left an estate valued at £4607.

Sources: P. Redfern, *The Story of the C.W.S.* (Manchester, [1913]); *Fiftieth Annual Co-operative Congress Report* (1918); P. Redfern, *The New History of the C.W.S.* (Manchester, 1938). OBIT. *Bury Times,* 19 Aug 1931; *Co-op News,* 22 Aug 1931.

H. F. BING

See also: Percy REDFERN, for Co-operative Wholesaling.

KING, William (1786–1865)
CO-OPERATIVE PIONEER

The son of the Rev. John King, Master of Ipswich Grammar School, William was born at Ipswich on 17 April 1786. He was educated first at the local grammar school, then Westminster School, and then for a short while at Oxford University, from where he later went to Cambridge University. He showed a special aptitude for mathematics, took a BA degree and became twelfth wrangler in 1809. Three years later he was elected to a Fellowship at Peterhouse. He then moved to London where he studied medicine at St Bartholomew's Hospital and attended medical lectures at Montpellier and Paris, obtaining his MD in 1819. In 1820, after completing his studies, he became a Fellow of the Royal College of Physicians.

In the following year, 1821, he married Mary Hooker, the daughter of an Anglican clergyman who was vicar of Rottingdean, Sussex, and King moved to Brighton, where he remained in medical practice for the remainder of his life. In Brighton he at once became active in charitable work. In 1823 he established a children's school, organised along the lines pioneered by Fellenberg at Hofwyl in Switzerland. He was a vigorous supporter of the Mechanics' Institute founded in Brighton in 1825, and although it lasted only three years, the contacts King made during these years exercised a considerable influence upon his social ideas, for it was from among the members of the Mechanics' Institute that the first Brighton Co-operative Society was created.

By the second half of the 1820s King was already known in Brighton as 'the Poor Man's Doctor'; and it was in this connection that Lady Noel Byron first heard his name. Lady Byron was to spend much of her life, after the break-up of her marriage, at either Tunbridge Wells or Brighton, and from 1826 she became closely associated with William King. Like him, Lady Byron insisted upon education as the central reforming agency of society, and they were both greatly influenced by the teaching and the practice of Philipp Emanuel von Fellenberg, the Swiss educationalist, with whom they corresponded at length. At the same time, King was equally attracted to the ideas of Robert Owen and he saw co-operation above all as an educational movement. King was, however, a deeply religious man, and the differences between his religious understanding of co-operation, as the will of God, and the anti-clericalism and irreligiosity of many of his Owenite contemporaries were to prove a major source of conflict in later years.

In 1827 King, together with William Bryan, a skilled mechanic, with whom he had worked in the founding of the Mechanics' Institute, established the Brighton Benevolent Fund Association. With the proceeds of weekly contributions, the Association opened a retail shop, and encouraged various educational and social activities. A plot of land some nine miles from Brighton was acquired for market gardening, and there were plans, as funds accumulated, for employing members in various handicraft trades. Other societies in the Brighton area were established, all inspired by this example; although none lasted long. William Byran left for America in the autumn of 1829, and by the beginning of 1830 the original society had ceased trading.

As a model, however, the Brighton society was to have a national influence, largely through the columns of the *Co-operator*. This was a monthly journal whose first number appeared on 1 May 1828, and it was edited and almost entirely written by William King. The *Co-operator* sold for one penny, and its last number appeared on 1 August 1830. It had an extraordinary influence on the development of co-operation in Britain. For the first fifteen months of its existence, the journal strongly reflected the influence of Robert Owen, King summarising Owenite doctrines in his columns in vigorous and uncompromising terms. In the first number King listed four other co-operative societies (two in Brighton, one in Worthing and one in London) that were operating on the principles he was recommending: 'viz. that of accumulating a common Capital, and investing it in Trade, and so making TEN per cent of it, instead of investing it in the FUNDS, at only four or four and a half, with the intention of ultimately purchasing land, and living in COMMUNITY . . .' and by the time the last number of the *Co-operator* (August 1830) was published, King stated that there were now some three hundred societies in existence.

King's advocacy of Owenite ideas was meeting increased hostility in his own town throughout 1828 and 1829, and this may well have been a factor influencing him in the direction of a less uncompromising position; but he was also beginning to take an increasingly vigorous objection to the militant political and anti-clerical views of many of the leading Owenites. From the early months of 1830, and until the journal closed down in August, a breach began to widen between King himself and the majority of Owenite co-operators. A letter of John Rickman, published in the *Co-operator* in February 1830, which recommended, *inter alia*, middle-class patronage of co-operative societies as a means of knitting 'together all classes in a common effort for the comfort and moral improvement of all mankind', was especially severely criticised by the rest of the co-operative press.

With the closing down of the *Co-operator*

William King virtually severed his connection with the Owenite movement, although he still professed a warm regard for Robert Owen himself. King continued in medical practice and remained a personality of some importance in Brighton. He showed some interest in the work of the Christian Socialists of 1848 [see his long letter in *Christian Socialist*, 11 October 1851] and his correspondence in 1864–5 with Henry Pitman, editor of the newly-established *Co-operator*, is interesting for his continued sympathy with the ideals of the later co-operative movement. To the end of his life he interested himself in various social reforms, although at the time of his death he was hardly known to the general public. He died at his home in Brighton on 19 October 1865, and was buried in Hove Parish Church. His wife survived him.

Writings: 'A letter on the subject of Mechanics' Institutions' from *Brighton Herald* (Brighton, 1825); *Observations on the Artificial Mineral Waters of Dr Struve, of Dresden, prepared at Brighton with cases* (Brighton, 1826); *The Co-operator* (Brighton, 1828–30); *The Institutions of De Fellenberg* (1842) P; *Medical Essays read before the Brighton and Sussex Medico-Chirurgical Society* (Brighton, 1850); *Cemeteries: two lectures delivered before the members of the Brighton Medico-Chirurgical Society* (Brighton, 1853); *Thoughts and Suggestions on the Teaching of Christ* (published posthumously, 1872).

Sources: The most useful accounts are: W. H. Brown, *Brighton's Co-operative Advance, 1828–1938* (Manchester, 1938); T. W. Mercer, *Co-operation's Prophet. The Life and Letters of Dr William King of Brighton, with a Reprint of The Co-operator, 1828–1830* (Manchester, 1947); Sidney Pollard, *Dr William King of Ipswich: A Co-operative Pioneer* (Co-operative College Papers, no. 6: Loughborough, 1959) 17–33. See also: *DNB 11*; *Aphorisms and Reflections of Dr William King*, selected and arr. by T. W. Mercer (Manchester, 1922); B. Jones, *Co-operative Production* (2 vols 1894; 1 vol. New York, 1968); F. Podmore, *Robert Owen. A Biography* (2 vols 1906; repr. in 1 vol. New

York, 1968); Hans Müller, 'Dr William King and his Place in the History of Co-operation', *Year Book of International Co-operation* (1913); J. J. Dent, *The Co-operative Ideals of Dr William King* (Manchester, 1921) 14 pp.; G. D. H. Cole, *A Century of Co-operation* (Manchester, [1945?]); A. Bonner, *British Co-operation* (Manchester, 1961); J. F. C. Harrison, *Robert Owen and the Owenites in Britain and America* (1969). OBIT. *Gentleman's Magazine* 2 (1865) 797.

H. F. BING
JOHN SAVILLE

See also: *Lady Noel BYRON; E. T. CRAIG; *Robert OWEN; James SMITHIES.

LANG, James (1870–1966)
TRADE UNIONIST AND CO-OPERATOR

Born on 6 September 1870 at Paisley, the son of Alexander Lang, a shoemaker, a native of Maybole, Ayrshire, who had settled in Paisley about 1868, James Lang was educated at the parish school in Paisley. He found his first employment in the neighbouring royal burgh of Renfrew with the first Lord Blythswood, a leading scientist, but subsequently became an engineer in the local shipyards. His parents had died when he was eighteen leaving him with the responsibility for bringing up a younger brother and sister. He had a passion for service, not of the kind that would bring him publicity but a single-minded desire to help working people to a life of more comfort. He remained throughout his long life a man of the people with an accent that was clear and couthie. He joined the Amalgamated Society of Engineers in 1895, was in the forefront of the disputes between employers and engineers in the last years of the century and the beginning of the twentieth century, and retained his membership until his death.

His desire to serve humanity was further satisfied through the co-operative movement which later in his life became his main field of activity. He was made president of the now defunct Renfrew Equitable Co-operative Society and from there was elected to the board of the United Co-operative Baking Society in 1926. In 1932 he became president of this society, holding the office for twenty-eight years until his retirement in 1960 at the age of ninety. His conduct of the quarterly meetings during that long period was noted for the good sense and humour with which he dealt with questioners and critics.

In local government he first became a Renfrew councillor in 1918 and later held the office of dean of guild and ultimately provost of the burgh during the Second World War, retiring from the council in 1945 after twenty-seven years' continuous service. He was also a local magistrate. In religion he was a kirk elder and office bearer for sixty-five years of the Renfrew North Church, a constituent of the Church of Scotland. When, at the age of ninety, he decided to retire from co-operative work and public life, he was made a freeman of the burgh: the first working man to receive that honour. He was a personal friend of Patrick Gallagher (known as Paddy the Cope), for whom Lang obtained assistance from Scottish co-operators to help him in his struggles against vested interests in Ireland.

He had married, in 1894, Christina Hutchison Craig who predeceased him in 1951, but he was survived by five of his family of seven children. He died at the home of one of his sons Mr Alex. Lang in Laurieston, Castle Douglas, on 19 October 1966 and was cremated on 22 October at Paisley.

Sources: J. B. Jefferys, *The Story of the Engineers 1800–1945* [1945]; personal information: Robert C. Lang, of Renfrew, son. OBIT. *Co-op. News*, 29 Oct 1966; *Scottish Co-operator*, 29 Oct 1966.

H. F. BING

See also: William ALLAN, for New Model Unionism; Patrick GALLAGHER; W. MAXWELL, for Scottish Co-operation.

LEE, Frank (1867–1941)
MINERS' LEADER AND LABOUR MP

Born 8 November 1867 at Pinxton, Derbyshire, the son of Thomas Lee, a miner, and his wife Catherine (née Burrows), he moved to Tibshelf, Derbyshire, with his parents in 1878. He began work in the pit at the age of thirteen and became a checkweighman in 1896. As a member of the Derbyshire Miners' Association he was treasurer of the Tibshelf No. 1 lodge, a delegate to the Council and acted as minute clerk to the Council and executive committee from 1908. He remained a checkweigher until he was elected assistant secretary and compensation agent of the Association in 1914 in succession to Barnet Kenyon. In 1918 he was relieved of some of his work to give him more time for political activities and he became compensation agent. In 1920 he was made assistant general and financial secretary.

Lee's political sympathies were Liberal until the MFGB became affiliated with the Labour Party in 1909. He was registration officer and sub-agent for the Mid-Derbyshire Liberal Association and one of its vice-presidents. After affiliation he became a loyal supporter of the Labour Party. In 1918 he unsuccessfully contested North-East Derbyshire as an official Labour candidate. In the 1922 general election he again contested the same constituency and was declared elected after numerous recounts. It was then discovered that some ballot papers were missing and Lee's Liberal opponent, Stanley Holmes, petitioned against the decision of the returning officer. Lee's election was not confirmed until April 1923. In 1924 he held the seat with 13,420 votes against 9914 for Major Bowden (Conservative). Philip Guedalla was the Liberal candidate.

In 1928 Lee unsuccessfully contested the general secretaryship of the Derbyshire Miners' Association when Henry Hicken was elected. He was not prepared to abandon his parliamentary career to serve as full-time assistant secretary but was prepared to do so if he could enjoy the prestige of being general secretary of the Association. He continued to serve as unpaid assistant secretary until he lost his seat in Parliament in the general election of 1931 and he was then employed as a full-time official until 1935, when he again became MP for North-East Derbyshire until his death.

Lee was a moderate trade union leader

who did much valuable routine work in his early days. In 1904 he became secretary of the Derbyshire Miners' Convalescent Home at Skegness. During the 1912 dispute he helped to organise the distribution of strike payments; and after the 1926 General Strike he was a vigorous opponent of Spencerism. He also played a prominent part in local affairs. He was overseer of the poor, school manager and parochial trustee, parish councillor, secretary of the Tibshelf Technical Education Committee and secretary of the Tibshelf Colliery field fund (sick club) with 2000 members.

Lee was a Wesleyan and, like many miners' leaders of his day, a local preacher. He was a trustee of the local church, for twenty-seven years secretary of the Sunday school and for twenty years the choirmaster of his church. He was also a Sunday school superintendent, the secretary of the Mansfield Wesleyan Circuit School Union and a JP. He died on 21 December 1941 at his Chesterfield home and was survived by his wife, three sons and two daughters; he left £1225 in his will.

Sources: (1) MSS: Minutes of the Derbyshire Miners' Association, 1908–41 (NUM, Saltergate, Chesterfield); (2) Printed: *Derbyshire Times*, 1914–41; *Parliamentary Debates*, 1922–31, 1935–41; (3) Secondary: J. E. Williams, 'The Political Activities of a Trade Union', *Int. Rev. Social Hist.* 2 (1957) 1–21; idem, *The Derbyshire Miners* (1962). Obit. *Times*, 22 Dec 1941; *Derbyshire Times*, 26 Dec 1941.

J. E. WILLIAMS

See also: Thomas Ashton, for Mining Trade Unionism, 1900–14; *A. J. Cook, for Mining Trade Unionism, 1915–26; *Peter Lee, for Mining Trade Unionism, 1927–44.

LEES, James (1806–91)
CO-OPERATOR

Born the son of a handloom weaver at Hollins, Oldham, in Lancashire in 1806; and he began work at home as a weaver before being apprenticed as a hatter. In 1830, after moving to Oldham, he became a member of the Foresters' Confidence Court Lodge until its dissolution in 1887. He was secretary of the lodge for thirty-seven years and of the court of the society's Oldham district for thirty years, holding at various times all the offices of the Foresters' Order.

Lees was an active supporter of William Cobbett and John Fielden in the Oldham parliamentary election of 1833 and also a follower of Robert Owen, becoming a member of the local Socialist Society. Some time during the 1830s he and a number of associates founded a co-operative retailing society in Oldham which collapsed when the manager absconded with £25 (c. 1838). He was also a shareholder in a co-operative hat manufacturing society at Denton (1841–3); but this also failed through a combination of fraud and depression in trade.

Lees helped to promote the Oldham Industrial Co-operative Society in November 1850, becoming a trustee with a seat on the committee. He was the first shop manager (unpaid), treasurer (1852–60) and later again served on the committee (1865–6 and 1871–5). He was twice president (October 1864–January 1865 and April–July 1866) and was a member of the Society's education committee.

In 1865 he was a promoter and first president of the Oldham Building and Manufacturing Co. Ltd (later the Sun Mill Co. Ltd), the first limited liability company in Oldham. The company had close connections with the Oldham Industrial Co-operative Society, which invested quite heavily in the project. In 1871 Lees helped to promote the private enterprise Central Spinning Co. Ltd although he remained an advocate of the principles of co-operation until his death on 11 January 1891.

Sources: *Oldham Chronicle*, 8 Nov 1884; *Oldham Industrial Co-operative Society Record*, *1*, no. 8 (Dec 1894); J. T. Taylor, *Jubilee History of the Oldham Industrial Co-operative Society Ltd 1850–1900* (Manchester, 1900). OBIT. *Oldham Standard*, 14 Jan 1891.

R. E. TYSON

See also: G. J. HOLYOAKE, for Retail Co-operation – Nineteenth Century.

LEWIS, Richard James (1900–66)
TRADE UNIONIST, CO-OPERATOR AND
LABOUR PARTY WORKER

Richard Lewis was born on 4 October 1900 at Tavern Spite, near Whitland in Pembrokeshire, South Wales, the son of Thomas Lewis, a miner. At an early age he went with his parents to the Rhondda Valley where he was educated at the Treorchy Grammar School. At fourteen he started in the pit where he continued working until he went to the Central Labour College in London in 1921 as a nominee of the SWMF. After two years there he returned to the Rhondda Valley and played a leading part during the 1926 General Strike. In the following year he was elected to the Rhondda UDC.

After a prolonged period of unemployment he went to London in 1928 where he became tutor organiser to the National Council of Labour Colleges. In this connection, he frequently visited East Anglia and, in 1930, was appointed education secretary of Ipswich Co-operative Society, holding this post until his retirement in October 1965 on attaining the age of sixty-five. Education was to him not merely a necessary process of earning a living, but the right of everyone to the enjoyment of as full a life as possible. In addition to his educational work for the Ipswich Society, 'Dick' Lewis (as he was always called) was a member of the southern section education council of the Co-operative Union. He served on the national education executive of the Co-operative Union from its formation, and was vice-chairman from 1949 until his death. Lewis was a vigorous and colourful character and was always a prominent figure for many years at the Co-operative Union's annual education convention. He was also a member of the executive committee of the British Federation of Young Co-operators, the National Council of Labour Colleges, and the governing body of Ruskin College.

He was also active in local affairs at Ipswich. In 1940 he assisted in the initiation of the 'Ipswich committee against malnutrition': an organisation which provided cheap milk for children and the elderly, financed by Richard Stokes MP. This service was the forerunner to the national scheme. Lewis served on the Ipswich Town Council from 1942, became in time an alderman and was mayor of Ipswich in 1959–60. During his year of office he inaugurated the Ipswich Council of Social Service. He was also on the governing body of the Ipswich Civic College: he helped to introduce comprehensive education in the city, and he was a member of the board of governors of the University of East Anglia. He made three unsuccessful attempts to enter Parliament: in 1945 as a Labour candidate and in 1951 and 1955 as a Labour and Co-operative candidate for the Sudbury and Woodbridge Division of Suffolk.

Following an operation in a London hospital, he was transferred to the East Suffolk Hospital where he died on 20 January 1966. He was buried on 25 January and a widely attended memorial service was held on 28 January. He left an estate valued at £2531. As a token of respect for his services to Ipswich, donations sent following his death have been used for the conversion of a house into flatlets for the elderly. He was survived by his wife, Mrs L. E. Lewis (née Varley), whom he had married in 1940. Mrs Lewis, a JP for Ipswich and vice-president of the Ipswich branch of the WEA, was a sister of Mr Frank Varley, MP for Mansfield, and a Nottinghamshire miners' leader.

Sources: W. W. Craik, *The Central Labour College, 1909–29: a chapter in the history of adult working class education* (1964); *Suffolk Chronicle and Mercury,* 20 June 1951 and 6 Feb 1959; personal information: Mrs L. Eveline Lewis, Ipswich, widow. OBIT. *Evening Star,* 20 Jan 1966; *Co-op. Gazette,* 25 Jan 1966; *Co-op. News,* 29 Jan 1966; *Platform,* March 1966.

JOYCE BELLAMY
H. F. BING

See also: T. R. BIRD; A. BONNER, for Co-operation, 1945–70; Fred HALL, for Co-operative Education; Fred HAYWARD, for Co-operative Union.

LEWIS, Thomas (Tommy) (1873–1962)
TRADE UNIONIST, BOROUGH ALDERMAN AND LABOUR MP

Thomas Lewis was born on 12 December 1873 in the St Mary's district of Southampton. His father John Lewis was a dock labourer, from Jersey in the Channel Islands. In the early days the family were poor and Tommy Lewis had to leave the Eastern District Board School, Southampton, when he was eleven years of age. He worked as a watchmaker and jeweller in St Mary's Street, Southampton, and later as a Friendly Society officer. He had over forty years' association with the friendly society world, having enrolled as a member of the Hearts of Oak Benefit Society in 1899. In 1905 he was elected to represent Southampton on the Board of Delegates, a position he held for thirty-one years, and in 1907 he was first elected to the executive council, becoming chairman in 1918 and again in 1930, and president in 1924. In 1936 he was elected a trustee from which position he retired at the age of seventy in 1944. In 1920–1 he was president of the National Conference of Friendly Societies.

His first bid for public office (?1892), as socialist candidate for the Board of Guardians, was unsuccessful. He was not yet twenty-one years of age and had he been elected would have been liable to prosecution for a false declaration of age in his nomination paper. He was later elected to the Board of Guardians and was associated with its work until it finally wound up. Some time in the early 1890s Lewis made another unsuccessful bid for public office as a Social Democratic Federation candidate, for the St Mary's Ward, in the Southampton Borough Council elections. In 1895, when he was only twenty-two years of age, he acted as the election agent for Mr C. A. Gibson, the SDF parliamentary candidate in Southampton. The SDF were bottom of the poll with only 274 votes. The successful Liberal candidate received 5555 votes. Lewis was a member of the SDF executive for nine years.

In 1901 Lewis successfully contested the

St Mary's Ward in the Borough Council election and became the first Labour Councillor in the history of the town. This was the beginning of a long association with Southampton local government, a record of service unsurpassed and unlikely to be equalled either in that town or many others. He served on the Borough Council for nearly sixty years, from 1901 until May 1961, with only two short breaks of service totalling eighteen months. He was leader of the Labour Group from the time of its formation until May 1957 and elected alderman in 1929. He served on many Council committees and represented the town on Southampton Harbour Board for sixty years. In this latter capacity he was successful in compelling the board to pay the town its legitimate share of harbour revenues. The town was generous in recognising his great services and in 1944 he was given the Honorary Freedom of the County Borough. On his retirement from public office in June 1961 he was elected to the unprecedented distinction of Honorary Alderman. By his own choice Alderman Lewis was never mayor of his home town.

Tommy Lewis was active in the wider trade union and labour movement as well as in the affairs of local government. His service in the cause of trade unionism and particularly of merchant seamen is itself a notable record of effort. He was a member of Southampton Trades Council for over fifty years, and a leading figure in forming local branches of the Dock, Wharf, Riverside and General Workers' Union (he was chairman of the Southampton Branch of this union for two years), the Ships' Stewards' Union, the Shop Assistants' Union and the British Seafarers' Union. This latter organisation was a breakaway from the National Sailors' and Firemen's Union of Havelock Wilson. After the 1911 seamen's strike the Southampton Branch of the National Sailors' and Firemen's Union refused to remit its funds to Head Office until a full investigation into the financial affairs of the union had been undertaken. The outcome of this dispute was the breakaway of the Southampton Branch of the National Sailors' and Fire-

men's Union and the founding of the British Seafarers' Union. They were later joined by a similar breakaway branch in Glasgow led by Emanuel Shinwell. The BSU (later the Amalgamated Marine Workers' Union) was in continual and intensely bitter conflict with Havelock Wilson and the National Sailors' and Firemen's Union (NUS) from 1911 until 1927 when Wilson won the final battle and the AMWU had to wind up its affairs. During this long struggle between the militant BSU and Wilson, the influence of Lewis's leadership was of great importance. The BSU journal, The British Seafarer (1913–22), is an excellent example of trade union journalism. It was produced in Southampton and it seems likely that Lewis was directly associated with the editorship. From 1911 until 1922 Lewis was honorary president of the BSU and after the amalgamation of the BSU and Joe Cotter's Ships' Stewards to form the AMWU Lewis became honorary treasurer, a post he held until 1926.

In national politics Lewis had an interesting, if less colourful, record. Apart from his time as SDF election agent he himself contested no less than eight parliamentary elections. In 1910 he was selected as the Labour candidate for the Southampton Constituency but the Party could not raise the funds to contest the election. He did stand unsuccessfully in 1918, 1922, 1923 and 1924 (these last two in dual harness with the Rev. R. W. Sorenson). In 1929, on his fifth attempt, he was finally elected to the House of Commons but was defeated and lost his seat in the National Government election of 1931. In 1931 he received 26,425 votes. Four years later, in 1935, his vote increased to 30,751 but he was again unsuccessful. The post-war election of 1945 witnessed the Labour Party's landslide victory and Tommy Lewis, now seventy-two years old, was elected again to Parliament with a majority of 13,000. In 1950 Lewis did not contest the Southampton constituency again but voluntarily retired from the national political arena to concentrate his efforts in local government. His record as an MP was not outstanding. He had been elected too late in his career to hold office, but he had the reputation of being a 'good constituency man' with a willingness to fight for local issues. He acted as parliamentary agent to the Hearts of Oak Benefit Society and to the National Conference of Friendly Societies.

Tommy Lewis was an excellent speaker and ruthless in debate. For over seventy years he used these skills to fight the cause of the labouring man. He had two great loyalties in his life: Socialism and Southampton, and he served both well. The time span of his activity was phenomenal and compares with that of his old comrade in the seamen's cause, Emanuel Shinwell. But Lewis was essentially a local man; a socialist pioneer who married his ideals to practical purposes. Southampton seamen long recognised him as the champion of their cause, and he was the obvious choice to represent them following the *Titanic* disaster in 1912. His political position was always uncompromising in its general principles. Before 1914, when he was an active member of the SDF he disliked the ILP for what he thought was their sentimental and often sloppy approach to Socialism; and the fact that he was an atheist may have further accounted for his rejection of ILP attitudes. After 1918 Lewis was always a firm Labour Party man. On the one side he opposed Tories and Liberals as 'enemies of the masses' and on the other he would have no truck with the Communist Party or with any organisation the CP was involved with. Thus he had no connection with the Minority Movement in the 1920s or with the National Unemployed Workers' Movement in the 1930s, although he always took a leading part in pressing the claims of the unemployed. Nor did Lewis support activist movements inside the Labour Party such as the Socialist League. He never married, was a staunch teetotaller and non-smoker, was respected by his opponents and much loved and admired by his own people.

He was awarded the CBE in 1950 for his public service. In 1955 the University of Southampton conferred on him the Honorary Doctorate of Laws, for his service to the University. He had been a member of College and University Council for more than fifty years, and an active worker for the University status which came with the granting of a Charter in 1952.

The best obituary to Tommy Lewis is a quotation from a speech he made in 1950 – he was then seventy-seven – when presented with a cheque raised by public subscription to mark his fifty years of service to the town. (The money was used to buy books on economics and politics for the Borough library.) 'I shall not give up just because you have honoured me tonight. I shall go on working. There is still much to be done. I shall never give up.' Among the audience there were a few ex-members of the old SDF, septuagenarians who had worked with Tommy in the 1890s. He died on 28 February 1962 at the Southampton home of friends with whom he had lived for ten years since the death of his sister. He left an estate valued at £21,588 (net, before duty paid).

Sources: *The British Seafarer* (1913–22); *The Marine Worker 1* no. 2 (Mar 1922); J. H. Wilson, *My Stormy Voyage through Life* (1925); H. W. Lee and E. Archbold, *Social-Democracy in Britain* (1935); *Presentation to Alderman Thomas Lewis CBE, JP recording the Resolution of the Town Council bestowing the Freedom of the Borough* (26 Oct 1945); *Southern Daily Echo*, 27 Oct 1945; *Presentation to Alderman Thomas Lewis CBE, JP to commemorate his 50 years' Service in the Public Life of Southampton* (17 Oct 1950); B. Mogridge, 'Militancy and Inter-Union Rivalries in British Shipping 1911–1929', *Int. Rev. Social Hist.* 6 part 3 (1961) 375–412; W. Kendall, *The Revolutionary Movement in Britain 1900–21: the origins of British Communism* (1969). Biographical information: Secretary, Hearts of Oak Benefit Society; personal information: H. T. Willcock, Labour Party agent in Southampton, who also lent various documents; Sir James Matthews. OBIT. *Southern Evening Echo*, 28 Feb 1962 and 19 Mar 1962; *Hearts of Oak J.* (June 1962).

JAMES MACFARLANE
JOHN SAVILLE

See also: *C. R. ATTLEE, for British Labour Party, 1931–51; Arthur HENDERSON, for

British Labour Party, 1914–31; *J. HAVE-LOCK WILSON.

LIDDLE, Thomas (1863–1954)
TRADE UNIONIST AND CO-OPERATOR

Born at Middlesbrough on 26 April 1863, the son of John Liddle, a journeyman joiner, the young Thomas Liddle was apprenticed to a carpenter. He became interested in trade unionism in his youth and in 1896 was elected full-time organiser of the Amalgamated Society of Carpenters and Joiners. He resigned in 1910 to become the first manger of Sunderland Labour Exchange and for his services in connection with Labour Exchanges during the First World War was awarded the MBE. In later life he was elected president of the National Federation of Employment Exchange Managers' Associations. He was made a JP in 1906.

Liddle was a keen co-operator, a member of Hartlepools Co-operative Society and its president from 1905 to 1936, playing an important part in its development and expansion. He was chairman of the District Association, 1912–20, and of the first wages board in the northern section. In 1919 he was one of the eight representatives of retail societies in the Special Inquiry Committee to consider a general pension scheme for all co-operative employees. He was elected to the board of the Co-operative Wholesale Society in 1920 and retired (under the age rule) in 1932, serving on the grocery committee and representing the CWS on the New Zealand Produce Association. He was also a director of the English and Scottish Joint Co-operative Wholesale Society 1924–31 and in 1930 was elected president of the Co-operative Congress at York.

Liddle was also active in local government. He was a member of the West Hartlepool School Board and sat on the Hartlepool Town Council for eight years from 1903 to 1911, was a member of the Local Education Authority and chairman of the first Juvenile Court. He also served as chairman of the Port Sanitary Authority, was a governor of the local hospitals and a member of the Memorial Homes Committee. In religion he was a Primitive Methodist.

After a life of great public activity, he resided for many years in retirement at Leigh-on-Sea and died there on 2 July 1954, aged ninety-one, leaving a widow, two sons and two daughters.

Sources: *Co-op. Congress Report* (Manchester, 1930); P. Redfern, *The New History of the C.W.S.* (Manchester, 1938); personal information: Hartlepools Co-operative Society Ltd, and the Librarian, Co-operative Union. OBIT. *Times*, 7 July 1954; *Co-op. News*, 10 July 1954.

H. F. BING

See also: W. H. BROWN, for Retail Co-operation, 1900–45; Percy REDFERN, for Co-operative Wholesaling.

LOWERY, Matthew Hedley (1858–1918)
MINING TRADE UNION LEADER

Born on 23 December 1858 at Low Fell, Gateshead. Lowery's father died when he was young and his mother moved with her family to the Blyth area. He began work at the Cambois Colliery as a blacksmith's apprentice but was unwilling to comply with the regulations of the yearly bond whereby colliery workers were tied to the same employer for a year. He then went to Seaton Burn but soon moved to Widdrington at the request of Mr Jos. Wedderburn, a former Cambois blacksmith who was foreman blacksmith at Widdrington. In his youth he was a gambler but promised his mother, on her deathbed, that he would reform his way of life. He became a close friend of William Straker and together they organised an educational class which met twice weekly. Lowery moved to Stobswood Colliery and then to Pegswood where he remained until his death twenty-seven years later. He took an active part in the Northumberland Colliery Mechanics' Union and for many years was a member of the executive committee of the Union. In 1905 he was elected to the joint committee of the Northumberland and Durham Mechanics'

Union and in 1915 became president of the Union. (The association of the colliery mechanics operated independently from the miners' unions for the two counties.)

Apart from his trade union activities, Lowery was president of the Pegswood Co-operative Society for many years; he was also a Primitive Methodist who occasionally undertook lay preaching. Married with at least one son and one daughter, he died on 22 July 1918 at Pegswood, Morpeth. He left effects valued at £330.

Sources: S. Webb, *The Story of the Durham Miners (1662–1921)* (1921); E. Welbourne, *The Miners' Unions of Northumberland and Durham* (Cambridge, 1923); W. S. Hall, *A Historical Survey of the Durham Colliery Mechanics' Association 1879–1929* (Durham, 1929). OBIT. *NMA* (1918).

ANTHONY MASON

See also: *W. STRAKER; J. W. TAYLOR.

MACDONALD, Alexander (1821–81)
MINERS' LEADER AND MP

The eldest of seven sons, Alexander Macdonald was born on 21 June 1821 at Dalmacoulter, New Monkland, Lanarkshire. His father had been a sailor for eighteen years but then left the sea to work in the mines, and Alexander followed him into the pits at the age of eight. He worked continuously as a miner in both coal and ironstone mines for the following sixteen years, supplementing a limited formal education by evening classes, including the study of Latin and Greek, and much private reading. At an early age he was enthused and inspired by newspaper accounts of Richard Oastler's struggle for the limitation of hours of work of factory children. He took part in the Lanarkshire strike of 1842, at the end of which, in his own words, 'I was one of those that was selected as a victim for the tyranny of the employers.' In 1846 he began attending Glasgow University in the winter session, paying for his tuition from his savings and returning to the pits in the summer; and he continued his university courses in the following two sessions. In 1849 and 1850 he worked as a mine mana-ger and then in 1851 he opened a school in which he continued for about five years. From 1855 or thereabouts (the date being given differently in different sources) he left teaching and began to devote himself wholly to the improvement of miners' conditions. This he was able to do having acquired a modest fortune by commercial speculation; but the nature of the business that he was engaged in is so far unknown. His financial resources were later added to by collections and donations made to him by his fellow miners.

In these early years as a full-time worker for the cause of the miners, Macdonald was a vigorous advocate of strike action under certain conditions to demonstrate solidarity and purpose. At the same time he was always a believer in parliamentary action and insisted that only through government intervention, and parliamentary legislation, could the mining community expect a permanent redress of their grievances. His own words from a much quoted speech in 1873 best indicate the changes he was seeking to achieve from the middle 1850s on:

It was in 1856 that I crossed the border first to advocate a better Mines Act, true weighing, the education of the young, the restriction of the age to twelve years, the reduction of the working hours to eight in every twenty-four, the training of managers, the payment of wages weekly in the coin of the realm, no truck, and many other useful things too numerous to mention here. Shortly after that, bone began to come to bone, and by 1858 we were in full action for better laws.

In October 1855, following a series of strikes in Lanarkshire, Macdonald issued a public appeal to Scottish miners to join a Coal and Iron Miners' Association of which he was the interim secretary. By the end of 1855 the Association had met with a considerable response. The immediate issue was the Special Rules under the Mines Act of 1855 but in the early spring of 1856 a severe wage cut led to a widespread strike which lasted from April to early June. It ended in failure, the fortunes of the Association slumped, and despite Macdonald's attempt to build up the union once again by mid-1859 there was little left of the original Association. During the same period however Macdonald had continued his assiduous lobbying of Parliament and the important Mines Act of 1860 which *inter alia* allowed the election of checkweighmen by the miners themselves was in large measure due to his persistence. In the same year, 1860, he acquired a controlling interest in the *Glasgow Sentinel*, on which Alexander Campbell was already working as industrial reporter. Among other important campaigns conducted by the *Sentinel*, that for the repeal of the Master and Servant Laws is the best known: in which Campbell worked closely with George Newton, the secretary of the Glasgow Trades Council. Macdonald attended the famous national conference in May 1864 to discuss the basis of a national campaign against the unequal laws which were especially severely interpreted by the Scottish courts.

The most important event in Macdonald's career in the 1860s was the five-day meeting of miners at Leeds in November 1863. He had previously organised in 1858, at Ashton-under-Lyne, a meeting that was intended to be national in its representation, but not until the Leeds meeting was a truly representative gathering brought together. From the Leeds meeting emerged the Miners' National Association with Macdonald as president, a position which he retained in the organisation until his death. Much of the preliminary work for this founding conference had been done by John Towers, the editor of the *British Miner* (later the *Miner and Workman's Advocate*); and the bitter hostility between Towers and Macdonald dates from this time. W. P. Roberts, the radical attorney, was also deeply involved in the controversy against Macdonald, and among the consequences of the quarrel, which was both a matter of personalities as well as a wide-ranging argument about tactics and strategy, was the establishment of the little-known, and short-lived, Practical Miners, as a breakaway from the Miners' National Association in November 1864 [Challinor (1967–8)].

Macdonald took an important part in all the many aspects of trade union and political activity that were developing in the 1860s, and was associated in many campaigns with George Potter. He gave evidence before the S.C. on Regulation and Inspection of Mines and Miners' Complaints and the S.C. on Contracts between Masters and Servants, both in 1866; before the R.C. on Trade Unions, 1868–9; and the S.C. on Present Dearness and Scarcity of Coal in 1873. By the late 1860s Macdonald was modifying his political attitudes, and showing tendencies to compromise in matters of parliamentary legislation, for which he was vigorously criticised by Beesly as well as by Marx and Engels. He was a candidate for Kilmarnock in the election of 1868 but withdrew in favour of Edwin Chadwick, for whom he spoke in support before the electors. He had close relations with Lord Elcho (later the Earl of Wemyss), who was closely involved in both the Master and Servant controversy as well as mining legislation, and Macdonald became known in some quarters as 'Elcho's Limited'. But mining conditions remained his central interest and he was active in the great movement in Scotland which began with a one-day strike in May 1870 and culminated in the winning of the eight-hour day in Fife. At the gala day on 5 June 1871, organised to mark the first anniversary of the eight-hours victory, Macdonald was presented with a purse of sovereigns. To celebrate the passing of the Mines Act of 1872 another public presentation was made to him: a total of £780 being handed over, of which the Scottish contribution was £680.

Macdonald was elected to the first parliamentary committee of the TUC in 1871 and was chairman in 1872 and 1873. These were the years of intensive debate and lobbying over the Liberal Government's Criminal Law Amendment Act. Macdonald at this time worked closely with George Howell, the secretary of the parliamentary committee, and they were both trying to play the tactic of private negotiations within the committee rooms and lobbies of the House of Commons. Events, however, were against them and Howell in particular came under severe criticism, both in the labour press and at the January 1873 Congress of the TUC. When the new Conservative Government appointed a R.C. on the Labour Laws in 1874, the parliamentary committee held a special meeting to which were invited A. J. Mundella, Frederic Harrison, Tom Hughes and other middle-class supporters. A statement was issued denying the need for a Royal Commission and urging immediate remedial legislation. The next day Burt and Tom Hughes were offered places on the Commission, and, time being short, they discussed the matter with Macdonald. It was agreed that the latter should take the place of Hughes and after the parliamentary committee had again reaffirmed its opposition to any collaboration by the trade union movement, Macdonald resigned as chairman of the parliamentary committee. He submitted a minority report to the main report of the R.C.

At the general election of 1874 which returned the Conservative Party to office, Macdonald was returned to the Commons as member for Stafford and he was re-elected in 1880; most of his time being now taken up with parliamentary affairs. He introduced a private member's bill on workmen's compensation in 1875, and was a most persistent questioner of ministers on all aspects of mining conditions. He was vigorous in his sympathy with the Irish and strongly opposed to the Irish Coercion Bill of the Gladstone Government in February 1881. In the field of mining trade unionism, which in the second half of the 1870s was confronted with falling prices and declining membership, Macdonald was in favour of the sliding scale, restriction of output to raise prices and therefore wages, and of emigration as the way to reduce an overstocked labour market. But he still had his dramatic moments, as when the official inquiry into the great Blantyre explosion of October 1877 allowed him to make a vigorous denunciation of the absence of adequate safety precautions.

Macdonald was a flamboyant personality with an excellent platform manner. In his later years he exhibited the social snobbery by no means uncommon among many labour leaders of the past century: one critic writing in 1875 that he simmered with satisfaction at 'holding easy converse with a live lord' [Hinton (1875) 156]. In his political attitudes in his last years he was never as firmly committed to the Liberal Party as were the great majority of his colleagues, and during his years in Parliament he showed himself not unwilling to get on to terms with Benjamin Disraeli, then leader of the Conservative Party. His reputation, however, does not rest upon the last decade of his life: it is as a pioneer of mining trade unionism and mining legislation that his memory remained green for generations of miners. Each year on the anniversary of his death miners gathered in procession, particularly from North Lanarkshire, to go to the churchyard to pay tribute with flowers: a custom which lasted for sixty years until disrupted by the Second World War.

Towards the end of his days Macdonald bought a small estate at Wellhall, near Hamilton, and here he died on 31 October 1881, being buried in the churchyard at New Monkland. He left an estate valued at £3487.

Sources: Evidence before the S.C. on Regulation and Inspection of Mines and Miners' Complaints 1866 XIV Qs 6573–7277; 7868–882; 8366–453; S.C. on Contracts between Master and Servant 1866 XIII Qs 283–453; R.C. on Trade Unions 1868–9 XXXI Qs 15020–1; 15237–762; 16330–53; 16518–27; S.C. on Present Dearness and Scarcity of Coal 1873 X Qs 4488–945; R. J. Hinton, *English Radical Leaders* (New York, 1875) 142–60; *Dod* (1880); Lloyd Jones, 'Alexander Macdonald', *Newcastle Daily Chronicle*, 17 Nov 1883 [most of which is reproduced in J. M. Baernreither, *English Associations of Working Men* (1893) 409–11]; S. and B. Webb, *The History of Trade Unionism* (1894); A. S. Cunningham, *Reminiscences of Alex M'Donald, the Miners' Friend* (repr. from *Dunfermline Journal*: Dunfermline, 1902); A. J. Youngson Brown, 'Trade Union Policy in the Scottish Coalfields 1855–1885', *Econ. Hist. Rev.* 6 ser. 2 (1953) 35–50; D. Simon, 'Master and Servant', in *Democracy and the Labour Movement*, ed. John

Saville (1954); R. Page Arnot, *The Scottish Miners* (1955); B. C. Roberts, *The Trades Union Congress, 1868–1921* (1958); J. E. Williams, *The Derbyshire Miners* (1962); H. A. Clegg et al., *A History of British Trade Unions since 1889* vol. *1: 1889–1910* (1964); Royden Harrison, *Before the Socialists* (1965); R. Challinor, *Alexander Macdonald and the Miners*, Our History series, no. 48 (winter 1967–8) 34 pp. OBIT. *Times*, 1 Nov 1881; *Airdrie and Coatbridge Advertiser*, 5 Nov 1881; *Hamilton Advertiser*, 12 Nov 1881.

JOHN SAVILLE

See also: William ABRAHAM, for Welsh Mining Trade Unionism; Thomas ASHTON, for Mining Trade Unionism, 1900–14; Alexander CAMPBELL; Benjamin PICKARD, for Mining Trade Unionism, 1880–99; *Robert SMILLIE, for Scottish Mining Trade Unionism; and below: Mining Trade Unionism, 1850–79.

Mining Trade Unionism, 1850–79: R. Bayldon, *The London Lock-out and the Methley Miners* (Leeds, 1860) 16 pp.; H. H. Burke, *Black Diamonds: or the Gospel in a colliery district* (1861); Anon., *Life amongst the Colliers* (1862); 'Ignotus', *The Last Thirty Years in a Mining District* (1867); F. Wemyss-Charteris-Douglas, *Lord Elcho and the Miners* (1867) 16 pp.; R. Fynes, *The Miners of Northumberland and Durham* (Sunderland, 1873, repr. 1923); G. Howell, *Labour Legislation, Labour Movements and Labour Leaders* (1902); P. Sweezy, *Monopoly and Competition in the English Coal Trade, 1550–1850* (Camb., Mass., 1938); H. Scott, 'The History of the Miner's Bond in Northumberland and Durham: with special reference to its influence on industrial disputes' (Manchester MA, 1946); H. Scott, 'The Miner's Bond in Northumberland and Durham', *Proc. Soc. Antiquaries of Newcastle upon Tyne 11* ser. 4 (1946–50) 55–78, 87–98; R. Page Arnot, *The Miners: a history of the Miners' Federation of Great Britain* (1949); A. J. Taylor, 'The Miners' Association of Gt Britain and Ireland, 1842–48', *Economica, 22* (1955) 45–60; B. McCormick and J. E. Williams, 'The Miners and the Eight-Hour Day, 1863–1910', *Econ. Hist.*

Rev. 12 ser. 2 (1959–60) 222–37; A. J. Taylor, 'Labour Productivity and Technological Innovation in the British Coal Industry, 1850–1914', *Econ. Hist. Rev. 14* ser. 2 (1961–2) 48–70; R. Challinor and B. Ripley, *The Miners' Association: a trade union in the age of the Chartists* (1968); J. E. Williams, *The Derbyshire Miners* (1692); R. Challinor, *Alexander Macdonald and the Miners*, Our History series, no. 48 (winter 1967–8) 34 pp.; J. B. Smethurst, 'Lancashire and the Miners' Association of Great Britain and Ireland', *Trans. of the Eccles and District History Society* (1968–69); A. R. Griffin, *Mining in the East Midlands 1550–1947* (1971).

MacDONALD, James Ramsay (1866–1937)
LABOUR LEADER AND FIRST LABOUR PRIME MINISTER

Born on 12 October 1866, in Lossiemouth, Morayshire, out of wedlock, and brought up by his mother Anne Ramsay and his grandmother; his father, John MacDonald, was head ploughman at a farm near Elgin at which his mother had worked. The Ramsay household of two women and the boy was poor but not destitute, and Mac-Donald received a good Scots village schooling at Drainie School, latterly serving as pupil teacher. In 1885, at the age of eighteen, he took the road of the ambitious Scot to England, and worked for a few months in Bristol, but returned to Lossiemouth before settling in London. He established himself with great difficulty, living for a time on nothing but oatmeal and hot water, and it was not till 1888, after an enforced return home through ill-health, that he secured steady employment as private secretary to Thomas Lough, subsequently a Liberal MP. He joined the Fabian Society in 1886, whose members mistook him from his handsome appearance and bearing for an army officer. In 1888 he became a member of the SDF in London, and was London secretary of the Scottish Home Rule Association. He joined the ILP in 1894, a year after its founding, doing so in disgust at the Liberals' refusal to adopt a Trades Council candidate for the Attercliffe (Sheffield) by-election. By this time he was supporting himself by journalism, writing among other things several articles for the new *Dictionary of National Biography*. He rapidly achieved a national reputation inside the ILP – he was first elected to the National Administrative Council in 1896 – and by 1900 he was the ILP's most prolific writer and propagandist. The first major political crisis of his career occurred as the result of the Boer War, during which he took a pro-Boer line. His resignation from the Fabian Society on the war issue, and his unequivocal denunciation of the war in his election campaign in Leicester in 1900 (where, although he was defeated, he achieved a high poll) all seemed to increase his popularity with the ILP rank and file.

MacDonald's life was transformed by his marriage in 1896 to Margaret Ethel Gladstone, daughter of Professor J. H. Gladstone, FRS, a distinguished chemist, and grand-niece of Lord Kelvin. She had been a school manager and voluntary social worker in Hoxton, and had met him as a result of his unsuccessful candidacy for Parliament for Southampton in the election of 1895. Marriage gave MacDonald an assured income and status within the middle class to which, by instinct, he belonged; it brought him within the English status system from which, as a poor Scot, he was excluded; and of equal importance it gave him the security and love of a happy marriage and family. The MacDonalds' home, 3 Lincoln's Inn Fields, became a meeting-place for socialists from far and wide, including many from India and elsewhere whom MacDonald and his wife met on their various travels.

MacDonald's importance in the labour movement as a speaker and writer was recognised by his election as secretary of the Labour Representation Committee at the founding conference in Memorial Hall, Farringdon Street, London, in February 1900. The Committee, whose object was 'to establish a distinct Labour group in Parliament', depended upon attracting affiliations of trade unions, but these came slowly until after the Taff Vale decision of 1901; an initial membership of 232,000 rose

to 847,000 by early 1903. MacDonald's careful advocacy of the new organisation played a large part in its growth. Some arrangement to prevent rival Liberal and Labour candidacies in critical working-class constituencies was clearly necessary, and was mooted as early as March 1900. In 1903 MacDonald negotiated with Herbert Gladstone, the Liberal Whip, a pact by which Liberals and LRC would refrain from opposing each other in certain English constituencies; this secret *entente* was supported by Keir Hardie and other leaders of the LRC when overtures came from the Liberals, who were pessimistic about their chances of gaining power after their two defeats in 1895 and 1900. In the 1906 election, in which twenty-nine LRC candidates were elected (nineteen for seats in which the pact operated, eleven of these being in two-member constituencies), MacDonald was returned, along with a Liberal, for Leicester. He early stood forth as one of the leaders of the Parliamentary Labour Party, and served as chairman from 1911 until the outbreak of war. He was an able parliamentarian and an effective speaker in a somewhat flowery, Gladstonian style; but his reputation among the Left of the labour movement had seriously diminished by 1914 as a result of what was widely felt to be his easy accommodation within the Liberal Party in Parliament. To this period belong his main writings on Socialism, in which he expounded his evolutionary, non-Marxist creed. Socialism is 'a theory of Social organisation, which reconciles the individual to Society': it 'is the creed of those who . . . seek to build up a social organisation which will include in its activities the management of those economic instruments such as land and industrial capital that cannot be left safely in the hands of individuals'. It would come gradually: '*solvitur ambulando*, not *sic volo* – laboratory experiment, not revolution – is the method of Socialism emerged from the Utopian and pseudo-scientific stages'. His writings show a love of metaphor and analogy; he is always much stronger in his criticism of capitalism and its wastefulness and selfishness than in describing what is to take its place; but he is hardly alone in this. Certain of his political writings, especially in the years after 1900 – *Socialism and Society* (1905) for example – served a very practical need in that he was trying to provide a theoretical justification for the existence of the Labour Alliance, by no means wholly approved of by his own power base in the ILP. He was much given to biological analogy in his socialist writings, believing that a society is an organism which had developed from the primitive and undifferentiated to the advanced and complex. Almost everything in society is related to each other and to its proper functioning in general, although there are certain alien elements which are not only deeply disruptive of its working, but also immoral; class hatred and poverty, for example. An understanding of the direction of social change – and the willingness to use that knowledge in practical affairs – is a necessary prerequisite of positive social reform. MacDonald's political philosophy never advanced beyond these ideas, and it is possible to interpret his career as a gradual unfolding of the conservative implications of his theory.

MacDonald's career was shaken off course by two things. The first was his wife's death in 1911, which reinforced his loneliness and his impatience of criticism, his self-pity and his restlessness in social intercourse. He had few friends among his Labour colleagues, but enjoyed a wide acquaintanceship in London society, where his taste for travel, paintings and old furniture was admired. His elder daughter, Ishbel, served in later years as hostess for him. His family consisted of six children, three sons (one of whom died in 1910) and three daughters. Malcolm, his second son, had a distinguished career within and, after 1931, outside the Labour Party, and was British High Commissioner in Canada during the Second World War.

The other factor controlling MacDonald's career was his attitude to the war of 1914–18. In his speech in Parliament on 3 August 1914, MacDonald opposed the declaration of war, arguing that the outcome was unforeseeable and that friendship with France did not demand it. The Parliamentary Labour Party had passed a resolution in favour of staying out of the war four days previously; but now MacDonald found himself in a small minority within the Party and resigned the chairmanship. He remained a member of the Party, and continued to serve as treasurer (1912–24). The grounds for his opposition to the war were broadly those of the Union of Democratic Control. He was a founding member of the UDC, and his was the first signature on the UDC's first public statement. He was opposed to secret diplomacy and rightly sceptical of promises of a better world. But he was no pacifist, and though he refused to make recruiting speeches in Leicester he wrote that 'those who can enlist ought to enlist'. He was much vilified for his stand, and when he sought to serve in an ambulance unit in France in December 1914 he was immediately sent home. The effect of his wartime experiences was to make MacDonald seem much more a man of the Left than he really was; for it threw him into the cause of the ILP and of advanced internationalists (many of them ex-Liberals who subsequently joined the Labour Party) with whom he co-operated in the Union of Democratic Control and other bodies working for a just peace. He took part (along with Philip Snowden) in the Leeds Convention, an unofficial gathering held to hail the Russian Revolution in June 1917. In the previous month he set off for Petrograd with a Labour delegation to visit the new Kerensky government, but was prevented from sailing by Havelock Wilson's seamen's union, whose members refused to allow him on board.

In the 'coupon election' of December 1918 MacDonald lost his seat at Leicester. For the next few years he was active in the ILP and won much support in Scotland by his vigorous fortnightly column in Tom Johnston's *Forward*. He attended the International Socialist Conference at Berne in February 1919 at which the division between the Communists and the older socialist movement became clear; thereafter he used his influence to dissuade the ILP (at its Glasgow and Southport conferences in 1920 and 1921) and the Labour Party from affiliating with the Communist International. His moderating counsel helped to keep the ILP and the Labour Party from diverging at this time, when the latter, with its new constitution and local branches, was entering into competition with the former for individual members. His prominence was enhanced when he narrowly lost the East Woolwich by-election in 1921, when his wartime conduct was bitterly attacked. In the general election of November 1922 he was returned for Aberavon, and when Parliament met he was elected chairman of the Parliamentary Labour Party by sixty-one votes to fifty-seven, with the strong support of the newly elected Clydesiders. He proved to be an effective Leader of the Opposition, though often angered by the obstructive tactics of the left-wingers, as when James Maxton and three other Clydesiders were suspended in a debate on 28 June 1923.

In the general election of December 1923 there were 191 Labour members returned as compared with 158 Liberals and 258 Conservatives. When Parliament met in January the Liberals supported the Labour amendment declaring no confidence in the Conservative Government of Stanley Baldwin. MacDonald, as leader of the next largest party in the Commons, was asked to form a Government on 22 January, just after he had been sworn a member of the Privy Council. He combined the offices of Prime Minister and Foreign Secretary, which led to much overwork but also to his main success in the first Labour Government, his chairmanship of the London Conference in July which ended the French occupation of the Ruhr and secured the adoption of the Dawes plan for German reparations payments. MacDonald led the British delegation to the League of Nations Assembly in September, the first British Prime Minister to do so. In home affairs MacDonald's Government was much less successful, hampered by its minority position and the dissatisfaction of the left-wingers with MacDonald's cautious policies and orthodox Cabinet (which included only John Wheatley and F. W. Jowett from the Left among

several ex-Liberals and one Conservative). His concern, as he told Lord Parmoor, was to 'gain the confidence of the country'. The fall of the Government on 8 October 1924 occurred when the Liberals joined the Conservatives in demanding a select committee to inquire into the 'Campbell case' (the withdrawal of prosecution of J. R. Campbell for an allegedly seditious article in the Communist *Weekly Worker*). MacDonald, perhaps partly from tiredness and irritation with personal attacks on himself, made this a vote of confidence, with the Cabinet's support. He may have preferred to challenge the Opposition on this issue rather than over the controversial treaties with Russia concluded on 8 August. MacDonald's role in the Campbell case was vigorously criticised at the time and is still a matter of debate among historians; it is worth noting that the (1969) publication of Tom Jones's *Whitehall Diary* offers a critical assessment of MacDonald in this matter.

In the resulting general election of October 1924 Labour had a net loss of forty-two seats though it increased its poll by over one million votes. The Conservative victory may have owed something to the publication, four days before polling, of the 'Zinoviev letter' purporting to give the British Communists Russian advice about subversive activities. It was published by the Foreign Office (but the *Daily Mail* had a copy which it was threatening to publish) with an official protest which MacDonald had revised in draft but not signed. MacDonald's handling of the letter, which was complicated by his busy speaking tour in the country, has been severely criticised; he never accepted the letter's authenticity as proved, but he defended the Foreign Office's conduct in publishing it.

MacDonald continued as leader of the party and leader of the Opposition during the Baldwin Government of 1924–9. Snowden urged Henderson to replace him, but Henderson had no such ambition, and there was no obvious alternative to MacDonald, whose grip on the party remained strong, particularly at the annual conferences. The acceptance of the new programme, *Labour and the Nation*, by the Birmingham Conference in 1928 owed much to his skilful chairmanship. During the General Strike he was critical of the Government's tactics and worked behind the scenes to get negotiations going to end the strike. In the same year, 1926, he became further alienated from the ILP when it passed into the control of Maxton and adopted the programme *Socialism in Our Time*, which MacDonald criticised as 'sanctification of phrases of no definite meaning'.

The general election of May 1929 again put MacDonald in office as Prime Minister in the second minority Labour Government (Labour, 287; Conservatives, 261; Liberals, 59). MacDonald's constituency was now Seaham, County Durham. This time he did not take over the Foreign Office, though he retained control of policy towards the United States, paying an unprecedented visit to President Hoover in October 1929 and presiding over the London Naval Conference in January 1930. MacDonald was at his best at such conferences; he presided over the first Indian Round Table Conference in November 1930 and attended the Assembly of the League in September 1929. His Government was dogged by the problem of unemployment which began to grow steadily in 1930, reaching $2\frac{1}{2}$ million by December. No large schemes to meet it were produced; instead the Government was forced to ask for successive increases in the borrowing powers of the Unemployment Insurance Fund and, latterly, to introduce an unpopular bill to correct certain 'anomalies' in benefits. Sir Oswald Mosley's Memorandum of February 1930 proposed various schemes (control of credit, tariffs, development of agriculture and of imperial trade) to revive employment; the Cabinet's rejection of it led to Mosley's resignation and a continued passive policy on the government's part. On legislation concerning the coalmines, electoral reform, the raising of the school-leaving age, the repeal of the repressive Trade Disputes Act of 1927, the Government was in difficulties with the Liberals and its own supporters, and accomplished little. On 24 August 1931, it resigned following disagreement within the Cabinet over economies to

be adopted to balance an emergency budget (the stumbling-block was a cut in unemployment payments). The emergency was caused by the publication of the report of the Economy Committee appointed under Sir George May's chairmanship, which predicted a budgetary deficit of £120 million and intensified a 'run on the Pound' which had begun as part of the world economic crisis.

To the general surprise of the Labour Party and especially of his Ministerial colleagues, MacDonald remained Prime Minister in a 'National' Government of Conservatives, Liberals, and fifteen Labour members (including Snowden and J. H. Thomas). MacDonald was expelled from the Labour Party, and was condemned by many as a traitor to the cause. He seems to have regarded his action as a temporary measure which was essential to save the country from the disaster of a rapidly depreciating currency (in fact the ending of the gold standard on 21 September had no such result), and to have expected that, as in 1914, it would produce no personal breach.

The National Government was confirmed in office in the general election of October 1931. The election has become notorious for the wild abuse directed against the Labour Party, and in this both MacDonald and Snowden took a leading part against their former colleagues. The result was an enormous majority for the National Government, and the catastrophic decline in the numbers of the Parliamentary Labour Party to a total of forty-six, compared with 289 in 1929. MacDonald's position in the new Government was unhappy, since his National Labour supporters numbered only thirteen (including his son Malcolm), and 472 of the Government's 556 members were Conservatives. His health began to decline, and though he still presided ably at conferences and great occasions and attempted to help on the work of the Disarmament Conference in 1932–3, he saw the real leadership in the Government pass to Baldwin and, even more, to the Chancellor of the Exchequer, Neville Chamberlain. His last important act was his signing of the Defence White

Paper on rearmament in March 1935. In June 1935 he handed over the Prime Ministership to Baldwin and became Lord President of the Council, a post he held until Chamberlain became Prime Minister in May 1937. He was defeated at Seaham by Emanuel Shinwell in a bitter campaign in the general election of October 1935, but subsequently returned to Parliament as member for the Scottish Universities. He died while on a voyage to South America on 9 November 1937.

MacDonald was a man of handsome appearance and good bearing with, in latter days, a fine head of white hair. He had a good speaking voice with a soft Scots brogue, and at his best could hold large audiences spellbound. Indeed, it has often been difficult for later generations to understand the magnetic attraction Ramsay MacDonald had for his contemporaries in the British labour movement. Yet his hold over the Labour Party in the 1920s was quite extraordinary. He was a good, businesslike chairman. He possessed charm, but little warmth or intimacy, at least for most of his political colleagues. His pride, his touchiness at criticism, a certain deviousness which to some seemed like treachery, and an unwillingness to come to grips with hard questions of economic policy handicapped him as a leader and perhaps justified Beatrice Webb's characterisation of him as 'a magnificent substitute for a leader'. In the 1920s he was quite consciously trying to win over the 'middle ground' of political opinion, and most of the decisions he took on political issues followed from that attempt. Whatever the criticisms, his moderating leadership kept the new and restive party reasonably united, helped to school it to office and parliamentary methods, and saved it from rancorous divisions over dogma or class. The first Labour Prime Minister made the party respectable to the public and gave a sense of pride and achievement to its rank and file which his later career did not erase. At the same time there have been few politicians, of any party, whose reputation has sunk so low in the opinions of succeeding generations; and although some professional historians began

in the 1960s to modify the harsh judgement passed upon MacDonald in the previous thirty years, it is still fair to say that the overwhelming majority of the Labour movement have not, so far, altered their traditional verdict.

The National Portrait Gallery, London, has a portrait by Lavery (1931), and a bronze bust by Epstein. MacDonald left an estate valued at just over £25,000 and bequeathed all his personal letters, diaries and other documents to his son Malcolm to be used at the latter's discretion.

Writings: J. Ramsay MacDonald's principal books are: *What I saw in South Africa Sep and Oct 1902* [1902]; *Socialism and Society* (Socialist Library, vol. 2 ILP, 1905); *Socialism* (1907); *Labour and Empire* (1907); *The Awakening of India* (1910); *The Socialist Movement* (1911); *Syndicalism: a critical examination* (1912); *Margaret Ethel MacDonald* (1912 and later editions); *The Social Unrest: its cause and solution* (1913); *National Defence: a study in militarism* (1917); *Socialism after the War* (1917); *The Government of India* (1919); *Parliament and Revolution* (Manchester, 1919); *A Policy for the Labour Party* (1920); *Socialism: critical and constructive* (1921); Introduction to W. Stewart, *J. Keir Hardie* (1921); *Wanderings and Excursions* (1925); *At Home and Abroad* (1936). He wrote many pamphlets and articles in periodicals [see Benjamin Sachs, *J. Ramsay MacDonald in Thought and Action* (Albuquerque, New Mexico, 1952]. The following is a selection of his more important periodical writings not mentioned in Sachs's bibliography: 'Labor Politics in Great Britain', *Int. Soc. Rev. 3* (June 1903) 713–17; 'Socialism and the Labour Party', *Soc. Rev. 1* (Mar 1908) 13–23; 'Let us reform the Labour Party: a rejoinder', *Soc. Rev. 6* (Dec 1910) 301–5; 'What is Liberalism?: a review', *Soc. Rev. 8* (Sep 1911) 46–53; 'Socialism during War', *Soc. Rev. 12* (Oct–Dec 1914) 344–53; 'The Fabian Society', *Soc. Rev. 13* (Aug 1916) 245–50; 'The ILP and the Labour Party', *Soc. Rev. 15* (Apr 1918) 185–94; 'The Case for a Liberal Party, II The Labor View', *Nation* (Lond) 27 (May 1920) 272–4; 'How I won Aberavon', *Nation* (Lond) *32* (Nov 1922) 309–10; 'The Great Strike', *Soc. Rev.* no. 5 ser. 2 (June 1926) 1–8; 'Were the Miners let down?', *Soc. Rev.* no. 6 ser. 2 (July 1926) 1–7.

Sources:
(1) MSS: The MacDonald papers in the possession of the family are not generally available for research; and are currently (1971) being used for a biography by David Marquand MP. The main MS sources are: Herbert Gladstone Papers, Campbell-Bannerman Papers, British Museum; executive minutes, Fabian Society; Keir Hardie correspondence and ILP National Administrative Council minutes, Francis Johnson; a few items in British Library of Political and Economic Science (LSE), which also include the papers of Clifford Allen and George Lansbury, and the minutes of the Labour Representation Committee.

(2) Biographies: M. A. Hamilton, *The Man of Tomorrow* (1923) and *James Ramsay MacDonald, 1923–1925* (1925), reprinted together as *J. Ramsay MacDonald* (1929); H. H. Tiltman, *J. Ramsay MacDonald: Labor's man of destiny* (New York, 1929); L. M. Weir, *The Tragedy of Ramsay MacDonald* (1938); G. Elton, *Life of James Ramsay MacDonald (1866–1919)* (1939); *DNB* (1931–40) [by Lord Elton].

(3) Other: For an assessment of MacDonald that is more favourable than the traditional view see: R. Bassett, *Nineteen Thirty One: Political Crisis* (1958) and A. J. P. Taylor, *English History, 1914–1945* (Oxford, 1965). Other works include: M. A. Hamilton, 'Rt Hon. J. Ramsay MacDonald MP: Labour's First Prime Minister', in *The Book of the Labour Party*, ed. H. Tracey [1925] 118–41; J. Scanlon, *Decline and Fall of the Labour Party* (1932); P. Snowden, *Autobiography*, 2 vols (1934); A. Hutt, *The Post War History of the British Working Class Movement* (1937); J. R. Clynes, *Memoirs*, 2 vols (1937–8); M. A. Hamilton, *Arthur Henderson* (1938); A. F. Brockway, *Inside the Left* (1941); M. A. Hamilton, *Remembering my Good Friends* (1944); G. D. H. Cole, *History of the Labour Party from 1914* (1948);

H. Tracey ed., *The British Labour Party: its history, growth, policy and leaders* (1948) 209–18; Beatrice Webb, *Our Partnership* (1948); Margaret Cole, *Growing up into Revolution* (1949); R. Postgate, *George Lansbury* (1951); Beatrice Webb, *Diaries 1912–1924*, ed. Margaret Cole (1952); idem, *Diaries 1924–1932*, edited and with an Introduction by Margaret Cole (1956); H. Nicolson, *King George the Fifth: his life and reign* (1952); H. Dalton, *Call back Yesterday* (1953) and *The Fateful Years* (1957); H. Pelling, *The Origins of the Labour Party, 1880–1900* (1954, 2nd ed. revised 1965); C. L. Mowat, *Britain between the Wars* (1955); J. H. S. Reid, *Origins of the British Labour Party* (Minneapolis, 1955); R. W. Lyman, *The First Labour Government 1924* (1957); F. Bealey and H. Pelling, *Labour and Politics 1900–1906* (1958); G. D. H. Cole, *Communism and Social Democracy, 1914–1931* (1961); Margaret Cole, *The Story of Fabian Socialism* (1961); R. Miliband, *Parliamentary Socialism* (1961); M. Foot, *Aneurin Bevan 1: 1897–1945* (1962); R. W. Lyman, 'James Ramsay MacDonald and the leadership of the Labour Party, 1918–22', *J. of British Studies 2*, no. 1 (Nov 1962) 132–60; L. Woolf, *Beginning Again* (1964); A. Marwick, *Clifford Allen* (1965); H. Pelling, *A Short History of the Labour Party* (1965); F. Williams, *A Pattern of Rulers* (1965); H. W. Richardson, *Economic Recovery in Britain 1932–1939* (1967); R. J. A. Skidelsky, *Politicians and the Slump: the Labour Government of 1929–31* (1967); *Thomas Jones: Whitehall Diary*, ed. K. Middlemas (Oxford, 1969): D. Carlton, *MacDonald versus Henderson: the foreign policy of the second Labour Government* (1970); C. L. Mowat, 'Ramsay MacDonald and the Labour Party', in *Essays in Labour History 2: 1886–1923*, ed. A. Briggs and J. Saville (1971) 129–51; R. I. McKibbin, 'James Ramsay MacDonald and the Problem of the Independence of the Labour Party, 1910–1914', *J. of Modern History 42* (Sep 1970) 216–35; M. Cowling, *The Impact of Labour 1920–1924: the beginning of modern British politics* (Cambridge, 1971). Among the works of European observers of British politics, see: Jacques Bardoux, *J. Ramsay MacDonald*

(Paris, 1924); idem, *Le Socialisme au pouvoir. L'expérience de 1924. Le dialogue J. Ramsay MacDonald–Edouard Herriot* (Paris, 1930); J. de Gruyter, *MacDonald et le Labour Party* (traduit du néerlandais, Paris, 1929); E. Wertheimer, *Portrait of the Labour Party* (1929, 2nd ed. 1930). OBIT. *Manchester Guardian* and *Times*, 10 Nov 1937.

CHARLES LOCH MOWAT

NOTE: This entry has been amended by the editors following C. L. Mowat's death, and they are much obliged to Mr David Marquand MP for his helpful comments and suggestions.

See also: *C. R. ATTLEE, for British Labour Party, 1931–51; * J. R. CLYNES; *J. Keir HARDIE; Arthur HENDERSON, for British Labour Party, 1914–31; *George LANSBURY; *Philip SNOWDEN; *J. H. THOMAS.

McGHEE, Henry George (1898–1959)
LABOUR MP

Born on 3 July 1898 at Lurgan, County Armagh, Northern Ireland, Henry George McGhee was the son of Richard McGhee and his wife Mary Campbell. His father sat for South Louth from 1896 to 1900 as a Home Ruler and from 1910 until the 1920 Government of Ireland Act represented Mid-Tyrone as a Nationalist. A radical, he had helped to found the National Union of Dock Labourers at Glasgow in 1889 and worked with Henry George to advocate the 'single tax' [Barker (1955)]. Richard McGhee named his son after the American land reformer. H. G. McGhee was educated at Lurgan and Glasgow Technical College and practised as a dentist, first at Omagh, County Tyrone, then in England where he settled in 1922. Most of his life he lived in Sheffield, where he followed his profession. A lifelong Socialist, he joined the Labour Party in 1920 and was also a member of the National Union of General and Municipal Workers for over a quarter of a century.

In 1930 and 1931 he unsuccessfully contested the Crookesmoor Ward of Sheffield and, in the general election of 1931, the Conservative stronghold of Sheffield, Hallam. He became a JP in 1935. At the parliamentary election of 1935 McGhee was returned as Member for the Penistone division of the West Riding of Yorkshire with a majority of just over three thousand. The seat had previously been held by Labour, but had been lost in the 1931 landslide; at subsequent elections McGhee was returned with large majorities and he represented the constituency until his death. He never rose to ministerial office, though he served as Parliamentary Private Secretary to Richard Stokes, a personal friend, when Stokes was Minister of Works in 1950 and Lord Privy Seal in 1951. McGhee was noted as a conscientious and hard-working back-bencher. His main political interests were the advocacy of land reform, and in particular the taxation of land values, pacifism and temperance, and he was also a member of Labour Party groups on health and finance. In 1950 he criticised General MacArthur's forceful methods in Korea and spoke in favour of the establishment of an International Police Force. At a ceremony in 1956 to mark the completion of twenty-one years' service as Member for Penistone, James Griffiths presented him with a cheque for £40 which McGhee asked should be handed over to the Hungarian Relief Fund. In a message from Hugh Gaitskell read at this ceremony, the Labour Party leader declared of McGhee: 'He stands firm by his principles, standing for right first and everything after.'

McGhee died from a heart attack at his home in Millhouses, Sheffield, on 6 February 1959 and was cremated at Sheffield on 10 February when the service was conducted by a friend, J. H. Hudson, a former MP for North Ealing. A Presbyterian, in 1927 he had married Elizabeth Shelmerdine who bore him two sons (one named Henry George) and two daughters. This marriage was dissolved; his first wife and children survived him, as did his second wife, Mrs Marjorie Mary McGhee. In his will he left effects to the value of £13,096. At a by-election in June 1959 the Penistone seat was retained for Labour by J. J. Mendelson.

Sources: C. Bunker, *Who's Who in Parliament* [1946]; *WWW* (1951–60); C. A.

Barker, *Henry George* (New York, 1955); *Dod* (1958); *Labour Party Report* (1959); personal information: Miss C. McGhee of Sheffield, sister. OBIT. *Sheffield Telegraph*, 7 Feb 1959; *Times*, 7 Feb 1959; *Barnsley Chronicle*, 14 Feb 1959.

DAVID E. MARTIN

See also: *C. R. ATTLEE, for British Labour Party, 1931–51; Arthur HENDERSON, for British Labour Party, 1914–31.

MANN, Amos (1855–1939)
CO-OPERATOR

Amos Mann was born in Leicester on 16 January 1855, the son of William Mann, a slater. He attended St Mary's and Laxton Street Church Schools but started work at nine years of age in a match factory, where he earned 1s 6d a week. He extended his education through night schools and his own appetite for reading. Social, political and religious reform appealed to him in early life and he took a keen interest in the campaign preceding the passing of the 1870 Education Bill. He joined the Church of Christ, whose members preach and teach without a minister and, being a gifted speaker, became an acceptable preacher of the Church so that he was among the early converts of the Restoration Movement in Leicester. The Church of Christ, being run by the laity, strengthened his belief in democracy and in his preaching he acquired a fluency and mastery of language as well as an idealism which never left him. With other brethren he assisted in the formation of a Church of Christ at the Humberstone Garden Suburb of Leicester where he was a regular attender. He subsequently became active in the co-operative, temperance, trade union and adult education movements.

His first official connection with the co-operative movement was as one of the founders of the Leicester Anchor Boot and Shoe Co-operative Productive Society, of which he became the second president and held office for more than twenty years. He was outstanding among the pioneers of the Anchor Tenants Ltd, creators of the Humberstone Garden Suburb, being both a

shareholder and a committee member, and he resided there during the latter part of his life.

Amos Mann became a member of the Leicester Co-operative Society general committee in 1898 but retired in 1900. Then in 1908 he was successful in being elected president of the society in competition with two members of the committee. He was re-elected annually to the presidency until his death in 1939. In 1922 he was elected to the central board of the Co-operative Union from which he retired in 1936, serving on the united board, the publications and statistical committee and the committee convening trade and business conferences. He also served on the boycott defence committee of the Co-operative Union.

Mann was one of Britain's leading advocates of producers' co-operation. For over thirty years he was treasurer of the Co-operative Productive Federation, and was one of its representatives on the joint exhibition committee of the Co-operative Union and on the co-operative inquiry committee set up by the Co-operative Congress in Dublin (1914). In 1911 he was elected president of the Labour Co-partnership Association and in his last years he acted as organising secretary of this association. In 1907 when the British Association met in Leicester he read a paper before the economic section on 'Co-operative Production from the Labour Co-partnership Standpoint' which called forth warm praise from A. J. Balfour. Under the auspices of the Labour Co-partnership Association, and later the Co-operative Co-partnership Propaganda Committee, he lectured extensively, visiting most places of any size in the country, and he also contributed many articles to co-operative periodicals. One result of his lecture tours was a very much enjoyed series of travel articles which he contributed to the *Leicester Co-operative Society Magazine*. The Leicester Basket Makers benefited from his special knowledge in the field of co-operative production when he became their president.

He was elected to the Leicester Town Council as a Liberal in 1897 for the West Humberstone Ward and, during his period of office to 1908, he served on the Watch, Parks, Tramways and Distress Committees. He was sympathetic towards the claims of labour and was, in fact, adopted as a Labour candidate for South Leicester Parliamentary constituency but withdrew in deference to the attitude of the co-operative society towards his candidature. He believed that all progressive forces should unite, and he was a strong opponent of class privilege. Other local interests included a life governorship of the Leicester Royal Infirmary, membership of the grand council of the Wycliffe Society for the Blind and treasurer of the Leicester free Christmas dinner fund. He was also a JP. It was said that there was something prophetic in his being christened Amos, for he turned out to resemble that ancient Hebrew utopian reformer and idealist.

He died on 25 December 1939 at the age of eighty-four and the funeral service was held at the Church of Christ, Humberstone, Leicester. His wife, formerly Miss Emma Leavesley, whom he had married in 1876, had predeceased him in 1937. She also had been a member of the Church of Christ and was the daughter of a pioneer of the movement. Mann left effects valued at £621.

Writings: *Democracy in Industry: the story of twenty-one years' work of the Leicester Anchor Boot and Shoe Productive Society Ltd* (Leicester, 1914); articles in *Leicester Co-operative Society Magazine* and other co-operative periodicals.

Sources: *Trade Union Congress Souvenir* (1903); *Leicester Co-op. Congress Souvenir* (1915); *Labour Who's Who* (1927); Co-operative Productive Federation records: Hull University Library ref. DCF; personal information: Leicester City Library, Leicester Co-operative Society and the Town Clerk, Leicester. OBIT. *Leicester Mercury*, 27 Dec 1939; *Christian Advocate*, 19 Jan 1940; *Co-op. Productive Rev.*, Jan 1940; J. J. Worley, 'Passing of a Great Co-operator', *Leicester Co-op. Society Mag.* (1940); *Co-op. Congress Report* (1940).

H. F. BING

See also: W. H. BROWN, for Retail Co-operation, 1900–45; Fred HAYWARD, for Co-operative Union; Benjamin JONES, for Co-operative Production; H. H. VIVIAN.

MARCROFT, William (1822–94)
CO-OPERATOR

Born 15 July 1822 at Heywood, Lancashire, William Marcroft was the illegitimate son of Sally Marcroft, farm servant, and Richard Howard, weaver. He began work at the age of eight as a piecer in a cotton mill, and was later apprenticed to a fustian cutter. He married Jane Smith in 1844 and moved to Oldham in the same year, finding employment as a grinder in the textile machinery firm of Hibberts and Platts. He was later promoted to foreman, but in 1861, having been entirely self-educated, he became a dentist.

Marcroft was a teetotaller, a member of the Rechabites and Oddfellows, and in politics an active supporter of W. J. Fox, the radical MP for Oldham (1847–63); but his central interest was in co-operation, especially co-operative production. He helped to promote the Oldham Industrial Co-operative Society in 1850; and in 1858 the Oldham Building and Manufacturing Co. Ltd, which later became the Sun Mill Co. Ltd. He was a director of the Sun Mill Co. 1859–61, 1862–4, 1865–71, 1875–7; and treasurer 1861–2. He was a consistent advocate of the principles of co-operative production against the majority of the board.

Other societies that he helped to promote included the Co-operative Insurance Society (1867); the Oldham House and Mill Co. Ltd (1867); the Star Corn Mill (1868); the Central Mill Co. Ltd (1871); Federative Insurance Co. Ltd (1875); Oldham Limited Liability Association (1875); Cotton Buying Co. Ltd (1881).

Marcroft was a vigorous advocate of a co-operative wholesale society, and he was present at the Rochdale Conference of November 1860, being appointed a member of the committee to inquire into appropriate legislation for co-operative wholesaling. When the CWS was established, the rules being submitted to the Registrar in August 1863, Marcroft was elected to the first directorate, although he soon resigned because his own Oldham society refused to join. He later, 1867-71, rejoined the board.

He was a frequent contributor to the columns of the *Co-operative News*, *Oldham Chronicle* and *Oldham Standard*. He spoke extensively on behalf of the movement and travelled widely in the USA, France and Belgium. He died on 8 September 1894, leaving four sons and one daughter and estate valued at £14,753.

Writings: *Sun Mill Company Limited: its commercial and social history from 1858 to 1877* (Oldham, 1877); *The Companies Circular* (Oldham, 1879); *Our Hives of Industry – The Central Mill, Oldham* (Oldham, 1882); *The Inner Circle of Family Life* (Manchester, 1886); *The Marcroft Family: a history of strange events* (Manchester, 1886) 44 pp.; *A Co-operative Village: how to conduct it and where to form it* (Manchester, [1888]) 20 pp.; *Ups and Downs: life in a machine-making works* (Manchester, 1889).

Sources: *Oldham Industrial Co-op. Society Record*, July 1894; B. Jones, *Co-operative Production* (Oxford, 1894); J. T. Taylor, *The Jubilee History of the Oldham Industrial Co-operative Society Limited, 1850-1900* (Manchester, 1900); P. Redfern, *The Story of the C.W.S.* (Manchester, [1913]); R. E. Tyson, 'The Sun Mill Company Limited: a study in democratic investment, 1858-1959' (Manchester MA, 1962). OBIT. *Oldham Chronicle*, 10 Sep 1894; *Oldham Standard*, 10 Sep 1894; *Co-op. News*, 15 Sep 1894.

JOHN SAVILLE
R. E. TYSON

See also: Benjamin JONES, for Co-operative Production; G. J. HOLYOAKE, for Retail Co-operation – Nineteenth Century; Percy REDFERN, for Co-operative Wholesaling.

MARLOW, Arnold (1891-1939)
CO-OPERATOR

Arnold Marlow was born on 12 March 1891 at Desborough, Northamptonshire, the son of Harry Marlow, an employee of the Crompton Boot Manufacturers, Desborough,

a co-operative co-partnership factory. The father was a staunch Wesleyan Methodist and lay preacher. Arnold started work as a half-timer at the boot factory at the age of twelve while continuing his education at the local council school for a further year, after which he was employed full-time at the factory. He worked systematically at his own self-education.

In 1904 he joined the office staff of the Desborough Co-operative Society and later began to study in his spare time for the Methodist ministry. The First World War prevented him from pursuing this career but his interest in Methodism continued throughout his life: he was a lay preacher for twenty-eight years and held most of the offices open to laymen in his own district. The opportunities for his career in the co-operative movement increased. In 1915 he was appointed educational secretary of the Desborough Society and promoted to cashier of the Society in 1916. In 1923 he was appointed general secretary of the Kettering Industrial Co-operative Society in succession to Percy Loake but resigned from this position in 1933 on being elected to the board of the Co-operative Wholesale Society when Sir Thomas Allen retired. As a CWS director and chairman of one of the board's committees he gave evidence before the committee of inquiry into the constitution and method of election of the CWS board (1936-7). He was re-elected in 1938 but died in the following year. Marlow held a number of Co-operative Union certificates and taught co-operative employees in his own county and Leicester. Until his election to the CWS board, he was an active member of the Co-operative Secretaries' Association.

In addition to his co-operative interests and his work for the Methodists, he was also a founder member of the Kettering Rotary Club. Politically he inclined to Liberalism but he was never active in the movement. He married Miss Gertrude Alice Mobbs of Pytchley, near Kettering, on Christmas Day 1913 and they had two sons and a daughter. He died on 3 January 1939 at the early age of forty-seven, the funeral service being held at Desborough Methodist Chapel on 6 January. His wife and family survived him. He left an estate valued at £2828.

Sources: S. York, compiler, *Achievement: the diamond jubilee history of the Kettering Industrial Co-operative Society* (Kettering, 1926); P. Redfern, *The New History of the C.W.S.* (Manchester, 1938); personal information: Mrs A. Marlow, widow, Mrs J. Sims, daughter, both of Kettering, and A. N. Marlow, Manchester, son. OBIT. *Kettering Leader and Guardian*, 6 Jan 1939; *Co-op. News*, 7 Jan 1939.

JOYCE BELLAMY
H. F. BING

See also: W. H. BROWN, for Retail Co-operation, 1900–45; Percy REDFERN, for Co-operative Wholesaling.

MARTIN, James (1850–1933)
MINERS' LEADER

Born at Basford, Nottingham, on 6 May 1850, he went to Staveley, Derbyshire, with his parents at the age of nine and started work in the pit as a door-trapper at the Speedwell Colliery, later becoming a driver. Martin received his only formal education at a night school which he attended regularly and became an enthusiastic reader. He took a leading part in trade union activities from the time William Brown tried to organise the Derbyshire miners in 1866–7 and in 1874 was elected delegate for the Staveley lodge to the council of the South Yorkshire Miners' Association which at that time organised the Derbyshire miners. From 1876 he was secretary of his lodge and after the formation of the Derbyshire Miners' Association in 1880 continued to be active in the new organisation. He had been appointed a sub-checkweighman at Fairwell Colliery in 1876 and went to Ireland Colliery as a checkweighman in 1882, becoming secretary of the Ireland lodge. His work for the miners was recognised by his election as president of the Association in 1906 in succession to Barnet Kenyon, a position he held until he resigned on health grounds in 1917.

In politics Martin began as a Liberal, was president of the North-East Derbyshire Liberal Association and Liberal sub-agent for Staveley from 1869 to 1914 when, with the MFGB having a few years earlier affiliated with the Labour Party, Martin was nominated as a Labour candidate for North-East Derbyshire. This prevented his collaboration with the Liberals and precluded him from their support even though he maintained a personal affiliation to the Party: an official Liberal candidate contested the seat which split the vote and enabled the Unionist candidate to be elected.

Like many miners' leaders of his day, Martin was an ardent Primitive Methodist and local preacher. For about forty years he was superintendent of Staveley Zion Primitive Methodist Church Sunday School, was also Band of Hope Superintendent and vice-president of the Free Church Council. He first attended the Sunday school in 1864 and two years later was appointed a local preacher. He was also active in local government affairs: in 1894 was elected vice-chairman of the Staveley Parish Council and for seventeen years prior to 1913 presided over the Council. He represented the Council on the local Church School, was a governor of Netherthorpe Grammar School and a member of the local technical education committee. He served on other committees of the Council, was treasurer to the Staveley Co-operative Society for forty years and also to the colliery sick club of 950 members. He was a JP for the county from 1909.

Martin died at a Sheffield nursing home on 1 November 1933 and was survived by two sons and a daughter.

Sources: (1) MSS: Minutes of the Derbyshire Miners' Association, 1906–17 (NUM, Saltergate, Chesterfield); (2) *Derbyshire Times*, 1906–17; J. E. Williams, 'The Political Activities of a Trade Union, 1906–14', *Int. Rev. Social Hist.* 2 (1957) 1–21; idem, *The Derbyshire Miners* (1962). OBIT. *Derbyshire Times*, 4 Nov 1933.

J. E. WILLIAMS

See also: Thomas ASHTON, for Mining Trade Unionism, 1900–14; Alexander MACDONALD, for Mining Trade Unionism,

1850–79; Benjamin PICKARD, for Mining Trade Unionism, 1880–99.

MAXWELL, Sir William (1841–1929)
CO-OPERATOR

Born on 30 November 1841 in Glasgow, the son of a coachmaker who was a local Chartist leader, Maxwell's parents moved to Paisley in his early youth and it was here that he received his first education. He returned to Glasgow when he was ten and at the age of twelve was apprenticed to a coachbuilder. During his spare time he attended evening classes at the Glasgow School of Design and after completing his apprenticeship he travelled throughout Britain. This was in the early 1860s. He returned to Scotland, resuming his work in Glasgow, where he became treasurer of his local trade union branch. His connection with the co-operative movement commenced when he moved to Edinburgh in the early 1870s. In 1874 he joined the St Cuthbert's Co-operative Society there and four years later became its secretary, a position he held until 1882. He devoted much of his time to propaganda work in the east of Scotland. In 1880 he was elected to the board of the Scottish CWS and from 1908 served this organisation as president. His interests lay especially in producers' co-operation and, following a visit to America in 1884, he planned the Shield-hall Co-operative Productive Works which brought together on one site a number of factories manufacturing goods for the Scottish Co-operative Wholesale Society. He was in addition a vigorous promoter of new retail societies, and was also among the founders of the Scottish Women's Co-operative Guild. On two occasions, in 1897 and 1905, he was president of the Co-operative Congress and in 1883 and 1890 presided over part of the Congresses in those years.

He was also active in the international co-operative sphere. He succeeded Henry Wolff as president of the ICA in 1907, having been a member of the executive committee of the Alliance since 1902, and held office until 1921 when illness compelled him to resign from the presidency. He was a man of great dignity and calmness whose influence on the ICA was considerable, and the author of several pamphlets and articles on co-operation, national and international: his most important literary work was his *History of Co-operation in Scotland*, published in 1910. He was in general much influenced by the work of Lloyd Jones and Alexander Campbell and was a personal friend of J. T. W. Mitchell.

Maxwell was active on the political side of the co-operative movement and strongly advocated parliamentary representation for co-operators. He contested as a Liberal candidate the Tradeston Division of Glasgow at the 1900 general election but was defeated. His local work was recognised first by his appointment as a JP and later by a knighthood which was conferred on him in 1919. He gave evidence to the Royal Commission on Labour in 1892 and before the Joint Select Committee on Municipal Trading in 1900.

He lived at Rothesay during his retirement and it was at his home there that he died on 9 February 1929. He was thrice married, first in 1884 to Ann Forrest of Glasgow who died in 1892, secondly in 1894 to Agnes Sutherland who died in 1924 and finally to Mary Emily Bowers, daughter of Capt. Bowers and sister of Lieut Bowers of the Scott Antarctic Expedition, who survived him. He left an estate valued at £1005.

Writings: *Wholesale Co-operation a Necessity* (Manchester, 1888) 28 pp.; *The Relation of Employees to the Co-operative Movement* (Manchester, 1893) 14 pp.; 'The Late John Thomas Whitehead Mitchell, JP', *CWS Annual* (1896) 392–414; *The I.C.A. – its claims* (Glasgow, 1909) 16 pp.; *First Fifty Years of St Cuthbert's Co-operative Association Ltd*, edited by W. Maxwell (Edinburgh, 1909); *The History of Co-operation in Scotland* (Glasgow, 1910); 'The Late John Shillito, JP, FRGS', *CWS Annual* (1916) 427–460; Evidence before the R.C. on Labour, 1893-4 XXXIX pt I, Qs 406–940.

Sources: *Co-op. Congress Report* (1893);

Handbooks to Co-operative Congresses for 1897 and 1905; D. Robertson, 'William Maxwell, JP', *Millgate Monthly*, Mar 1908, 329–35; J. Flanagan, *Wholesale Co-operation in Scotland* (Glasgow, 1920); J. Lucas, *Co-operation in Scotland* (Manchester, 1920); S. R. Elliott, *Sir William Maxwell: A pioneer of national and international co-operation* (Manchester, 1923). OBIT. *Glasgow Herald*, 11 Feb 1929; *Times*, 11 Feb 1929; *Co-op. News*, 16 Feb 1929; *RIC*, Mar 1929.

MAI ALMAN
JOYCE BELLAMY

See also: *J. A. FLANAGAN; Benjamin JONES, for Co-operative Production; H. J. MAY, for International Co-operative Alliance; and below: Scottish Co-operation.

Scottish Co-operation: J. Campsie, *Glimpses of Co-operative Land, including an Account of the Largest Bakery in the World* (Glasgow, 1899); W. Maxwell ed., *History of St Cuthbert's Co-operative Association Ltd: 1859–1909* (Edinburgh, 1909); W. Maxwell, *The History of Co-operation in Scotland: its inception and its leaders* (Glasgow, 1910); A. Buchan, *History of the Scottish Co-operative Women's Guild, 1892–1913* (Glasgow, 1913); J. Lucas, *Co-operation in Scotland* (Manchester, 1920); J. A. Flanagan, *Wholesale Co-operation in Scotland: the fruits of fifty years' efforts (1868–1918)* (Glasgow, 1920); Committee on Agricultural Co-operation in Scotland, *Report*, Cmd 3567 (1930); N. S. Beaton, 'Co-operation in Scotland', in *London-Scottish Self-Government Commission: the new Scotland (1942)* 74–81; E. Orr, *Co-operation in the Highlands and Islands* (Glasgow, 1946) 20 pp.; K. M. Callen, *History of the Scottish Co-operative Women's Guild, 1892–1952* (Glasgow, [1952?]); A. Himeimy, 'The Development and Organisation of the Scottish Co-operative Movement' (Edinburgh PhD, 1955).

For the histories of individual retail societies, most of which are not listed above, see: *An Interim Bibliography of the Scottish Working Class*, ed. I. McDougall (Edinburgh, 1965) 43–50, and *Studies in Scottish Business History*, ed. P. L. Payne (1967) 96–8.

MAY, Henry John (1867–1939)
CO-OPERATOR

Born at Woolwich, London, on 16 July 1867, the son of an engineer. He was educated at an elementary school, and his first job was as a junior with the Royal Arsenal Co-operative Society from 1880 to 1885. At the age of seventeen he left to become an engineering apprentice at the Royal Arsenal. He joined the Amalgamated Engineering Union after serving his time and retained membership till his death. But it was co-operation with which he was always most concerned, his parents having been long associated with the Royal Arsenal Co-operative Society. At this time he came under the influence of Thomas Blandford, an enthusiastic pioneer of Co-operative production, who saw in his young protégé intimations of a great career ahead. Before long May was a member of the Royal Arsenal Society's board of management, editor of the Society's magazine *Comradeship* and a leading platform exponent of the cause, determined that the South should no longer remain 'a co-operative desert'.

In 1898 May was elected to the central board of the Co-operative Union and from 1905 to 1913 was secretary of the southern sectional board of the Co-operative Union. He believed that the co-operative movement should participate directly in politics. In 1909 he was elected secretary of the joint parliamentary committee of the Co-operative Congress, an office he held until 1919. In 1917 the Co-operative Parliamentary Representation Committee was formed, signalising the entry of the movement into politics. May became the Committee's first secretary, and its first candidate, by contesting a by-election at Prestwich in the same year. He was defeated by a strong Coalition candidate; and in the Khaki election of 1918 he contested Clackmannan and East Stirlingshire in the Co-operative Party interest but was again defeated.

On the eve of the Glasgow Congress of the International Co-operative Alliance in 1913, Dr Hans Müller, Secretary of the ICA, was suddenly taken ill. May, at short notice, assumed direction of affairs and it was not unexpected that shortly afterwards he was elected secretary of the ICA, an office which he held till his death in 1939. He had hardly entered upon his new duties, which included the editing of the ICA *Bulletin*, when he was faced with the catastrophe of the First World War but he maintained contact with co-operators in enemy countries through neutral countries. With the ending of hostilities he quickly restored the international character of the movement and organised a full international congress at Basle in 1921. For the rest of his life the development of the ICA was his main work. During the twelve years of comparative peace (1921–33) he built up the International into an efficient and influential organ of the world-wide co-operative movement. The renewal of international tension and the hostility of fascist and national-socialist governments to the co-operative movement in the period 1933–9 found him ready for the challenge. Contacts with Germany, Austria, Spain, Czechoslovakia, Poland, became increasingly difficult but May showed great resource in maintaining what links were possible and in organising relief for many of his former colleagues who were now refugees.

In the meantime the British co-operative movement had shown its appreciation of him by conferring upon him the presidency of Congress at Torquay in 1929. He was also a keen supporter of movements working for peace and international understanding: he was a member of the National Peace Council, of the executive committee of Viscount Cecil's International Peace Campaign and an observer at the World Disarmament Conference at Geneva in 1932.

May's work for the international co-operative movement cannot be over-estimated. He was, as a colleague wrote just after his death, 'a veritable missionary of Co-operation and a practitioner of it as well'. He could be tactful in approaching opponents but almost brutally frank in talking to his fellow co-operators: always insisting on the observance of principle at the expense of temporary success. He represented the ICA at the World Economic Congress at Geneva in 1932, intervened with the Austrian Chancellor in 1934 on behalf of the

Austrian co-operative movement and organised relief for Spanish co-operators in 1938.

In his own country he served the co-operative movement in many ways. He was interested in co-operative co-partnership and was a member of the board of the Co-operative Printing Society. During the First World War he led a number of deputations to the Cabinet, and forced them to recognise co-operative rights and privileges and in particular what was widely regarded as unfair taxation of the movement. He served for a time on the War Emergency Workers' National Committee. From 1919 to 1920 he was a member of the Royal Commission on Income Tax, and from 1921 he was a member of the National Wages Board (Railways) and later a member of the Railways Staff National Tribunal. The award of the OBE and his appointment as a JP were public recognition of his services.

He died on Sunday 19 November 1939 following an operation in hospital on 16 November. The funeral took place at the South London Crematorium at Streatham on Friday 24 November. He was survived by his wife and left an estate valued at £7873. The December 1939 and July 1940 issues of *The Review of International Co-operation* (official organ of the ICA) contained tributes to the life and work of H. J. May from thirty leaders of national co-operative movements in Europe, Asia and America; as well as tributes from Viscount Cecil of Chelwood (President, International Peace Campaign) and Sir Arthur Salter (Chairman, Railway Staff National Tribunal), who also contributed his obituary notice in the *Times*.

Writings: *Scope and Methods of District Work* (1910) 12 pp.; *The Relation of Co-operation to other Working Class Movements* (1912) 16 pp.; *The International Co-operative Alliance and the War* (1915) 24 pp.; *Co-operative Societies and Income Tax* (1916) 24 pp.; *Co-operators and the National Insurance Act* (n.d.) 20 pp. H. J. May, as general secretary of the ICA, was also editor from 1913 to 1939 of the *International Co-operative Bulletin* (*ICB*) which became the *Review of International Co-operation* (*RIC*) in April 1928. This was the journal of the International

Co-operative Alliance and, from the beginning of 1914 until November 1939, May wrote in it almost every month. His articles relating directly to the work of the ICA are cited in the separate ICA bibliography below but the following articles are a selection of May's writings which appeared in the *Bulletin* or the *Review*: 'Democracy and the International Peace', Feb-Mar 1914, 29–33; 'Co-operation and Taxation in Great Britain', Mar 1916, 45–9; 'The Russian Situation', Feb 1920, 37–8; 'The World Peace Congress at The Hague', Jan 1923, 1–5; 'The Recent Dispute at the Works of the English C.W.S.', Oct 1923, 241–5; 'The All-Russian Co-operative Congress at Moscow and 25th Anniversary of Centrosoyus, Moscow', Dec 1923, 276; 'Co-operation versus Fascism', Apr 1926, 97–102; 'International Wheat Pool Conference at Regina, Canada', July 1928, 233–9; 'Sir William Maxwell 1841–1929', Mar 1929, 81–4; 'The Canadian Wheat Pools and the Present Crisis', Feb 1931, 48–9; 'Charles Gide 1847–1932', Apr 1932, 121–4; 'Albert Thomas 1878–1932', June 1932, 217–19; 'Antonio Vergnanini 1861–1934', June 1934, 187–91; 'Michael Avramovitch – A Yugoslav Pioneer', Feb 1935, 46–7; 'James Deans of Scotland 1845–1935', May 1935, 161–2; 'Victor Serwy – An Appreciation', Aug 1935, 281–3; 'A. Honora Enfield', Sep 1935, 324–5; 'Is the Co-operative Movement extinct in the U.S.S.R.?', Mar 1936, 81–6; 'The Spanish situation: the results of the ICA Appeal', Dec 1936, 443–5; 'Sir Robert Stewart', June 1937, 204; 'Why I support the International Peace Campaign', Oct 1937, 393–4; 'James A. Flanagan', Jan 1938, 6–8; 'In Memoriam – Elemer de Bologh 1871–1938 and Mr Fred Hall 1879–1938', Sep 1938, 426–30; 'Robert Fleming', Oct 1939, 469–70.

Sources: *Co-op. Congress Report* (1929); T. W. Mercer, *Towards the Co-operative Commonwealth* (Manchester, 1936); Royden Harrison, 'The War Emergency Workers' National Committee', in *Essays in Labour History*, vol. 2: *1886–1923*, ed. A. Briggs and J. Saville (1971) 211–59; personal information: Miss G. F. Polley, general secretary of

ICA (retired 1964). OBIT. *Times*, 23 Nov 1939; *Co-op. News*, 25 Nov and 2 Dec 1939; *Co-op. Rev.*, Dec 1939; *RIC* Dec 1939; *Co-op. Congress Report* (1940); *RIC*, July 1940.

H. F. BING

See also: A. V. ALEXANDER, for Co-operative Party; Fred HAYWARD, for Co-operative Union; and below: International Co-operative Alliance.

International Co-operative Alliance: E. O. Greening and E. V. Neale, *Proposals for an International Alliance of the Friends of Co-operative Production* (1892) 12 pp.; E. O. Greening, *International Co-operation and the Constitution of the International Co-operative Alliance* (1895) 12 pp.; H. W. Wolff, 'The Co-operative Alliance at work', *Econ. Rev. 5* (1896) 503–9; J. Halford, *The International Co-operative Alliance: its aims and work* (1904) 20 pp.; W. Maxwell, *The ICA: its claims* (Glasgow, 1909) 16 pp.; H. Müller, *The International Co-operative Alliance and its Importance to the Co-operative Movement* (1909) 12 pp.; D. McInness, *The International Co-operative Alliance* (1912) 16 pp.; H. J. May, 'The ICA and the War. Conference in London', *ICB* (May 1915) 77–84; 'The ICA and the War, the War of Ideas', *ICB* (Sep 1915) 169–73; C. Gide, *The International Co-operative Alliance* [1917?] 12 pp.; H. J. May, 'The 10th International Congress at Basle: Summary of Proceedings', *ICB* (Sep 1921) 217–47; idem, 'The New President of the ICA: G. J. D. C. Goedhart', *ICB* (Oct 1921) 249–51; idem, 'The International Co-operative Delegation to Russia', *ICB* (May–June 1922) 97–107; *Fabian Essays on Co-operation*, edited by L. S. Woolf (1923); H. J. May, 'The International Co-operative Congress at Ghent', *ICB* (Sep 1924) 257–64 and (Oct 1924) 291–301; idem, 'International Co-operation in 1925', *ICB* (Jan 1926) 2–5; idem, 'The ICA – Its History, Aims, Constitution and Government', *ICB* (Dec 1926) 353–62; idem, 'The ICA in 1926', *ICB* (Feb 1927) 33–6; idem, 'The ICA Congress at Stockholm', *ICB* (Sep 1927) 257–82; idem, 'Soviet Co-operation and the ICA', *ICB* (Dec 1927) 369–72; idem, 'The ICA in 1927', *ICB*

(Feb 1928) 41–5; idem, 'The ICA in 1928', *RIC* (Feb 1929) 57–60; idem, 'The ICA in 1929', *RIC* (Feb 1930) 41–6; idem, 'Thirteenth Congress of the ICA at Vienna', *RIC* (Sep 1930) 333–45; idem, 'The ICA in 1930', *RIC* (Feb 1931) 41–7; idem, 'The ICA and the Gold Standard', *RIC* (Jan 1932) 2–3; idem, 'The ICA in 1931', *RIC* (Apr 1932) 125–33; idem, 'The Progress of the ICA', *RIC* (Nov 1932) 417–21; idem, 'International Co-operation in Light of the World Economic Crisis', *People's Year Book* (1932) 182–92; idem, 'ICA Special Conference at Basle' *RIC* (June 1933) 201–6; idem, 'The Basle Conference and after', *RIC* (July 1933) 241–9 and (Aug 1933) 281–4; idem, 'Whither the ICA?', *RIC* (Sep 1933) 321–3; idem, 'The I.C. Review confiscated', *RIC* (Nov 1933) 402–3; idem, 'The Tasks of the ICA', *RIC* (Aug 1934) 257–61; idem, 'Fourteenth Congress of the ICA in London', *RIC* (Oct 1934) 329–44; idem, 'The Orientation of the International Co-operative Movement', *RIC* (July 1935) 244–51; idem, 'The 40th Year of the ICA', *RIC* (Sep 1935) 321–3; T. W. Mercer, *Towards the Co-operative Commonwealth: why poverty in the midst of plenty?* (Manchester, 1936); H. J. May, '15th Congress of the ICA in Paris', *RIC* (Sep 1937) 341–61; idem, 'What should be the Role of the ICA in the Present World Situation?', *RIC* (Mar 1938) 105–10; idem, 'The International Co-operative Alliance in Retrospect and Prospect', *RIC* (Sep 1938) 435–45; idem, 'Czechoslovakia and the ICA', *RIC* (Nov 1938) 521–3; idem, 'Does the ICA still stand for Freedom?', *RIC* (Mar 1939) 105–7; idem, 'The Present Position of the ICA', *RIC* (Sep 1939) 423–32; idem, 'The War-time Tasks of the ICA', *RIC* (Nov 1939) 513–21; R. A. Palmer, *Progress and Future of the International Co-operative Alliance* (Manchester, [1942]) 47 pp.; D. Flanagan, 'Britain's Role in International Co-operation' in *The Co-operative Movement in Labour Britain*, ed. N. Barou (1948) 110–23; M. Digby, *The World Co-operative Movement* (1948) rev. ed. (1960); A. Bonner, *British Co-operation* (1961) 421–60; ICA Commission, *Report of the ICA Commission on Co-operative Principles* (1967) 40 pp.

MERCER, Thomas William (1884–1947)

CO-OPERATIVE AUTHOR AND JOURNALIST

Born on 20 July 1884 at Old School, Nutfield, near Redhill, Surrey, the son of Thomas William Mercer, a farm labourer. He began work in the local grocer's shop at the age of twelve and in 1899 was apprenticed to a Quaker firm of grocers in Croydon. During his stay in Croydon he extended his reading by using the facilities provided by the public library and when he entered co-operative service in his early twenties he was comparatively well read. His first co-operative position was as a grocer with the Reigate Industrial Society where he became branch manager, but after a few years left to take charge of the Epsom Society. Before the end of the First World War he had transferred to Plymouth where he became secretary to the education department, which developed into one of the most comprehensive in the country. At Plymouth he became political agent to W. T. Gay, who contested the Sutton Division of Plymouth as a Labour candidate at the 1918 general election, and at a by-election in the following year.

Mercer then moved to the north of England to become one of the first members of staff at the Co-operative College under Professor Hall. In November 1922 he contested the Moss Side Division of Manchester at the general election but was not elected. In the same year he was made editor of the *Co-operative Review* and for the remainder of his life he worked in journalism. In 1927 he was appointed as the southern representative of the *Co-operative News*; for a time he joined the staff of *Reynolds News* but returned to the *Co-operative News* in 1937 and after the outbreak of the Second World War was transferred to the Manchester staff of that paper. He was a lively and prolific writer and up to his retirement in 1945 his 'Random Thoughts' and other writings in his own name and under the pseudonyms of Lawrence Graham and John Sheridan gave much pleasure to readers of the *News*. At various times he edited the *Co-operative Official*, *Millgate* and *Guildsman* and wrote numerous pamphlets and several larger works, his best-known book being *Towards a Co-operative Commonwealth* (1936).

He took part in a number of other co-operative activities, notably as a prominent member of the Shop Assistants' Union and the Amalgamated Union of Co-operative Employees, both forerunners to NUDAW (later USDAW). He served on the central committee of the National Co-operative Men's Guild and was its representative on the national committee of the Co-operative Party. He was also a member of the central committee of the WEA for about ten years. He edited a book about Dr William King of Brighton, published in 1922, but then undertook further research and after his retirement produced a second volume on Dr King. This was published in the year of his death. Mercer had been ill for a considerable time and died in hospital on 3 March 1947. He left an estate valued at £2564.

Writings: (with J. Hallsworth) *The Need for Trade Unionism in the Co-operative Movement* (Manchester, 1909) 8 pp.; (with E. F. Hobley) *The Adult School Movement: what it is and what it may become* [1911]; *Co-operative Movement and a Minimum Wage for its Employees* (Manchester, 1913) 10 pp.; *The Co-operative Movement in Politics: a statement of the case for and against the proposed Labour and Co-operative Political Alliance* (Manchester, 1920) 15 pp.; *The Proposed National Co-operative Society* (Manchester, 1920) 16 pp.; *The Income Tax Menace* (Manchester, 1920) 8 pp.; *The Co-operative Survey Committee and its work* (Manchester, 1920) 12 pp.; 'Co-operative Politics and Co-operative Progress', *People's Year Book* (1921) 77–87; *The Relation of Co-operative Education and Co-operative Politics* (Manchester, 1921) 14 pp.; *Co-operative Policy in relation to the Organisation of Retail Trade*, rev. and ed. T. W. Mercer (1921); *William Thompson: an early co-operative economist* (1922) 24 pp.; *The Principles and Purpose of Co-operative Trade* (Manchester, 1922) 12 pp.; *International Co-operative Trading* (Manchester, 1922) 12 pp.; *Dr William King and 'The Co-operator' 1828–1830*, with an Introduction and Notes by T. W. Mercer (Manchester,

1922); *Aphorisms and Reflections of Dr William King*, selected and arranged by T. W. Mercer (Manchester, 1922) 11 pp.; *John Stuart Mill and Co-operation: his place in co-operative history*, repr. from *Co-operative News* (Manchester, 1923) 8 pp.; *The Co-operative Union: its organisation and work* (Manchester, 1923) 20 pp.; *Co-operative Representatives in Parliament* (Manchester, 1924) 37 pp.; *District Work and its Development* (Manchester, 1925) 16 pp.; *The Men's Guild and the Co-operative Movement: guildmen and their value as a body of volunteers* (Manchester, 1926) 8 pp.; *Co-operative Literature: how to push sales* (Manchester, 1926) 16 pp.; *The Co-operative Press and its Development* (Manchester, 1927) 18 pp.; *Co-operative Policy in relation to Municipal Trading*, repr. from *Leicester Co-operative Mag.* (Manchester, 1927) 20 pp.; *Interim Dividends: notes on co-operation* (Leicester, 1928) 22 pp.; *Servants of Democracy: reflections on co-operative employment and co-operative employees* (Manchester, 1929) 24 pp.; *Richard Carlile on Co-operation: a century-old criticism*, repr. from *Co-op. Rev.* (1929) 11 pp.; *Steps toward Standardisation in Co-operative Retail Selling* (Manchester, 1929) 16 pp.; *First Essentials of Co-operative Industry* (1930) 22 pp.; *Sixty Years of Co-operative Printing: 1869–1929* (1930); *Our Road to Manhood* (Manchester, 1932); *Economic Foundations of Consumers' Co-operation* (Manchester, [1934]) 8 pp.; *Towards the Co-operative Commonwealth. Why poverty in the midst of plenty?* [A history of the co-operative movement] (Manchester, 1936); *Co-operation's Prophet. The Life and Letters of Dr William King of Brighton with a reprint of 'The Co-operator', 1828–1830* (Manchester, 1947).

Sources: A. Bonner, *British Co-operation* (Manchester, 1961). OBIT. *Co-op. News*, 8 Mar 1947; *Co-op. Rev.*, Mar 1947.

JOYCE BELLAMY

See also: W. H. BROWN, for Retail Co-operation, 1900–45; Fred HALL, for Co-operative Education.

MILLERCHIP, William (1863–1939)
TRADE UNIONIST AND CO-OPERATOR

Born on 29 January 1863 at Dale Street, Palfrey, Walsall, the son of Thomas Millership, a journeyman locksmith. When the spelling of his name was altered to Millerchip is not known; although registered at birth as Millership, the form used by his father, William's obituary notices and his death certificate gave Millerchip. He followed his father into the lock trade as a half-timer at the age of ten, and on leaving Wesley School, Ablewell Street, Walsall, followed this occupation full-time. He was employed by the Walsall Locks and Cart Gear Company Limited, a successful enterprise run on co-partnership lines. During this early period of his life he continued his education at night school and later became a Methodist Sunday school teacher at the Dale Street and Corporation Street Schools. He played a leading part in the debating society run by these schools and his interest in social and municipal questions may have stemmed from this.

Millerchip became chairman of the directors of Walsall Locks and Cart Gear at the age of twenty-four. He resigned this position in 1902, on becoming the general secretary of the Lock and Keysmiths' Union, because the co-partnership constitution of the company made employment an essential qualification for holding a directorship. He retained an interest in the company as a shareholder until the end of his life.

Millerchip was also closely associated with the Walsall and District Co-operative Society Limited. He was present at the original meeting in the YMCA lecture room on 10 August 1885 and from 1896 to 1910 he was president of the Society. He was a member of the central board of the Co-operative Union from 1913 until Whitsuntide 1938, when he retired on grounds of ill-health. He was also a member of the Midland sectional board. During his lifetime the value of the annual trade of Walsall Co-op. rose from £500 to £1 million.

Millerchip's leadership of the Lock and Keysmiths' Union led naturally to a close involvement with the Midland Counties Trades Federation, established in 1886 by Richard Juggins. He was president of the Federation from 1898 to 1901, and again from 1902 to 1904. He represented the Federation at many congresses and conferences both in this country and abroad.

In 1898 he became one of the first Labour members of Walsall Town Council, being elected for Pleck ward in November. He was mayor in 1908–9 and a magistrate from 1906. During this period on the Council he was an energetic advocate of municipal tramways, and a prominent member of the Education Committee, and on resigning from the Town Council in 1910 he became a co-opted member of the Higher Education sub-committee.

His resignation from the Council was occasioned by his appointment as the first manager of Walsall Labour Exchange, a position he held until January 1927 when he reached superannuation age. During his time as manager the number of clerks employed at the Labour Exchange increased from one to sixty, and it became well known locally as a model of its kind. On his resignation as manager, Millerchip was awarded the MBE for his services, the first Walsall citizen to be so honoured.

After being surprisingly defeated for the Bloxwich ward in 1928, Millerchip returned to the Town Council in 1931 when he was elected in Palfrey ward. In April 1937 he became an alderman. In addition to his varied career in public life he was also a founder member of Walsall Rotary Club.

He married in 1889 and was survived by his wife, three sons, one daughter, eight grandchildren and one great-grandchild. He died at his home, Beatrice Street, Leamore, Walsall, on 9 January 1939 and was buried in Bloxwich Cemetery. He left effects valued at £909.

Sources: Reports of activities of Lock and Keysmiths' Union and Midland Counties Trades Federation in *Walsall Observer* and *Wolverhampton Chronicle* (1898–1910); *Walsall Red Book* (1909) [photograph in Mayor's robes]; F. Hall, *From Acorn to Oak, being the History of the Walsall and District Co-operative Society Limited 1886–1936* (Birmingham, 1936). OBIT. *Co-op. News*, 14 Jan 1939; *Walsall Observer*, 14 Jan 1939; *Co-op. Congress Report* (1939).

ERIC TAYLOR

See also: W. H. BROWN, for Retail Co-operation, 1900–45; E. O. GREENING, for Co-partnership; G. J. HOLYOAKE, for Retail Co-operation – Nineteenth Century; Richard JUGGINS.

MITCHELL, John Thomas Whitehead (1828–95)
CO-OPERATOR

The illegitimate son of a working woman, Mitchell was born at Rochdale on 18 October 1828. He rarely spoke of his early life except to indicate that it was hard both for his mother and himself. He acquired some education at the Red Cross Street National School and this was extended by attendance at a Sunday school. His first job was as a piecer in a Rochdale cotton mill where he worked from 6 am to 7 pm for 1s 6d per week. At seventeen, encouraged by his mother, he joined a young men's class at the Providence Independent Chapel in the town and in the following year signed the teetotal pledge. He remained faithful to this cause for the remainder of his life during which he became an office-holder in the Sons of Temperance organisation.

The leader of the young men's class, a local flannel manufacturer, impressed by Mitchell's anxiety to learn, gave him a job in 1848 in his own warehouse where Mitchell stayed for two decades, rising ultimately to the position of manager. The religious teaching of the Sunday school inspired Mitchell with the desire to help others and this he was able to do through the local co-operative movement. Mitchell's maternal grandfather had lost money in an earlier co-operative store about ten years before the opening of the Toad Lane Store by the Rochdale Pioneers' Society in 1844, and in later years Mitchell impressed on audiences that the Pioneers were not the inventors of co-operation but demonstrators of its successful principles.

Mitchell joined the Pioneers' Society in 1853 and by 1856 was on the committee, becoming its part-time secretary in the following year. He had now found his life's main work. In 1854 he assisted the Pioneers' leaders to promote the Rochdale Co-opera-tive Manufacturing Society, serving on the Society's committee and becoming chairman, a position he held for several years up to 1870. In 1867 he left the flannel warehouse and started in business on his own as a flannel dealer. Travelling around the country in connection with his work, he sold cotton cloth woven at the mills of the Society and at the same time gave his services to assist the co-operative, political, religious and temperance movements in which he was interested.

His experience at the warehouse had given him an insight into the textile trade and had demonstrated an ability to manage men: talents which he used in the service of the co-operative movement. He attended the first Co-operative Congress in 1869 as a delegate from the Rochdale Pioneers' Society and the impact of his energy and ideas was soon apparent on the movement. He inaugurated district conferences of the Co-operative Union and proposed manufacturing activities by the CWS. In 1874 he was elected to the board of the Co-operative Union and in the same year to the chairmanship of the CWS. For the next twenty years – until his death in 1895 – he was the strongest and most vigorous personality in the whole co-operative movement.

It was during his chairmanship that the Wholesale Society experienced financial difficulties which brought him face to face with the conflicts of approach developing among other leaders of the co-operative movement. Unlike Hughes, Sedley Taylor, Holyoake and Neale, who favoured co-partnership and profit-sharing among the employees, Mitchell was more concerned with the welfare of the consumer and was a supporter of industrial production by the Wholesale Society, the profits being divided among the customers: although he conceded, when giving evidence before the R.C. on Labour in October 1892, that he did not object to independent productive societies if they were the best method. Regarded by the intellectuals of the movement as a 'materialist', Mitchell nevertheless, in theory at least, envisaged a future when the whole economy would be organised on a co-operative basis. He emphasised this theme of 'the common good for all' when he delivered his presidential address at the Co-operative Congress of 1892. In this address he summed up his ideals in a well-known statement: 'The three great forces for the improvement of mankind are religion, temperance and co-operation; and, as a commercial force, supported and sustained by the other two, co-operation is the greatest, noblest and most likely to be successful in the redemption of the industrial classes.' This quotation is engraved on a granite monument in Rochdale Cemetery erected in his memory by the CWS. Mitchell was of considerable assistance to Beatrice Potter (Mrs Sidney Webb) when she sought information on the co-operative movement and when her book was published in 1891 it revealed a sympathy with Mitchell's view of the role of the CWS in industrial production. In her autobiography, *My Apprenticeship* (1926), Mrs Webb described him as 'the most remarkable personality that the British co-operative movement has thrown up'.

Among Mitchell's other activities associated with the co-operative movement was his work as liquidator of the Lancashire and Yorkshire Productive Society which had flannel mills near Rochdale. He was appointed to this task in 1878 and kept the mills going by means of a loan from the CWS bank. After his death the CWS took over the works which by that time was a prospering concern. With William Maxwell and others he went to America in 1884 on CWS business concerned mainly with visits to meat packers; in the following year he and his fellow directors of the CWS supported the project for a Manchester Ship Canal and £20,000 was contributed from CWS funds. In 1893 the trading services rendered by the CWS to Greece were recognised by the award to Mitchell of the Order of the Golden Cross from the King of Greece.

As early as 1877 Mitchell saw the necessity for the co-operative movement to be represented in Parliament, a point which he again reiterated in 1891. He had been a member of a pre-franchise Non-electors' Association in Rochdale and later of a Radical Reform Association, and in 1893,

when he was made a JP, and unsuccessfully contested a local by-election for the Rochdale Council, he still represented the Liberals. Even so he had, according to his biographer, Percy Redfern, admitted 'that in the past Conservatives had done more good than Liberals', which suggests that his political sympathies did not dogmatically follow party lines. He again failed to win a seat on the local council in 1894.

Throughout his life Mitchell was a regular attender at the Milton Congregational Church, Rochdale, where from 1854 he taught in the Sunday school and where later he became superintendent until his death. He never married and despite his considerable business ability he died a poor man, leaving only £350 in his will. His death occurred at his Rochdale home on 16 March 1895 and following a service at Milton Church on 20 March he was buried in Rochdale Cemetery. In addition to the monument erected in the cemetery, his memory is also commemorated by the Mitchell Hall at the headquarters of the CWS in Manchester.

Writings: Inaugural address, *Co-op. Congress Report* (1892); Evidence before R.C. on Labour 1893-4 XXXIX pt I, Qs 1–405.

Sources: W. Maxwell, 'The late John Thomas Whitehead Mitchell, JP', *CWS Annual* (1896) 392–414; P. Redfern, *The Story of the C.W.S.* (Manchester, [1913]); idem, *John T. W. Mitchell: pioneer of consumers' co-operation* (Manchester, 1923); idem, *The New History of the C.W.S.* (Manchester, 1938); G. D. H. Cole, *A Century of Co-operation* [1945?]; Margaret Cole, *Makers of the Modern Labour Movement* (1948); E. C. Mack and W. H. G. Armytage, *Thomas Hughes* (1952). OBIT. *Co-op. News*, 23 Mar 1895.

JOYCE BELLAMY
JOHN SAVILLE

See also: Benjamin JONES, for Co-operative Production; Abraham GREENWOOD; G. J. HOLYOAKE, for Retail Co-operation – Nineteenth Century; Percy REDFERN, for Co-operative Wholesaling.

MOLESWORTH, William Nassau
(1816–90)

ANGLICAN, HISTORIAN AND CO-OPERATOR

Born on 8 November 1816 at Millbrook, near Southampton, William Nassau Molesworth was the eldest son of the Rev. John Edward Nassau Molesworth DD, curate of Millbrook and later, for many years, vicar of Rochdale. He was educated at King's School, Canterbury, and at St John's and Pembroke Colleges, Cambridge, where he won the Latin prize in 1838, graduating in the Senior Optime list in 1839 and receiving his MA in 1842. Ordained in 1839, the year in which his father was made the vicar of Rochdale, William Nassau became curate there but from 1841 to 1844 he was vicar of St Andrew's, Ancoats, Manchester, and in 1844 became vicar of St Clement's, Spotland, Rochdale, which position he retained until his resignation on grounds of failing health in 1889. In 1881 he was made an honorary canon of Manchester Cathedral and in 1883 received the LL.D from the University of Glasgow.

Molesworth was a High Church Anglican but in politics he was a radical and an enthusiastic advocate of the co-operative movement. A personal friend of both Richard Cobden and John Bright, he was one of the first to recognise the importance of co-operation: thereby incurring much unpopularity on account of his vigorous support of it in speech and writing. His services in this field were recognised when the education committee of the Rochdale Equitable Pioneers' Society presented him in 1861 with a copy of the English 'Hexapla' as a testimonial of his services to the Society and co-operation generally. Molesworth had spoken at the opening of the Spotland branch of the Society in 1859, and later he helped at the festive opening of the new central premises of the Society in Toad Lane, Rochdale, in 1867. He read a paper at the first Co-operative Congress in 1869 in which he urged the establishment of a co-operative bank. He participated actively in the second Congress, held in Manchester in 1870, where he presided on the second

day and contributed to various discussions, especially on banking, education and the Co-operative Press. At the tenth Congress, again held in Manchester, he preached a sermon on co-operation in the cathedral and again presided over one day of the Congress. His services to the Rochdale Society were extensive. He first suggested to the Pioneers the advantage of legal protection for their members; he was for some years a member of the science and art classes conducted by the Society and in 1862 became arbitrator for the Society. For a time he was president of the Rochdale Literary and Scientific Society.

In addition to his work for the co-operative movement he became well known for his historical writings, his principal work being a history of England from 1830 until the early 1870s. He married on 3 September 1844 Margaret, daughter of George Murray of Ancoats Hall, Manchester, by whom he had six sons and a daughter. He died at his Rochdale home on 19 December 1890 and was buried at Spotland. He left a personal estate of £65,774.

Writings: *A Strong Man disturbed in his Palace: a sermon preached at . . . Dobcross, on behalf of the National Society for the Education of the Poor in the Principles of the Established Church*, 28 Feb 1841, Rochdale [1841]; (with J. E. N. Molesworth) ed. *Common Sense* (1842–3); *A Lecture on the System of Religious Education established by the Reformers* (1849); *Secular Instruction an Important Element of Religious Education* (Manchester, 1857); *Essay on the French Alliance* [which won the Emertonian prize in 1860]; *The Progress of Co-operation in Rochdale* (1861); *Plain Lectures on Astronomy* (Manchester, [1862]); *On the History of Industrial Progress* [Rochdale Pioneers' Society Lect.: Manchester, 1864?]; *The History of the Reform Bill of 1832* (1865); *On the Great Importance of an Improved System of Education for the Upper and Middle Classes* [prize essay] (1867); 'The Best Means of making Co-operative Societies mutually helpful', *Co-op. Congress Report* (1869) 62–3; *The History of England 1830–1874*, 3 vols (1874); *History of the Church of England from 1660* (1882); *History of the Free and Open Church Movement* (n.d.).

Sources: *Co-op. Congress Reports* (1870 and 1878); *DNB 13*; G. J. Holyoake, *History of Co-operation*, 2 vols (1906); P. Redfern, *The Story of the C.W.S.* (Manchester, [1913]); W. H. Brown, *The Rochdale Pioneers* (Rochdale 1944); G. D. H. Cole, *A Century of Co-operation* (Manchester, [1945?]); A. Bonner, *British Co-operation* (Manchester, 1961). OBIT. *Manchester Guardian*, 20 Dec 1890; *Times*, 20 Dec 1890; *Co-op. News*, 27 Dec 1890.

H. F. BING

See also: G. J. HOLYOAKE, for Retail Co-operation – Nineteenth Century.

MOORHOUSE, Thomas Edwin (1854–1922)
CO-OPERATOR AND RADICAL

Born on 21 January 1854 near Bilberry Reservoir, Austonley, Holmfirth, Yorkshire, the son of John Moorhouse, a farmer, T. E. Moorhouse entered business as a newsagent and stationer in the Delph district adjacent to the Lancashire border. He was a founder and trustee of the Delph Mechanics Institute and when he acted as its librarian was said to have read every book in the library twice through. He also served the Ashton-under-Lyne weekly newspaper, the *Ashton Reporter*, as correspondent. A lifelong co-operator, he became a member of the Delph Co-operative Society committee in December 1883 and a year later was elected chairman, a position he held until his death, being only once opposed in the election for chairmanship during those thirty-seven years. He edited the Delph *Wheatsheaf* for a time and in 1889 was elected to the CWS board, being the longest-serving member when he died. He served on the drapery committee, of which he was chairman in 1921, and was a member of various CWS deputations abroad, one of his last visits being to Japan in 1919. He was said to have been twice round the world on CWS business. At the Co-operative Congress in 1921 he defended the action of the CWS, which had been accused of lack of sympathy with Russia, by pointing out that it was impossible to continue sending goods unless there was some guarantee of payment.

He had many interests outside the co-operative movement. From about 1890 he served for twenty years on the Saddleworth Board of Guardians, was a trustee of the Wesleyan Church and the first secretary of the Liberal Club. With the formation of the Labour Party he severed his connection with Liberalism and became a staunch supporter of Tom Mann and later worked for Victor Grayson. For twenty-seven years he was a member of the Saddleworth Urban District Council, was one of its first Labour members and held office until his death. He was chairman of the local Labour Party and of the Trades Council; from 1919 he sat on the local bench. He also acted as chairman of the housing committee of Saddleworth, was president of the Woollen Weavers' Textile Association and chairman of the Delph Brass Band.

While on CWS business in Belgium in 1921 he contracted an illness and died at his Delph home on 1 January 1922, the funeral taking place at the Independent Church, Delph, on 5 January. He left effects valued at £1954.

Sources: P. Redfern, *The Story of the C.W.S.* (Manchester, [1913]); idem, *The New History of the C.W.S.* (Manchester, 1938). OBIT. *Oldham Chronicle*, 7 Jan 1922; *Wheatsheaf*, Feb 1922.

JOYCE BELLAMY
H. F. BING

See also: *George LANSBURY, for British Labour Party, 1900–13; Percy REDFERN, for Co-operative Wholesaling.

MORGAN, David (Dai o'r Nant) (1840–1900)
MINERS' LEADER

Born at Cefu, near Merthyr, South Wales, on 14 February 1840, he attended a Unitarian school until the age of seven, and then entered the Cyfarthfa mines. At eighteen he transferred to Mountain Ash, where he worked in the Nixon and Powell–Dyffryn Collieries. His career as a miners' leader began in 1867 but it was not until 1871 that he became prominent in Thomas Halliday's

Amalgamated Association of Miners. At the Swansea half-yearly conference of the AAM on 6 April 1875, Dai o'r Nant was appointed secretary. The experience of the two stoppages of 1873 and 1875 converted him to the principle of the sliding scale and he was a member of the committee in the latter year which operated the first sliding-scale agreement. Thus he was one of the five signatories including William Abraham, Henry Mitchard, John Prosses and Thomas Halliday who signed the first Award of 12 February 1876. Dai o'r Nant was one of the eight signatories of the sliding-scale agreement of 17 January 1880, one of seven on 6 June 1882, one of ten to the agreement of 15 January 1890, one of eleven to that of 1 January 1892, and one of seven to that of 17 February 1893. But he did not sign the agreement of 7 November 1887 modifying the 1882 sliding scale; and neither he nor Isaac Evans signed the agreement of 28 March 1895 recommending the continuance of the 1892 sliding scale.

After the collapse of the Amalgamated Association at the end of the 1870s he helped found the Aberdare Miners' Association, and became its agent in 1882; although the Association, like others in South Wales at this time, was so bound by the sliding-scale agreement that it could not be considered a trade union in the accepted meaning of the term. He gave evidence before three Royal Commissions: on Accidents in Mines in 1881, and on Mining Royalties and on Labour in 1891.

Morgan was always active in his own community. He was a prominent Baptist in religion, and a deacon of his chapel for twenty-two years. In March 1883 he was elected to Aberdare School board, and three years later went on to the school management and finance committee, in which position he remained until his death. In 1892 he was returned unopposed for the county council and served on the finance and sanitary committees. At the time of his death he was an alderman.

David Morgan was a lean, ascetic man, a teetotaller all his life, who lacked the temperament to compromise; and he could be bitter in his animosities. He was beginning

to be known nationally in the 1880s. Thus he represented 17,000 miners from Aberdare and Dowlais at the six-day national conference of November 1886 at Manchester; and he again represented Aberdare at the national conference in Manchester which began on 20 April 1887. The main business of the conference was to consider the Mines Regulation Bill, and it was Dai o'r Nant who proposed the successful amendment enlarging the scope of the provision for local inspectors. Later in the same year, at a conference of the miners of England, Scotland and Wales in Edinburgh (11–14 October), he and William Abraham together represented 60,000 miners from the valleys of Aberdare, Merthyr and Rhondda. He attended the famous conference at Newport of November 1889 which established the MFGB. Although he was one of the ten signatories of the manifesto denouncing the miners who came out in the hauliers' strike of August 1893, he was gradually becoming opposed to the sliding scale, and for this and other reasons he found himself increasingly at loggerheads with many of the other Welsh mining leaders. A six months' notice to end the sliding-scale agreement began on 1 October 1897, the employers intimating their intention to declare a lock-out as from 1 April 1898, while at the same time they made it a condition of negotiations that the dozen workmen's representatives be given plenary powers. Against this the minority, headed by Dai o'r Nant, were for the miners themselves having the final say. At two conferences on 14 March and 28 March 1898 plenary powers were opposed by William Brace and Dai o'r Nant and their proposal for a ballot was carried by a large majority (44,872 votes to 14,500); and this majority by mid-April had risen to 74,548 against 20,538. At the special conference of the MFGB attended by Brace, Mabon, Richards, Williams and Dai o'r Nant the last-named put the case for the strikers in a speech, a minuted extract of which ran as follows (26 April 1898):

Mr D. Morgan stated that the South Wales and Monmouthshire miners were now out seeking to obtain a ten per cent advance. They were quite destitute of funds. It must be admitted that trade unionism in South Wales had been very feeble, and was only very feeble as yet. Some may say they were very foolish to come out with no money at their backs. Their reply to that was that they as leaders had done all they could to organise the men. He had been a great advocate of the sliding scale, and he must say he would be that day if the principle was not abused so extremely. However, he had come to the conclusion that the sliding scale was unpracticable. They must admit that they stood that day at the mercy of the world, and they appealed to the Federation to support them. They asked support from the Federation not only from the Central Fund but to permit them to send men to the different localities because their experience was that in South Wales coalfields, even where they had little organisation, much more money was got by men visiting localities than the contributions paid to the General Fund. They asked permission to go to different localities. They had plenty of men prepared to go up and down the country, and they hoped the Federation would consider their case with favour. It must be admitted if they did that, it did not mean repaying what they had done to them previously, but when they were in Scotland and the Midlands they did what they could at the time. They were destitute of funds at the present. Had they good funds at their backs they would not have made this appeal, but it was essential to put this appeal to them. No working man who lived upon his own labour in South Wales ever earned 14/– per day except contractors, and some of them who had as many as 300 men employed had been audacious enough to admit that they were not paid unless they got 3d per man from the workmen for looking after him. Out of 100,000 men there were 157 earning 5/– a day. The others were making about 3/6 or 4/– a day in South Wales. Instead of the owners giving way they had put their

claims, which meant a reduction and not an advance in wages. They asked for bread and were offered stones.

As a result of incidents in the lock-out of 1898 Morgan was arrested and sentenced to two months' imprisonment in August. He was released after a month and received an enthusiastic welcome on his return to Aberdare and Merthyr. Subsequently he lost much of his popularity when, in expressing his dissatisfaction with the peace terms, he accused the negotiators of having been bribed to end the strike, but failed to substantiate the claim; although the *Labour Leader* continued to write sympathetically of Morgan's position (27 August 1898).

After the establishment of the South Wales Miners' Federation on 11 October 1898, Morgan was compelled to resign from the executive committee in the following March. He died, a dispirited man, on 5 July 1900 and left £627 in his will. His wife, by whom he had seven daughters and a son, had predeceased him in November 1899. There is a bust and a portrait of Morgan in Aberdare library.

Sources: Evidence before R.C. on Accidents in Mines 1881 XXVI Qs 8412–576; Mining Royalties 1890–1 XLI Qs 10846–1178; Labour 1892 XXXIV Qs 3942–4387; biographical information: Dr E. W. Evans. OBIT. *Times*, 6 July 1900; *Western Mail*, 6 July 1900.

JOHN SAVILLE

See also: William ABRAHAM, for Welsh Mining Trade Unionism; Alexander MACDONALD, for Mining Trade Unionism, 1850–79; Benjamin PICKARD, for Mining Trade Unionism, 1880–99.

MORGAN, David Watts (1867–1933)
MINERS' LEADER AND LABOUR MP

Born on 18 December 1867 at Skewen, Neath, the son of Thomas and Margaret Morgan, he was educated at elementary schools in Skewen, Neath and Swansea. He began working in the mines when he was eleven but continued to extend his education through evening classes in Glamorgan. These enabled him to qualify as a mine manager but he did not in fact ever hold such an appointment, although, from 1900 to 1914, he worked as a mining engineer, experience which qualified him for rescue work with which he was to be much involved, and which included the saving of eighteen men at the Senghenydd Colliery disaster of 1913. He was active also in trade union work and in 1898 was appointed a miners' agent in the no. 1 Rhondda district, working with Mabon whom he succeeded as chief agent when the latter retired. Morgan held this post until 1920 and remained advisory agent until his death. During the First World War he volunteered to serve as a private in the Welsh regiment in 1914 but later transferred to the Labour Corps. He recruited many miners for the Army, served in France, was mentioned three times in dispatches and promoted to Lt-Col; in 1918 he was awarded the DSO and in 1920 the CBE.

He was elected unopposed in 1918 as Labour MP for the Rhondda East constituency and he held the seat until his death. For many years he was chairman of the Welsh members of the Parliamentrary Labour Party; served on several parliamentary committees during his term of office and was noted for his strong anti-Communist views. In October 1928 he offered to resign his seat and fight a by-election with Arthur Horner, a well-known Communist who had been elected to the executive of the MFGB in 1927 as one of the South Wales representatives. Horner did in fact contest Rhondda East in 1929 and again in 1931 and was easily defeated. Morgan was also very active in local government as a member of Glamorgan County Council for twenty-four years, and as chairman of the Roads and Bridges Committee he was concerned with a large road construction programme in the county. An alderman of the Council and chairman of it in 1926-8, he was also a JP for the county and a Freemason.

He was twice married and had a family of two sons and four daughters. He died on 23 February 1933 at his Porth home, leaving £203 (net) in his will.

Writings: *Compensation Act* (n.d.); *Safety in Mines* (n.d.); *Miners' Tables on Wages* (n.d.); Evidence before R.C. on Mines, vol. III 1908 XX Qs 30413–909.

Sources: S. V. Bracher, *The Herald Book of Labour Members* (1923); *Labour Who's Who* (1927); *Kelly* (1932); *Dod* (1933); *WWW* (1928–40); E. D. Lewis, *The Rhondda Valleys* (1959); *Times*, 17 May 1933. OBIT. *Times*, 24 Feb 1933; *Weekly Mail and Cardiff Times*, 25 Feb 1933; *Labour Party Report* (1933).

JOYCE BELLAMY

See also: William ABRAHAM, for Welsh Mining Trade Unionism; *A. HORNER.

MORGAN, John Minter (1782–1854)
CHRISTIAN OWENITE AND PHILANTHROPIST

Born in 1782, probably in London, Minter Morgan was the eldest son of John Morgan, a wholesale stationer, who died in 1807. The intellectual development which resulted in Minter Morgan becoming a defender and popular expositor of Robert Owen is not yet fully established, but he was much influenced by Dugald Stewart's *Elements of the Philosophy of the Human Mind* (1792) and Charles Hall's *The Effects of Civilization* (1805). In August 1817 Minter Morgan attended Owen's meetings at the City of London Tavern, and eighteen months later he published, under the pseudonym of Philanthropos, the *Remarks on the Practicability of Mr Robert Owen's Plan to Improve the Condition of the Lower Classes*, a faithful reproduction of Owen's views of 1817, except in the matter of religion. Minter Morgan never lost his Christian faith, and he convinced himself, from his first encounter with Owen's views, that Owen's practical proposals, which naturally emphasised the crucial importance of environment upon character formation, could be the means of spreading 'true Christian benevolence'. Since Owen himself, and many of his followers, deduced anti-clerical conclusions from the emphasis upon character formation as the product of social environment (thereby denying original sin and moral accountability), Minter

Morgan's Christian acceptance of Owenite ideas established an important precedent. Morgan developed a portrait of his ideal Owenite hero in *Hampden in the Nineteenth Century* (1834), parts of which are probably autobiographical.

Earlier, in 1826, he had published what was to become one of the best known popularisations of Owenism: *The Revolt of the Bees*, which went through five editions between 1826 and 1849 and was serialised in the *Co-operative Magazine* (1826–9). It is probable that this book, and its frontispiece, suggested the 'Beehive' as a symbol of co-operation that was to be widely adopted by the later co-operative movement.

Minter Morgan remained close to Owen's views during the 1830s, while always distinguishing between the central meaning of Owenism and what he regarded as Owen's personal idiosyncrasies, such as his anti-clericalism. Morgan's intellectual position can be derived from his *Letters to the Bishop of London* (1830) and from a series of articles he wrote in the *Crisis*, 24 May to 25 August 1832, under his old pseudonym of Philanthropos. Because of a passionate interest in education, Morgan was intellectually influenced by J. P. Greaves, and by the intellectual contacts between Greaves and Pestalozzi.

At the end of the 1830s Morgan began to move away from the main Owenite movement. His purpose was now to reconcile Owenite communitarianism with the Established Church; and on 22 June 1841 he launched a scheme to establish 'self-supporting villages' under the supervision of the Church of England. He secured some support from members of the upper classes, and he persuaded W. F. Cooper, nephew of Lord Melbourne, to present a petition in favour of his scheme to Parliament in July 1842. Among others who provided active support was James Silk Buckingham, and his two main lieutenants were the Rev. Joseph Brown (chaplain to the Poor Law Schools at Norwood) and the Rev. E. R. Lanken. The latter had been much influenced by Fourier, and was to collaborate later, in 1845, with James Hole and David Green in the formation of the Leeds Redemption Society. Throughout the decade of the 1840s Morgan persevered with his plans and continued to meet with much verbal agreement; and his influence upon his contemporaries was considerable. He travelled on the Continent, explaining his ideas, and in 1846 interviewed Pius IX with a view to getting papal approval and/or sponsorship for his Christianised communities. In 1849 he founded a national orphan home near his own home on Ham Common for children left destitute by the cholera epidemic. In order to raise money for his community schemes he published the Phoenix library in 1850: a collection of his own writings, but also including a second edition of Charles Hall's *The Effects of Civilization*.

The failure of the Chartist movement in 1848, the collapse of the Christian Socialist schemes of the early 1850s, and the new political and intellectual buoyancy symbolised in the Great Exhibition of 1851, all helped to produce a much sharper criticism of the theory and practice of associationism than had been the case in the previous decade. Morgan remained untouched by an increasingly hostile reaction to his ideas, and published in 1851 *The Triumph, or the Coming Age of Christianity*, an enthusiastic collection of essays by supporters of community life.

He died on 26 December 1854 at his London house and was buried in the church on Ham Common on 3 January 1855. Among other bequests, he left £12,000 in trust for his sister and her children.

Writings: *Remarks on the Practicability of Mr Robert Owen's Plan to improve the Condition of the Lower Classes* (1819); *The Revolt of the Bees* (published anonymously, 1826); *Hampden in the Nineteenth Century: or colloquies on the errors and improvements of society* (1834) [held by Holyoake to be his most extensively read book]; *Colloquies on Religion . . . Being a Supplement to Hampden in the Nineteenth Century* (1837); *Religion and Crime: or the condition of the people* (1840) 32 pp.; A translation of Napoleon III's essay, *Extinction du Pauperism*, edited by J. M. Morgan (1849); *Extracts for Schools and Families in*

Aid of Moral and Religious Training (1850); *The Phoenix Library, a Series of Original and Reprinted Works bearing on the Renovation and Progress of Society in Religion, Morality and Science*, selected by J. M. Morgan, 13 vols (1850); *The Triumph or the Coming Age of Christianity: selections from authors, chiefly religious and philosophical on the necessity of early and consistent training, no less than teaching*, ed. J. M. Morgan (1851). Among his lesser writings may be mentioned: *The Reproof of Brutus* [a Poem] (1830); *Address to the Proprietors of the University of London* [*in favour of the endowment of a Professorship of Education and the Establishment of a Hospital*] (1833); *A brief Account of the Stockport Sunday School and on Sunday Schools in Rural Districts* (1838); *The Christian Commonwealth* (1845); *Letters to a Clergyman on Institutions for Ameliorating the Condition of the People* (1846: 3rd ed. 1851); *A Tour through Switzerland and Italy in the years 1846–7* (1851) [first printed in the Phoenix Library in 1850].

Sources:

(1) MSS: Robert Owen correspondence, Co-operative Union, Manchester.

(2) Secondary: *DNB 12*; *Boase 2*; G. J. Holyoake, *The History of Co-operation*, 2 vols (1875 and 1879); Spencer T. Hall, *Biographical Sketches of Remarkable People* (Burnley, 1881); M. Beer, *History of British Socialism*, 2 vols (1919); G. D. H. Cole, *A Century of Co-operation* (Manchester [1945?]); J. F. C. Harrison, *Social Reforms in Victorian Leeds: the work of James Hole, 1820–1895* (Leeds, 1954); W. H. G. Armytage, 'John Minter Morgan, 1782–1854', *J. of Education 86* (Dec 1954) 550, 552; idem, 'John Minter Morgan's Schemes, 1841–1845', *Int. Rev. Social Hist. 3* (1958) 26–42; A. Bonner, *British Co-operation* (Manchester, 1961); W. H. G. Armytage, *Heavens Below* (1961); J. F. C. Harrison, *Robert Owen and the Owenites in Britain and America* (1969).

JOHN SAVILLE

See also: *J. Pierrepont GREAVES; *James HOLE; *J. M. F. LUDLOW, for Christian Socialism, 1848–54; *Robert OWEN, *J. E. 'Shepherd' SMITH.

MUDIE, George (1788?–?)
OWENITE

Little is known of his early life. He was in Edinburgh in 1812 where he was a member of a discussion group that used to meet in St Andrew's Chapel; and he came to London about 1820. By trade he was a printer and a journalist. On 23 January 1821 he brought together a group composed mainly of printers to discuss the establishment of a community. George Hinde was in the chair and Henry Hetherington was a member. A committee appointed at the meeting began to raise money for the project and to publicise its aims. Mudie then began publishing the weekly *Economist*, the first number of which appeared on 27 January 1821. He was also at this time editor of the *Sun*.

The pages of the *Economist* were devoted to an exposition of Robert Owen's ideas in general, and to the particular scheme of local community-building that Mudie was encouraging. A 'Co-operative and Economical Society' was formed and by the autumn of 1821 the society had acquired several houses in the Spa Fields district, and families began to move in. A fixed charge for maintenance was agreed, and domestic, educational and recreational activities were organised on a communal basis. Each member chose a 'monitor' whose duty it was to criticise the behaviour of the member in question in order to further general harmony among the community as a whole. The Society advertised publicly various services and goods provided by their members – including boots and shoes, millinery, book-binding – and they announced (January 1822) that a school, run on Fellenberg lines, would soon be opened. There are four main sources for the community: the files of the *Economist* (1821–2); Southey's *Sir Thomas More*, 134–9; the 1821 pamphlet *Report of the Committee Appointed . . .*; and the MS correspondence at the Co-operative Union, Holyoake House, Manchester.

The *Economist* was the first co-operative journal to be published in England and is an important source for both early Owenite ideas and Owenite experiments. The last number appeared on 9 March 1822, but the community seems to have lasted for another two years. Then, according to Mudie's own account, the proprietors of the *Sun* (of which Mudie was still editor) offered him the choice of either resigning from the editorial chair or abandoning the community. He chose the latter and the Spa Fields community came to an end. In 1823 he edited the *Political Economist and Universal Philanthropist*.

When the Orbiston community was established in 1825 Mudie resigned from the *Sun* and joined Abram Combe, investing all his capital in the venture. But he quarrelled with what he described as Combe's dictatorial pretensions and left the community before Combe's death in 1827. He then published from Edinburgh *The Advocate of the Working Classes* (1826–7) and does not appear to have been heard of again until 1840. In that year, living in the Strand in London, he published his *Grammar of the English Language*, and he was still in London in 1848–9 when he published *A Solution of the Portentous Enigma of Modern Civilisation* in which he was still arguing the case for self-sufficient communities. For his career after this there is still no evidence, and the date of his death is unknown. The detailed schedules of the 1851 Population Census show George Mudie living at 23 Parr Street, Hoxton, London, with his wife Louisa and a niece. Mudie gave his age as sixty-three, his birthplace as Scotland and described himself as author, translator and master printer. His wife was sixty-two and born in Middlesex.

Writings: *A Few Particulars Respecting the Secret History of the Late Forum* (Edinburgh, 1812); *Report of the Committee Appointed at a Meeting of Journeymen . . .* (2nd ed. 1821); *The Grammar of the English Language, truly made Easy and Amusing by the Invention of Three Hundred Moveable Parts of Speech* (1840); *A Solution of the Portentous Enigma of Modern Civilisation* (1849).

Sources: R. Southey, *Sir Thomas More: or Colloquies on the Progress and Prospects of Society*, 2 vols (1829); G. J. Holyoake, *History of Co-operation*, 2 vols (1875 and 1879); F. Podmore, *Robert Owen*, 2 vols (1906; and reprinted 1 vol. New York, 1968); M. Beer, *History of British Socialism* (1920); G. D. H. Cole, *A Century of Co-operation* (Manchester, [1945?]); W. H. G. Armytage, 'George Mudie: journalist and utopian', *Notes and Queries 202* (May 1957) 214–16; idem, *Heavens Below* (1961); J. F. C. Harrison, *Robert Owen and the Owenites in Britain and America* (1969) with comprehensive bibliography of Owenism.

H. F. BING
JOHN SAVILLE

See also: *Abram COMBE; H. HETHERING-TON; *Robert OWEN.

MURRAY, Robert (1869–1950)
CO-OPERATOR AND LABOUR MP

Born 30 June 1869 at Barrhead, Renfrewshire, into a family with long traditions in the labour movement. His maternal grandfather, David Stark, was a millwright employed at Robert Owen's New Lanark Mills and David's daughter, Marion, was educated at the New Lanark School. She married a Robert Murray of Bridgeton, a cotton yarn warper, later a tenter, who played a prominent part in the co-operative activities of the Barrhead community. In 1880 he was made a director of the SCWS although his service on the board was of short duration. He died at the age of eighty-one in 1912 and Marion died in 1891.

There were three sons of the marriage including Robert, the subject of this entry, and all played a part in local politics, including terms on the parish council and the Town Council. One of their early protégés was James Maxton, whose father was headmaster of one of the schools attended by Robert. He went first to the local elementary school known as Jamiesons and then to a school in Cross Arthurlie, a suburb of Barrhead. At the age of nine he worked in Stewart's cotton mill, as a half-timer, but was subsequently trained as a brass-finisher and pattern-maker, and for some time worked at the sanitary ware firm of Shanks.

He extended his early education by learning shorthand and, having a considerable literary ability, became a journalist and edited a local newspaper. He also started his own newsagency and bookselling business and wrote articles for literary periodicals. He was one of the earliest members of the ILP and as already noticed he took a keen interest in local government affairs, being elected to the Neilston parish council on its inception in 1894 and serving continuously until 1922, for six years of this period as chairman. On his retirement from the council, he was succeeded by his wife, formerly Margaret McKinlay, whom he had married in 1894 and whose father had also been a director of the SCWS in the years 1886-8.

Murray's first attempt to enter Parliament was in 1918 when he unsuccessfully contested West Renfrewshire in the Labour interest. In 1922 he stood again for the same seat and was elected in that year, and again in 1923. In the Labour Government of 1924 he served as a parliamentary secretary to the Scottish Office but was defeated at the next general election which returned the Conservative Party to office. Murray was subsequently appointed to the Extra-Parliamentary Commission which dealt with legislation under the Private Legislation (Scotland) Act.

An accomplished speaker and a prolific writer, his life was devoted to the spreading of co-operative ideas and furthering the cause of Socialism. It was especially in his work for the co-operative movement that he was particularly well known. He used his literary talents to write several histories of Scottish co-operative societies, the first of these, relating to his local Barrhead Society, being published in 1911. His journalistic ability led to his appointment in 1918 as associate editor of the Scottish Co-operator, and when he left Parliament in 1924 he was appointed to the editorial chair in succession to William Reid, and he held the position until August 1927. In the latter year he was made a director of the SCWS and served continuously until his retirement in 1939. During these years he travelled widely on behalf of the Society and remained an ardent propagandist for the movement. Towards the end of his period of service he represented the SCWS on the committee of academics and co-operators whose researches led to the publication of a standard work on the movement: Consumers' Co-operation in Great Britain by Carr-Saunders, Sargant Florence and Robert Peers, published in 1938. Apart from his co-operative writings, Murray published a work on land nationalisation in 1922, a book of poems in 1936, and his last major work was The Annals of Barrhead in 1942. He was a JP for Renfrew County. An active member of the Evangelical Union Congregational Church for much of his life, in his later years he ceased his connection and became an agnostic.

He died on 9 August 1950 at Johnstone Nursing Home and his funeral service was held at the Woodside Crematorium, Paisley. His wife had predeceased him in 1944 but he was survived by three daughters and a son, Dr D. Stark Murray, a prominent socialist and president for nineteen years of the Socialist Medical Association. He left an estate valued at £3464. One of his daughters married Neil Maclean, a solicitor and son of Neil Maclean, MP for Govan 1918-50. A great-grandfather of the Maclean family is also known to have worked at the New Lanark Mills.

Writings: *History of the Barrhead Co-operative Society 1861-1911* (Barrhead, 1911) and *1911-1936* (Barrhead, 1937); *History of London Road Co-operative Society 1872-1922* (1922) 32 pp.; *The Land Question Solved*, with a foreword by R. Smillie (1922); *History of Fife and Kinross Co-operative Society 1877-1927* (Glasgow, 1927) 32 pp.; *Stirling Co-operative Society: a historical sketch 1880-1930* (Glasgow, 1930) and *1930-1940* (Glasgow, 1940); *The Deil and John Knox* [collected poems] (1936); *The Annals of Barrhead* (Glasgow, 1942); *The House of Memories* (Glasgow, 1944).

Sources: J. A. Flanagan, *Wholesale Co-operation in Scotland: the fruits of fifty years' efforts (1868-1918)* (Glasgow, 1920); *Scottish Co-operator*, 3 Sep 1927; A. M. Carr-

Saunders et al., *Consumers' Co-operation in Great Britain: an examination of the British co-operative movement* (1938); personal information: Dr D. Stark Murray (son). OBIT. *Barrhead News*, 10 Aug 1950; *Scottish Co-operator*, 12 Aug 1950; *Times*, 12 Aug 1950; *Barrhead News*, 13 Aug 1950; *Scottish Newsagent*, Aug 1950.

JOYCE BELLAMY
JOHN SAVILLE

See also: W. MAXWELL, for Scottish Co-operation.

NEALE, Edward Vansittart (1810–92)
CHRISTIAN SOCIALIST AND CO-OPERATOR

Born 2 April 1810, at Royal Crescent in Bath. Oliver Cromwell was numbered among his ancestors; and his living relatives included William Wilberforce and Nicholas Vansittart, Chancellor of the Exchequer during Liverpool's administration. His father was the Rev. Edward Neale, LL.B, evangelical Rector of Taplow, Bucks.

Evangelical Christianity was the most significant influence in Neale's early life; the fact that he was educated by his father, rather than being sent to public school, served to accentuate its effect. In 1828 Neale entered Oriel College, Oxford, where J. H. (later Cardinal) Newman became his tutor. Influenced by the critical tradition of the Noetics as well as by Newman, he gradually abandoned his evangelical convictions and with them the idea of a career in the Church. On 16 January 1832 he began studies at Lincoln's Inn and became a Chancery Barrister, being called to the Bar on 4 May 1837. From the standpoint of his future career as a co-operator, Neale's marriage (14 June 1837) was an unfortunate one. His wife, Frances Sarah Farrer, was half-sister to the 2nd Earl of Eldon (grandson of the Lord Chancellor, 1801–27) and thus connected with a family notorious for its reactionary political and social ideas.

Neale was only moderately successful as a lawyer as his main interests lay elsewhere. Seeking a satisfactory substitute for evangelical Christianity, he mastered the works of the German philosophers and French

socialists, becoming by 1841 a disciple of Fourier. He was also influenced by the proposed land reforms of Jeremy Bentham and Lord Brougham as evidenced in both *The Real Property Acts of 1845* and the *Thoughts on the Registration of the Title to Land*, books which he published in 1845 and 1849 respectively. In 1850, attracted by the Working Tailors' Association, Neale joined the Christian Socialists and was appointed by F. D. Maurice to the Council of Promoters of that organisation. While a Christian Socialist he invested heavily in co-operative workshops (established along lines pioneered by Benjamin Buchez and Louis Blanc), which all, however, failed. In these and other co-operative ventures Neale lost a sum of money in excess of £40,000; but certain of his efforts during this period were of lasting significance. In 1851 Neale founded the Central Co-operative Agency, a wholesale depot which was a progenitor of the later Co-operative Wholesale Society in Manchester; and a year afterwards, in 1852, he aided the passage of the Industrial and Provident Societies Act, the so-called 'Magna Carta of Co-operation'.

Neale was the most prominent leader at a series of co-operative conferences (1852–4) launched by John Ludlow and himself, at which he strove unsuccessfully to bring about a federal union of British co-operators. As a result of his efforts the Conference Executive published the *Co-operative Commercial Circular* (1853–5) now a rare and valuable source of information on co-operation during these years.

Neale founded the Co-operative League in 1852. Composed largely of Owenites, it was intended as a forum for the exchange of co-operative ideas and held regular public meetings at one of which Owen gave an address: 'On the Science of Society'. The organisation sponsored a periodical called the *Transactions of the Co-operative League* (published in three parts in 1852) under Neale's direction.

He was one of the leading figures in the development of co-operation as an organised movement. Striving to bring uniformity, he drew up numerous editions of model rules for the individual societies. The

Industrial and Provident Societies Act of 1862, which among other benefits made provision for joint action by many societies, was Neale's handiwork. Its passage led directly to the establishment of the Co-operative Wholesale Society. This latter organisation plus the Co-operative Insurance Society (1867) and the Co-operative Congress (1869) owed a great deal to him. He provided much of the initial inspiration for these great federal bodies, worked as a trusted consultant and legal adviser with the committees that originated them, and finally was responsible for formulating the rules, articles of association, etc., under which they commenced operation. Finally, in 1873, Neale became general secretary of the Co-operative Union.

During the years after 1873 Neale led a group, including G. J. Holyoake, Thomas Hughes and E. O. Greening, which wished to turn the movement away from its exclusive concern with retail co-operation. Neale envisaged the creation of stores and wholesale societies as only the first step towards the more important business of establishing co-operative workshops and, ultimately, home colonies. He wanted the CWS to establish semi-autonomous producers' societies – where workers participated in management and shared profits – which would ultimately supply all of the products demanded by co-operative consumers. Neale's enthusiasm for co-operative production remained unabated throughout his life. He helped to establish a myriad of independent productive enterprises, including the Agricultural and Horticultural Association (1867) and the Hebden Bridge Fustian Manufacturing Society (1870).

Neale was a prolific propagandist. He inspired a generation of co-operative leaders, including such personalities as Mrs Mary Lawrenson (a founder of the Women's Co-operative Guild) and William Nuttall (prominent director of the CWS and a founder of the Co-operative Newspaper Society). From its origins in 1871, Neale contributed to the *Co-operative News* on almost a weekly basis, if not always a major article then a letter to the editor or legal note. He edited the Annual Congress reports, writing a lengthy preface for each, and published numerous co-operative pamphlets. He wrote, with less distinction, in the fields of religion, science and philosophy. His most important work in this sphere, *The Analogy of Thought and Nature* (1863), was a ponderously long and elaborate philosophical structure in defence of the Utopian Socialists' dogma of association; the theme was built on a broad Hegelian foundation.

In 1875 Neale created the Mississippi Valley Trading Company to facilitate the exchange of products between American Grangers and British Co-operators, and travelled to America on its behalf. Although it failed, the plan was instrumental in popularising (for the first time on an extensive scale) the Rochdale Plan of Co-operation in America. Neale continued to be a mentor for Americans (he was, for example, involved in converting the Knights of Labor to co-operation in the early 1880s) and was influential in helping to establish congresses and unions of co-operators in France and Italy.

Neale always undervalued political reform, which he considered to be building with the point of the pyramid downwards, and found himself out of phase with the renewed interest in state socialism after 1880. His philosophy precluded violence; he preferred to avoid the political route and begin with gradual social and economic change. Neale called himself a Conservative but was almost unrecognisable as such for he shunned dogmatism and frequently aligned himself with radicals. He had vigorously supported the engineers' strike in 1852, and in 1867 he was favourable to the enfranchisement of the working men by the Second Reform Bill. His ability to work for the CWS while strenuously criticising its abandonment of profit-sharing was typical of his pragmatic approach. Neale's consistency lay in his willingness to support everything capable of advancing the cause of labour.

In 1885 Neale inherited the family estate, Bisham Abbey on the Thames near Marlow, yet he remained at Manchester working as general secretary of the Co-operative Union until his retirement in 1891. On 16 September 1892 Neale died in a nursing home in London and was buried in Bisham Churchyard. He was survived by his wife Frances, two daughters, Constance and Edith, and a son, Henry, who, like his father, had been for some years active in co-operative work. Neale left an estate valued at £14,533, but before his death part of the estate had already come into the hands of his son, Henry. Bisham Abbey, for example, was jointly owned.

Writings:

(1) Books: *Feasts and Fasts. An Essay on ... the Laws relating to Sundays and Other Holidays* (1845); *The Real Property Acts of 1845* (1845); *Thoughts on the Registration of the Title to Land* (1849); *The Analogy of Thought and Nature* (1863); (with T. Hughes) *A Manual for Co-operators* (1881).

(2) Pamphlets and shorter published works: *Memoir relating to the Position and Prospects of the Associations* (1850) 11 pp.; *Scheme for Formation of the Working Associations into a General Union* [1851] 15 pp.; *The Characteristic Features of some of the Principal Systems of Socialism* (1851) 44 pp.; *Laws for the Government of the Society for the Formation of Co-operative Stores* (1851) 11 pp.; *Report of a Meeting for the Establishment of the Central Co-operative Agency . . . May 30 1851* (1851) 24 pp.; *Sketch of a General Establishment for the Realization of Industrial Reform to be called the Co-operative Agency* [1851] 8 pp.; *Suggestions to Aid in the Formation of a Legal Constitution for Working Men's Associations* (1852) 34 pp.; *Labour and Capital . . .* (1852) 34 pp.; *May I not do what I will with my own? Considerations on the Present Contest between the Operative Engineers and their Employers* (1852); *Prize Essay on the Best Means of Employing the Surplus Funds of the Amalgamated Society of Engineers etc. in Associative or Other Productive Objects* (1855) 32 pp.; *The Co-operators Handbook, containing the Laws relating to a Company of Limited Liability with Model Articles of Association suitable for Co-operative Purposes* (1860) 32 pp.; 'On Typical Selection, as a Means of removing the Difficulties attending the Doctrine of the Origin of the Species by Natural Selection', *Proc. of the Zoological Society of London* (Jan 1861) 1–11; *The Doctrine of the Logos*, reprinted from the *Theological Review* (Oct 1867) 28 pp.; 'State, Prospects and Objects of Co-operation', *Co-op. Congress Report* (1870); *Does Morality depend on Longevity?* (1871) 17 pp.; *The New Bible Commentary and the Ten Commandments* (1872) 15 pp.; *The Mythical Element in Christianity* [printed 1872] 60 pp.; *The Central Co-operative Board* (1874) 8 pp.; *The Distinction between Joint Stockism and Co-operation* (Manchester, 1874) 8 pp.; *Reason, Religion, and Revelation* (1875) 31 pp.; *The Principle of Unity* (Manchester, 1875) 8 pp.; *True Refinement* [Manchester, 1877] 15 pp.; *What is Co-operation?* [1877] 8 pp.; *Why should the Rich interest themselves in Co-operation? and how can they promote it?* (Manchester, 1877) 15 pp.; *The 'Co-operative News' and why Co-operators should support it* (Manchester, 1878) 12 pp.; *Associated Homes* (1880) 29 pp.; 'Self Help', *Co-op. News*, 2 Oct 1880; *Association and Education* (1882) 16 pp.; *The Economic Aspect of Co-operation* [Manchester, 1884] 11 pp.; 'What is the Social Condition of the Working Classes in 1884 as compared with 1857 when the First Meeting of the National Association for the Promotion of Social Science was held in Birmingham; and in What Way can the Working Classes best utilize their Savings?', *Trans Nat. Assn for the Promotion of Social Science* (1884) 607–34; *The Economics of Co-operation* (1885) 30 pp.; *The Labour Association for promoting Co-operative Production based on the Co-partnership of the Workers; its principles, objects and methods* (1885) 12 pp.; [another edition (1913) with a portrait and short account of E. V. Neale, 16 pp.]; (with J. Woodcock) *Copyhold Tenure and Copyhold Enfranchisement* (Manchester, 1885) 16 pp.; *The Common Sense of Co-operation* [Manchester, 1886] 8 pp.; *The Social Aspects of Co-operation* (Manchester, 1887); *Land, Labour and Machinery* [1888?] 22 pp.; (with T. Hughes) *Co-operative Faith and Practice* (1892) 15 pp.; 'Thoughts on Social Problems and their Solution', *Econ. Rev.* 2 (Oct 1892) 518–37; *The Principles of Rating applied to Co-operative Stores* (Manchester, n.d.); *The Right of Nomination* (Manchester, n.d.) 8 pp.

(3) Evidence by E. V. Neale to the S.C. on Investment for the Savings of the Middle and Working Classes, *M. of E.* 1850 XIX Qs 145–245, 389–91.

Sources:

(1) MSS: E. V. Neale's personal papers, with family, Bisham Grange, Marlow, Bucks; Mississippi Valley Trading Company papers; Robert Owen, G. J. Holyoake and E. O. Greening collections; misc. letters and papers on Neale, Co-operative Union Library, Manchester; John M. F. Ludlow MSS, Cambridge University Library; Ludlow tracts, Goldsmiths Library, University of London; Richard T. Ely papers, Wisconsin Historical Society, Madison; John Samuel papers, Wisconsin Historical Society, Madison; E. R. A. Seligman collection, Columbia University, New York City. Letters on Associated Homes between Col. Henry Clinton and E. V. Neale (1861) 18 pp. (Goldsmiths' Library, London).

(2) Secondary: A. J. L. St André, *Five Years in the Land of Refuge* (1854); W.H.R., *Edward Vansittart Neale and the Christian Socialists* (n.d.) 14 pp.; *DNB 14*, 138–41; T. Hughes, 'Edward Vansittart Neale as a Christian Socialist', *Econ. Rev. 3* (1893) 38–49, 174–89; J. M. Ludlow, 'Some of the Christian Socialists of 1848 and the Following Years', *Econ. Rev. 3* (Oct 1893) 486–500; idem, *Econ. Rev. 4* (Jan 1894) 24–42; *Memorial of Edward Vansittart Neale*, ed. H. Pitman (1894), which is the most important work to date; S. and B. Webb, *The History of Trade Unionism* (1894); H. W. Lee, *Edward Vansittart Neale: his co-operative life and work* (1908); J. McCabe, *Life and Letters of George Jacob Holyoake*, 2 vols (1908); C. E. Raven, *Christian Socialism, 1848–1854* (1920); W. M. Bamford, *Our Fifty Years* (1921); E. O. Greening, 'Some Makers of Co-operation III: memories of Edward Vansittart Neale', *Co-op. Official 4* (1923) 71–2; G. D. H. Cole, *A Century of Co-operation* [1945?]; J. B. Jefferys, *The Story of the Engineers* [1945]; E. C. Mack and W. H. G. Armytage, *Thomas Hughes* (1952); C. K. Yearly, *Britons in American Labor* (1957); T. Christensen, *The Origin and*

History of Christian Socialism, 1848–1854 (1962); N. Masterman, *John Malcolm Ludlow* (1963); R. G. Garnett, *A Century of Co-operative Insurance* (1968). OBIT. *Times*, 17 Sep 1892; J. M. Ludlow, 'Obituary, Edward Vansittart Neale', *Econ. J.* (Dec 1892) 752–4.

Other standard works on co-operation, especially those by E. O. Greening, are of value. Useful periodicals include: 1850–4, *The Christian Socialist*, *The Co-operative Commercial Circular*, *The Journal of Association*, *The Leader*, *Notes to the People*, *The Operative*, *Trans of the Co-operative League*; 1860–71, *The Co-operator*, *Industrial Partnership's Record*, *The Reader*, *Social Economist*; 1871–92, *Annual Reports of the Co-operative Congress*, and *Co-op. News.*

P. N. BACKSTROM

See also: E. O. GREENING, for Co-partnership; Fred HAYWARD, for Co-operative Union; G. J. HOLYOAKE, for Retail Co-operation – Nineteenth Century; Benjamin JONES, for Co-operative Production; *J. M. F. LUDLOW, for Christian Socialism, 1848–54; Percy REDFERN, for Co-operative Wholesaling.

NORMANSELL, John (1830–75)
MINERS' LEADER

Born in December 1830 at Torkington, near Stockport, the eldest of four children whose father, a colliery banksman, was earning 2s 6d a day when John was born. Soon after the birth of the last child the mother died, to be followed two years later by the father. The children thus orphaned were brought up by an aunt and grandparents, although only John survived into manhood. He attended a Wesleyan Sunday school, the only education he received before he began work in the mines, at Clayton and Brook's Colliery near Stockport, at the age of seven, being paid 6d a day as a 'hurrier'. At fourteen he began working underground continuously. He married at twenty-two and was at that time still unable to sign his name. But his wife could read and write and John was determined to learn, and he began attending evening classes.

Soon after his marriage he moved to Derbyshire where he worked for two and a half years before starting work at the South Yorkshire colliery of Wharncliffe Silkstone in 1856; and in the following year he was elected checkweighman. This was before the Coal Mines Regulation Act of 1860 which, *inter alia*, permitted miners to elect their own representatives to check the weights of coal; but even with the passing of the Act it was years before the right was fully safeguarded against employers' victimisation. Normansell himself was involved in a bitter incident in 1863 when he was sacked from employment and only reinstated after a court case had decided that he had been legally appointed under the 1860 Act. He had been out of work for seven months.

There had been a miners' organisation in the Barnsley district in the early 1840s but this had gone out of existence in 1844. Normansell was actively concerned with the beginnings of a new South Yorkshire Miners' Association in 1858, whose first secretary was Richard Mitchell. It grew quite rapidly for the first three years of its life but then declined; and the nineteen weeks' lock-out of 1864 left the union in a state of disarray. The Association was reorganised in October 1864, at which time the number of members was only 1748, and Normansell was appointed secretary on 20 December. Together with Philip Casey, who became assistant secretary in January 1867, the two leaders rebuilt the Association on an efficient basis and at the time of Normansell's death in 1875 membership was over 20,000. In the year following his appointment as secretary the first of the annual galas of the South Yorkshire Miners was held, on 4 September 1865. Normansell presided and the main speakers were Ernest Jones and Alexander Macdonald of the Miners' National Union. Normansell was a close collaborator of Macdonald and he was elected vice-president of Macdonald's union in 1870, in which year they both represented the miners at the Trades Union Congress.

The Webbs characterised Normansell as 'second only to Macdonald as a leader of the miners between 1863 and 1875'. He was a man of fine presence who spoke with authority and persuasiveness. As one of the earliest miners' leaders his opinions were sought by a number of government committees. He gave evidence before the S.C. on Coal in 1866; the S.C. on Contracts of Service between Master and Servant 1866; the R.C. on Trade Unions 1868-9; and the R.C. on the Labour Laws 1874-5. He was one of two miners' delegates at the first meeting of the Trades Union Congress in 1869 where he read a paper on direct representation of Labour in the House of Commons. He was personally friendly with A. J. Mundella, who urged him in 1869 to follow up the Trade Union's Commission's report and press for an arbitration court to be established. Mundella had been elected MP for Sheffield in 1868 and became closely connected with the South Yorkshire Miners' Association. Mundella had strongly advocated his Nottingham system before the R.C. on Trades Unions and Normansell was among many prominent trade union leaders who became apostles of the arbitration principle.

The Association grew rapidly during the boom years of the early 1870s. In October 1871 Normansell stood unsuccessfully for the Barnsley Council but was elected in 1872: the first working man to achieve that position, made possible by the deposit of £1000 by the Association in a local bank in Normansell's name. He served only for three years and did not offer himself for re-election. The last two years of his life were difficult and unhappy. The decline in general prices which became noticeable in 1874, and continued thereafter, brought to an end the period of rising coal prices and wages. Great bitterness developed in South Yorkshire and elsewhere when the miners' leaders recommended the acceptance of wage reductions, and in Normansell's case the issues were confounded by accusations of improper bookkeeping of the finances of the Association. Early in 1875 he threatened to resign but was persuaded to continue in office. He died at the early age of forty-five on 24 December 1875 leaving a widow and seven children. Alexander Macdonald spoke at the funeral service, which was held in the Wesleyan chapel. The South Yorkshire Miners' Association passed over to his widow the £1000 which had been banked in her husband's name, and a Normansell Family Fund was established. His effects were under £450.

Sources: Evidence before the S.C. on Regulation and Inspection of Mines and Miners' Complaints 1866 XIV Qs 3014–716; 12792–5; 14198–231; S.C. on Contracts of Service between Master and Servant 1866 XII Qs 890–1048; R.C. on Trade Unions 1868–9 XXXI Qs 16092–329; S.C. on Present Dearness and Scarcity of Coal 1873 X Qs 7354–514; and the R.C. on the Labour Laws 1874–5 XXX Qs 536–60; *Bee-Hive*, 19 July 1873; *The Life and Labours of John Normansell* (repr. from *Barnsley Chronicle*, 1 Jan 1876); S. and B. Webb, *The History of Trade Unionism* (1894); R. Page Arnot, *The Miners* (1949); W. H. G. Armytage, *A. J. Mundella 1825–1897* (1951); F. Machin, *The Yorkshire Miners* (Barnsley, 1958); J. E. Williams, *The Derbyshire Miners* (1962); H. A. Clegg et al., *A History of British Trade Unions since 1889* (1964). OBIT. *Times*, 29 Dec 1875; *Barnsley Chronicle*, 1 Jan 1876.

JOYCE BELLAMY
JOHN SAVILLE

See also: Alexander MACDONALD, for Mining Trade Unionism, 1850–79.

NUTTALL, William (1835–1905)
CO-OPERATOR

Born in the Oldham district in 1835, he began his working life as an apprentice shoemaker, becoming a self-employed master shoemaker. While still a young man, he studied mathematics and other subjects at evening classes, and in 1863 he was appointed the first paid secretary of the Oldham Equitable Society. He was also the first secretary of the Star Corn Mill in 1868. Nuttall remained with the Oldham Equitable for two years and then resigned to take up a position in the accountants' department of the North of England Co-operative Wholesale Society (the forerunner of the CWS). He was also made a director of the CWS (1865–6) and later, 1868–70, became its cashier.

The demand for a general representative organisation embracing all aspects of the co-operative movement had been growing steadily in the last years of the 1860s. William Pare was continually urging the idea in the columns of Henry Pitman's *Co-operator* and in May 1869 the first of the regular series of Co-operative Congresses was held in London. A second national congress was organised at Whitsuntide 1870 in Manchester and it was agreed to set up a Co-operative Central Board out of which gradually developed the Co-operative Union. Nuttall undertook secretarial duties for the Central Board on a part-time basis with William Pare, and his appointment is one indication of the way in which his general organising ability kept him very much at the centre of new developments in these years. He was, for example, a founder and committee member of the Co-operative Printing Society (1869) and a founder of the *Co-operative News* in 1871. Nuttall, with other officers of the Co-operative Printing Society, at first shared the editorial duties, but the arrangements were not satisfactory and debts accumulated. It was only when Samuel Bamford became editor in 1875 that the *News* began to improve its circulation and become an intellectual force in the movement.

Having already been auditor of a number of co-operative enterprises including the Oldham Twist Co. Ltd and the Sun Mill Co. Ltd, 'the great Joint Stock laid hold on him' and from the closing years of the sixties Nuttall became the leading promoter of limited liability cotton-spinning companies in the Oldham district. These were the so-called 'Working-Class Limiteds'. By 1875 Nuttall claimed association with twelve of these companies and he argued at the Co-operative Congress of that year that the companies were part of the co-operative movement because the majority of their share capital was held by members of the working class. Undeterred by widespread criticism of this view, he continued to promote companies not only in cotton spinning but also in coalmining, iron production, paper manufacturing, as well as the abortive Mississippi Valley Trading Company (for which see E. V. NEALE). Nuttall lost heavily on these ventures, and in December 1883 he emigrated to Australia. His last main service to the co-operative movement was the editorship of the *CWS Annual*. Prior to 1883 the CWS had issued an annual publication, made up of *Whitaker's Almanac* together with statistics relating to the progress of the CWS. Nuttall took over the idea and produced, for 1883, a large annual wholly devoted to co-operative matters. It was almost entirely compiled and written by him and before he left England he had already put together the 1884 volume.

In Australia Nuttall lived on a small farm near Melbourne, and he became secretary to the newly-formed Melbourne Industrial Co-operative Society. In 1900 he returned with his wife to England and settled in Manchester. He continued to attend co-operative gatherings and was often in the offices in Balloon Street. He died on Thursday 26 October 1905 at his Manchester home, his considerable services to the co-operative movement having been largely forgotten, although the *Co-operative News* gave him a full obituary notice. He was buried at the Manchester Southern Cemetery on 30 October.

Writings: 'The North of England Co-operative Wholesale Society', *Co-op. Congress Report* (1869); 'Co-operative Cottage Building', *Co-op. Congress Report* (1870); 'Co-operative Check System', *Co-op. Congress Report* (1872); 'The best means of propagating Co-operation in Large Towns', *Co-op. Congress Report* (1883).

Sources: B. Jones, *Co-operative Production*, 2 vols (1894, reprinted in one volume, New York, 1968); *Oldham Industrial Co-operative Society Record, 4*, no. 10 (Oct 1898); C. Walters, *History of Oldham Industrial Equitable Co-operative Society* (Manchester, 1900); P. Redfern, *The Story of the C.W.S.* (Manchester, [1913]); G. D. H. Cole, *A Century of Co-operation* (Manchester, [1945?]); *Co-op. Rev.* Sep 1947. OBIT. *Oldham Chronicle*, 28 Oct 1905; *Co-op. News*, 4 Nov 1905; *Oldham Industrial Co-operative Society Record, 7*, no. 23 (Nov 1905).

JOHN SAVILLE
R. E. TYSON

See also: G. J. HOLYOAKE, for Retail Co-operation – Nineteenth Century; Benjamin JONES, for Co-operative Production; Percy REDFERN, for Co-operative Wholesaling.

OLIVER, John (1861–1942)
CO-OPERATOR

Born on 8 July 1861 at Gateshead, the son of Thomas Oliver, an engine fitter, John Oliver was apprenticed at the Greenesfield works of the North Eastern Railway Company. He rose to be a railway claims inspector before leaving railway service in 1915 on becoming a CWS director. He played an active part in establishing a pensions society for North Eastern Railway workers and at a later date was vice-chairman of the Railway Employees' Pension Fund. He spent the whole of his life in Gateshead.

In 1895 he was elected a scrutineer of the Gateshead Co-operative Society; in 1903 he was elected to the management committee and was president of the society from 1907 to 1916. He was elected to the board of the Co-operative Wholesale Society in 1915 and remained on the board until his retirement under the age rule at the age of seventy in 1931, being vice-president of the board during his last years of office. He served on the drapery committee, and represented the CWS on the Gilsland Convalescent Home Committee and the committee of Newcastle Royal Infirmary. He was also a member of the general committee of the Co-operative Insurance Society. He was one of three northern CWS directors appointed to help manage Middlesbrough Co-operative Society from 1924 to 1930 when it got into financial difficulty owing to local economic depression. In December 1930 the members of the Middlesbrough Society made a presentation to Mr Oliver and his two colleagues for their 'immeasurable assistance in the restoration of our Society'.

John Oliver was the first working man to be appointed JP for Gateshead in 1907. He was chairman of the Gateshead Unemployment Committee (Ministry of Labour) and served on the Juvenile Committee, the Juvenile Court and the Probation Committee. He was a member of the National Advisory Committee for Juvenile Unemployment and in the 1934 Birthday Honours list was given the OBE in recognition of his work as chairman of the Gateshead Juvenile Advisory Committee. He was a Methodist local preacher for over fifty years from 1887 onwards, and was for many years vice-president, and, from 1931, president of the Gateshead Brotherhood. He was a Freemason and a member of the Saltwell Masonic Lodge.

On 7 April 1887 he married Miss Jennie Thompson, daughter of James Macdonald Thompson, a glass-maker, at the United Methodist Free Church, Durham Road, Gateshead, of which they were both members. They had two daughters and a son, the latter being killed in action in France in April 1917. John Oliver died on 3 October 1942 and was buried at Saltwell Cemetery on 7 October. He left an estate valued at £4395.

Sources: P. Redfern, *The New History of the C.W.S.* (Manchester, 1938); Co-operative Press records, Manchester; personal information: Borough Librarian, Gateshead. OBIT. *Newcastle Journal* and *North Mail*, 5 Oct 1942; *Co-op. News*, 17 Oct 1942.

H. F. BING

See also: W. H. BROWN, for Retail Co-operation, 1900–45; Percy REDFERN, for Co-operative Wholesaling.

ONIONS, Alfred (1858–1921)
MINERS' LEADER AND LABOUR MP

Born 30 October 1858 at St Georges, Salop, the son of Jabez Onions, a miner, he was educated at St George's Church School which he left at the age of ten and a half. Soon afterwards the family moved to North Staffordshire and at thirteen, Onions started to work in the mines. When he was twenty he began to extend his early education through night classes organised by the North Staffs Adult Education Society. He transferred to South Wales in 1883 where he worked as a miner at Black Vein Colliery, Risca. When the colliery closed two years

later he went for a short time to the Rhondda, returning to Abercarn where he worked as a timber-man for two years before being appointed a checkweigher at the Abercarn Colliery in 1887. This was the starting-point of his subsequent career as a miners' leader. In the following year he was made secretary of the Monmouth District, one of the many individual unions formed in the South Wales coalfield in the last decades of the century. In 1891 he represented the South Wales miners at the International Miners' Conference in Paris and in 1892 joined other miners' leaders on the sliding-scale committee which regulated wages in the South Wales coalfield at this period. At the national conference of miners' representatives of England, Scotland and Wales in January 1893 (the so-called 'Hen and Chickens' conference after the name of the hotel in Birmingham in which the meeting took place) Onions opposed the MFGB policy on the regulation of wages and defended the sliding scale.

Onions was one of the ten union leaders who signed the famous manifesto during the hauliers' strike of 1893 urging the men to work; and he continued to support the principle of the sliding scale until it was superseded. In the same year (on 3 March) he was a member of the formidable deputation of miners' representatives who crowded into No. 10 Downing Street to urge shorter hours legislation upon the Prime Minister, W. E. Gladstone. Onions was one of four speakers chosen to put the case for the eight-hour day. In addition to the usual arguments then current Onions said: 'Another reason I think why the Legislature should step in is because in those districts where the short hours are worked, generally speaking again, there is not the loss of life from working per man employed, or per thousand men employed, or per thousand tons of minerals raised, as in those districts where the long hours are in existence.'

In 1898 Onions was appointed agent for the Sirhowy Valley. During the 1898 strike, which marked the beginning of the end of the sliding-scale tradition in South Wales, Onions was responsible for the collection and distribution of strike funds amounting to

£120,000. The aftermath of the strike led to the formation of the South Wales Miners' Federation (Onions being elected treasurer) and to the entry of the SWMF into the MFGB. Onions held the position of treasurer until his death. He was a member of the Conciliation Board formed in 1903 when the sliding-scale method of wage payment was discontinued. He was one of the moderate Welsh leaders who represented the South Wales miners on the MFGB executive from 1904 to 1910; during this time he was actively concerned in the campaign against a proposed export tax on coal and was one of three (the others being William Straker and John Weir) who presented the miners' case to the Chancellor of the Exchequer. Along with William Brace and Tom Richards, however, he lost his seat on the MFGB executive in 1911 when the miners' dissatisfaction with the handling of the Cambrian Miners' dispute and lock-out of 1910–11 was reflected in the election of more militant leaders.

Apart from his work for the miners, which included giving evidence before the R.C. on Labour in 1891 and the Inquiry into the Senghenydd Colliery disaster in 1914, Onions played an active part in local affairs. A member of two school boards – that of Mynyddyslwyn in 1888 and Bedwellty in 1899 – he was also first chairman of the Risca Urban District Council, a JP, a member of the Monmouth County Council for eighteen years, an alderman from 1919 and chairman of the Council. Finally he represented the Caerphilly Division of Glamorganshire as Labour MP from 1918 until his death at his Tredegar home on 5 July 1921. He had married Miss S. A. Dix, a miner's daughter, in 1887 and had two sons, one of whom was killed in action, and a daughter. His wife, a son and a daughter survived him. Following a service in Risca Methodist Church, he was buried in Risca Cemetery on 9 July. He left an estate valued at £3627 (gross).

Writings: Evidence before R.C. on Labour 1892 XXXIV Qs 4958–5423; articles to the press.

Sources: *Dod* (1919) and (1921); *WWW* (1916–28); biographical information: Dr E. W. Evans. OBIT. *Times*, 7 July 1921; *Western Mail*, 7 July 1921.

JOYCE BELLAMY

See also: William ABRAHAM, for Welsh Mining Trade Unionism.

PARE, William (1805–73)
OWENITE

Born in 1805 in Birmingham, the son of John Pare, an upholsterer and cabinet-maker. He received his education at a local grammar school and was first apprenticed to his father but later engaged in business as a tobacco and cigar retailer. He became interested in politics in his teens, and continued his education at the Birmingham Mechanics' Institute when it opened in 1826; and within two years had become a convert to co-operation and to Owenism, largely through reading William Thompson's *An Inquiry into the Principles of the Distribution of Wealth most Conducive to Human Happiness*. The practical example of Dr William King of Brighton encouraged Pare to form the first co-operative society at Birmingham in November 1828. A journal, the *Birmingham Co-operative Herald*, was published between April 1829 and October 1830 with Pare as editor; and this marks the beginning of a lifelong involvement as an Owenite propagandist within the co-operative movement.

He undertook the first of a number of Owenite missionary speaking tours in 1830 and in May of the same year he attended the first of the Co-operative Congresses, being present at all the succeeding ones. After the opening of the London National Equitable Labour Exchange in September 1832, the leading Owenites in Birmingham – William Pare, William Hawkes Smith and John Rabone – agreed to establish a similar exchange in their own city; and they succeeded in interesting Thomas Attwood, of the Political Union, and G. F. Muntz. Robert Owen came to Birmingham on a very successful visit in November 1832 and to prepare the ground, Pare distributed 10,000 leaflets explaining the principles involved. The *Birmingham Labour Exchange Gazette*, a short-lived journal, appeared in January 1833, but the Labour Exchange did not open its doors until July 1833. Reports of its activities by Charles West, the secretary, appeared at intervals in the *Crisis*, but turnover was on a more modest scale than the London Labour Exchange; and the Birmingham Exchange closed down in the early summer of 1834. Pare in later years provided a typically Owenite analysis of the experiment: which did not end because of 'any inherent defect in the principle' but because 'those who availed themselves of it were too ignorant, too selfish, too dishonest; added to which the whole forces of a vast erroneous system were against us'.

Pare's commitment to Owenite socialism in no way inhibited his business and professional career, nor did it interfere with other political and social activities. As a young man he joined in the agitation for the repeal of the Test and Corporation Acts and for Catholic emancipation. He joined the Birmingham Political Union when it was founded in 1829 and became a member of its council, advocating an extension of the suffrage, vote by ballot and shorter parliaments. He became secretary of the Reformers' Registration Society when it was established in 1835, and was elected to the first town council in 1838. After the passing of the Births, Deaths and Marriages Act of 1837 he became the first registrar in Birmingham, a position that was later to be the subject of violent attack. He was elected Poor Law Guardian and was active in the campaign against church rates.

Throughout the 1830s Pare was centrally involved in the activities of the Owenite movement. He paid a few days' visit to the Co-operative agricultural community at Ralahine and nearly three decades later, in 1870, he was to publish his account of Ralahine – *Co-operative Agriculture: A Solution to the Land Question* – at a time when the problems of rural society, in England as well as Ireland, were well to the front in the public mind. William Thompson died in 1833 and Pare was a trustee of the estate which Thompson intended to be used to assist in founding communities; a trust which involved Pare in a long and in the end unsuc-

cessful legal struggle with relatives who contested the will.

When Owen established *The New Moral World* in 1834 as the successor to the *Crisis* Pare was active in many departments of the journal's life. He was a member of the Birmingham branch of the National Community Friendly Society and in 1838 he became vice-president of the Central Board which co-ordinated the work of the NCFS and the Association of All Classes of All Nations (founded 1835). These two bodies were amalgamated in May 1839 to form the Universal Community Society of Rational Religionists (UCSRR); and it was Pare's leading position in the national Owenite movement that brought upon him the Bishop of Exeter's much publicised attack in the House of Lords in January–February 1840.

The closing years of the 1830s witnessed a growing awareness by many conservative and religious individuals and groups of Owenite doctrines and organisation. The Owenite involvement with the working-class movement, especially the trade unions, had already ended, and public opinion was now alarmed at what was regarded as an organised movement concerned with subverting organised religion. From about 1837 on, a number of religious champions went about the country delivering lectures against the atheistical Owenites, and debating with any who would accept their challenge; and from their side, a number of leading Owenites, as well as Robert Owen himself, were equally willing to expound their ideas. The attack upon the irreligion of the movement intensified as a result of the House of Lords debates and it undoubtedly helped to encourage the spate of blasphemy prosecutions in the first half of the 1840s. Pare, who had been mentioned by name, indeed specially singled out by the Bishop of Exeter in January 1840, tendered his resignation as the Birmingham registrar.

He left Birmingham in November 1842, being presented with a public testimonial, and for the next two years he was acting governor of the Harmony Hall community at Queenwood, Hampshire. He remained there until the 1844 annual congress voted John Buxton as governor, and Pare then returned to his business affairs. From 1844 to 1846 he lived in London, being frequently employed as a statistician in railway promotion work, and then in 1846 he removed to Dublin where he bought and managed the Seville ironworks. His work for the Owenite movement continued; he played a major part in settling the quarrels of the Queenwood community, and for many years after Pare tried to achieve a reasonable settlement of its affairs. Eventually, he had to bring an action in the Courts in 1861 in order to compel the trustees to publish the full accounts.

He remained close to Robert Owen until the latter's death in 1858, and Owen named Pare as his literary executor. At the time of Pare's own death he was still working on his life of Owen, on which he had been engaged for many years. In the last quarter-century of his life Pare hardly changed his basic ideas: and in this he was similar to Henry Travis, another Owenite who also lived on into a period of history quite different from that of the early beginnings of the movement. Pare continued to lecture before academic and business as well as popular audiences and he wrote widely. His *Equitable Commerce, or Cost the Limit of Price*, which was read before the British Association in 1855, explained and defended the principles of Owen's labour exchanges. He published a fair amount in Henry Pitman's *Co-operator* and to the end of his life he argued for a return to the principles of Owen, and away from co-operative shopkeeping. He moved from Dublin to London in 1866, helped establish a co-operative ironworks in Norway in 1868 and in the following year became the secretary of the committee which convened the first modern Co-operative Congress in 1869. He acted as the first secretary to the Central Co-operative Board (later the Co-operative Union) and remained as fertile in ideas as always: advocating co-operative banking, insurance and newspapers and laying especial emphasis upon his lifelong advocacy of a co-operative educational college for the young. He presided at the Owen centenary celebrations in 1871.

William Pare was a man of equable temperament, wholly disinterested and utterly dedicated to the ideals he had accepted as a young man. In a movement which inevitably attracted its full share of fanatics and cranks he was notable for his common sense and reasonableness.

His health deteriorated seriously during 1872 and he died, after a long illness, on 18 June 1873 at the house of his son in Croydon; and was buried in Shirley Churchyard. He had married Ann Oakes, of Market Drayton, Shropshire, who died in 1886, and there were one son and two daughters of the marriage. His effects were valued at under £14,000.

Writings: *An Address delivered at the Opening of the Birmingham Co-operative Society, November 17, 1828, by a Member. To which is added the Laws of the Society* (Birmingham, [1828]); *An Address to the Working Classes of Liverpool, on the Formation of Co-operative Societies or Working Unions* [1829] n.p.; *A Full and authentic Report of the Great Catholic Meeting, which took place in the Town Hall, Birmingham . . . November the 23rd, 1835* (Birmingham, [1835]); Preface to the second edition of William Thompson, *An Inquiry into the Principles of the Distribution of Wealth most Conducive to Human Happiness* (1850; 1st ed. 1824); *The Claims of Capital and Labour: with a sketch of practical measures for their conciliation. A paper read before the Dublin Statistical Society* (1854); *Equitable Commerce, as practised in the Equity Villages of the United States . . .* (1856; reprinted from the Journal of the Statistical Society, June 1856); *A Plan for the Suppression of the Predatory Classes: a paper read before the Third Department of the 'National Association for the Promotion of Social Science', London Meeting, 1862 . . . reprinted . . . with additional matter from the volume of 'Transactions of the Association'* (1862); *Co-operative Agriculture: a solution of the Land Question, as exemplified in the history of the Ralahine Co-operative Agricultural Association, County Clare, Ireland* (1870).

Sources: The *DNB* has an article by W. A. S. Hewins who was given family information by Pare's son. There is a modern account by R. G. Garnett, *Co-op. Rev.* (May 1964) 145–9, and see the same author's *The Ideology of the Early Co-operative Movement* (University of Kent, 1966) 18 pp. The most comprehensive source book for Owenism in all its aspects is J. F. C. Harrison, *Robert Owen and the Owenites in Britain and America* (1969). See also: Hansard, Commons 3rd ser. vol. *51*, 6 Feb 1840 col. 1342ff; *Report of Festival in Commemoration of the Centenary Birthday of Robert Owen* . . . (London, 1871); G. J. Holyoake, *The History of Co-operation* (1st ed. 1875 and 1879; many later editions); F. Podmore, *Robert Owen*, 2 vols (1906); *Dictionary of Political Economy* (ed. Palgrave, 1908) s.v. Pare, William; G. D. H. Cole, *A Century of Co-operation* (Manchester, [1945?]); R. K. P. Pankhurst, *William Thompson, 1775–1833* (1954). OBIT. *Co-op. News*, 5 July and 19 Aug 1873.

JOHN SAVILLE

See also: E. T. CRAIG; John FINCH; E. O. GREENING; *Thomas HUGHES; *William THOMPSON; Henry TRAVIS.

PARKINSON, Tom Bamford (1865–1939)
TRADE UNIONIST AND CO-OPERATOR

Born at Rochdale on 9 June 1865, the son of Thomas Parkinson, an engineer, he was apprenticed to the engineering firm of John Petrie on leaving school. After finishing his time, he visited America on two separate occasions, and then came back to his home town where he worked at his trade. He joined the Rochdale branch of the ASE in August 1891, became local secretary in 1901 and Rochdale district secretary in 1912. In 1917 this position was made full-time and Parkinson continued as district secretary until the end of 1931. He became a superannuated member of the AEU on 11 January 1932.

During the First World War he was appointed to the armaments committee in Manchester and later, when the Rochdale munitions committee was set up, he was co-opted upon it, and served until the war ended. He was a member of the local Court of Referees, set up under the Unemployment Insurance Act, and he was also a member for many years of the local employment committee; of this body he acted as chairman for three or four years.

He had a long association with the co-operative movement both locally and nationally. With the exception of one break of three months he was a member of the board of management of the Rochdale Pioneers' Society for twenty-eight years. He served two periods of office as president of the society, the second period being from 1928 until late in 1938 when he retired under the age-limit for membership of the board. During his presidency the merging of the Pioneers' Society and the Provident Society took place. He acted as secretary of the Rochdale District Association, secretary of the Rochdale and District Co-operative Hours and Wages Board, and represented the wages board on the sectional council. He was a member of the north-western sectional board from 1929 and a member of the central board of the Co-operative Union, the latter position involving membership of many important national committees of the union. In 1931 he was elected the sectional board's representative on the Co-operative Party national committee and was still a member of that committee at the time of his death.

Parkinson made four unsuccessful attempts to enter the Rochdale town council as a Labour member, in 1919, 1923, 1926 and 1927. He was appointed JP in 1920. He died on 3 February 1939, and was survived by his wife, son and daughter. He left an estate valued at £1372.

Sources: J. B. Jefferys, *The Story of the Engineers 1800–1945* [1945]; personal information: Amalgamated Union of Engineering and Foundry Workers. OBIT. *Rochdale Observer*, 4 Feb 1939; *Co-op. News*, 11 Feb 1939; *Co-op. Congress Report* (1939).
H. F. BING
JOHN SAVILLE

See also: Fred HAYWARD, for Co-operative Union.

PATTERSON, William Hammond (1847–96)
MINERS' LEADER

Born on 14 February 1847 at Durham, the son of Thomas Patterson, a quarryman. Little is known of his early life but one report speaks of him as a local preacher at the age of sixteen for the Methodist New Connexion. About 1864 or 1865 he encouraged the miners at Heworth Colliery to form a union lodge of which he became secretary. He was in the chair at the great meeting on 25 September 1869 at which the decision was taken to establish a separate organisation for Durham miners, and he helped to draw up its rules and regulations. He became a member of the first executive of the DMA and on 4 June 1870 was appointed agent for South-west Durham. Later in the same year, on 3 December, he was made vice-president. On 6 December 1878 Patterson was elected a member of the first County Mining Federation Board; and for some years he represented the DMA on the General Arrangement Committee of the TUC. He gave evidence before the Royal Commission on Labour in 1891. From 1872 to 1890 he served as financial secretary, and on the death of William Crawford, with whom he had been closely associated for many years, he became general secretary of the DMA, and retained the position until his death.

Patterson was a radical in politics: in 1884 he was elected to the Durham School Board; and from 1889 to 1892 he represented Tanfield on the Durham County Council. In 1892 he was made an alderman. In 1874 he had been appointed a member of the management committee of the co-operative company set up to run Monkwood Colliery [for which see Benjamin Jones, *Co-operative Production*]. Patterson was always interested in education for the miners and did much work in connection with the Durham Mechanics' Institute. He was also, like Crawford, a prominent Freemason.

In most respects he was a lesser man than Crawford, under whose shadow he had worked for many years. His main and important contribution to the union in its formative years was to help establish it on a sound basis of organisation and financial stability. He died on 16 July 1896.

Sources: Evidence before R.C. on Labour 1892 XXXIV Qs 1–383; B. Jones, *Co-operative Production*, 2 vols (1894: reprinted New York, 1968); J. Wilson, *A History of the Dur-*

ham *Miners' Association, 1870–1904* (1907); E. Welbourne, *The Miners' Union of Northumberland and Durham* (Cambridge, 1923); R. F. Wearmouth, *The Social and Political Influence of Methodism in the Twentieth Century* (1957). OBIT. *Durham County Advertiser,* 17 and 24 July 1896.

ANTHONY MASON

See also: Thomas BURT; William CRAWFORD; John FORMAN; Alexander MACDONALD, for Mining Trade Unionism, 1850–79; Benjamin PICKARD, for Mining Trade Unionism, 1880–99; J. H. RUTHERFORD.

PATTISON, Lewis (1873–1956)
CO-OPERATOR AND LABOUR PARTY WORKER

Born at Laisterdyke, Bradford, Yorkshire, on 17 February 1873, son of Stephen and Mary Pattison, his father being a plate roller at the Bowling Iron Works in Bradford. Lewis attended an elementary school until the age of ten. He then became a half-timer, working alternate weeks in the mornings from 6.30 am to 12.30 pm and in the afternoons from 1.10 pm to 5.40 pm, the remainder of each week being spent at school, until at thirteen he began full-time work. His earnings were six shillings and sixpence per week, and becoming dissatisfied with factory work he took employment in 1888 with the Bradford Co-operative Society. In 1894 he started a butchery business of his own to assist the family since his father had died in 1890. He was, however, anxious to get back into the co-operative movement and in 1895 accepted the post of first provision hand with the Twerton Co-operative Society near Bath. In 1897 he was appointed manager of the Stoke-on-Trent Co-operative Society and later in the same year transferred to Walsall Co-operative Society as general manager. In 1911 he was appointed general manager of Long Eaton Co-operative Society, Derbyshire, and under a rearrangement of offices in 1928 became general manager and secretary until he retired in 1938.

At Long Eaton, Pattison pursued a vigorous policy of expansion and modernisation of premises, together with a consolidation of assets which very greatly increased the Society's trade and influence. It was largely due to his personal effort that the Society successfully weathered the storms of the First World War. In addition to being an efficient manager and organiser, Pattison was a forceful speaker on co-operative platforms and had a remarkable record as a teacher of classes in management and salesmanship under the auspices of the Co-operative Union in different parts of the country. He himself held first-class certificates in book-keeping, co-operation and general management, and was said to have trained more men in the co-operative movement in the Midlands than any other man, many of his pupils going on to hold positions of high responsibility. Positions he himself held in the co-operative movement included those of chairman of the National Co-operative Milk Retailers' Federation, and member of executive of the National Union of Co-operative Officials.

The co-operative movement did not absorb the whole of Pattison's energies, and he devoted a considerable part of his leisure time to serving the community in religious, public and social activities. In 1927 he was elected to the Shardlow Board of Guardians. Subsequently he became chairman of Long Eaton School managers, a member of the Derbyshire County Education Committee and of the South East Derbyshire Divisional Executive, and a member of the Trent River Catchment Board. From 1933 to 1948 he was a Labour member of the Long Eaton Urban District Council and its chairman in 1942-3. He was appointed a JP in 1935. From 1939 to 1952 he was a member of the Derbyshire County Council and during the Second World War acted as an honorary fuel overseer for Long Eaton and district.

Lewis Pattison was a Methodist and had always taken an interest in religious work. In his early youth he joined the Ebenezer Church, Bradford, and during his stay in Walsall from 1897 to 1911 was a member of the Stafford Street Wesleyan Chapel. At Long Eaton he was connected with the Central Methodist Church where he was both a teacher and a trustee. He died in Long Eaton on 24 February 1956. His wife, formerly Sarah Elizabeth Marsden, whom he

had married in 1897, predeceased him in 1948 but he was survived by four sons. He left an estate valued at £10,549.

Sources: G. R. Lane and R. Bowley, *Through Six Decades: The story of co-operation in Long Eaton and District 1868-1928* (Manchester, 1929); F. Hall, *From Acorn to Oak being the History of the Walsall and District Co-operative Society Limited 1886-1936* (Birmingham, 1936); G. Kingscott, *A Centenary History 1868-1968* (Long Eaton Co-operative Society Ltd) (Nottingham [1968]); personal information: A. E. Pattison, of Long Eaton, son.

H. F. BING

See also: W. H. BROWN, for Retail Co-operation, 1900-45; Fred HAYWARD, for Co-operative Union.

PENNY, John (1870-1938)
CO-OPERATOR AND SOCIALIST

Born at Preston on 30 October 1870, the son of Daniel Penny, a coachbuilder, John Penny grew up in an atmosphere highly charged with the spirit of reform and social progress. He became a pupil teacher in a Wesleyan day school at the age of fourteen and secured the necessary qualifications to become headmaster of an elementary school in that town. In 1892 he took part in the formation of a Fabian Society in Preston. This was soon transformed into a branch of the newly constituted Independent Labour Party, of which Penny became the secretary and later on secretary of the Lancashire and Cheshire Federation of that party. Also in 1892, in spite of the opposition of his parents who were private traders in the town, he joined the Co-operative Society in Preston.

In 1892 he left the teaching profession to become editor of the *Preston Advertiser* and three years later was invited to become assistant secretary of the ILP with Tom Mann as general secretary. Penny became national secretary of the ILP when Mann resigned at the 1898 Conference, and he retained this position until 1903 when he resigned for personal reasons. His appointment to the secretaryship involved removal to London and in his new work he met Miss

Edna Frank whom he married and who later became well known in co-operative circles as Mrs E. M. Penny, secretary of the National Guild of Co-operators. (The Guild was formed in 1926, its object being 'to provide a meeting ground for all men and women interested in the working and development of the co-operative movement, irrespective of class or sex' [Carr-Saunders et al. (1938) 240].) In his political work Penny acquired that clear, lucid speech and power of logical argument which stood him in such good stead in many circumstances. He had an easy manner and would face any amount of heckling with cheerful and friendly calm.

Although his main interest at this time was in politics he found time for co-operative work. London was at that time a backward co-operative area and in 1898 his London home was used as a store in an unsuccessful attempt to launch a co-operative society. His great achievement from a co-operative point of view, however, was his part in the formation of the Planet Friendly Society in 1905. For a time he acted as voluntary organiser and appointed agents in various parts of the country. Subsequently he acted as superintendent of the Sheffield district of the society and later district manager. He played a big part in the negotiations which merged the Planet Society with the Co-operative Insurance Society, a move which cleared the way for the considerable growth of co-operative insurance after the First World War.

Penny moved to Sheffield in 1908 and at once joined the Sheffield and Ecclesall Co-operative Society. In 1909 he was elected to its board of management and remained a member, with one short interval, until 1924 when owing to his duties as a CWS director he decided not to seek re-election. He was a member of the building sub-committee which was responsible for much of the detailed work in connection with the erection of the new central arcade premises (1913); and he was elected at the top of the poll for the Manchester district on the special committee of inquiry appointed to consider a pensions scheme for co-operative employees, 1919.

In 1921 Penny was elected to the board of the Co-operative Wholesale Society and continued a member until his sudden death in 1938. He was an advocate of the centralisation and modernisation of CWS furniture manufacture in 1934. In 1935 he became chairman of the drapery committee of the board of which he had been a member since his election. He was the senior member of the board at the time of his death. He also took a great interest in the National Co-operative Men's Guild. He was a member of its central council for eighteen years (1918–36) and national chairman in 1928. He died suddenly on 9 January 1938 and was cremated at Leeds Crematorium on 12 January 1938. He left an estate valued at £6406.

Writings: *The Political Labour Movement* (Clarion Pamphlet no. 41, [1904?]); *Collective Buying: Co-operative methods and their relation to income tax* (1920) 8 pp.

Sources: W. Rose, *History of the Sheffield and Ecclesall Co-operative Society Ltd, 1874–1913* (Sheffield, 1913); A. M. Carr-Saunders et al., *Consumers' Co-operation in Great Britain* (1938); P. Redfern, *The New History of the C.W.S.* (Manchester, 1938); H. Pelling, *The Origins of the Labour Party* (2nd ed. Oxford, 1965); R. G. Garnett, *A Century of Co-operative Insurance* (1968); personal information: Secretary, Sheffield and Ecclesall Co-operative Society.

H. F. BING

See also: W. H. BROWN, for Retail Co-operation, 1900–45; *F. W. JOWETT, for Independent Labour Party, 1893–1914; T. W. MERCER.

PERKINS, George Leydon (1885–1961)
TRADE UNIONIST, CO-OPERATOR AND LABOUR PARTY WORKER

George Perkins was born at Kingsweston, Bath, on 30 December 1885, the son of Mark Thomas Perkins, a coachman and farmworker, and his wife Honorah Leydon. He was educated at the village school at Leonard Stanley, Gloucestershire, and joined the clerical staff of the Midland Railway in Bristol in 1899. His working life was spent in the service of the railway company – subsequently in the capacity of a commercial representative – until his retirement in 1946. He became an active trade unionist when he joined the Railway Clerks' Association in the early 1900s, holding various offices such as branch secretary and chairman, divisional council officer, and Midland Railway sectional councillor. He played a prominent role at annual conferences of the Association and served on the national executive of the RCA from 1916–22. Apart from his work for the RCA he was well known as a pioneer of the labour movement in Bristol. He had attended the same adult school in Bristol as Ernest Bevin and worked with him to establish the Bristol Trades Council on a sound footing. Bevin, who was chairman of the Trades Council, brought in the dockers and general workers and Perkins, who served as the Council's secretary, brought in the railwaymen. He also served on the Bristol City Council as a Labour Party representative for the Bedminster East ward when he won the seat from the Liberals on 1 November 1920. During his term of office, which lasted until his resignation two years later, he served on several of the Council's committees: Estates and General Purposes, Libraries, Small Holdings and Allotments, City Lands and Tramways. His contemporaries in Bristol remember him as a very able and popular man and describe him as 'an old type trade union leader'.

In 1922 he left Bristol for Winchester where he continued to work for the railway and began to play an active role in the local co-operative movement. He joined the Winchester and District Industrial Co-operative Society and was a regular attender at the Society's quarterly meetings. His constructive abilities were recognised by his election to the management committee and in 1929 he was elected by the societies in the southern section to the central board of the Co-operative Union. He was a member of the southern sectional board from 1929 to 1953 and served for a time as its chairman. In 1944 he was chairman of the Co-operative Union's central executive and in 1947

reached the highest position in the co-operative movement when he was elected president of the Brighton Congress. Other co-operative service included membership of the District Association, the District Hours and Wages Board and the chairmanship of the National Co-operative Laundry Trade Association in which he helped to develop the co-operative laundry industry on federal lines. He served for a time on the central committee of the International Co-operative Alliance visiting, immediately after the Second World War, Norway, Czechoslovakia, Yugoslavia (where he met President Tito), Switzerland, France and Poland; he also visited Iceland and Sweden. He collaborated with Lord Rusholme, former secretary of the Co-operative Union, in ICA work.

Apart from his trade union and co-operative interests, Perkins was well known in Freemasonry circles as a member of the Caer Gwent Lodge; he had been chairman and secretary of the Winchester Allotment Holders' Society and in his later years he was active in the Old Age Pensioners' Association. When the gas industry was nationalised in 1949, he was elected a part-time member of the Southern Area Gas Board. An Anglican by religion, he served on the parochial council of St Luke's Church, Winchester, where for some years he was vicar's warden. He died at his home, 60 Cromwell Road, Winchester, on 21 May 1961. Following a funeral service at St Luke's, Winchester, he was cremated at Southampton on 24 May. He was survived by his wife, formerly Miss Alice Workman of Dursley, Gloucestershire, whom he married in 1909, and by two sons and a daughter. He left effects valued at £1085.

Writings: 'The Co-operative Union's Future Services', *People's Year Book* (1945) 20–4.

Sources: *Railway Service Journal* (Mar 1946); *Co-op. Congress Report* (1947); W. H. Brown, *Winchester's Co-operative Golden Jubilee: 1900–1950* (Winchester, 1950); biographical information: Bristol City Library; personal information: Miss I. Lobb and Ald. J. Knight, Bristol; G. M. H. Morris (formerly of TSSA) and H. G. Perkins, Winchester,

son. OBIT. *Hampshire Chronicle*, 27 May 1961;
Co-op. News, 3 June 1961.

JOYCE BELLAMY
H. F. BING

See also: W. H. BROWN, for Retail Co-
operation; Fred HAYWARD, for Co-operative
Union; *George LANSBURY, for British
Labour Party, 1900–13; H. J. MAY, for
International Co-operative Alliance.

PICKARD, Benjamin (1842–1904)
MINERS' LEADER AND LIB-LAB MP

Ben Pickard was the eldest son of Thomas
Pickard, a miner. He was born on 28
February 1842 at Kippax, Yorkshire, and
was educated up to the age of twelve at
Kippax Grammar School; he then began
work as a 'hurrier' in the pit. He became
active in mining trade unionism early in life
and was secretary of his local lodge when he
was eighteen. In 1873 he was elected assistant secretary of the West Yorkshire Miners'
Association and secretary in 1876, and was
the main architect of the establishment of
the Yorkshire Miners' Federation in 1881.
By the 1870s he was already well known in
the British coalfields, becoming by 1877 vice-
president of the Miners' National Union;
the president of which was Alexander
Macdonald.

Pickard was a man of the most stubborn
and pugnacious character, an extremely
skilled negotiator, and utterly dedicated to
the cause of mining trade unionism. He was
a strict Protestant belonging to the Wesleyan
sect, a firm supporter of the Lord's Rest Day
Association and for the greater part of his
life a rigid teetotaller and non-smoker. He
was an aloof and rather distant personality,
known to his contemporaries and later
generations of miners as the 'iron man'.

His outstanding achievement was the
successful establishment of the Miners'
Federation of Great Britain in 1889, the first
fully effective national organisation. Mining
trade unionism during the years of falling
prices from the middle 1870s had experienced
marked fluctuations and although most coalfields maintained some organisation, membership was often only a fraction of the total

of working miners. Towards the end of the
1880s the vigorous economic boom which
then developed brought with it rising prices
for coal. Between 1851, when export duties
on coal were abolished, and 1901, when they
were reimposed (for six years), declared
values at the ports fluctuated for over thirty
years, touching their zenith of 20s 6d in 1873,
and by 1887 reaching their nadir of 8s 2d a
ton. Average price per ton at the pithead
rose from 4s 10d in 1886 and 1887, to 5s 1d in
1888, to 6s 4d in 1889 and 8s 3d in 1890. To
this the miners responded with demands
for higher wages. During 1888 demands for
wage increases and strikes were common
throughout all the mining areas and, out of
the national conferences which were called
to organise concerted action, there emerged
the strong belief that a closer grouping of
the county unions was both desirable and
possible. During late 1888 and through 1889
a series of conferences were held and in
November 1889, at a conference at Newport,
there emerged the Miners' Federation of
Great Britain. Pickard was the dominant
personality at the Conference and he was
elected president, a position he held
until his death. Other officials appointed
were Sam Woods, vice-president, Enoch
Edwards, treasurer, and Thomas Ashton,
secretary.

The dominating question in the early
years of the Miners' Federation was the
eight-hour day. The matter was already
being widely discussed in the trade union
and labour movement. At the Trades Union
Congress of 1887 Keir Hardie had strongly
attacked Henry Broadhurst for the latter's
speech and vote against the eight-hour
principle in the House of Commons. Hardie
at this time failed to win any substantial
support, and the liberal-minded members
of the parliamentary committee of the Trades
Union Congress were vigorously opposed to
State legislation on this question. The
miners' leaders were in a rather odd position.
They too were liberal in outlook and were
against *general* legislation establishing the
eight-hour day, but they regarded their own
industry as a special and exceptional case.
The districts of Durham and Northumberland were, however, in opposition. John

Wilson and Thomas Burt, the leaders respectively of these two areas, fought inside the trade union movement as well as within the House of Commons against the eight-hour day principle, believing that all matters relating to wages and conditions of work must be left to the unions themselves bargaining with their employers. They were further supported in their opposition to a statutory eight-hour day by the fact that the hours of work for adults in the north-eastern coalfields had already been reduced to seven in 1890.

Pickard was also active in the formation of an International Federation of Mineworkers. The first coming together of miners in Western Europe was at Jolimont, in Belgium, in May 1890. Among those who attended from Britain was Keir Hardie. Because of the rivalry in the British delegation between the Federation and Durham and Northumberland it was agreed that Pickard and Burt should preside on alternate days. When the issue of the eight-hour day was discussed, Burt and his group were easily voted down. The second international conference was held at the end of March 1891 in Paris; the third in June 1892 in London; and the fourth in May 1893 in Brussels. With this fourth Conference the International Federation of Miners was formally established and it had accepted the eight-hour day as one of its central aims. In all the work of the International Federation Pickard had taken a leading part.

At home the first severe test of the Miners' Federation came in 1893 when most of the central coalfields of England were involved in a great strike and lock-out between July and November. It was ended by the direct intervention of the Liberal Government and one of its consequences was the establishment of the Miners' Conciliation Board. Pickard had led the executive throughout and its successful conclusion further strengthened his already powerful hold over the affairs of the Federation. The success of the Federation in general, moreover, led to an important shift in the balance of forces within the Trades Union Congress. Ned Cowey displaced John Wilson, the opponent of the eight-hour principle, from the par-

liamentary committee of the Trades Union Congress in 1893, and the next year Sam Woods, the vice-president of the Federation, became secretary of the parliamentary committee of the TUC in place of Charles Fenwick. Henceforth, therefore, Pickard and his colleagues were at the centre of power in the whole movement.

Although often uncompromising in trade union affairs, Pickard was always a Liberal in politics. He was elected on the Liberal ticket for the mining constituency of Normanton in 1885, he vigorously opposed socialist candidates standing against Liberals in parliamentary elections, and he was highly dubious about the usefulness of the Labour Representation Committee. The most bitter episode in this context was the Barnsley by-election in the autumn of 1897, when Pete Curran stood as ILP candidate in opposition to the Liberal candidate who was supported by Pickard, Cowey and other Yorkshire leaders. Like most Lib-Labs, however, Pickard was firm in support of the need for more working-class representations in the House of Commons and he was in full support of the Miners' Federation in 1901 when a Labour Election Fund was created. What he did not encourage was political independence from the Liberal Party.

Pickard was not a success as an MP: it was the Miners' Union that was at the centre of his interests. He did, however, play an active part in local affairs, being elected to the Wakefield School Board in 1881 and an alderman of the West Riding CC in 1889. He married in 1864.

Pickard died on 3 February 1904, in London, after giving evidence to a Board of Trade inquiry into the Denaby Main strike. His body was brought back to Yorkshire and he was buried in Barnsley Cemetery. He left an estate valued at £2019 (net). He had fought valiantly for the Miners' Federation of Great Britain, and he had sustained and encouraged the International Federation. His whole being was centred in the coalfields. The best epitaph on his life and work is his own words, spoken a few months before his death: 'I have to confess to you I love this Federation of Miners more than any one man I know.'

Writings: *Organisation and Co-operation* (n.d.); *Biography of the late John Dixon, Miners' Secretary* (n.d.); speeches in *Hansard* (1885–1903) *passim*.

Sources: *Dod* (1886); W. Hallam, *Miners' Leaders* (1894) [with portrait]; *WW* (1897); A. E. P. Duffy, 'The Growth of Trade Unionism in England from 1867 to 1906 in its Political Aspects' (London PhD, 1956); F. Machin, *The Yorkshire Miners: a history*, vol. *1* (Barnsley, 1958). OBIT. *Times*, 4 Feb 1904.

JOHN SAVILLE

See also: William ABRAHAM, for Welsh Mining Trade Unionism; Thomas ASHTON, for Mining Trade Unionism, 1900–14; T. BURT; E. COWEY; C. FENWICK; Alexander MACDONALD, for Mining Trade Unionism, 1850–79; *Robert SMILLIE, for Scottish Mining Trade Unionism; and below: Mining Trade Unionism, 1880–99.

Mining Trade Unionism, 1880–99: Miners' National Conference, *Proceedings of a Conference of the Miners of the UK ... Birmingham ... 1885* (1885) 15 pp.; T. Mann, *What a Compulsory Eight Hour Day means to the Workers* (1886); J. Young, *The Organisation of Labour with Special Reference to the Mining Industry* (Newmilns, 1886) 16 pp.; S. Woods, *Visions of the Mine: sketches of real life at our collieries* (Wigan, 1891); R.C. on Labour (1891–4) *passim*; R. N. Boyd, *Coal Pits and Pitmen* (1892); M. Gilbert-Boucher, *Étude sur les 'Trade-Unions'. Un député ouvrier Anglais* (Paris, 1892); F. B. Jevons, 'The Strike of the Durham Miners', *Econ. Rev. 2* (Apr 1892) 251–2; J. W. Cunliffe, 'Modern Industrial Warfare', *West. Rev. 140* (Aug 1893) 109–14; Durham Miners' Association, *Joint Committee Decisions, Agreements, Awards, Reports, Practices, Rules etc.*, 1875–98 (Durham, 1893); C. Edwards, 'The Lock-out in the Coal Trade', *Econ. J. 3* (Dec 1893) 650–7; I. S. Jeans, 'The Coal Crisis and the Paralysis of British Industry', *19th C. 34* (Nov 1893) 791–801; V. Nash, 'The Lock-out in the Coal Trade', *Fortn. Rev. 60* (Nov 1893) 604–15; S. Olivier, 'The Miners' Battle – and after', *Cont. Rev. 64* (Nov 1893) 749–64; C. M. Percy, 'Coal

Dispute of 1893: its history, policy and warnings', *Econ. J. 3* (Dec 1893) 644–9; J. Rae, 'The Eight Hour Movement in England', *Social Econ. 4* (May 1893) 267–76; H. H. L. Bellot, 'The Coal Question and the Nationalisation of Mines', *West. Rev. 141* (1893–4) 117–25; T. Ashton, *Three Big Strikes in the Coal Industry* (Manchester, [1894?]); E. Bainbridge, 'The Coal Strike of 1893', *Cont. Rev. 65* (Jan 1894) 1–15; J. Chadburn, 'The Coal War: Lancashire', *Econ. Rev. 4* (Jan 1894) 80–6; R. N. Grier, 'The Coal War: Cannock Chase', *Econ. Rev. 4* (Jan 1894) 68–79; W. Hallam, *Miners' Leaders: thirty portraits and biographical sketches* (1894); R. H. Hooker, 'On the Relation between Wages and the Numbers employed in the Coal Mining Industry', *J.R.S.S. 57* (1894) 627–42; T. Horne, *'Victimised': a story of pit village life in South Yorkshire* (Rotherham, 1894) 32 pp.; F. D. Longe, 'The Coal Strike and a Minimum Wage', *Econ. J. 4* (Mar 1894) 25–34; J. E. C. Munro, 'Some Economic Aspects of the Coal Dispute, 1893', *Econ. J.* (Mar 1894) 14–24; W. T. Thomson, 'The Miners' Eight Hour Question', *West. Rev. 141* (June 1894) 593–600; T. R. Threlfall, 'The Political Future of Labour', *19th C. 35* (Feb 1894) 203–16; S. and B. Webb, *The History of Trade Unionism* (1894: revised ed. 1920); K. Hardie, *A Word with our Collier Laddies* (Glasgow, [1895?]) 7 pp.; F. U. Lacock, *Good Trade and a Living Wage* (1896); A. Paddon, *The Coal-Miner's Heaven* (Wrexham, 1896) 21 pp.; P. de Rousiers, *The Labour Question in Britain* (1896); S. Fothergill, 'Trades Union Tactics in Relation to Law and Order: The Colliery Strikes of 1892–1893', *West. Rev. 149* (Jan 1898) 82–93; R. Page Arnot, *The Miners: a history of the Miners' Federation of Great Britain, 1889–1910* (1949); B. McCormick and J. E. Williams, 'The Miners and the Eight-Hour Day, 1863–1910', *Econ. Hist. Rev. 12* ser. 2 (1959–60) 222–37; A. J. Taylor, 'Labour Productivity and Technological Innovation in the British Coal Industry, 1850–1914', *Econ. Hist. Rev. 14* ser. 2 (1961–2) 48–70; J. E. Williams, *The Derbyshire Miners* (1962); A. R. Griffin, *Mining in the East Midlands 1550–1947* (1971).

PICKARD, William (1821-87)
MINERS' LEADER

Born on 10 February 1821, in the neighbourhood of Aspull Moor, near Wigan, and left fatherless when three years old. Pickard had little formal education and entered the mines at an early age in order to assist his mother and two younger children. He was unable to read or write at the time of his marriage to a pit-girl but he became involved in trade union activities and soon achieved a leading position in his own district. He was a delegate from the Wigan District Miners' Union to the 1863 Conference of the National Association of Coal, Lime and Ironstone Miners of Great Britain which was held in Leeds and was chosen as vice-president from the fifty-one delegates present. In the following year he was elected agent for the Wigan, Pemberton, Standish, Aspull and Blackrod Miners' Union and two years later he brought money from the National Association of Miners to assist Derbyshire Miners during a strike at Staveley. He gave evidence before the S.C. on the Regulation and Inspection of Mines and Miners' Complaints 1866, the R.C. on Trade Unions 1868 and the S.C. on Present Dearness and Scarcity of Coal 1873. He was involved in the formation of the short-lived Amalgamated Association of Miners (1869–75) (for which see Thomas HALLIDAY). At the nine-day conference at Swansea in April 1875, Pickard as treasurer, after the reading of a long letter to the conference from Alexander Macdonald, paid a tribute saying: 'Such a sensible and prudent letter showed Mr Macdonald to be in his right place in the House of Commons.' Pickard contested Wigan for the Labour Representation League at the parliamentary election of 1874 as one of five candidates, and came fourth with 1134 votes, immediately below the Liberal candidate who was also not elected.

Wigan became notorious for its mining accidents in the late 1860s and early 1870s, and Pickard became famous for his skill and courage in rescue work and for an unrivalled knowledge of mining problems. After the 1874 election Pickard remained active in the miners' cause and as a moderate social reformer. He was especially concerned with the problem of financial help to the dependants of miners killed in pit accidents. In 1885 he was appointed a borough magistrate, and in the following year was elected to the Board of Guardians, and soon after to the School Board. In his industrial activities he searched always for the decent compromise between employers and men. He remained agent for the Wigan miners until his death on 21 October 1887. His wife survived him and he left a personal estate of £4134.

In May 1887 there appeared a short sketch of Pickard in Keir Hardie's *The Miner*: 'In appearance Mr Pickard is the very *beau idéal* of the old English squire in song and story. A real John Bull cast of countenance without the ferocity so often attached thereto, a large fund of common sense, a fair delivery in speaking, and a considerable spice of humour. Such is the man.'

Sources: Evidence before the S.C. on the Regulation and Inspection of Mines and Miners' Complaints 1866 XIV Qs 1584–821, 1932–2422; R.C. on Trade Unions 1867–8 XXXIX Qs 12115–57, 15763–6091; S.C. on Coal 1873 X Qs 3966–4218; *Dod* (1874); R. P. Arnot, *The Miners* (1949); F. Machin, *The Yorkshire Miners* (Barnsley, 1958); J. E. Williams, *The Derbyshire Miners* (1962). OBIT. *Wigan Observer*, 22 Oct 1887.

JOYCE BELLAMY

See also: *Thomas HALLIDAY; Alexander MACDONALD, for Mining Trade Unionism, 1850–79.

PITMAN, Henry (1826-1909)
CO-OPERATOR AND SOCIAL REFORMER

Born at Trowbridge in 1826, Henry Pitman was the tenth and youngest child of Samuel and Maria Pitman. His father was first an overseer in a large weaving factory and later set up on his own. Henry's eldest brother was Isaac Pitman [s.v. *DNB 22*] the inventor of the system of shorthand that goes under the family name. Henry attended a nonconformist school at Wotton-under-Edge where Isaac was master, and from about his twentieth year Henry began lecturing on the Pitman system. As a shorthand writer he was to have few equals, and it was probably as a teacher of phonography that he became best known. (The 1st edition of Pitman's Shorthand was published in 1837; the 3rd and much improved edition of 1840 was entitled: *Phonography, or Writing by Sound, being also a new and Natural System of Short-hand.*)

From his early years Henry was a strict vegetarian and he reported the formation of the Vegetarian Society at Ramsgate in 1847; subsequently reporting every annual conference until the week or so before his death. He was also a strong supporter of temperance reform and for many years worked within the United Kingdom Alliance. About the year 1848 he moved to Manchester where for some time he was chief reporter on the *Manchester Examiner and Times* and for a brief period served also on the staff of the *Manchester Guardian*. In the late 1850s and early 1860s he edited *The Popular Lecturer*, an educational journal.

In 1860 *The Co-operator* was launched to provide a discussion platform for the movement. Its first editor was E. Longfield but after nine months Henry Pitman took it over, including its liabilities, and he continued to edit the journal until its demise. *The Co-operator* has an honoured place in the history of co-operative journalism, and it was in its correspondence columns that William Pare in particular argued the case for a representative body which would embrace the whole of the co-operative movement. Pitman supported the argument in his editorial articles, and the journal served as a sounding-board for those who were to bring into existence the Co-operative Congress and the Central Board. *The Co-operator* had a distinguished list of contributors, among them Dr King of Brighton, Charles Kingsley, Matthew Davenport Hill and William Howitt. The paper was never, however, out of financial difficulties. It began as an eight-page penny monthly in June 1860, increased to sixteen pages in July and was turned into a fortnightly in June 1865. In 1866 William Cooper became its treasurer but at no time does it

seem to have paid its way, Ben Jones (p. 596) estimating that its subsidies (from open financial appeals) amounted to an average of £150 a year for the decade of its existence.

Henry Pitman was an ardent co-operator, but he was also a fervent teetotaller, vegetarian, anti-tobacco and anti-vaccinationist, and these matters were given full coverage in his journal. The result was a growing dissatisfaction within the movement and in the late 1860s many discussions were held on the advisability of a more representative and a more soundly based paper. In the event, the three existing journals (*Scottish Co-operator*, *Social Economist* and *Co-operator*) were persuaded to suspend publication in order to give a clear field to a single representative organ, and on 2 September 1871 appeared the first issue of the *Co-operative News*, printed by the newly established (1869) Co-operative Printing Society. *The Co-operator* changed its name to the *Anti-Vaccinator* and then ceased publication on 2 December 1871. Pitman's debts, amounting to £572, were finally cleared in 1872, the largest amount being subscribed by the Wholesale Society.

Pitman continued to work within and for the co-operative movement, as one of the many kinds of reforming groups he was interested in. He reported co-operative meetings for the *Co-operative News* and for many years he was the official reporter of the annual congresses of the Co-operative Union. He was as eccentric in dress as in some of his ideas, and appeared always in a grey suit: open coat, knickerbockers and velvet cap. For his opposition to vaccination he once spent six months in prison.

He seriously considered emigrating to California in 1886, but friends and acquaintances came to his aid with a gift of several hundred pounds, and he was persuaded to stay in Britain. He died on 25 October 1909 at Cropthorne, Pershore, Worcester, the home of a married daughter, Rosie Pitman Hime. He had married Helen Tate of Sunderland and there were eight children by the marriage; he left personal effects valued at £481.

Writings: *The Popular Lecturer*, vols 1–9

n.s. compiled and edited by H. Pitman (1856–64); *Hints on Teaching and Lecturing on Phonography* (1885); 'Spelling Reform and Phonography', *CWS Annual* (1890) 236–72; *Memorial of Edward Vansittart Neale* (Manchester, 1894); 'Sanitation, Health and Long Life', *CWS Annual* (1896) 374–87.

Sources: *Co-operator's Handbook* (Manchester, 1874); B. Jones, *Co-operative Production*, 2 vols (1894; reprinted in 1 vol., New York, 1968); G. J. Holyoake, *History of Co-operation* (rev. ed. 1906); P. Redfern, *The Story of the C.W.S.* (Manchester, [1913]); G. D. H. Cole, *A Century of Co-operation* (Manchester, [1945?]). OBIT. *Co-op. News*, 30 Oct 1909.

JOHN SAVILLE

See also: Fred HAYWARD, for Co-operative Union; G. J. HOLYOAKE, for Retail Co-operation – Nineteenth Century.

POLLARD, William (1832/3?–1909)
CO-OPERATOR

William Pollard was born in Burnley, Lancashire, in the early 1830s and moved to Gloucester in 1855. A bookbinder by trade, he went into partnership with Mr Edward Power as printers and bookbinders. The business was purchased in 1863 by John Bellows, and Pollard remained in the firm for forty-four years, retiring in 1906.

William Pollard is chiefly remembered as one of the pioneers of the Gloucester Co-operative and Industrial Society Ltd. His name appears in the first list of subscribers and at the first general meeting, held at the Hope Inn, Barton Street, Gloucester, 17 July 1860, he was elected president of the Society for the year ending February 1861. He acted as secretary *pro tem.* in 1862, and continued to be active in the Society's affairs till his death. Working in the centre of the city, he was called upon to do many things that his colleagues on the management committee (many of them railwaymen) were unable to do because of their occupation. The authors of the Jubilee History of the Gloucester Society record that he was sometimes at the treasurer's house before 6 am to

get a cheque: then home for breakfast and to the mill to order flour before work: at lunch a hurried meal before going to Samuel Bowly's warehouse to taste and order cheese; and then after work carrying goods to customers in all parts of the city, and ending his evenings, on occasion, with bookwork for the Society's secretary.

The early records of the Society are full of his activities and of his self-sacrifice of time and money. A member of the Society of Friends, he later also joined the Good Templars and was a member of the Jesse Sessions Lodge. He died of influenza at his Gloucester home on 26 February 1909, aged seventy-seven years, and was survived by four sons and three daughters. He left effects valued at £289.

Sources: F. Purnell and H. W. Williams, *Jubilee History of the Gloucester Co-operative and Industrial Society Ltd* (Gloucester, 1910); personal information: G. Wilkins, Gloucester Co-operative Society. OBIT. *Gloucester Journal*, 6 Mar 1909.

H. F. BING

See also: G. J. HOLYOAKE, for Retail Co-operation – Nineteenth Century.

PRATT, Hodgson (1824–1907)
SOCIAL REFORMER AND CO-OPERATOR

Born on 10 January 1824 at Bath, the eldest of five sons of Samuel Peace Pratt. His family were middle class, and he was educated at Haileybury College and London University. In 1846 he was nominated for service with the East India Company and he arrived in India on Christmas Day 1846. Two years later he was appointed an assistant magistrate and collector at Moorshedabad and in 1851 he became superintendent of the Land Revenue Survey of Monghyr. In 1853 he was made joint magistrate and deputy collector of the same district and in the following year he became an under-secretary to the Government of Bengal. In 1855, following Sir Charles Wood's establishment of a system of national education for India, Pratt became inspector of public instruction for the Lower Provinces; and he retained this position until he returned to England in 1858 on long furlough because of the serious illness of his father. He finally resigned from the Indian Civil Service in 1863.

Hodgson Pratt early developed the social conscience which took him into many reforming movements during his lifetime. As a boy he had been stimulated by the discussions and debates of the Chartist movement in Bath and the neighbouring town of Bristol, and in India he worked strenuously for much closer and more sympathetic contacts by the British administration with the Indian peoples. In 1851 he helped establish a Vernacular Literature Society, of which he became the joint honorary secretary, and later he established a school of Industrial Art in Calcutta. When he returned to England Pratt wrote voluminously on Indian questions and he was associated with Mary Carpenter in the formation of the National Indian Association, and he retained a close connection with the Association until 1905. In his later years he applauded the political efforts of the Indian nationalists in their demands for self-government.

His return to England offered him new opportunities for his reforming zeal. He met the Rev. Henry Solly in 1864, and was drawn into the Working Men's Club and Institute Union, which Solly and others had formed two years previously [B. T. Hall, *Our Fifty Years*]. But although he gave many devoted years' service to the Club movement he became even better known for his contribution to the co-operative movement.

It was, initially, his work in the Club movement that brought him into contact with leading advocates of co-operation such as Vansittart Neale, Thomas Hughes, J. M. F. Ludlow and G. J. Holyoake; and with Neale and Holyoake in particular he developed very close personal ties. Pratt was a member of the committee which organised the first Co-operative Congress in 1869 and he was appointed a member of the first central board. In 1870, along with other middle-class sympathisers (including Thomas Hughes) he was one of the guarantors of the capital required to establish the London Co-operative Agency, founded to supply co-operative stores in the south of

England with goods at wholesale prices, there being no branch of the CWS in London; and it was owing to Pratt's efforts, among others, that a London branch of the CWS was established in 1874. Throughout the 1870s and 1880s Pratt worked with Vansittart Neale to promote co-operative societies in London and the suburbs.

In 1878 Pratt suggested to the sectional board that the principles of co-operation should be more widely disseminated and the Guild of Co-operators was founded, with Thomas Hughes as president, Pratt as chairman of the council, and Ben Jones as honorary secretary. The Guild was inaugurated with a public lecture by Thomas Hughes, and for a number of years the Guild organised its propaganda work from accommodation offered by the Club and Institute Union in the Strand. When Ben Jones resigned as secretary, Pratt succeeded him, until failing eyesight compelled him, for a time, to give up active work. In the early 1890s he was one of the originators of the idea of the International Co-operative Alliance.

He was also a warm supporter of the Labour Co-partnership Association, in which Thomas Blandford and Henry Vivian were among the leading spirits; and he was one of the founders, in 1884, of the Co-operative Permanent Building Society. He was a vigorous supporter of all forms of education for working people, and particularly of the training needs of co-operative employees. He was an early advocate of a Co-operative College and enthusiast for craft and technical training, and in the last years of his life he warmly commended the founding of the WEA.

The most important part of the many-sided activities in the last three decades of his life was probably the international peace movement. He worked assiduously for the provisional international peace conference held in Paris in 1881, and in 1883 there was formed the International Arbitration and Peace Association of which Pratt was the first president. He was active in the 1880s in both France and Germany, encouraging the formation of peace societies, and he was fervent in his opposition to militarism and

PURCELL 275

war. He never became a socialist, but remained to the end of his years a mid-Victorian radical.

A few years before his death, Pratt retired to the village of Le Pecq, not far from Paris, from which retreat he continued to conduct an immense correspondence. He died there on 26 February 1907, his wife and a daughter surviving him. He was buried at Highgate Cemetery and left an estate valued at £27,718. A Hodgson Pratt Memorial Fund was established in 1910 and each year the money was used to support a variety of causes for which Pratt had worked, including scholarships to the Co-operative College and to Ruskin College, prizes for essays on peace and war, grants to the WEA, etc. In 1931 the Fund was transferred to the Co-operative Union and a Hodgson Pratt Memorial Lecture was founded; the first address being given by J. J. Dent on 19 November 1932. The executive report of the Co-operative Union in 1967 showed the Fund was worth £4295 on 31 December 1966.

Writings: *A Selection of Articles and Letters on Various Indian Questions, including Remarks on European Parties in Bengal, Social Policy and Missions in India and the Use of the Bible in Government Schools Contributed to the English Press* (1857); *A Few Words on the Question of Teaching the Bible in Government Schools in India* (1859); *University Education in England for Natives of India – Considered with a View to Qualify them for the Learned Professions or the Public Service* (1860); *Bengal Planters and Ryots,* repr. *National Review* (1862); *Notes of a Tour among Clubs: or warnings and examples, including a notice of the Trades Hall at Liverpool and the 'Model' Club at Wisbech* (1872); *A New Industrial World* (Labour Co-partnership Association, 1893); *International Arbitration: its necessity and its practicability,* repr. from *The Reformer* (1898) 13 pp.

Sources: *The Reformers' Year Book* (1904); H. Evans, *Sir Randal Cremer: his life and work* (1909); B. T. Hall, *Our Fifty Years: the story of the Working Men's Club and Institute Union* (1912); J. J. Dent, *Hodgson Pratt, Reformer: an outline of his work* (First Hodgson Pratt Memorial Lect.: Manchester, 1932) 20 pp.;

A. Bonner, *British Co-operation* (Manchester, 1961). Obit. *Co-op. News,* 2 and 9 Mar 1907; *Times,* 5 Mar 1907.

JOHN SAVILLE

See also: G. J. HOLYOAKE, for Retail Co-operation – Nineteenth Century; E. V. NEALE.

PURCELL, Albert Arthur (1872–1935)
TRADE UNIONIST AND LABOUR MP

Born on 3 November 1872 in Hoxton, East London, the son of Albert Duncan Purcell, a French polisher, and his wife Charlotte (née Alleway), Purcell was educated at a Keighley, Yorkshire, elementary school before starting work at the age of nine as a half-timer in a woollen mill. He was apprenticed to his father's trade in 1890 back in Hoxton and became active in the London French Polishers' Union, of which he later became president. In 1898 he was elected general secretary of the Amalgamated Society of French Polishers. When in 1910 his Society merged with the Amalgamated Furnishing Trades Association, Purcell became the chief organiser of the latter. He had joined the SDF in the 1890s and was also a member of the ILP, for it was not uncommon at the time for a man to belong to both. In 1893 he joined the Legal Eight Hours and International Labour League, established by the Avelings in July 1890 [Tsuzuki (1967) 205].

In the early years of the twentieth century Purcell moved to Manchester. The first mention of him there was as a delegate from the Manchester branch of the Amalgamated Society of French Polishers to the Manchester and Salford Trades Council for the year 1903, and this probably happened soon after he arrived. He remained a branch delegate until 1922. After the union merger of 1910, his branch was known as the French Polishers' Branch (Manchester no. 112) of the National Furnishing Trades Association. In 1905 and again in 1906, he was president of the Manchester and Salford Trades and Labour Council, a position he also held from 1917 to 1919 and in 1922. He was vice-president from 1914 to 19 and was a member of the executive committee from 1910 to 1922. For many years after 1911 along with Tom Fox he was a Trade Council representative to both the Co-operative Union and the Lancashire and Cheshire Federation of Trades Councils. At this time Purcell lived in the Broughton district of Salford and later in the Pendleton district, and from 1907 to 1912 he was an ILP member of the Salford Borough Council. In the general election of January 1910 he contested Salford West as an Independent Labour candidate but was bottom of the poll.

Purcell was closely associated with Tom Mann in the work of the Industrial Syndicalist League, formed in 1910, and he acted as chairman of a conference on industrial syndicalism held at the Coal Exchange, Manchester, on 26 November 1910. During the war Purcell remained with the majority of the British Socialist Party who opposed the war as imperialist, rather than with the pro-war faction, headed by Hyndman, that walked out of the Caxton Hall, Salford, conference in April 1916. In the years immediately after the war he was caught up in the Guild Movement and in 1922 he began the Furnishing Guild, an interesting but short-lived experiment that was started in Manchester.

It was in the immediate post-war years that Purcell first attained national prominence, and it was in these years also that he was at his most militant, especially in his support for the Russian Revolution. Purcell had been closely involved in the long negotiations that preceded the Communist Unity Conference of 31 July and 1 August 1920, which he attended as delegate from the South Salford branch of the BSP, and it was he who proposed the resolution that a British Communist Party be established. Two months earlier he had visited the Soviet Union as a member of an oddly-assorted Labour Party delegation (which included Ben Turner, Margaret Bondfield and Ethel Snowden). Their report was published on 12 June 1920. Purcell was prominent in the 'Hands off Russia' movement from November 1919, when the first committee was established and he continued active right through 1920 until the British Government

in late August 1920 finally acknowledged the strength of the Labour movement's opposition to intervention. When the 'Hands off Russia' committee turned itself into the Anglo-Russian Parliamentary Committee in 1924 Purcell became chairman and W. P. Coates secretary. By this time, however, he had already resigned from the Communist Party – in April 1922, following a split in the Salford branch, centred largely around the resolutions of the recent congress of the Communist International.

In 1919 Purcell was elected to the parliamentary committee of the TUC (after 1921, the general council) and he continued in this office until 1927. He was president of the 1924 Congress, held in Hull. In the 1920s much of his work was directed towards the establishment of a single trade union international, and he was in agreement with the formation of the Red International of Labour Unions, although he later objected to what he considered to be the unrestrained Russian hostility to the Amsterdam International (the social democratic International Federation of Trade Unions), to which his own union was affiliated. When the Labour Government came to office in 1924, J. H. Thomas resigned his office as president of the IFTU and Purcell was nominated by the TUC as his successor. In November and December 1924 Purcell headed a ten-member TUC delegation to Russia; the party included Tillett, Fred Bramley, A. A. H. Findlay, John Turner and Herbert Smith, and returned with hopes of bringing the Russians back into the international fold. There followed the episodes of the Anglo-Russian Trade Union Alliance of 1924, Purcell being a member of the Anglo-Russian Unity Committee, and the polemics between the British and continental unions in the IFTU over the admission of the Russians. In this dispute Purcell played a leading part.

In December 1923 he was elected Labour MP for Coventry. He was never very prominent on the back benches but on a number of issues he came out strongly against the government leadership. He was highly critical of the Dawes Plan, for example, and used his presidential address to the TUC to condemn it for placing the burden of reparations on the German working class. The most publicised event of his career in the 1924 Parliament was the part he played with five Labour colleagues in re-starting negotiations with the Russians after the breakdown of talks between the British and Russian delegations in early August 1924. E. D. Morel, another leading participant, published a fairly full and substantially accurate account in *Forward*, 23 August 1924. Purcell was defeated at the general election of October 1924, in which the Zinoviev letter scare exercised considerable influence, but he returned to the Commons in July 1925, following a striking victory in a by-election in the Forest of Dean. He secured a record poll despite his uncompromising left-wing views and an absence of support from Ramsay MacDonald, who refused to speak during the election or even write a public letter in support of Purcell's candidature. While member for the Forest of Dean the most sensational episode – quite unconnected with politics – was his support for a Mrs Pace who was accused of poisoning her husband. Purcell secured Norman Birkett as her defending counsel, and he sat in court throughout the trial, which ended with Mrs Pace's acquittal.

In 1925 Purcell founded the journal *Trade Union Unity* which for the relatively short period of its existence obtained a considerable influence. He was chairman of its editorial board and wrote many of its editorials and other articles. He also at this time became a contributor to *Labour Monthly*. In 1925 he attended and spoke at the Atlantic City Congress of the American Federation of Labor, and in the following year he visited Mexico to assist in the work of trade unions there. In Britain, as a member of the TUC general council he was prominent in all the discussions leading up to the General Strike of 1926, and with Ernest Bevin he was in charge of the Strike Organisation Committee, at one stage believing that he was on the point of being arrested by the Government. When the strike was called off, he was, reputedly, the 'most disappointed man in the country'. Although he had up till this time shown sympathy with such Communist-led organisations as the National Minority Movement (although never himself an active participant), following the strike he was vigorously attacked by R. Page Arnot and J. T. Murphy in the *Communist Review* (July 1927) for what was described as his capitulating attitude.

Soviet attacks on the British TUC following the General Strike and the belief that the miners had been betrayed placed a severe strain on the alliance between the British and Russian trade unions. At the Paris congress of the IFTU in 1927, however, Purcell repeated his belief in international trade union unity, which he felt 'must take preference over everything'. The implications of this presidential address, involving as it did Russian membership of the Amsterdam International, resulted in a sharp quarrel between the British delegates and those of the continental countries, who refused to have Purcell, whom they described as a 'Communist', again as president. He was rebuked for his friendliness towards the Russians, and also for his visit the previous year to the socialist unions of Mexico. The continental unions succeeded in keeping him off the IFTU executive, for which he was automatically nominated at the end of his term of office as president, electing George Hicks as British representative against the latter's own wish. Purcell's quarrel with the IFTU arose largely because he felt the International was too parochial and in particular because the western unions were doing nothing to encourage trade unionism among the newly industrialised countries of the East. His view was so far taken by the TUC that in 1927 he and J. Hallsworth were sent out to India to report on labour conditions and the scope for trade unionism. Purcell was thereafter always active on behalf of the Indian workers and the Indian trade union movement.

At the general election of 1929 he left the Forest of Dean to stand as Labour candidate for the Moss Side division of Manchester, but he failed to secure election. By this time he had ceased to be eligible for membership of the TUC owing to changes within his own union, the exact circumstances of which are not clear. Purcell now moved from national politics to trade union and political affairs at local level, and the declension involved has been unusual for leading personalities of the British labour movement. Shortly after his defeat in the 1929 election, Purcell succeeded Councillor William Mellor as secretary of the Manchester and Salford Trades Council, a position he held until his death in 1935. It says much for his strength of character and belief in socialist principles that he was able to make a return to the relatively ordinary existence of a trades council secretary, important though Manchester and Salford was as a centre of working-class political and industrial activity. Purcell, a man of great physical vigour, invested the position of secretary to the trades council with new life and a new authority. His office in Manchester was constantly filled with poor people seeking his help. He became an authority on rents, mortgages and housing problems generally and established a Manchester and Salford Tenants' Defence Association. In 1931 he led an extensive campaign in the Manchester area against high rents, in the course of which he visited many hundreds of working-class homes to investigate cases of alleged exploitation. At this time also he became active on behalf of the unemployed in Manchester and Salford, and was responsible for the holding of a major demonstration in the two cities in April 1932 to demand the provision of public works for the unemployed. A similar demonstration was held in 1935. In May 1931 he organised a 'People's Congress', held in the Free Trade Hall, Manchester, attended by more than 2100 delegates from trade unions, Labour parties and co-operative organisations throughout Great Britain. Seven Lancashire MPs were present and the speakers included Ernest Bevin, J. R. Clynes, Walter Citrine, George Hicks, Ben Tillett and A. J. Cook. Resolutions and declarations passed by the congress included topics such as 'Economy and the Social Services', 'The War Danger', 'The Building and Strengthening of the Labour Movement' and 'Unemployment'. He published a large number of pamphlets in these years and shortly before his death began a campaign for road safety, and was the author of a manifesto on road deaths published by the Trades Council a fortnight before he died.

It was said of Purcell that his whole life revolved around the theme of working-class unity. He was an agitator who, as the *Manchester Guardian* wrote of him, 'often talked of revolution and looked the part'; but he also had a long record as a trade union negotiator. The story was often told how Purcell, in November 1919, presiding over negotiations between workers and employers in the Co-operative movement, kept the discussions going for twenty-three and a half hours before a settlement was reached. He was undoubtedly one of the most striking personalities of the trade union movement of his day, and it was a considerable loss to the trade union movement that from 1929 he was no longer a national figure. He was, indeed, remarkable in many ways. An excellent amateur boxer, he did a good deal to improve the lot of young recruits to this profession. He married, in 1895, Sarah Elizabeth, daughter of George Thomas Fidler, an engine driver of Edmonton, London, and had a son, who died in infancy, and three daughters.

Purcell died at his home, 24 Kendall Road, Higher Crumpsall, Manchester, on Christmas Eve 1935, aged 63. He had been unwell the previous day but his illness was not considered serious. His funeral took place at Manchester Crematorium on 28 December 1935 and was attended by hundreds of representatives from almost every trade union branch in Manchester and Salford as well as representatives from local Labour parties and branches of the Co-operative Union. There was, according to one report, a whole coach full of wreaths, including one from the Soviet embassy with the inscription 'To A. A. Purcell; Champion of Anglo-Soviet friendship'. Funeral orations were given by W. P. Coates, J. Hallsworth of the TUC general council, and F. Harrison, the president of the Manchester and Salford Trades Council. He had left effects valued at £775 and a fund to provide for Purcell's wife and children was established by the Trades Council: something over £1200 was subscribed.

Writings: Purcell wrote numerous short articles and pamphlets, including frequent contributions to *Trade Union Unity* in 1925-6. Among his other publications are: preface to Edo Fimmen, *Labour's Alternative: The United States of Europe or Europe Limited* (1924); (with E. D. Morel) *The Workers and the Anglo-Russian Treaty: why the treaty must be ratified* (n.d. [1924]) 7 pp.; four articles in the *Lab. Mon.*: 'Towards a New Policy – V', *6* (1924) 268-70; 'The Burning Question of International Unity', *7* (1925) 524-9; 'Capital and Labour in U.S.A.', *8* (1926) 93-8; 'The Importance of May Day', ibid., 208-11; foreword to National Joint Council, *Report of the Committee of Inquiry into Production etc., The Waste of Capitalism* (n.d. [1924?]); *Workers of the World – Unite!* (n.d. [1927?]) with a foreword by James Maxton, 19 pp.; *Moss Side Parliamentary Election: a souvenir* (Manchester, 1929) 8 pp.; (with A. M. Wall) foreword to S. G. Hobson, *The House of Industry: a new estate of the realm* (1931); 'Agitate for Lower Rents', *Lab. Mag. 10* (1932) 464-6; a number of pamphlets by Purcell were issued by the Manchester and Salford Trades Council between 1930 and 1935, including: *The Trades Councils and Local Working-class Movement* (an address delivered to the York Trades Council 13 Dec 1931, with a foreword by Ben Tillett) 14 pp.; *The Economics of a Madhouse* (1931) 12 pp.; *Onward to Socialism* (n.d. [1931?]) 12 pp.; *Our Poverty – Your Responsibility* (n.d. [1932]) 12 pp.; *Days in Leningrad: notes on a visit to Leningrad, August 1933* (n.d. [1933]) 4 pp.; *The Workers' Battle for Livelihood and Life: being the story of trade unionism during the past 25 years* (1935) 32 pp.; *The Massacre on the Roads* (1935) 4 pp.

Sources: Manchester and Salford Trades Council, *Annual Reports* (1902-35); ILP *Reports* (1907-11); *Industrial Syndicalist Monthly 1* no. 4 (Oct 1910), no. 11 (May 1911); Communist Unity Convention, *Official Report* (1920); *Dod* (1924-9); TUC *Report* (1924); *Russia: The Official Report of the British Trade Union Delegation to Russia and Caucasia Nov and Dec 1924* (1925); *WWW* (1929-40); Manchester and Salford Trades Council, *The People's Congress* (Manchester, 1931); *DNB* (1931-40) by J. S. Middleton; *Labour Party Report* (1936); J. A. Mahon, 'A. A. Purcell: A Champion of Working Class Unity', *Labour Monthly 18* (Feb 1936) 101-9; W. J. Munro, 'Albert Arthur Purcell: A Short Biography', in Manchester and Salford Trades Council, *Annual Report* (1935-6) 10-13; A. Hutt, *The Post-War History of the British Working Class* (1937); W. P. and Z. K. Coates, *A History of Anglo-Soviet Relations* (1944); G. D. H. Cole, *A History of the Labour Party from 1914* (1948); C. L. Mowat, *Britain between the Wars 1918-40* (1955); L. Bather, 'History of the Manchester and Salford Trades Council' (Manchester PhD, 1956); *Beatrice Webb's Diaries 1924-32*, ed. Margaret Cole (1956); S. R. Graubard, *British Labour and the Russian Revolution 1917-1924* (Cambridge, Mass., 1956); R. W. Lyman, *The First Labour Government 1924* [1957]; W. Citrine, *Men and Work: an autobiography* (1964); H. M. Hyde, *Norman Birkett: the life of Lord Birkett of Ulverston* (1964); L. J. Macfarlane, *The British Communist Party: its origin and development until 1929* (1966); C. Tsuzuki, *The Life of Eleanor Marx 1855-1898: a socialist tragedy* (Oxford, 1967); J. Klugmann, *History of the Communist Party of Great Britain 1: 1919-24* (1968), *2: 1925-7* (1969); W. Kendall, *The Revolutionary Movement in Britain 1900-21: the origins of British Communism* (1969); R. Martin, *Communism and the British Trade Unions: a study of the National Minority Movement* (Oxford, 1969); R. H. C. Hayburn, 'The Response to Unemployment in the 1930s, with particular reference to SE Lancashire' (Hull PhD, 1970); personal information: R. and E. Frow; John Mahon. OBIT. *The Citizen*, 27 Dec 1935; *Daily Despatch*, 27 Dec 1935; *Manchester Guardian*, 27 Dec 1935; *Times*, 27 Dec 1935; *Manchester City News*, 28 Dec 1935 (also 17 Jan 1936); *Manchester Evening Chronicle*, 28 Dec 1935.

RALPH HAYBURN
DAVID E. MARTIN
JOHN SAVILLE

See also: Arthur HENDERSON, for British Labour Party, 1914-31; *E. D. MOREL; *J. T. MURPHY.

RAMSAY, Thomas (Tommy) (1810/11–73)
MINERS' LEADER

Tommy Ramsay's exact date of birth is not known and the only record we have is from his death certificate which gave his age as sixty-two. Of his early life little has survived and the first reference to his trade union activities comes in 1832 when he joined the widespread strike of that year organised by the Pitmen's Union of the Tyne and Wear, led by Tommy Hepburn. Ramsay was also active in the great strike of 1844, and in the short revival of the union in 1863 and 1864, and throughout the bitter decades of the middle of the century he remained a vigorous and uncompromising advocate of the union. He fought steadily against the yearly bond and he was victimised on many occasions. Welbourne has a graphic description of Old Tommy:

> In the Miners' Hall at Durham there is a picture of this old warrior, who for years tramped from village to village, preaching the need for combination. There he stands, in his Sunday Blacks and his top hat, a roll of hand-bills in one hand, the 'Corn-Crake of Union' in the other, that policeman's rattle which was used to attract the men from their houses and the inn parlours. Mostly he preached from the same text: 'Lads, combine, and better your condition. When eggs are scarce, eggs are dear. When men are scarce, men are dear.'

Ramsay was an earnest Christian, almost certainly a chapelgoer. His homely oratory, full of rough humour, usually clothed in biblical imagery, was delivered in the broadest dialect of the pits. At the end of his life he was being refused employment from one end of the county to the other; and after the formation of the DMA he was appointed an assistant agent at a wage of 28s a week. Less than a year before he died he attended the first annual demonstration of miners and their families on Durham race-course on 15 June 1872; and looking over the great crowd of about 30,000 from one of the platforms Ramsay spoke with feeling and emotion:

'Lord, now let thy servant depart in peace, for mine eyes have seen Thy salvation.' He died in the following year on 8 May 1873 at Winlaton, near Blaydon. In 1874 the officials of the DMA proposed the building of a hall as a memorial to their indomitable brother; and he remains commemorated in miners' songs and on their colliery banners.

Sources: R. Fynes, *The Miners of Northumberland and Durham* (Blyth, 1873, repr. Sunderland, 1923); J. Wilson, *A History of the Durham Miners' Association 1870–1904* (Durham, 1907); S. Webb, *The Story of the Durham Miners (1662–1921)* (London, 1921); E. Welbourne, *The Miners' Union of Northumberland and Durham* (Cambridge, 1923). OBIT. *Newcastle Weekly Chronicle*, 10 May 1873.

JOYCE BELLAMY
JOHN SAVILLE

See also: *T. HEPBURN; *M. JUDE; Alexander MACDONALD, for Mining Trade Unionism, 1850–79.

REDFERN, Percy (1875–1958)
CO-OPERATIVE JOURNALIST AND AUTHOR

Born in 1875, the illegitimate son of a housekeeper, Percy Redfern was brought up by his father and a stepmother in Leicester, where he first attended a dame school. His subsequent education was acquired at seven different schools including a church school, a London boarding school, the Nottingham Grammar School and finally a new secondary school. At fourteen he was apprenticed to a draper in Nottingham but left to seek employment in London and Coventry. In the latter city he joined the SDF and contributed socialist verses to the Federation's weekly paper *Justice*. In 1895 he transferred to London where he also associated with SDF members but shortly afterwards returned to the North and settled in Huddersfield in 1896 where he joined an active branch of the ILP. It was there that he met Philip Snowden with whom he was to associate during the famous by-election in Colne Valley in 1907 which sent Victor Grayson as an independent Socialist MP to Westminster.

Redfern had a succession of jobs which

included travelling for a wholesaler, store-keeping for the Vegetarian Society of Manchester and a clerical post with a man whom Redfern himself described as a usurer; but his socialist spirit conflicted with working for private gain and in 1899 he took a clerical position with the CWS in Manchester. Within two years his writing talents were being utilised in the position of a sub-editor of the Society's monthly magazine, the *Wheatsheaf*, of which he subsequently became editor. This journal, with a circulation in the 1920s and 1930s of over 700,000, included local items relating to some 500 retail societies in addition to articles of general interest. Redfern combined co-operative journalism with more academic publications mainly bearing on the co-operative movement and among his best known works are his two histories of the CWS, the first published in 1913 and the second in 1938. He played a large part in improving the *People's Year Book* and introduced many leaders of the labour, trade union and pacifist movements to co-operators through the columns of periodicals sponsored by the CWS. In the mid-1920s he promoted the Self and Society series of pamphlets in an endeavour to increase public understanding of the movement and was encouraged in this project by Sidney and Beatrice Webb. These essays, written by distinguished people, were intended to emphasise the widening sphere of consumer co-operation. Redfern retired from the CWS in 1938 although he continued his literary work until the end of his life, and he will be remembered as one of the leading historians of the co-operative movement in the first half of the twentieth century.

In his early life a Freethinker, Redfern later joined the Society of Friends and his autobiography, *Journey to Understanding*, reveals much of his personal philosophy of life. He married in 1905 and had a happy family life. He lived at Marple Bridge, Cheshire, for many years but on retirement he went to live in the south. He died, however, in a York hospital on 11 February 1958 and was buried at the Southern Cemetery, Manchester, a memorial service being held at the Manchester Friends' Meeting House. He left an estate valued at £1826.

Writings: 'The Social Teaching of Tolstoy', *CWS Annual* (1906) 202–36; *Tolstoy: a study* (1907); 'The Conflict of Capitalism', *CWS Annual* (1910) 191–218; *The Story of the CWS: being the jubilee history of the Co-operative Wholesale Society 1863–1913* (Manchester, [1913]); *Co-operation for All* (Manchester, 1914); *Ideas of Progress in Co-operation* (1915) 12 pp.; 'The Wholesale in Recent Years: The Story of the C.W.S. 1913–1917', *CWS Annual* (1918) 245–50; *Consumers' Place in Society* (Manchester, 1920); *Wholesale Co-operation at work* (1921) 12 pp.; *John T. W. Mitchell, Pioneer of Consumers' Co-operation* (Manchester, 1923); *Rights and Responsibilities of Consumers* (Manchester, 1924) 8 pp.; *Twenty Faces the World* (1929) 32 pp.; Article on Co-operation in *Encyclopaedia Britannica*, 14th ed. (1929); *Twenty-four essays on social and economic problems from the hitherto neglected point of the consumer* (Self and Society series) ed. P. Redfern 2 vols (1930); *South and West Wales: souvenir of Co-operative Congress 1935* ed. P. Redfern [1935]; *Northern England: Co-operative Congress 1936* (Manchester, [1936]); *The New History of the CWS* (Manchester, 1938); *Journey to Understanding* (1946).

Sources: *Co-op. Rev.*, Oct 1946; personal information: A. L. Sugar, Publications Manager, Co-operative Union Ltd; and below: Co-operative Wholesaling. OBIT. *Manchester Guardian*, 12 Feb 1958; *Co-op. News*, 22 Feb 1958; *Co-op. Rev.* Mar 1958.

JOYCE BELLAMY

See also: W. H. BROWN, for Co-operative Retailing, 1900–45; Fred HALL, for Co-operative Education.

Co-operative Wholesaling: W. Nuttall, 'The North of England Co-operative Wholesale Society', *Co-op. Congress Report* (1869) 39–42; J. Borrowman, 'On the Extension of Wholesale Co-operative Societies', *Co-op. Congress Report* (1872) 55–7; L. Jones, 'Wholesale Co-operation', *Co-op. Congress Report* (1880) 49–53; J. Watts, 'The Co-operative Scheme and the Function of the Wholesale Society therein', *CWS Annual* (1884) 1–17; Anon., 'The Crisis in Co-operation', *Spectator*

60 (1887) 760–1; E. Copland and C. Shufflebotham, 'Ought Productive Works to be carried on as Departments of Wholesale Societies; if so, under what Conditions?', *Co-op. Congress Report* (1888) 83–7; W. Maxwell, *Wholesale Co-operation a necessity* (Manchester, 1888) 28 pp.; G. E. Quirk and C. Shufflebotham, 'What should be the True Relations between the Wholesale Distributive Society and the Productive Societies whose Work it may sell?', *Co-op. Congress Report* (1888) 16–22; J. Wilson, *The Wholesale and Our Relation to it* (Manchester, [1888]) 8 pp.; H. R. Bailey, 'The Advantages and Necessity of a Co-operative Wholesale Centre of Supply as established in the Organisation of the English and Scottish Wholesale Societies', *CWS Annual* (1889) 377–89; Anon., 'The Productive Departments of the Co-operative Wholesale Society', *CWS Annual* (1892) 430–73; R.C. on Labour, 1893–4 XXXIX Pt I, *Minutes of Evidence* J. T. W. Mitchell, Qs 1–405; B.J., L.B., 'The Wholesale Co-operative Societies and Their Relations to the Retail Co-operative Societies', *CWS Annual* (1896) 209–31; Anon., 'Co-operative Wholesale Societies' Tea Estates', *CWS Annual* (1903) 359–64; P. Redfern, *The Story of the C.W.S.: the jubilee history of the Co-operative Wholesale Society Limited, 1863–1913* (Manchester, [1913]); idem, 'The Wholesale in Recent Years: the story of the C.W.S. 1913–1917', *CWS Annual* (1918) 245–50; idem, *Wholesale Co-operation at work* (1921) 12 pp.; Co-operative Press Agency, *The Growth of the C.W.S.* (Manchester, 1923) 39 pp.; idem, *Sixty Years of the C.W.S.* (Manchester, [1923]) 22 pp.; C.W.S. Ltd, *The Survey of the C.W.S. Ltd: some comments on the report* (Manchester, 1929) 12 pp.; G. Darling, *The C.W.S. of Today: a survey of achievements* (Manchester, [1932]) 32 pp.; C.W.S. Ltd, *The C.W.S. Past and Present* (Manchester, 1933); E. Jackson, *Service for Democracy or Fifty Years with the C.W.S.* (Manchester, 1937); P. Redfern, *The New History of the CWS* (Manchester, 1938); G. D. H. Cole, *A Century of Co-operation* (Manchester, [1945?]); H. L. Jennings, 'The Co-operative Wholesale Society', *ACE 20* (Jan–Apr 1949) 25–43; C.W.S. Ltd, *A Consumers' Democracy: an account of the origins and growth of the Society and a survey of its present structure and its major activities* [Stockport, 1951]; Co-operative Independent Commission, *Report* (1958); A. Bonner, *British Co-operation: the history, principles and organisation of the British co-operative movement* (Manchester, 1961; revised edition, 1970); Co-operative Union, *Report on integration of the Co-operative Wholesale Society and the Co-operative Union* (Manchester, 1970) 45 pp.

REEVES, Samuel (1862–1930)
SOCIALIST AND LABOUR PARTY WORKER

Born in 1862, probably in Glasgow (although that is not wholly certain) but educated in church schools in Liverpool, where he spent the remainder of his life. Of his parents nothing appears to be known. He left school at an early age and went to work on the new docks being constructed at the north end in Bootle. In 1879 he became apprenticed as a coremaker (ironmoulder) with David Crawford & Sons with whom he remained until 1895. His hands had been hardened by the craft and it was said that 'his whole appearance bore witness to a daily struggle with the hard facts of nature'. Yet he had travelled on the Continent and, for a working man, was remarkably widely read – not only the solid fare of Marx and Herbert Spencer's works, but also he would discourse fluently on Bacon's *New Atlantis* and Campanella's *City of the Sun*. He was a ravenous reader of socialist and economic works. It is recorded that when he was unemployed for three months he would set out early each morning and search for work from 6 to 10 am, after which he went to the public library and devoured Ruskin until the building closed. In 1895 he left the trade of the ironmoulder in order to devote more time to socialist activities and to enable him to fulfil his duties should he succeed in being elected to public office. He took over a newsagent and tobacconist shop, first in Scotland Road and later in Bootle, and remained in this occupation for the rest of his life. A political opponent in later years referred to him as 'a measly little shopkeeper'.

He was an unbending and vigorous advocate of the rights of industrial workers and was promoter of the first eight-hour day demonstration in Liverpool. On public platforms in 1889–90 he stressed the importance of organising unskilled labour throughout the country. During this period he was active in the foundation and establishment of new trade unions; in particular, the Liverpool Coremakers Society, of which he was president and delegate to the Trades Council, and the local assembly of the Knights of Labour in Bootle, with a highly variegated membership, in which he held the office of 'Inside Esquire'. He was often chairman and a frequent lecturer at meetings of the Knights where he attacked 'sectional' trade unionism, favoured arbitration in place of strikes and strongly denounced the use of female labour which, he asserted, was supplanting male labour in many branches of trade. If women did equal work then they should have equal wages. In 1890 he represented the assembly at the Labour Electoral Association Convention at Hanley. He became president of the Liverpool Trades Council in 1894 and had represented it at the Newcastle Trades Union Congress (1891). At the end of 1892 he spoke in favour of the Liverpool Association of the Unemployed, created with active local Socialist support, and against its ostracism by the Trades Council mainly on account of its militant views. Reeves maintained that the Council had thereby 'abandoned its own class'.

His political activities were equally diffuse and energetic. Throughout the 1880s he was the leader of the socialist movement on Merseyside and in this period his voice was heard at every important meeting of Liverpool working men. In 1882 he was one of the founders of the Democratic Federation in Liverpool (the SDF after 1884) and kept the branch going until 1887 when it was dissolved. The branch was resuscitated in 1892 but with J. B. Goodman, a printer, former secretary of both the Liverpool Trades Council and of the 1890 Liverpool Trades Union Congress, as its moving spirit. (In 1894 it brought H. M. Hyndman to speak in Liverpool.) Reeves was no longer connected with the Federation branch after it was re-formed, devoting himself instead to

the Fabians and ILP, which was considered by Goodman to be 'weak kneed and boneless'.

From 1889 to 1892 Reeves was secretary of the Liverpool Socialist Society which met weekly in a dimly-lit café off Dale Street. Under its auspices packed public meetings were addressed by leading figures such as Robert Blatchford (in November 1891). In June 1892 the Socialist Society became absorbed into the well-established Liverpool Fabian Society, in which Reeves was elected a vice-president. He took a leading part in the formation of the Independent Labour Party in Liverpool in 1893 becoming chairman of the District Federal Council in the following year. Indeed, in Liverpool the Fabians and ILP were closely interwoven: as well as Reeves three of the other founder members of the ILP branch, John Edwards, R. T. Manson and J. W. T. Morrissey, were also leading members of the Fabian Society and, in their own right, personalities in the Liverpool labour movement. For many years Reeves stood repeatedly, and unsuccessfully, under ILP sponsorship in the municipal elections.

As a pioneer Reeves had to face an active and undisguised hostility and many a promising meeting ended in a rush for safety. He had been stoned in 1887 by a crowd of Orange roughs while speaking with J. Hunter Watts (SDF) at a meeting in front of St George's Hall at which Home Rule was advocated, and at an early election in the Edge Hill ward he received seven votes and a black eye. Yet he never wavered in his convictions. In 1891 he first contested, as an independent, elections for the School Board which was virtually dominated by the religious bodies, and finished at the bottom of the poll. In later years his candidacy for the School Board came to be backed by the Secular Society. In 1891 Reeves argued forcefully on the Trades Council that Liberals could no longer be relied upon to accommodate working-men candidates and that trade unionists ought now to fend for themselves. He favoured direct labour representation in place of the entrenched Lib-Lab orthodoxy and in the following year attacked the candidacy of

T. R. Threlfall for the Kirkdale parliamentary constituency, which had Trades Council support. Reeves was at that time president of the Kirkdale Labour Electoral Association but had become disenchanted because he claimed that as soon as the members of that Association had secured the adoption of Threlfall they 'returned to the Liberal ranks from whence they had come'. He maintained throughout his lifetime that both Tory and Liberal opponents were 'but one dog with two names'. The persistence of Reeves and his followers in favour of independent political action by the Trades Council was largely responsible for setting up the Liverpool Labour Representation Committee under the combined sponsorship of the Trades Council and the ILP, SDF and Fabians early in 1894. Its function was to help secure direct worker representation on public boards and councils by avoiding a clash of interests. However, the Trades Council, always wary of association with the Socialists, abandoned the principle of direct representation and withdrew from the Committee in 1896 after two disastrous showings in the municipal elections. By 1900, however, the Socialist contingent on the Trades Council had been sufficiently reinforced to secure the Council's participation, along with the ILP, SDF, Fabians and two local Labour clubs, in the establishment of a Workers' Municipal Committee – to further direct representation and to share election expenses. Reeves was nominated by this Committee for the School Board elections. The support of the Trades Council for the WMC (the forerunner of the Liverpool Labour Party) and even of those individual unions previously averse to direct labour representation was strongly confirmed after the Taff Vale decision. Political action was now seen as essential to labour's defence. In such political preoccupations as the Trades Council had, up to that time, permitted itself Reeves was leader of the 'advanced' group until the arrival of James Sexton on the Council in 1893, and again after 1894 when Sexton's Dock Labourers' Union seceded from the Council. Many years later Reeves was a member of the amalgamation committee which eventually (1921) fused the Trades Council and Labour Party in Liverpool. At the time of the First World War he was opposed to nations fighting each other 'like wild beasts' and he came into conflict with Sexton's union which had asserted that the Trades Council was a pacifist body. In the early 1920s Reeves endorsed the programme of the local Labour Party and supported its official candidates in elections. He was intensely suspicious of 'Bolshevik aspirations'. In 1923 he successfully moved the expulsion of R. Tissyman from the Liverpool Trades Council and Labour Party as a result of his nomination as a candidate of the Unemployed in the municipal elections, against the official nominee of the Labour Party. Tissyman was at that time the figurehead of the Liverpool Unemployed Workers' Committee Movement, whose executive had strong Communist representation.

Reeves never became a national figure although he was on intimate terms with Keir Hardie, Bernard Shaw, Sidney Webb and Ramsay MacDonald. In 1918 he stood for Labour against a coalition candidate in the new Lancashire parliamentary division of Waterloo but was not successful and, indeed, scarcely saved his deposit. He did, however, achieve belated local recognition. He became a city auditor and in 1920 was made a magistrate. During the war (1915) he was co-opted on to the West Derby Board of Guardians as Labour's first representative and became vitally interested in the administration of the poor law, being made also a member of the Bootle Public Assistance Committee. In 1928 he was finally elected a member of the Bootle town council, at the top of the poll. The hero of forty-two public elections, he was victor in only one. An old campaigner, he described himself towards the end of his career as 'a Democrat in politics and a Socialist in economics'. He died suddenly on 9 September 1930 at his home 316 Derby Road, Bootle, and, at his own request, his funeral was without ostentation or mourning. He had married in 1893 and was survived by his two sons.

Solid and immovable in his principles, noted for his uncompromising views, he was one of the most respected and active figures in the Liverpool labour movement for over two generations of local trade unionism and politics.

Sources: Minutes of the Liverpool Labour Representation Committee and of the Liverpool Trades Council (1890–1900), Liverpool Record Office; *Halfpenny Weekly* (Liverpool, 1890); *Porcupine* (Liverpool, 1891); *Labour Annual* (1895); *Labour Chronicle* (Liverpool, 1895, 1897); *Waterloo and Crosby Herald* (1918); *Bootle Times* (*passim*); J. Sexton, *Sir James Sexton, Agitator* (1936); W. Hamling, *A Short History of the Liverpool Trades Council 1848–1948* (Liverpool, 1948); H. Pelling, 'The Knights of Labor in Britain, 1880–1901', *Econ. Hist. Rev. 9* (Dec 1956) 313–31; M. Toole, *Mrs Bessie Braddock M.P.* (1957); C. Tsuzuki, *H. M. Hyndman and British Socialism* (1961). OBIT. *Liverpool Echo*, 9 Sep 1930; *Bootle Times*, 12 Sep 1930.

RON BEAN

See also: *John BRADDOCK; *J. Keir HARDIE; *James SEXTON.

RICHARDS, Thomas (1859–1931)
MINERS' LEADER AND LABOUR MP

Born on 8 June 1859 at Beaufort, Ebbw Vale, South Wales, the son of Thomas and Mary Richards, he was educated at Beaufort British School and started work at Pwyllgaer Colliery when he was twelve. When this pit closed he left for Ebbw Vale where he worked at the Victoria Colliery. In 1884, while still working at the coal face and at a time when the South Wales coalfield was largely unorganised, Richards formed the Ebbw Vale Miners' Association. He was secretary of this body until his appointment as miners' agent of the Ebbw Vale District four years later, a position he held until 1901. Within four years of becoming agent he was a member of the South Wales sliding-scale committee: a joint committee of employers and workmen concerned with operating sliding-scale agreements which controlled wage rates in the South Wales coalfield at this period. He was one of ten union leaders who signed the manifesto during the important hauliers' strike of 1893 urging the men to go

back to work; and he does not seem to have opposed the principle of the sliding scale until it was superseded. Towards the end of the 1890s Richards played a prominent role in the establishment of the SWMF and was appointed general secretary from its commencement in 1898, a position he held until his death. From 1898 also he was joint secretary of the South Wales District Board responsible for the regulation of wages. He gave evidence before two Royal Commissions: in 1891 (Labour) and 1907 (Mines).

Richards's approach to wage disputes was essentially that of a moderate man who favoured negotiations. He worked closely with Mabon but at times he could be much tougher with the coalowners, although in the decade before 1914 he came under increasing criticism from the younger militant elements among the South Wales miners who were identified with the Plebs League and the Central Labour College. Richards represented South Wales on the executive of the MFGB from 1903 to 1911, but in 1911 he was replaced along with William Brace and Alfred Onions by Vernon Hartshorn, C. B. Stanton and George Barker, following the widespread dissatisfaction with the results of the Cambrian Combine lock-out and strike of 1910. Richards, however, had a strength and determination in his trade union work which retained for him the respect of most of the militant personalities in the coalfield. He resumed his direct association with the MFGB in 1921 and served on the executive continuously from that time until his death. From 1924 to 1930 he was also vice-president of the MFGB and in the latter year succeeded Herbert Smith as president, and also as president of the Miners' International.

In his seventieth year the presidency of the Miners' Federation of Great Britain, then undergoing severe difficulties, was thrust upon him. The effect of the contraction of the coalmining industry that had set in after the First World War, and particularly in South Wales after 1924, had been accentuated in the years after 1927 by the fall in markets and the introduction of mechanisation with a resultant mass unemployment such as never before had been a feature of the coalmining industry. The effect of the new legislation proposed by the Labour Government of 1929 to 1931, which was to result in the Coal Mines Act of 1930, had shaken to its foundations the Miners' Federation already fragmented by the score of distinct District agreements following on the seven months' lock-out of 1926. In particular the Yorkshire Miners' Association, from which had stemmed the whole conception forty years earlier of unitary negotiations and unitary agreements over the British coalfields, now found itself opposed not only to the government and to the coalowners, but to the rest of the Federation; and its chief representative, Herbert Smith, felt compelled to resign the presidency of the National Federation. It was in these conditions, when the whole national organisation seemed in danger of dissolution, that Thomas Richards left his largely nominal position of vice-president and stepped into the breach.

The next year both the debates and discussions on the Coal Mines Act of 1930, and particularly the amendment to the Bill successfully introduced in the House of Lords by Lord Gainford (then vice-chairman of the Coal Mining Association of Great Britain) caused additional trouble. The Bill had provided for the reduction of the eighthour day (imposed in 1926) to seven and a half hours. It was productive of further dissension within the Federation, with which secretary A. J. Cook found it difficult to cope: and the dissension eventuated in several strikes, notably one in South Wales at the beginning of January 1931. At the same time the troubles of the mining industry were enormously accentuated by the spread of the world economic crisis (1929 to 1933) with the result that the general level of unemployment in the UK standing at the very high figure of 11 per cent in December 1929, just after Richards took office, mounted rapidly and was doubled in two years. In the case of South Wales and other mining areas the figure of unemployment was far higher so that at the depth of the crisis two colliers out of every five were out of work. In these catastrophic conditions Richards took on the onerous task of resisting as far as was possible the conditions that

made life so hard and sought remedies which would lead them out of what in his Conference opening speech of 19 March 1931 was succinctly described by him in the words: 'What a horrible condition we are in as a Federation generally!' This involved him with very difficult negotiations with the Ramsay MacDonald administration in his endeavour to induce them to bring forward an effective Minimum Wage Act updating the Act of twenty years earlier after the great strike of 1912. He was, however, forced to resign from the presidency in June 1931 because of ill-health.

Richards was invited to be a miners' candidate for the West Monmouth constituency in 1904 and he informed the Liberals that he would not join the ILP group. He thereby obtained Liberal support. At that time the MFGB did not require its candidates to be attached to any party but Richards did indicate to the Federation his willingness to join the Labour Group since a resolution had been passed favouring affiliation to the Party. In 1906 the LRC did not endorse his candidature, since he was regarded as a Lib-Lab, and when elected he still accepted the Liberal whip. In 1909, however, when the MFGB affiliated to the Labour Party he was the first of the miners' representatives in Parliament to announce his support of the new party. He served for a number of years on the national executive of the Labour Party, and retained the Ebbw Vale seat in the Labour interest until 1920 when he resigned owing to pressure of trade union work. Unlike many of his Welsh colleagues in the leadership of the South Wales miners, Richards was in no way a polished orator: but he had a winning manner of putting forward his views whenever he found it necessary to speak. In his personal contacts he was very effective and disarming, as is clear from an anecdote told by Arthur Horner. After the latter had made a vigorous attack upon him at a coalfield conference, in the restaurant afterwards Tom Richards came and sat down beside Horner and said: 'I can see you are thinking of stepping into my shoes. So you will some day. But not yet: your feet are not big enough!'

An active worker for the Congregational Church, Richards was also involved in local affairs in Monmouthshire: as a member of the Ebbw Vale District Council from 1895, of which he became chairman, and as an alderman of the Monmouthshire County Council from 1904 of which he was chairman in 1924. From 1907 he was a JP for the counties of Brecon and Monmouth, served on two school boards and was a director of the St John Ambulance Association for Wales, being made a Knight of Grace of St John of Jerusalem in 1918. He was made a Privy Councillor in the same year.

He had married in 1880 Elizabeth, daughter of David Thomas of Beaufort, and he died on 8 November 1931 at his Cardiff home. His wife had predeceased him but he was survived by four sons and five daughters. Following a memorial service at Roath Park Congregational Church, Cardiff, he was buried at Cardiff Cemetery on 11 November. He left £1528 (net).

Richards up to the last was a picture of good health, always looking hale and hearty, an effect that was scarcely belied by the way his trembling hands gave an impression of infirmity – probably Parkinson's disease. A special meeting on 11 November, then described as Armistice Day, to celebrate the end of the First World War thirteen years earlier, was given over by the executive council 'to express their own feelings of what seemed to be an irreparable loss to the coalfield'. Each strand of opinion within the South Wales miners was woven into that meeting of the council, ending with Noah Ablett saying: 'We have lost the greatest man in the Federation; the greatest man in Wales.' John Thomas, speaking in Welsh, said he was 'a safe leader' and added: 'He was a son of Peace, but the sons of Peace might be the sons of Thunder, like Mr Richards, who had given his life for the men.' S. O. Davies, afterwards MP for Merthyr Tydfil (1934 onwards), said that 'Richards's personality was incarnated in the lives of the whole of the people', and finally W. H. Mainwaring, afterwards MP for Rhondda (1933–59), said briefly: 'The life of Mr Richards was the life of industrial Wales.'

Sources: Evidence before R.C. on Labour 1892 XXXIV Qs 5424–520 and R.C. on Mines III 1908 XX Qs 19621–20216; Dod (1905) and (1919); Pall Mall Gazette, New House of Commons (1911); Labour Who's Who (1927); R. Page Arnot, The Miners, vol. 1 (1949); vol. 2 (1953); F. Bealey and H. Pelling, Labour and Politics 1900–1906 (1958); E. W. Evans, The Miners of South Wales (Cardiff, 1961); R. Page Arnot, The South Wales Miners 1898–1914 (1967). Obit. Times, 9 Nov 1931; Western Mail, 9 Nov 1931; Lab. Mag. 10 (Nov 1931) 317–18.

R. Page Arnot
Joyce Bellamy

See also: William Abraham, for Welsh Mining Trade Unionism.

ROBINSON, Richard (1879–1937)
CO-OPERATOR AND TRADE UNIONIST

Born in Bury, Lancashire, on 14 May 1879, the son of Alfred Robinson, a billiard marker, Richard Robinson was left fatherless at the age of ten and largely dependent upon his own ability to earn a living. He sold newspapers in the streets of Bury mornings and evenings. Following a period as 'reacher-in' at a local cotton mill he became an apprentice engineer and rose to local eminence as district secretary of the Amalgamated Society of Engineers (later the Amalgamated Engineering Union). An accident to one of his eyes ended his employment in the engineering trade and he became a school attendance officer, a post he held for seventeen years, and which his real love of children enabled him to perform with great satisfaction to all concerned.

Richard Robinson became actively associated with the co-operative movement. He was a member of the Bury District Co-operative Society for thirty-five years, serving on the management committee from 1917 to 1922 and re-elected the following year until 1929. He was president, 1919–22 and 1924–8, and during the eight years of his presidency the society's progress owed much to his shrewd guidance with new branches being opened and the Bury Head Office rebuilt. In 1928 he was nominated for the board of the Co-operative Wholesale

Society and apparently elected, when Burslem Society lodged a complaint that he had violated the rule concerning canvassing. The complaint was upheld and Robinson was disqualified though maintaining that every other candidate had equally broken the rule. He stood again in 1929 and was returned at the top of the poll and continued to serve until his death. He was a member of the finance and wages committees and gave evidence before the special committee of inquiry set up in 1936 to review the constitution of the CWS board, its method of election and the basis of representation of districts. He represented the CWS on the boards of the Co-operative Insurance Society and the English and Scottish Joint CWS. On several foreign delegations he did much to strengthen CWS trading activity overseas. He was also associated with the Manchester Chamber of Commerce, the Industrial Institute Council and the Roads Improvement Association.

In the sporting world, Robinson was a national figure as chairman of the famous Bury Football Club for many years up to his death. Next to the co-operative movement the Bury team was his second love. He was also well known locally as chairman of the Bury Allotment Holders' and Horticultural Society.

His wife predeceased him by seven years. They had no children. Robinson died suddenly of pneumonia at his home at Elton, Bury, on 3 April 1937 and he was buried at Bury Cemetery on Wednesday 7 April. He left an estate valued at £5271 (net).

Sources: P. Redfern, *The New History of the CWS* (Manchester, 1938). OBIT. *Bury Times*, 10 Apr 1937; *Co-op. News*, 10 Apr 1937.
H. F. BING

See also: W. H. BROWN, for Retail Co-operation, 1900–45; Percy REDFERN, for Co-operative Wholesaling.

ROGERS, Frederick (1846–1915)
JOURNALIST AND TRADE UNIONIST

Born in Whitechapel, London, on 27 April 1846, the eldest of five children of Frederick Rogers, labourer, sailor and linen-draper's assistant, and Susan Bartrup or Barltrop. He left school at the age of ten or earlier to become an errand boy. Subsequently he became a vellum bookbinder, a member of a trade which specialised in the binding of account books. He was associated with this trade in one capacity or another for nearly forty years and was a skilful craftsman.

During his youth Rogers was constantly ill, especially with spinal trouble. This involved four years of treatment between 5.0 and 7.30 in the morning. Though he was troubled by ill-health later in life, Rogers was always proud of having overcome the two obstacles of physical weakness and lack of education. During his youth and middle age Rogers was concerned with four main activities outside his work: working-class education, journalism, religion and trade unionism.

In the early years of the university extension movement in East London, beginning in 1877, Rogers was the movement's co-secretary, his colleague being Alfred Milner. He was also involved with the London School Board in its early years, both as a school manager and as an election worker; and he further took an active part in the educational aspects of working-men's clubs in East London.

Rogers believed strongly in an educated democracy, giving equal opportunities to everyone for full self-development. This belief, and a related conviction that class jealousy and hatred were to be opposed, led to Rogers's early involvement in the settlement movement. In the autumn of 1883 he spoke at a series of lectures organised by socially conscious undergraduates at Oxford. His paper, which dealt with artisan life in East London, was enthusiastically received and undoubtedly helped to influence the decision to found Toynbee Hall, the first settlement, in 1884.

Once the settlement was founded Rogers became active in its life and remained so for thirty years. In 1886 he was elected one of the first forty non-resident Associates of Toynbee Hall, serving on its Education Committee from 1890 to 1898. During these years Rogers was also concerned with the developments which led to the foundation of the People's Palace, the educational-cum-social establishment in the Mile End Road.

Rogers was a highly educated man, deeply read in many periods of English literature. His taste was orthodox (he expressed a dislike for Ibsen), and his particular interests lay with the Elizabethans and the poetry of Robert Browning. For many years he was active in the Elizabethan Literary Society. This body, which met at Toynbee Hall until 1913, was founded in 1884, and Rogers became its vice-president and effective leader in 1886. He retained this position until his death, meeting thereby many of the leading literary figures of his day. In most of his own writing Rogers made a point of quoting classic English writers and an anonymous writer in the *Railway Review* called him 'the most scholarly man I know of in the Labour movement' (12 Nov 1909).

Rogers was an active journalist for many years, his first printed work being a competition entry published in the *Paper and Printing Trades Journal* on the influence of cheap literature on the working classes (June 1876). He wrote for a variety of journals, dailies, weeklies, monthlies, religious papers, trade union and other journals. By the end of his life his occupation was effectively that of journalist, and he was so described in his death certificate. His most effective writing was in the 1880s when he published regular articles in the *Weekly Dispatch* under the pseudonym 'An Artisan'. He later claimed that in articles in the *Dispatch* (8 Feb 1885 and 8 Aug 1886) he had been the first man to advocate the idea of a separate Labour Party. Although the claim to precedence is not quite accurate, Rogers was certainly a pioneer in the field. His intention was summarised in an answer to correspondents [29 Aug 1886]:

A labour party in the House of Commons, strong enough to compel the respect of either party, and strong enough, if need be, to hold the balance of power between the parties, would put an end at once and for ever to the power of landowners and capitalists there.

Rogers's mother was a strict Baptist.

Influenced by her, Rogers was a Nonconformist in his youth. He was a follower of the radical Congregationalist James Allanson Picton, who was a member of the London School Board and later a Member of Parliament. (Rogers wrote Picton's entry in the *Dictionary of National Biography*.) During the 1890s however, Rogers was converted to Anglo-Catholicism, under the influence of Arthur Henry Stanton (1839–1913), the famous ritualist curate of St Alban the Martyr, Holborn. His religious convictions were shared by few of his working-class contemporaries, though his willingness to work with men of other faiths was shown by his continued collaboration with the Broad Churchman Samuel Barnett of Toynbee Hall and the Congregationalist F. H. Stead of Browning Hall. But his Anglo-Catholicism gradually turned him against the Nonconformists, of whom he wrote splenetically in his autobiography, and against the Nonconformist-dominated Liberal Party.

Rogers joined the Vellum (Account Book) Binders' Trade Society in the early 1870s, and had an active career as a trade unionist, especially during the 1890s. The union, which had a continuous existence from 1823, had a tiny membership and the conditions of the vellum binders were worse than those of the letterpress binders. During the binders' strike for an eight-hour day in 1891–2, Rogers was a foreman in the binding department of the Co-operative Printing Society; not himself on strike, he was able to be an effective leader without fear of dismissal. The strike failed despite Rogers's leadership, but it had repercussions both in the union's life and his own. The union nearly foundered, its membership of over 800 falling by over half and its funds being almost wiped out. In 1911 the Vellum Binders amalgamated with the three letterpress binders' unions to form the National Union of Bookbinders and Machine Rulers.

The consequences of the strike for Rogers himself were happier. In 1892 he became the president of the Vellum Binders, holding the office until 1898. From this position came developments which were to make him a man of some importance. He represented the Vellum Binders at the Trades Union

Congress in 1892 and in 1895–8, and while he failed three times to secure election to the Parliamentary Committee, he became well known in trade union circles as an able and informed speaker on a variety of topics. It was his trade union activity during these years which caused him to be chosen as the secretary of the National Committee of Organised Labour for the achievement of old age pensions. A final trade union activity was Rogers's membership of the executive committee of the London Trades Council between 1901 and 1903.

The National Committee of Organised Labour was established in 1899, and it was in July of that year that Rogers was elected its organising secretary at a salary of £4 a week. The choice of Rogers was unexpected, but not surprising. He was a capable writer and a fine speaker, a good organiser, a man with a middle-of-the-road labour background and a religious person with access to clerical support. All these were excellent qualifications.

During the agitation for pensions, which lasted for nearly ten years, the National Committee kept up a continuous agitation, publishing some twenty-five pamphlets and leaflets (fifteen of them by Rogers), lobbying members of Parliament, political and religious leaders and holding large numbers of meetings. Rogers travelled all over the country, especially in the early years, when the Committee's activities were at their height. Rogers's fellow worker for pensions, F. H. Stead (warden of Browning Hall, the centre of the pensions agitation), wrote of these years:

Mr Rogers was indefatigable. He passed to and fro throughout the country like a flame of fire, kindling everywhere an enthusiasm responsive to his own. It might be a great Conference of associated wage-earners gathered from a wide area, it might be a working men's debating club, or a lecture in an out-of-the-way colliery village or rustic hamlet – it mattered not. Wherever men asked to hear of Pensions, there Mr Rogers went, eloquent, stimulating, conclusive. Old age he always championed, but he never failed to make

it the centre of a wide horizon of ennobling thought. The principles he expounded laid the train for more extended reforms [*How Old Age Pensions Began to Be* [1909] 89].

Trade union support for pensions and for the National Committee were not as great as had been hoped, and Rogers went without salary for a year, being paid for work connected with Joseph Rowntree's and Arthur Sherwell's publications on temperance (1904–5). The ultimate success of pensions, however, occasioned a well-publicised dinner to Rogers in November 1909 at which he was presented with a cheque for £161.

At the founding conference of the Labour Representation Committee in February 1900 Rogers represented the Vellum Binders. It was probably his work for old age pensions which made him sufficiently prominent to be elected, bottom of the poll, to the trade union section of the Committee's executive. By a majority of five to three he was chosen the Committee's first chairman, an election which earned him a mention in most histories of the Labour Party.

Rogers's period of service on the LRC was short and took second place to his pensions work; in the Committee's second year he was an executive committee member and in its third year the treasurer. But his service during these years is particularly interesting, not only because of the important period of Labour history with which he was associated, but because it is from this period alone that Rogers's manuscripts survive. These consist of sixty-three letters and postcards, most of them addressed to J. Ramsay Mac-Donald, the Committee's secretary.

What comes out of the correspondence is Rogers's pride in Labour and Labour representation, his opposition to dependence on other political parties (despite the fact that he was never a Socialist), and his scepticism about the working-class voter. He was depressed by support for the Boer War rather than social reform, condemning the workman (in a letter of 14 Jan 1901) 'who won't vote for representatives of his own order, because he believes their ideas visionary and impracticable'. In these letters and elsewhere he pointed out that trade unionists were essentially conservative people and that they could not be expected to advance revolutionary views. At the same time: 'The ideals of the Labour movement make more for national righteousness and national progress than those of any other party' [*Fabian News*, Nov 1902].

Gradually Rogers drifted away from party politics, an important cause of his break with the party system being the education struggle of 1901–6, in which he found himself opposed to most Liberals and Socialists. Eventually he came, without ever abandoning his faith in Labour representation, to believe that party politics were 'simply sectarianism in politics'. His gradual drift away from radicalism was illustrated by his acceptance of a Conservative nomination as an alderman of the London County Council during 1910–11. He sat on the Council ostensibly as a non-party figure, but he normally voted with the Conservative Municipal Reformers. His connections with organised Labour gradually weakened, and in the entry Rogers wrote for *Who's Who* at the end of his life he did not mention his connection with the LRC.

In 1913 Rogers published his autobiography, which had earlier been serialised in the Anglo-Catholic illustrated monthly, the *Treasury*. From an obituary we catch a glimpse of Rogers in his declining years: he began, wrote *Fellowship*, organ of the Browning Settlement:

to take somewhat gloomy views of tendencies in faith and morals. He deplored the popularity of negative preachers. They were his pet abomination. Young men, he said, were growing pleasure-loving, unbelieving, frivolous. Young women he described in terms that were positively savage. But when the world-war broke out the magnificent response which England made to the call of justice and freedom simply transfigured Rogers. It renewed his youth. He felt England was herself again, back once more in the spacious days of great Elizabeth. . . . Now that England called he flung himself without reserve into her service. He went

anywhere, reciting patriotic poetry and appealing for recruits, in music halls, picture palaces, theatres [15 Dec 1915].

Rogers never married. He lived with his parents until their deaths in 1907 and 1908, and at the time of his death lived with his sister, Susan. His nephew Frank, whom Rogers had looked upon as a son, died at the battle of Loos in September 1915. This news deeply affected Rogers, whose own death followed on 16 November 1915. The obituary notices were generous, one of the most notable being by Canon Henry Scott Holland, an old acquaintance of Rogers, in the *Commonwealth*:

No one could have guessed from the outside the kind of man who lay behind the face and form of Frederick Rogers. These suggested something strange and blurred. But the man himself was all sound-hearted, sound-minded, sound-tempered, straight, clear, simple, good. He was the most companionable of fellow-workers, so reliable, so steady, so ready, so right.

The funeral service was held at the church of St John the Divine, Kennington, to whose former vicar, the well-known Anglo-Catholic, Charles Edward Brooke, Rogers had had a strong attachment. He was buried in Nunhead Cemetery, not far from his home in New Cross, to which he had moved from East London in 1901. His net estate of £615 11s 6d was left mainly to his sister Susan; and his literary remains were left to his friend, the civil servant Arthur Canler Hayward, a fellow member of the Elizabethan Literary Society. Rogers's papers, with those of Hayward, were almost certainly destroyed by fire during the Second World War. All other remains, apart from the letters in the Labour Party files, seem to have disappeared.

Writings: (1) Individual books and pamphlets: *James Allanson Picton, A Biographical Sketch* (1883) 20 pp.; *The New Movement at the Universities and what may come of it* (n.d. [1886]) 4 pp.; *The Art of Bookbinding* (1894) 32 pp.; (with F. Millar) *Old Age Pensions: are they desirable and practicable?* (1903); *The*

Early Environment of Robert Browning (1904) 20 pp.; *The Seven Deadly Sins* (1907); *Cowper in the Temple* (1907); *Labour, Life and Literature; Some Memories of Sixty Years* (1913); *The Church in the Modern State* (1914); (2) Contributions to the Proceedings of the Browning Hall Labour Weeks: 'Religion an Answer to the Problem of Life', in *Labour and Religion* (1910); 'The Bond of Unity', in *Christ and Labour* (1911); 'The Rights of a Man', in *The Gospel of Labour* (1912); 'The Logic of Sin', in *The Soul of Labour* (1914) [these four works were published by W. A. Hammond]; (3) Pamphlets and Leaflets published by or on behalf of the National Committee of Organised Labour: *Manifesto in The Times* [reprinted as a leaflet, 1900] 3 pp.; *Old Age Pensions. A Memorandum submitted to the Rt Hon. A. J. Balfour, MP* (1900) 10 pp.; *The Worn-out Workman: what is to be done with him?* [1900?] 2 pp.; *Old Age Pensions for All. An appeal to the Electors* [1900?] 2 pp.; *The Old Age Pension Movement. Interim Report* (1901) 4 pp.; *Why we should not subsidize the Friendly Societies to get Old Age Pensions* [1902?] 2 pp.; *Society and its Worn-out Workers* (1902) 16 pp.; *Poverty and the Aged* (1903) 2 pp.; *The Present Position of Old Age Pensions* (1903) 4 pp.; *Politicians and Old-Age Pensions* [1903?] 4 pp.; *Our Aged Fellow Subjects* [1903?] 2 pp.; *Parliamentary Candidates and Old Age Pensions* [1904?] 2 pp.; *The Care of the Aged in Other Countries and in England* (1905) 24 pp.; *A Plea for Old-age Pensions* (1906) 18 pp.; *Some facts concerning Age and Poverty* [1906?] 2 pp.; *Ten Years' Work for Old Age Pensions, 1899–1909* (1909).

Sources: W. F. Aitken, *Canon Barnett, Warden of Toynbee Hall: his mission and its relation to social movements* (1902, republished 1906 as *Thirty Years in the East End, a Marvellous Story of Mission Work*); F. H. Stead, *How Old Age Pensions began to be* [n.d. 1909]; *Old Age Pensions and Mr Frederick Rogers: a report of the proceedings at a public presentation made to Mr Frederick Rogers at Browning Hall, York Street, Walworth, on Friday November 5 1909 with some press opinions* (privately printed, 1910); *WWW* (1897–1915), 2nd ed. addenda; *WW* (1916); H. Barnett, *Canon Barnett, His Life, Work and Friends*, 2 vols

(1918); G. N. Barnes, *From Workshop to War Cabinet* (1924); *The Book of the Labour Party 1*, ed. H. Tracey [1925]; F. Boas, 'The Elizabethan Literary Society, 1884–1934', *Q. Rev. 262* (Apr 1934) 242–57; J. A. R. Pimlott, *Toynbee Hall, Fifty Years of Social Progress, 1884–1934* (1935); F. Williams, *Fifty Years March: the rise of the Labour Party* [n.d. 1949]; J. Middleton, 'Labour's First Chairman: appreciation of the late Fred Rogers of Whitechapel', *East End News*, 3 Feb 1950; F. Bealey and H. Pelling, *Labour and Politics, 1900–1906: a history of the Labour Representation Committee* (1958); B. B. Gilbert, *The Evolution of National Insurance in Great Britain: the Origins of the Welfare State* (1966); P. d'A. Jones, *The Christian Socialist Revival 1877–1914* (New Jersey, 1968). OBIT. *Times*, 17 Nov 1915; *Guardian*, 18 Nov 1915; *Church Times*, 19 Nov 1915; *Fellowship*, 15 Dec 1915; *Commonwealth*, Dec 1915; *Toynbee Record*, Dec 1915.

DAVID RUBINSTEIN

See also: *George BARNES; *Francis H. STEAD.

ROWLINSON, George Henry (1852–1937)
MINERS' LEADER

George Rowlinson was born in July 1852 at James Bridge, near Walsall, Staffordshire, one of twelve children of Samuel Rowlinson, a coalminer. Confirmation of his date of birth has not been obtained. He declined an opportunity for a good education (which he later regretted) and at the age of nearly eight years went to work in the Silver Thread Stone Mine in the Hopyard district between Walsall and Willenhall. He then entered coalmining and was working at the coal face before he was sixteen. In 1872, when he married Miss Sarah Lane of Cheltenham, he could hardly read or write but commenced studying in his spare time. He became a local preacher for the Primitive Methodists in 1873 and maintained a lifelong association with the movement. In 1880 he emigrated to America intending to work for part of the year and then continue his education but a health breakdown compelled his return to

England where he became an active trade unionist. He obtained employment as an overman in a colliery and in 1881 became president of the West Bromwich District Miners' Association. At the same time he acted as secretary of the local branches of the South Staffordshire and East Worcestershire Permanent Provident Society. He continued his work at the pit until 1884, when following a strike he was victimised. He then joined with others in the establishment of the *Labour Tribune* in 1886.

While travelling to promote sales of this journal in mining districts he visited the Forest of Dean and was there invited by the miners to be their agent. When he was appointed to this position on 16 August 1886 only fifty out of 5000 miners belonged to the Miners' Union but Rowlinson succeeded after four years' work among the miners in obtaining a 100 per cent response. A member of the MFGB executive committee in 1891 and again in 1914, he organised the Forest of Dean miners over a period of thirty-one years into a strong union. During the First World War he adopted a patriotic line and encouraged recruits to the Armed Forces. But in 1917 he was out-voted from his union position and was succeeded by H. W. Booth. In 1922, Jack Williams from the Garw Valley was elected secretary, and later put on record that he found the Union 'in a thoroughly corrupt condition'.

In addition to his work for the miners he was active in local affairs as a member of the school board; chairman of the East Dean Grammar School and of the Dilke Memorial Hospital for a number of years. He continued to serve the Primitive Methodist church as a local preacher and for a long period was an active member of the Liberal Party. His work for the Board of Guardians was of long standing; first elected in 1887 to the Westbury Board, he continued to serve until 1930. A Freemason, he had held office in the craft lodge and was also a Senior Deacon. He was a JP and had been awarded the MBE.

He died on 23 May 1937 at the Dilke Memorial Hospital which he had helped to found and of which he had been honorary secretary since its establishment in 1911. He was survived by his wife, two sons and a daughter; another son and a daughter had predeceased him. He left effects valued at £755.

Sources: W. Hallam, *Miners' Leaders* (1894). OBIT. *Dean Forest Mercury*, 28 May 1937.

JOYCE BELLAMY

See also: Benjamin PICKARD, for Mining Trade Unionism, 1880–99; Thomas ASHTON, for Mining Trade Unionism, 1900–14.

RUTHERFORD, John Hunter (1826–90)
SOCIAL REFORMER AND CO-OPERATOR

Born at Jedburgh on 19 February 1826, John Rutherford was educated at the Grammar School there before entering St Andrews University in 1839 where he studied in the arts faculty for four years but did not graduate. After leaving the University he became an evangelist proclaiming the Morisonian doctrine of a free gospel for all, in opposition to the stricter form of Calvinism. He first became an itinerant preacher in the Cheviots and the Lake District but in 1849 he settled in Newcastle where he already had a number of active supporters. For many years Rutherford had no chapel of his own but continued to preach at street corners and from pulpits of friendly ministers: those of the Primitive Methodist Connexion being the most sympathetic. The Lecture Room, Nelson Street, Newcastle, was finally taken for regular services and in 1860 his supporters decided to build the Bath Lane Church as a permanent centre for his ministry.

Rutherford was an ardent educationalist, and he achieved a national reputation for his success in developing elementary and higher grade schools, especially the well-known Bath Lane schools. He became one of the first members of the Newcastle School Board and maintained an unbroken connection with the Board from the early 1870s until his death in 1890. He was also vigorous in his encouragement of educational opportunities beyond the normal school age. On 21

November 1877 Joseph Cowen laid the foundation stone of the School of Science and Art in Corporation Street, and in 1886 a further step was taken with the establishment of a technical college, first accommodated in buildings in Diana Street. A number of scholarships for the School of Science and Art were also established – available to scholars in public elementary schools throughout England; and in all these efforts and activities Rutherford was the leading figure. His name is commemorated today in the Rutherford College of Technology. In politics, Rutherford was a mid-Victorian radical. He joined the Northern Reform Union (1858–62) and the Reform League in the middle 1860s; was a vigorous supporter of Joseph Cowen, and in 1874 he was a member of Thomas Burt's election committee in Morpeth.

His reforming interest extended to the temperance movement, and in order to be able to speak with authority on the physiological aspects of abstinence he decided to study medicine. After attending the Newcastle Medical School, he took the degrees of LRCP and LRCS at Edinburgh University in 1867, and on his return to Newcastle conducted a medical practice among members of his congregation, and others. His medical knowledge encouraged a special interest in public health problems, and in 1866, following a personal investigation, he presented a report on public health in Newcastle, which was then discussed at length in the town council. On the same subject he read a paper at the Social Science Congress held in Newcastle in 1870. He tried unsuccessfully, on at least one occasion, to enter the Newcastle Town Council, but he did serve for several years on the Board of Guardians.

He became associated with the co-operative movement at the time of the engineers' Nine Hours Movement in the early 1870s. It was the famous strike of 1871 that led, under Rutherford's initiative, to the establishment of the Ouseburn Co-operative Engine Works Company, with a capital of £100,000, in £5 shares. Every workman employed had to become a shareholder, and the articles of association provided for profits, after the excess of 10 per cent on paid-up capital, to be distributed equally between labour and capital. Rutherford was both the chairman and managing director of the company, the story of which is told in Ben Jones, Co-operative Production, pp. 446ff. The enterprise, which was widely supported by working-class organisations in the Newcastle region, went into voluntary liquidation in 1875; as did the Industrial Bank which Rutherford had also helped to float. The engineering works were acquired jointly by the CWS and several co-operative societies but they finally closed down in 1881.

Despite considerable criticism Rutherford's general standing in the co-operative movement does not seem to have been affected by his connection with these industrial and banking failures, and he continued to be a prominent figure at Co-operative Congresses.

He took a great interest in the Mississippi Valley Trading Company, created by E. V. Neale, and with whom he visited the United States to pronounce on the feasibility of the project. He seems also to have maintained his connections with the wider labour movement for at the time of his death he was a trustee of the National Labourers' Society. He died, following a very short illness, on 21 March 1890, and was survived by his wife and a family of three sons and two daughters. He was buried at Elswick Cemetery on 24 March 1890 and left an estate valued at £1499.

Writings: (with G. J. Holyoake) *Christianity versus Secularism* (1854); 'The Public Health of Newcastle-upon-Tyne in 1866 and 1869', *Trans. NAPSS* (1870) 414–20; 'Proposal of a National Industrial Orphanage', *Co-op. Congress Report* (1875); 'A Co-operative Orphanage', *Co-op. Congress Report* (1879).

Sources: J. Burnett, *The Nine Hours' Movement: a history of the Engineers' Strike in Newcastle and Gateshead* (1872); *Bee-Hive*, 19 June 1875; B. Jones, *Co-operative Production* (Oxford, 1894; repr. New York, 1968); R. Welford, *Men of Mark Twixt Tyne and Tweed* 3 (1895); W. E. Adams, *Memoirs of a Social Atom*, 2 vols (1903; repr. with an introduction by John Saville: New York, 1968); P. Redfern, *The Story of the C.W.S.* (Manchester, [1913]); G. D. H. Cole, *A Century of Co-operation* [1945?]; J. B. Jefferys, *The Story of the Engineers* [1945]; E. C. Mack and W. H. G. Armytage, *Thomas Hughes* (1952); C. Muris, 'The Northern Reform Union, 1858–1862' (Newcastle MA, 1953); personal information: R. G. Cant, St Andrews University. OBIT. *Newcastle Daily Chronicle*, 22 Mar 1890; *Co-op. News*, 29 Mar 1890; *Newcastle Weekly Chronicle*, 29 Mar 1890.

JOYCE BELLAMY
JOHN SAVILLE

See also: Joseph COWEN; Benjamin JONES, for Co-operative Production; E. V. NEALE; W. H. PATTERSON.

SEWELL, William (1852–1948)
MINERS' LEADER

Born at Worksop on 22 September 1852, the son of Charles Sewell, a labourer, he moved to Derbyshire in 1861 to work as a miner at the Renishaw and Holbrook collieries. He joined the Eckington lodge of the South Yorkshire Miners' Association which organised the Derbyshire miners in the 1870s and later played a prominent part in the Derbyshire Miners' Association, helping to form the Holbrook lodge and serving as a delegate to the council. A member of the executive committee of the council for nearly thirty years, he gave evidence before the R.C. on Mines in 1907 and in the same year was elected vice-president of the Derbyshire Miners' Association, an office which he held until he became president in 1918. Towards the end of 1924, on account of his age, he decided not to stand for presidency in the following year. At the age of sixty-six he was still working at the coal face, had been a stallman for many years and was a member of the Derby and Midland Fatal Accident Society.

In politics Sewell was a Liberal who was reluctant to support the Labour Party after the affiliation of the MFGB. He was active in local affairs: as a member of the Eckington parish council from its inception in 1894 and several times its chairman, and of the Eckington Burial Board and Old-Age Pen-

sions Committee. His name was repeatedly recommended for the position of county magistrate but he was never selected.

Sewell died on 24 May 1948, aged ninety-five, at his Halfway, near Sheffield, home and was buried in Eckington Cemetery on 29 May.

Sources: (1) MSS: Minutes of the Derbyshire Miners' Association, 1907–24 (NUM, Saltergate, Chesterfield); (2) Evidence before the R.C. on Mines vol. III 1908 XX Qs 24146–392; *Derbyshire Times*, 1907–24; ibid., 12 Jan 1918; J. E. Williams, 'The Political Activities of a Trade Union, 1906–14', *Int. Rev. Social Hist.* 2 (1957) 1–21; idem, *The Derbyshire Miners* (1962).

J. E. WILLIAMS

See also: Thomas ASHTON, for Mining Trade Unionism, 1900–14; *A. J. COOK, for Mining Trade Unionism, 1915–26; Benjamin PICKARD, for Mining Trade Unionism, 1880–99.

SHALLARD, George (1877–1958)
SOCIAL REFORMER AND LABOUR COUNCILLOR

Born on 29 March 1877, at Crew's Hole, Barton Regis, a small semi-rural community on the eastern outskirts of Bristol. He was the son of a baker, Charles Shallard, and was brought up within a family that was centred on the local – somewhat unorthodox – Methodist chapel. Shallard's religious faith and chapel activities were central to his whole life and gave meaning and direction to his social and political work. He was a lay preacher for nearly sixty years in the Kingswood circuit and from 1905 was president of the Crew's Hole Methodist Bible class until nearly the end of his life.

He was educated at the local board school and at the age of thirteen was apprenticed to the letterpress printing trade. When he was twenty-four he set up in business on his own account but after meeting the simple material needs of his family, he was more concerned with social problems than with achieving commercial success. At an early age he had accompanied his father to the Ratepayer's Protection Society and he quickly interested himself in public affairs.

He followed at first his family's devotion to Mr Gladstone and became a member of the East Bristol Liberal Association; and early in his life he became interested in the temperance movement. His deeper concern with social realities was fostered by his close acquaintance with the slums of East Bristol. He joined the Independent Labour Party, vigorously opposed the Boer War and during the First World War claimed unconditional exemption from military service as a pacifist. His claim was rejected, and although fully prepared to go to prison for his beliefs he was offered and accepted agricultural work, returning after the war to rebuild his almost defunct business. In all these activities during the war years he faced much abuse and personal opposition but although a quiet and soft-spoken man, he was inwardly fearless, and never allowed himself to be deflected from either the expression of his views or the practice of his political opinions.

After the First World War he joined the Labour Party and stood unsuccessfully for the Bristol Council. On a second occasion, in November 1921, he was elected and thereafter always held his seat. He was made an alderman in 1936, was a JP for twenty-seven years and served on many committees, taking an especial interest in education. At the age of twenty-five he married Edith Bretton, by whom he had two daughters, Winifred and Elizabeth, who shared many of their father's interests and activities. He died on 18 September 1958 at the age of eighty-one, having lived in the same neighbourhood all his life. He left an estate valued at £4631.

Sources: Personal information: Elizabeth Radnedge (daughter). OBIT. *Bristol Evening Post*, 19 Sep 1958; *Western Daily Press*, 19 Sep 1958.

H. F. BING
JOHN SAVILLE

See also: G. L. PERKINS.

SHARP, Andrew (1841–1919)
MINERS' LEADER

Born at Ellenport, near Maryport, on 26 April 1841, Andrew Sharp was the youngest of nine children whose families on both sides had been engaged in mining in Cumberland for several generations. Only fifteen months old when his father died, he was helping his sisters in the fields at an early age and occasionally went to help his elder brothers on the night shift at the pit. He commenced full-time employment when he was ten, working as a pony driver, and by the time he was eighteen he was a hewer at the coal face. Through self study he became a well-informed and fluent speaker and from early youth he was involved in trade union activity. Victimisation followed and for a time he left Cumberland for Durham, but returned to his native county in 1872.

With John Milburn and John Bell he attended as a delegate from West Cumberland the conference of the Amalgamated Association of Miners held at Walsall from Tuesday 1 October to 9 October 1872. There were altogether in attendance 125 delegates, the three leading officers of the association being Tom Halliday, president; Luke Walkden, treasurer; and John Worrall, secretary. It was largely due to Sharp's efforts that the Cumberland Miners' Association was formed; and at the 1874 conference of the AAM, held at Birmingham on 6–15 October 1874, he was representing some 1500 West Cumberland miners. In the same year he had become agent to the Cumberland Miners' Association, a position he held until his retirement on 22 December 1916, when he was succeeded by Thomas Cape. Shortly after his appointment he was faced with a prolonged strike, the outcome of which was the adoption of a sliding scale in 1879. Sharp was one of the early members of the MFGB executive, on which he represented the Cumberland miners in 1891–2, 1897, 1899, 1903, 1909 and 1912. He was a regular attender at national and international conferences of miners; and was a member of the board of examiners for colliery managers' certificates. After his retirement he was granted a pension of £1 per week.

Although he held Liberal views he adopted an unusually independent policy on political questions, believing that, as his Association contained men of all shades of opinion, he should not exert his influence on either side. He spoke frequently, however, on Liberal platforms; but when the miners affiliated to the Labour Party, Sharp went with them and became an advocate of nationalisation. He unsuccessfully contested the Whitehaven constituency in the January 1910 general election as a Labour candidate, having been nominated by the Whitehaven Trades Council. Sharp had been elected to the Cumberland County Council when it was first constituted as a member for Ellenborough and subsequently sat for West Seaton. He also served on the Maryport Urban District Council and was a poor law overseer in the town.

He died at his Maryport home on 14 October 1919 and was buried at Maryport Cemetery on 18 October. His wife, two sons and two daughters survived him. His estate was valued at £3658.

Sources: Evidence before R.C. on Mining Royalties 1890–1 XLI Qs 13247–389; W. Hallam, *Miners' Leaders* (1894) [inc. portrait of Sharp]; biographical information: M. W. Rowe, Secretary NUM (Cumberland). OBIT. *Whitehaven News*, 16 Oct 1919.
                                    JOYCE BELLAMY

See also: Thomas ASHTON, for Mining Trade Unionism, 1900–14; *Tom HALLIDAY; Alexander MACDONALD, for Mining Trade Unionism, 1850–79; Benjamin PICKARD, for Mining Trade Unionism, 1880–99.

SHILLITO, John (1832–1915)
CO-OPERATOR

Born at Upper Brear, Northowram, near Halifax, on 19 January 1832, the son of a farm labourer, George Shillito, and his wife Jane. He received a short education at the village dame school. Between the age of six and eight years he assisted his mother at home card setting and then helped his father in the fields where he earned two shillings a week for working from 7 am until 8 pm. He acquired a great love of natural history during his agricultural work, an interest which became lifelong. In 1846 he was apprenticed to his father's employer who had a small wiredrawing business in Lower Brear but had

to complete his apprenticeship at Cleckheaton when the firm went bankrupt. He attended classes at the Northowram Mechanics' Institute and, after his apprenticeship ended, he took employment with a firm of Halifax card makers, Gaukroger Bros, and also continued his studies at the Mechanics' Institute there. In addition to his interest in natural history he was also passionately interested in physical geography and geology and in 1896 was admitted to Fellowship of the Royal Geographical Society.

Shillito's connection with the co-operative movement commenced when he joined the Halifax Industrial Co-operative Society in 1861. He served as vice-chairman of the Society for some years and maintained his association with it until his death. His abilities were early recognised by the co-operative movement and in November 1870 he was elected to the board of the CWS. He was compelled to retire in the following year owing to the difficulty of attending meetings but in 1883 he resigned from his full-time employment with Gaukroger Bros where he was foreman, in order to devote all his time to work for the co-operative movement. In 1892 he was elected vice-chairman of the CWS and he succeeded J. T. W. Mitchell as chairman following the latter's death in 1895, a position he held until his own death twenty years later in his eighty-fourth year. During his term of office sales more than trebled – from £10 million in 1895 to £35 million in the year prior to his death. He was president of the Co-operative Congress in 1903 and his work for the CWS involved him in extensive travelling throughout Europe and he also visited America and Ceylon. He represented the Society on the Cotton Growers' Association and was also a director of the Heckmondwike Manufacturing Company for over forty years, being chairman of the Company at the time of his death.

Politically an advanced Liberal, he was closely connected with the West Ward Liberal Club in Halifax of which he was a past president. He served on the Halifax School Board, 1889–95, and in 1892 was appointed a JP, his election as a working-class magistrate being due in large measure to his service for the co-operative movement. He was a Unitarian in religion and had attended the Northgate End Chapel for over forty years.

After a short illness he died at his Halifax home on 12 February 1915 and was buried at All Saints' Cemetery, Halifax, on 16 February following a service at the Unitarian Chapel. He was survived by his wife, formerly Frances Sykes of Lightcliff, whom he married in 1856, and by four sons and a daughter, a second daughter having died in infancy. He left an estate valued at £6073.

Sources: *Co-op. Congress Report* (1903); P. Redfern, *The Story of the C.W.S.* (Manchester, [1913]); and *The New History of the C.W.S.* (Manchester, 1938). OBIT. *Halifax Courier*, 13 Feb 1915; *Halifax Guardian*, 13 Feb 1915; *Co-op. News*, 20 Feb 1915; W. Maxwell, 'The Late John Shillito, JP, FRGS', *CWS Annual* (1916).

JOYCE BELLAMY

See also: J. T. W. MITCHELL; Percy REDFERN, for Co-operative Wholesaling.

SIMPSON, James (1826–95)
CO-OPERATOR AND TRADE UNIONIST

Nothing is known of his early life except that he was born on 7 March 1826 and that he worked for the Greenock Foundry Company in his youth. He remained with the Company for forty years and in his later years was foreman engineer. He was prominently associated with the co-operative movement in Greenock and was among a small group of enthusiasts who succeeded in reconstructing a co-operative society, which had been formed by a group of workmen in the early 1860s but which failed after a few years. In 1870 this new society, the Greenock Industrial Co-operative Society, was formed and James Simpson appointed first president, a position he held for thirty years. From 1884 until his death Simpson was president of the Renfrewshire Conference Association and was a director of the Paisley Manufacturing Society and the Scottish Co-operative Farming Association.

Apart from his interest in co-operation which was the central concern of his life, he was an ardent temperance advocate and he also served the Amalgamated Society of Engineers in an official capacity for a number of years. By religion he was a member of the Reformed Presbyterian Church, in which he served as an Elder. He died at his home in Greenock on 22 July 1895 and was buried in Greenock Cemetery where, in 1896, a memorial stone was erected by the Renfrewshire Co-operative Conference Association as a tribute to his loyalty and work for the movement. William Maxwell gave the address at the unveiling ceremony, at which members of the Simpson family, including James's son David, were present.

Sources: M. S. Swan, *Jubilee History of the Greenock Central Co-operative Society Ltd* (1930). OBIT. *Greenock Telegraph*, 24 July 1895; *Co-op. News*, 10 Aug 1895; *Greenock Telegraph*, 16 Mar 1896.

JOYCE BELLAMY

See also: W. MAXWELL, for Scottish Co-operation.

SITCH, Thomas (1852–1923)
TRADE UNION LEADER

Born on 23 July 1852 at Lomeytown in Cradley Heath, Staffordshire, the son of a chainmaker. He started work at the age of eight, blowing bellows in a chain shop, before moving with his family to Tipton near Dudley, where he became a very young chain striker at the works of Parkes and Company. At the age of seventeen he moved, again with his family, to Newcastle upon Tyne where he worked as a small chainmaker. The strength of union organisation in the north-east, as compared with the 'mushroom' unionism of his native Black Country, made a profound and lasting impression on him. While living in Newcastle he married Elizabeth Young in 1877 and he also became the youngest member of the Trades Council. He won a local reputation as an outstanding club cricketer by heading the batting averages of the Heaton Club for seven successive years.

From Newcastle, Sitch and his wife moved to Chester where he worked on government contracts at the factory of

Wood and Company. Here, in July 1889, he established the Saltney, Pontypridd and Staffordshire Chainmakers' and Strikers' Association. The initial membership was just fifteen, all drawn from Wood's factory. By 1894 membership had grown to 360 and Sitch returned to Cradley Heath, the established centre of the chain trade, as full-time secretary of the Association. By virtue of its place of origin the union became known in South Staffordshire as the 'Chester Society', and on the twenty-fifth anniversary of its inauguration, in 1914, members and their families travelled to Chester by two special trains on a celebration excursion. By this time membership had grown to over 1300, and included every employee in the factory branch of the chain trade, where the Association in effect had a closed shop. Sitch was thus in the position of being probably the most powerful individual in the South Staffs trade, which had virtually a world monopoly of a vital product. It was a position he never abused. He was always prepared to recognise that there were two sides to every dispute. In consequence relations with the employers were consistently harmonious, and the industry was virtually strike-free.

In spite of the union's success in raising wages and improving conditions (the average wage in the factory branch of the chain trade rose from 18s to 40s per week between 1890 and 1914), Sitch was always keenly aware of the limitations of industrial action. He was the main inspiration behind the union's long and ultimately successful struggles to end the scandal of bogus certificates in the trade, and to secure the application of the Particulars Clause to outworkers in chain and other trades. He also ensured that the 'Chester Society' played a leading part in the long agitation which resulted in the inclusion of the hammered and dollied branches of the chain trade in the Trade Boards Act of 1909. In all these struggles Sitch and the union had the full support of the Midland Counties Trades Federation, of which he was treasurer for six years. He represented the Federation and his own Association at many national conferences, and at international congresses in Paris, Berlin, Amsterdam, Brussels and Pittsburg.

He also once travelled abroad on a 'rescue' mission. In 1906 two Cradley Heath chainmakers and four strikers were lured away to Duisburg to reveal the secrets of their trade to their German counterparts. Sitch and a member of the Employers' Association followed them, and at the second attempt persuaded them to see the error of their ways, smuggled them out of the country and back to England.

In politics he was for most of his life a Liberal. In 1918, however, his third son Charles was adopted as the Labour candidate for the Kingswinford division, whereupon his father changed his allegiance, and in fact became the first president of Cradley Heath Labour Club. Charles was duly elected, and held the seat until 1931. He also succeeded his father as union secretary in 1923. Thomas himself declined a number of opportunities to stand as a parliamentary candidate. As a practical man he had little time for political theories, and felt that as an MP his ideals of personal service would suffer by his being too remote from his constituents. These ideals may have stemmed from his Baptist convictions.

He did, however, play a notable part in local government. From 1898 to 1913 he was a member of Rowley Regis Urban District Council. He became chairman of the Education Committee and was chairman of the Council in 1911. In 1913 he relinquished his seat to allow Charles to stand and be elected for his ward, Cradley Heath. In this year he became a JP and was returned unopposed to Staffordshire County Council. In 1918 he returned to the Rowley Regis Urban District Council to fill the vacancy for the Cradley Heath ward occasioned by Charles's election to Parliament. He remained a member of both Councils until his death. Also in 1918 he became chairman of the local Labour Employment Committee.

Sitch retired from his position as secretary of the Chainmakers' Association, which now had a membership of 2000 at the end of 1922, honoured by many handsome tributes from his union and from the employers in the chain trade. He was not, however, to enjoy a long retirement. He died on 23 April

1923 at his home, Unity Villa, Sydney Road, Cradley Heath, which had been built for him by the union as a combined residence and office. His wife, four daughters and four of his five sons survived him, the eldest son having died from pneumonia, contracted while on active service, in 1916. Sitch left effects valued at £1104.

Sources: Reports of activities of Association and Midland Counties Trades Federation in *Wolverhampton Chronicle, Dudley Herald, Stourbridge County Express, Brierley Hill Advertiser* (1894–1922); *Souvenir of Chainmakers' and Strikers' Association Semi-Jubilee* (1914); G. C. Allen, *The Industrial Development of Birmingham and the Black Country 1860–1927* (1929); *Souvenir of Chainmakers' and Strikers' Association Jubilee* (1939) [in Dudley Public Library: photographs in these *Souvenirs*]; personal information: A. E. Head, secretary of Chainmakers' and Strikers' Association (Nov 1970 by interview). OBIT. *Times,* 27 Apr 1923; *Dudley Herald,* 28 Apr 1923; *Stourbridge County Express,* 28 Apr 1923.

ERIC TAYLOR

See also: Richard JUGGINS; William MILLERCHIP.

SKEVINGTON, John (1801–50)
OWENITE AND CHARTIST

John Skevington, born in 1801 in Loughborough, Leicestershire, was the son of Joseph Skevington (probably identical with the Joseph Skivington, manufacturer of twist lace in Derby Road, Loughborough, mentioned in Pigot's *Directory of Leicestershire,* 1830). Joseph Skevington was one of the founders of the Primitive Methodist Connexion in Loughborough and in 1819 became one of the trustees of the first Chapel in the town in Dead Lane. At the age of fourteen, John Skevington acquired fame as 'the boy preacher' in the Primitive Methodist Loughborough Plan and shortly afterwards became a travelling preacher. In 1822, 1823 and 1824 he travelled successfully at Halifax, Barnsley and Bradwell. He then ceased 'to travel' mainly because of his lameness, and returned to Loughborough where he con-

tinued as a leader and preacher in his native circuit and was employed in recording minutes and drafting resolutions for district meetings. He severed his connection with the Primitive Methodists in 1836 owing to troubles over the Dead Lane Chapel, of which he was Trust treasurer. The property was sold and demolished in 1837. Towards the end of his life he sought to re-enter the Primitive Methodist Church but was refused and joined another communion. [Kendall vol. *1* 337] considered that Skevington ought not to have been allowed to leave the Connexion in 1836 over the Dead Lane affair; and he also thought it possible that it was Hugh Bourne who was responsible for the refusal to readmit Skevington into the Primitive fold: Bourne being vigorously hostile to political Radicals.

While still active among the Primitive Methodists, John Skevington had become interested in the early Owenite movement. He attended, as a delegate from Loughborough, the First Co-operative Congress, in Manchester, on 26–27 May 1831 and moved a resolution for the election of a chairman (E. Dixon) and twelve members (including Robert Owen, William Pare, and William Thompson) to be the committee for the coming year. At the Third Co-operative Congress, held in London on 23 April to 1 May 1832, during a discussion on Robert Owen's religious views John Skevington told the Congress that he had not been sent to discuss metaphysical questions and that his society would not sanction or receive any doctrine which aimed at the subversion of Christian principles. He was again present at the Fourth Co-operative Congress held at Liverpool in October 1832, when he represented the Hathern, Leicester, Loughborough and Wymeswold Co-operative Societies. (In the Congress report his address is given as J. Skevington and Co., top of Market Place, Loughborough.) At this Congress a report was given of the North-West of England Co-operative Company, established in December 1831, of which Skevington and four others were trustees.

It was shortly after he left the Primitive Methodists that Skevington became associated with the Chartist movement, which was then in its beginnings in his region. 'From early life', he wrote, 'I advocated the rights of the many.' He was already widely known as a democrat and spoke frequently on the hustings at elections; and when Chartism began to grow he was regarded as its natural leader in Loughborough. He had great influence among the working classes and always used his power to prevent violence, being no insurrectionist. Towards the end of his life he wrote: 'As an advocate of the principles of the People's Charter, I found nothing on inspection to condemn in them, nor in my advocacy of the same, but a firm conviction that though a man may be a Chartist and not a Christian, a man cannot be a Christian and not a Chartist unless through ignorance.'

Skevington took the chair at a meeting in late August 1838 to form a Loughborough District Association of the National Union, which had its headquarters in Birmingham; and two months later he chaired a mass meeting variously estimated at between 3000 and 7000 people. On 19 November 1838 he spoke in the morning at a mass meeting in Leicester for the official adoption of the Charter and in the evening took the chair and made the opening speech at a dinner in the Town Hall attended by 250 people, at which Feargus O'Connor was the guest of honour. In 1839 Skevington was Loughborough delegate to the National Convention, along with T. R. Smart for Leicester, and they both reported back to a public meeting on Whit Monday held on a piece of open land in Belvoir Street, Leicester. At the Convention in July Skevington protested against O'Brien's motion calling off the National Holiday, but when it came to the vote, he supported the motion. On 6 September, he was one of those who voted for the dissolution of the Convention.

All this activity had drawn upon him the attention of the authorities. On 30 January 1839, one of the Loughborough JPs, C. M. Phillips of Garendon Hall, in a report to the Home Secretary, described Skevington as 'the husband of a respectable bonnet maker' and had gone on to say that he and Smart were 'both reckless men, destitute of character'. (Slater's *National and Commercial Directory, Leicestershire*, 1849, includes, under Straw Bonnet Makers, Emma Skevington of Market Place, Loughborough, and under Hatters, John Skevington of Market Place, Loughborough.)

The activity of the Chartist movement in Leicester and the surrounding villages increased greatly with the assumption of leadership by Thomas Cooper, who had arrived in the town in November 1840. By the autumn of 1841 two rival Chartist organisations were in existence: the larger, the Shakespearean Association led by Thomas Cooper; and John Markham's group (Markham being a radical leader of long standing in the town). In January 1842 a meeting was held in the Town Hall to try to settle the quarrel, with John Skevington, as so often, in the chair. During the summer of 1842 he was conducting vigorous propaganda for the Charter in the north Leicestershire villages, and the climax of political activity in the whole country was reached with first a colliers' strike, and then a strike of stockingers. The turnout in Loughborough was complete and Skevington and Charles Jarratt, the latter a framework knitter, then turned their attention to the surrounding villages. Both were then arrested on a charge of using inflammatory language. Skevington was ultimately allowed out on sureties, and he was bound over to keep the peace.

Thomas Cooper was imprisoned in May 1843 and in the town and the county political activity declined sharply during the middle years of the decade. The split between those who followed Cooper, and the rest of the Chartist body, was gradually overcome, and the old leaders, T. R. Smart, John Markham and Skevington himself, remained active, coming into prominence again during the more excited months of 1848. The failure of the 10 April meeting on Kennington Common made no impact upon the Leicestershire movement, and during the succeeding months the militant spirit of the local Chartists was as vigorous as it ever had been. Skevington was at the centre of the movement's leadership, but it is doubtful whether he countenanced the growing spirit of physical force which was now beginning to pervade the mass of the Chartist followers. For this growing mood of militancy, among other pieces of evidence, we have John Sketchley's reminiscences, written nearly thirty years later.

In 1848 Skevington's followers in Loughborough presented him with a testimonial, and his portrait in oils, 'for his great services to the cause of liberty'. He died on 4 January 1850 at the age of forty-nine. He had inherited money from his father and was always prepared to spend it to further the causes he was interested in. He named his son Feargus, after O'Connor.

Sources: MSS: Home office papers: PRO 40/44; 41/19 Skevington; Pigot's *Directory of Leicestershire* (1830); *Report of Fourth Co-operative Congress* (Liverpool, 1832); *Leicester Journal and Midlands Counties General Advertiser*, 26 Aug 1842; Slater's *National and Commercial Directory, Leicestershire* (1849); G. R. Searson, *A Quarter of a Century's Liberalism in Leicester, 1826–1850* (Leicester, n.d.); *The Life of Thomas Cooper. Written by himself* (1872); John Sketchley, 'Personal Experiences in the Chartist Movement', *Today* (July 1884) 20–9; H. B. Kendall, *The Origin and History of the Primitive Methodist Church 1* (n.d.); A. Temple Patterson, *Radical Leicester. A History of Leicester, 1780–1850* (Leicester, 1954); J. F. C. Harrison, 'Chartism in Leicester', in *Chartist Studies*, ed. Asa Briggs (1959) 99–146; A. Bonner, *British Co-operation* (Manchester, 1961); H. F. Bing, 'John Skevington: a Loughborough Radical', *Bull. of the Loughborough and District Archaeological Soc.*, no. 11 (1970) 6–9; personal information: Fergus Stevens, Narborough, son of Elizabeth Skevington and great-grandson of John Skevington; there is a portrait of Skevington in Newark House Museum, Leicester.

H. F. Bing
John Saville

See also: *Thomas Cooper; *Feargus O'Connor, for Chartism, 1840–8.

SMITHIES, James (1819–69)
OWENITE AND ROCHDALE PIONEER

Born at Huddersfield in 1819, James Smithies had a fairly good education for those times and was good at figures. Moving to Rochdale, he became apprenticed to a wool stapler there and, when he had served his time, set up in business on his own in the top storey of a house in Lord Street, which he called 'Henland'. His home became the meeting-place of all sorts of people. Rochdale was a lively town in the first half of the century, with many religious and social sects discussing and debating their points of view, and Owenism took root quite early, there being a propagandist society already by 1830. Smithies had a bound copy of Dr William King's *Co-operator* which was certainly read and discussed, and Smithies must have been a member of the Rochdale branch, no. 24, of the Rational Society (for which see Charles Howarth). In personal terms Smithies made a most important contribution to the small group of Owenites and radicals who were later to become the Co-operative Pioneers, for his was a happy nature and he had great patience and tolerance; and all the records of these years bear witness to the strength and solidity which he brought to the early co-operative movement. His house was the place to which visitors went. G. J. Holyoake was a well-known visitor, and when J. M. F. Ludlow toured the northern co-operative organisations in 1851, it was Smithies who showed him round Rochdale.

The original meeting which led to the formation of the Rochdale Society of Equitable Pioneers was held at Smithies's house in 1844 and, when the Society was formally established on 15 August 1844, he was elected one of the four directors. At the opening of the Toad Lane Store on 21 December, Smithies took down the shutters. He later held the offices of president, secretary and superintendent of the Society. He initiated the textile trade of the Society in 1847 and he was active in promoting the Rochdale Co-operative Manufacturing Society (1854). He became a town councillor of Rochdale, the only one of the Pioneers to reach municipal office. In 1855–6 the Rochdale Pioneers' Society became involved in income tax complications and Smithies cheerfully accepted the Society's request to contest the issue in the Courts and before the Commissioners of Inland Revenue.

Smithies also played an important part in the development of the Co-operative Wholesale Society. In 1851 a conference at Bury passed a resolution in favour of a central trading department and appointed a committee of four (Smithies being one) to draw up a report which was presented to a conference of representatives of co-operative societies from Lancashire and Yorkshire at Manchester in June 1851. This report, said to have been drawn up largely by Lloyd Jones, survives in Smithies's handwriting. In 1854 Smithies wrote to the Central Co-operative Agency in London that the Rochdale Society was willing to become a central depot for the North and would, as hitherto, supply neighbouring societies with goods at cost price on a commission basis to cover expenses. In March 1856 he was one of the Rochdale Society's delegates at a conference in Rochdale which decided to convert the Rochdale wholesale department into a federal agency. In November 1860 he was appointed at a Rochdale conference to be a member of a committee to discuss amendments to the Industrial and Provident Societies Acts, which would facilitate the establishment of a wholesale society, and he went to London with Abraham Greenwood to promote the Amending Bill. When the North of England Co-operative Wholesale Industrial Provident Society Ltd was established in 1863, Smithies was enrolled as one of twelve individual members and appointed treasurer. He also became secretary of the Rochdale Co-operative Land and Building Company which by 1864 had built twenty-five houses; and he attended the conference on Good Friday 1867 to form the Co-operative Insurance Company and was a witness to the signatures of the seven original members.

Conscious of the fact that he had had more education than most of his fellow co-operators, Smithies was always anxious to promote educational opportunities. He learned from books as well as experience and distributed his knowledge freely to all. He taught in the Toad Lane Store on Sunday mornings. In his speech at the opening of the new Rochdale Central Store on 28 September 1867, he said they would have provided schools for their children had the proposed rule for the allocation of one-tenth of the profits to education been allowed by the Registrar. His daughter regularly used the Reading Room of the Rochdale Society in the 1870s, something which required courage at a time when women played practically no part in public, or even co-operative, affairs.

In May 1869, although unwell, Smithies insisted on attending a CWS board meeting in Manchester. Returning home, he had to remain in bed, where he was visited by friends, and his last message to one of his old colleagues was: 'Stick to Toad Lane.' He died on Thursday 27 May and was buried in Rochdale Cemetery on Monday 31 May and was mourned at the CWS quarterly meeting in August. Thomas Hughes at the end of his presidential address to the Co-operative Congress (31 May 1869) referred to the death of James Smithies, whose friendship he had enjoyed for twenty years, and expressed the sympathy of Congress with his relatives. Smithies's effects were valued at under £600.

Sources: Anon., 'Co-operative Stores', Chambers' Edinburgh J. n.s. 14 (Nov 1850) 346–8; P.G., 'The Rochdale Pioneers', Frasers Mag. 61 (June 1860) 861–72; Anon. [one of the twenty-eight], 'The Rochdale Twenty-eight', All the Year Round, 19, 29 Feb 1868, 274–6; Co-op. Congress Report (1869); G. J. Holyoake, History of Co-operation, 2 vols (1875–9); idem, Self-help by the People: thirty-three years of co-operation in Rochdale (1882); W. Robertson, 'Rochdale: the birthplace of modern co-operation' in Handbook of the Co-operative Congress (1892); G. J. Holyoake, 'The History of the Rochdale Pioneers', Co-operation, 1 (1909–11); P. Redfern, The Story of the C.W.S. (Manchester, [1913]: new ed. 1938); E. O. Greening, Memories of Robert Owen and the Rochdale Pioneers (Manchester, 1925); W. H. Brown, The Rochdale Pioneers (Manchester, 1944); G. D. H. Cole, A Century of Co-operation (Manchester [1945?]); A. Bonner, British Co-operation (Manchester, 1961).

H. F. BING

See also: William COOPER; James DALY; Charles HOWARTH; *James STANDRING.

SPENCER, George Alfred (1873–1957)
MINERS' LEADER AND LABOUR MP

Born on 13 December 1873 at Sutton-in-Ashfield, Nottinghamshire, the second son of eighteen children of a miner. His date of birth was given by his son but no record of this was found at Somerset House, nor for the year 1872, the date given in *WWW*. Spencer's parents moved about a good deal in his early days, and at one time they kept a public house at South Normanton, Derbyshire. At the age of eight he began working in the fields (presumably after school hours) and when he was eleven he worked as a 'half-timer' at Pleasley Colliery, going underground at Blackwell Colliery a year later (both in Derbyshire). His childhood education had been much interrupted because of the frequent moves by his family to new homes, and in the decade before 1914 he attended WEA evening classes for some seven years to extend and deepen his general education.

Spencer began to be involved in trade union affairs as a young man. He was elected checkweighman at New Hucknall Colliery near Sutton-in-Ashfield some time before the First World War, although the exact date is not known, and was of sufficient standing in the Nottinghamshire coalfield to be nominated by the local miners as one of the arbitrators over the introduction of cutting machines at Eastwood Collieries, afterwards centre of the No. 5 Area of the East Midlands Division. This was in 1910, and in the same year he came second to W. Carter in the poll for the assistant secretary-ship of the Nottingham Miners' Association. He was elected president of this Association in 1912 and also in the same year began to represent the Association on the Joint District Board.

He took a moderate pro-war position during the First World War and was already showing some of the political and industrial attitudes that became more strongly marked at a later stage in his career. In 1915, for instance, he supported the unsuccessful attempt made by J. G. Hancock MP to disaffiliate the Notts Miners' Association politically from the MFGB; and in 1918 he spoke strongly at a delegate conference of the MFGB against a proposal for national wage negotiation, preferring to retain the Federated District Conciliation Board which covered all the inland coalfields. Spencer was always highly conscious of Nottinghamshire's own interests as a district, not least because it was one of the more prosperous mining areas and he wanted to retain the quasi-national Federated District (of all inland coalfields). The actual, though unintended, effect of the left-wing campaign for national negotiations was the break-up of the Federated District.

Responding to the militancy of the rank and file in the post-war years he opposed intervention in Russia and called for the withdrawal of British troops from Ireland; and during the years 1919–21 he spoke in favour of some measure of direct action, though whether he ever believed in it is doubtful. Spencer had joined the ILP about 1900 and became the first Labour MP for the Broxtowe division at the general election of 1918. His opponents were Sir Charles Seely (Liberal) and H. H. Whaite (Coalition National Democratic Party). Spencer held the seat at subsequent elections until his last contest in 1924, when he had a majority of 2963 over the Liberal candidate. He resigned just before the 1929 general election. At the time when he was first elected to Parliament, Spencer was a moderate, orthodox miners' leader. He seconded the resolution on nationalisation at the annual conference of the MFGB in 1920 and his political opinions in 1918 would be well in line with middle of the road opinion inside the LP. The increasing problems of the coal industry, however, and the industrial tensions which were their accompaniment, encouraged a steady shift to the right in Spencer's attitudes and outlook. He vigorously attacked A. J. Cook for the latter's revolutionary talk in 1925 and his own policies and statements came under increasing criticism from the left wing in the Notts Miners' Association. Spencer was supported in his general position by Frank Varley MP, although the personal relations between the two men are said to have been very difficult [Arnot (1961) 201].

The turning-point in Spencer's career came with the General Strike and the long-drawn-out miners' lock-out. The Notts Miners' Association on the eve of the General Strike had only just liquidated the large debt accumulated during the 1921 lock-out; it had 33,000 members of whom 6000 were in arrears with their subscriptions; and some 23,000 miners in the country remained outside the union. The Association was not, therefore, in a strong position to engage in a long struggle, and from early on it was clear that Nottinghamshire was a weak link in the national miners' chain, and this for a number of reasons, some of which have already been indicated. Spencer himself had been against a strike from the beginning, and both in the House of Commons and outside he had argued for a sympathetic understanding of the Samuel Report.· The problem for Nottinghamshire was that relatively favourable terms for settlement could without much difficulty have been arranged, and the presence of Spencer and Varley, among others, in the top leadership of the Association undoubtedly encouraged sectional feeling in the coalfield. Even so on 16 August 1926 the number of men working underground in Nottinghamshire was estimated at only 1700, although the number working outcrops was increasing quite rapidly. On 6 August the owners wrote to the Notts Miners' Association suggesting a joint meeting to discuss a return to work, and throughout August there were growing contacts between unofficial groups of miners, whose leaders were members of the British Workers' League, and the local colliery owners, particularly the Bolsover Colliery Company with an annual output of three-and-a-half million tons and 10,562 employees in 1925. The latter company had supported the British Workers' League before 1926. The League, founded as an ultra-patriotic organisation, had become prominent during 1917 and 1918. Its main aim was the separation of the trade unions from the Labour Party by the establishment of an 'independent' trade union party. The League had probably some connection in its early days with the British Commonwealth Union founded about 1917 by prominent industrial-

ists and public figures (among them Sir Vincent Caillard of Vickers and W. A. S. Hewins); and in any case it seems certain that the League was supported throughout its life by financial contributions from employers. In Nottinghamshire the League members formed a breakaway organisation and met the Bolsover company to negotiate a settlement on 19 August 1926. This was before Spencer joined the organisation. Both Varley and Spencer were attacked for their sectionalism at national meetings of the MFGB but up to September 1926 all the permanent officials of the Association were still publicly supporting the policy of the MFGB, except that Spencer in the House of Commons at the end of August 1926 made clear that his standpoint differed from that of his mining colleagues in a speech which won him warm praise from the coalowner members of Parliament who followed him in the debate. What was exacerbating the situation, itself much encouraged by the known doubts of many of the Nottinghamshire leaders, was the steady drift back to work. By the end of September the Association estimated that some 32,000 to 33,000 men were back in the pits [Griffin (1962) 183].

On 5 October Spencer was the speaker at a meeting of the Digby and New London lodge which agreed on an immediate return to work of the minority of men still out. Spencer did not negotiate terms: these were already fixed unilaterally by the owners [Griffin (1962) 201–2]. He agreed, however, to negotiate with the management for the right of the remaining unionists to return to their old jobs. This he did the next day and, since this was in clear opposition to MFGB policy, on 7 October he was summoned before a national conference. He duly appeared on 8 October to make his explanation which was not accepted but indeed was followed by a debate unprecedented in the thirty-five years of the Miners' Federation conferences. From the chair Herbert Smith denounced Spencer as 'a coward' and secretary A. J. Cook also asked that he be condemned, saying 'Mr Spencer is a blackleg of the worst order: a conscious blackleg.' On the proposition that 'Mr Spencer be asked to leave the conference and the matter be referred to the Nottinghamshire District' the vote was overwhelming, Spencer's explanation being rejected by 759 votes to four. The council of the Notts Miners' Association met on 16 October and Spencer was suspended until the council itself was reconstituted. These two events precipitated the decision for Spencer to lead a breakaway union from the Notts Association, and from the beginning of November the organisation began to take shape. On 20 November a formal agreement was reached between the Nottinghamshire owners and Spencer's group [text in Griffin (1962) 217–20] and two days later the breakaway union was formally established. The Nottinghamshire and District Miners' Industrial Union had Ben Smith, formerly vice-president of the Notts Miners' Association, as president, Richard Gascoyne (later sacked by Spencer) as secretary and George Spencer as 'leader of the men at work represented'. After 1926 Spencer was on particularly close terms with the directors of the Bolsover Colliery Co. who maintained the 'Butty' system (in an acute form) until the Second World War years.

Spencer's Union lasted for just over ten years. One of its first acts was to persuade the owners to help subsidise a pension fund, and this proved a notably successful recruiting device. Yet the Union, at its most powerful, never organised more than a third of the Nottinghamshire miners and in most years the proportion was a good deal lower. But the Union was throughout vigorously supported by most of the owners and the Notts Miners' Association found itself incapable of obtaining elementary rights of organisation except at the mines of James Oakes and Co.; and partly because of this there was a steady fall in membership to the mid-thirties. Branches of the Spencer Union were opened in Scotland, Durham, Northumberland, Yorkshire, Derbyshire, Staffordshire and South Wales and by the end of 1928 the national total of branches was 273, but the membership of most of them was small. The national Non-Political Trade Union movement also achieved but meagre success outside Nottinghamshire and it was only

Havelock Wilson's energy and money together with some financial support also from some industrialists that helped keep any semblance of national organisation alive. Havelock Wilson was secretary of the National Union of Seamen: he had kept his union out of the General Strike, and when Spencer's organisation was established, Wilson backed it vigorously. For this he and the National Union of Seamen were excluded from the TUC late in 1927.

In the decade which followed the formation of Spencer's Union, although many attempts were made by the MFGB and the Notts Miners' Association to replace the Spencer Union none was successful. There were some inside the Notts Miners' Association – among them Herbert Booth – who believed that attempts should be made to negotiate a reunion and such an attempt was made with A. J. Cook's support when Emanuel Shinwell was at the Mines Department; but the majority were firm on their insistence on 'no compromise'. It was not until 1935 that there began a further effort to end what the MFGB characterised as company unionism in the Nottinghamshire coalfield. On 2 February 1935 three national officials of the MFGB – Joseph Jones, Will Lawther and Ebby Edwards – attended a full delegate council of the Notts Miners' Association and their report to the executive of the MFGB led to the beginnings of the campaign against Spencerism. In the course of the next two years the MFGB took negotiations into their own hands but really what precipitated matters was the dispute at Harworth Colliery which was to assume national importance and became notorious for the harsh prison sentences served on some of the local miners' leaders, including Michael Kane, chairman of the Harworth Branch of the Nottingham Miners' Association.

The story of Harworth and of the eventual fusion of the Notts Miners' Association with Spencer's Industrial Union is told in detail in both Arnot (1961) and Griffin (1962). Their approach and interpretation as well as some of their facts differ but there is no disagreement that the decision to merge the two organisations was more favourable initially to Spencer than to the Notts Miners' Association. In the long run, however, MFGB policies triumphed, with the formation of the National Union of Miners in 1944 and the nationalisation of the coal industry in 1946; both of which were strongly opposed by Spencer.

George Spencer became president of the new Nottinghamshire Miners' Federated Union, which came into existence officially on 1 September 1937, and he retired in 1945. During this last period of his career as a miners' leader he continued to play some part in national conferences and was on the executive of the MFGB in 1942. The bitterness in the Nottingham coalfield took many years to heal, although the greater prosperity of the war years and the immediate postwar period helped to moderate the hatreds of the inter-war period; but even as late as 1943 there were over 10,000 non-unionists in the county. The Pension Scheme initiated by Spencer was greatly improved upon after the formation of the Federated Union. It was financed in effect by a levy on the sale of coal and it continued to exist under nationalisation. Spencer was highly regarded by some, who otherwise disliked him, for forcing the Pension Scheme on the owners and for his expertise in workman's compensation and common law damages for industrial injuries.

In his earlier days Spencer, like many activist miners, took a prominent part in local politics. He was elected a member of Sutton-in-Ashfield Urban District Council and became its chairman. In religion he was a Wesleyan Methodist and was one of their lay preachers; but he left the chapel in his middle age and had ceased local preaching in the late twenties. In his last years he had no religious faith. His politics, as already noted, shifted steadily to the right after the First World War and especially in the years of his non-political union he was vigorously outspoken against Socialists and Communists. His interests, outside unionism and politics, were varied. He was an enthusiastic cricketer and in 1949–50 was president of the Nottinghamshire County Cricket Club; and he was interested in other sports including football as well as being a keen chess and

card player. He also invested in stock markets on the advice of colliery owners. He was a Deputy Lieutenant of Nottinghamshire from 1941, and a Freemason. Spencer always dressed smartly, usually in a dark formal suit, and he disliked the sloppy dress worn by many miners in his day (especially Herbert Smith's cloth cap). In his personal manners he was autocratic, and in later years he was a friend and confidant of Waldron Smithers, Conservative MP for Orpington.

He married in 1896 Emma, daughter of Richard Carlin of Sutton-in-Ashfield, and there was a son and a daughter of the marriage. He died on 21 November 1957 in the Nottingham City Hospital, being survived by his wife and family. He left an estate worth about £20,000.

Sources: The most detailed accounts of George Spencer's career as leader of a breakaway union are in R. Page Arnot, *The Miners: Years of Struggle* (1953) and *The Miners in Crisis and War* (1961) and Alan R. Griffin, *The Miners of Nottinghamshire, 1914–1944* (1962). See also: S. V. Bracher, *The Herald Book of Labour Members* (1923); *Dod* (1929); W. L. Ellis, 'The Miner's Struggle in Notts.', *Lab. Mon. 18* (Jan 1936) 34–9; *The Harworth Colliery Strike: A Report to the Executive Committee of the National Council for Civil Liberties* (NCCL, 1937) 16 pp.; *Kelly* (1952); *WWW* (1951–60); A. R. Griffin, *The Miners of Nottinghamshire: 1881–1914* (Nottingham, 1956); J. E. Williams, *The Derbyshire Miners* (1962); Anthony Mason, 'The Miners' Unions of Northumberland and Durham, 1918–1931, with special reference to the general strike of 1926' (Hull PhD, 1968); A. R. Griffin, *Mining in the East Midlands, 1550–1947* (1971); personal information: Dr A. R. Griffin, Dr John Spencer (son) and Dr C. H. Thompson. OBIT. *Nottingham Guardian Journal*, 22 Nov 1957; *Times*, 23 Oct 1957; *Colliery Guardian*, 28 Nov 1957.

JOHN SAVILLE

See also: *A. J. Cook, and for Mining Trade Unionism, 1915–26; *Peter Lee, for Mining Trade Unionism, 1927–44; *F. B. Varley.

SPENCER, John Samuel (1868–1943)
MINERS' LEADER

Born on 29 March 1868 at Castle Acre, Norfolk, the son of Thomas James Spencer, a farm labourer, he started work himself on the land when he was about eight years of age. When he was twenty he moved to Derbyshire to work at the Markham Colliery and was subsequently employed at the Glapwell and Pleasley Collieries. In the 1890s he helped to sink the Warsop Main Colliery and formed there a branch of the Nottinghamshire Miners' Association, which was eventually transferred to the Derbyshire Miners' Association. Spencer was elected checkweighman and delegate to the council of the Association. In 1918 he was elected vice-president of the Association and later in the same year became full-time general treasurer. In 1920 he took over the duties of compensation agent and held the office until his death.

Spencer was a militant trade unionist who did much to maintain the unity of the Derbyshire Miners' Association in the face of company unionism after the 1926 stoppage. He also played an active part in local government: as a representative for the Shirebrook district he was elected to the Derbyshire County Council in 1919 and was made an alderman in 1931. He also served as chairman of the Shirebrook parish council, was a member of the Blackwell Rural District Council and on the Mansfield Board of Guardians. In the early 1920s Spencer moved to Chesterfield and was appointed a magistrate on the Chesterfield Bench in 1929; he also served on the Chesterfield Town Council, 1933–5, as a representative of St Leonard's ward, was a co-opted member of the Chesterfield Education Committee and governor of the Chesterfield Grammar School, Girls' High School and Technical College and the Shirebrook Girls' Secondary School. For many years Spencer was associated with the Shirebrook Bourne Methodist Church.

He died on 28 January 1943 in Chesterfield Royal Hospital following an operation, and after a service at the Shirebrook Bourne Methodist Church he was buried at Shirebrook Cemetery. His wife had predeceased him by fourteen years but he was survived by two sons and two daughters. He left effects valued at £3875.

Sources: (1) Minutes of the Derbyshire Miners' Association, 1918–43 (NUM, Saltergate, Chesterfield); (2) *Derbyshire Times*, 1911–43; (3) Secondary: J. E. Williams, *The Derbyshire Miners* (1962). OBIT. *Derbyshire Times*, 5 Feb 1943.

J. E. WILLIAMS

See also: Thomas ASHTON, for Mining Trade Unionism, 1900–14; *A. J. COOK, for Mining Trade Unionism, 1915–26; *Peter LEE, for Mining Trade Unionism, 1927–44.

STANLEY, Albert (1862–1915)
MINERS' LEADER

Born on 7 June 1862 at Dark Lane, Madeley, Shropshire, the son of a coalminer. He was educated at a dame school and then a National School and he also attended the local Primitive Methodist Sunday school, his father being an active worker for the chapel. Stanley himself became known as the 'boy preacher' and at the age of fourteen was addressing large congregations. When he was eleven years old he began work alongside his father at the Stirchley Coal and Iron Company Colliery, but a few years later they transferred to Hednesford and young Stanley then obtained work at the West Cannock Colliery. He became interested in trade unionism and politics at an early age, and at fifteen was secretary of a young Liberal Association.

In 1883 he suffered a pit accident which prevented further work underground, but within a year he had been appointed agent to the Cannock Chase miners, probably the youngest ever to be entrusted with such a responsibility. The circumstances were unusual. Following upon a conference of miners held in Birmingham at the end of January 1884 at which Cannock Chase was reported among those that were poorly organised, a circular was issued by Joseph Southall, agent and secretary. This asked for nominations for election of officers, viz.

agent, members of conciliation board and representative committee. The nominations were to be in 'on Thursday evening, December 18th, 1884, at the Talbot Arms Inn, Fiveways, Cannock at 6 p.m.' In the circular Southall stated that six years earlier the Cannock Chase miners had been 'working under a sliding scale which gave a minimum wage of 2/9d per holer's stint'. This had given little satisfaction, 'the majority of the men declaring, in very strong language, that they could not be worse off without a scale'. The circular continued: 'Accordingly (against my advice) instructions were given by the workmen to give notice to terminate the same. This left us without any agreement, in the month of October 1878, which time I shall always look back upon with both· sorrow and pain.' Southall went on to relate how bit by bit ('and I was as usual called a "master's man" for my pains') wages had been brought down in the April following to 'the miserable pittance of 2/3d per stint, a wage unprecedented in the history of Cannock Chase'. He asked the miners not to try 'to put the blame on myself and your Representatives, whom I consider as honourable a body of Representatives as ever represented a body of men.... Every means short of a strike have been used to get an advance of wages, but hitherto without success, the Employers telling us distinctly that no advance will be given unless an advance takes place in the coal, which they tell us cannot be done in the present state of the markets.' Southall apparently was not elected and the very young Albert Stanley took his place.

The Cannock Chase Miners, Enginemen and Surfacemen's Union registered as a trade union in 1887, had a membership of 4000 in 1890 (when Stanley was its representative at the TUC). Its membership fluctuated thereafter around the 4000 figure down to 1905 (when it stood at 4003 according to an official return) and then increased to 5000 in 1906 and to 9400 in 1910, at which time there were thirty-four branches.

A few years after he had become agent of his own union Stanley also became secretary of the Midland Miners' Federation. The Federation, which had a rule book dating from 1882, is considered to have been definitely established in 1886, with Enoch Edwards as president and S. H. Whitehouse as secretary. It was the latter whom Stanley replaced. The Federation comprised seven unions in all with a membership around 20,000 to 1905, thereafter increasing to 36,500 in 1910, with Stanley remaining as its secretary up to the time of his death. (The seven unions were the Miners' Associations of North Staffordshire, South Staffordshire and East Staffordshire, Cannock Chase, Pelsall District, Old Hill and District, Shropshire and Warwickshire.)

He was present at the founding conference of the MFGB in late November 1889 and was elected to the first provisional committee. He served on the executive committee for many years: 1889–90, 1892, 1894, 1897, 1900, 1902, 1905, 1908, 1910 and 1912; and he was often called upon to speak for the miners at the national level. He gave evidence before the R.C. on Mining Royalties (1890–1), and was a member of the 1893 Rosebery conference and of the Conciliation Board which that conference agreed upon.

Stanley was a man of remarkably wide reading, and his early command of language developed into a florid style of oratory that gained a warm response from the Midland miners in the early 1890s. An example of his style at this time was his pamphlet *The Miner's International Congress*. Stanley had been one of the three dozen or so delegates from Britain to the first international conference at Jolimont on 20–24 May 1890. 'It has long been felt desirable', he wrote, 'in the minds of the leaders of the working classes that an international organisation of labour should be effected. It has been a dream, but alas, little more than a beautiful fantastic dream in the brain of every aspirant to the position of the leader of workmen.' His extensive and unusual reading in the literature of the labour movement showed itself in his second and third paragraphs, which ran:

The soundness of the principle of international action was first laid down by a French woman named Flora Tristan in 1843, in a wonderful pamphlet she published. She appears to have been one of those prophetic souls who, from the heights of the snowy mountain peaks, see the sun rise in the East long before the first bright ray gladdens the eyes of the toilers in the darkened vale below. She proclaimed the need for the internationalisation of labour, the recognition of universal unity of working men and women, and the abolition of national barriers and prejudices.

Later (1864) came the birth of the 'International' in London, inspired by Karl Marx and his noble little band of co-adjutors, that had for its object the mutual help, the progress, and complete emancipation of the working classes. Born in weakness and obscurity, hardly attracting the notice of a considerable portion of the wealthy classes it yet pursued its quiet course until it suddenly blazed up sky high in the Paris Commune. The flames of Paris were quenched in the blood of the insurgents, but the victims had accomplished their great purpose: the conscience of Europe was troubled; their blood, wreathed in letters of flame, wrote the doom of oppression and monopoly.

These are interesting words from one who remained a Liberal in politics throughout his life. Stanley was a dedicated Gladstonian Home Ruler, a founder-member of the Midland Liberal Federation in 1894, and in 1897 he refused, together with W. E. Harvey of Derbyshire, to stand on the same platform as Keir Hardie. He declined invitations to contest parliamentary seats in 1896 and 1900, but when the sitting member for North West Staffordshire died in 1907, Stanley easily won the by-election. During his election campaign he showed so much hostility to socialist ideas that the local ILP branches refused to support him in any way. Stanley, like so many Lib-Labs, had no difficulty in signing the Labour Party constitution in 1909, following the affiliation of the MFGB to the Labour Party, and the new label made no difference to him or to Enoch Edwards, who represented Hanley. Stanley retained his seat at both the general elections of 1910, and he continued to sit in the Com-

mons until his death. He played a prominent part in local affairs, was a member of the Cannock School Board, and in 1889 was elected to the newly established Staffordshire County Council. He became a JP in 1907. Stanley came very close to being elected secretary of the parliamentary committee of the TUC. In 1904 Sam Woods was taken ill and had to resign the position, which he had held for ten years. W. C. Steadman, of the Barge Builders' Union, was appointed to act in his place until the Congress election. The MFGB nominated Stanley but he lost by 752,000 votes to 770,000 for Steadman.

He was always a man of moderate views: well-informed, a voracious reader and during his lifetime he built up a private library of some 2000 books. He was active within the chapel throughout his days, and later in life he became a Freemason. He married in 1882 and there were four sons and two daughters of the marriage. He died on 17 December 1915 in a Northampton nursing home, and his funeral took place at Hednesford. His wife and children survived him. He left an estate valued at £3200 (gross).

Writings: *The Miners' International Congress, Jolimont, Belgium, May 1890* [Hednesford: Evans and Withington ... with preface containing remarks of the Rev. R. M. Grier in the Parish Magazine for July 1890] (1890) 32 pp.; Evidence before R.C. on Mining Royalties, 1890–1 XLI Qs 8281–488.

Sources: W. Hallam, *Miners' Leaders* (1894) [photograph]; *Dod* (1914); R. Page Arnot, *The Miners* (1949); J. E. Williams, *The Derbyshire Miners* (1962); H. Pelling, *Social Geography of British Elections, 1885–1910* (1967); R. Gregory, *The Miners and British Politics 1906–1914* (Oxford, 1968); C. N. Gattey, *Gauguin's Astonishing Grandmother* (1970: for Flora Tristan); biographical information: NUM (Stafford); R. Page Arnot. OBIT. *Staffordshire Sentinel*, 18 Dec 1915; *Times*, 18 Dec 1915; Minutes MFGB, Special Conference, London, 13 Jan 1916.

JOYCE BELLAMY
JOHN SAVILLE

See also: Thomas ASHTON, for Mining

Trade Unionism, 1900–14; Enoch ED-WARDS; Benjamin PICKARD, for Mining Trade Unionism, 1880–99.

STANTON, Charles Butt (1873–1946)
MINERS' LEADER AND MP

Born at Aberaman in 1873 and educated at the Aberaman British School. Little is known of his early life except that he had worked as a docker and miner before being appointed in 1900 successor to David Morgan (Dai o'r Nant) as miners' agent for Aberdare. By this time he was a revolutionary Socialist although how and in what way he had arrived at this political position remains unclear. He became adviser to the National Democratic League, established in 1900, of which Tom Mann was for a short period the full-time organiser. The League made little progress except in London and South Wales, the latter area having fourteen out of its seventy-one branches in the early years of its history.

During the first decade of the twentieth century, Stanton was among the most vigorous of the growing number of left-wing critics of the leadership of the South Wales miners. With Barker and Hartshorn in particular he sought to change the organisation and attitudes of the South Wales Miners' Federation leaders and at the time of the Cambrian Combine strike in 1910 told the pioneers of the miners' federation that 'they must move on or move out'. In 1911 Stanton was elected to the MFGB executive with Barker and Hartshorn, replacing the more moderate leaders Brace, Onions and Richards, but, unlike his collaborators, he was replaced on the executive the following year by Brace and did not again serve on the committee of the MFGB.

Stanton first attempted to enter Parliament at the December 1910 general election when he contested East Glamorgan. He was not endorsed by the MFGB and he was substantially defeated by Clem Edwards, the Liberal candidate, whose record on behalf of the trade unions was very well known. Stanton was at this time beginning radically to change his ideas from those of the fiery militant of the previous decade, although it was only in the year or so before August

1914 that he became the bellicose imperialist of the war years. In *Justice*, 13 April 1912, there was published an interview which Stanton had given to *L'Humanité* in which he had acknowledged his membership of the British Socialist Party, his opposition to *The Miners' Next Step* and to syndicalism in general, and his dismay that Tom Mann had accepted these ideas. By the outbreak of war Stanton was leading the crowds in howling down Keir Hardie's 'peace meetings' at Aberdare [K. O. Morgan (1963) 276]. The death of Keir Hardie early in 1915 caused a vacancy in the Merthyr Boroughs constituency. The executive council of the South Wales Miners' Federation decided to nominate a candidate under the MFGB parliamentary representation constitution; and having received nominations from their lodges submitted five names to a ballot vote, out of which vice-president James Winstone, a member of the ILP, was the choice, which in turn was approved by all the Labour organisations in the constituency. The MFGB decided to endorse his candidature and, when a contest arose, sent down James Robson of Durham and David Gilmour of Scotland to assist in the campaign. Stanton had vigorously supported the war from its beginning, and against the decision of the Union and in defiance of the wartime electoral truce, he stood as an Independent candidate, receiving support from members of the British Socialist Party as well as from Liberal and Conservative interests. The main issue in Stanton's campaign was unconditional victory over Germany and he won with a majority of over 4000. Stanton's views at this time were clearly expressed by him in his maiden speech in the House of Commons:

... The people of Merthyr Boroughs were good enough to elect me on the straight war ticket. They thoroughly understand it was not a sham electoral cry that I made, so as to try and sneak into the House. They knew me, and knew how I had sacrificed my position as miner's agent; and they understood what I was doing, not as a partisan to back up the war party, but to do all I could as a humble individual, in my lowly sphere of life, to try and bring this War through successfully, and to bring as much possible disaster, trouble and tribulation to the Germans and Huns. . . .

We ought to drop this sham, hypocritical, nonsensical talk about avoiding Conscription. In a country such as this is, with our Empire extending to the four corners of the earth, we have so much more than any other nation that, although I have stood up at street corners and told our people otherwise, I think I may venture to say that we have much for which to be thankful! It is at a time like this when we really find ourselves. I have been sneered at and reviled because I declared that I was a Britisher. I discovered it; I really did not know it. But I was a true Britisher when the hour of trouble came . . . [Hansard, LXXVII, col. 225ff, 21 December 1915].

Stanton became a vice-president of the British Workers' National League, formed in April 1916 as a labour organisation wholly devoted to the war effort. Signatories to its first manifesto (*Times*, 2 May 1916), in addition to Stanton, were Will Crooks, Charles Duncan, John Hodge, Stephen Walsh, A. Wilkie – all MPs – H. G. Wells, A. M. Thompson (chairman of the executive committee), J. A. Seddon (chairman of the organisation committee), and Victor Fisher (honorary secretary). A statement of the aims of the League was published in the *Times*, 15 May. He retained his parliamentary seat at the 1918 election, standing as a representative of the pro-coalition National Democratic Party.

In the early 1920s Stanton was a journalist and lecturer. He was awarded a CBE in 1920 and in the same year became a JP for Glamorgan. His political affiliations had swung from revolutionary Socialism to Liberalism and when he contested his parliamentary seat as a National Liberal at the November 1922 general election he was defeated by G. H. Hall, the Labour candidate. He became a governor of Cardiff and Aberystwyth University Colleges and formally joined the Liberal Party in 1928. Some time after losing his parliamentary

seat, he went to live in London where he took over an old inn in Hampstead. He was keenly interested in painting, music and reading. The walls of his inn were decorated by his own pictures of Welsh landscapes, and he was an accomplished violin player. He had married in 1893 Alice Maud Thomas of Aberdare and they had two sons, one of whom was killed in the First World War. He died in London on 6 December 1946 and was survived by his wife and son. His funeral took place at Golders Green Crematorium on 10 December. He left £437 in his will.

Writings: *Why we should agitate* (Aberdare, 1903); *Facts for Federationists* (Aberdare, 1907); *Maxims for Miners* (n.d.).

Sources: *Times*, 2 and 15 May 1916 [for British Workers' National League]; *Dod* (1916) (1918) (1919) (1922) (1923); *The Aberdare Division Labour News*, 11 Nov 1922; *WW* (1929) (1946); *WWW* (1941–50); *Kelly* (1932); F. Bealey and H. Pelling, *Labour and Politics 1900–1906* (1958); E. W. Evans, *Mabon* (Cardiff, 1959); K. O. Morgan, *Wales in British Politics 1868–1922* (Cardiff, 1963). OBIT. *Western Mail*, 9 Dec 1946.

JOYCE BELLAMY
JOHN SAVILLE

See also: William ABRAHAM, for Welsh Mining Trade Unionism; Thomas ASHTON, for Mining Trade Unionism, 1900–14; *Clement EDWARDS; *Tom MANN.

STEWART, Aaron (1845–1910)
MINERS' LEADER

Born on 5 October 1845 at Coleorton, a village in north Leicestershire, the son of a miner who had been victimised for his part in a strike in the 1840s, and who died when Aaron was two years old. He had little formal education and despite the provisions of the 1842 Act, he commenced work underground when he was only eight years old (working with two of his uncles). When he was eighteen he left Leicestershire and worked in mines in various parts of the country until 1870 when he began work at Annesley

Colliery in Nottinghamshire as a stallman. The failure of the Derbyshire and Nottinghamshire Miners' Association in the late 1860s left behind some measure of organisation in certain pits, of which Annesley was one; and Stewart appears to have been active in the cause of unionism soon after he began working there. In 1880 he was elected checkweighman and he played a part in the establishment of the Notts Miners' Association which was formerly inaugurated at a meeting at Kimberley in July 1881. He was on the platform at the first annual demonstration of the Notts miners in June 1884, when Thomas Burt MP and John Wilson MP were among the main speakers, with J. E. Ellis, a prominent Hucknall coalowner and future Liberal MP, in the chair. From 1884 to 1886 Stewart acted as part-time secretary to the Association, but progress in recruitment was slow. In 1886 he published a series of vigorously written letters in the *Labour Tribune* (6 March 1886–June 1894) in which he criticised sharply the general weakness of trade unionism among the Notts miners and emphasised particularly the absence of effective leadership. In the following year the dynamic William Bailey was appointed full-time secretary/agent and his drive and personality began to make a notable difference in the county. In 1888 Stewart became president of the Association and he held this position until 1897. He took an active part in the late eighties and early nineties in the agitation for the statutory eight-hour day, and fully supported the action of the Association in withdrawing their backing for Henry Broadhurst in the West Nottingham election of 1892 [Griffin (1956) 79–80; Pelling (1967) 208]. Stewart was present at the 1893 Rosebery conference and following the death of William Bailey in July 1896, he was appointed full-time secretary in January 1897 (J. G. Hancock having already been appointed agent/financial secretary). Stewart represented the Nottinghamshire miners on the MFGB executive on six occasions between 1898 and 1907 and he attended most national and some international conferences.

Stewart was a man of solid worth, a good organiser and dedicated to the cause of mining trade unionism. In politics he remained a Liberal throughout his life. He was mainly responsible for the local abolition of the machine known cynically among the miners as 'Billy Fair Play', responsible, so it was generally understood in the mining community, for men being mulcted of part of their wages because of this particular method of weighing slack. But Stewart lacked the personality of his predecessor William Bailey and his policies tended to be rather cautious. Throughout 1910 he was seriously ill and the Council of the Notts Miners' Association decided on 2 July to reduce his salary to 30s per week, and to ask the lodges whether he should be required to vacate his house, which was owned by the Association. Two months later, Stewart submitted his resignation, and on 9 September 1910 the Council recommended lodges to elect Mr C. Bunfield in his place. No resolution of appreciation of Stewart's long service on behalf of the Nottinghamshire miners was ever recorded. He died on 30 November 1910, leaving a widow and a large family, and £134 in his will.

Sources: W. Hallam, *Miners' Leaders* (1894) [photograph]; A. R. Griffin, *The Miners of Nottinghamshire 1: 1881–1914* (Nottingham, 1956); J. E. Williams, *The Derbyshire Miners* (1962); H. Pelling, *Social Geography of British Elections, 1885–1910* (1967). OBIT. *Nottingham Daily Express*, 1 Dec 1910; *Nottingham Guardian*, 2 Dec 1910.

JOYCE BELLAMY
JOHN SAVILLE

See also: Thomas ASHTON, for Mining Trade Unionism, 1900–14; *William BAILEY; Benjamin PICKARD, for Mining Trade Unionism, 1880–99.

TAYLOR, John Wilkinson (1855–1934)
MINERS' LEADER AND LABOUR MP

Born on 11 August 1855 at North Quay, Monkwearmouth, Sunderland, the son of John Wilkinson Taylor, a blacksmith and landlord of the Jolly Sailor Tavern. At the age of nine he began working for a newsagent and was subsequently apprenticed to a blacksmith. Both his parents died, however, when he was fourteen and he then lived with a married sister who moved to Annfield Plain in Durham where Taylor became a blacksmith at Bankfoot Colliery. He later worked at the coal face and became involved in trade union affairs, initially as the first secretary of the Annfield Plain Lodge of the Durham Colliery Mechanics' Association; and in 1882 he was elected to the executive committee of the Association. In 1891 Taylor was elected treasurer of the organisation and in 1897 was made general secretary, a position he held until his retirement in 1923. In the previous year he had represented group 1 Enginemen on the executive committee of the MFGB.

Apart from his work for the colliery mechanics, he was an ardent Primitive Methodist and a Labour Party worker. He dated his commitment to the Primitive Methodists from the age of nineteen when he heard an address on the 'Three Bs' – be ambitious, be studious, be prayerful – and for over fifty years he served the Burnopfield Methodist Church as an eloquent local preacher. He pioneered local government in Annfield Plain, whose Urban District Council was created in 1899, Taylor becoming its first chairman. He served on the Council continuously from 1899 to 1933, except for his period in Westminster. He was also one of the early pioneers of the ILP in County Durham. At the general election of January 1906 Taylor was nominated for the Chester-le-Street constituency. All previous candidates, for many years, had been attached to the Liberal Party, and Taylor's refusal to accept the colours of the Liberal Party started a major controversy. He stood as an independent Labour candidate sponsored by the miners, who had not, at that time, affiliated with the LRC; and when he was elected in a three-cornered fight, he applied immediately for the Labour Whip. Taylor held the seat at all subsequent elections, although after January 1910 he was unopposed. He retired from Parliament in 1919.

Taylor also served his local community in other ways. He was a member of the Colliery School Board and of the Lanchester Board of Guardians; was president of the Annfield Co-operative Society from 1905 to 1933; a member of the Durham County Council and a member of the Lanchester, Stanley and Consett magisterial benches, being chairman for a time of the Stanley bench and vice-chairman of the Consett bench. He was also chairman of the Durham Aged Mineworkers' Homes Association. He was a part proprietor (with his brother) of a printing business.

He had married a Miss Mason of Annfield Plain and they celebrated their golden wedding seven years prior to his death on 26 June 1934 at his Dipton home; his wife survived him. He left £998 (net).

Sources: Pall Mall Gazette Extra, *The New House of Commons* (1911); *Durham Chronicle*, 23 Feb 1924; 15 Mar and 23 Aug 1929; W. S. Hall, *A Historical Survey of the Durham Colliery Mechanics Association 1879–1929* (Durham, 1929); G. D. H. Cole, *A Short History of the British Working-Class Movement 1789–1947* (1948); R. F. Wearmouth, *The Social and Political Influence of Methodism in the Twentieth Century* (1957); F. Bealey and H. Pelling, *Labour and Politics 1900–1906* (1958); R. Gregory, *The Miners and British Politics 1906–1914* (1968). OBIT. *Durham County Advertiser* and *Durham Chronicle*, 29 June 1934.

JOYCE BELLAMY
ANTHONY MASON

See also: Thomas ASHTON, for Mining Trade Unionism, 1900–14; M. H. LOWERY.

THORNE, William James (1857–1946)
TRADE UNION LEADER AND LABOUR MP

Although for most of his life he was known simply as Will Thorne, following his birth on 8 October 1857 his name was registered as William James Thorn. He was born in the Hockley district of Birmingham, his father being Thomas Thorn, a brickmaker journeyman who in winter months often worked as a stoker at the Saltley Gas Works. His mother Emma Everiss, who also worked in the brickfields, was Thomas Thorn's second wife but was widowed in 1864 after her husband had died in a fight with a horse dealer. By this time Thorne, who had received no formal education, was already working from six in the morning to six at night with an hour and a half off for meals. This job, which he had taken at the age of six, involved turning a wheel for a rope and twine spinner at Rob's Rope Walk in the Vauxhall area of Birmingham. His wage was 2s 6d a week. On Saturdays when this work ended at one o'clock, Thorne earned an extra shilling by working for his uncle who was a barber. His widowed mother meanwhile attempted to support Will and his three sisters by sewing hooks and eyes on to cards, a common form of sweated labour. The meagre family income was further supplemented by a grant from the Birmingham Board of Guardians of four loaves and four shillings a week.

Thorne declared his first strike when the rope spinner sought to reduce his wage to 2s a week and he took another job, again working about seventy hours each week helping an uncle in the brickyards for a wage of 7s. In the next few years a variety of labouring jobs followed including work as a plumber's mate, as a lath splitter, in the cow- and pig-hair trade, and at an ammunition factory, where Thorne was involved in a strike. These jobs, which were always arduous and frequently harrowing and unhealthy, had a lasting impression on Thorne, not only on his mental outlook, but physically as his hands were burned with acid in the munitions factory. He later recorded that this work made him a rebel, and at the age of fifteen he swore to do all he could to help prevent other children from going through the same hardships.

In 1875 his mother married a carpenter and joiner whom Thorne described as 'a double-handed drinker' and whose violent temper led to Thorne leaving home to go on the tramp. For a time he became a navvy and gained further experience of life among the unskilled workers before returning to Birmingham and a job at Saltley Gas Works. Here he worked twelve hours a day for a seven-day week which included a twenty-four-hour shift each fortnight. After a summer in the brickfields he returned to the gasworks where he persuaded the men to allow him to head a deputation to request an end to Sunday work, a claim which the Gas Committee of Birmingham Corporation conceded. In 1879 Thorne married Harriet, daughter of John Hallam, a fellow gas stoker and an active radical; both Thorne and his wife were illiterate and could only make their mark on the marriage register. He tramped to London in November 1881, worked at the Old Kent Road Gasworks and returned to Birmingham the following summer. He again walked to London for the winter season, got a job at Beckton Gasworks, took rooms and then sent for his wife and three children (another son, one of twins, had died).

Thorne joined the SDF some two or three years after its formation in 1881 and when its total membership was only a handful. In the course of spreading socialist propaganda he met many prominent radicals and socialists, including Hyndman, Eleanor Marx (whose suicide in 1898 deeply affected him), Aveling, Shaw, Tom Mann, Quelch, Bradlaugh, Annie Besant, Liebnecht, Engels, Lafarge and Jaurès. Later Thorne's associates included Pete Curran, J. R. Clynes and the Countess of Warwick. During the 1880s Eleanor Marx, more than anyone, helped Thorne to improve his reading and writing. He came to consider himself a Marxist and read the works of Hyndman and others; and though he gradually moved towards the political right, he continued often to use the phrases of the class war.

As well as street-corner agitation with the SDF, Thorne was taking every opportunity to convince his fellow gas workers of the value of organisation. A union established in 1872 at the Beckton works had been crushed when the company brought conspiracy charges against the leaders and issued summonses under the Master and Servant Act; in 1884 Jack Monk had attempted to form a union, and in the following year George Angle had been appointed secretary of another short-lived society. A further opportunity came in March 1889 when, in conditions of good employment, a meeting was held to put the resolution that a union be formed with the eight-hour day as one of its objects. This meeting was addressed by Ben Tillett, Thorne and Harry Hobart, another member of the SDF. Within four months the National Union of Gas Workers and General Labourers of Great Britain and Ireland had twenty thousand members with forty-four London branches and over twenty provincial ones. As general secretary Thorne was paid £2 5s a week. It was decided that 2d should be the weekly membership contribution, 'Love, Unity, and Fidelity' was adopted as the union's motto and 'One Man, One Ticket, and every Man with a Ticket' as its slogan. It was further agreed that only one benefit would be paid – strike benefit. In the face of this organisation the gas companies accepted the union's eight-hour-day petition and agreed to introduce three shifts of eight hours instead of two of twelve. The success of the gas workers, first achieved before the London dock strike of August 1889, gave further impetus to the development of 'new unionism'. To follow the eight-hour day, the union then began to negotiate over double pay for Sunday work. George Livesey of the South Metropolitan Gas Company was prepared to accept this, but resisted the union's aim of a closed shop. He introduced a bonus scheme which required the workers to accept an annual contract. The union resisted the scheme on the grounds that, because of the terms of the 1875 Conspiracy and Protection of Property Act, the union would have had to give lengthy notice before withdrawing labour. The dispute led to a largely unsuccessful strike from December 1889 to February 1890 which cost the union £20,000 in funds.

Thorne was also directly involved in the 'Battle of Wortley Bridge' during the Leeds gas workers' bitter strike in the summer of 1890; Engels marked the event by presenting him with a copy of *Capital* inscribed 'To Will Thorne, the victor of the Leeds battle, with fraternal greetings from Frederick Engels.' The union's policy in these early years was to accept all who applied for membership and to insist that all who had a trade union ticket should be able to work anywhere without interference from any other union. This led to some friction and in particular to demarcation disputes with Tillett's dockers' union, but by encouraging members from all sections of the unskilled,

Thorne's union gained greater stability, being able to support one group on strike by the subscriptions from their members in other trades who were still at work. During its early days the union also had problems in its internal organisation; and here the SDF gave invaluable assistance, with Eleanor Marx especially important. She acted as secretary, for instance, at the first annual conference.

Thorne's union affiliated to the TUC in 1890 and in that year he was a delegate to the Trades Union Congress at Liverpool where he helped to carry a resolution in favour of the legal eight-hour day. Up to 1894 he supported James MacDonald, Hardie and Burns who were the leading spokesmen for the socialists in the TUC, but in that year he was elected to the parliamentary committee and from then on he became a loyal member. He sat on the parliamentary committee of the Congress from 1894 until 1921, when it became the general council and on this body until 1933. In 1897 and again in 1911–12 he acted as the chairman of the TUC parliamentary committee and at the annual Congress of 1912 he held the post of president.

Thorne served as general secretary of his union for a period of forty-five years. In the union's early days London members, and especially London gas workers, predominated; in 1892 it had some 40,000–50,000 members of whom 30,000 were gas workers. However, it embraced many other trades, and in his evidence before the R.C. on Labour, Thorne estimated the union had members in some seventy industries. Despite recruitment among groups such as shopworkers and telephone operators the union's early growth was not rapid, and its 32,000 members in 1910 represented a decline on earlier years. Numbers then rose to 70,000 in 1912 with a peak of 490,000 in 1920, before another period of falling membership in the early twenties. A response to this decline was the impetus given to amalgamation with two smaller unions, the National Amalgamated Union of Labour and the Municipal Employees' Association, which was concluded by 1924. The new union was then known by its modern title of the National Union of General and Municipal Workers, and in 1934, at the time of Thorne's retirement, it had 269,000 members. His union work also took him abroad and he attended several international congresses including the conference of the American Federation of Labor in 1898 when Thorne was a fraternal delegate, and in 1913 he was appointed the first delegate to attend the Canadian Trade Union Congress.

With others Thorne was responsible for bringing Keir Hardie to West Ham before the latter's election to Parliament in 1892. He was present at the conference which established the Labour Representation Committee in 1900 and in the general election of the same year he unsuccessfully fought West Ham South as a Labour candidate. In this election Thorne was one of the two SDF candidates supported by the LRC – Lansbury was the other – but when in 1903 the SDF left the LRC he remained a member of the latter by virtue of the continuing affiliation of the Gas Workers' Union. Some SDF members demanded his resignation, which he refused, and rather anomalously he kept up his membership long after the SDF had ceased to exercise any significant weight within the labour movement and long after his own militant views had mellowed into reformism.

Thorne continued to live in East London and was active in local politics. In 1891 he became a member of the West Ham town council and except for a break of three weeks in 1900 he sat as a councillor until 1910 when he was elected alderman, which he remained until his death. He was Deputy Mayor of West Ham in 1899 and Mayor in 1917–18. He was also a JP and in 1930 was created a Freeman of West Ham. At the 1906 general election he again contested the West Ham South constituency and this time was elected. He sat for the division until 1918 when he became member for Plaistow. At the 1918 general election in common with other NSP candidates (as the Hyndman group in the SDF was then known) he stood on the platform 'to kill – Bolshevism, Capitalism, Militarism'. He represented Plaistow until his retirement in 1945.

In the Commons Thorne was never at his best and though he could make an impact at Question Time he was not without detractors in his own party. In 1908 Thorne prepared a Bill proposing a Citizen's Army, the SDF's answer to Haldane's Territorial Reorganisation scheme of 1907, which they described as an 'attempt to militarise the nation'. Thorne's scheme, which sought to give military training to most males between eighteen and thirty and to operate along trade union lines, was the object of a widespread campaign, but other sections of the labour movement were hostile and in the *Labour Leader* and elsewhere Thorne was subjected to severe criticism. On the outbreak of war Thorne adopted a strongly patriotic attitude similar to Hyndman's. He joined the 1st Volunteer Battalion of the Essex Regiment and was given the rank of lieutenant-colonel. When the pro-war faction of the BSP set up a Socialist National Defence Committee, in the company of Hyndman, John Hodge, then chairman of the PLP, Tillett and others, Thorne spoke in support of the Allies. The activities of the SNDC widened the split within the BSP which resulted in Hyndman and his supporters walking out of the Salford conference of April 1916. Thorne's views also angered the pacifist wing of the Labour Party and he was particularly stung when in 1916 Snowden wrote of his 'unlettered ignorance and unfitness for Parliament'. It was an unhappy, and certainly unfair comment, but on many occasions Thorne infuriated his parliamentary colleagues, as when, in 1916, he described the *New Witness* as a 'very respectable journal'. The *New Witness* was edited by Cecil Chesterton, a former member of the Fabian Executive who had moved quite sharply to the right, and who at this time was running a heated campaign against the UDC.

Promoted to colonel, in 1917 Thorne went to Petrograd on a Labour delegation with James O'Grady and W. S. Sanders, the purpose of which was to encourage the Kerensky Government in its attempts to continue the war against Germany. On their return they made a secret report to the Cabinet. Thorne also discussed his findings with the King, which again indicated his own move to the right, for only four years earlier he had refused as a matter of principle to meet the King, who was visiting West Ham. By 1923, as a guest at Lady Astor's dinner table, he was reassuring the Prince of Wales that his approach to reform was strictly constitutional.

Having earlier refused honours, Thorne was awarded a CBE in 1930 – the same year in which he acted as chairman of the SDF – and in June 1945 he was made a Privy Councillor. With his fine constitution, which had fitted him for a lifetime's strenuous work, Thorne remained active into advanced old age. After the death of his first wife he had married in 1895 Emily Byford, whose father was the treasurer of the Gas Workers' Union. After she died Thorne married again in 1925, his third wife being Rebecca Sinclair, the daughter of a marine draughtsman. In 1926 she also died and four years later Beatrice Collins became his fourth wife; she survived him. Thorne had seven sons and six daughters; one son was killed at Ypres in 1917 and another, named Karl in honour of the prophet, died in 1924. Two sons and six daughters survived him.

Thorne died at his home, 1 Lawrence Road, London, E13, on 2 January 1946 after a heart attack. In 1906, when writing to W. T. Stead on the books that had influenced him, Thorne had declared that he belonged to no religious denomination, but after his death the Bishop of Barking stated that in his later years Thorne had attended St Mary's, Plaistow (and that his wife was an active church worker), and it was following a service at this church that the funeral took place at the East London Cemetery on 10 January. In his will Thorne left effects to the value of £7187.

Writings: Thorne's autobiography, *My Life's Battles*, with a foreword by J. R. Clynes MP (n.d. [1925]), is best on his early career; he also wrote many short articles for newspapers and magazines and contributed 'A Working Class View of Prohibition' to *Liberty*, ed. E. E. Williams (1917). He gave evidence before the R.C. on Labour in 1892, 1893-4 XXXIV Qs 24529-25418 and to

the Industrial Council Inquiry into Industrial Agreements, 1913 XXVIII Qs 9724-10071 [examined jointly with Fleming Eccles].

Sources: *Dod* (1907, 1944); *WWW* (1941-50); *Labour Party Report* (1946); *TUC Report* (1946); *DNB* (1941-50), by G. D. H. Cole; S. and B. Webb, *History of Trade Unionism* (1894); W. T. Stead, 'The Labour Party and the Books that Helped to Make It', *Review of Reviews 33* (June 1906) 568-82; W. Thorne, *My Life's Battles* [1925]; 'Will Thorne', *Labour Mag. 4* (Oct 1925) 242-5; H. W. Lee and E. Archbold, *Social-Democracy in Britain* (1935); Anon., *Fifty Years of the National Union of General and Municipal Workers* (1939); Anon., *Sixty Years of the National Union of General and Municipal Workers* (1949); D. W. Crowley, 'The Origins of the Revolt of the British Labour Movement from Liberalism, 1875-1906' (London PhD, 1952); H. A. Clegg, *General Union: a study of the National Union of General and Municipal Workers* (Oxford, 1954); S. R. Graubard, *British Labour and the Russian Revolution 1917-1924* (Cambridge, Mass., 1956); B. C. Roberts, *The Trades Union Congress 1868-1921* (1958); F. Bealey and H. Pelling, *Labour and Politics 1900-1906: a history of the Labour Representation Committee* (1958); P. P. Poirier, *The Advent of the Labour Party* (1958); E. H. P. Brown, *The Growth of British Industrial Relations: a study from the standpoint of 1906-14* (1959); E. P. Thompson, 'Homage to Tom Maguire', and J. Saville, 'Trade Unions and Free Labour: The Background to the Taff Vale Decision' both in *Essays in Labour History*, ed. A. Briggs and J. Saville (1960); A. Stafford, *A Match to Fire the Thames* (1961); C. Tsuzuki, *H. M. Hyndman and British Socialism* (Oxford, 1961); A. E. P. Duffy, 'New Unionism in Britain, 1889-1890: a reappraisal', *Econ. Hist. Rev. 14* (1961-2) 306-19; H. Pelling, *A History of British Trade Unionism* (Harmondsworth, 1963); H. A. Clegg, *General Union in a Changing Society: a short history of the National Union of General and Municipal Workers, 1889-1964* (Oxford, 1964); H. A. Clegg et al., *A History of British Trade Unionism since 1889, 1: 1889-1910* (Oxford, 1964); E. J. Hobsbawm,

'British Gas-workers, 1873–1914', and 'General Labour Unions in Britain, 1889–1914' both in *Labouring Men: studies in the history of labour* (1964); H. Pelling, *The Origins of the Labour Party, 1880–1900* (2nd ed., Oxford, 1965); P. Thompson, *Socialists, Liberals and Labour: the struggle for London, 1885–1914* (1967); C. Tsuzuki, *The Life of Eleanor Marx 1855–1898: a socialist tragedy* (Oxford, 1967); W. Kendall, *The Revolutionary Movement in Britain, 1900–21: the origins of British Communism* (1969); R. Hyman, *The Workers' Union* (Oxford, 1971). OBIT. *Times*, 3 Jan 1946; *Stratford Express*, 4 and 11 Jan 1946.

DAVID E. MARTIN

See also: *C. R. ATTLEE, for British Labour Party, 1931–51; *Charles DUKES; Arthur HENDERSON, for British Labour Party, 1914–31; *H. M. HYNDMAN; *Eleanor MARX; *Ben TILLETT, for New Unionism, 1889–93.

THORPE, George (1854–1945)
CO-OPERATOR

George Thorpe was born at Thornhill near Dewsbury in 1854 but no record of the birth has been found at Somerset House. He was the youngest of five sons of a quarry worker whose wage never exceeded eighteen shillings a week and who also had four daughters. Thorpe had no early formal education and a month before his eighth birthday (two years younger than the law allowed) be began work in a coalmine as a hurrier-boy. When he was twelve an explosion of fire-damp took place in the mine, resulting in loss of life. His parents refused to let him enter the mine again and soon afterwards he found employment in Messrs Cook and Wormald's woollen mill where he worked for three years, later going to Messrs Cardwell Bros where he became foreman.

Although he never went to day school, he learned a little from his mother and attended Sunday school. The family possessed a four-penny brown Testament and the boys and girls took turns in reading the verses. At twenty he began attending night school in Dewsbury, chiefly to learn mathematics of which he was then completely ignorant and two years later joined science classes at the

Mechanics' Institute, where he stayed for five years. His education was entirely due to his own efforts. At twenty-one he could not do an addition sum: at twenty-eight he passed three stages in mathematics and later successfully got through examinations in chemistry and other sciences. On the occasion of his being given the Freedom of his home town he told the story of how, as a young man, he had won a prize for chemistry. At the time he was working nightly until 8 pm in the mill, and he went straight from work to the prize distribution in the old Centenary Methodist Sunday school room in his clogs, fustian trousers and smock. He remembered what a trying ordeal it was when he answered his name and marched up to the platform to receive his prize before the crowded audience of 'ladies and gentlemen, all smartly dressed' [*Dewsbury Reporter*, 31 Oct 1942].

His introduction to the co-operative movement was early, for his mother used to send him four miles to fetch flour from the co-operative store. He married in 1872 when he was eighteen, on a Sunday because he could not afford to do it on any other day, joined the co-operative movement (the Dewsbury Pioneers' Industrial Society) on the Monday and on the following Sunday signed the Temperance pledge. He remained a total abstainer and non-smoker to the end of his life; and at the age of ninety he was the oldest trustee of the Dewsbury Gospel Temperance Society.

Thorpe was obviously a young man of great energy and ability. He served for ten years on the management committee of the Dewsbury Co-operative Society, including four years as president, and then, at the comparatively early age of forty-four, he was elected to the board of the CWS in 1898. He continued on the board until his retirement under the age rule in 1924. He became vice-president in 1919 and then president from 1920 to 1924, periods of office of great strain and difficulty. Before 1914 he travelled extensively abroad as a director of the CWS.

He served for four years on the central board of the Co-operative Union and in 1911 he was elected president of the annual Co-operative Congress. When he retired from the CWS board at the age of seventy-two he was still extraordinarily energetic, and he created something of a precedent by returning to active participation in the affairs of his own local society; and he served a second period of four years (the maximum consecutive period allowed under the rules) as President of the Dewsbury society from 1926 to 1930. He also continued to serve the movement nationally as speaker and adviser.

His other interests included membership of the Dewsbury Council from March 1903 to November 1906; he then retired from Council Service because of his CWS duties, but he became a JP in 1904. All his life a staunch Liberal, he was, for four years, president of the Dewsbury Liberal Association. Awarded the CBE in 1933, he was honoured locally in 1942, at the age of ninety, when he was presented with the Freedom of the Borough of Dewsbury, the third recipient in eighty years. His certificate was placed in a casket of Yorkshire-grown walnut as silver was not available owing to war conditions. He had learned to drive a car at the age of seventy-three and at ninety was still remarkably fit and active.

He died at his Dewsbury home on 1 March 1945, aged ninety-two years, and was buried on 6 March after a funeral service at Salem Chapel. He was survived by a daughter, Mrs H. Mitchell, her husband and another son-in-law, Mr Stabler. His estate was valued at £8824.

Writings: 'Can the Co-operative Movement govern the Output and Price of Commodities?', *Co-op. Congress Report* (1915).

Sources: *Bradford Co-op. Congress Souvenir* (Manchester, 1911); *Co-op. Congress Report* (1911); P. Redfern, *The Story of the C.W.S.* (Manchester, [1913]); *People's Year Book* (1921) 7; *Co-op. News*, 9 Aug 1924; P. Redfern, *The New History of the C.W.S.* (Manchester, 1938); *Dewsbury Reporter*, 31 Oct 1942; Co-operative Press records. OBIT. *Dewsbury Reporter*, 3 Mar 1945; *Co-op. News*, 10 Mar 1945.

H. F. BING

See also: Thomas ALLEN; Fred HAYWARD,

for Co-operative Union; Percy REDFERN, for Co-operative Wholesaling.

TOPHAM, Edward (1894–1966)
CO-OPERATIVE JOURNALIST, AUTHOR AND TRADE UNIONIST

Edward Topham was born on 9 September 1894 in Sheffield, the son of Edward and Harriet Topham, both of whom were engaged in the drapery business. Educated at Crookesmoor Elementary School, whose headmaster was a pioneer co-operator, Topham twice had the opportunity for free secondary education but family circumstances prevented him from pursuing it and he left school at the age of thirteen. Thereafter he extended his education by his own efforts. His first employment was packing sweets for eleven hours a day for 3s 6d a week but he had a variety of other jobs before starting at the age of seventeen in the office of the *Sheffield Independent* as news telegram sorter and night telephonist. His leisure hours had previously been spent in writing and his natural ability in this direction soon became apparent: he was given minor reporting jobs and after six months was appointed a full-time junior reporter. In September 1914 he enlisted in the RAMC and saw service in France, Macedonia and Bulgaria. While in France he started *The Leadswinger*, a famous duplicated trench journal which ran until the end of the war.

On demobilisation in 1919, Topham returned to the *Sheffield Independent* where he was sub-editor for several years. He then joined the *Sheffield Evening Mail*, a radical paper, as industrial correspondent. He became assistant editor and leader writer of this newspaper until his appointment in 1927 as publications editor of the Co-operative Union in succession to T. W. Mercer, a position he retained until his retirement in 1959. While serving with the *Sheffield Evening Mail* he had acted as correspondent for the *Co-operative News*, and wrote also for the *Sheffield Co-operator* and the *Scottish Co-operator*. From 1927 to 1930 he edited the *Co-operative Guildsman*, the organ of the National Co-operative Men's Guild, and contributed various articles to the journal. As editor of the *Co-operative Review* he transformed it from a rather staid journal published every two months to a lively monthly publication. In 1934 he edited a book on the co-operative movement, *British Co-operation To-day*, and in 1944 with John Hough he produced *The Co-operative Movement in Britain*, a pamphlet published by the British Council which ran through several English editions and was printed in ten languages, including Chinese, Arabic and Persian.

A keen publicity man, he was a founder member of the Co-operative Publicity Managers' Association (Northern and Midland section) when this was inaugurated in 1938. In 1939 this merged with the southern section, founded in 1937, to form a national organisation. During the Second World War he established the Co-operative Union's *Emergency Circular* which later became the *Co-operative Gazette*. The work of the department was considerably extended under his direction and as the Union's press relations officer, 'Top of the Co-op', as he was affectionately called by journalists, he provided an excellent information service on the co-operative movement's activities to the national and local press. In 1941 the Ministry of Information commissioned him to write a monthly article on the British Co-operative movement in wartime, first for publication in Sweden, and subsequently in other countries. He continued this series of articles over a long period.

An active trade unionist, Topham was chairman successively of both the Sheffield and Manchester branches of the National Union of Journalists and was honoured by the NUJ with life membership. A well-known speaker at the annual delegate meetings of the NUJ, he worked actively in support of the demand for a Royal Commission on the Press (which reported in 1962). He was president in 1949 of the Manchester Press Club.

A socialist from his youth, he took an active part in local and national Co-operative and Labour Party affairs. A man of strong left-wing sympathies and a forceful and witty speaker, he joined the Society for Socialist Inquiry and Propaganda when this was formed by G. D. H. Cole in the winter of 1930–1. With T. E. Bean (who later became general manager of the Royal Festival Hall) and A. L. Sugar (who became publications manager of the Co-operative Union in 1951) he produced an SSIP pamphlet exposing the right-wing bias of the press coverage of the Manchurian troubles in 1929. In 1930 he unsuccessfully contested the Chorlton-cum-Hardy ward in the Manchester City Council elections in opposition to Lady Simon.

He had married, in June 1922, Doris Adelaide Williams whom he met after he was demobilised and who was also employed on the *Sheffield Independent*. Both trade unionists, they were also both members of the Sheffield and Ecclesall Co-operative Society. Mrs Topham shared many of her husband's interests and became a county councillor and a JP. Edward Topham retired from the Co-operative Union in September 1959 and lived a further seven years at Romily in Cheshire. He died in Macclesfield Hospital on 2 November 1966 and was survived by his wife and a son, Edward Theodore Topham. He left an estate valued at £3644.

Writings: 'The Guild's Duty to the Democratic Ideal', *Co-op. Guildsman 3* (Dec 1930); *Your Co-operative Union: what it does for the movement and its members* (2nd rev. ed. Manchester, 1933) 23 pp.; *British Co-operation To-day*, ed. E. Topham (Manchester, [1934]); (with J. A. Hough) *The Co-operative Movement in Britain* (1944); articles in co-operative periodicals and various newspapers and also on the co-operative movement for the Ministry of Information 1941–5.

Sources: *Co-op. Guildsman 3* (Dec 1930); W. H. Brown, *The Trek of the Men: history, programme and policy, rules and standing orders of the National Co-operative Men's Guild* (Manchester, [1937] 24 pp.; *Co-op. News*, 12 Sep 1959; personal information: Mrs D. A. Topham (widow); A. L. Sugar, Publications Manager, Co-operative Union Ltd; H. J. Bradley OBE, National Union of Journalists. OBIT. *Hyde Reporter*, 12 Nov 1966; *Le Coopérateur Suisse* (Basle), 26 Nov 1966; *Co-op. Rev. 40* no. 11 (Nov 1966).

JOYCE BELLAMY
H. F. BING

See also: A. BONNER, for Co-operation, 1945–70; W. H. BROWN, for Retail Co-operation, 1900–45; Fred HAYWARD, for Co-operative Union; T. W. MERCER.

TRAVIS, Henry (1807–84)
OWENITE

Little is known of the details of the private life of Henry Travis. Like his father and grandfather before him, he was a physician from Scarborough (although the *Co-operative News* obituary notice speaks of him as having been born in Durham). Most of his life seems to have been spent in London. He became acquainted with the ideas of Robert Owen fairly early in his life and was one of Owen's most fervent and dedicated disciples. Like William Pare and John Finch, Travis was among those whose financial or professional position allowed them time and leisure to devote to the propagation of enthusiasms. He became chairman of the central board of the Universal Community Society of Rational Religionists in 1839–40 and for a short time went to Queenwood where, according to Podmore, he became secretary for a while. For a time (probably in the late 1840s) he became private physician to the 2nd Marquess of Ailesbury, and he also took a close interest in the Christian Socialist movement of F. D. Maurice and his colleagues. In the 1850s he remained close to Owen and assisted in a number of literary matters, including Owen's *Journal* 1850–2 and the publication of the two volumes of *Autobiography* in 1857–8. After Owen's death Travis was the self-appointed champion of his master's doctrines (he was also Owen's literary executor), and he preached his particular version of Owenism with increasing dogmatism and decreasing effectiveness to the end of his life in the 1880s.

On one matter only did he differ from Owen, whom he thought too rigidly determinist. Travis spent a good deal of his time and much of his considerable literary output in arguing the free will versus necessity thesis. Queenwood, in his view, failed not because of any flaw in the communitarian idea, but because of Owen's

faulty psychology. It was the denial of free will and responsibility that was sufficient both to account for the failures of the Owenite practical experiments in community living and the very restricted acceptance of Owenite ideas in general by the public at large. But apart from this important difference in the understanding of human nature, Travis was content to preach the unmodified doctrine of Robert Owen. He coined the phrase 'effectualism' to describe his system but otherwise there was no fundamental change in the approach. His last work, *English Socialism*, published in 1880, was a presentation of Owenism or 'Advanced Co-operation' to the working people. Like his friend Charles Bray he classified consumers' co-operation as a rudimentary form of co-operation, to be set against the higher form of communitarianism. When G. J. Holyoake's first volume on *The History of Co-operation* appeared in 1875 Travis vigorously attacked it for what he described as its misrepresentation of Robert Owen (*Co-operative News*, Oct 1875).

Travis was an indefatigable publicist, and in the 1860s and 1870s he had a considerable range of political and trade union contacts. On one occasion he referred 'to my good friend Mr George Potter'; to the delegates of the 1876 Newcastle TUC he distributed free 200 copies of his *Effectual Reform in Man and Society*; and he wrote in a number of working-class journals: including the *Co-operator, Co-operative News, Bee-Hive* and the *American Socialist* (1877–8). He helped organise in 1871 the centenary meeting to commemorate Owen's birth. Soon after his death the old Owenite, E. T. Craig, published a *Memoir* of him which brought together most of the known facts about his life. Craig himself was in his eighties when he published his memoir, which includes the following:

I have known many good men and have delineated many thousands of characters, both in public and in private life, but two of the noblest and best of men I have intimately known were the great Socialists, Dr Travis and Robert Owen. . . . There was a quiet dignity in our friend's manner, united to a modesty that was neither shrinking humility nor feeble weakness....

He was most orderly, punctual, and painstaking, and a marvel of industry in arranging the articles in portfolios which he devised. ... To show me his method of working he fetched from his bedroom a thick journal, 9 in. by 7 in. and 1 in. thick, of ruled pages, filled with the original compositions of his articles, as the thoughts had occurred to him when awake in the night. He had a bracket at the head of his bed on which he kept a benzoline lamp ready to be lighted, on awakening in the night, when he would resume his studies, and jot down his thoughts as they arose, and afterwards would correct and revise them, and hence his pages were crowded with fastidious corrections, interlineations, and marginal revisions.

Travis died on 4 February 1884, after a long and painful illness, at his Camden Town home, and was buried at Finchley on 8 February. He had married when young, but lost his wife during their first year of marriage. He never remarried. He left an estate valued at £12,003.

Writings: *Moral Freedom, reconciled with Causation, by the Analysis of the Process of Self-Determination. ... With a Postscript on Co-operation* (1865); *Free Will and Law in Perfect Harmony* (1868); 'Higher Aims of Co-operation and how to realise them', *Co-op. Congress Report* (1869); *The Co-operative System of Society; or the Change from Evil to Good* (1871); *The Coming Revolution* (1872); *Effectual Reform in Man and Society* (1875); *The End of the Free Will Controversy* (1875); *A Manual of Social Science for the Working Classes* (1877); *Advanced Co-operation and Tracts on English Socialism* (1880). Obit. *Lancet*, 9 Feb 1884, 281.

Sources: E. T. Craig, *Memoir and In Memorian of H. Travis, English Socialist* [1886?]; J. M. Wheeler, *A Biographical Dictionary of Freethinkers of all Ages and Nations* (1889); G. J. Holyoake, *History of Co-operation in England*, 2 vols (1875-9); T. W. Mercer,

Towards a Co-operative Commonwealth (Manchester, 1936); A. Bonner, *British Co-operation* (Manchester, 1961); F. Boase, *Modern English Biography 6* (1965); J. F. C. Harrison, *Robert Owen and the Owenites in Britain and America* (1969); Biographical information: the 7th Marquess of Ailesbury. Obit. *Co-op. News*, 16 Feb 1884.

JOHN SAVILLE

See also: E. T. CRAIG; *Robert OWEN; William PARE.

TWEDDELL, Thomas (1839-1916)
CO-OPERATOR

Born at Newcastle on Tyne on 5 August 1839, the son of George Tweddell, a papermaker, Thomas Tweddell was educated at Mr Kidman's Methodist Academy. His first employment was at York with the North Eastern Railway and afterwards with the same company at Hartlepool but he then left railway service to commence in business on his own as an auctioneer and fish salesman. He also participated actively in Hartlepool local affairs as a member of the town council, school board, board of guardians and as a supporter of Liberal interests.

His first direct association with the co-operative movement followed the Co-operative Congress of 1880 held in Newcastle, which drew Tweddell's attention to the role of co-operation in economic and social affairs. He was a prime mover in the establishment of the Hartlepool Co-operative Society in 1882, of which he was the first secretary, holding this position until his death. His administrative ability combined with enthusiasm for the movement was soon recognised by the CWS when he represented the Hartlepool Society at the Newcastle meetings of the wholesale society. In December 1887 he was elected a member of the Newcastle branch of the CWS and appointed chairman of the branch in 1893. In the following year he presided over the Co-operative Congress held in Sunderland, which marked the jubilee of the co-operative movement. A forceful speaker, he lectured throughout the North of England on behalf of the movement. In 1904, with J. C. Gray, he presented the case for co-operative societies to the Departmental Committee on Income Tax.

He was markedly sympathetic to the work of the Women's Co-operative Guild, and it was through him that a resolution in support of women's suffrage was brought before the Co-operative Congress of 1908. Margaret Llewelyn Davies wrote a graceful obituary notice of him, emphasising his help and sympathy, in the *Co-operative News*, 8 April 1916.

It was especially in the field of parliamentary representation that his work for the co-operative movement was outstanding. He represented the CWS on the joint parliamentary committee of the Co-operative Union and the two wholesale societies (CWS and SCWS) from 1899 and was a strong advocate of direct parliamentary representation for the movement. He read a paper on this subject at the Co-operative Congress at Paisley in 1905 and was then made chairman of the parliamentary committee, being re-elected, with one exception only, for each subsequent year until his death. He was the spokesman for the co-operative movement on delegations to Government departments, and was elected by the National Health Insurance Commissioners to represent the movement on the advisory committee appointed to assist in administering the new (1911) insurance legislation. Made vice-president of the CWS in 1905, he retained this position until his election to the chairmanship of the Society in 1915 but ill-health prevented him from fulfilling many duties in this latter capacity.

A JP for West Hartlepool, he had also been invited to contest the Hartlepools constituency in the Liberal interest, but had declined. He died at his West Hartlepool home on 23 March 1916 and was survived by his wife and family. Following a service in St Paul's Church he was buried in the Old Cemetery at West Hartlepool on 25 March. He left an estate valued at £11,239. Tributes to his work for the movement were published in the *Co-operative News* from representatives of British co-operators and the International Co-operative Alliance.

Writings: *Direct Representation in Parlia-ment* (Manchester, 1905) 20 pp.; rev. and brought up to date by W. H. Watkins (1918) 16 pp.; *The Co-operation of Consumers* (Paper to British Association: 1907).

Sources: *Co-op. Congress Handbook* (1894); P. Redfern, *The Story of the C.W.S.* (Manchester, [1913]); idem, *The New History of the C.W.S.* (Manchester, 1938); G. D. H. Cole, *A Century of Co-operation* (Manchester, [1945?]); S. Pollard, 'The Foundation of the Co-operative Party', in *Essays in Labour History 2: 1886–1923*, ed. A. Briggs and J. Saville (1971) 185–210. OBIT. *Newcastle Daily Chronicle*, 25 Mar 1916; *Co-op. News*, 1 and 8 Apr 1916; *CWS Annual* (1917) 294.

JOYCE BELLAMY

See also: A. V. ALEXANDER, for Co-operative Party; Percy REDFERN, for Co-operative Wholesaling.

TWIGG, Herbert James Thomas (1900–57)
CO-OPERATOR AND AUTHOR

Born on 28 September 1900 at Sheerness, Kent, the son of Thomas Richard Twigg, an engine fitter, and his wife Mary Ann Ada Twigg. (He never used his third christian name and was always known as H. J. Twigg.) Educated at an elementary school he obtained in 1910 both a Kent county scholarship and a Rochester Mathematical School scholarship but was unable to take up either owing to his father's unemployment at the time; and he became an engineering apprentice in Sheerness Dockyard from 1915 to 1922. His co-operative career commenced in 1919 when he became a member of the first education committee of Sheerness Economical Co-operative Society (just formed by the amalgamation of the Sheerness Economical Society, with which his parents had been actively associated, and the neighbouring Sheerness Co-operative Society, of which his grandfather had been for many years chairman). He gained useful experience in the engineering trade union to which he belonged, while study at summer schools and by correspondence courses eventually led to his obtaining a place at the Co-operative College, Manchester, with the Infans and Blandford Scholarships and a supplementary scholarship. He spent two years (1922–4) at the Co-operative College, obtaining the co-operative honours diploma, the diploma in co-operative secretaryship and a variety of prizes. In 1924 he was a prize-winner in an international essay competition sponsored by Ed. A. Filene of Boston, USA, on the subject 'How peace and prosperity can be restored to Europe through international co-operation'. It was at the Co-operative College that he met Edith Potter, whom he later married, then a member of the staff of the Co-operative Union Research Department.

After College, Twigg spent a short time with the CWS audit department in London and then moved to Manchester as a CWS bank employee. While there he gained second place in Great Britain in the examination of the Institute of Bankers and won the Gwyther Prize in Economics. This led to his receiving various offers of employment from the Commercial Banks, but out of loyalty to the co-operative movement he rejected them. In 1929 he won a £25 Essay Prize offered by the Bankers' Institute. In 1931, out of 500 candidates, he was appointed assistant labour adviser to the Co-operative Union and held this post till 1941 when he was appointed general secretary and chief executive officer of Plymouth Co-operative Society. Taking over at Plymouth six months after the society's central premises had been destroyed by enemy bombs, he guided the society through the difficult war years, supervised the rebuilding and replanning of the central premises after the war and saw the annual sales of the society increase from £2 million in 1941 to nearly £7 million at the time of his death in 1957.

While working at the CWS bank in Manchester, Twigg was elected to the education committee of Prestwich Co-operative Society (1926–34) and acted as secretary to the North-Western Sectional Co-operative Education Association for a number of years. He was vice-president of the Educational Secretaries' Association, member of the Manchester district executive and member of the North-Western Choral Association executive. He had already made a name for himself as a lecturer, teacher and writer. As assistant labour adviser to the Co-operative Union (1931–41) he was closely associated with the establishment of the co-operative hours and wages boards, gave evidence before government committees and commissions on behalf of co-operative interests, and served on the Boot Repairing Trade Board and Milk Distributive Trade Board, as well as various joint industrial councils for the retail trade. Despite his responsibilities as chief executive officer of Plymouth Society from 1941 he still found time to serve the co-operative movement nationally, and the city of Plymouth locally. He was chairman of the co-operative congress standing orders committee 1942–53, and in 1954 was elected president of the Scarborough Congress. Twigg was a highly competent economist and his views played an important part in shaping post-war co-operative financial policy. He served on the Mutual Aid Committee (1942–3), the Co-operative College Finance Inquiry Committee (1950–2) as chairman, and the Financial Policy and Dividend Policy Committees between 1951 and 1953.

His business ability was soon recognised in Plymouth after he settled there. In 1944 he became a member of the Plymouth Incorporated Mercantile Association and was one of a committee of six appointed by that body to report on the traders' mutual salvage scheme. Also in 1944 he was elected to the executive council of the Port of Plymouth Chamber of Commerce. His membership of both bodies lasted till his death.

In addition to his textbooks, listed below, H. J. Twigg was a prolific writer on co-operative subjects. He was a frequent contributor to the *Co-operative News, Co-operative Review, Co-operative Year Book, Co-operative Official* and other Co-operative publications. He was the anonymous author of 'General Managers' Notebook', a controversial feature which appeared regularly in the *Co-operative News* for nine years (1948–57) and in his later years also he was responsible for the 'Balance Sheet Survey' feature.

H. J. Twigg was known as the 'J. B.

Priestley of the Co-operative Movement' because of his resemblance in appearance and manner to the Yorkshire novelist, for whom he was frequently mistaken. He married Edith Potter on 15 September 1928 and they had one son and one daughter. He died of heart failure at his home, 46 Thorn Park, Plymouth, on 24 October 1957; and nearly 500 people gathered in the Methodist Central Hall, Plymouth, for the funeral service on Tuesday 29 October. He left an estate valued at £2978.

Writings: *Junior Co-operators and their Organisation* (Manchester, 1925) 21 pp. [first written as a thesis for the Honours Diploma in Co-operation: 1924]; *The Organisation and Extent of Co-operative Education* (Manchester, 1924); *The Economic Advance of British Co-operation 1913–1926* (Manchester, 1928; 2nd rev. ed. 1931; 3rd rev. ed. 1934).

Sources: *Co-op. Congress Report* (1954); *Co-op. News,* 19 Nov 1955; R. Briscoe, *Centenary History: a hundred years of co-operation in Plymouth* (Manchester, 1960); personal information: Mrs E. Twigg (widow); Co-operative Press records, Manchester. OBIT. *Western Evening Herald,* 25 Oct 1957; *Times,* 26 Oct 1957; *Western Morning News,* 25 and 30 Oct 1957; *Western Independent,* 27 Oct 1957; *Reynolds News,* 27 Oct 1957; *Co-op. News,* 7 Nov 1957; *Co-op. Rev.,* Nov 1957.

H. F. BING

See also: A. BONNER, for Co-operation, 1945–70; W. H. BROWN, for Retail Co-operation, 1900–45; Fred HALL, for Co-operative Education; Fred HAYWARD, for Co-operative Union.

VINCENT, Henry (1813–78)
CHARTIST AND RADICAL LECTURER

Vincent was the eldest son of a radical gold- and silversmith in Holborn, central London, who failed in business when Henry was eight. The family, now impoverished, moved to Hull, Yorkshire, where Henry was apprenticed to a printer in 1828. In 1829 his father, who was employed by the excise, died in the course of duty, leaving a widow and six children. Vincent was attracted into politics at an early age, first by the Catholic emancipation agitation and then by the 1830 revolution in France. He read widely in radical literature: Bentham, Cartwright, Richmond, Burdett, Fox and Cobbett. Tom Paine was the strongest influence over him at this time, but he often quoted Volney and later described Perronet Thompson as his 'political father'. At seventeen, Vincent was elected vice-president of a Painite young men's discussion group, which launched him on his long career as a public speaker. He was elected to the Hull Political Union, and during the reform crisis warmly advocated universal suffrage. When his apprenticeship was completed in 1833 he and his family returned to London. An opportune legacy freed him from responsibility for his mother, to whom he always remained dutiful. He joined the London compositors' union, and worked briefly for Spottiswoode, the King's printer, but in 1836 there was a dispute, and he and some sixty others left.

Vincent soon made contact with London radical circles. He met William Lovett, whom he always admired, and in November 1836 joined the London Working Men's Association. At the Crown and Anchor meeting of 28 February 1837 he denounced the 'aristocracy of money', according to O'Brien, 'with boldness, fluency, and a perfect command of his subject'. He became a political missionary for the LWMA, especially popular in the West country and in South Wales, particularly successful at meetings of female Chartists. At this time Gammage found him

much below the middle size. His person, however, was extremely graceful, and he appeared on the platform to considerable advantage. With a fine mellow flexible voice, a florid complexion, and, excepting in intervals of passion, a most winning expression he had only to present himself in order to win all hearts over to his side. His attitude was perhaps the most easy and graceful of any popular orator of the time. For fluency of speech he rivalled all his contemporaries, few of whom were anxious to stand beside him on the platform. His rare powers of imitation irresistibly drew peals of laughter from the gravest audience. His versatility, which enabled him to change from the grave to the gay and *vice versa*, and to assume a dozen various characters in almost as many minutes, was one of the secrets of his success . . . the Democrats of both sexes regarded him as the young Demosthenes of English Democracy [Gammage [1894] 11].

Vincent was among the several London craftsmen who, as Chartist leaders, were more influential in the provinces than in London. He seems to have begun active missionary work for the LWMA in summer 1837. In late August 1837 he and John Cleave addressed the meeting on Woodhouse Moor which originated the Leeds WMA. His private correspondence shows him really excited at the spontaneous radical zeal he encountered among northern working people. In October 1837 he made what was probably his first speech in Bath, where he held many meetings later as a Chartist leader. Banbury, Hull, the West country and Monmouthshire were four areas where Vincent dominated local Chartism. As LWMA missionary in Monmouthshire, he ensured that Chartism catered for the grievances of both nonconformists and miners, an alliance with far-reaching consequences for Welsh Chartism. He wanted the LWMA to become an ambitious reforming organisation, and favoured displays of strength. He was elected a delegate to the Chartist convention at the Palace Yard meeting of 17 September 1838, and his speeches became increasingly extreme, although he always recommended education and moral reform.

In December 1838 he strengthened his standing in the movement by founding the *Western Vindicator*, a weekly paper which became very popular among Chartists in the West country and South Wales. He represented Hull at the 1839 Chartist convention and was knocked senseless by a stone from a hostile mob at a Devizes meeting on 1 April 1839. He was arrested on 7 May 1839 for participating in a 'riotous assemblage' on 19 April, the first of the many Chartist

leaders to be imprisoned by the government. He was tried at Monmouth in August 1839, and was defended (in Vincent's view, unskilfully) by J. A. Roebuck. Imprisoned for a year, he was at first denied books. Until the *Western Vindicator* was closed down on 14 December 1839, he continued contributing somwhat excited articles. On 7 December 1839 the paper claimed that moral force strategies were now 'all HUMBUG' because government was stopping up the means of non-violent reforming pressure. Vincent urged Chartists to defend Frost, whom he admired, but it is curious that Frost should now be a better-known Chartist figure than Vincent, who was always far more prominent in the Chartist movement. 'We think it of importance', wrote J. S. Mill in the *Westminster Review* for 1839, 'that Mr Lovett and Mr Vincent should make themselves heard in St Stephen's as well as in Palace Yard, and that the legislature should not have to learn the sentiments of the working classes at second-hand.'

Vincent's persistence with his *Vindicator* and his refusal to sign a warning to Chartists against violence destroyed his chances of gaining improved prison conditions, early release, or freedom from prosecution for debt, but his conduct enabled him on public platforms in later years to enlarge upon his incorruptibility and integrity under government temptation. Vincent was tried again in March 1840 for conspiring with Frost. He ably defended himself, but was imprisoned for another year. Place, Duncombe, and Serjeant Talfourd urged more humane treatment and had him moved from Millbank to Oakham Gaol. There Place gave him a correspondence course in French, history and political economy, and impressed him with the importance of Godwin's ideas. Vincent told Place in August 1840 that he was determined 'not to remain the *fool* I am. My desire is *to learn*. . . .' But he still wrote angry letters to the Chartist press.

In September 1840, however, he welcomed the development of Christian Chartism in Scotland, and in December 1840 he signed an address denouncing drunkenness. He was released in January 1841, but he retained his ebullience and offended Place by resuming itinerant lecturing. He married Lucy, eldest daughter of John Cleave the Chartist leader, announced in February 1841 that 'the days of idle bombast and rant are gone by', and began a two months' campaign in the Midlands for teetotal Chartism. He had been a teetotaller for some years, and in his *Western Vindicator* for 20 July 1839 had issued an appeal to all Chartists to abandon intoxicants and tobacco so as to deprive the government of revenue. In 1841 this was still his motive, and in addition he aimed to stimulate working-class self-respect. He insisted that working-class ignorance scared away potential middle-class allies and prevented working people from gaining their freedom. His language was now more moderate, though he still attacked the 'system'. He often stressed the need for class harmony. He was inspired by the recent teetotal successes of Father Mathew in Ireland, but he never received much encouragement from temperance reformers. The pledge he administered to teetotal Chartists was too political in phrasing and intent for their tastes.

Vincent now realised that the government repression of 1839 had at last scaled down Chartists' notions of their own political power. Like Lovett, Stephens and several other Chartist leaders therefore, he came out of prison with a new political strategy. He now emphasised that the Frost rising had been a mistake, and had been organised by a few drunken Chartist dupes of government agents. He admired Lovett and Collins's *Chartism* (1840), and was a signed adherent of Lovett's 'new move'. But he feared that mass poverty would cause it to fail, and was never active in Lovett's National Association for Promoting the Improvement of the People. Bristol Chartists forced him publicly to declare that the 'new move' would be unwise if it split the Chartist movement. Vincent joined the National Charter Association, restarted his paper as the *National Vindicator*, and simultaneously promoted its sales and Chartism by his itinerant lecturing. But his teetotal Chartist campaign succumbed before attacks in the *Northern Star* on 3 April 1841 by Feargus O'Connor, who feared that his own personal authority over

the Chartist movement was being undermined. Vincent had never associated closely with O'Connor, but there was no immediate breach between them. Vincent stood as radical candidate at Banbury in the general election of July 1841 and the *Northern Star* described him as 'one of the most exciting and animating speakers belonging to our ranks'. He attracted much nonconformist support, but Francis Place refused aid both on this occasion and in 1842 when Vincent contested Ipswich, and Vincent was defeated.

At this time Vincent attacked the Anti-Corn Law League, though he denied doing so ten years later. This was because he distrusted its middle-class leaders, and not because he opposed free trade as such. He felt it better to agitate against all forms of aristocratic oppression rather than against merely one aspect of it. He ridiculed the fuss made over the birth of the Prince of Wales: 'titles and doll dresses excite our contempt'. He saw the Queen as an innocent pawn of aristocracy. Distressed at the misery prevalent in Lancashire industrial areas, he described the poor in April 1841 as 'slaves in the land of their birth'. They must recover their rights, for charity alone was insufficient: 'it would be far more benevolent so to frame our laws and institutions *as to render it impossible for any industrious healthy man to be in want*', he said in December 1841, 'and there ought to be comfortable provision made by law for those who, owing to sickness, or old age, or insanity, or loss of limbs, were unable to provide for themselves'. Yet Vincent did not have a welfare state in mind, for he soon joined the Complete Suffrage Union.

By November 1841 he was admiring the editorials in the *Nonconformist*. He still, however, went to the April 1842 CSU conference with some mistrust, but was soon convinced of the sincerity of its promoters. He tried to win the CSU to all six Chartist points, less from a belief in measures as extreme as annual parliaments than from a desire to convince Chartists that the CSU was in earnest. He valued franchise extension, if only because it must force government into supporting national education. He supported Lovett's demand that the Conference ensure the enactment of its principles by arranging for future conferences to be summoned. He blamed much working-class suffering on their own lack of political principle, and on their exaggerated deference to aristocracy: 'no man was fit to be a leader of the people unless he would tell them of their own errors'. For Vincent there seemed to be no contradiction between the aims of Chartists and CSU. Both attacked corruption and state pensions, favoured decentralisation, free trade, reduced taxation and religious and political liberty. Both were genuinely concerned to relieve popular suffering.

Immediately after the April 1842 conference, therefore, Vincent began active work for the CSU. The *National Vindicator* ceased publication in April, and Vincent supported Sturge at the Nottingham by-election. In May Vincent denounced O'Connor as a 'designing Demagogue', suspicious of plots and thirsty for admiration. O'Connor retaliated by calling Vincent a 'political pedlar' who changed his coat according to his audience. Chartists often heckled Vincent for several years subsequently. O'Brien defended him at the May 1842 Chartist convention ('as noble a little soul as ever breathed'), but many Chartists, especially Thomas Cooper, thought Vincent a traitor. At Leicester in July 1842 Cooper's Chartists disturbed Vincent's CSU meetings. 'To Vincent I never apologised', wrote Cooper in Gammage's *History*: 'I still think that, under the circumstances, he deserved what he got.' There may be something in popular suspicions that Vincent joined the CSU partly because he was short of money. By January 1842 he owed £250, and the demands of his new family probably accentuated his need for security. In his case, as with another Chartist leader Robert Lowery, his departure from the Chartist movement may owe something to a serious illness. He had been ill early in 1840 and again in November 1841. He fainted at Banbury after giving a speech there in May 1842, and at the CSU conference in December he abstained on the crucial division owing to 'a termination of blood to the head'.

But does the move into the CSU mark anything more than a tactical change? Vincent's speeches certainly became more moderate, more conciliatory to the middle classes. They dwelt less upon the conflict of interest between working men and shopocracy, and concentrated more on the need for moral reform. But there was no fundamental change in his ultimate political ideals. On his release from prison in 1841, Vincent indignantly told Hume that he would agitate for nothing less than universal suffrage, and unlike many radicals he held to this resolve for the rest of his life. He was, in fact, a Felix Holt who could have risen high in society, but who chose to spend a lifetime in morally elevating his order. He always distrusted Whigs and Tories, doubted the virtues of a two-party system, and wanted all classes to rally round a single reform party. This can be seen from studying his personal campaign to purify the English electoral system in his eight election contests between 1841 and 1852.

As an independent radical, Vincent unsuccessfully contested Banbury (1841), Ipswich (1842), Tavistock (1843), Kilmarnock (1844), Plymouth (1846), Ipswich (1847) and York (1848 and 1852). His aim was to educate the public in Liberal principles, to weaken the corrupting influence of the London political clubs, and to transform elections into debates on public policy rather than battles between local interests and personalities. Vincent lacked sufficient cash, but his well-mannered, uncorrupt and non-violent election campaigns won him respect even from his opponents. Whig wirepullers often obstructed him and accused him of splitting the anti-Tory vote, but Vincent always despised them as 'Tories in disguise' who added the vice of hypocrisy to their Tory policies. If he had got himself elected, Vincent's principles would probably have confined him to a merely 'protesting' role in parliament. His experience as an extra-parliamentary public speaker would not have helped him at Westminster, as the careers of James Silk Buckingham and George Thompson reveal. He would certainly have found effective reform more elusive than it seemed when viewed from outside.

In his election campaigns, Vincent

appealed strongly for nonconformist support. From 1842 to 1846 he lectured for the CSU and for other predominantly dissenting organisations, while his wife kept a genteel school for young ladies in Stoke Newington. He supported the temperance movement for its attacks on corruption and servility, and because it promoted harmony between middle and working class, though timid teetotal leaders were sometimes reluctant to admit him to their meetings. He also lectured for the Liberation Society, and his political career can be understood only against the background of a radicalism nourished equally by nonconformist manufacturers and tradesmen and by progressive artisans. Vincent always identified Liberalism with Christianity and Toryism with sin, and never ceased to emphasise that Christianity had first flourished among the common people. For the rest of his life he was prominent in the movements of combative dissent and eager to apply individual moral principles to public affairs. He opposed the Maynooth grant in 1845 because he believed that the state should not endow education, but in 1850 he warned nonconformists against betraying their traditions by persecuting Catholics. Education, not persecution, was the way to deal with Catholic superstition. Vincent joined no religious denomination, but he disliked priestcraft and admired the Quakers. O'Connor tried to embarrass him in the 1840s by citing from the 1830s irreligious statements which had sprung more from the intensity of his class feeling than from any loss of faith.

During the 1840s, Vincent's ideas settled into a self-help mould. He espoused religious freedom, decentralisation, direct taxation and free trade. In the 1840s he was as zealous a devotee of the policeman theory of government as Lord Salisbury was to be in the 1880s. He did not even advocate the modest degree of state control recommended by Paine his master, and envisaged the day when education and religion would so inculcate internal self-discipline that no central government would be needed. In 1843 he strongly opposed poor laws which aided 'the idle and worthless', and in 1844 he thought factory legislation would 'greatly injure' the working classes. Until 1839 he had concentrated on attacking jobbery and maldistribution of wealth, but in 1840 he was much puzzled on how to remedy industrial poverty. Self-help rapidly became his panacea, an opportunity society his objective. He strongly opposed Malthus before 1839, but told Place privately in 1840 that he was 'now thoroughly convinced of the soundness of the doctrines taught by Malthus and yourself'. But he did not say so publicly, and his views did not deter him from later having several children of his own. He was a lifelong opponent of socialism, and in 1841 he regarded competition as 'best adapted for developing the energies and talents of the human race'. He often severely attacked those who fell short of his self-reliant, upstandingly independent but compassionate ideal of conduct.

By 1848 Vincent had become a strong admirer of the Cobden whom in 1841 he had despised. He shared Cobden's belief that aristocrats 'got up' foreign wars in order to perpetuate domestic oppression, and that they developed the empire to provide their younger sons with jobs. Armies were recruited from the residuum and soldiers were 'mechanical automata' who bartered away both reason and conscience. Vincent strongly condemned public executions, partly from humanitarian distaste for capital punishment, partly because he feared gatherings of residuum. Politics for Vincent was a battle between 'old feudalism and young liberty', not between employer and employee. Commerce he regarded as the vehicle of peace, religious toleration and affluence. He wanted the existing party system superseded by principled politicians, and often stressed that revolutions resulted only from governments which were deaf to the demands of their subjects. He feared London mobs, and in 1848 privately urged Cobden to divert discontent into parliamentary channels by starting up a new League agitation: 'If you free traders don't help to do this peacefully, the people, the mass, will by-and-by win the suffrage in a passion, and then we shall fall before Communists, and a mob of social quacks who will derange everything.' Vincent joined Lovett's People's League, and was convinced that reform could be effective only if it was gradual and peaceable. He preferred public meetings to barricades. By the 1850s he was praising the Great Exhibition and apologising for his extremist statements of the 1830s.

Henceforward Vincent was less in the public eye. After the decline of the CSU, he became a freelance lecturer, frequently performing for mutual improvement organisations. His lecturing career could only have been pursued in an urban society which had rejected the old rural sports without yet acquiring the new urban mass recreations. Short but graceful in appearance, pleasant in features, mellow but vigorous in speech, he was a brilliant mimic who could entertain and enthral his audiences. His character-sketches resemble those in Dickens and in contemporary music-hall performances. He took a delight in ridiculing ignorant rustics, pompous and self-interested ecclesiastics, effete aristocrats, and feather-headed young people enslaved to conformity and fashion. His speeches were jaunty and boisterous, but also moralistic, culminating in high-flown rhetoric. Vincent was in fact a cheerful puritan. 'He was a humorist, with a funny little chuckle when he said something intended to cause laughter, a keen satirist, and an excellent mimic' [H. J. Jennings [1920] 38]. W. E. Adams heard him at Newcastle in the 1860s and found him 'a man of fine presence, of powerful voice, of impressive delivery', whose 'torrent of words, poured forth with the skill of a master, brought down thunders of applause' [Adams [1903] 194]. Vincent was a master of the dramatic peroration, replete with mixed metaphors and an antique style involving repeated 'O's, 'thees' and 'thous'. Logic was not his *forte*, but he became well known for his setpiece orations, particularly on historical topics, at a time when history was the customary training for politicians, when oratory was highly-prized among the arts, and when events in seventeenth-century England were still matters of present politics.

Vincent's earliest Chartist speeches reflect his deep interest in English history, which was for him the story of progress and the rise of Liberalism. He idealised Anglo-Saxon liberties and Magna Carta, and shared Cobden's desire for a social history which would show how the masses lived. History was not for him a story of kings and battles. He attacked feudal brutality, and when commenting on late medieval history in 1844 took a delight in singling out for discussion, not Crécy or Poitiers, but 'the gradual rise of commerce, diffusing in its operations a spirit of sociability among the people, and increasing the comforts and growth of towns and communities'. He believed that medieval Catholicism defended liberty against despotism, but worshipped Wyclif and the Reformation martyrs, and eloquently praised the effects of the discovery of printing. He helped to pioneer the early Victorian revaluation of Cromwell by attacking Hume's historical interpretation, and by seeing Cromwell as the seventeenth century's 'man of principle'. Spellbound by his Cromwell lectures 'you could hear the sound of the great man's jack boots', said J. B. Leno. Vincent urged his audiences to follow the example set by the Whig heroes Russell and Hampden. Wyclif, Wesley and Whitfield were for him the pioneers of voluntarism, and he urged his audiences to respect them not merely by praising them but by emulating today the courageous independence they had displayed yesterday. Vincent's ideas after 1839 were influenced more by the English revolution than by the French. For him, French revolutions did no more than create political opportunities for English radicalism to pursue its own independent and superior course.

Once established as a lecturer, Vincent concentrated far more heavily on the need for self-reform. He idealised women, whose sphere was decidedly in the home, but he scorned the idea that they should be mere ornaments. He himself enjoyed a very happy family life, and wrote home daily when away. He favoured aristocracies only of virtue and talent, and enjoyed ridiculing a subservient rustic peasantry. He attacked money-worship, affectation, snobbery, extravagance, flippancy and belief in luck. He had always attacked pauperism at both ends of society, but whereas in the 1830s his attention had been concentrated on aristocratic paupers, he later focused as much on the self-indulgence and idleness of the very poor. 'There were two classes of hereditary paupers in this country,' he said in 1871, 'one at the top and the other at the bottom of the social scale.' He despised unprincipled, easygoing individuals, and ridiculed working-class Conservatives. The world owed everything, he believed, to the nonconformers. He promoted the Liberal ideal of the alert citizen and lacked the Owenite's environmentalist perspective. He thought that his home-centred ideal society could be created primarily through individual moral effort.

In later life he was more concerned with questions of foreign policy than with domestic social questions, though he still advocated franchise extension and always stressed the need for individual moral reform. He greatly admired Mazzini, Cavour and Garibaldi, delighted in the Pope's discomfiture in the 1860s, and rebuked Louis Napoleon for defending him. Throughout the American Civil War he consistently defended North against South, and greatly admired Abraham Lincoln and American political institutions He lectured successfully in America in 1866, 1867, 1869 and 1875. In the *Bee-Hive* he defended Americans against European accusations that they were noisy and vulgar, urged ambitious and hardworking labourers to emigrate, and rejoiced at meeting in America prosperous and respected ex-Chartists who as Englishmen in the 1830s had been poverty-stricken and despised. He spoke at the unveiling of Cobden's statue in Camden Town, and lived nearby for many years. In July 1870 he was a council member of the Land Tenure Reform Association, which aimed at abolishing the law of primogeniture, at taxing unearned increases in land values and at democratising property ownership. He was convinced, in 1871, of the need for monarchy to be more useful and popular if it was to survive, but his later speeches breathe a pride in England's prosperity and libertarian institutions. He welcomed the collapse of the Second Empire, the unification of Germany, and the retreat of priestcraft all over Europe. He was enthusiastic for the Bulgarian atrocities agitation of 1876: 'we have certainly put the hook through the Tory nose on the Eastern

Question', he told Lloyd Garrison privately, and his correspondence at this time shows him as jauntily self-confident and optimistic as he had ever been in the 1830s. In his last speech at Barrow in 1878, he vigorously attacked Beaconsfieldism, defended free trade, urged reduced taxation, and called on his audience to rally round the Liberal standard. But he caught a chill and, after three weeks' illness, died on 29 December 1878. Vincent's effects were valued at under £450.

His biographer's assessment that Vincent was 'a co-worker together with God' is unverifiable, but his career certainly displays earnestness, courage, independence and energy. He never lost his distrust of authority or his sympathy with the oppressed. But his speeches by the 1870s had become repetitive and somewhat vacuous. 'It was a fine performance,' said W. E. Adams of his Newcastle speech in the 1860s, 'splendid as a piece of declamation, but neither pregnant with thought nor of much value as a literary effort.' His speeches in Lancashire in 1871 contrast interestingly with those of J. R. Stephens in the same year. Vincent's speech on home politics favours nothing more than self-help, licensing legislation, land law reform, disestablishment, housing reform, the ballot, House of Lords reform, and unsectarian education. Stephens, on the other hand, condemns industrial society, and focuses rather on the need for a living wage and for factory legislation. And whereas Stephens condoned popular recreations as a respite from exhausting and montonous work, Vincent feared the continued prosperity of sports old and new, for these were frustrating too many of the objectives of an early Victorian radical.

Vincent was therefore a lively but unoriginal spokesman of radicalism, and displayed in his last speeches the bankruptcy of late-Victorian *laissez-faire* Liberals when Little Englandism and the Great Depression were shaking the popular basis of their support, and when libertarian concessions had begun to erode the radicalism of nonconformity. If the classless society could be realised at all, Vincent believed that it would congeal round bourgeoisie rather than proletariat. 'The English working-class . . .', wrote Marx disgustedly in 1878, 'had at last got to the point when it was nothing more than the tail of the Great Liberal Party, *i.e.*, of its *oppressors*, the capitalists.' Labour historians will praise Vincent for stimulating working-class self-respect and political awareness throughout his life, and even for stimulating working-class consciousness in the 1830s. 'I constantly console myself with my old motto "The road to Liberty lies through the jail" ', wrote Vincent in 1877, recalling his Chartist days in a letter to W. L. Garrison. But Vincent's consistent Liberalism after the 1830s may well seem an anticlimax to historians who underestimate the radical achievement in transforming the mid-Victorian Whig-Liberal Party, and who exaggerate the affinities between Chartism and the Labour Party. Vincent did not himself feel that his Chartist past had been betrayed by his later conduct. Crucial to an understanding of his career is a recognition of the centrality in nineteenth-century working-class politics of two divisions: the geographical division between working men in town and country, and the cultural division between the rough and the respectable.

Writings: Several of Vincent's speeches are kept in the Vincent Coll. of newspaper clippings, Labour Party Library, Transport House, London. His writings also appear in issues of the *Western Vindicator*, 23 Feb–30 Nov 1839, Newport Public Library; 7–14 Dec 1839, Transport House; *National Vindicator*, 18 Sep 1841, Newport Public Library; 13 Nov 1841–8 Jan 1842, 22 and 29 Jan 1842, Transport House; 12 Feb 1842, Newport Public Library; 23 Apr 1842, Francis Place Newspaper Coll., Set 56 (Apr–June 1842) 115, BM; but there does not appear to be a complete set. Some of Vincent's 1841 election material is in the Rusher Coll., Banbury Public Library.

Sources:
(1) MSS: Cobden: 43667 f. 211; Place: 35151, ff. 227–9, 327–9, 343–5, 360–2; Place Newspaper Coll., Set 56 (Oct 1840–Feb 1841) Appendix: all at BM; Lovett Coll.,

vol. 1 pp. 44, 129, 202, 282; vol. 11 p. 242, Birmingham City Library; Garrison-Vincent Correspondence in Boston (USA) Public Library; Vincent-Miniken Correspondence in Transport House; Banbury Elections 1841–3 (G.A. Oxon. b. 101) [election squibs], Bodleian Library, Oxford; Glyde Coll. [election squibs 1842], Ipswich City Library.

(2) Newspapers and journals: *London Mercury*, 5 Mar 1837; *London Dispatch*, 26 Mar 1837; *Bradford Observer*, 7 Sep 1837; *Northern Liberator*, Aug 1838; *Hansard's Parliamentary Debates*, 1839–41; *Northern Star*, 1839–48; *Western Star*, 3 Oct 1840; *True Scotsman*, Nov 1840; *Chartist Circular* (ed. W. Thomson) Dec 1840; *Midland Counties Illuminator*, Feb–Apr 1841; *Leicestershire Mercury*, Mar–Apr 1841, 30 July 1842; *Liverpool Mercury*, Mar–Apr 1841; *Leicester Chronicle*, Mar 1841; *Nottingham Review*, 9 Apr 1841; *Cheltenham Free Press*, Apr 1841, Mar 1843; *Glamorgan, Monmouth & Brecon Gazette*, June 1841; *Oxford City & County Chronicle*, July 1841; *Hull Rockingham, Yorkshire & Lincolnshire Gazette*, 6 Nov 1841; *Nonconformist*, 1841–54; *English Chartist Circular*, vol. 1, nos. 5, 11, 17 (1841); vol. 2, no. 90 (1842); *Report of the Proceedings at the Conference of Delegates, of the Middle and Working Classes, held at Birmingham, 5 Apr 1842, and three following days* (1842) 15–16, 39, 52, 67; *British Statesman*, 1842–3; *Birmingham Journal*, Apr, June 1842; *Derby & Chesterfield Reporter*, 21 July 1842; *Suffolk Chronicle*, Aug 1842, June–July 1847; *Sheffield & Rotherham Independent*, Sep 1842, 26 Sep 1846; *Leeds Times*, Oct 1842, Mar 1844; *Plymouth, Devonport & Stonehouse Herald*, Mar, June 1843; *Plymouth & Devonport Weekly J.*, Mar, Aug 1843, July 1846; *Manchester Times*, May 1843; *Metropolitan Temperance Intelligencer & Journal*, July 1843; *Sentinel*, 2 and 4 Sep 1843; *Somerset County Gazette*, Sep 1843, July 1844; *Bolton Free Press*, Dec 1843; *Edinburgh Weekly Chronicle*, Apr, June 1844; *Kilmarnock J.*, May, Aug 1844; *National Temperance Chronicle*, Feb 1845; *Berkshire Chronicle*, 16 May 1846; *Carlisle J.*, Mar 1848; *York Herald*, May, July, Dec 1848, 26 Jan 1850, Apr–July 1852, June 1857; *Yorkshireman*, June 1848; *Bristol*

Examiner, 9 Mar 1850; *Preston Guardian*, 13 Apr 1850, 20 Apr 1850, 18 Jan 1851; *Oxford Chronicle*, 25 May, 1 June, 26 Oct 1850, 23 Nov 1872; *Reading Mercury*, 28 June 1851; *Falkirk Herald*, Nov 1853; *Greenwich & West Kent Observer*, Apr 1854; *Cambridge Independent Press*, May 1854; *Halifax Courier*, May 1854; *Staffordshire Sentinel*, Mar 1857; *Oldham Advertiser*, Dec 1857; *Bath Herald,* 7 July 1861; *Monmouthshire Merlin*, 10 Jan 1863; *Wolverhampton Spirit of the Times*, 1 July 1865; *Bee-Hive*, 14 Mar 1868, 18 Apr 1868; *Ashton Reporter*, 18 Mar 1871, 28 Oct 1871, 12 Oct 1872; *Christian World*, 11 Aug 1871; *Barrow Herald,* Dec 1878; *Barrow Times,* Dec 1878.

(3) Secondary: W. Dorling, *Henry Vincent: a biographical sketch* (1879); D. Burns, *Temperance History*, 2 vols (1889); J. B. Leno, *The Aftermath* (1892); G. J. Holyoake, *Sixty Years of an Agitator's Life*, 2 vols (1893); H. Solly, *These Eighty Years*, 2 vols (1893); R. G. Gammage, *History of the Chartist Movement* (1894; reprinted with an introduction by John Saville, New York, 1969); W. E. Adams, *Memoirs of a Social Atom*, 2 vols (1903; reprinted in one volume, with an introduction by John Saville, New York, 1967); M. Hovell, *The Chartist Movement* (Manchester, 1918); G. Wallas, *The Life of Francis Place* (1918); H. J. Jennings, *Chestnuts and Small Beer* (1920); J. West, *History of the Chartist Movement* (1920; repr. New York, 1968); D. Williams, *John Frost: a study in Chartism* (Cardiff, 1939); A. R. Schoyen, *The Chartist Challenge* (1958); *Chartist Studies*, ed. Asa Briggs (1959), *passim*, but especially H. Fearn, 'Chartism in Suffolk', R. B. Pugh, 'Chartism in Somerset and Wiltshire', D. Williams, 'Chartism in Wales'; C. Tucker, 'The Prisoner in Monmouth Jail: a study of Henry Vincent (1813–1878)', *Presenting Monmouthshire* (J. Monmouthshire Local History Council) no. 20 (Autumn 1965); B. Harrison and P. Hollis, 'Chartism, Liberalism and the Life of Robert Lowery', *English Historical Review, 82* (July 1967) 503–35.

BRIAN HARRISON

See also: *William LOVETT, for Chartism to 1840; *Francis PLACE; *Feargus O'CONNOR, for Chartism, 1840–8; * J. R. STEPHENS.

VIVIAN, Henry Harvey (1868–1930)
CO-PARTNERSHIP ADVOCATE AND MP

Born on 20 April 1868 at Cornwood, South Devon, the son of William Henry Vivian, a carpenter, and his wife Mary, he was educated at Cornwood National School and then apprenticed to a Plymouth carpenter. In his early youth he went to London where he engaged actively in trade union affairs as a member of the Amalgamated Society of Carpenters and Joiners and served as president of the Pimlico branch. A strike and lock-out of joiners in 1890 convinced him of the need to introduce co-partnership as a means of averting industrial strife. There was already a movement in existence. The Co-operative Productive Federation (CPF) had been founded in 1882 to bring together for purposes of mutual assistance the individual producers' societies. Two years later the Labour Association was established, concerned solely with education and propaganda, leaving the CPF to concentrate upon the business affairs of the societies. E. O. Greening and Thomas Blandford were the leading personalities of the movement in the 1880s and Vivian became close friends with both and especially with Blandford.

In 1890 he was made secretary of the Labour Association and in January 1893 he gave evidence before the Royal Commission on Labour, which, together with the evidence of Joseph Greenwood relating to the Hebden Bridge Fustian Works (Qs 962–1107) represent a comprehensive statement of the contemporary co-partnership situation. Vivian defined the Labour Association as 'purely a propagandist body' and as 'the representative of that party in the co-operative movement which seeks to establish workshops in which the workers share in profits and participate in the management, as opposed to the workshops called "co-operative" which are organisations of stores employing wage-paid labour, and the mills called "co-operative" which are merely organisations of small capitalists hiring labour on ordinary competitive terms' (Q. 7526). At the time that he was speaking, E. O. Greening was treasurer of the Labour Association and there were about thirty co-partnership societies affiliated, together with two hundred individual members.

Vivian remained secretary of the Labour Association until 1909; he served as honorary secretary in 1909–10 and was a member of its executive committee until his death. In 1902 the Association was renamed the Labour Co-partnership Association and in 1927 its title was further changed to Industrial Co-partnership Association.

Thomas Blandford died at an early age in 1899, and about the same time Vivian entered upon a new phase of his career. He had established General Builders Ltd in 1891 as a co-partnership enterprise, and by 1897 it had seventeen branches. Vivian now began to apply co-partnership principles directly to housing development. There had been an early attempt in 1888 when Tenant Co-operators Ltd was established but Vivian improved on this model by forming the Ealing Tenants Ltd in 1901, a society which linked profit-sharing with the provision of social amenities on the estates. The background was the rapidly growing interest in town planning and new types of suburban developments and garden villages. Ebenezer Howard published *Tomorrow: A Peaceful Path to Real Reform* in 1898 and this was re-issued under the better-known title *Garden Cities of Tomorrow* in 1902. Vivian served as chairman of Ealing Tenants until 1911 and during his term of office advised, sometimes with the help of E. O. Greening, on the formation of several tenant societies, and in certain cases initiated the schemes. In 1907 he became chairman of Co-partnership Tenants Ltd, created to advise societies on financial matters and estate layout. Initially it had eight affiliated societies and Vivian was a considerable influence in the planning of a number of garden villages and suburban developments, including Hampstead Garden Suburb and developments at Birmingham, Derwentwater, Letchworth, Manchester and Wolverhampton. He was consulted, for example, when Joseph Rowntree founded the Rowntree Village Trust in 1904. He visited Canada in 1910 at the invitation of Lord Grey, the Governor-General, in order to discuss town planning and housing matters

and again, invited by Grey's successor, the Duke of Connaught, in 1912.

In 1906 Vivian entered Parliament as a Lib-Lab member for Birkenhead and served on the R.C. on Canals and Waterways, the S.C. on Housing and Town Planning and the Departmental Committee on Accidents in Factories and Workshops. He and Fred Maddison, another Lib-Lab MP, were against the decision to join the Labour Party in 1908 and had been censured by the Trades Union Congress in the previous year for opposing Pete Curran's candidature at the Jarrow by-election in July 1907. Vivian lost his seat at the December 1910 general election and when he contested the South Somerset constituency in the Liberal interest at a by-election in 1911 he was also defeated. On two subsequent occasions – at Edmonton in 1918 and Northampton in 1922 – he contested parliamentary constituencies without success, but in 1923 he was elected as a Liberal member for the Totnes division of Devon although he lost this seat in the following year.

Vivian was a Liberal of the free-trade school. John Stuart Mill was probably the most important intellectual influence in his life, and Vivian was active in Liberal political circles from the 1890s on. He was at one time or another a member of the committee of the National Liberal Club, vice-chairman of its Political Committee and a member of the executive committee of the Cobden Club. After 1918, in the anti-militarist Cobdenite tradition he became an enthusiastic advocate of the principles of the League of Nations and he was chairman of a very successful Hornsey (North London) branch of the League. He was also, in the 1920s, active in the Hornsey Liberal Association. He had been appointed a JP for Middlesex in 1907, and he sat occasionally on the bench at Wood Green and Highgate. His main recreation was playing bowls.

Vivian was apparently not associated with any religious sect or group. He died at his Crouch End, Hornsey, home on 30 May 1930 and his funeral took place at Golders Green Crematorium on 3 June. His wife survived him. Fred Maddison, a colleague of many years' standing, and at the time secretary of the International Arbitration League and a member of the executive committee of the Industrial Co-partnership Association, was among those who delivered a funeral address at the cremation ceremony. He left an estate valued at £17,275.

Writings: Evidence before the R.C. on Labour, 1893–4 XXXIX Pt I Qs 7523–688; (with A. Williams) 'The Co-partnership of Labour', *Econ. Rev. 4* (July 1894) 297–317; *True Position of Employees in the Co-operative Movement* (1894); *What Co-operative Production is doing* (1894); *Some Aspects of the Co-operative Movement* (1894); 'A Novel Attempt at Co-operative Production in the Building Trades', *Econ. J. 6* (June 1896) 270–2; *What is Co-partnership?* [1896] 4 pp.; *Co-operators and the thorough Cultivation of the Land* (Newcastle, 1898) 11 pp.; *Partnership of Capital and Labour as a Solution of the Conflict between them* [1898] 11 pp.; *Co-operative Stores and Labour Co-partnership* (1899) 8 pp.; *The Efficient Organisation of Industry* (1901); 'An Interesting Co-operative Housing Experiment', *Co-operators' Year Book* (1902) 119; *Industrial Democracy* (1903) 8 pp.; *Co-operation and Trade Unionism* (1903); *The Labour Co-partnership Movement* (1904) 10 pp.; 'Co-partnership in Housing', *Econ. J. 15* (June 1905) 254–7, *Econ. Rev. 16* (Jan 1906) 76–81 and *West. Rev. 168* (Dec 1907) 615–21; *A New Chapter in the History of Co-operation and Labour: The North Wales Quarries Ltd* (1906) 20 pp.; *Co-partnership in Housing* [1910] 8 pp.; *Problems of Finance with Special Reference to the Co-partnership Movement* [1912] 15 pp.; 'The Co-partnership Tenants' Movement', *Garden Suburbs, Villages and Homes*, no. 2 (Summer 1912) 29–36; 'Garden Cities, Housing and Town Planning', *Q. Rev. 216* (1912) 493–515; *Some Experiments in Community Making* [1912] 19 pp.; A. Wood, *Co-partnership Housing*, with an introduction by H. Vivian (1913).

Sources: H. M. Lloyd, *Labor Co-partnership* (1898); Times, *House of Commons* (1910); *Dod's Parliamentary Companion* (1909) and (1924); G. D. H. Cole, *British Working Class Politics 1832–1914* (1950); J. W. R. Adam, *Modern Town and Country Planning* (1952); W. Ashworth, *The Genesis of Modern British Town*

Planning (1954); A. Bonner, *British Co-operation* (Manchester, 1961); H. A. Clegg et al., *A History of British Trade Unions since 1889* (1964); M. Timms, *Ealing Tenants Ltd: pioneers of co-partnership* (Ealing Local History Society, Members' Papers, no. 8: 1966); *WWW* (1929–40); personal information: Mrs I. S. Ramsey, secretary, Industrial Co-partnership Association; Co-operative Productive Federation records: Hull University Library ref. DCF. OBIT. *Times*, 31 May 1930; *Co-partnership*, June 1930; *Hornsey Journal*, 6 June 1930.

JOYCE BELLAMY

See also: T. BLANDFORD; E. O. GREENING, for Co-partnership; Benjamin JONES, for Co-operative Production.

WADSWORTH, John (1850–1921)
MINERS' LEADER AND LIB-LAB MP

Born 4 February 1850 at West Melton Fields, near Wath-on-Dearne, Yorkshire, and educated at Brampton School, John Wadsworth commenced work in a coalmine at an early age. In the early 1860s he went to New Biggin, near Chapeltown, Sheffield, where he was employed in the Drift Pit of Newton, Chambers and Co. at Thorncliffe until the lock-out of 1869. He then moved to the Wombwell Main Colliery and in the following year obtained work at Wharncliffe Silkstone Colliery, Tankersley, near Barnsley. Here the miners elected him checkweighman in 1883, a position he retained until 1904, during which time he acted as secretary and then president and also as delegate for the Wharncliffe Silkstone branch of the Yorkshire Miners' Association. For fifteen years of this period he served as vice-president of the YMA and was elected in 1903 to succeed Edward Cowey as president. In 1905 he succeeded William Parrott as general secretary of the association, a position he held until his death. He served on the MFGB executive in 1891 and again from 1903 to 1911 and was a member of the Conciliation Board appointed in 1894. For some years in the 1890s (the dates are not quite certain) he was the local correspondent to the Labour Department of the Board of Trade for the

Yorkshire mining districts, excepting Cleveland.

An outspoken speaker, he was a strong opponent of extremist policies and belonged to the Lib-Lab group of mining MPs when he was elected to serve the Hallamshire Division of West Yorkshire at the 1906 general election as a MFGB nominee. He subsequently held the seat in the Labour interest until 1918 when he retired from Parliament on health grounds. He declined invitations to be a candidate for elections to a school board, local board and the county council preferring to devote his life to work for the miners, although he did become a magistrate for the West Riding.

He had married, in 1872, Annie Eliza Bell of New Biggin, near Sheffield. He died on 10 July 1921 at his Barnsley home and was survived by a son and two daughters. He left an estate valued at £3633. Wadsworth was buried at Barnsley Cemetery on 13 July when Herbert Smith paid tribute to his work for the Yorkshire miners.

Sources: W. Hallam, *Miners' Leaders* (includes a portrait of Wadsworth) (1894); *Dod* (1909) and (1918); *WWW* (1916–28); F. Bealing and H. Pelling, *Labour and Politics, 1900–1906* (1958). OBIT. *Barnsley Chronicle*, 16 July 1921.

JOYCE BELLAMY

See also: Thomas ASHTON, for Mining Trade Unionism, 1900–14; Benjamin PICKARD, for Mining Trade Unionism, 1880–99.

WALKER, Benjamin (1803/4?–83)
SOCIAL REFORMER AND CO-OPERATOR

Of Benjamin Walker's early life little is known except that he was born at Stretton near Burton on Trent in the early years of the century and left his native village as a young man for Lenton, near Nottingham, where he established a firm of lace manufacturers. A Baptist, ardent supporter of the temperance movement and politically an advanced Liberal, he was a benevolent employer interested in the welfare of his workers and described locally as 'a Robert Owen of Nottingham'. As a staunch nonconformist he opposed the monopoly of the Church School in Lenton and decided with his fellow industrialist, Thomas Bayley, a tanner, to open a reading room in Lenton which became known as Mr Bayley's Reading Room. Walker's interest in temperance was reflected in his chairing of a meeting at the Reading Room on 31 August 1858 which led to the formation of the Lenton Temperance Society on 14 September 1858 and his membership of the Society's management committee. As president of the Society in 1861 he provided members with a room at the rear of the New Inn and later furnished the new Lenton Temperance Reading Room in Wollaton Street. In the same year he was appointed treasurer of a Savings Bank run by the Lenton Temperance Society.

In 1863 at a meeting in the Temperance Reading Room, Messrs Walker and Bayley introduced the subject of co-operation, having visited Lancashire and learned of its method of operation in that county. As a result of this meeting a committee was formed which included the two speakers and J. Keeton as secretary to explore the possibility of establishing a co-operative store in Lenton. A meeting on 10 April 1863 approved the formation of the Lenton Co-operative Society (the forerunner of the Nottingham Co-operative Society). On 12 May 1863, at a members' meeting of the newly established Lenton Industrial and Provident Society Ltd, Benjamin Walker was elected secretary and Thomas Bayley president. On 5 January 1869 Walker replaced Bayley as president. He guided the Society during a period of financial crisis but resigned his presidency in 1878 when the majority report of the committee on the Society's financial affairs, which he had supported, was rejected at a members' meeting in favour of a more radical minority report. On his death in 1883 his eldest son received a letter of condolence which referred to 'his incessant and unselfish service ... over a long period of years to the cause of co-operation'.

Walker had returned to his native Stretton a few years before his death and had been ill for some time before he died on 3 February 1883 in his eightieth year. Following a funeral service in Nottingham, he was buried in Nottingham Cemetery. Memorial services were held at Stretton and Burton. At the Stretton memorial service, the preacher advised the congregation to look on the good that Walker did and ignore 'the peculiarities of his life'; a reference presumably to Walker's advanced political and social views. He left an estate valued at £31,072.

Sources: F. W. Leeman, *Co-operation in Nottingham* (Nottingham Co-operative Society Ltd, 1963); personal information: John A. Walker, Nottingham. OBIT. *Burton Chronicle*, 8 and 15 Feb 1883.

JOYCE BELLAMY
H. F. BING

See also: Thomas BAYLEY; G. J. HOLYOAKE, for Retail Co-operation – Nineteenth Century.

WALSHAM, Cornelius (1880–1958)
CO-OPERATOR AND TRADE UNIONIST

The son of Jonas Walsham, a farm labourer, Cornelius was born on 16 April 1880 near Horncastle, Lincolnshire, and was educated at the local Church of England school. He left school about the age of twelve to become a farm labourer. Later he was a locomotive driver and from 1926 to 1945 (when he retired) was manager of the Scunthorpe Co-operative Dairies. 'Corney' (as he was familiarly known) was first elected to the management committee of the Scunthorpe Mutual Co-operative and Industrial Society in 1914, and except for a period of eighteen months he remained on the committee for the rest of his working life. He was for many years secretary of the Society's education committee and was president of the Society in 1921–2 and subsequently vice-president.

During and after the First World War he was chairman of the Lindsey War Pensions Committee. He was made a JP in 1920 and served on the bench for thirty-five years, retiring under the age rule in April 1955. He served as chairman of the domestic court for many years and was concerned with the administration of the Mental Health Acts

for nearly twenty years. Among his other activities, Walsham was for some time secretary of the Scunthorpe Trades and Labour Council, and was associated with bodies dealing with the training of disabled soldiers and post-war unemployment questions. His main recreational hobby was playing bowls.

He died on 25 October 1958, at the home of his daughter, Mrs Edith Brown, having been predeceased by his wife some years earlier.

Sources: A. Ginns, *Jubilee History of the Scunthorpe Mutual Co-operative and Industrial Society Ltd* (Manchester, 1924); *Scunthorpe Evening Telegraph*, 7 Apr 1955; personal information: Mrs Edith Brown. OBIT. *Scunthorpe Evening Telegraph*, 28 Oct 1958; *Scunthorpe Star*, 31 Oct 1958.

H. F. BING

See also: Frederick BOND; Fred CLARK.

WATKINS, William Henry (1862–1924)
CO-OPERATOR

Born on 19 March 1862 at Plymouth, the son of John Watkins, a cabinet-maker, and his wife Eliza, William Watkins was educated at Plymouth Public School and the Apprentices School at Plymouth Dockyard. He widened his education through university extension classes where he studied politics and economics and passed examinations in these subjects. After his early working career as an apprentice shipwright, he served as a clerical assistant in naval stores during the years 1883–1912. He was at Chatham initially but after a few years transferred to Devonport and from 1910 to 1912 was at Portsmouth.

Throughout his whole life his spare time was largely devoted to the co-operative movement and his association with it began in 1887 when he joined the Plymouth Society. He attended classes arranged by the Co-operative Union and in 1891, following considerable success in the Union's examinations, he was awarded a scholarship at the university extension meeting held at Oxford. In the following year he taught co-operative subjects at local classes and continued to do so for some ten years while at the same time pursuing his own studies until he had passed with distinction in most subjects then taught by the Co-operative Union. He held almost all of the Union's certificates including that awarded to students passing at the 'honours' level. He later acted as teacher for the correspondence classes arranged by the Co-operative Union. In 1907 he urged the central education committee of the Union to extend its teaching by correspondence and to establish an educational monthly paper – a proposal which subsequently gave rise to the publication of the *Co-operative Educator*. He proposed the appointment of an educational organiser and the employment of lecturers in a paper read to the Newport Congress in 1908 and played an important role in the formation of the Co-operative Students' Fellowship, of which he was joint secretary for a number of years.

Watkins was also active in the promotion of other co-operative ventures, especially in the co-partnership sphere. In 1894 he was among the founders of a local Co-operative House Painting and Decorating Society and he also helped to establish the Plymouth Printers Ltd. From 1903 to 1908 he served on the management committee of the Plymouth Co-operative Society. In rapid succession he became secretary of the South-Western Co-operative Education Association which he had helped to form, a member of the Devon District Co-operative Conference Association, and of the south-western sectional board of the Co-operative Union. He first served on the central board of the Co-operative Union from 1906 to 1909 and was soon chosen to fill several of the principal offices of the Union, being in turn a member of the united board, of the central education committee, the publications committee and the joint parliamentary committee. In 1910 he gave the presidential address at the Co-operative Congress, held that year in Plymouth. He was president of the Plymouth Co-operative Society from 1914 to 1919 and a member of the central board of the Co-operative Union from 1914 until his death in

1924. He became a member of the general co-operative survey committee when this was appointed in 1914.

Watkins was always keenly interested in political affairs and during the early war years he was a member of the Joint Parliamentary Committee as one of the representatives of the co-operative movement. He had long been an ardent advocate of parliamentary representation, and he was one of the leaders of the agitation which finally brought the co-operative movement into national politics in 1917; and from 1919 until his death he was chairman of the Co-operative Party. From 1918 to 1920 he was on the Ministry of Food's Consumer Council and he also sat on the Special Committee on Trusts.

In addition to his work for the Plymouth Society, the Co-operative Union and the Co-operative Party, he helped to form the National Men's Co-operative Guild, over whose central committee he presided for thirteen years. He was also joint secretary of the Co-operative Students' Fellowship for several years. He travelled widely for the co-operative movement and wrote pamphlets and articles on the subject. While his life was largely devoted to co-operative affairs, in his later years he was a Labour member of Plymouth City Council from 1919 to 1924.

Following a short illness he died at his Plymouth home on 29 July 1924 and was buried at Eggbuckland Cemetery on 31 July. He left an estate valued at £2650 and was survived by his son, W. P. Watkins, a member of the teaching staff of the Co-operative Union.

Writings: *Co-operative Teaching* (Manchester, 1907) 16 pp.; *Present Co-operative Educational Resources and some Immediate Needs* (Manchester, 1908) 24 pp.; *Formation of Co-operative Character* (Manchester, 1914) 14 pp.; *Co-operation in Cornwall* (Manchester, 1917) 12 pp.; *Trade Associations and Combinations* (Manchester, 1919) 12 pp.; *The Co-operative Party: its aims and work* (Manchester, 1921) 14 pp.; *Development of Co-operative Resources and Services* (Manchester, 1921) 16 pp.; *The Co-operative Party: its policy, activities and needs* (Manchester, 1922) 8 pp.

Sources: *Congress Handbook* (1910); T. W. Mercer, *Towards a Co-operative Commonwealth* (Manchester, 1936); R. Briscoe, *Centenary History: the story of the Plymouth Co-operative Society* (Manchester, 1960); A. Bonner, *British Co-operation* (Manchester, 1961); S. Pollard, 'The Foundation of the Co-operative Party', in *Essays in Labour History 2: 1886–1923*, ed. A. Briggs and J. Saville (1971) 185–210. Obit. *Western Morning News*, 30 July 1924; *Times*, 31 July 1924; *Co-op. News*, 2 and 9 Aug 1924; *Co-op. Congress Report* (1925).

JOYCE BELLAMY

See also: A. V. ALEXANDER, for Co-operative Party; Fred HALL, for Co-operative Education.

WATTS, John (1818–87)
OWENITE AND SOCIAL REFORMER

Born at Coventry on 24 March 1818, one of twelve children of a ribbon weaver, he had a severe illness at the age of five which left him partially paralysed on the left side. He received his early education at a Coventry charity school and when he was eleven he became a scholar in Trinity Church Sunday School and subsequently taught in the school. His physical disability prevented him from taking manual work and he was sent to the local Mechanics' Institute where from the age of thirteen to twenty he served in various capacities: as general assistant, librarian and assistant secretary. But he was, at the same time, extending his own education and about the age of twenty became converted to Owenism, was appointed a social missionary and in May 1840 went to Manchester where he delivered his first lecture. He then visited most of the towns in Lancashire and Cheshire lecturing and holding public discussions. Towards the end of the year he went to Glasgow and subsequently lectured in many Scottish towns before returning to Manchester in July 1841, where for three years he conducted educational classes at the Hall of Science. In 1842 he published *The Facts and Fictions of the Political Economists*, an Owenite analysis which condemned all appropriation as unjust and rent as robbery, and he suc-

cessfully presented a second edition of this volume as a doctoral thesis in the University of Giessen in 1844. By this time, however, he had become disillusioned with the practicality of Owen's schemes. Necessity required him to earn his own living and he developed an insurance business but he also devoted much of his life to a wide variety of social reform movements of strictly utilitarian and practical purposes.

Following his break with the Owenites, Watts immediately began working for local reform issues in the Manchester area. In 1845 he joined the movement which led to the establishment of three public parks in Manchester and Salford; in 1847 he joined and soon became a leading figure in the Lancashire (afterwards the National) Public School Association which campaigned for the provision of free, secular and rate-supported schools. Of this system he became the foremost advocate and held more than a hundred public meetings in towns from Newcastle upon Tyne to Brighton. Educational reform remained a major cause with which Watts was associated all his life. He also joined at this time the movement for the repeal of Taxes on Knowledge and during the late 1840s and throughout the fifties was a major figure in the agitation. He was a vigorous supporter of the Anti-Corn Law movement; an important influence in the establishment of the Manchester Central Library; and during 1848 a persistent advocate of moral force during the revived Chartist agitation.

Watts seems to have touched most of the reform movements of the next thirty years, and in many of them he played an important part. In the 1850s he continued his activity within the campaign for the removal of the newspaper advertisement, paper and stamp taxes (the so-called Taxes on Knowledge); he gave a warm welcome to the emergence and development of consumers' co-operation; and in February 1858 he attended the political reform conference called together by Ernest Jones (*People's Paper*, 13 and 20 February 1858). In 1853 he helped to promote a life assurance society, removed to London to take his place as one of the board of directors and in 1857 returned to Manchester as local manager. In the next ten years the company amalgamated with many others, a large number of which were actuarially unsound, and it came to a disastrous end in the later years of the 1860s, causing the loss of savings to thousands. Watts was deeply affected by the experience. In part as restitution to those who had placed their confidence in his company because of his own association with it, Watts wrote the first draft of what later became the Life Assurance Act of 1870, and campaigned actively for its acceptance by Parliament.

The American Civil War provided Watts with further opportunities for his philanthropic and reforming zeal. He sat as a member of the famous relief committee, whose history he recorded in his well-known *The Facts of the Cotton Famine*; and he became secretary of the Cotton Famine Convalescent Fund. In 1867, in the midst of the anxieties and worries over the collapse of his assurance company, a public subscription was got up and a presentation made to Watts of £3600 from friends and well-wishers in Lancashire. Thomas Ashton was chairman of the organising committee.

With the passing of the Education Act of 1870, Watts began a new phase of his career. He was elected to the first school board in Manchester as an Unsectarian candidate, and he continued to be re-elected at all subsequent elections. Until the end of his life educational matters now occupied a major part of his political social activity. In the same period his work for the co-operative movement increased in its range. He had been a member of the Manchester and Salford Equitable Society from its beginnings in 1860, and he spoke often at the annual meetings of the society. He read a paper to the 1869 Co-operative Congress, and when the *Co-operative News* was established in September 1872 he became a frequent contributor to its columns and was the principal leading article writer during the first year of the journal's existence. Among his other activities may be mentioned his quarter-century service as chairman of the Manchester Botanical and Horticultural Society; the secretaryship of the Owens College Extension Scheme; his important contribution

to the establishment in 1875 of the Provident Dispensaries branch of the Manchester and Salford Provident Society. He was a constant attender at the meetings of the Manchester Statistical Society, to which he contributed several papers, and over which he presided for the term of one year. He was a contributor to many journals, periodicals and newspapers, wrote a number of pamphlets and books and served as secretary of the Manchester Reform Club which had a membership of upwards of twelve hundred.

Watts was a gentle man, very determined, always fair-minded. He had an excellent platform manner and was an effective speaker. In political attitudes he moved a long way from his early Owenism but he always retained a sense of compassion and understanding within a moderate radical framework. An essay of his on 'Strikes', read to the British Association in 1861, provoked much hostile comment from advanced working-class circles; and it was to other forms of working-class self-help that his sympathies were mostly given. He married Catherine Shaw in 1844 and they had seven children, three of whom predeceased him. He died at his Old Trafford, Manchester, home on 7 February 1887 and was buried at Bowden, Cheshire. He left an estate valued at £12,133. The most useful short account of his life is the obituary notice published by the *Manchester Guardian*.

Writings: *The Facts and Fictions of Political Economists: being a review of the principles of the science etc.* (1842); *Robert Owen, 'The Visionary', a lecture* [3rd anniversary of Manchester Hall of Science] (Manchester, 1843) 12 pp.; *The Alphabet of Political Economy* (1847) 36 pp.; *On National Education, considered as a Question of Political and Financial Economy* (Public School Association, 1850); 'On Strikes and their Effects on Wages, Profits and Accumulations', *JRSS* 24 (1861) 498–506; *The Workman's Bane and Antidote: comprising the essay on strikes, read at the British Association* (1861); *The History of a Mistake: being a tale of the Colne strike, 1860–1* [and a lecture on the power and influence of co-operative effort] [1864]; *The Facts of the Cotton Famine* (1866); *The Catechism of Wages and Capital* [1867];

'Co-operation: how to secure safe progress therein', *Co-op. Congress Report* (1869); *On Co-operation considered as an Economic Element in Society* (Manchester Statistical Soc., 1872) 19 pp.; *The Power and Influence of Co-operative Effort: a lecture* (1872); *The Working Man: a problem* (Mechanics' Institution lect.: Manchester, 1875) 26 pp.; *What are the Social Effects of Trades Unions, Strikes and Lockouts?* (1878) 21 pp.; *The Loss of Wealth by the Loss of Health*, a lecture [1879]; 'Primary Education in England', *CWS Annual* (1885) 395–404.

Sources: *Bee-Hive*, 14 Aug 1875 [emended by Watts, 28 Sep 1876: Manchester City Library]; *DNB 20*; B. Jones, *Co-operative Production* (2 vols, Oxford, 1894; repr. in one vol., New York, 1968); C. D. Collet, *History of the Taxes on Knowledge*, 2 vols (1899); P. Redfern, *The Story of the C.W.S.* (Manchester, [1913]); 'The History of Dr John Watts', *City News*, 6 Nov 1920; F. E. Gillespie, *Labor and Politics in England, 1850–1867* (Duke University Press, 1927); W. O. Henderson, *The Lancashire Cotton Famine 1861–1865* (Manchester, 1934); M. Tylecote, *The Mechanics' Institutes of Lancashire and Yorkshire before 1851* (Manchester, 1957); B. Simon, *Education and the Labour Movement 1870–1920* (1965); J. F. C. Harrison, *Robert Owen and the Owenites* (1969); personal information: University of Giessen. OBIT. *Manchester Evening News*, 8 Feb 1887; *Manchester Guardian*, 8 Feb 1887; *Times*, 9 Feb 1887; *Co-op. News*, 12 Feb 1887.

JOHN SAVILLE

See also: *Robert OWEN.

WEBB, Simeon (1864–1929)
TRADE UNIONIST

Born on 30 April 1864 at Kates Hill, Dudley, the son of a miner. He was educated at St John's School, Dudley, and on leaving school became a pupil teacher with the intention of entering the teaching profession. Family circumstances prevented him from achieving this ambition, however, and on moving to Yorkshire with his family he followed his father into the mines. He remained a miner until he was in his middle twenties, by which time he and his family had returned to the Dudley area. On leaving the mines he went to work for Hill and Smith Ltd of Tividale, near Dudley, makers of sheet and galvanised hollow-ware. He was closely associated with the galvanising trade for the rest of his life and it is no exaggeration to say that his efforts as trade union organiser and negotiator were a main factor in transforming conditions in what was a sweated industry.

In 1898 he was elected president of the Galvanised Hollow-ware, Sheetmetal Workers and Braziers Association, and in 1901 became general secretary of the society. From 1897 to 1904 he served on the executive committee of the Midland Counties Trades Federation and when the Galvanised Hollow-ware Association amalgamated with the National Amalgamated Sheet Metal Workers in 1910 Webb was appointed a member of the Management Committee, a position he occupied until his death. From 1921 to 1925 he was a member of the National Executive Committee and from 1925 to 1927 he was general president of what had now become the National Union of Sheet Metal Workers and Braziers. In these various capacities he represented his union many times at the TUC, Labour Party Conference and the International Metal Workers Conference.

Webb also played a notable part in local government. For thirteen years he was a member of the Tipton Urban District Council, twice being chairman of the Education Committee. In 1910 he was elected to the Dudley Board of Poor Law Guardians and from 1920 to 1925 was its chairman. During his occupancy of the chair he became well known as an advocate of the view that care of the unemployed was properly a national obligation, not a responsibility of the Poor Law authorities. He resigned from the Tipton branch of the Labour Party over this issue, but remained a loyal supporter of the Party. In 1919 he became a JP.

Webb was an active member of both the Rowley Regis and Dudley Trades Councils, being president of the former body for two years, and a vice-president of the latter. In 1917 he served as Labour representative on the Enlistment Complaints sub-committee for the Dudley area, and for ten years he was the Labour representative on the Staffordshire Teachers Advisory Committee.

Webb was a prominent layman of the Primitive Methodist Church for over forty years, and on many occasions he represented his circuit in the West Midland synods of the Connexion. He was a very popular lay preacher. In March 1929 Webb was awarded the OBE for his many public services. By this time his health was failing and he died at his home, 37 Burnt Tree, Tipton, on 29 June 1929. The funeral service was at Dudley Port Methodist Chapel and he was buried at Tipton Cemetery. At Webb's request the pall-bearers were six members of the teaching profession. His wife, one son and five daughters survived him and he left effects valued at £1114.

Sources: A. L. Kidd, *History of the Tinplate Workers and Sheet Metal Workers and Braziers Societies* (1949). OBIT. *Wolverhampton Chronicle*, 3 July 1929 [photograph]; *Dudley Herald*, 6 July 1929; *Stourbridge County Express*, 6 July 1929.

ERIC TAYLOR

See also: Richard JUGGINS; Thomas SITCH.

WEBB, Thomas Edward (1829–96)
CO-OPERATOR AND RADICAL

Thomas Edward Webb was born in Battersea in July 1829 of a very poor family, and after being apprenticed worked until 1878 as a coppersmith at Price's Candle Factory, at Belmont, Vauxhall. Price's became well known in the early 1850s for the philanthropic attitudes of its managers – Tom Hughes and the Christian Socialists once played cricket against a works team – and in 1854 Webb helped to promote the Sherwood Friendly Society at the factory, and in later years also played a part in introducing a profit-sharing scheme. In the same year he joined with some other workers in founding the Battersea and Wandsworth Co-operative Society, the oldest in the metropolitan area; and from then until his death he was the most prominent worker for the Society, serving on the committee 1854–60, as chair-

man 1860–74, and as secretary 1874–8. From 1878 to 1890 he was full-time secretary and manager of the Society and subsequently president until his death. He attended every half-yearly meeting for forty-two years.

Despite the physical handicap of deafness throughout his life he devoted himself to movements for the well-being of his fellow men. A strong temperance advocate, he spent the money saved by abstaining from drink on an annual excursion into various parts of the country and was always willing to invest small sums in co-operative productive societies. He was among the founders of the People's Co-operative Society in 1894, which was a special effort for store organisation in the London area made by the CWS in collaboration with the Co-operative Union, but it was wound up in 1899. He was an unfailing advocate of the Women's Co-operative Guild with which his daughter, Catherine Webb, was prominently associated, and his other co-operative interests included chairmanship of the Co-operative Building Society from 1884, and membership of the board of the Co-operative Printing Society from 1866. From 1874 until his death he was a director of the CWS.

In politics he was a radical and for some years worked actively in the local government of Battersea, being from 1885 to 1888 a member of the Board of Works and of the Battersea Vestry from 1882 to 1891. He served for many years in the ranks of the Volunteers. He died at his Raynes Park home on 2 December 1896 and was buried at St Mary's Cemetery, Battersea, on 8 December. The funeral was attended by nearly a thousand people, including representatives of the many co-operative and other organisations with which he had been associated, and by John Burns MP. His wife, who had warmly supported his ideals, and four children survived him. He left effects valued at £889. His will and his daughter's birth certificate recorded a third Christian name of Burgess but only 'Thomas Edward' is noted on his death certificate.

Sources: 'Special Report by the Directors to the Proprietors of Price's Patent Candle

Company, April 5th 1852' [Vauxhall Factory Schools], *Q. Rev. 92* (1853) 1–18; Board of Trade, *Workman's Co-operative Societies* (1901); P. Redfern, *The New History of the C.W.S.* (Manchester, 1938); C. Wilson, 'Pioneering in Education: an industrial experiment' [Price's Patent Candle Company], *Progress 44* (Summer, 1954) 18–22. OBIT. *Co-op. News*, 5 and 12 Dec 1896; *South Western Star* [London], 11 Dec 1896.

H. F. BING

See also: G. J. HOLYOAKE, for Retail Co-operation – Nineteenth Century; Percy REDFERN, for Co-operative Wholesaling.

WEIR, John (1851–1908)
MINERS' LEADER

Born on 1 May 1851 at Parkneuk, near Dunfermline, the son of a mining family. His father died when John was four years old and the eldest of three children, and he entered the pit on his eleventh birthday. Throughout his life he continued to educate himself, being a voracious reader, and his outstanding abilities were recognised early. In the mid-1860s he was associating with the Free Colliers or 'brothered miners' movement: a colourful, rather strange semi-union development which persisted in Fife until the late sixties. After the Fife and Kinross Miners' Association had been formed in 1870, Weir was a delegate to their meetings from the Wellwood Colliery. In 1874 or 1875 he was elected president of the union, and resigned only after the great lock-out of the Fife and Clackmannan miners in 1877. Weir then left Scotland for Lancashire in January 1878, and he worked for some two and a half years in a paper-mill. He still kept contact with his mining friends, and in July 1880, on the death of the Fife Miners' secretary, Henry Cook, Weir was invited to take his place. When Weir took office in September 1880 the union had less than 1000 members, but under his vigorous direction membership increased steadily and by 1888 numbers had quadrupled; and Fife remained one of the strongest districts of the Scottish miners until the second half of the twentieth century. A few months after Weir had become secretary James Innes succeeded John Burt as

president, and this was the beginning of a close association between the two men which was broken only with the retirement of Innes after twenty-two years of office.

The Fife miners had pioneered the eight-hour day in 1870, secured on 5 June 1870 after a stay-down strike: a victory that was marked by an annual gala in commemoration. The outstanding event during Weir's years as secretary was the great strike of 1894. Before it broke out the Scottish Miners' Federation had been formed in March 1894, with Robert Smillie as president, R. Chisholm Robertson of the Stirlingshire Miners as secretary and Weir as treasurer. (Weir had been one of the promoters of an earlier Federation in 1886, but it had lasted only one year.) A special conference of the MFGB promised support to the Scottish miners in their refusal to accept wage reductions, and a ballot of the Scottish miners showed a majority in favour of strike action. The strike began on 26 June 1894 and lasted for fourteen weeks in the West of Scotland and the Lothians, and sixteen weeks in Fife. Weir had been dubious about the outcome of the strike from its early days, but he carried out his instructions faithfully. Despite the considerable help from the MFGB the strike was defeated, wages were reduced, and the membership of the Scottish Miners' Federation, which stood at 35,900 in 1894, was halved within two years and by 1897 had fallen to 15,700. One result of the strike was the establishment in Fife and Kinross of conciliation machinery, and later in 1899 of a Scottish conciliation board. Weir also became a member of the conciliation board for the federated district of England established on 1 February 1894 [Arnot (1949) 263ff].

By the end of the 1880s Weir had become a nationally respected figure in mining trade unionism; and with the convening of international conferences he became known in Western Europe. At the fourth international congress, held in Brussels in May 1893, Weir moved one of a series of resolutions put forward by the MFGB as follows: 'That if necessary, owing to the various Parliaments refusing a legal Eight Hours Day a universal strike be resorted to to obtain the same.'

Despite, however, his vigour in trade union affairs he was a Lib-Lab in politics, and his inclination to compromise and resort to conciliation procedures tended to deepen with the passing years. He declined nomination three times as candidate for Fife on the grounds that he did not wish to split the Liberal vote; and he was against affiliation to the Labour Representation Committee. Outside mining affairs, Weir was an active public figure, being an effective speaker both on the platform and in committee. He was a member of Dunfermline Town Council for eighteen years (1885–1903) during the last six of which he was one of the Burgh Bailies. He served for nine years on the local school board, was a JP for Fife, and a manager of the local hospital. He was a life member of the Carnegie Dunfermline Trust, the huge benefaction bestowed on his native town by the Scots-American multi-millionaire steel magnate, and of the Hero Fund Trust, and a member also of the committee which administered the collection of monies for the survivors and relatives of those involved in mining disasters in the county. He was also prominent in local Freemasonry circles. He died on 20 December 1908, and was survived by his wife, a daughter and four sons. He left an estate valued at £1956.

Sources: Evidence to R.C. on Labour, 1892 XXXIV, Qs 3707–941; W. Hallam, *Miners' Leaders* (1894); R. P. Arnot, *The Miners* (1949); idem, *A History of the Scottish Miners* (1955). OBIT. *Dunfermline Press*, 26 Dec 1908.

JOYCE BELLAMY
JOHN SAVILLE

See also: Thomas ASHTON, for Mining Trade Unionism, 1900–14; Alexander MAC-DONALD, for Mining Trade Unionism, 1850–79; Benjamin PICKARD, for Mining Trade Unionism, 1880–99; *Robert SMILLIE, for Scottish Mining Trade Unionism.

WHITEHEAD, Alfred (1862–1945)
CO-OPERATOR

Born on 14 January 1862 at Newton Heath, Manchester, the son of Abraham Whitehead, a labourer at a print works, who was an original member of the Failsworth Co-operative Society, Alfred started his working life in a textile mill in 1872. He joined the staff of the central board of the Co-operative Union in 1886 where he undertook clerical duties and worked with E. V. Neale, who was secretary of the board. For several years Whitehead acted as secretary of the north-western section and was appointed assistant secretary of the Union when J. C. Gray succeeded E. V. Neale in 1895. After Gray's death in 1912, Whitehead became secretary of the Union. In 1928 he was president of the Co-operative Congress and in the following year he retired from the Union having served the organisation for over forty years.

His interests also extended to the international field and in 1910 he was elected to the ICA executive committee, having previously acted as auditor to the association. At the Basle Congress of the ICA in 1921 he was elected vice-president, an office he held until his retirement. Like J. C. Gray, he was an advocate of a national co-operative society. Outside the co-operative movement he was a temperance worker and a Sunday school teacher. Little is known of his politics and indeed he seems not to have been actively engaged in political activity, although in 1915 he did join the Union of Democratic Control, itself a useful index to his views during the years of the First World War. He died on 21 February 1945 at Cheadle Hulme, Cheshire, his wife having predeceased him in 1939. He left an estate valued at £5237.

Sources: *Co-op. Congress Handbooks* (1905, 1913, 1914, 1917); T. W. Mercer, *Towards a Co-operative Commonwealth* (Manchester, 1936); P. Redfern, *The New History of the C.W.S.* (Manchester, 1938); G. D. H. Cole, *A Century of Co-operation* (Manchester, [1945?]); *Co-op. Rev.*, Sep 1947; UDC Papers: Hull University Library. OBIT. *Co-op. News*, 24 Feb 1945; *Co-op. Congress Report* (1945).

JOYCE BELLAMY

See also: Fred HAYWARD, for Co-operative Union; H. J. MAY, for International Co-operative Alliance.

WILLIAMS, Aneurin (1859-1924)
CO-OPERATOR, AUTHOR AND LIBERAL MP

Born at Dowlais, Glamorgan, on 11 October 1859, the second son of Edward Williams, a civil engineer and manager of the Dowlais Iron Works, Aneurin was educated privately and later at St John's College, Cambridge, where he obtained an MA degree in 1880. His father had meantime transferred to Middlesbrough where he had entered business as an ironmaster. After completing his legal studies, Aneurin was called to the Bar at the Inner Temple in 1884 but did not practise as a lawyer. For a time he travelled widely in Europe and also lectured in economic subjects in London but from 1886 to 1890 he was one of the acting partners of the Linthorpe Iron Works, Middlesbrough. He was greatly attracted to the co-partnership movement and he joined the Labour Association, devoting much of his time from 1892 to the work of this organisation which he served as president, treasurer and joint honorary secretary. He wrote articles and the well-known Home University Library volume on profit sharing and co-partnership, was first editor of the journal *Co-partnership* and *inter alia* translated from the French two works on co-partnership at Guise: he also contributed the article on 'Co-operative Societies' to the 10th and 11th editions of the *Encyclopaedia Britannica*.

Williams's initial contact with the work of the International Co-operative Alliance was at its first Congress, held in London in 1895, which he attended as a delegate of a society affiliated to the Labour Association. He was included on the provisional central committee and appointed assistant honorary secretary. Re-elected to both offices at the Paris Congress in 1896, he subsequently resigned but resumed his close connection with the ICA in 1907 when he was elected as one of the British representatives on the central committee and a member of the executive. He served as chairman of the ICA executive from 1907 until 1920.

Williams's interests extended to the political field, contesting mid-Kent in 1906 but before his actual election to Parliament as a Liberal for Plymouth in January 1910, his experience in a variety of allied activities proved a useful apprenticeship to his later career. In 1902 he was a member of the South African Conciliation Committee for establishing peace between Dutch and English South Africa, he was on the executive of the League of Liberals against Militarism and Aggression and chairman, for some years, of the Land Nationalisation Society established in 1881. He was also chairman of the Proportional Representation Society and was attracted by the garden city movement in which his co-partnership associate, Henry Vivian, played an active part. Williams was a director of the Pioneer Society formed to locate a suitable site and was later elected president of the first garden city of Letchworth.

His first membership of Parliament was short-lived and he lost his seat at the second December election in 1910; in 1914 he was returned for North-West Durham which he served until the 1918 general election when the constituency was reconstituted. He retained his seat for the new area designated as the Consett Division of Co. Durham and served this constituency until 1922. He was a member of the UDC by February 1915 and was very interested in the work of the League of Nations Society which he helped to form in 1915 and which he served as honorary secretary. Other spheres of activity which benefited from his support included smallholdings, and he was especially concerned with the problems of the Armenian refugees.

He had married, in 1888, Helen Elizabeth, daughter of John Pattinson of Gateshead, by whom he had a son and daughter. Williams died at his Hindhead, Surrey, home on 20 January 1924 and was interred at Grayshott Cemetery on 23 January. His wife had predeceased him in 1922 but he was survived by his son and daughter. He left an estate valued at £102,386.

Writings: *Home Rule: a plea for conciliation and a national settlement* (1893) 12 pp.; (with H. Vivian) 'The Co-partnership of Labour', *Econ. Rev. 4* (July 1894) 297-317; 'The International Co-operative Congress', *Econ. J. 5* (1895) 456-60; 'British Co-operative Congress, 1896', *Econ. J.* (Sep 1896) 455–60; *The Relation of the Co-operative Movement to National and International Commerce* (Manchester, [1896]) 23 pp.; *Government by the Fit* (Labour Co-part. Assn, 1897); *A Better Way. Some Facts and Suggestions as to Introducing the Partnership of Labour with Capital into Established Business* (Labour Co-part. Assn, 1899); (with H. Vivian) 'Recent Progress of Labour Co-partnership', *Econ. Rev. 11* (Apr 1901) 201–17; 'The National Co-operative Festival', *Econ. Rev. 12* (Oct 1902) 472–6; *Labour Co-partnership: its theory and practice* (Labour Co-part. Assn, 1903); *Twenty years of Co-partnership at Guise*, translated from the French by A. Williams (1903); *History and Present Position of Labour Co-partnership* (Labour Co-part. Assn, 1904); 'Twenty Years of Co-partnership', *Econ. Rev. 15* (Jan 1905) 15–27; *Twenty-one Years' Work for Co-partnership* (Labour Co-part. Assn, 1905); 'Co-operation in Housing and Town Building', *Co-op. Congress Report* (1907) 379–98; *Twenty-eight Years of Co-partnership at Guise*, translated by A. Williams (1908); 'Proportional Representation', *CWS Annual* (1913) 179–200; *Co-partnership and Profit Sharing* (1913); *Proposal for a League of Peace and Mutual Protection among Nations*, reprinted from *Cont. Rev.* (Nov 1914) (Letchworth, 1915) 13 pp.; 'The Future Policy of Co-operation: national and international', *Co-op. Congress Report* (1915) 544–67.

Sources: *Times, House of Commons* (1910); *Dod* (1915) and (1919); *Int. Co-op. Bull.* (Oct–Nov 1920) 286–8; *WWW* (1916–28); A. J. Peacock, 'Land Reform 1880–1919, a study of the activities of the English Restoration League and the Land Nationalisation Society' (University of Southampton MA, 1962); Co-operative Productive Association records, Hull University Library, ref. DCF. OBIT. *Int. Co-op. Bull.* (1924) 47; *Times*, 21 Jan 1924.

JOYCE BELLAMY

See also: E. O. GREENING, for Co-partnership; H. J. MAY, for International Co-operative Alliance; H. H. VIVIAN.

WILLIAMS, John (1861–1922)
MINERS' LEADER AND LABOUR MP

Born in 1861 at Aberaman, the son of Davie Williams, a collier, he was educated at the British School there. He started work at the age of twelve as a door boy at the Plough Colliery, Aberaman, and after eight years in underground employment became a checkweigher at the Lady Windsor Colliery at Ynysybwl. A gifted platform speaker and a leader of men, he was ordained as a Welsh Baptist preacher but continued his work in mining and in 1890 was appointed general secretary of the Amalgamated Society of South Wales Colliery Workers – an attempt to bring local unions together in a federal organisation before the establishment of the SWMF in 1898. He also succeeded Isaac Evans, who died in 1897, as advisory agent to the Western District Miners' Association, a post he held until his own death. He was also agent of the small Saundersfoot District in East Pembroke during its fitful existence. He opposed the sliding scales but was among the more moderate of the Welsh leaders and with Mabon, Brace and Richards was opposed to the growth of Marxism and Syndicalism among the South Wales miners in the early years of the twentieth century. Williams served on the executive committee of the SWMF from its foundation and was one of the senior members of the workman's side of the Conciliation Board, appointed in 1905, following the ending of the sliding-scale agreement in 1903.

A fervent Welsh nationalist and poet, he had acquired an extensive knowledge of Welsh and English literature in his youth, and had won his bardic title of 'Eryr Glan Gwawr' in 1885, which entitled him to a place in the Gorsedd circle. In later years he studied and lectured in economics and in 1902 was chosen as prospective candidate for the Gower parliamentary constituency. Essentially a Lib-Lab, he had to fight a three-cornered contest as a Labour man in 1906 against a Liberal and a Unionist but he won the seat, without LRC endorsement, by about 300 votes. He retained this subsequently (after the MFGB affiliation to the Labour Party in 1909) in the Labour interest until his death. In the election of 1900 he had used his influence to help defeat John Hodge, secretary of the Steel Smelters' Union and a member of the LRC. The candidate elected was an orthodox Liberal.

Williams was highly respected in West Wales where for years he had been a local preacher: equally fluent in Welsh and in English. He was a governor of the University of Wales, a JP for Glamorganshire and served on the Mountain Ash Council. He died at his Sketty home on 20 June 1922 after a long illness and was survived by his wife, four sons and five daughters. He left an estate valued at £2460.

Writings: Welsh poetry.

Sources: *Review of Reviews 33* (Jan–June 1906) 581; *Dod* (1909) and (1922); *WWW* (1916–28); F. Bealey and H. Pelling, *Labour and Politics 1900–1906* (1958); E. W. Evans, *The Miners of South Wales* (Cardiff, 1961); R. Page Arnot, *The South Wales Miners* (1967). OBIT. *Times*, 21 June 1922; *Western Mail*, 21 June 1922.

JOYCE BELLAMY

See also: William ABRAHAM, for Welsh Mining Trade Unionism; W. BRACE.

WILSON, John (1837–1915)
MINERS' LEADER AND LIB-LAB MP

Born on 26 June 1837 at Greatham, near Hartlepool, Co. Durham, the son of Christopher Wilson, a labourer, and his wife Hannah (née Sponton) of Hamsterley. His father, who had shot a man while poaching, had to keep on the move and his mother having died when John was four and a half, he travelled around with his father. Educated at various dame schools, he became a voracious reader in his early youth, a habit he continued in later life. When he was ten or eleven he joined his father who was then working at Stanhope quarries, but after his father's death from cholera during the epidemic of 1849 Wilson obtained work at a colliery and during the next few years was employed at several Durham pits. (The exact date of the father's death is uncertain,

Wilson himself giving different dates at different times in his later career.) When he was sixteen he led a successful agitation for a wage increase but was victimised in 1853 for his part in a Sherburn Hill strike and went to sea for a time. On his return he went to Haswell Colliery as a hewer but declined an offer to become secretary of a union lodge when this was formed in 1863. In the following year he emigrated with his wife, Margaret Firth, whom he married in 1862. He worked in mines in Pennsylvania and Illinois but in July 1867 returned to England and to coal hewing at Haswell. In 1869 he played a prominent role in the formation of the Durham Miners' Association.

At this stage in his career he was both a gambler and a drinker but he became converted to Primitive Methodism and on 11 June 1870 became a local preacher. In that year he was an assistant to three checkweighmen at Haswell and was also working as part-time secretary at the local co-operative store. On account of his trade union and other activities the colliery manager would not re-engage him at the time of the Yearly Bond – the practice of annual hirings adopted in the Durham coalfield but discontinued in 1872 – so he became full-time secretary of the Haswell Co-operative Society. The colliery manager then threatened the co-operative officials, who were also miners, with the sack unless Wilson left; so he resigned and went to Wheatley Hill where he organised a lodge of the DMA and became its chairman. In 1877 the colliery company went bankrupt and Wilson was not engaged when the pit was reopened. He then started a stationery shop in Wheatley Hill where he was assisted by his wife, and in the following year (1878) the Miners' National Association conference selected him as an organiser for the Midlands where he spent about four years working in North Staffordshire, Warwickshire and Leicestershire.

He returned to Durham in 1882 when the DMA appointed him as their agent and treasurer; he was made financial secretary in 1890 and secretary of the Association in 1896, a position he held until his death. He gave evidence before several government committees including the R.C. on Mining

Royalties in 1890 when he favoured the nationalisation of mine royalties. He took a leading part in opposing the eight-hour day agitation within the trade union movement from 1888. Neither Durham nor Northumberland joined the MFGB on its foundation in 1889 as miners in these counties objected to the Federation's eight-hour-day policy and Wilson was the mainspring of their refusal. He also favoured local trade union activity and did not submit to the famous Rule 20 of the Federation which enabled united action on a national basis to be taken in the event of a dispute with the employers. Wilson, rather than Burt or Fenwick, was the most formidable opponent of the MFGB policies put forward by Ben Pickard, including the hope for a single Conciliation Board for all the British coalfields: a position not reached until 1943, four years before nationalisation came into effect.

In addition to his trade union activities for the miners, he was a keen political worker. In 1874 he assisted the Liberal Party at an election in Hetton-le-Hole; in 1875 he was secretary of the County Franchise Association in Durham; and from 1875 to 1885 was secretary of the Miners' Political Reform Association. In 1884 he was a member of a franchise deputation to Gladstone and in the following year he was elecfed Liberal MP for Houghton-le-Spring but was defeated in 1886. In 1890 he succeeded William Crawford as MP for the Mid-Durham Division and held the seat until his death. When the TUC in 1886 established the Labour Electoral Association, on the motion of T. R. Threlfall, John Wilson was one of the representatives of the North on the committee, and at its first meeting he was elected its chairman. Wilson had for some years been in favour of such an organisation, and at the 1884 TUC he had brought forward a resolution regretting that so few working men had been returned to Parliament, although he was strongly opposed to the independent labour representation in the House of Commons which occurred in the first decade of the twentieth century. To socialist ideas he was consistently hostile, his imagination being captured by a vision of permanent accord between labour and capital. In this he was greatly influenced by Brooke Foss Westcott, Bishop of Durham [Clayton (1906)]. In the event, the Labour Electoral Association became increasingly identified with the Liberal Party and its last Congress was held in 1895.

Wilson always remained deeply Lib-Lab in his general attitudes and in 1909, when the MFGB was accepted into membership of the Labour Party, Wilson, along with Burt and Fenwick, declined the Labour Whip – the only parliamentary representatives of the Federation to abstain. Wilson was constantly emphasising to his own miners the social progress which had occurred in his own lifetime, and the opportunities which were opening for working men in the future. Like many contemporary trade union leaders, he was firmly committed to arbitration in international affairs and in 1887 was a member of a delegation to America which urged upon the US President the necessity of a treaty of arbitration between the two countries. In the House of Commons he was a ready and effective speaker and a good committee man. He played an important part in local politics, was made an alderman of Durham County Council and in 1906 was awarded an honorary DCL by the University of Durham.

Wilson made an interesting statement about the intellectual influences in his life in reply to W. T. Stead's inquiry [*Review of Reviews* (1906)]:

When I reached man's estate I felt the need of a wider and more solid reading. I took grammar and logic. In the poets I read Homer, Milton, Shakespeare, Whittier and Lowell. Political economy – J. S. Mill, H. George and Walker of America. History – Rollin, Green, Molesworth and Macaulay. Speaking of novels, my favourite is Scott, with Dickens and Lytton. In addition, I have tried to keep myself up to an acquaintance with modern literature in various forms. Starting from a meagre point, being left an orphan at nine and a half, commencing work at that time and having to battle my way up amongst strangers, I had to adopt a severe mode of self-education after I married. I used to take an hour or two before I went to work or after I came home, the time of study depending upon the shift I was in. I oft-times took an old grammar to the pit with me, and when I had a minute I committed a portion to memory.

He had a family of one son and four daughters and died in London on 24 March 1915, his wife having predeceased him by seven years. He left an estate valued at £4888 (net) which included a bequest of £100 to the Durham Aged Mine Workers' Homes Association and £50 to the Primitive Methodist Chapel in North Road, Durham.

Writings: Evidence before the R.C. on Mining Royalties 1890–1 XLI Qs 8835–96; the R.C. on Labour 1892 XXXIV Qs 384–692 and the R.C. on Mines 1908 XX Qs 35372–914; *History of the Durham Miners' Association, 1870–1904* (Durham, 1907); *Memories of a Labour Leader: autobiography of J. Wilson MP* (1910).

Sources: (1) MSS: Minutes of the Durham Miners' Association; (2) Secondary: R. Fynes, *The Miners of Northumberland and Durham* (Sunderland, 1873); W. Hallam, *Miners' Leaders* (1894); *Durham Chronicle*, 21 Aug 1896; *Dod* (1905); J. Clayton, *Bishop Westcott* (1906); *Review of Reviews, 33* (Jan–June 1906) 582; J. Wilson, *Autobiography* (see Writings above); *Dod* (1914); *WWW* (1897–1916); S. Webb, *The Story of the Durham Miners* (1921); E. Welbourne, *The Miners' Unions of Northumberland and Durham* (1923); R. Page Arnot, *The Miners* (1949); F. Bealey and H. Pelling, *Labour and Politics 1900–1906* (1958); H. A. Clegg et al., *A History of British Trade Unions since 1889*, vol. *1: 1889–1910* (1964). OBIT. *Times*, 25 and 29 Mar 1915; *Durham Chronicle*, 26 Mar 1915; G. J. Bowran, 'Dr John Wilson MP', *Holborn Rev.* (July 1915) 321–34; *NMA* (1915).

ANTHONY MASON
JOHN SAVILLE

See also: W. ABRAHAM; Thomas ASHTON; W. BRACE; T. BURT; E. COWEY; W. CRAWFORD; C. FENWICK; Alexander MACDONALD, for Mining Trade Unionism, 1850–79; Benjamin PICKARD, for Mining Trade Unionism, 1880–99; Samuel WOODS.

WINSTONE, James (1863–1921)
MINERS' LEADER

Born on 9 February 1863 at Machen Lower, Risca, Monmouthshire, the son of William Winstone, a master mason, and his wife Hannah. His father having died when James was quite young he had to leave school when he was eight and first went to work at a brickworks. He then became a colliery boy at Risca Colliery where he worked as a miner for some fourteen years. During this time he became involved in trade unionism and for a time was victimised and had to leave the mine. He later returned as a checkweigher at Risca and collaborated with William Brace in the struggle against the sliding-scale method of wage payment. He was a very popular choice for miners' agent of the Eastern Valleys District when this position became vacant in 1891; he was one of the founders of the SWMF and the first executive member from the Tredegar District.

During the early years of the SWMF, Winstone became increasingly critical of the conciliatory attitude adopted by its leaders and he joined with other left-wing reformers and in particular with Barker, Hartshorn and Stanton in attempts to reorganise the Federation. In 1910 he stated that 'the federation is much too tame – through the medium of the conciliation board has become practically inert as a fighting force. Instead of trying to reconcile capitalism and labour it should show the impossibility of such a reconciliation.' In 1912 Winstone was elected vice-president of the SWMF, taking the place of William Brace, who moved up to president following Mabon's resignation. Winstone succeeded Brace as acting-president when the latter was given leave of absence from June 1915 to December 1918, and after Brace's resignation in November 1920 he was appointed president, a position he held until his death some eighteen months later. He represented the South Wales miners on the MFGB executive from 1915 to 1918 and again from 1920 to 1921. He had given evidence before the R.C. on Mines in 1907 and was a witness before the Sankey Commission in 1919 when he advocated the nationalisation of the mines.

When the Plebs League, formed by supporters of the Central Labour College to promote independent working-class education, set up a South Wales wing, Winstone became president. By religion a Baptist he was always active in nonconformist and temperance movements and like most South Wales trade union leaders took an active part in local politics. Winstone was especially involved in local government throughout his life, strongly advocating municipal housing. While a checkweigher at Risca he was elected to the local council and became its chairman, and when he removed to the eastern valleys as agent at Pontnewynydd he became a member of the Abersychan District Council, of which he was made chairman in 1911. His advanced ideas on local and national government frequently conflicted with the more moderate views of many of the local people, which may account for his failure to enter Parliament.

He contested three parliamentary elections. The first was in 1906 when he stood as LRC candidate for Monmouth District, the first occasion on which there was a close association between the miners and the LRC. He polled well in the Alexandra ward of Newport where the dock labourers, mostly Irish, were a substantial part of the electorate, but the strong Liberal tradition elsewhere defeated him and the Conservative candidate. In 1915 the death of Keir Hardie – a close friend of Winstone – caused a vacancy in the double-barrelled constituency of Merthyr Boroughs, and Winstone was put forward as candidate by ballot vote of the SWMF, and was adopted by the Labour Party. But the wartime electoral truce was broken by C. B. Stanton, who forsook his miners' agency at Aberdare to enter the contest on a jingoist platform. Winstone, himself a staunch member of the ILP, invited Ramsay MacDonald MP and F. W. Jowett MP, both then very unpopular among the jingo sections of the population, to speak for him; and Stanton won easily. At the time of the general election of 1918 the Representation of the People Act of that year had divided Merthyr Tydfil into two constituencies: Aberdare, where C. B. Stanton representing the National Democratic Party

defeated the Labour candidate (the Rev. T. E. Nicholas) by 22,824 votes to 6229, a majority of over 16,000; and Merthyr, where Sir Edgar Jones, Coalition Liberal, defeated James Winstone by 14,127 votes to 12,682, a majority of only 1445.

Among his other local government activities was election to the Monmouth County Council in 1906. He was made a county council alderman in 1919 and became chairman in 1920. He had also served for a time on the Pontypool Board of Guardians, was a JP for the county of Monmouth and in his later years was a governor of the University of Wales. He had married Sarah Jane Iven in 1886 and had seven children, two of whom died in infancy. Following an operation, he died in London on 27 July 1921; he left £249 in his will. The death of the SWMF treasurer, Alfred Onions, preceded that of Winstone, and in an editorial the *Western Mail* praised the former as 'a clear and capable thinker' and denigrated the latter. The *Times* recorded that 25,000 attended the funeral.

Sources: Evidence before R.C. on Mines vol. III 1908 XX Qs 34698–864; before R.C. on the Coal Industry (Sankey Commission) vol. II 1919 XII Qs 22623–740, 22853–3765; F. Bealey and H. Pelling, *Labour and Politics* (1958); *Dictionary of Welsh Biography* (1959); E. W. Evans, *Mabon* (1959); R. Page Arnot, *The South Wales Miners: a history of the South Wales Miners' Federation 1898–1914* (1967); H. Pelling, *Social Geography of British Elections, 1885–1910* (1967). OBIT. *Times*, 28 July 1921; *Western Mail*, 28 July 1921.

JOYCE BELLAMY
JOHN SAVILLE

See also: William ABRAHAM, for Welsh Mining Trade Unionism; Thomas ASHTON, for Mining Trade Unionism, 1900–14; W. BRACE; C. B. STANTON.

WOODS, Samuel (1846–1915)
MINERS' LEADER AND LIB-LAB MP

Born on 10 May 1846 at Sutton near St Helens, the son of Thomas Woods, a miner, and his wife Margaret (née Rothwell) who also worked in the mines up to 1840. Samuel's grandfather was also a collier. His education began at the age of six but was interrupted when his father changed his place of work and took his young son into the mines with him. At nine he was again attending school but at thirteen he obtained regular employment in the pits, for the first two years with the pit ponies. He supplemented his formal education by attending night classes given by a Baptist minister, Rev. F. J. Greening, and Woods was baptised in 1863 and later became a lay preacher within the Baptist Connexion. He was also a total abstainer. He worked in the mines until he was twenty-nine and was then elected checkweighman: three years later, in 1878, he began to organise the miners in the St Helens and Haydock districts.

He was appointed agent to the Ashton and Haydock Miners' Association in 1881 and in 1884 he became the first president of the Lancashire Miners' Federation, a position he held until his death. In 1886 he obtained a first-class certificate in mining management from Owens College, Manchester. When the MFGB was established in 1889 Woods was elected vice-president and he retained this office until 1909. With Ben Pickard and Thomas Ashton, he was deeply involved in the controversy between the MFGB and the county unions of Northumberland and Durham over the issue of the eight-hour day. At the TUC of 1892 he moved the vote of censure on the parliamentary committee and its secretary, Charles Fenwick, for not carrying out the instructions of Congress and giving full support to the Eight Hours Bill in Parliament; and when Fenwick was defeated on this matter in the election for secretary of the parliamentary committee in 1894, Woods succeeded him. In the year which followed Woods was a member of the committee set up to revise the standing orders of the TUC which, *inter alia*, took away the right of trades councils' representation, introduced the block vote and excluded as delegates all those who were not working at a trade, or who were not permanent officials of a trade union. The new standing orders were introduced at the 1895 Congress.

The work of the parliamentary committee increased steadily throughout the 1890s and in the first few years Woods showed a considerable improvement over Fenwick in his handling of business; but the volume of work became too much for him and because of illness he was succeeded as secretary in 1904 by W. C. Steadman of the Barge Builders' Union. Woods was not a man of outstanding ability but he was well liked by his colleagues, being characterised by William Brace, many years after his death, as 'a dapper, gentle kind of soul'. He gave evidence before the R.C. on Mining Royalties; was a delegate to the Rosebery conference of 1893, and a member of the Conciliation Board in 1894. In politics he was an advanced Liberal, being in favour of the legislative eight-hour day for miners, the nationalisation of royalties, home rule for Ireland, compulsory employers' liability and the payment of MPs. He stood successfully as a Lib-Lab candidate in the general election of 1892, being elected for the Ince division of Lancashire; was unsuccessful in 1895 but at a by-election in 1897 he won the Walthamstow constituency, being defeated again in 1900. He was unable to stand again for health reasons. After 1900 he was associated for some time with the National Democratic League.

When Pickard died early in 1904, Enoch Edwards succeeded him as president because Woods was too ill; but the annual conference decided to retain him as vice-president despite his infirmity, the alternative being Robert Smillie who was unacceptable to the majority because of his outspoken socialist views. Although Woods's health made him incapable of attending either conferences or executive committee meetings for some years before he actually retired, he continued to be elected until 1909, when Smillie replaced him, and Woods was then given an honorary position. For many years he had been active in local politics, being elected to the Ashton District Council in 1895. He had married a miner's daughter, Sarah Lee, in 1867 and they had twelve children. He died at his home near Wigan on 23 November 1915 and left £235 in his will.

Sources: *St Helens Lantern*, 26 Oct 1888; Evidence before the R.C. on Mining Royalties 1890–1 XLI Qs 8489–636; *Dod* (1892) and (1900); A. W. Humphrey, *A History of Labour Representation* (1912); R. Page Arnot, *The Miners* (1949). OBIT. *Times*, 24 Nov 1915; *St Helens Newspaper*, 26 Nov 1915.

JOYCE BELLAMY

See also: William ABRAHAM, for Welsh Mining Trade Unionism; Benjamin PICK-ARD, for Mining Trade Unionism, 1880–99.

WORLEY, Joseph James (1876–1944)
CO-OPERATOR AND TRADE UNIONIST

Born at Devonport on 23 May 1876, the son of Henry Yorn Worley, an engine fitter, whose father had pioneered the Devonport Dock Society, Joseph Worley entered the service of the co-operative movement at the age of fourteen when he joined the Plymouth Co-operative Society. From his earliest years in the movement, Worley extended his education in co-operative history and allied subjects. He was a regular attender at co-operative summer schools, first as a student (at the first co-operative summer school in Castleton in 1913) and then as a teacher. He took an active part, also from very early in his career, in the practical affairs of his own society. In 1899 he helped to establish the Plymouth Printers, a co-operative venture, and he served as chairman of the education committee of the Plymouth Society. In 1905 he was appointed secretary of the Bridgwater Co-operative Society and in 1909 transferred to the Plympton, becoming their manager-secretary. Worley was always to the left of centre – later in life he lectured for the National Council of Labour Colleges – and he showed his political attitudes in an early commitment to the cause of unionism among co-operative employees. He joined the Associated Union of Co-operative Employees on the formation of the Plymouth branch in 1900 and when a district council was formed for the West country, Worley was elected president. Later, after he had moved to Leicester, he sat on the Midland district council. In 1915 he was elected to the executive council and continued to serve until 1917 when army service caused his retirement.

It was his appointment in 1910, as the first propaganda agent for the Co-operative Productive Federation (for which see H. H. VIVIAN), which brought him into prominence in the national movement. Within a few years he was generally regarded as an ambassador for co-operative production throughout Europe and he represented the CPF at the first Russian Co-operative Congress after the Revolution. In 1922 he succeeded Robert Halstead as secretary of the Federation, a position he held until his death in 1944. Also in 1922 he was elected to the central committee of the International Co-operative Alliance and he represented Britain for many years at international conferences. He served on the board of the Leicester Society from 1922 until 1937, when he retired for reasons of health; he was a member of the joint parliamentary committee for many years; a director of the Co-operative Press, and president of the Co-operative Congress in 1938. In 1930 he was chairman of the special committee of inquiry which recommended the establishment of a National Co-operative Authority, and he was himself a member of the Authority from the time of its formation. At this time he was editing *The Co-operator's Year Book* and the *Co-operative Productive Review*. A fluent speaker, he also expressed in writing his lifetime of experience in the co-operative movement in *A Social Philosophy of Co-operation*, which was published two years before his death.

His last public act was typical of the man. He moved the vote of thanks to the chairman at a public meeting called jointly by the education department of the Leicester Co-operative Society and the British-Soviet Friendship Society, addressed by the Dean of Canterbury (the Very Rev. Hewlett Johnson), while the Second World War was still being fought. The Leicester Labour Party had threatened to discipline one of their aldermen, Sydney Taylor, for taking the chair and J.J., as he was always known, was present in Taylor's support. He died within two hours of reaching his Leicester home on 18 November 1944 and was buried at Welford Road Cemetery on 22 November. His wife and a son survived him. He left an estate valued at £3161.

Writings: *The Producers' Theory of Co-operation* (Leicester, 1928) 10 pp.; *A Social Philosophy of Co-operation* (Manchester, 1942); *Thomas Blandford, the Man and his Message* (Leicester, 1943) 12 pp.

Sources: *Co-partnership 28* (1922); *The New Dawn* (1922); *Co-op. Year Book* (1923); *Millgate Monthly* (Mar 1925); T. W. Mercer, *Towards a Co-operative Commonwealth* (Manchester, 1936); *Co-op. News*, 28 May 1938; *Co-op. Rev.* (Feb 1970); Co-operative Productive Federation records, Hull University Library, ref. DCF. OBIT. *Reynolds News*, 19 Nov 1944; *Leicester Mercury*, 20 Nov 1944; *Co-op. News*, 25 Nov 1944; *Co-op. Rev.* (1944).

JOYCE BELLAMY
JOHN SAVILLE

See also: E. O. GREENING, for Co-partnership; Benjamin JONES, for Co-operative Production; H. J. MAY, for International Co-operative Alliance.

WRIGHT, Oliver Walter (1886–1938)
MINERS' LEADER

Born at Swanwick, Derbyshire, on 29 July 1886, the son of Percy Edward Wright, a foundry labourer. Oliver Wright began work as a miner at the age of twelve at the Butterley Co.'s Britain Colliery and continued in that employment for twenty-eight years. In 1920 he was elected secretary of the Britain lodge of the Derbyshire Miners' Association and a delegate to the council; he was also one of the Association's trustees. He was a militant trade unionist and fearlessly exposed the miners' grievances during the 1921 and 1926 strikes. After the latter stoppage he was an outspoken critic of Mondism and company unionism both at the TUC and at conferences of the MFGB. In March 1928 he was elected treasurer of the Derbyshire Miners' Association in succession to Henry Hicken who had become general secretary, and he held this position until his death.

Like his father, Wright was an active worker in his local Labour Party at Swanwick and with Frank Varley, MP for Mansfield, pioneered the Labour cause in the Belper Division of Derbyshire. As a nominee of the Derbyshire Miners' Association, Wright twice unsuccessfully contested the Belper Parliamentary Division in 1922 and 1923. An active co-operator, he undertook much propaganda work on behalf of the Ripley Co-operative Society.

Apart from his mining, co-operative and political interests, Wright also engaged in local government work. He was elected to the Chesterfield Town Council in 1928, on which his wife also served, and he represented Whittington Moor in the Labour interest until his death. He quickly established the reputation of being one of the ablest speakers on the Council and was recognised as the official spokesman of the Labour group. He served on the Finance and Special Purposes Committee, the Improvements and Highways Committee, the Sewage Disposal and Cleansing Committee and the Parks and Cemeteries Committee. For several years he was chairman of the Housing Committee.

He died at Chesterfield on 21 January 1938 and following a service at Brampton Congregational Church was buried at Boythorpe Cemetery, Chesterfield, on 25 January.

Sources: (1) MSS: Minutes of the Derbyshire Miners' Association, 1928–38 (NUM, Saltergate, Chesterfield); (2) *Derbyshire Times*, 1928–38; *Minutes of the Miners' Federation of Great Britain*, 1928–38; *TUC Reports*, 1928–38; (3) Secondary: J. E. Williams, *The Derbyshire Miners* (1962). OBIT. *Derbyshire Advertiser*, 28 Jan 1938; *Derbyshire Times*, 28 Jan 1938.

J. E. WILLIAMS

See also: *A. J. COOK, for Mining Trade Unionism, 1915–26; *Peter LEE, for Mining Trade Unionism, 1927–44; *Frank VARLEY.

List of Names

ABBOTTS, William (1873–1930)
ABRAHAM, William (Mabon) (1842–1922)
ACLAND, Alice Sophia (1849–1935)
ACLAND, Sir Arthur Herbert Dyke (1847–1926)
ADAMS, John Jackson, 1st Baron Adams of Ennerdale (1890–1960)
ADAMS, William Thomas (1884–1949)
ALEXANDER, Albert Victor (Earl Alexander of Hillsborough) (1885–1965)
ALLAN, William (1813–74)
ALLEN, Robert (1827–77)
ALLEN, Sir Thomas William (1864–1943)
AMMON, Charles (Charlie) George (Lord Ammon of Camberwell) (1873–1960)
ANDERSON, Frank (1889–1959)
ARCH, Joseph (1826–1919)
ARNOLD, Thomas George (1866–1944)
ASHTON, Thomas (1844–1927)
ASHWORTH, Samuel (1825–71)
ASPINWALL, Thomas (1846–1901)

BALLARD, William (1858–1928)
BAMFORD, Samuel (1846–98)
BARKER, George (1858–1936)
BARNETT, William (1840–1909)
BARTON, Eleanor (1872–1960)
BATES, William (1833–1908)
BATEY, John (1852–1925)
BAYLEY, Thomas (1813–74)
BEATON, Neil Scobie (1880–1960)
BIRD, Thomas Richard (1877–1965)
BLAIR, William Richard (1874–1932)
BLAND, Thomas (1825–1908)
BLANDFORD, Thomas (1861–99)
BOND, Frederick (1865–1951)
BONNER, Arnold (1904–66)
BOYLE, Hugh (1850–1907)
BOYNTON, Arthur John (1863–1922)
BRACE, William (1865–1947)

BROWN, James (1862–1939)
BROWN, William Henry (1867/8–1950)
BUGG, Frederick John (1830–1900)
BURT, Thomas (1837–1922)
BUTCHER, John (1833–1921)
BUTCHER, John (1847–1936)

CAMPBELL, Alexander (1796–1870)
CANN, Thomas Henry (1858–1924)
CARTER, William (1862–1932)
CATCHPOLE, John (1843–1919)
CHARTER, Walter Thomas (1871–1932)
CHEETHAM, Thomas (1828–1901)
CIAPPESSONI, Francis Antonio (1859–1912)
CLARK, Fred (1878–1947)
CLARKE, Andrew Bathgate (1868–1940)
CLAY, Joseph (1826–1901)
COCHRANE, William (1872–1924)
COOPER, William (1822–68)
COURT, Sir Josiah (1841–1938)
COWEN, Joseph (1829–1900)
COWEY, Edward (Ned) (1839–1903)
CRABTREE, James (1831–1917)
CRAIG, Edward Thomas (1804–94)
CRAWFORD, William (1833–90)

DALLAWAY, William (1857–1939)
DALY, James (?–1849)
DARCH, Charles Thomas (1876–1934)
DAVIES, Margaret Llewelyn (1861–1944)
DAVISON, John (1846–1930)
DEAN, Benjamin (1839–1910)
DEANS, James (1843/4?–1935)
DEANS, Robert (1904–59)
DENT, John James (1856–1936)
DIXON, John (1828–76)
DRAKE, Henry John (1878–1934)
DUDLEY, Sir William Edward (1868–1938)
DYE, Sidney (1900–58)
DYSON, James (1822/3–1902)

EDWARDS, Enoch (1852–1912)
EDWARDS, John Charles (1833–81)
EDWARDS, Wyndham Ivor (1878–1938)
ENFIELD, Alice Honora (1882–1935)
EVANS, Isaac (1847?–97)
EVANS, Jonah (1826–1907)

FENWICK, Charles (1850–1918)
FINCH, John (1784–1857)
FINNEY, Samuel (1857–1935)
FISHWICK, Jonathan (1832–1908)
FLEMING, Robert (1869–1939)
FORMAN, John (1822/3–1900)
FOSTER, William (1887–1947)
FOULGER, Sydney (1863–1919)
FOWE, Thomas (1832/3?–94)
FOX, James Challinor (1837–77)
FRITH, John (1837–1904)

GALBRAITH, Samuel (1853–1936)
GALLAGHER, Patrick (Paddy the Cope) (1871–1966)
GANLEY, Caroline Selina (1879–1966)
GLOVER, Thomas (1852–1913)
GOLIGHTLY, Alfred William (1857–1948)
GOODY, Joseph (1816/17–91)
GRAHAM, Duncan MacGregor (1867–1942)
GRAY, Jesse Clement (1854–1912)
GREENALL, Thomas (1857–1937)
GREENING, Edward Owen (1836–1923)
GREENWOOD, Abraham (1824–1911)
GREENWOOD, Joseph (1833–1924)

HALL, Frank (1861–1927)
HALL, Fred (1878–1938)
HALLAM, William (1856–1902)
HARDERN, Francis (Frank) (1846–1913)
HARES, Edward Charles (1897–1966)
HARTSHORN, Vernon (1872–1931)
HARVEY, William Edwin (1852–1914)
HASLAM, James (1842–1913)
HASLAM, James (1869–1937)
HAWKINS, George (1844–1908)
HAYHURST, George (1862–1936)
HAYWARD, Sir Fred (1876–1944)
HENDERSON, Arthur (1863–1935)
HETHERINGTON, Henry (1792–1849)
HIBBERT, Charles (1828–1902)
HICKEN, Henry (1882–1964)
HILTON, James (1814–90)

HINES, George Lelly (1839–1914)
HOBSON, John Atkinson (1858–1940)
HOLYOAKE, Austin (1826–74)
HOLYOAKE, George Jacob (1817–1906)
HOOSON, Edward (1825–69)
HOWARTH, Charles (1814–68)
HUGHES, Hugh (1878–1932)

JACKSON, Henry (1840–1920)
JARVIS, Henry (1839–1907)
JENKINS, Hubert (1866–1943)
JOHN, William (1878–1955)
JOHNSON, John (1850–1910)
JONES, Benjamin (1847–1942)
JONES, Patrick Lloyd (1811–86)
JUGGINS, Richard (1843–95)

KENYON, Barnet (1850–1930)
KILLON, Thomas (1853–1931)
KING, William (1786–1865)

LANG, James (1870–1966)
LEE, Frank (1867–1941)
LEES, James (1806–91)
LEWIS, Richard James (1900–66)
LEWIS, Thomas (Tommy) (1873–1962)
LIDDLE, Thomas (1863–1954)
LOWERY, Matthew Hedley (1858–1918)

MACDONALD, Alexander (1821–81)
MacDONALD, James Ramsay (1866–1937)
McGHEE, Henry George (1898–1959)
MANN, Amos (1855–1939)
MARCROFT, William (1822–94)
MARLOW, Arnold (1891–1939)
MARTIN, James (1850–1933)
MAXWELL, Sir William (1841–1929)
MAY, Henry John (1867–1939)
MERCER, Thomas William (1884–1947)
MILLERCHIP, William (1863–1939)
MITCHELL, John Thomas Whitehead (1828–95)
MOLESWORTH, William Nassau (1816–90)
MOORHOUSE, Thomas Edwin (1854–1922)
MORGAN, David (Dai o'r Nant) (1840–1900)
MORGAN, David Watts (1867–1933)
MORGAN, John Minter (1782–1854)

MUDIE, George (1788?-?)
MURRAY, Robert (1869-1950)

NEALE, Edward Vansittart (1810-92)
NORMANSELL, John (1830-75)
NUTTALL, William (1835-1905)

OLIVER, John (1861-1942)
ONIONS, Alfred (1858-1921)

PARE, William (1805-73)
PARKINSON, Tom Bamford (1865-1939)
PATTERSON, William Hammond (1847-96)
PATTISON, Lewis (1873-1956)
PENNY, John (1870-1938)
PERKINS, George Leydon (1885-1961)
PICKARD, Benjamin (1842-1904)
PICKARD, William (1821-87)
PITMAN, Henry (1826-1909)
POLLARD, William (1832/3?-1909)
PRATT, Hodgson (1824-1907)
PURCELL, Albert Arthur (1872-1935)

RAMSAY, Thomas (Tommy) (1810/11-1873)
REDFERN, Percy (1875-1958)
REEVES, Samuel (1862-1930)
RICHARDS, Thomas (1859-1931)
ROBINSON, Richard (1879-1937)
ROGERS, Frederick (1846-1915)
ROWLINSON, George Henry (1852-1937)
RUTHERFORD, John Hunter (1826-90)

SEWELL, William (1852-1948)
SHALLARD, George (1877-1958)
SHARP, Andrew (1841-1919)

SHILLITO, John (1832-1915)
SIMPSON, James (1826-95)
SITCH, Thomas (1852-1923)
SKEVINGTON, John (1801-50)
SMITHIES, James (1819-69)
SPENCER, George Alfred (1873-1957)
SPENCER, John Samuel (1868-1943)
STANLEY, Albert (1862-1915)
STANTON, Charles Butt (1873-1946)
STEWART, Aaron (1845-1910)

TAYLOR, John Wilkinson (1855-1934)
THORNE, William James (1857-1946)
THORPE, George (1854-1945)
TOPHAM, Edward (1894-1966)
TRAVIS, Henry (1807-84)
TWEDDELL, Thomas (1839-1916)
TWIGG, Herbert James Thomas (1900-1957)

VINCENT, Henry (1813-78)
VIVIAN, Henry Harvey (1868-1930)

WADSWORTH, John (1850-1921)
WALKER, Benjamin (1803/4?-83)
WALSHAM, Cornelius (1880-1958)
WATKINS, William Henry (1862-1924)
WATTS, John (1818-87)
WEBB, Simeon (1864-1929)
WEBB, Thomas Edward (1829-96)
WEIR, John (1851-1908)
WHITEHEAD, Alfred (1862-1945)
WILLIAMS, Aneurin (1859-1924)
WILLIAMS, John (1861-1922)
WILSON, John (1837-1915)
WINSTONE, James (1863-1921)
WOODS, Samuel (1846-1915)
WORLEY, Joseph James (1876-1944)
WRIGHT, Oliver Walter (1886-1938)

General Index

Compiled by V. J. Morris and G. D. Weston
Numbers in bold type refer to biographical entries

Abbotts, William, **1**
Aberaman, 311, 347
Aberdare, 245
Abertillery, 20
Ablett, Noah, 37, 151
Abraham, William, **1-4**, 52, 110, 114, 151, 195, 245, 247, 285, 347, 350
Abram (Lancs.), 123-4
Accrington, 157, 158
Ackroyd, E., 203
Acland, Lady Alice Sophia, **5-6**, 7, 36
Acland, Sir Arthur Herbert Dyke, 5, **6-8**, 36, 197
Acland, Sir Francis, 6
Acts of Parliament: see Parliamentary Acts
Adams, John Jackson (later Lord Adams of Ennerdale), **8-11**, 25
Adams, William Edwin, 83
Adams, William Thomas, **11**
Adult School Movement, 96, 230, 259
Advocate of the Working Classes, 250
AE: see Russell, George William
Agricultural and Horticultural Association, 137-8, 253
Agricultural Economist, 137
Airdrie, 133
Alcott House Community, 66. See also Owenism
Aldam, Heaton, 119
Alexander, Albert Victor (later Earl Alexander of Hillsborough), **11-14**, 159
Allan, William, **14-19**
Allen, Clifford (later Lord Allen of Hurtwood), 179
Allen, Miss E. H. J., 5
Allen, Robert, **19-20**
Allen, Sir Thomas William, **20-1**, 45, 71, 158, 232
Allerton Burn (Northumberland), 123
Altrincham, 38
Amalgamated Association of Miners; see Miner's Unions – Local and Regional
Amalgamated Engineering Union, 132, 235,

263. See also Amalgamated Society of Engineers
Amalgamated Furnishing Trades Association, 275
Amalgamated Marine Workers' Union, 216
Amalgamated Society of Carpenters and Joiners, 47, 218, 334
Amalgamated Society of Engineers, 15-17, 76, 119, 131-2, 212, 263, 287, 298
Amalgamated Society of French Polishers, 275
Amalgamated Union of Co-operative Employees, 109, 239
American Civil War, British attitudes towards, 40, 66-7, 72, 78, 111, 137, 189, 203, 332, 341
American Federation of Labor, 22, 121, 277, 317
American Socialist, 91, 322
Ammon, Charles George (later Lord Ammon of Camberwell), **21-4**
Amsterdam International: see International Federation of Trade Unions
Anchor Tenants Ltd, 230
Anderson, Sir Alan Garrett, 45
Anderson, Frank, **24-6**
Anderson, Mary Elizabeth, 25
Anderson, William Crawford, 22, 162
Angell, Sir Norman, 179
Angle, George, 315
Anglican Church: see Churches: Church of England
Anglo-Baltic Produce Association, 21
Anglo-Russian Parliamentary Committee, 276
Anglo-Russian Trade Union Alliance, 276
Anglo-Russian Unity Committee, 276
Ankylostomiasis (miners' anaemia), 80-1
Annfield Plain (Durham), 314
Anti-Corn Law League, 328, 340
Anti-Persecution Union, 170, 183
Anti-Prosecution Union (later Anti-Persecution Union), 170

and local government, 11, 29–30, 39, 43–6, 64–5, 73–4, 84, 98, 100–1, 106, 112, 129, 132, 143, 150, 157, 160, 212, 215, 218, 230–1, 240, 242, 244, 251, 263, 265, 267, 302, 320, 323, 339, 343
and Owenism, 32, 36, 65–8, 40–2, 94–5, 118–19, 167, 169–71, 182–4, 190, 201–2, 210–11, 214, 252, 260–2, 300–302, 322, 340, 341
and phrenology, 91
and religion
 Baptist, 12, 20, 35, 42, 76, 337
 Church of England, 6, 49, 78, 106, 121, 157, 243, 252, 267, 337
 Church of Scotland, 212
 Congregationalist, 38, 46, 78, 149, 198, 241, 242, 251
 Methodist, 71, 74, 105, 127, 240, 259, 265
 Presbyterian, 298
 Primitive Methodist, 100, 218, 300
 Roman Catholic, 73, 97–8, 118, 209
 Society of Friends (Quakers), 113, 137, 273, 281
 Unitarian, 32, 55, 73, 78, 94, 118, 124, 139, 146, 175, 182, 298
 Wesleyan Methodist, 19, 36, 41, 65, 78, 158, 213, 232, 244
Co-operators' Year Book, 47, 353
Co-partnership, 346
Co-partnership, 47, 97, 137–8, 143, 184, 204, 230, 232, 236, 240, 274, 334–5, 339, 346
Co-partnership Tenants Ltd, 335
Cornwood (Devon), 334
Cost of Living Inquiry Committee (1936), 130
Cotton Factory Times, 155, 156
Cotton Growers' Association, 297
Council of Protestant Churches, 13
Counsellor, 78
Court, Sir Josiah, **79–81**
Coventry, 280, 340
Coventry Express, 91
Cowen, Joseph, **81–6**, 183, 204, 294
Cowey, Edward, **86–8**, 126, 269, 336
Crabtree, James, **88–9**, 108
Crabtree, Joseph, 88
Cradley Heath (Staffs.), 298
Craig, Edward Thomas, **89–93**, 137, 201, 322
Craig, Mrs E. T., 90

Cramlington (Northumberland), 115
Crawford, William, 31, 60, **93–4**, 203, 264
Crewe, 15
Cripps, Sir R. Stafford, 13, 45
Crisis, 91, 248, 261
Crompton Boot Manufacturers, 232
Crooks, William, 110, 117, 312
Cross, E. R., 178
Cross Keys (Monmouth), 150
Crowther, John, & Sons (Milnsbridge), 11
Crystal Palace Co-operative Productions Exhibition, 47
Cumberland Development Council, 9, 25
Cunningham, Alice Sophia: *see* Acland, Lady Alice Sophia
Cunninghame Graham, Robert Bontine, 3, 61, 114
Curragh (Kildare), 47
Curran, Pete, 87, 269, 315, 335
Cuthbertson, John, 66
Cwmavon (Glamorgan), 1, 112

Dai o'r Nant: *see* Morgan, David
Daily Express, 13
Daily News, 137
Dallaway, William, **94**
Dalton, Hugh (*later* Lord Dalton), 9, 13, 163, 178
Daly, James, 77, **94–5**
Darch, Charles Thomas, **95–6**
Darlaston, 206–7
Darlington, 161
Davies, Henry, 114
Davies, John Llewelyn, 96
Davies, Margaret Llewelyn, 39, **96–9**, 113, 324
Davis, William John, 207
Davison, John, **99–100**
Davitt, Michael, 114, 128
Dawes Plan, 276
Dean, Benjamin, **100–1**
Deans, James, **101–2**
Deans, Robert, **102–3**
Delph (Yorks.), 244
Democratic Committee for Poland's Regeneration, 170
Democratic Committee of Observation on the French Revolution (1848), 170
Democratic Federation: *see* Social Democratic Federation
Denaby Main Case, 87–8, 126, 269
Dent, John James, **103–4**